The L/L Research Channeling Archives

Transcripts of the Meditation Sessions

Volume 3
June 22, 1980 to April 5, 1981

Don Elkins   Jim McCarty   Carla L. Rueckert

Copyright © 2009 L/L Research

All rights reserved. No part of this book may be reproduced or used in any form or by any means—graphic, electronic or mechanical, including photocopying or information storage and retrieval systems—without written permission from the copyright holder.

ISBN: 978-0-945007-77-7

Published by L/L Research
Box 5195
Louisville, Kentucky 40255-0195

E-mail: contact@llresearch.org
www.llresearch.org

About the cover photo: *This photograph of Jim McCarty and Carla L. Rueckert was taken during an L/L Research channeling session on August 4, 2009, in the living room of their Louisville, Kentucky home. Jim always holds hands with Carla when she channels, following the Ra group's advice on how she can avoid any possibility of astral travel.*

Dedication

These archive volumes are dedicated to Hal and Jo Price, who faithfully and lovingly hosted this group's weekly meditation meetings from 1962 to 1975,

to Walt Rogers, whose work with the research group Man, Consciousness and Understanding of Detroit offered the information needed to begin this ongoing channeling experiment,

and to the Confederation of Angels and Planets in the Service of the Infinite Creator, for sharing their love and wisdom with us so generously through the years.

Table of Contents

Introduction 7
Year 1980 9
    June 22, 1980 10
    June 29, 1980 14
    July 27, 1980 19
    August 3, 1980 28
    August 10, 1980 35
    August 23, 1980 43
    August 24, 1980 47
    August 27, 1980 51
    August 31, 1980 54
    September 2, 1980 57
    September 3, 1980 60
    September 4, 1980 63
    September 6, 1980 66
    September 6, 1980 68
    September 7, 1980 70
    September 8, 1980 75
    September 9, 1980 78
    September 14, 1980 80
    September 16, 1980 85
    September 28, 1980 87
    October 5, 1980 91
    October 15, 1980 97
    October 16, 1980 100
    October 19, 1980 102
    October 26, 1980 104
    November 9, 1980 107
    November 16, 1980 110
    November 30, 1980 113
    December 7, 1980 118
    December 14, 1980 122
    December 28, 1980 127
    December 31, 1980 129
Year 1981 132
    January 4, 1981 133
    January 5, 1981 137
    January 11, 1981 140
    January 15, 1981 144

January 15, 1981	148
January 15, 1981	151
January 18, 1981	155
January 20, 1981	159
January 21, 1981	163
January 21, 1981	167
January 22, 1981	171
January 23, 1981	175
January 24, 1981	177
January 24, 1981	181
January 25, 1981	183
January 25, 1981	186
January 26, 1981	190
January 26, 1981	192
January 27, 1981	197
January 27, 1981	200
January 27, 1981	204
January 28, 1981	205
January 28, 1981	208
January 28, 1981	212
January 28, 1981	216
January 29, 1981	219
January 29, 1981	223
January 30, 1981	228
January 30, 1981	232
January 31, 1981	233
January 31, 1981	239
February 3, 1981	240
February 3, 1981	246
February 4, 1981	248
February 4, 1981	252
February 4, 1981	256
February 8, 1981	261
February 9, 1981	266
February 10, 1981	271
February 10, 1981	274
February 10, 1981	275
February 10, 1981	279
February 11, 1981	281
February 11, 1981	285
February 15, 1981	286
February 15, 1981	289

FEBRUARY 16, 1981	291
FEBRUARY 16, 1981	293
FEBRUARY 17, 1981	295
FEBRUARY 17, 1981	301
FEBRUARY 21, 1981	302
FEBRUARY 21, 1981	305
FEBRUARY 22, 1981	307
FEBRUARY 23, 1981	311
FEBRUARY 23, 1981	315
FEBRUARY 24, 1981	316
FEBRUARY 24, 1981	319
FEBRUARY 25, 1981	320
FEBRUARY 27, 1981	325
FEBRUARY 27, 1981	328
MARCH 1, 1981	330
MARCH 4, 1981	334
MARCH 4, 1981	338
MARCH 6, 1981	340
MARCH 8, 1981	343
MARCH 10, 1981	346
MARCH 10, 1981	350
MARCH 12, 1981	352
MARCH 12, 1981	354
MARCH 13, 1981	357
MARCH 13, 1981	360
MARCH 16, 1981	362
MARCH 16, 1981	365
MARCH 18, 1981	367
MARCH 20, 1981	371
MARCH 22, 1981	376
MARCH 22, 1981	380
MARCH 22, 1981	384
MARCH 24, 1981	386
MARCH 28, 1981	390
MARCH 29, 1981	394
APRIL 5, 1981	398

Introduction

Welcome to this volume of the *L/L Research Channeling Archives*. This series of publications represents the collection of channeling sessions recorded by L/L Research during the period from the early seventies to the present day. The sessions are also available on the L/L Research website, www.llresearch.org.

Starting in the mid-1950s, Don Elkins, a professor of physics and engineering at Speed Scientific School, had begun researching the paranormal in general and UFOs in particular. Elkins was a pilot as well as a professor and he flew his small plane to meet with many of the UFO contactees of the period.

Hal Price had been a part of a UFO-contactee channeling circle in Detroit called "The Detroit Group." When Price was transferred from Detroit's Ford plant to its Louisville truck plant, mutual friends discovered that Price also was a UFO researcher and put the two men together. Hal introduced Elkins to material called *The Brown Notebook* which contained instructions on how to create a group and receive UFO contactee information. In January of 1962 they decided to put the instructions to use and began holding silent meditation meetings on Sunday nights just across the Ohio River in the southern Indiana home of Hal and his wife, Jo. This was the beginning of what was called the "Louisville Group."

I was an original member of that group, along with a dozen of Elkins' physics students. However, I did not learn to channel until 1974. Before that date, almost none of our weekly channeling sessions were recorded or transcribed. After I began improving as a channel, Elkins decided for the first time to record all the sessions and transcribe them.

During the first eighteen months or so of my studying channeling and producing material, we tended to reuse the tapes as soon as the transcriptions were finished. Since those were typewriter days, we had no record of the work that could be reopened and used again, as we do now with computers. And I used up the original and the carbon copy of my transcriptions putting together a manuscript, *Voices of the Gods*, which has not yet been published. It remains as almost the only record of Don Elkins' and my channeling of that period.

We learned from this experience to retain the original tapes of all of our sessions, and during the remainder of the seventies and through the eighties, our "Louisville Group" was prolific. The "Louisville Group" became "L/L Research" after Elkins and I published a book in 1976, *Secrets of the UFO*, using that publishing name. At first we met almost every night. In later years, we met gradually less often, and the number of sessions recorded by our group in a year accordingly went down. Eventually, the group began taking three months off from channeling during the summer. And after 2000, we began having channeling meditations only twice a month. The volume of sessions dropped to its present output of eighteen or so each year.

These sessions feature channeling from sources which call themselves members of the Confederation of Planets in the Service of the Infinite Creator. At first we enjoyed hearing from many different voices: Hatonn, Laitos, Oxal, L/Leema and Yadda being just a few of them. As I improved my tuning techniques, and became the sole senior channel in L/L Research, the number of contacts dwindled. When I began asking for "the highest and best contact which I can receive of Jesus the Christ's vibration of unconditional love in a conscious and stable manner," the entity offering its thoughts through our group was almost always Q'uo. This remains true as our group continues to channel on an ongoing basis.

The channelings are always about love and unity, enunciating "The Law of One" in one aspect or another. Seekers who are working with spiritual principles often find the material a good resource. We hope that you will as well. As time has gone on the questions have shifted somewhat, but in general the content of the channeling is metaphysical and focused on helping seekers find the love in the moment and the Creator in the love.

At first, I transcribed our channeling sessions. I got busier, as our little group became more widely known, and got hopelessly behind on transcribing. Two early transcribers who took that job off my hands were Kim

Howard and Judy Dunn, both of whom masterfully transcribed literally hundreds of sessions through the eighties and early nineties.

Then Ian Jaffray volunteered to create a web site for these transcriptions, and single-handedly unified the many different formats that the transcripts were in at that time and made them available online. This additional exposure prompted more volunteers to join the ranks of our transcribers, and now there are a dozen or so who help with this. Our thanks go out to all of these kind volunteers, early and late, who have made it possible for our webguy to make these archives available.

Around the turn of the millennium, I decided to commit to editing each session after it had been transcribed. So the later transcripts have fewer errata than the earlier ones, which are quite imperfect in places. One day, perhaps, those earlier sessions will be revisited and corrections will be made to the transcripts. It would be a large task, since there are well over 1500 channeling sessions as of this date, and counting. We apologize for the imperfections in those transcripts, and trust that you can ascertain the sense of them regardless of a mistake here and there.

Blessings, dear reader! Enjoy these "humble thoughts" from the Confederation of Planets. May they prove good companions to your spiritual seeking. ♣

For all of us at L/L Research,

Carla L. Rueckert

Louisville, Kentucky

July 16, 2009

Year 1980

June 22, 1980 to December 31, 1980

Sunday Meditation
June 22, 1980

(Carla channeling)

I am Oxal, and I greet you in the love and the light of the infinite Creator. We of Oxal are members of the Confederation of Planets in the Service of the Infinite Creator and we, like the man whom you call John the Baptist, are drawn to you as messengers to bear witness to the truth as we know it. We are very grateful to be with you this evening and greet each of you and especially the one known as *(inaudible)* who is new to this group. We hope that we may say those things which you may need at this time to hear with your outer ears in order that your inner ears, the ears of your spirit, may be awakened to those vibrations which you have the most need of at this time. For although we speak through these instruments in intellectual patterns, the truth that we bring to you is so simple that it is difficult for your intellectual mind to accept it. Therefore, we attempt to find many different methods by which we may present this simple truth.

(Pause)

We are sorry for the pause, my friends, but this instrument was distracted. We now again have good contact again with this instrument. We do not speak to your group very often, but because we are of the vibration of light and yet closely connected with the vibrations of love, we are drawn to you on these days when your planetary sphere is bathed in more light than at any other time during the year.

We speak of a simple truth and we would express it to you by saying that to serve the Creator is perfect freedom. This, my friends, is a universe of love. The entities upon your sphere, being co-creators, have distorted that love in many ways. But if you can look about you to see the world the Creator has made for you, you can learn the lessons of love, of service to others that we bring to you.

The sun that rules your daytime and shines upon you so abundantly at this time of your planet's travel about that sun offers its nearly infinite supply of light in service to all who dwell upon this planet that you call Earth. Without it your ability to survive would be negative for you are creatures developed in your physical vehicles to be adapted to that which the sun can give, its warmth and the life that it brings to plants, the evaporation that it gives to water so that there may be rain.

Yes, my friends, even your nights are illuminated by the reflection of the light of the sun. There is a darkness that exists in your density in order that you may understand the light. As it has been written in one of your holy works, light may come into a dark world and the world may not comprehend it, but still, my friends, it exists. The light of which we speak is love. For when we of the Confederation greet you in light and love we are saying the two manifestations of the one thing that animates all of creation.

And what is your role as you bear witness to a world of duality, darkness and light? For those of you who seek to know the truth, your role is one of seeking the light. For in the light is unity. In the light is love. And these things speak to the inner self of a deeper reality. Yes, my friends, it is true that some seek the dark and separate themselves from the rest of your kind and attempt to gain power over others of their kind. There is indeed power in darkness. The power that is in love, the power that is in light, is like the flaming wheel that moves eternally, unifying all those who seek its wisdom and its warmth. It is necessary that you gain firsthand knowledge of this light and this love through meditation or prayer. It is not enough, my friends, that you study, for study will not bear fruit without the catalyst of understanding. And spiritual understanding comes in silence.

Seek, then, within yourself that spark of the infinite love and light of the Creator and then, my friends, we ask you to make the giant step, to cease being observers of your own light, and to speak, when asked, of those things in which you may believe. We do not ask you to volunteer information or to press thoughts and ideas upon people who may not request these concepts, for each student is ready in his own time. But when you are asked, be courageous and speak of those things which are within you, bearing witness to the light in your own way and with your own words. For the kingdom which is called heaven by many on your planet is within you. And as you manifest it in your love, light begins to shine from you, and your being begins to touch those who may need you.

This, my friends, is the kindliest service that you can perform for your fellow beings. So be aware when someone asks for your aid, and plant the seed of thought where you may. It does not matter whether or not you may think that they have borne fruit for that is not within your provenance. It matters only that you have been true to the understanding that you now possess, just as we are true to the understanding that we now possess in sharing our thoughts with you.

We have greatly enjoyed speaking to you through this instrument. It has been some time since we used this instrument and we thank her for allowing us speak through her at this time. We will leave this instrument now. We feel the rhythmic exhalations of your spirits as they sway in gentle harmonious waves of meditation and we thank you for allowing us to mingle our meditation with yours. I am known to you as Oxal. I leave you in the love and the light of our infinite Creator. Adonai vasu.

(Carla channeling

I am Latwii, and I greet you in the love and the light of the infinite Creator. I send you the greetings and love of the entities of Hatonn and am standing in [for] him as a pinch hitter and am very glad to be with you at this time. At this time I would like to ask for questions.

Jim: I would like to know what the relationship between the mind and the brain and the will is, how they function together.

Ah, my brother Jim, you ask a difficult question. However, we are aware of the question and will attempt to answer it. The brain is a type of computer with various stages of programming. The deepest programs which have been termed metaprograms by some of your authors are those involving your survival, the reproduction of your species, your social position, and other items that are very big on the agenda of third-density living.

The mind is a function of the spirit which is an amalgam of the effects that a wealth of experiences in various incarnations have had upon the basic spiritual personality. This mind is a collection of biases, emotions and feelings. Depending upon the uses to which the mind has been put in prior incarnations, it may consist of [a] large intellectual factor or little intellect. It is, however, a mind function rather than a brain function. However, standing between mind and brain is that which you call the will. If a person does not use the faculty of his will there will go into effect an automatic metaprogram which will cause that person's mind to become linked to his brain in a fashion predetermined by his circumstances.

Thus, native intellect, native biases, native emotions, which are brought in from the immortal spirit may be completely buried in the personality of the brain due to lack of will. However, in some instances the faculty of will is developed in the individual and in those cases the mind is able to impress its own metaprogramming much more carefully over the basic metaprogramming of third-density survival mechanisms. Any changes in metaprogramming will be developed and successfully completed by the use of the will.

As you sit here this evening you are exercising the faculty of will. It has been written, "Seek and ye shall find, ask and it shall be opened unto you." The will is that faculty of seeking, desiring and wishing. When it is developed to perfection, the will of the individual becomes the will of the Creator and you become a clear channel so that you may function through your mind and not through the lower programmings.

Do you wish to question us further on this subject, my friend?

Jim: Just one follow-up. It seems occasionally when I think intellectually on a topic that I wish to share with someone—my feelings of that—and then forget that topic for a while—hours or days—and then speak to them later without thinking of it, a continuous flow of information occasionally occurs that I was not aware it was there. Is that the release of the information of the mind and has the will been used there in that process?

I am Latwii. That is correct, my brother. As you yourself described, preliminary to the experience of the information flow, you had the desire to share this information. What you desire you will get. Thus, we always remind you to take care in your desires. For you will receive all that you desire before you leave this density.

Does that answer your question, my brother?

Jim: Yes. Thank you.

We thank you. Is there another question at this time?

Questioner: May I ask what level you come from?

We are happy to share with you our level, however we cannot take it as seriously as some. We are at a level you would call six. You are at a level called three. We are honored to be able to speak to you. We have not been able to speak to a group before this and are enjoying the contact very much, although we realize we still sound a bit awkward. Do you wish us to speak more about the level six?

Questioner: Yes.

What would you wish to know, for as you can imagine there is much to say about any vibration or dimension of existence.

Questioner: Does level six as opposed to level three have to do with understanding?

I am Latwii. No, my sister. Level six is not the level of understanding. Level six is a level of light or enlightenment. We do not any longer understand. Rather, we are. We exist as light and dwell as light beings. Our ability to be has made us into what you would call scientists within the Confederation. We are attempting to monitor and understand or feel, as you would say, all of the sub-densities of light that are within your planetary sphere in each of the seven octaves of your density.

We are enjoying this greatly, for [you] see, because in the end all things are one, those who feel become the best technicians, as you would say, and those who are the best at what you would call understanding or wisdom work best with philosophy and the understanding of the personality. This would be backwards from what your vocational advisors would tell you in your high school. However, as one becomes more experienced one learns that the skills that seemed to be the best for scientific endeavors are those best suited for abstract thought and vice versa.

Thus, we who are light beings feel your universe and are able to place that feeling or enlightenment about your creation into our central bank of thought which you might call a very, very vast computer. The dimension of love is level four. The dimension of understanding is level five. The dimension of unity is level six. Our teachers come from the dimension of unity. We do not know if there is an end to the progression for our teachers do not know this. But that is what we can tell you.

Does this aid you in your understanding, my sister?

Questioner: Yes, thank you.

We indeed are grateful to you for allowing us to share with you what little we do know. Is there another question at this time?

Questioner: I would like to ask a question. Is there truth in the science of astrology?

Ah, my brother, there is truth in everything, but truth with a capital T is found in nothing. We are aware we must be more specific but this is a very important principle which we would like to share with you. There is no truth in your density. There are intimations of the mystery of truth which you can find in every rock, in every scene, in every face, in every word that you may hear. But truth, as this instrument would see the cartoon character standing upon a pedestal marked "TRVTH" does not exist in your illusion or maya.

Now to astrology. The planetary configurations are as they are. And this in itself is a truth. That there are basic confluences and influences having to do with the stars and the planets and the relationship to each individual is also true. The confusion comes in most cases when one attempts to find too much truth in what is only the type of predictive statement, "Cats like to chase mice." Well, my friends, this is quite true of many cats. However the cat seated upon this instrument's lap runs from mice and indeed most other things.

Just so with the indications of an astrological chart. The chart is one of a general geography. It may show what particular material you might best work upon in smoothing out a rough personality, in determining the dynamics of a personality conflict between two people, and this sort of general use. However, to use it predictably is to assume that the universe is mechanical and predetermined and this is patently false. The universe is in the process of being made at all times and you have complete free will. Regardless of the road map you can always strike off cross-country. You can develop your own version of yourself. Again the question of will, as the one known as Jim brought up, is very relevant here. To the one who does not exercise his will, influences such as those of the stars will, along with the influences of mother and father and friends and experiences of all kinds, shape the individual pattern. With meditation and the application of the will, those things which are desired, freedom from any confines, astrological or otherwise, is assured.

Does this answer your question, my friend?

Questioner: Yes. Thanks.

We are pleased. We see further in your mind, however, that there is something we should [answer] which is not particularly relevant to astrology but is relevant instead to a general mass of predictive pseudo-sciences which are grouped under the term occult or metaphysical.

You must understand that there are individuals whose psychic abilities may remain largely unknown even to themselves but who use astrology or Tarot or other occult mechanisms in order to focus their abilities to see clearly those things which may help the individual. In those cases the so-called astrologer sees much more than in a chart, the reader of Tarot reads much more than cards, and so forth. When you run across an individual such as this, recognize that individual for what he or she may be and treat the information accordingly without putting too much stress upon the mechanism by which this information …

(Tape ends.)

Sunday Meditation
June 29, 1980

(The recording on this tape is very noisy.)

(Carla channeling

I am Oxal, and I greet you in the love and the light of our infinite Creator. It is, as always, our privilege to greet each of you and send you our blessings and our gratitude at being able to share these moments of *(inaudible)* with you. This instrument was not aware of the reason for her desire to play the music which she played while you were tuning the group. However, it is our desire that the message of those particular songs [simply leave their] message, for we feel that it is very much in the mind of each of you that this is the time to consider each designed journey and how you shall make it.

We have listened to you speak about those things that are to come and those things are happening now in fulfillment of messages that this group has received in the past. We are sorry, my friends, that your peoples are never able to understand that the friction between them is the true cause of the planetary change. This the scientists cannot understand no matter how they shuffle their papers or hone their computers, but it is true, my friends. Your transition into fourth density has occurred, though apparently being somewhat difficult. Each of you, my friends, has a program of action to carry out at this time, and we say this not only to those in this room but to each person upon your sorrowing planet.

For some, a very few, my friends, there is the program of the shepherd, and those of you who have made contact with that portion of what you may call your oversoul that allows you to be a shepherd that guards the sheep will find it very compelling at this time to take some sort of action in order to better establish yourself that you may survive. We confirm those feelings that you have at this time although we cannot tell you specifically, as you know what you must do. We can urge you only to be aware of your own program. We do not wish to be the element among those things which you have heard that causes you to become estranged from those whom you may love. We do not wish to encourage or discourage any specific action. We know that each of you has more urgency of the feelings of wanting to help and of thinking of the past. The time has come to activate whatever there is in your program.

We do confirm that we wish to be of help *(inaudible)*, but it is the time when many will seek out those who can give them hope or understanding of any kind. The great majority of you, my friends, are what you would call the sheep, because they have not yet become consciously aware that they are programmed entities programmed by their higher selves for service to others and for learning in this illusion. They move through the illusion easily herded by any and all forces that surround them. When trouble comes near, those sheep that have some hope of being awakened to themselves will be your charges. Thus, we ask you to be aware of who you are and of what you wish to be.

It may seem very strange for us to speak to you on a calm evening, for trouble is not now. You are peaceful, you are not hungry. But, my friends, in some variations of your future things have already happened. You are hungry and you are not peaceful. Because of your free will, we do not know which of the many futures is yours, but a very large percentage of them include what you would call catastrophe. Therefore, my friends, look to yourselves, cherish each other and serve the Father. There may be many whom you cannot help just as there are many now that you cannot help, and even the stimulus of trauma will not be enough to awaken those who sleep to the miracle of creation, and they will sleep on while their lives and their consciousnesses pass before them and they do not budge. You must let these go, my friends, secure in the knowledge that each sphere has an infinite amount of time to discover the desire to know the Creator.

The path leads to love but it may be a long one. You cannot help and you must accept this and open yourself always to those who ask for help. Many people ask for help in such a way that you cannot truly comprehend what they wish, for help comes in many different shapes and sizes, types and varieties. Therefore, instead of following the golden rule we ask you to listen to the requests of those about you and do unto others as they would have you do unto them, not as you would have them do unto you, for what you need may not be what they need. And always, my friends, be grounded in meditation, spending time in a tabernacle, seated with the blessed One who comes in the name of the Lord. This is written in your holy works and it refers to consciousness, the consciousness of love. And this consciousness is most [peaceful] and without it you as a shepherd will grow very lean. Thus, do not forget to minister to yourself by meditation and awareness of the blessing of love.

I will at this time leave this instrument so that my brother Laitos may speak. I leave you in the love and the light of the infinite Creator. I am known to you as Oxal. Adonai.

(Carla channeling

I am Laitos, and am delighted to greet you in the love and light of the infinite Creator. We are sorry that we were unable to speak through the one known as *(inaudible)*. However, it is our desire that [we] do something quite unusual and *(inaudible)* he is of a *(inaudible)* valuable in channeling. However, it will mean a great deal to me if he is able to speak without being assigned *(inaudible)*. Therefore, we attempt to contact him. This is not our usual method, but each time that *(inaudible)* comes a little closer to channeling we feel that he is gaining confidence in a way that is *(inaudible)* to him. *(Inaudible)* We would like now to transfer to the one known as C. I am Laitos.

(Carla channeling

I am again with this instrument. I am Laitos. We have good in contact with the one known as C. However, he is somewhat fatigued and also seems to *(inaudible)* the context which we give him. We will continue working with him *(inaudible)*. We would like at this time to transfer the contact to the one known as Jim. I am Laitos.

(Jim channeling

I am Laitos, and I am with this instrument. It is again a pleasure and a joy to share our thoughts and our feelings through this new instrument. It is not always the easiest task to put aside the analyzing portion of the mind, but when this is done it is a very simple matter to be able to pick up and receive our thoughts. We know that this instrument desires very much to be of that type of service and it is with joy that we are able to assist this instrument in that endeavor. Again, we would like to say that we are adjusting our [beam.] The instrument is so pleased to be channeling that he also wishes to analyze. We again remind him of the necessity to refrain from such dual endeavors. And now we would again transfer to the one known as Carla. I am Laitos.

(Carla channeling

I am Laitos, and I am again with this instrument. We are very happy to *(inaudible)* contact *(inaudible)*. We would like to briefly touch and condition the one known as M, if she would allow herself at this time to refrain from *(inaudible)*. If she would make *(inaudible)* we will attempt to make our presence known. I am Laitos.

(Carla channeling

I am again with this instrument. I am Laitos, and we *(inaudible)*. *(Inaudible)*. I am Laitos. I leave you love *(inaudible)*. Adonai.

(Carla channeling

I am Latwii. I have been waiting for my chance to speak with you and greet you also in the name of the Father. We have come to offer ourselves to you in case you wish to ask us any questions. Is there a question?

C: *(The question is mostly inaudible, but it was about tiredness.)*

I am Latwii. I understand your question, my brother, and far be it from us to attempt to influence …

(Side one of tape ends.)

(Carla channeling

… the vital energy of the universe which some call *prana* and [some] call *shiva* filling your lungs and your blood with this life-giving force. And when you exhale, my brother, picture all the weariness, all the carbon dioxide that stifles your muscles and your mind flowing away from your body so that it may be used by the plant life which in turn gives you back the oxygen. This is the cycle of being that aids you both. In meditation you tune in to the infinity and the strength of this source of energy. You can also open yourselves to the teachings and the understandings which you need to have hour by hour and day by day. If you do this in a waking state then your lack of sleep will not be so fatiguing because, as we have said before, your main need for sleep is so that you may be in harmony with the teaching which you need in order for your spirit to be whole.

Does this aid you, my brother?

C: Yes. I have another question *(inaudible)* during the daylight hours *(inaudible)* sleep *(inaudible)* mostly awake *(inaudible)* any difference *(inaudible)*?

I am Latwii. My brother, there is a substantial physiological difference between night sleep and day sleep among your species due to the diurnal rhythms of *(inaudible)*. It is possible to lessen severity of the damage caused by turning your schedule …

(Pause)

(Carla channeling

I am Latwii, and extend greetings to the one known as [Carla.] We will continue through this instrument. It is possible to lessen the severity of the effect of these changes in diurnal rhythm by means of creating as darkened a portion of the living area as possible for the purpose of day sleeping. There are very heavy drapes, heavy shades or even that which in your density is known as black gardening plastic which may be attached to windows close to your bed so that you may feel darkness instead of light. This will help. However, the diurnal rhythms are such that a person cannot make a complete adjustment to that particular turnaround unless that person has for reasons of growth a particular affinity for the night. There are such people. We can see clearly that you are not one of them.

May we answer further, my brother?

C: No.

Is there another question?

Questioner: I'm going to be leaving Kentucky soon and moving to Oregon in the next few weeks. I would like to be able to take this skill of channeling with me so that I might be able to share the message of love and light to any who are open to it. Can you tell me any additional exercises with meditation or besides meditation that might aid me in acquiring this skill before I leave?

I am Latwii. There are two skills to learn in addition to daily meditation. One is humility. When you have learned to meditate you will understand that you cannot speak. Therefore, you are free to be a channel. Humility is one of the greatest freedoms in the universe and relieves the fever of many problems. In humility you understand what you may or may not do. When you see messengers of light, whether in a *(inaudible)*, you may speak without being concerned as to whether or not you are part of the evil. And we say to you, my brothers, you are part of the evil, for we are all one. The universe is one Being in love and in service to Itself. Many parts of that universe have become very confused, but this does not alter base reality.

There is another habit that, if embellished, may cause you to become better and better at being a clear and prayerful channel for the Creator. This, my brother, is resolve. We are aware that you have a very strong resolve for this service. Nurture that desire as you would a plant, a [cactus.] Nurture its purity, its strength. Nurture it knowing that many would rather sleep. *(Inaudible)*. As it is written in your Proverbs, "When those who turn away have done so, shake the dust from your feet and move on." For your desire must be nurtured and this can only be done by yourself. Let it burn within you, not consuming you, but flowing freely like a river of love that you may be the channel which you wish to be.

This instrument which speaks to you now prays before each channeling the prayer of St. Francis. It begins. "Lord, make me an instrument of Thy peace." It is possible that you too would find that particular arrangement of words, one which strengthens your resolve, which says use it or whatever else you may need to use in order to appreciate and conserve the desire that is within you, your soul.

Does this answer your question?

Questioner: Yes, very well. Thank you.

We thank you, my brother, very much. Is there another question?

Questioner: I was wondering, is it possible to receive information similar to what we are receiving now in a hypnotic state?

I am Latwii. We greet you, my brother. We are sorry that you missed out on all the good stuff and have to be *(inaudible)*, but we will attempt the answer to your question, for it is simply done. It is possible to hear the message of love and light riding in your car, talking with friends, going to your place of worship, sitting in a redneck bar, or in a bathroom. It is also possible in a hypnotic state. This information is not to be learned. This information is already part of you, merely something of which you may become aware. The techniques of becoming aware of this information include the use of channels such as this one and entities such as we are, but there are so many ways to begin to understand love that it is quite amazing to us that your peoples called us to come with a cry so loud it shook the heavens.

Why do you [sorrow,] where is your grief? For the answers are all about you. We only speak the most simple truths, for it is the simple truths that are the whole truth. Complexity has no part of the truth. It is written in the holy works of those of your planet with whom you are not familiar, "The way that is known is not familiar." You must go beyond any information that you get from us, any information that you get in your bathtub, or in your regular form of *(inaudible)*. Wherever you get it, my friends, go further, go beyond the ways to refine that which is unspeakable, unknowable and ineffable, and that will be the heart of love.

Does this aid you, my brother?

Questioner: Yes, it does. One more question. Are there ones who use this method to, say, send bad information and lead us away from *(inaudible)*?

I am Latwii. Yes, my brother. It is a very crowded universe. We can understand your troubled mind. That is why we emphasized before to go beyond the rules, whatever they may be. The crowded planetary spheres which you inhabit contain many, many souls whose chief delight in consciousness is to baffle, confound and confuse those who are seeking for spiritual truth, because those who seek the truth must be gullible to a certain extent. Thus, you may think of yourself as being part of "Gullible's Travels."

Therefore, if you allow hypnosis, which is often an uncontrolled situation instead of a controlled situation where you have tuned as a group and where you have experienced channels to guide you, you may well come up with some bozo from the lower astral planes who will tell you anything that you want to hear in order to speak to you. It happens quite often, especially with what this instrument would call a ouija board. Thus, we have cautioned this group before not to use the ouija board because, unfortunately, they do work. It is much better to develop one's abilities in an orderly manner, not going beyond one's ability to cope with the information they receive.

May we help you further, my brother?

Questioner: That satisfies my questions.

We are grateful to you. Is there another question at this time?

Questioner: I have one other question. In my studies I have come across a person who has known an altered state of consciousness called [Zen.] It's like *(inaudible)* has taken a person's will and *(inaudible)*. Is this what it appears to be? Am I stating it correctly?

Yes. Do you wish to understand further in this area?

Questioner: Is there anything you can add to that?

You realize, my brother, that we are very careful to maintain total free will with our own conscience. We do this for a simple reason. We care for you. The entities who manifest through instruments, putting them in a "trance" state or a state without free will, may or may not have a tendency not to care to any great extent about the precious life-force of the instrument as that particular entity understands it. Thus, we are more comfortable using the method we use.

There are very positively-oriented entities who use those who have prayed to be used in a "trance-oid" state. We are sure you are familiar with the one known as Edgar Cayce. It was his prayer to be used as he was used, and ultimately he died because of the extraordinary strain of such constant trance channeling had upon his physical being. Any entity in the spectrums of positive to negative can be an instrument who is capable of trance and there are many who get into a situation of this [kind] without realizing they haven't ability nor have they any protections necessary or any tuning provided them.

Have we helped you, my brother?

Questioner: Yes. Thank you.

Is there another question at this time?

(Pause)

We are receiving an unspoken question and would like to send a concept to the one who asks at this time, if he will be patient.

(Pause)

I am Latwii. We thank you for your patience. Sometimes there is desire *(inaudible)*. This is not a question that we wish to verbally give the answer to. Is there another question at this time?

(Pause)

I am Latwii. My friends, we thank you. We would close through the instrument known as Jim. I will transfer at this time.

(Jim channeling)

I am Latwii, and we would say in closing that the tasks which each of you have set for yourselves are worthy tasks, and we would aid you in every way that it is possible for us to do so in the accomplishing of your tasks. Your work will not be easy, but you will discover the greatest rewards in serving your brothers and sisters on your planet at this time. Your world has never needed your service more, and it is with this knowledge that you must go forth each in your own way and be of whatever service you can be. I am known to you as Latwii and I leave you in the light and love of our infinite Creator. Adonai, my friends. ♣

L/L Research

L/L Research is a subsidiary of Rock Creek Research & Development Laboratories, Inc.

P.O. Box 5195
Louisville, KY 40255-0195

www.llresearch.org

Rock Creek is a non-profit corporation dedicated to discovering and sharing information which may aid in the spiritual evolution of humankind.

ABOUT THE CONTENTS OF THIS TRANSCRIPT: This telepathic channeling has been taken from transcriptions of the weekly study and meditation meetings of the Rock Creek Research & Development Laboratories and L/L Research. It is offered in the hope that it may be useful to you. As the Confederation entities always make a point of saying, please use your discrimination and judgment in assessing this material. If something rings true to you, fine. If something does not resonate, please leave it behind, for neither we nor those of the Confederation would wish to be a stumbling block for any.

CAVEAT: This transcript is being published by L/L Research in a not yet final form. It has, however, been edited and any obvious errors have been corrected. When it is in a final form, this caveat will be removed.

© 2009 L/L Research

Meditation Meeting
July 27, 1980

(Carla channeling)

I am Hatonn, and I greet you in the love and light of the infinite Creator. We were attempting to contact the one known as E, and feel that we made good contact, and are happy that we are continuing to progress in giving him confidence at this time.

It is my great blessing to share with you in the stream of your life at this time. We have been too long away from you, my friends, not in thought, but in our work, and it is truly a great blessing to us to return to you.

There are several thoughts we would like to share with you this evening, as there have been some things upon people's minds that they may wish to think about. We will attempt to work with a few of them.

We know that you are all familiar with a prayer that many of you have learned as children which is called "The Lord's Prayer," and we wonder if you might not reconsider this prayer with the understanding that we may have to offer, for it is truly a central and worthwhile teaching of one of your great teachers, but it has been much misunderstood by your peoples, for it has led them to believe that there is an entity outside of themselves, bearing no resemblance or connection to themselves, to whom they pray and beseech assistance. My friends, to the best of our understanding, this is not so.

This prayer begins, "Our Father, which art in heaven." That is to say "Love, which is in light."

"Hallowed be Thy name." This is to say "Holy be the name of Creation"—the word that means "all that there is."

"Thy Kingdom come"—the Kingdom of love, "Thy will be done"—the will of love, "on Earth as it is in Heaven"—as it is in Heaven, the kingdom of love."

"Give us this day our daily bread." You must ask this, my friends, as a symbol for all of the needs and supplies of the illusion, for in the physical body you have many needs which must be fulfilled—food and drink and shelter. But love is the source of all supply, and it is *(inaudible)*.

"Forgive us our trespasses, as we forgive those who trespass against us." May love prevail, both in the giving of forgiveness and the gracious acceptance of the forgiveness of others for the wrongs which you have done.

This, my friends, is perhaps the hardest of the phrases to live. *(Inaudible)*. For some it is difficult to forgive, but for most it is easier to forgive than be forgiven, for you do not wish to understand this love, and to understand that you are in need of love, that you have not, without love, become the perfect being that you can be and that you are in reality. You are [so] caught up in the illusion, my friends, that you forget how foolish it is, and how foolish each entity is as he reacts within that illusion. But we ask you to forgive and, more than this, we ask you to accept your own failings, and to accept the forgiveness of yourself and others when you have failed to manifest perfection.

"Lead us not into temptation, but deliver us from evil." You are aware, my friends, that you yourself planned the lessons that you would learn in this lifetime. Each of those lessons requires a testing, and each testing will be difficult. As you pray to love, it is not that you ask to avoid the lessons, but that you ask the grace of love, the spirit of that which is light, to enter into you and to lead you into a wiser, higher self, that protects you from misunderstanding the test, and from misperceiving the testing.

"For Thine is the Kingdom, and the Power, and the Glory forever." And whose is "Thine," my friends? To whom do we think of? The Kingdom is part of ourselves. That which you know as Christ-consciousness is a spark that dwells within each of us. To center yourself upon the Christ within is to then be perfectly poised for action in any direction, in any way that may be needed. It is to have your burden lifted, that you may be light of heart, and merry, and full of love for mankind.

We ask you in your meditations and your actions, my friends, to find this love, and to see this love, not only in your friends, but in the homeless, and those who have no friends, and those who are troubled. They need Christ's love, and you can offer yourself. You need not say or do anything to be radiant with the love of Christ-consciousness as you may wish to call it, for if you are centered in service and in love, all those who need you will be drawn to you, and all that they need from you will be given.

I would transfer this contact to the instrument known as Jim.

(Jim channeling

I am Hatonn, and I greet you once again in the love and light of the infinite Creator. We have been talking about those things that have been on the minds of many of you over the past few days and weeks, and we would continue in this vein and speak of another of what may be termed your concerns in these ever-changing days that each of your people are experiencing now in your world. It is said that we must know who we are in reality in order to become one with all that is, with each of our fellow creatures in the universe. We say to you that your identity is of utmost importance to you at this time, your true identity that resides in every cell of your being and every part of the universe. This identity is one which you have carried with you throughout eons of what you call time and it is an identity that you shall continue to carry with you and that you shall continue to realize more and more fully as you evolve in your conscious awareness. It is an identity that is ever-expanding love. It is at its core, love, which manifests in as many ways as can be imagined.

Each of you, as you perceive the world around you, as you perceive the means of the interaction that you share with your brothers and sisters, each of you has within your being that central source of love. And each of you perceives this in your own unique way. We would ask that you search more and more diligently and finely, for that identity of love within yourself. We would ask you to look carefully and intently as to how that central source of love resides within your being, and more, how that central source of love is manifested in your daily interaction with your brothers and sisters, with all creatures, and all creations of your reality, for we say to you that this central source of love which is within your being is also within the being of each of your brothers and sisters, in fact, is within the being of each particle of creation upon your plane.

When you fully realize this simple fact, that all about you is the creation of the Father, then you have the understanding and the realization to carry forth that manifestation of that love on a conscious level in each of your interactions with all whom you meet in your daily life. It is this carrying into action of the realization of love at the core of your life, at the core of your identity, that is the key to your growth individually and as a people in your reality.

Each of you now seeks in your own way to know more fully that identity that is yours and how you uniquely manifest that which is love. We seek to aid you in your efforts in every way possible.

We suggest that at any time you might wish our assistance in your meditations, in your realization of your identity, that you simply call upon our aid and we will be with you to give our aid in whatever way is possible.

Seek to know more and more fully that central source of your self which is love. Seek and ye shall find. Ye shall find that it is an ever-expanding joy, an ever-expanding mystery.

We would now transfer this contact to the one known as Carla. I am Hatonn.

(Carla channeling)

I am again with this instrument. We will pause at this time that I and my brother Laitos may pass among you to aid you in your conditioning. If you will mentally request our presence we will be with each of you. I am Hatonn.

(Pause)

I am again with this instrument. I am Hatonn, and I greet you again in love and light. Before I leave this instrument I would attempt to exercise a few of those who are here. I would attempt to speak a few sentences through the one known as C. I would transfer to him at this time if he will relax. I am Hatonn.

(Carla channeling)

I am again with this instrument. We would now attempt to condition the one known as E and speak a few sentences through him if he would relax and refrain from analysis. I am Hatonn.

(E channeling)

I am Hatonn, and I greet you in love and light of the infinite Creator. It is a pleasure to use this instrument to share our thoughts with you. I am Hatonn.

(Carla channeling)

I am Hatonn. I am again with this instrument. It is a pleasure to have made vocal contact with the one known as E. And we thank him for his service. I would at this time attempt to condition and speak a few words through the one known as L *(inaudible)* if he would relax and refrain from analysis and speak the thoughts which come into his head. I am Hatonn.

(Pause)

I am again with this instrument. We are finding the one known as S to be a very sensitive instrument, therefore we must make adjustments in our vibratory contact to be more comfortable to the one known as S. We will do so at this time. We will again transfer to the one known as S. I am Hatonn.

(Pause)

I am again with this instrument. I am Hatonn. And I thank each of you for allowing us to work with you. It is a great privilege for us to do so. We would leave this time commending you always to the love and light of the One Who is all Creation. Look into your own eyes and you will see Him, for in all of us He dwells, the Father of love, the Mother of light. I leave you in all that there is, for indeed you have nowhere else to be. We are with you there. Adonai, my friends. I am known to you as Hatonn.

I am Latwii, and I greet this assemblage with great happiness in the love and light of the infinite Creator. It is my privilege to be asked by the brothers and sisters of Hatonn to be with you in case you would like to ask any questions at this time. Please speak forth if you have a question.

Questioner: I would like to know if there is any way that you can aid in the physical diagnosis *(inaudible)*?

We of the Confederation, my sister, cannot work with the specific diagnosis of ailments having to do with the physical vehicle, although we are able to lend our healing light to those who are troubled in healing spirit, though we have planetary consciousnesses as the one known as Nona who sometimes do work with those who have need of spiritual healing. However, because of the necessity for complete free will in your illusion, we cannot ask the patterns to be changed. You yourself are responsible for your own physical vehicle, as is this instrument and as are each of you. Thus each of you is ultimately responsible for healing yourselves if that is to be done.

There are consciousnesses within your planetary vibration which can be requested by what you would call angelic means, and these levels of consciousness may help in diagnosis. They have the right to do that because they are part of your planetary consciousness and therefore may deal with the various components of planetary consciousness as it is found in your illusion. Thus we suggest in your meditations that you ask for that level of help which aided those healers such as the man you know as Edgar Cayce. This level will be of much more help to you than that aid which we can give which heals the spirit and gives the spirit then the task of rallying and beginning to work on the pattern which has developed from its electrical body.

May we answer you further, my sister?

Questioner: No.

Is there another question at this time?

Questioner: Along those lines, I have a friend who is a psychologist and she feels that she sees some of her clients while she sleeps and feels that they might be traveling to her astrally. I'm wondering if it is possible or even natural for those in our healing professions to heal some of their clients while they sleep as well?

I am aware of your question. There is a subtle difference between what is occurring and what you have said which we will attempt to give to this instrument.

The healing process is, as we have said, caused totally by the patient, with the healer acting as a spiritual friend who, in dialogue, stimulates the patient in the art of realization of the self and thus the patient begins to mend. During the waking context much occurs on many levels. There is much disappointment due to the fact that each patient expects the healer to be wiser or better than the patient. This is not so, for we are all children along the same path. These disappointments, when understood correctly, can break through great blocks which have blocked the growth of the individual spiritually, mentally or physically. When the patient begins to understand the vulnerability of the healer, begins to feel the friendship of two pilgrims on the path, he can then begin to forgive others for disappointments in the past and begin the self-healing process that starts with the soul and only ends with the body.

In sleep, the patient and the healer are working out on deeper levels those conflicts which will aid both the patient and the healer. For does the healer not learn as much from the patient as the patient learns from the healer?

May we answer you further, my brother?

Questioner: No. Thank you very much.

We thank you. Is there another question at this time?

Questioner: Along those same lines, I would like more specific information on those angelic spirits who will aid us if we request them to during our meditations for healing our spirits.

I am Latwii. Ah, my brother, you want information about angels. This is a big subject and has been the cause of many a theologian to write great things throughout the centuries. But it is basically very simple. There are those who have gone through [cycles] on this planet in your third density, who have learned the ways of service and of love, and who have graduated from your third density. Some of them have graduated from the next density and some even the next but have chosen to stay with your planet. These are what you would call angelic beings. Some of them are most high. All of them are totally oriented towards service, and they are available to those who seek them—as teachers, as guides, as healers.

If you quest for spiritual healing you may ask of the Confederation that the one known as Nona come to you and this entity which you would call female will be with you and you will feel a touch as soft as the softest dream *(inaudible)*. You also have a great deal of help from your own angelic presences, for you have your own guardian and as you become more aware of them you will be able to ask them for help. We cannot tell you who they are, but if you ask to see them, their faces will come to you in meditation and you will be aware of their kindly selves.

There are also inner masters whom you seek through silence, through self-discipline, and through constancy of the ideas that you have set for yourself on your path. These masters will make themselves known to you only as you are ready and we urge you not to request their path unless you wish to commit yourself to a truly straight and narrow path, for the work of the initiate bears the heavy consequences of knowledge. That is to say, that which is known must be acted upon. If you know and do not act the consequences are as grave as if you threw a live grenade and it was thrown back at you.

(Pause)

I am Latwii, and we understand from scanning this instrument's mind that there used to be a lot of conditioning in these meetings, but now the only conditioning occurs in your tape recorders. If you are through clicking we will once again open the meeting to questions.

Is there another question at this time?

Questioner: I have a question from M. He would like to know what his homeopathic constitutional remedy is and how much of it he should take.

We greet your friend and our brother and ask you to explain to him that Latwii does not make house calls. You must understand that we cannot deal with this type of information using this type of contact. We are sorry.

Is there another question?

Questioner: Can you tell me anything about the planet called Krishnaloca?

Yes, my sister, we can tell you some but not all that you wish to know. The vibration of which you speak is a high one, far from your density and all vibrations have their place in the universe. In this density planets, suns and even galaxies are not named but the vibration is extremely full of the heavenly consciousness of love. Let us say that it is very near the end of the spectrum of maya, the very end of the spectrum which you call in one of your languages Kamaloca and the vibration of which you speak is very close to that of power, the power of love and the fire of light.

May we answer you further?

Questioner: Yes, one more question. How are you related in time to that place which you just mentioned—Kamaloca? Is that how you pronounced it?

That is close, my sister. We are using this instrument's vocabulary and she is aware of a term Kamaloca. It is not precise, but we have difficulty dealing with precise vibrational names and this is what we are dealing with here, for each word is a vibration. Thus, even our name itself has been chosen by us to vibrate in a certain light or love pattern that may blend in with your meditation in such a way as to be beneficial to you.

Our relationship to that which is Kamaloca is that we are in a light density which is less than full of perfect light. It would seem perfect to those who have not seen beyond where we are, but we know that there is more to learn and more, shall we say, to lose, for we wish to become the sea and at present we are still bubbles upon the waves. We retain an individual consciousness and although we experience the blending of our consciousness with what you would call the divine energy of love and light we find ourselves frequently back in our self. We find ourselves from time to time still engaged in duality, thus we have not yet reached what this instrument would call Kamaloca, but are in one of the myriads of universes which dwell within the Father's creation, somewhat below perfection; somewhat more advanced in understanding than your density, but, most importantly, beings like yourself. We are all one. You may be whoever you wish.

May we answer you further?

Questioner: No.

We thank you. Is there another question at this time?

Questioner: Can you tell me what some of the earth tremors portend?

As you know, my sister, the earth tremors are a part of the pattern that we, as members of the Confederation, have been speaking of for years, so that the fundamental causes are generally widely known. That is, the internal heat of the planet has become intense and unbalanced due to the friction between the peoples of this plane. The immediate cause of the tremors has to do with a series of shocks which travel along the various faults which span this continent and are being activated by the volcanic eruptions in your northwest. There are also difficulties, as we have said before, which may very probably show up more to the south and to the east. Does this answer your question?

Questioner: Yes.

Is there another question at this time?

S: *(Mostly inaudible. The sense of the question was, "Do you see California sliding into the ocean in the near future?")*

I am Latwii. That is correct. The coast of what you call California will in all probability not remain intact for very many more years. This is widely known by your government, which has been relocating to the east for some time. The disaster, as it will be called by your people, will be profound. However, it will not precisely slip into the sea, never to be seen again. There will be islands which remain above sea level, so that it shall not completely disappear. However, we would not advise long-term planning on that particular part of the continent unless you have a great desire to experience this transition, for it has some probability for rearranging the molecules of your physical body in such a way that you will change densities.

(Laughter)

S: Thank you, Latwii. I love the Coast, but not enough to sacrifice my physical body.

My sister, we believe that you have time for the trip you have in mind.

(Laughter)

S: Whewww!

Is there another question at this time?

L: I would like to ask a question. I have recently learned that our area sits atop a major fault. Is there any information that you can give us about the future events concerning earthquakes along that fault?

I am Latwii. We do not wish for you to take this information without a grain of salt, for you must understand that we deal at this time with a multiple timeline, for in actuality, there is no time. But your people have not at this time—but your people have not decided what your particular future, shall we say, should be. We are looking at this point at probability, not certainty. It will occur during some point in the late, what this instrument would term, '80s or early '90s, that you will have a profound rearrangement of some of the valleys in which you live. However, observing these timelines, it is also a large probability that other factors will profoundly affect this area before natural disasters cause great difficulties.

That is to say, the economic, as you would call it, difficulties, due to the delicacy of your transportation system, and your system of bartering, cause your society to be in some danger of breaking down. Many of you feel that without knowing why, and, therefore, are in your own way preparing to live a simple life, being of help to others, being as self-sufficient as possible, and learning to do without some of those things to which you have been accustomed in your orderly life. We feel that this instinct is a good one, and, if you wish to survive in physical form, we encourage you in following these feelings that you may have.

You must understand that we do not have a bias towards the preservation of your physical vehicle. And we ask you to understand that, in the days that are ahead, you must feel in your own heart what the Creator wishes of you on any day. If you are to pass from this density, let it be a joyful passing, and let no thought of disaster cross your mind, for this is an illusion, my friends, and if you walk through the valley of death, it is truly written that you need fear no evil, for you are not alone, and those faithful to you always will wait for you.

Some of you have long lives to live upon this sphere at this time during the transition, but you must take it a day at a time, letting each day be guided by the Creator within. As my brother, Hatonn, has said, your identity is that which is love within you. You will know what to do. The Father has work for you to do. Therefore do not be attached to living, to surviving, or to any facet of the illusion, but only to remembrance of love, and your devotion to keeping that spark within you, which is love, radiant and radiating.

We realize that many of you are wondering whether this area is a good one for ultimate survival. We must say to you that, although this area is relatively good, there is no area which is totally safe, because most of your future lines contain the certainty of a polar shift, making it highly probable that, within your lifetime, the polarity of the planet will alter. There will not be a safe place at that moment of time. Thus, enjoy yourselves. Do what you can, for yourselves and others, but we do not urge you to go heavy on the freeze-dried foods, as this instrument would say, but rather look to service to others, for what you need will be provided if your heart is full of the Creator.

May we answer you further, my brother?

L: I will ask one more question. I can understand the effects of the Earth change, but not the order. Can you explain that to me?

I am Latwii. We wish we had a better instrument for this one, but we will attempt to use this philosophical, unscientific one for this contact. We are showing her a spinning top. It spins, but it is not straight. Therefore, it wobbles. Do you understand this concept?

L: Yes

That is the status of your planet at this time. During the shift of polarity, the wobble will increase to the point where it will be self-correcting. At that point, the entire top, shall we say, will change its orientation with respect to your solar body.

Do you understand this concept, my brother?

L: Yes, thank you.

We thank you for understanding us through this instrument. Is there another question at this time?

E: Latwii, can you tell us of where the new—geographically, where the new north and south poles will be? Is that within your power?

Yes, my brother, it is within our power, but this instrument is so weak in geography that we will have difficulty in communicating.

(Pause)

We are having difficulty communicating this concept. This instrument is able to see both of your poles being somewhat warm, and your temperate zones being somewhat cold.

(Laughter)

But she does not know the names of the places that the magnetic north will be. We are sorry we cannot use this instrument. We will attempt at this time to transfer to the one known as Jim, for his mind is better furnished for an answer to this question. I am Latwii.

(Jim channeling)

I am Latwii. I am with this instrument. We are attempting to show this instrument a more precise location of the poles.

(Pause)

But, again, we must conclude that the instrument would benefit by more study of geography.

(Laughter)

We are sorry that we are not able to give you a definite location of the poles after they shift. We will now transfer the contact back to the one known as Carla. I am Latwii.

(Carla channeling)

I am Latwii. I do not know what to do with these people.

(Laughter)

I am sorry that we cannot give you this information, for it is not, as you would say, classified or particularly important, since when the shift comes it will not matter where you stand, but we simply cannot speak through these instruments. There is the further problem that, by the year in which this in all probability will occur, there will be in all probability significant changes in the land masses. So we do not wish to give these instruments too hard a time.

(Laughter)

Is there another question?

E: *(The following is paraphrased.)* We've read a book called *The Earthquake Generation*. In that there's a description of 200 m.p.h. winds for about three days or so after the polar shift. Is that correct?

You understand, my brother, that we of Latwii speak only of possibilities. The probability is that that is a modest estimate of these facts, and that the effects of the shift would be even harsher. We would ask that you realize that those things that are written in scientific writings such as the one that you mentioned and in books such as Revelation are both accurate and unimportant; accurate in that they speak of something that may happen within your illusion, unimportant because you must follow that which you will retain in your person as you progress on your infinite journey. Thus, seek first the Kingdom, and all else will follow. We realize that this is a cliché, but we cannot emphasize it enough, my brother.

May we answer you further?

E: Not at this time, Latwii. Thank you.

We thank you. Is there another question at this time?

S: *(The following is paraphrased.)* Yes, Latwii. I have seen reports of many UFOs in Brazil. Why are there so many space ships in Brazil? Is Brazil a special place, or are the people more ready to have the experience, or what?

My sister, there are two reasons for the appearance of our craft in the skies and in the waters of your country. In the first place, we are able to manifest much more freely to cultures who do not disbelieve our presence or feel threatened or confused by it. Among your people, it is understood that we are ships of light and that we have to do with the vibrations of the sun. Therefore, we can appear much more often. There is a portion of our survey group, which is connected with the Confederation, but which does not speak with groups such as yours, which has an underwater base off the coast of your country, and therefore, these ships are quite often seen by your people, entering the water. It would not be possible to occur in a culture which is so filled with the skepticism that the culture of this particular area offers.

Is there any other question at this time?

S: *(The following is paraphrased)* Yes. I felt your presence before but I could not speak any words. I don't know what happened, but I felt your presence and I knew that you were coming through, but I could not speak. My English is not so good.

Yes, my sister. I am Latwii. I am aware of your question. You were perfectly correct in that we were speaking to you and that you were receiving. If you had channeled in your native tongue, you would have been able to say our words. However, you did not wish to confuse the group, so it was simply the fault of our brothers and sisters of Hatonn that they did not encourage you to speak a few words in your native tongue before you attempted English. We will, in any future contact, encourage you to speak first in your mother language, and then, and only then, in a learned language. We understand it is difficult for you. Does this answer your question?

S: Yes, thank you very much.

Is there another question at this time?

Jim: I have a question about relationships that I've been wondering about for some time. It seems that learning happens so much quicker in a relationship with another person, a mated type of relationship, but then it seems that there might also be times when not being in a relationship, being alone, might be proper. I'm wondering if there might be any generalized rules or laws of learning that would recommend being in relationships or not being in relationships. Is there one better way of learning? Alone, or with another?

I am Latwii. I do not know if I have the wisdom to answer this question properly, but I will attempt it.

There is an infinity of individualized persons of the one Consciousness. Each individualized person of the one Consciousness is placed by free will into this particular illusion to learn certain lessons. These have to do with love, the understanding of love, and with giving of love by dwelling in service with others. There are some people who cannot learn alone, for they do not have the keys to wisdom, and thus they must study the ways of love. There are some who do not have the keys to love, but must dwell alone and study the ways of wisdom. Love and wisdom are the two poles.

Perhaps we might say that the most balanced of the ways of learning is to find in a relationship both the companionship that enables two individuals to be of service to each other, and the understanding that enables each to be, along with his or her needs for wisdom, for aloneness, for meditation, or for whatever he or she needs that the other cannot give.

No two individuals are created alike, so there is no one answer to your question. Not all are made to be mated, nor are all made to dwell along the lonely paths of the one who walks alone. There are many shades of learning, of love, and of wisdom. You may take your choice. You will find, in a mated relationship, the most powerful means of balancing your own nature, so that the love and the wisdom become balanced, for truly it is only when this occurs that you can become what you would call a master.

But in most cases, one person does not become a master, but two, helping each other. This you have already intuited, and yet you wonder at your need to be alone, and at the fate which seems to ask you to be alone. Relax, for all is well. The creation gives you what you need. And when you have absorbed what you need, from this one environment, there will be a powerful attraction to the next phase of your learning, and you will not have to seek it out by thought and analysis, for it shall, as this instrument would say, "hit you between the eyes." For that is the way of the Creator. If you can be patient, your way will always be made quite, quite clear.

May we answer you further, my brother?

Jim: No. Thank you very much.

Is there another question at this time?

(Pause)

I am Latwii, and it has been a great privilege for me to share my thoughts with you, foolish as they are. I ask you all also to be foolish: to love without reason, to be happy without cause, and to give without receiving. Feel free, my children, for you are all one with the infinite source of love. We leave you in that light and love. I am known to you as Latwii. Adonai vasu borragus.

L/L Research

Meditation Meeting
August 3, 1980

(Carla channeling

I am Hatonn, and I greet you in the love and the light of the infinite Creator. It gives me great pleasure to welcome each of you and especially those who are new to this group, for it is a great privilege to be able to make contact with our brothers upon your sphere who are seeking to know the same truth that we are seeking to know. We look down upon your sphere at this time from a distance of approximately, as this instrument would say, eight of your miles. It is mostly in shadow at this time from our vantage point. Within those shadows, my friends, are many, many peoples who have largely concluded their business for the day. Many are sleeping. Many are not yet sleeping, but are distracting themselves. Some contemplate the weighty problems of their possessions and a few, my friends, like you seek to know the truth.

We hope that we can tell you enough that you can find the key to the door on the other side of which lies the truth. That is our highest hope. No more than that can we hope to do, for you have the key already, but you have largely lost the ability and the will to use it. You must understand that so much, my friends, of what you think and do is in vain, pertaining only to a daily life that is transient. What of your wisdom have you not found turned to folly? Of how many of your possessions have you not grown tired? How many of your words remain shining, and how many have become tarnished or forgotten? How many lives have you touched today, my friends?

You see, my friends, within the illusion that you now enjoy, it is useless to attempt to be of service by yourself. You cannot store up enough possessions to be of service to yourself or to others. You cannot store up enough goodwill in your heart to be pleasant of your own accord. For those of us with free will, my friends, have that fatal weakness of those with free will: we are separated from infinity by our self-consciousness.

The way to discover the key of which we spoke … ah yes, my friends, that lies beyond the illusion. That is not in vain, nor it is a striving after shadows, although it may seem to be the only thing that you do that is not real, and that my friends, is of course, meditation. In meditation, day by day, month by month, year by year, you develop within yourself a certain bias or means of approaching the illusion. You find yourself equipped with a connection to infinite supplies of patience, goodwill, kindness and the many other fruits of love.

Look at your life, my friends. You are looking at a looney tune. It is not your fault, that is your vibration. Put the captions under the comics, smile to yourself, and proceed, for there is more. There is something behind the cartoon. There *is* a reality which is unnameable, unknowable, ineffable and unspeakable. However, my friends, it can be experienced and shared, and this is where we go beyond, and I say far beyond, my friends, the wisdom of your peoples. For they do not believe that there is a possibility that your life could possibly mean anything. Many of your peoples honestly cannot conceive of a reality greater than the vanity and the folly which they now enjoy.

We assure you, my brothers and sisters, there is a reality, and then another, and then another—each one clearer than the last, each one truer to the original Thought of love. And as you meditate, as your mind and your heart become accustomed to the vibrations of silence and inward possession of yourself, you will begin to ascend more and more into these realms of higher reality until you yourself may see, without being disturbed, the folly of this particular vibration. You will not be disturbed because you will see it as an opportunity to witness, by the love that you show forth, the name of the Creator which you carry in your eyes and in your hands, as you give and receive love and service with each other.

It is written in your holy works, "Store not up for yourselves treasures upon Earth where moth and rust corrupt and thieves may break in and steal, but rather store up for yourselves treasures in heaven and you will have the better part." Have you stored up treasures, my friends? Which department do they fit into? In your daily life, take the time to give of yourself in meditation to the Creator who never leaves you. As you give yourself to that consciousness, It will give Itself too in infinite amount to you.

At this time, I would speak a few words through the one known as E. I am Hatonn.

(E channeling

I am Hatonn, and I greet you in the love and the light of the infinite Creator and it is a pleasure to speak to you through this instrument. I am Hatonn.

I am Laitos, and I also greet you in love and light as do my brothers and sisters of Hatonn. It is my privilege to work with each of you who request our conditioning and aid in deepening your meditative state. If you will mentally request the presence of Laitos, I will at this time move among you and make my presence known to each of you. I am Laitos.

(Carla channeling

I am again with this instrument. We have been attempting to speak to the one known as Jim without using this instrument to transfer contact. We feel we came very close to making the transfer without any intermediate help and we are very glad. At this time we will transfer to the one known as Jim. I am Laitos.

(Jim channeling

I am Laitos, and I am with this instrument. It is once again a pleasure to be able to share a few of our thoughts through this instrument. We have always offered our assistance and will continue to offer our assistance to any who ask for our conditioning while in meditation. We seek to serve those of your people by introducing them to our vibrations. This allows those who request our aid to experience a deeper and more probing meditation. It is a way of, shall we say, stepping up the frequency of your vibrations and opening a doorway, or as this instrument would say, a channel for our thoughts to flow through.

By aiding any who ask in their meditations, we are grateful to be able to aid each in their journey to their source. For each of your peoples now, in some way, are feeling the necessity for making that pilgrimage to their own inner knowing, their own well-known, yet long-forgotten, home. It is always a joy for us to be of service to such pilgrims who wish to make this most meaningful of all journeys, the journeys to the infinite Creator, from which we all spring and draw our energies.

May we say once again that should you request our aid at any time in your meditations, we will be most happy to lend that aid, for such service is our purpose among your people now, and is a great joy for us to give. For as you all know, and are discovering in more fullness, the more you give unto your brothers and sisters, unto all creation, the more you receive in knowledge and growth and love. For are we not all one, and when we give to another, do we not also receive in some degree?

We would now transfer our contact to the one known as Carla. I am Laitos.

(Carla channeling

I am with this instrument. I am Laitos. I thank you for allowing us to work with you and urge you to call upon us at any time. We are but those who wish you well. Adonai, my friends. We leave you in love and light and are always with you if you request it in meditation. I am Laitos.

I am Latwii. I must adjust this instrument. I am too strong for this instrument, if you will be patient. I … I … I am Latwii. I am Latwii. How are you all this evening, my friends? We are so very happy to be here. We greet you in love and light. Halleluiah, my friends, we think this is wonderful. Hello, how are you? We greet you. Thank you. We are so glad to be with you.

We have been listening to the messages of our brothers as they come through these instruments and we have been very inspired. We find that your peoples, even though they are much too serious, certainly do mean well, and we think that you are very good people. We were wondering if we could perhaps be of service to you this evening by answering your questions, even though we realize that since we are all one being, it is like a stomach asking an ear, "How are you today?" but still, we would like to offer ourselves to you at this time. For what little knowledge that we may have, may we invoke the light and love of the Creator in our honest attempt to be of service to you.

Is there a question at this time?

Questioner: It has come to my attention that many of my friends and myself have found difficulty in emotional relationships within the past week. Is there a special form of work being done on the Earth that is causing this effect?

I am Latwii. My brother, we must answer you in two parts. The first is that there are methods being worked on which will alter the emotional state of individuals. However, my brother, these are instruments of war and are not used on civilians in the locality in which you are now residing at this time.

For the most part, my brother, difficulties in emotional relationships must indicate to the serious student of himself that there is work to be done upon the self. You must understand that there are no problems outside of the self and that if you find a difficulty in dealing with what you perceive as another person, this is because you have not yet realized that not only is that other person yourself, but that you are creating in your mind a scenario or a play in which this problem takes place. This can be rewritten. You have the free choice at any moment of time to perceive the game, the play, the scenario, and rewrite your lines. This will take a bit of time, some effort upon your part, some well-directed meditation, and contemplation following meditation. However, you will find that it is an unerring fact that all problems are of your own manufacture. The world in which each of you live, my brothers and sisters, is your own private universe. Nothing from the outside may come in to harm you; only your own perceptions and thoughts can harm you. If you are being hurt, you must examine those thoughts and those perceptions and discover the separation that is producing disharmony.

Does this answer your question, my brother?

Questioner: Yes, it does.

Is there another question at this time?

Questioner: Yes, Latwii, in relation to what you just said, does that apply to everyone on this planet?

I am Latwii. Yes, my brother. All living things are responsible for their own individual perceptions. We feel that there is more to this question than you have expressed, and we are open to a further question if you wish.

Questioner: Well, I have a question in regards to that, and that is then, as there is so much suffering in this world, I would like to know if many entities incarnating on this planet were in need of the suffering.

That is correct, my brother. Many people, as you call them, choose situations which seem to be of some degree of suffering. This is because they will learn what they need to learn, not in this illusion which is evanescent, but in a higher understanding, which is not so short-lived. They choose these situations for the learning. However, during the process of incarnation, the oversoul blankets itself as does a man in a shroud, hiding in the shadows, so that the individual does not remember why he desired the lessons that he is now attempting to learn. Therefore, the challenge to understand the lesson and to learn the lesson that is presented by the situation in which you find yourself. The lesson is always one away from separation and towards love; away from attachment and towards love; away from what you call love and towards the burning desire and joy that is truly love.

You have a birthright of freedom. There is no situation, no matter how ghastly to the senses of your physical eyes and ears that is not rich in possibility to the immortal soul. Suffering is but for the moment and is full of purpose. There are those who do not need to learn lessons involved with suffering; they need instead to learn to conquer idleness, wealthiness, or some other desire which in the past has karmically led them to working out on this plane the desires that have held them back and kept them from being free. Therefore, you may see many things as forms of suffering that are not understood in your world as suffering, and you may see many things that seem to be filled with suffering that in truth are being used to learn precious lessons that will aid the traveler a bit more along what is truly a straightened path, narrow and rocky, but full nevertheless of the joy of learning and of sharing.

We understand, my brother, your compassion for those who suffer. Suffer then also; let them fully into your heart and feel what they feel. That is what the teacher known as Jesus did. It was a simple act, but it seems to mean a great deal to your peoples. He could not take the suffering away. He could share it, and one look at those sad eyes would help many to understand why those who knew this teacher were so devoted to him.

Does this answer your question, my brother?

Questioner: Yes, thank you, Latwii.

I thank you, my brother. Is there another question at this time?

Questioner: I have a question about the type of contact that is made in channeling. It is said that the ideal contact is made up of 30% of the instrument's own thoughts and experiences and words, and 70% from the Confederation. I am wondering, of the instrument's 30%, where does this information come from. Is it from the conscious, the subconscious, the memory? Could you shed some light on that?

We can, my brother, but it may not be totally sensible. Because of the fact that each individual's mind works so differently, that when we work in an individual's mind, it is like learning an entirely new computer system, shall we say. The electrical impulses are not in any two cases formed in the same way. There are minds whose intuition is linked very closely with conscious thought. There are other minds who have almost no memory, but whose day-by-day sensations and thoughts are as clear as a brook and we can use those things. Other minds are wired in such a way that there is a very large amount to retrieve from memory of those things thought and read. This instrument is of that type, which among your peoples would be called intellectual. The only unfortunate thing about this instrument is that her fields of knowledge are not particularly those of the Renaissance person and so many questions go completely from one ear to the other without stopping in any way shape or form. Therefore, we have difficulty.

In each case, we use what there is to use. We begin with a vocabulary that must be the instrument's, for we give to the instrument only concepts. The instrument must find the words to speak what is given. We also attempt to scan the instrument's knowledge, books, experiences and thoughts to find the closest to which we would call "enlightenment," so that we may use certain touchstones within that person's experience upon which to hang a more complex framework, a more varied tapestry of thoughts.

We do this in order that we may touch as many different minds as possible in whatever size group to which we speak, so that in each mind we have struck a chord which may cause a small transformation in thinking; which may in turn cause a feeling of joy, peace or happiness; which may in turn cause each person to seek. Our desire is to challenge your desire.

Thus, we start with the instrument and we proceed therefrom, touching with the instrument's mind again, and then again, as we scan—we will correct this instrument—as we scan the minds of those within the circle to find what they may wish to listen to.

May we answer you further, my brother?

Questioner: Just one additional question. How does the number of people in the meditation group affect the clarity of the message?

This instrument understands the question.

(Side one of tape ends.)

Questioner: How do you provide the concepts? How do they come into our minds? Are they verbal or nonverbal? How do we recognize them?

I am Latwii. The nature of thought is not understood by your peoples. It is electrical in nature and is a function of your connection with what you would call your oversoul. How do you think, my brother? When you think something, how has it come into your mind. We assure you that prior to thought, you are dealing with concepts. Then, as these concepts reach a conscious state of mind, you are obliged to voice them internally in a semblance or cloak made of the words which you have learned as you have grown from a young child to a grown person. Then you are able to use these words to express this thought. However, prior to the words was the concept.

Therefore, we use that part of your connection with the oversoul, which is deep within you, and allow the concepts to rise to your mind consciously, seemingly your own thoughts. We do this in order that you may at any time refuse to speak, for we do not wish to cause you to speak if you do not wish to. There are those who use what are called trance mediums and they speak whether or not they may wish to speak. However, we prefer to provide you with a constant choice between our thoughts and silence. Even when we speak through this instrument, at any moment she could simply stop speaking. We would retire, gracefully we hope, and come again when there was a request for our presence.

Always we use the concepts and this is the nature of telepathic contact. Thus, if you wished to telepathically speak to one among your peoples who speaks in another language, you could send the word in your language and the person would receive it in his language.

Do you wish to question us further on this phenomenon, my brother?

Questioner: Not at this time, Latwii.

Is there another question at this time?

Questioner: I'd like to ask another question, Latwii, and it goes back to the information you just gave. And that is, when I'm channeling, then instead of looking for words, what I should be doing is opening up to concepts? Is that correct?

Ahh, my brother, you have been doing very well, but you must not worry about doing anything. When you channel, you speak. When a ball is thrown, you catch. Is this not so? You do not think about, "Ah, I shall place my hand here; no, I shall place my hand there; no, no, I shall move my feet and then I shall swing my hips over here and then my shoulders will be here and my elbow will be cocked this way, and then I will catch the ball." By that time, my brother, the ball will be upon the grass.

Therefore, you do not think when you catch a ball. And when we send to you a concept, it is sent and you catch, and then you throw. By this we mean you speak, and when you speak, your hand is free. That is, your mind is empty. And again you catch and again you throw. Many times this instrument has been in stark terror because someone from the Confederation, usually our brother, Hatonn, who is a little pedantic, will say, "There are three reasons why," and this instrument does not know any reasons why, and therefore she must trust that Hatonn will pull her through and tell her all three reasons.

This is what you must face when you channel—[it] is simply nothing. You do not know what will occur. Therefore, you are empty-handed, that is empty-minded, and when you think of something that feels very much like your own thought, but you know that you are not thinking, you say it. And if you say it, you will receive another thought. You have mastered this basic technique without achieving a feeling of grace while doing so. Therefore, we encourage you to relax and allow your natural, shall we say, sense of rhythm to take over and let you play the game of channeling, for it is a game that is, we hope, of some service among your peoples.

Does this answer your question, my brother?

Questioner: Yes, it does.

Is there another question at this time?

Questioner: Yes, I have a question. When I was down at the farm a long time ago, I astral-projected to the top of the ridge and when I was there, there was somebody standing on the other side of me, but something kept me from looking one way or the other to see who they were, and I was wondering if you could shed some light on it *(inaudible)*.

I am Latwii. My brother, you just made a joke. However, it would be difficult to explain to you. We are light beings. We can say to you only that you were experiencing not two, but three, of the ones who are with you. They are what you would term "angelic entities," much as we are. However, they are of your planetary sphere. When you need to understand, you are always aided by these particles of your oversoul which appear as guides or helpers. In the projected state you were able to see them. However, due to your carefully balanced projection, you were not able to move freely in your new environment. We realize that you basically already understood this and are glad to be of some help in confirming.

Does this answer your question in full, my brother?

Questioner: Yes, thank you. One more thing. I haven't been able to project in quite a while now, and I was wondering in that it used to happen to me, just, you know, just seemingly for no special reason; it just happened. I was wondering if there was any method I could use to increase the possibility of this *(inaudible)* to astral project?

I am Latwii. My brother, we do not wish to give you a hard time, but we might suggest sending your children to college. Unfortunately for your more esoteric desires, the rewards of the hard work and responsibility of loving and caring for a family will cause your physical body to need its contact with these very entities in a very deep and subconscious state. You are grasping your lessons while you sleep as quickly as you can. Therefore, you being starved, shall we say, for this vibration *(inaudible)* you do simply not have the time, as you would say, to consciously project.

If you were to find a way to spend a few hours in an environment which was conducive to relaxation on a regular basis so that you were completely rested and continually meditated each day, you would then find yourself in a more appropriate position to reawaken this particular skill which to some extent is natural for you, although not for everyone. However, it is just a trick and not particularly enlightening, so we say to you, you are learning much more by being of service than by projecting. We, however, wish you the good feelings that you experience during those moments.

Does this answer your question, my brother?

Questioner: Yes.

Is there another question at this time?

Questioner: I have a question. Several years ago I experienced the sensation of being in space. The experience has returned to my thoughts very recently. I feel that there is more that I'm supposed to learn from this experience. Is there anything you can contribute?

I am Latwii. We scan this for you. We cannot speak fully to you for you do, indeed, have some to learn and we will not, shall we say, pass out the answers before the ten-minute quiz. We simply say to you that consciousness is infinite and you will come to understand that more and more.

Is there another question at this time?

Questioner: Yes. *(Inaudible).*

I am Latwii. We are not in the correct density to see your weather. We will, if you like, zip down a couple and check it out for you.

Questioner: That's all right, it's not necessary *(inaudible).*

We can see many colors as we look through the densities, but each density colors the one below it so that we would have trouble seeing the vibrations of your weather systems until we were somewhat closer to your density.

Is there another question, my brother?

Questioner: Speaking of colors, Latwii, I remember your saying that we perceive less than one octave of color. I was under the impression that red to violet was an octave, so that or that rather, violet was the next octave higher vibration of red. Apparently, I was mistaken. Could you elaborate on that?

Only insofar as this instrument can use our concepts, my brother. You must understand that from x-ray to ultraviolet, although it is not considered to be of one octave in your physics, is indeed part of one octave in our understanding, which we would hesitate to call physics, because we understand both thought and thing as vibration. We are not sure whether we should call ourselves vibrators, due to this instrument's unfortunate connotations with that word.

However, we will not call ourselves physicists, although in your language that would be our specialty. Indeed, your octave reaches beyond what your instruments detect at this time along the ultraviolet, as you call it, although your peoples have a rather murderous understanding of the red end of the octave, which is imperceptible to the human eye beyond a certain vibration.

May we answer you further?

Questioner: Not at this time, Latwii.

Is there another question?

Questioner: Yes, I have a question. Are you familiar with, associated with the Comforter of which Jesus spoke?

I am a voice which you may call Comforter. The one which your teacher known as Jesus, or Jehoshua, spoke meant simply spirit. We are messengers of that spirit and as messengers are part of that spirit. And we are sent to comfort you, as are a host of others.

May we answer you further, my brother?

Questioner: And are you comforted as well by this spirit?

We live and breathe and are completely sustained by this spirit. We know no life but joy.

We let this sink to your heart, my brother, and then ask, may we speak further to you?

Questioner: My mouth would say yes, but I'm not sure my conscience would say it.

We leave you in the peace that you seek, my brother, for it is within you, without you, about you, and forever surrounding you.

Is there another question at this time?

I am Latwii. This instrument is growing fatigued and we feel that we have answered enough of your questions that we may take leave of her at this time.

We leave you in the glories of your sixth density. It is a beautiful place and we are watching a yellow vibration at this time, you would call it. We are traveling between yellow and a violet. It is truly beautiful as we watch them lap together. We leave you in a circle of love and joy. Let it never leave you, my friends. Let it lift you ever higher. Come join us, my friends. The kingdom awaits. Love awaits. Adonai, my friends. We leave you in love and light. I am known to you as Latwii.

Sunday Meditation
August 10, 1980

(Carla channeling

I am Latwii, and I greet you, my brothers and sisters, in the love and the light of our infinite Creator.

One of our brothers of *(inaudible)* has been working with the channels known as Jim and E, in order that they may gain confidence to be able to begin a contact without another channel being present. We hope that this has been of aid. One of these days, my brothers, you will get up your nerve and speak out, and you will find that this instrument is only playing a fair game of softball with her thoughts.

We are aware that you wonder about the oldest teacher of your group, the entity known to you as Hatonn. Again Hatonn has moved back into temporary assignment elsewhere and is at this time working with some of the leaders of the continent which you know as Africa. Therefore, it is our privilege to speak to you of philosophy for a little while, although we cannot do so with as much grace as the brothers and sisters of Hatonn. We will share what we can and with great pleasure.

We realize that there is a great priority in the lives of each of you to become a better instrument of the Creator's will, and we realize that in the vast supermarket of books and paraphernalia having to do with various people's opinions of how to achieve that goal, you may have become thoroughly confused. There are those who believe in a very strict dietary regimen, and have made that almost a necessity for leading any sort of spiritual journey.

You are aware, my friends, that you do have physical bodies and that they function very efficiently as a type of furnace with an exhaust system for the by-products. We are sure that you understand that this particular type of furnace that is your body can burn some types of fuel better than others. However, my friends, we would urge you to keep your contemplation of the importance of diet on that level, for it is truly written in one of your holy works that it is not what goeth into the mouth of a man that defileth him, but that which issues therefrom.

There are many ways of living, both secular and spiritually-oriented, whose ethics are very strict and abstemious. My friends, we say again to you [that] you were born into this experience with a physical vehicle. It is a tool. When you consider how to use it, attempt to use it with purity, with love and with no degradation to the Creator within.

We ask that you keep considerations upon this level. In other words, my friends, we are trying to cut through a great deal of dogma, as this instrument would call it, that has grown up about what might be termed the spiritual trip. You must avoid mystiques, avoid the appearance of wisdom, for my friends, in reality you do not have wisdom, the

Creator is wisdom and, insofar as you realize your part in that perfection, you *are* wisdom.

But you are as wise as a grape or a mountain or the sea. Would, my friends, sometimes that you were as quiet, as beautiful, and of as much service to others. You know, beyond a shadow of a doubt, we are sure, that because you have chosen consciously to follow a spiritual path, you are different. We have spoken of this many times, as has our brother Hatonn, and our brother *(inaudible)*. However, my friends, that difference is that you have become a servant, you have become a fool, *you* have become the one who forgives when, to the eyes of the world, there is no forgiving. You have become the one who, when there is no hope, still has faith of things unseen.

Be triumphantly foolish, my friends, and let any reputation that you may have be a lost possession, for that, my friends, is a lost treasure and a false friend. We ask you to remember what a teacher known to you as Jesus suggested to his disciples: "Go forth," he said to them, "with one robe and one pair of sandals and offer yourselves to your neighbors along the journey and, if they welcome you, give them of your substance, of your thoughts, of your love. If they do not welcome you, move on."

There is no room in those instructions for self-justification—or even a suitcase, my friends. We realize, in this day and age, your illusion has become more complex and more things are considered necessary for the simple life than were considered necessary two thousand years in the past. But as we speak about the physical plane and its influence upon your spiritual journey, we can only echo the words of one of your great writers: "Simplify, simplify, simplify."

You will, my friends, make mistakes. Remember you are fools. You will misunderstand situations, you will attempt to be of service and find that you are not truly of service, you will be too warm-hearted or too cold-hearted, and you will learn. But if you desire to be of service to others, and if you then remove from your mind the paraphernalia of excessive, complex rules and regulations, and follow instead the simple lines of purity of spirit, of honesty and love, and of totality in desire to know the Creator and to serve Him wherever He may be, then, my friends, whatever mistakes you make, it shall make no difference.

Let us move up from the physical plane to the mental. How can you become a more effective spiritual seeker by using your mind? Like your body, my friends, your mind is a tool. Unlike your body, your mind contains elements of your infinite personality, it contains biases and feelings which you have gained by experiences prior to this incarnation. Consequently, your mind is an enhanced tool, capable when used properly of aiding you greatly.

Picture a seesaw, my friends, opinion on one end, experience on the other. There will come a balance when experience has informed opinion and a lesson has been learned. Coming to that balance may be difficult or painful, but you must remain true to the effort to balance your seesaw until your experience has been met with understanding. At that point, it is time for you to take a new direction and the more sensitive that you are to your inner self, the more able your mind will be in aiding you in discovering the new vector, and then you will climb upon another seesaw, and you will have trouble and you will learn.

It is very difficult, my friends, to learn if you do not have trouble because it is difficult to get the attention of those within the physical unless they have some stimulus. Difficulties, problems and troubles are the way that this incarnation which you have chosen works in order to give you the lessons that you need. Let your mind analyze the material which you meet, let it find the balances, and let it choose the new experiences with an eye towards enhancing your own understanding and that of those around you.

The emotions, my friends, we must only give a profound but simple bow to, for they are the purest thing in your density. Attempt, then, not to have mixed emotions but to have each emotion in turn purely and beautifully, little by little, extinguishing the fires that burn out of control in anger and negativity, little by little discovering the beautiful rainbow of colors of emotions that are positive.

Lastly, we come to the wellspring of spiritual growth, and that is, of course, the spiritual self which is your connection to your primary and true personality. Stimulate that connection with regularity, and though you may not hear what the silence speaks, the connection having been made will bear fruit. You may consider your spiritual self as a great protector, for once you align yourself with it, it will shade you, feed you, and supply you with your needs. Again it was written that the one known as Jesus said, "I have food and drink that you know not of." Yes, my friends, all of you have nourishment to an infinite degree. The bread of the Kingdom awaits your attention.

There is only one catch to all this, my friends, one thing to keep you from falling asleep while we talk philosophy, and that is the uncertain nature of the spiritual path. You must see this path as a great cartoon: there will be many blank squares and then in one square there will be the Creator, and you will find enlightenment. Shall you be asleep when that edition of the funny papers comes to your house? Yes, my friends, it is an illusion but the Creator is hidden and He will pop in on you if you are awaiting Him. Therefore be ready; be ready daily.

I will leave this instrument for a brief period so that my brother *(inaudible)*, who has been with us since the beginning of the meeting, may work with the newer instruments. I am Latwii.

(Pause)

I am *(inaudible)*. I am with this instrument, I am very pleased to be with you and greet you in love and light.

We are aware of the myth of the lions that guard the temple in one of your continents. However, we have been unable to get past the lions at the gates of the temple of the mind of the one known as Jim. We had a very good contact and wish him to know that he was, indeed, being given the contact to start the channeling for us.

The vocal channel does not have an easy time beginning to channel, due to the very lack of experience that he is attempting to overcome. For, because our thoughts and your thoughts feel the same, we have only conditioning to convince the newer channel that he or she is indeed receiving a contact. And this conditioning must be requested. However, we believe that if we attempt again, we will be able to make a good contact with the one known as Jim. I am *(inaudible)*.

(Pause)

(Jim channeling

I am *(inaudible)*, and I am with this instrument. It is once again a pleasure and a privilege to be able to share with you our thoughts through this instrument. It is not always the easiest task to remove the lions from the gate of the mind, for those lions have been stationed at this gate, and the gates of many of your people, for eons of time, so to speak. These lions are those thought-forms and images which you manufacture in your daily existence to serve as a form of guide or protection, as it were, against that world which seems to be, at times, ranging from inhospitable to incomprehensible. And lions stationed at the gates of the mind frequently are seen by those who employ them as a buffering or shielding device that will protect you [from] the world or perhaps explain that world to you in a way which will set your mind at ease.

We would suggest to you, each and every one of your people, to remove these lions from your employ and to let them go their way, for you need them not. They are ornaments which are unnecessary in the architecture of your life. It is, we would suggest, a more wise choice to allow the gate to your mind and to your being and to your heart to remain open, that all which you experience in your consciousness may flow freely through this gate.

We would suggest a pause for a moment …

(Pause)

I am *(inaudible)*, and I am again with this instrument, and we greet the one known as S to our meditation.

To continue in our train of thought, we would suggest that you leave this gate to your mind and to your being and to your heart unguarded, that each experience which comes your way might be fully experienced and might become a part of that lesson of learning love which, in some way, you have chosen with each experience which you encounter in your daily lives. The lions are not needed, my friends; rather become open in all of your being, in all of your experience, become open that you might become penetrated with the love of the infinite Creator which surrounds you each and every day of your life, with every experience that you come in contact with.

We are sure that, for many of you and indeed for most at some time, you will feel a great deal of insecurity, not knowing what is coming as a lesson and a learning in your lives. But we assure you that these feelings of insecurity soon shall fade as you look at every event that occurs in your life as a learning, and you will discover that you have nothing to fear in this universe, that every event, each occurrence, is planned as part of the infinite Creator's plan, to teach you a newer or better way to find your path inward to the Creator which resides within your being. Again, may we suggest that by removing these guards from your mind, that you will learn each of those lessons which are part of your path and your way to your home, to your source, to the center of all creation.

We would now transfer this contact to the one known as Carla. I am *(inaudible)*.

(Carla channeling

I am *(inaudible)*. I am now with this instrument, and wish again to express our thanks to the instrument known as Jim, for it is truly a joy to be able to share our thoughts with you and, to us, each mind which is offered to us in love is a treasure-trove of experiences and memories and thoughts upon which we can impress our concepts, so that each instrument has a unique place and a unique function. We may say various things through various instruments that perhaps one person in the group may need to hear. For this reason we thank each of you for attempting to speak our words.

At this time we would transfer to the instrument known as E, if he would relax. I am *(inaudible)*.

(Carla channeling

I am again with this instrument. We have good contact with the one known as E. However, we are meeting some friction and will attempt at this time to make a more comfortable contact that will not be so uncomfortable. I am *(inaudible)*.

Carla: Somebody might make contact with the door.

(Carla channeling

I am *(inaudible)*. We find that we have difficulty making a good clear contact with the mind of the one known as E, and due to a somewhat fatigued and perhaps less than clear state of mind. Therefore, we send to our brother our love and thanks for working with us. We would now contact the one known as S, if he will relax, and speak our thoughts as they occur to him without hesitation. I am *(inaudible)*.

(S channeling

I am *(inaudible)*. I am with this instrument. If the instrument will relax …

(Side one of tape ends.)

(S channeling

It is a pleasure to work with those who *(inaudible)* to be able to work with ones such as yourselves. We thank the one known as S for letting us work with him at this time, and at this time we will transfer the contact back to the instrument known as Carla. I am *(inaudible)*.

(Carla channeling

I am again with this instrument. May we thank each of you for your patience as we work with these new instruments. We would wish to work with two more, and then we will work with all of you upon the conditioning ray.

First we would like to attempt to make our presence known to the one known as B, if he would relax and mentally request our contact. He may hear a word or a phrase. If he does, and if he wishes to pursue this service, we encourage him to speak up and find what the experience may hold for him. I will now transfer to the one known as B. I am *(inaudible)*.

(Carla channeling

I am again with this instrument. We find that we are slightly overloading the one known as B and therefore we will work with him at his request and at his convenience at any time he may wish to ask for our help so that we may balance our vibrations with his.

At this time we would attempt to contact the instrument known as C if he also would relax and let our thoughts move into his consciousness and into speech without hindrance. I am *(inaudible)*.

(Carla channeling

We are again with the instrument. I am *(inaudible)*. We thank the one known as C and assure him that, as this instrument would say, the first *(inaudible)* is always the hardest to get out of the bottle. This is a stage that you may surely get beyond with constant application.

We would touch with each of the others in this group, some of whom desire to be channels such as this one, some of whom desire only to feel our presence and to deepen their own meditations, for we may act as a sort of carrier wave strengthening your own individual vibration. We touch, therefore, at this time and attempt to make our presence known, if it is wished, to Jim and to C, to M.

(Pause)

And now to the one known as L, our contact and our encouragement.

(Pause)

My friends, it is a great privilege to work with this group and we leave you with the request that you do ask for us if you have a spare few minutes. Never think that it is too short a time for meditation, for if you can look carefully at one blade of grass, or the beauty of the sky or your own task as you pursue it well, then you can meditate in that brief period as the clock strikes, as a car goes by, as a bird sings, as you hear the life-giving sound of water. Let all things be signals to meditate upon the beauty of the Creation of the Father. We are always with you, you need but ask us.

I am known to you as *(inaudible)*, and will leave this instrument at this time. Adonai, my friends. Adonai.

(Carla channeling

I am Latwii, and am again with this instrument. We took a flyer at the one known as Jim but he is not yet ready to answer questions for a large group. We think that he is, but he does not think that he is, but we will work that out in the future, as you would call it. Actually, to us it is a kind of past but that is difficult to go into with this instrument. May we ask at this time if there are any questions? If you have one, please ask it.

Questioner: Yes. First, I want to thank you for *(inaudible)* questions that I already had in my head. But, while *(inaudible)* was attempting contact with me, I know that during that thoughts passed through my head *(inaudible)* but *(inaudible)*. I just felt a flurry of activity going on in my mind, nothing in particular, just images, almost like *(inaudible)* was trying to block it out, *(inaudible)* block it all of a sudden with a flurry of activity.

We realize, my brother, that that is not precisely a question, however, we will make it into one because we know that which you speak of. It is a common occurrence with one who has not yet totally vanquished the old habits of the body. We will state that in such a way that you do not feel that, because you eat spaghetti, you cannot channel. The habit of the body is to be active. Unless the body is asleep, it is most often active, even while watching one of your television shows, the body will be active and will attempt to feed itself or move about or have some sort of pastime. It is very seldom that the mind and the body are without activity; such is your culture. Thus, when you begin to meditate, and especially when you realize that it would be a good idea for you to have a good meditative state in order to be able to achieve a goal which you desire, that of vocal channeling, your mind and your body will conspire against you to reinstate the older habits of activity.

In some cases those who meditate for a while will become ill, they may get what is known to you as a headache or stomachache, or they may see, as you do, images of varying kinds. It is a distraction which, if pursued, will eventually subside. Perhaps several months, and this experience will no longer be part of your repertoire, because you will have become used to neither physical nor mental activity. In other words, you will have learned to become passive.

This is easy for those trained in Eastern ways but very difficult for those trained in what this instrument would call the Occident. However, you must not be disheartened because you have, shall we say, "Occidentally" been born in the wrong place, but simply persist and this phenomenon will diminish and disappear.

Is there another question?

Questioner: Yes, I have another one. It's concerning the relationship of the body with the mind. It seems, or I find it *(inaudible)* taking an inordinate amount of sweets, and sugar is present in large amounts in my body, that my thought processes tend towards a more depressed kind of state, that I feel I wind up *(inaudible)* more prey to the ego games that we play in our lives, and more of a feeling of selfishness, and less of giving. Is there a relationship to the state of the body to the mind that such things occur?

My brother, that is indeed correct. As we said before, there are various degrees of perfection in the combustibility of nutrients that enter the furnace that is your physical vehicle. Those things which are of the sugar family are very unfortunate in their tendencies towards causing the person to become more within his or her own personality structure. It is, as this instrument would say, a downer. It is intended to give energy, however it does not, it removes energy from the electrical field of the body.

You see, there is a concept of inwardness and outwardness, and that which you know as sugar in many of its forms is an inward-looking combustible. Therefore, when ingested it will produce more consciousness of the self and therefore more tendency towards pettiness and, as you said, game-playing. On the other hand, there is an even greater difficulty; that is that as the body craves balance, and as all things crave balance, so a very inward food will request that the body ingest a very outward food, that which causes the body to gain the energy which it has lost, and therefore this will encourage the body to eat an equally large amount of what you would call red meat. This is an imperfectly burned substance, and should be used in your furnace with some caution, for the byproducts are often difficult to deal with when taken in excess, and you need to have some of your filters replaced after a long period of using these substances.

Thus, there is indeed a great deal of connection between mind and body for the simple reason that your mind dwells within the confines of the physical body while it is awake, unless of course you are fasting for a long period, in which case it might not stay with the body at all.

That, incidentally, is one of the purposes of fasting. Contrary to some modern beliefs, it is not a method of losing excess *avoirdupois* but rather a means of transcending the physical illusion and ascending to a more fine and well-tuned illusion. Thus the teacher known as Jesus fasted, as did many others in your holy works and others throughout the world.

May we answer your question further, my brother?

Questioner: Ah, yes. I have done some *(inaudible)* fasting and it does … I have achieved, a better state of being but in regards to—if the diet is changed in such a way that foods are taken in in a balanced amount … this question is on my mind [because] my wife received a book which stresses either eating habits as a way of preventing disease, curing ailments, and achieving a better balance within the body, therefore achieving a better state of mind. That is the premise behind the book. Would a diet that is fully balanced help you achieve a state similar to that achieved by fasting and taking the impurities out of the body that way?

I am Latwii. My brother, the effect of fasting is a loosening of the cord that ties the consciousness to the body. Thus, no matter how balanced the diet, the cord would remain tight as long as you are eating. The followers of ecstasy, such as Sufis and saints, have often used fasting as a means of loosening their consciousness from their body, that they may see visions and seek the Creator within. This, however, has little to do with a balanced diet.

It is healthy, for the body's sake, shall we say, speaking only on the physical plane, to fast if one finds oneself having bad reactions to seemingly something one has eaten. Then one may perhaps isolate the difficulty and remove it from one's diet.

As to a balanced diet, you must understand, my brother, that this is what we were cautioning you against, those who believe in one way for all peoples. If you will close your eyes and truly picture that you feel will make you healthy, then continue and eat that which you see, your body will inform you of that which it needs. There are foods, certainly, which are unhealthy to all peoples, but there are many, many foods to choose from, and in some cases foods, which may be harmful to one, would be greatly helpful to another.

Thus, you cannot learn your diet from a book, but from experiencing your feelings as you eat and as you live. Attempt, indeed, the advice given in a book, take what seems to work for you, and then go onward. We ask only that you do not become bogged down in the deep details of this and that and the other thing, for you will find that for every this, that and the other thing in one way of thinking, there will be a diametrically opposed this, that and yet another thing in another book that sounds equally plausible. Therefore, if you truly attempt to remain healthy on the physical plane by reading books, you will find that you might as well have eaten the paper.

We do not usually become involved in discussions of this sort because it is indeed physical plane activity and we do not achieve an enormous amount of joy therefrom. However, we realize that it was upon your mind at this time. Is there another question?

S: I have a question. This week I saw something very unusual. I saw a number in a very unusual way, an unnatural way. Is there some significance that I should be looking for connected to this number?

Carla: I'm just getting a "no," S.

This instrument is receiving correctly—no. Is there another question?

Questioner: Could I ask a little bit further on my "no"? It was so perfect, I don't think it could ever occur that way naturally. Could I have influenced it mentally myself? Can you offer a suggestion?

Yes, my brother, we can offer a suggestion: we suggest that you laugh for one half of an hour, and at the end of that time, you will be much closer to understanding the significance of all subjective proof.

Is there another question?

Questioner: I have a question. After learning of the cataclysmic events that will, in all likelihood, occur on this planet in the future, my mind just turned to finding ways of surviving that war; another way might be expressed as myself and my friends to circumvent the events. I'm confused as to what my responsibilities are to my body, whether I should put energy into trying to ensure its survival. On one hand I feel I should and on the other hand I feel that I'm wasting energy, concerning myself with something that is merely physical. Could you give me some help with this?

I am Latwii. Yes, my brother, I believe that we can give you some slight help. You understand that you are dealing with the physical vehicle that is a complete illusion. In the normal course of events, you would concern yourself with a retirement, you would concern yourself with the physical accouterments of comfort for yourself and for those whom you love. These events are far in the future, retirement, comfort without a working income, but indeed these would fill your mind and this is normal for your peoples, for unlike some societies your children will not be expected to take you in.

Therefore, you must concern yourselves with these things. You would not need to concern yourselves with these things if you decided not to. You may perhaps feel that it is irresponsible not to attempt to adjust your future for the comfort of your beloved family but you must look at the future and realize that it is the future that simply may turn out differently than your retirement. You may need, instead, to retire early and go to farming so that you may eat. There is nothing particularly foolish about deciding that you would like to survive the discomforts of dying in this city. In some aspects of your future, this would indeed be possible.

You may, on the other hand, adopt a purer ideal which those whom you love may not understand at all, and that is to say, "I will trust to the Creator that all things will be provided which I need, and I will do whatever work He has for me to do." Surprisingly enough, you may find that whichever route you take, you may end up on a farm, growing food so that you may eat.

Therefore, we suggest that, just as in your decisions about a long faraway retirement, you do precisely what you wish, because it is the future and you are trapped in the present, and when the present moves in its little boat down the stream of time in your dimension to that point in the future, you will then know what has happened.

We are sorry that we cannot tell you that it is either smart or stupid to provide for the future, given the cataclysms. However, it is totally a matter of your free choice. There is no shame in attempting to survive in the physical body in which you now experience this incarnation. The cataclysms which will come prior to the polar shift—that is some time off—there will be much to do before then. There is also no shame in leaving oneself completely open to the opportunities at hand wherever you may be. Some people are moved to plan and do in advance those things for their families which may give them the best chance of survival. Others are moved to blow with the winds, flow with the tides, and only be a lingering breath on the surface of the land. You will know as you listen to these words which type you are. We cannot tell you, but we assure you that there is goodness and righteousness in either path, and no shame to the secure or the wanderer.

May we ask if this answers your question adequately?

Questioner: It has both answered my question and given me great comfort. I thank you.

I thank you, my brother. Is there another question at this time?

Questioner: I have a question about something that was mentioned earlier. It seems that on our plane we learn from suffering and pain. I'm wondering if there might also be some other methods of learning that would not involve suffering, or if suffering is the quickest way of learning in our density?

I am Latwii. Each individual, my brother, is in a completely different universe. In many of those universes, suffering is the quickest way to learn. In some few universes, happiness, joy, delight and the total sharing of experience are the quickest ways to learn. It simply depends upon the vibration of the individual, and what lessons he has chosen for himself. There is no premium upon suffering. It is simply a very efficient tool for learning the lessons of patience and cheerfulness. When you can be patient, when you can be cheerful in the face of adversity, then you have become a potentially loving person. If you have come into the world with patience and with happiness, then whatever suffering you may have may not be for your learning at all, but only, shall we say, to hold you down, to keep you fixed upon your goal.

So if you find yourself cheerful and do not feel the need of suffering, and yet you find that you have some degree of emotional, mental, spiritual or physical pain, you might examine it in order to learn what limitations this would indicate, and willingly accept it. Then you can go back to being joyful, delighted and ecstatic as a means of learning. You see, you have the complete range of methods of learning. It is absolutely not necessary to suffer in order to learn. It is simply that the trauma introduced by these methods is often very effective in causing individuals to stop and ask themselves "why." That question is the beginning. The desire to know why is the beginning of all that you can learn about the Creator and His Love in this dimension.

May we answer you further, my brother?

Questioner: No, that was very good, I have food for thought now. Thank you.

We are glad to provide you with a late snack. We are sorry that we could not give you a more substantial meal.

Is there another question at this time?

Questioner: I have one other question on another area. I would like to know if such a thing as twin souls do exist and what they might be. I understand the concept of soulmates, which suggests people who have been together as mates before, but I understand also that twin souls are something else yet [again.] Could you shed any light on this concept?

Yes, my brother. It is a simple concept and part of the Father's plan as we know it. The twin soul is part of the oversoul of that individual personality. Thus, two souls have incarnated working with one basic unit of awareness. Soulmates, upon the other hand, are those who as whole individuals have chosen to work together in order to achieve mastery of third-dimension planes of existence.

(Tape ends.)

Meditation Session

August 23, 1980

(Unknown channeling)

I am Hatonn, and I greet you in the love and the light of the infinite Creator. It is my great pleasure to return to this group and be welcomed in your domicile at this time. We greet each of you with infinite blessings.

The hunter goes forth, my friends, and knows the manner of his prey. His weapons he has carefully provided for himself and fastidiously placed in the prime condition, that they may do their work. The hunter has a single mind and knows his prey. Is it the dark of the moon? Even so, the hunter stalks. Is it damp and cold in the dawning hours? Even so, the hunter waits watchfully, for the hunter knows his prey.

Each of you, my friends, dwells within the body as a hunter, but seldom, my friends, do you fully understand the nature of your prey. What wonder is it, then, that your weapons lay rusty, tarnished or broken, or that you lie beside them, asleep?

I would, at this time, transfer this contact. I am Hatonn.

(Unknown channeling)

My friends, I am now with *(inaudible)*. I am Hatonn. We have spoken of the hunter, for my friends, is he not the aggressor? But yet, we can break this aggressiveness down to yet two more *(inaudible)*.

What we are saying, my friends, is never allow yourselves to become idle once you have set yourself up to be found. For, my friends, there is such an important role for all. Through your training, you will allow yourself to become *(inaudible)* one that *(inaudible)*. For, my friends, therein lies your reward.

As you look about you, you will see the very fiber of what is known to you as existence unravel. But, my friends, through your meditation you will find a yet stronger bond. And though it is hard for you to see, it is there for you all, my friends. Do not settle for the role of being found, for in such a greater role through the intense vibration that you all experience, you will find it yet easier to project yourself to *(inaudible)* consciousness. My friends, open up yourselves and allow yourselves to experience yet other universes than those around you.

I will now *(inaudible)* this instrument. I am Hatonn.

(Unknown channeling)

I am Hatonn, and I am again with this instrument. We have been attempting to contact the one known as Don, but he is analyzing our contact and, therefore, we find it impossible to continue at this time through him. We will, therefore, conclude this particular thought through this instrument.

To continue—as we have said, it is all too easy to look upon yourselves as passive receivers of spiritual food. If you do so look upon yourself, you will find your progress to be slow. It is the hunter who seeks nothing but his prey who will achieve his goal, and you, therefore, must be hunters after your prey—aggressive, cunning and well-armed.

And what, then, is your prey, my friends? All of you can answer that question. You seek love. To say it another way, you seek the Creator. To say it another way, you seek the original Thought. And yet another way, you seek yourself. Only the single of mind will achieve the end of the trail, will find the prey that he desires.

And what, then, are your weapons? Perhaps you, yourself, know them better than we could ever tell you, but we say to you that those gifts that are given to you in meditation—a merry heart, a kindly and affectionate spirit, a gentle manner, and an ability to look at a larger picture, at a greater design than perhaps you have in the past—perhaps these are some of the things you gain in meditation, for in meditation you dwell, as it were, in a tabernacle with that which is divine, and you take away those elements to which you have opened yourself, to which you no longer have resistance, concerning which you no longer have reservations. There is a great deal of cleansing of the mind from bitterness and negative emotions that needs to be done in order for you to be able to gradually love yourself in a greater self, a self in which you have become the confident aggressor, seeking after love fearlessly, your weapons ready, your hands open.

At this time, since we are aware there are some questions, we would like to transfer this contact to the one known as Jim. I am Hatonn.

(Jim channeling)

I am Hatonn, and I am with this instrument. It is a pleasure, shall we say, to be able to speak through this instrument and to ask if there are any questions?

Questioner: I was wondering, Hatonn, how your efforts went with the leaders with whom you were working.

My sister, we must answer you by saying, again, our efforts have been, for the most part, unable and—we should say—we have been unable to achieve the breakthroughs and the inspiration of the leaders whom we have been working with. We have sought to increase the awareness of certain leaders of your world to the vibration of love, that vibration which we have to share and which we bring as our service to your people. We have found that the polarities of differences of opinions and projections of intentions on the part of most of the leaders whom we have attempted to contact … this polarity is so great that it, should we say, absorbs our efforts and vibrations of love and reflects them back to us in a manner which leads us to believe that your leaders are unable to comprehend the concept of love as they go about their work of leading the nations of your world.

It has been our hope to open somewhat their hearts and souls to the experience of the infinite Creator. And though that spark of recognition does, indeed, reside within each of the people of your planet and your leaders, in some it is buried so deeply beneath the desire for power and the gain of money that we are unable to be of much assistance in uncovering their own recognition of their divinity and the divinity of those whom they lead. So, my sister, it has again been necessary for us to take a brief respite from this effort, for it is somewhat taxing for our beings to continually receive the reflection of our efforts shined back at us, shall we say.

May we answer you further, my sister?

Questioner: I have some other questions, but perhaps some others do, too.

Is there another question?

Questioner: I've got one. I'm not really sure how to put it into words, but this concerns morality and the bond between a man and a woman who have made this bond about sex with someone else. *(Inaudible)* put into words. How do you feel about that?

My brother, we would answer you by saying that the bond that a man and a woman make between themselves is a sacred agreement; that, according to the terms of that agreement, as they are understood by each party of the agreement, these terms are binding upon each party and it must be understood by each that the agreement as it is stated should be kept.

But as to the terms of the agreement, in specific areas—for example, sex, as you have mentioned—the agreement must also be made clearly, so that both understand its terms, and we would suggest to you that the morality of a union between two people depends upon the people and their agreement and what they wish to attain with their relationship. We cannot be extremely specific and say this or that action is right or wrong, moral or immoral, for those are terms which imply an agreement of one nature or another.

So may we say to you that as long as both parties in the relationship understand what the terms of the relationship are, and as long as both keep the terms of the relationship, then they have lived up to the terms of their agreement and are faithful to the purpose of the agreement, and this would include any action which fits within the terms, as long as both have openly agreed that this is what they seek.

We would also add, however, that it is, or at least, hopefully, should be apparent to each who would enter into such agreements, that they can determine what they wish to achieve in their relationship, and that there are what might be called high ideals of spiritual seeking together, which can be what you might call a "high morality": both seeking to help the other achieve oneness with the Creator. And that whatever means are used to achieve that oneness, as long as they hurt no others, then these might be used in good faith to achieve that union with the Creator, and that union with each other and that union with the Self, for we are all one, my brother.

May we answer you further?

Questioner: I really have trouble understanding such a long answer, so to try this once—is there a higher reward for an agreement kept like this, or is this just something between two people? Just a "yes" or "no" will do.

My brother, we would suggest that the reward for any agreement is within the agreement, and there is …

We suggest a pause for a moment as we deepen the contact with this instrument.

(Pause)

I am Hatonn, and I am again with this instrument. My brother, we would suggest that you will decide for yourself what the reward for an agreement kept is.

Can we answer you further?

Questioner: One other question. Is this agreement—does it outweigh any karmic responsibilities to someone else?

I am Hatonn, and I would suggest that your karmic responsibilities are fulfilled by your own conscious decisions as you enter into relationships with those you find yourself in agreements with.

Can we answer you further?

Questioner: Is a relationship like this of a—I realize it isn't always the case—but, would it be a real high spiritual vibration if you enter into—two spiritual people—it gives me the feeling that it's just not as spiritual as I've always imagined, and I was just wondering, is it a highly spiritual thing or is it just down, maybe down a few rungs?

I am Hatonn. My brother, we would suggest that each activity you undertake is of the highest spiritual nature, if you will open yourself to that possibility.

May we answer you further?

Questioner: I think that'll do it, thank you.

Is there another question?

Questioner: Yes, but I don't know whether this deserves an answer or not, so you just let me know—but every once in awhile, I have a really severe ache, usually in the same place, that doesn't seem to be connected with any physical activity or anything that I can put my finger on, and I wondered whether its cause was emotional or something I'm not aware of, like distant weather patterns, or whether fate had just turned up my number, or what might be going on that I'm not aware of, because I would like to maintain as healthy an aspect as I can, and it is something that I'd like to understand better so that I can avoid it. Is that for me to know, or for me to ponder?

I am Hatonn. We can best answer you, my sister, by saying that your physical ailment is somewhat a riddle, as you are aware, and this riddle concerns the nature of your relationship to your physical vehicle, and it is a riddle which you are expending a good deal of effort to unravel. We would suggest that it might be revealing to you to meditate daily for a period of time upon the nature of your physical ailments, and to ask yourself what the reason is for the recurring nature of this physical ailment. We cannot give you specific information, for this would be to do your work for you, and that we cannot do. We would suggest, in your meditations, to use a visualization process to allow healing energy to enter within your physical vehicle, and that you attempt to release your own healing energies as you also ponder the cause of your physical ailments.

May we answer you further?

Questioner: No, thank you, Hatonn.

We thank you. Is there another question?

Questioner: Not for now.

I am Hatonn. If there are no further questions, then we would leave this instrument at this time. May we say that it has been a pleasure and a privilege to be able to share a few of our thoughts with your group this evening. We are always honored to be able to make the contact with your meditation group. We leave you, as always, in the love and the light of the infinite Creator. I am Hatonn. Adonai, my friends.

Sunday Meditation
August 24, 1980

(Carla channeling)

I am Hatonn, and I greet you in the love and the light of the infinite Creator. It gives us great pleasure to greet each of you in the name of love, and to wish each the blessing of light. Tonight, we would speak with you about a subject which some of you have been concerned with, and which all are interested in at this time. We will tell you a little story in order to give you some food for thought.

It came to pass in those days that the Earth was without water, and the seas were dried up. The Creator stayed His hand and war took place in great abundance among the beings of your planet. And then came the rains, and it was worse than the drought. And the Earth trembled and was lost in great abysses which opened in a moment. A remnant remained to know the ending of the rain and the beginning of a new cycle. Many of you in this room can cast your minds back in a subconscious manner to these sad happenings, for they marked the transition between the last cycle and this one upon your Earth-world.

There was great destruction, my friends, and many who lived were lost to their physical life, and what, my friends, had it booted[1] them to live? Perhaps this is the central question that we would ask each of you now, for you have your chance again, in this incarnation, for you are near the closing of another cycle. We have said to you many times: meditate, my friends. For the puzzle that this illusion is, is endless. Only the Creator is unified. Only love is simple.

What is the purpose? What is the point of being in your physical bodies at this time? What are you seeking, my friends? We know that each of you cares not only for yourself, but for the planet. And we have asked this group many times before to meditate on behalf of your Earth-world whenever you can, for the planetary consciousness is in great need of love. But for yourself, in order to obtain clarity and to attain that which you desire in this incarnation, you must then search out those things that you truly desire and pursue them. We do not mean to be shouting "Fire!" in a crowded theater, for my friends, those whom this instrument would call "existentialists" were correct: there is no exit. We ourselves are in an illusion. We can see many things which you cannot, and among them is the fact that one illusion follows another in an infinite variety and pattern. So, what does it gain us to be conscious? What is real?

I would, at this time, transfer this contact. I am Hatonn.

---

[1] booted: to avail, profit or benefit.

(Unknown channeling)

I am Hatonn. And I am with this instrument. We have been speaking to you about your reality and what is real to you. We ask this question because so often, among your people, what is considered to be real is of so little true substance. We see when we observe your people that they concern themselves greatly with such things as money, material pursuits, image, position and other such items which we would suggest only divert the attention of the seeker. We do not mean that those things and materials which your world has to offer you are completely unimportant; for of course, you have physical vehicles which need a certain amount of maintenance and attention. But we would suggest that when you continue to focus only upon the material reality of your world, that you miss the substance of what is real. For what shall see you through the end of this Age? Can you ride upon an airplane, or in an automobile, or even upon a horse into the New Age? Will your credit cards be accepted when the New Age dawns?

No, my friends, these things have their place. But at the center of your being and at the center of your focus is the spiritual path, the journey inward which, when traveled, shall bring you through this closing of the old and the beginning of the new. We say to you, seek within for the real substance of your being. Seek within for what is real. Look into your hearts, my friends. Find the love of the Creator which is there. Shine that love as you look about you in your world, in your everyday activities. Remember that love when you speak to strangers. Remember that love when you see discord. Remember that love when you are in doubt, when you are unsure and when you need strength, for you shall need strength in the days ahead. And that strength cannot be found at a McDonald's hamburger or upon a freeway, for the sunset which you will ride into is the sun—that great, central sun that is within you. Therefore, we ask you constantly to make meditation a part of every day that you have to spend upon your planet. For you shall discover that those realities within yourself which you find in meditation are the substance and the strength that shall see you through that which is an illusion, but which so many take for real.

We say these words to you, hoping that you will find the devotion within yourself to make this journey, this spiritual journey, and make it your everyday life. For soon, it shall be so.

At this time, we would transfer this contact back to the one known as Carla. I am Hatonn.

(Carla channeling)

I am Hatonn. I am again with this instrument. Again, we greet you in love and light. I and my brother, Laitos, would like to pause momentarily in order to share with each of those present the energies of the conditioning ray. If you will open yourself to us, we will make our presence known to you. I am Hatonn.

(Pause)

I am Latwii, and I greet each of you, especially the one known as C. We welcome him back to our circle. We are very glad to be with you, and are enjoying speaking to you no end, and wish you all the love and the light of the infinite Creator.

We would like to open the meeting to questions, but if the one known as Jim would accept our contact, we would like to use him at this time. I am Latwii.

(Jim channeling)

I am Latwii. And I am with this instrument, and we would now like to ask if anyone has a question they would like to ask. We shall do our best to make an answer. Are there any questions?

Questioner: I have a question. About a week ago, I asked if I could find out the name of one of my spiritual guides, and I was wondering if the name I received was correct.

I am Latwii. And we are having some difficulty discerning the name which you refer to. Could you be more specific, my sister?

Questioner: Do you mean you want me to tell you the name I thought it was?

That is correct.

Questioner: Millicent.

We are checking with the computer. We are unable to confirm the correct identity of this name which you have given. We would suggest checking again to be sure. We wish that we could be of more assistance, but are unable at this time.

Questioner: Thank you.

We thank you. Is there another question? Perhaps we could do better on our second try.

Questioner: I have a question. I know a very bright 13-year-old boy who is dealing with the question of death and suffering. Is there a most appropriate way to enable this boy to have the most help that it's possible for a human being to give? Is there a most supportive behavior towards such a boy?

I am Latwii, and I am aware of your question … concerning the subject of death with one who is young, with any who are grappling with this subject for the first time, and perhaps because it has become a reality in their life. We would suggest *(inaudible)*. We would suggest speaking of the natural rhythm of nature, of all the creatures that inhabit your planet. We are speaking specifically of the butterfly, which is born of the cocoon, which is born of the caterpillar. To enable one who is young to discern that movement of the life force from one stage to another is important, for at such an age, one can easily conceive that death means the end of all being. This is a great fear among many of your people, among the young, because they have no experience with this concept, usually, and must encounter it when it becomes real, for few in your world care to discuss the reality of death before it happens to one who is close.

We would suggest assuring, through any allegory or story which you would wish to tell demonstrating a natural life cycle, that the life force, the spirit within the physical vehicle, does indeed go on, does indeed continue, as always it has, and always it shall. You may use stories of animals, such as the butterfly, if the child has interests in other areas. In science, for example, you may use a variation of what is known in your laws of physics that energy can be created, but cannot be destroyed; that it can be transformed and change its nature, but always, it shall continue; that any being which has existed in any form, always exists, even after it has left many forms behind.

Does this help you in your help, my sister?

Questioner: I have listened carefully, and it helps me somewhat, but the thing that troubles me most about this young boy is his bitterness because of his mother's suffering. Death does not seem to be nearly as traumatic to him as the continued suffering of his mother. When I have spoken with him, I have simply said that it is, indeed, as I put it, a "crock." He is convinced that everything is an illusion. He has that solidly in mind; but if everything is an illusion, he then realizes with quite a clear eye that there may not be any meaning at all to life or death or suffering.

Consequently, I have only been able to respond by agreeing with him that all is illusion, and is sometimes very unfair, and that the only reality that I believe in is love and being kind to people. And I understand that this is precisely the reaction that his father has had to the same problem. It grieves me that I cannot think of a more appropriate response. Perhaps I, myself, do not understand well enough how to express the propriety of suffering in the world.

I am Latwii. And we would suggest that for the matter of suffering and the unfairness of suffering for those who must endure its pain, that each of the beings upon your planet are beings of light in reality. Many have chosen certain roles to play upon this stage in this illusion. They have chosen these roles for purposes, to learn certain lessons. Some lessons require certain props, perhaps pain. It is a common prop and lesson upon your planet. Many, many lessons and insights and truths can be learned by those who suffer. Suffering focuses consciousness to a fine degree, and even though the one who suffers in the physical vehicle may be unaware of the profound lesson being learned, we would assure you, and help you assure the young child, that the lesson which his mother is learning is incredibly important, or else, she would not endure such suffering.

Can we answer you further, my sister?

Questioner: That did it. That will do just fine, thank you very much.

We thank you. Is there another question?

Questioner: I'd like to know if there's any method to help develop the use of human energy *(inaudible)* life energies, or *(inaudible)*.

I am Latwii. My sister, we would answer you by saying, there is, indeed, a way for each, perhaps many ways for each person to awaken those healing energies that are within each of the beings upon your planet. And it is also true that some of the beings upon your planet have particular gifts or tendencies in the healing areas.

For those who wish to initiate the healing energy flow through their vehicles, we would suggest again, in meditation, to create an image within your mind, an image of light descending from the stars, descending into your brain, descending into your body, filling your body with light, with healing light, to feel your self, your heart open and to feel this light pour forth, and to open yourself to service as you shine this light, to seek not only the light, but to seek the desire to serve.

This light is the healing energy which is within each of you—we will correct this instrument—is within each of your people upon this planet. The image of the light descending from the stars, the image of the heart opening, will help you to release the energy which is within your being.

May we answer you further?

Questioner: Not right now, thank you.

Is there another question?

(Pause)

We are surprised. This is usually quite a group for questions, but if there are no further questions, we would leave you in the love and the light that is all about you, that is within you, and we would, again, suggest to you that you seek this love and this light daily, in meditation, and make it more a part of your day. I am known to you as Latwii. Adonai vasu borragus.

(Carla channeling

I am Nona. I have difficulty speaking through this instrument, for I am not used to speech. But I greet each of you in the love and the light of the infinite Creator. We of the vibration Nona are healers, and have been drawn to your group because of our sister, known as C. We would offer our consciousness and our vibratory aid in her work, and in order to acquaint her with our vibration, we will speak as we normally do through this instrument, so that the one known as C may be familiar with us. We shall speak no more words through this channel. Therefore, as all members of the Confederation do, we say farewell in the love and the light of the infinite Creator.

(Singing until the end of the tape.) ♣

Meditation Meeting
August 27, 1980

(Unknown channeling)

I am Hatonn. I greet you, my friends, in the love and the light of our infinite Creator. It is a very great privilege to be with you this evening.

It is a very great privilege to be with you at all times, for you see, my friends, we are inseparable, for we are one. Yes, we are one, just as you are one with all. Everything, as we have said many times, is but one thing: the Creation, or the Creator. Either is correct, for one is the other. This concept is the concept which the people of your planet must understand if they are to progress. It is unfortunate that this concept has not been communicated, in general, to most of the peoples of your planet. It is the lack of this concept that creates what they see as their present problems. A full understanding and application of this concept immediately eradicates all problems. This probably seems much too simple, but in truth, this is all that is necessary to be known. If you can greet each entity with whom you come in contact as you would greet yourself, if you could greet yourself, and love that person as you should love yourself, then, my friends, all of what you call your problems would be nonexistent.

We of the Confederation of Planets in the Service of our Infinite Creator have said this many times, through channels such as this one, and through other mechanisms. It has been put in writing many, many ways, and been communicated in many forms, through classifications of philosophy that you term "religion." Unfortunately, but few of the population of your planet have been able to understand this simple teaching. Some have understood it intellectually, and yet, they have not understood, for they have been unable to apply this simple concept.

The reason for the lack of ability to apply this simple concept, my friends, is primarily due to a lack of meditation. We have also, many, many times talked to you of the necessity for meditation. To sum it up, my friends, the concept of unity brought to your total awareness through the process of meditation is all that is necessary for the growth of the peoples of your planet at this time. If you find yourself straying from this awareness, remind yourself to relax and seek the truth that we bring you through the process of meditation. Reestablish, shall we say, your point of view, and then look at your environment and your fellow beings in a different light—in the true light. The light that simply states that everything that exists is one thing. Understand that that which is annoying or foreign to you is caused only by a lack of understanding of this simple, simple truth.

Many of your peoples will not be able to make the transition which is so close upon them that, as it has been said, they could reach out and touch it. They will require a longer period of learning. This is unfortunate, and yet, it is not as unfortunate as you might think, for it is their choice to experience the set of conditions that they will experience.

My friends, you have a terrific opportunity. If you are able at this time to fully understand and then apply this simple truth of unity, if you are in every action, every word, every deed, able to reflect this understanding, then, my friends, you will have achieved what you set out to achieve. Consider this point well, my friends, for all that you experience in the physical will fade away and no longer be with you. All that you will transport through time and space to eternity is your thinking. Develop that, my friends, for that is the only thing you have of any value at all.

It has been a very great privilege to speak to you through this instrument. I will leave this instrument at this time and contact another instrument. I am Hatonn.

(Unknown channeling)

I am Hatonn. We will speak briefly through this instrument and greet you again, in love and light. This instrument was rejecting our contact because she was analyzing.

Within yourselves, my friends, you have a simple understanding that all of the parts of your body make one entity. Without each member, the body would be maimed. It is in this fashion that you may grasp the concept of unity with your brothers and sisters of all dimensions and all densities, especially those who share your physical illusion at this time. You cannot be comfortable about choosing whom to accept as a brother or sister, for all beings are part of an organic whole. You cannot turn your back upon a member of an organic whole without pathetically reducing the efficiency of the whole.

Then, if you meet those situations and circumstances in which you find yourself in any judgment or incapacity to feel unity, we ask that you harken back to our words, for if you can vibrate upon the original Thought with your friends, that is a good thing. If you can send the same vibration to those with whom you are disaffected, you will have done a far harder thing and a thing which you will receive back a thousandfold. For many times, those beings who are inharmonious are just so because they expect the reception which they receive and so, become even more offensive in defense.

Look upon those people, my friends, as one being, and you stop a great wheel that is grinding down an entity whose soul is in pain. You stop a wheel and free a soul to be a perfect part of a perfect creation that, in truth, all of you are.

At this time, I would transfer this contact. I am Hatonn.

(Unknown channeling)

I am Hatonn, and I am with this instrument. And we greet you again, in the love and light of our infinite Creator.

We have been talking this evening, my friends, about the realization that each of your people must make if they are to make the transition into the New Age that is to come. We have been speaking about the necessity for each person to turn inward and seek for the Creator, to seek for love within, my friends.

So many of your people seek, in the world around them, for meaning. They look to friends, they look to their everyday jobs. They look to what your society offers as models of excellence. They look to the material world that surrounds them in such seeming abundance of wealth, and they look inside, in materials that they surround themselves with, and seek for answers to fill up their whole being with meaning.

Long have we watched this process of running to and fro, like worried ants, hoping to find a morsel of meaning dropped somewhere on the ground, so that they might quench their thirst and hunger for one more meal, then to be hungry, again. It grieves us to see such futility. We have hoped through many means to be able to be of service to your people and to help your people awaken that spark of the Creator that resides within. We send our love to each of your people, hoping that when a person feels the vibration of love within, that this feeling would be a clue as to the direction of their search. We have attempted through instruments such as are here this evening, at meditations such as this one, to share our philosophy of love with as many of your people as would listen.

We always hope that meditations such as this will become a common occurrence upon your planet in the days that lie ahead for your people. But the time is short, my friends. It is necessary for us to ask those of your people who have heard our message to rekindle their efforts to awaken their fellow beings to the truth of the unity of all creation. We can only do so much, and then, must pass the effort and the flame of truth on to others such as yourselves, and hope that you will pass it still further, that the spark of the divine Creator within each of your people might be rekindled. We ask each of you to consider these words and to consider your response as you go your way, each in your own way, and meet your fellow creatures in your everyday life. Remember, my friends, that when you meet another, you meet yourself; that when you meet another, you meet the Creator. Be in awe of this truth. For then, you shall be open to further discovery of the truth of the oneness of all creation. We have said this many times through instruments such as this, to many people. We hope that our words have made an impression upon your being, for we seek to serve and to awaken within each of your people the truth of love.

We would now leave this instrument, and transfer our contact to the one known as Carla. I am Hatonn.

(Carla channeling

I am Hatonn. If you will be patient, I am deepening this instrument's contact. Ommmmmmmmm. I am Hatonn. I will turn to this instrument to inquire if we may answer any questions at this time.

We are aware that there is a question that is unspoken, that this instrument is not fond of dealing with the answers to unspoken questions. We, therefore, would have a difficult time speaking through this instrument. May we say that we did work with this instrument in order to speak on an unanswered question, and if she will open herself to us, we will say a few words.

We give to this instrument a concept of a very deep and very vast sky. It is not the sky that is seen from the surface of the planet, it is that which is seen from deep space, in those magic spaces between the galaxies where the dimensions merge. We wish the asker of the question to place himself in that area, and to feel the ecstasy of touching the infinity of dimensions and creations that spread out like a rainbow from that point.

The Creator's universe is a beautiful thing. In your microcosmic, planetary world, you see a tiny part of it, and much of what you see has been mishandled by your peoples. This does not mean, my friends, that the Creator has in some way become tarnished. There are those things which endure, and it is those things in which you may rest as a bird floating upon the wind, or a sea creature resting at the ocean's bottom, touching an infinity of beauty that is all one tapestry of light. Please know, my friends, that this being of infinite light connects you with all that there is—not upon this plane, but upon a finer one. The knowledge of this oneness cannot get you through the illusion if you attempt to apply it consciously. The magic of creation can only be expressed spontaneously. Therefore, we ask you to lift your consciousness to deep space, and look back on the microscopic dot in a minor galaxy which is called Earth.

I would, at this time, transfer this contact. I am Hatonn.

I am again with this instrument. I am Hatonn. Because we are aware of the nature of the question that this instrument wishes to ask, we would leave this instrument so that our brother, Latwii, may speak. I leave you, my friends, in love and light. It has been an enormous privilege to be with you. Adonai, my friends. I am Hatonn.

Questioner: Anybody picking up Latwii?

(Tape ends.)

Sunday Meditation
August 31, 1980

(Carla channeling)

I am known to you as Hatonn, and I greet you in the love and the light of our infinite Creator. It is a great privilege to share your meditation and to enjoy each of your vibrations, and we thank you most gratefully for this opportunity to share our thoughts with you. Tonight we would like to speak about the sphere that you call Earth, and the experience that you call your life, and its relationship to what we may describe as love.

We would begin by telling a little story, the story of a young girl who felt that those about her were not speaking the truth. She listened to her parents, to her teachers, she listened to the words in books of intellect, of philosophy, of religion, and all seemed to be of no essence. All things seemed to her to partake of a kind of translucence—she could indeed see through each statement, each belief, and see that there was lacking a central truth. Within herself, she inquired as to the truth and found that she was not equipped by her studies, her observations, or her experience to answer this question, nor did she know to whom to turn.

One fine Fall day, as the sun filtered through the *(inaudible)* blue of the sky, through the golden and tawny blaze of the autumn leaves, and lit her upturned face, she began to have a feeling that perhaps she had not been looking for her answers in the proper manner, and so she began to observe the sky and the trees and the wind. And, as time passed, these things which she had formerly never noticed became her teachers, for she found that no matter what the news of the day, what the worries and the folly of the hour, the wind and the trees and the sky had their seasons and their cycles, and they moved to a rhythm given by the Creator.

It is said in one of your holy works that faith is the hope of things unseen, and yet many people have faith that the sun will rise, that the deciduous trees will lose their leaves and regain them again in the Spring, that winds will blow and rains will come, that the seasons will revolve. This the little girl thought, and as she became a young woman, she became grounded in the creation of the Father, and when she looked at the creation of man, a creation that had become very distorted from the original Thought, she could view it [and] in some way [was] able to understand that no matter how distorted, how difficult, or how illusory those things of the mind and the physical life may be, there is always a bedrock, a connection, that is as close as the nearest patch of ground, for truly, my friends, she discovered that she was grounded in the creation of the Father.

This Creation is a creation of love. The trees offer to mankind their shade, their beauty, the very oxygen that your peoples need to breathe. The winds carry the rains needed to make your wildlife grow and your crops mature. The sun beams always so that those upon your planet may live, for without it they would surely die. Each natural individual possesses in its individuality the simple bias of service to the creation by beauty, by use.

All things may be discovered to have some use in the natural creation. You yourselves, my friends, are part of that creation. When you become able through simplification of your complex thought processes to become aware of the one original Thought of love, you then rejoin the creation of the Father and stop co-creating the more complex creation of man.

And how can you become aware of this original Thought, my friends?

At this time I would transfer this contact to another instrument. I am Hatonn.

(Unknown channeling

I am Hatonn, and I am with this instrument. We are very pleased to be able to speak a few words through this instrument.

We are speaking of becoming aware of the love of the Father. How may your people, each and every one, become aware of that love of the Father? Of course, as we have suggested, many, many times in many previous messages, meditation, my friends, is the surest and the quickest way to become aware of the love which the infinite Creator has planted as a seed within each of your beings. Each of your people are as a garden to the Father, each provides certain ingredients and requirements analogous to the soil and the rain and the wind and the sun of your Earth. Each of your people provide the atmosphere and the surroundings for this seed of love to grow, to germinate, to come to full maturity, and to be harvested as the fruit of the Father. Each of you, as you live in this world of illusion, by your attitudes and your actions, as you greet each new day, as you greet each new friend, promotes the growth for the death of that seed. Each moment that you spend consciously awake nourishes that seed, provides a watering of devotion that is necessary to cause it to grow.

Each time you forget the grand drama in which you partake, each time you forget that it is the Creator whom you meet every day, each day with every person and situation which you come in contact with, each experience either causes the seed to grow or hinders its growth, depending upon whether or not you remember that it is the love of the Father that is within you and each of your fellow creatures. When you forget, you hinder the growth of the seed. We would suggest daily meditation to help you to remember that you have within your being the spark of the divine Creator. And when you focus upon that reality, the reality within, you bring a light to the world, a light that shall shine and help others to see within their own being their own sparks.

By your actions, by your attitudes, you shall help those of your people who are open to growing; you shall help each to water their seeds of love. Together as a people you create either a garden of Eden within your being or you create further illusions that, by your own creation, build a wall around your garden of Eden and keep you from tasting of the fruit of love, the fruit of life.

We hope that in some way messages such as this will help those of you who are open to service and seeking within, to grow and to nourish those seeds, those sparks which are your Divine inheritance. For we wish for all of your people to inherit the kingdom of love that is within your grasp, within your being.

We would at this time transfer this contact to the one known as Carla. I am Hatonn.

(Carla channeling

I am again with this instrument. Our brothers and sisters of *(inaudible)* are with us at this time and we would like to work with you, if you would wish it, on your conditioning. We will move among you. We would start with the one known as L. If he would relax, we will make our presence known to him at this time.

(Pause)

We will move now to the one known as M1, and if he would request it we will work with him briefly.

(Pause)

Moving now to the one known as T.

(Pause)

We would now touch our sister M2, that she may know our presence.

(Pause)

We would now move to the one known as E, and after a period of conditioning we will contact him and speak a few words through him, if he would relax and allow our thoughts to flow freely through him. I am Hatonn.

(Pause)

(Carla channeling

I am again with this instrument. I am Hatonn. We have a good contact with the one known as E, but he is analyzing due to a fear that he is not receiving our thoughts. Therefore, we will again contact him. I am Hatonn.

(E channeling

I am Hatonn, and I greet you in love and the light of the infinite Creator. It is always a pleasure to work with a new channel. We are pleased with your progress. You have been with analyzing. I am Hatonn, and I will speak now through the one known as Carla.

(Carla channeling

I am again with this instrument. I am Hatonn. We pause so that the clicking would be happening between our words. We would share our vibration now with the one known as K, if she would request it mentally.

(Pause)

I am again with this instrument. We would now work to deepen our vibration and contact with the one known as Jim.

(Pause)

We now work briefly with this instrument.

(Pause)

We send blessings all around, my friends, and ask you to understand that although we are not very wise compared to those who are truly wise in our creation, yet we do indeed love our brothers and sisters upon your planet. We would leave this instrument now, that the one known as Oxal may speak. We leave you in the hope of things unseen, in the knowledge of the invisible power of the creation of love, of which we are all an unique and perfect part. We leave you in the light and the love of the One Who is the creation. Adonai, my friends. I am known to you as Hatonn.

I am Oxal, and I, like my brothers, greet you in the love and the light of the infinite Creator. We are attempting to make our vibration known to the instrument known as Jim. Therefore we would use this method of assuring this instrument of the fact that this particular vibration that he is receiving is the Oxal vibration and if he would perhaps be able to attune himself to this vibration, we would like to speak a few words through him at this time. I am Oxal.

(Side one of tape ends.)

(Transcript ends.) ❧

Tuesday Mediation
September 2, 1980

(Unknown channeling

I am Hatonn. I greet you, my friends, in the love and in the light of our infinite Creator. It is once again a very great privilege to be with you. It is unfortunate that we have some difficulty fully communicating *(inaudible)* concepts to you. This, of course, is because your language is not adequate for those concepts that we would give you. However, we intend to circumnavigate the intellectual mind through communications with you during your meditation.

During these meditations, concepts we impress should be relatively easy to understand. You have been conditioned for what you call a lifetime, you have been conditioned to think about certain things and certain of these things you consider important, others you consider unimportant, some you don't consider at all. From our perspective, most of the things that the people of Earth consider important are not important at all, or of no consequence. Those things that they don't consider at all often are the most important.

If you would like to discover what is important and what isn't, the process is relatively simple.
(Inaudible) the following tests: first, is the concept involved with what you are considering of a lasting nature, that is, 100, 1000 or 10,000 years from now, will what you are considering and examining be of any consequence at all. This is the first and possibly the most important test. If you are putting considerable time and effort into a concept which will have no meaning in 100 or 1000 years, or even a few years, then, of course, it is of no importance at all from our point of view, for from our point of view your relatively short span of existence on the surface of your planet is but a brief experience in a much, much greater *(inaudible)*.

If you examine those things most of your people are fascinated with at this time, you will find them to be of a transient nature, and it will be obvious that almost everything which concerns them at this time will not even be worth putting in your history books 100 years from now. And, my friends, the material in your history books is of no consequence, for, my friends, there is only one thing of real consequence, and that, my friends, is the development of your thinking, not thinking about politics, not thinking about ecology, not thinking about evolution, but the simple process of growth through self-analysis, and even more important, your relationships with your fellow beings.

This, my friends, is the only thing of lasting importance. This is what develops you as a personality, develops you as a universal being, which is the only thing that you carry with you through the illusion of space and time which you call the creation. It is not necessary to be complex, it is not necessary to be intellectually bright or knowledgeable or well-informed. It is necessary, my friends, to know, why you react as you do to your fellow man, and it is necessary, my friends, to then, having analyzed your reactions, to improve them.

This is first necessary for you as an individual, to understand, to know and to apply. It is then necessary, if you have achieved your objective, to by demonstration of this knowledge, spread this knowledge to others. But by demonstration, my friends, by demonstration, for truly this is the only method you have available to you in your present state of existence. We have observed many on your planet attempting to do good through word of mouth, and yet, my friends, without the necessary demonstration of what they knew to be true, their words were hollow. It is far better to say nothing and to demonstrate through deed and action the unity that you embrace than it is to speak it, to teach it, without the demonstration.

Spiritual growth, my friends, is a very simple thing, it is almost too simple. You cannot possibly intellectually explain or understand any facet of spiritual growth. When you have reached the next step in the development of your awareness, you will then understand fully what was so impossible to explain before you had arrived at your new position of knowledge. But to explain it, my friends, if we could do this, our task would be very, very simple. We would explain to you how to grow spiritually, you would grow, we would all rejoice, and our task would be complete.

But why, my friends, then, is it so very, very difficult, why have we used so many, many words expressing in your language a direction, a technique that is unreachable? We say, "Know yourself," and yet do you follow our instructions.

We will attempt through this instrument *(inaudible)* and meetings to follow this one, to give you more specific and exact instructions *(inaudible)* exercises *(inaudible)* personal techniques for reaching that goal that each of you desires. We will also through the other instruments present do the same thing. We would hope that we will be able to praise in your language *(inaudible)* our instructions, and that you will be able to utilize them. They would be meaningless to a less advanced group, for they are a bit unusual and would seem, I am afraid, somewhat ridiculous to a group of lesser advanced in their seeking. We are limited, as you know, by the group we contact. We will attempt through another instrument at this time to give you some instruction. At this time I will transfer this contact.

(Unknown channeling

I am Hatonn. This instrument is in deep contact, and we do not wish to disturb her state. Therefore, we will speak more slowly than is usual through this instrument.

Step number one: question yourself as follows. Situation: "I am the Christ." Further situation: "This circumstance occurs." Question: "What shall I do for my people?" There will be no hedging in your identification with the one whom you call Jesus, a carpenter known to his fellow men as *(inaudible)*. You are *(inaudible)*, a carpenter, you have Christ consciousness, you are Christ. What will you do? In seventy years a gospel will be written. What shall be your sayings? What legacy leave you? There are times to remove your being from this illusion. However, the moment of contact with any spiritual being is your moment of Christhood. Who are you? You are Christ. Speak, therefore, in parables if so the need is, but speak as Christ, for this is the beginning, the entryway, the gate into your being and only in process, only as you kneel to wash the feet of your fellow beings, only as you humble yourself in servitude to all of those who are the extensions of the Father, will you begin to receive yourself unto yourself.

In your identity lies your question. We, your brothers and sisters, promise you no answers but promise that you can learn to live the question until there is no answer necessary. Growth is not what it seems, my friends. Seek ye therefore not with the mind, not with the predisposition, not with the suspicion half-formed of what to expect, for we shall attempt to aid you in the exploration of that which is unexplored. Flexibility, therefore, is your ally.

I will leave this instrument at this time that my sister may speak through another instrument. I leave you in the love and the light of the Christ consciousness, which is the manifestation of the Father, the Creation and love itself. I am known to you as Hatonn. Do not call me master; I am your brother and your sister; I am the Christ, and I speak to myself. Adonai *(inaudible)*.

Carla: Do you come in the name of the Christ?

(Singing)

(Unknown channeling

I am with the instrument.

(Transcript ends.) ❧

Wednesday Meditation
September 3, 1980

(Unknown channeling)

[I am Hatonn.] We will be able to speak to your meditation group this evening. We are aware that there are many concerns upon your minds, and we would speak to some of these concerns. We are aware that you each and every one present this evening are attempting each in your own way to decide the proper paths and method of proceeding down that path. We hope always that our messages are of some use as you journey down your path.

We have spoken many times to your meditation group. Always we have suggested that the journey which your people are embarking upon is a journey which each of you are responsible in some way for completing within yourself. We would hope that as you consider the proper path to take that you will always keep foremost in your mind and your heart and your soul the knowledge that you do not walk alone; that many beings of light are with you and walk beside you; that wherever you shall journey, there will be assistance available, and you are always encouraged to seek that assistance, for the Creator does not send the shepherds out without their staff, and we would suggest to you, each one, that you not be afraid to lean upon the staff from time to time.

Of course, as we have suggested many times in many messages to your group meditation, upon a daily basis is the most efficient way to call upon that inner strength that is the love of the infinite Creator. We realize that we need not suggest too many times to such a group as this that meditation is again the answer to questions and directions. We would, in this contact, suggest that you are accompanied always be those beings of light who are your guides and who have offered many directions and much love upon your path in the past and shall continue to do so in the future. We offer these words of hope and encouragement, for often it seems as though there is nowhere to turn when one has looked long upon the path which they travel, has looked long for ways to serve, and has hoped for more avenues to open. We would suggest once again that the seeking is the key to finding and those who seek always are always assured of finding.

We would at this time transfer this contact. I am Hatonn.

(Unknown channeling)

I am with this instrument. I am known to you as Hatonn, and I greet you in love and light through this instrument. We give to this instrument the image of a dog, a loyal and faithful dog who has been lost when his family was moving from plate to place. It is well known among your peoples that some animals lost in such a manner travel hundreds of miles to find their master. What is in the mind of this conscious being? What causes this creature of limited consciousness to seek and to seek and to seek? If his paws are cracked, he walks on bleeding feet; if there is no food, he continues starving; he finds water on leaves; he barely survives, but he never doubts for one instant his desire, for his mind is simple. The mind of man has become all too complex. And yet we say to you, learn what you desire, and once you have learned, seek it.

In your race of beings, you have no Earthly masters. Therefore, unlike a dog, you will never find precisely what you seek if what you seek is your master. For you could sit in the domicile in which you sit alone for the rest of this incarnation and you would never be away from your master. It is easy for us to tell you that life itself is your master, but this is not so, my friends; life is the catalyst by which you come to know the master. But you must begin with yourself to have faith in your feelings, in your desires, to be discriminating in all of your reactions. These things are important, but the road that you are on will be peopled with disappointing people until you realize that that which you desire is your master, love itself.

To an animal, the master is the incarnation of love. To a person, everything can be seen as an incarnation of love. The path that you take is relatively unimportant, as long as you remember what you desire. If you remember the Creator, those things which you need spiritually will not only fall into your life, but will give you a completely new slant on disappointments or feelings of discomfort concerning any whom you thought to be masters. You dwell upon a plane in which the jest of which you have discussed constantly calls the *(inaudible)*. The trickster plays his tricks. The prankster is not idle. What then can you seek in such an illusion, in such a maze, in such a meander, in such a labyrinth? Do not worry, my friends, do not be concerned, for the path, though seeming crooked, is straight. Though seeming narrow, is wide enough.

At this time we would transfer this contact. I am Hatonn.

(Unknown channeling

We are having difficulty with the instrument known as Don for he is extremely fatigued. I therefore will close through this instrument. Speak ye of guides? Nay, my friends, know that the hosts of the kingdom are yours as you polarize towards the love and the light of the Creator. In meditation, in action, in words, in touch, in caring, be aware that this is the Creator's work and that you are only an instrument. You do not simply channel at times such as these, your life is a channeled message. What will that message be? What say you of the love of the Creator, of the unity of the Creation? Dwell in the shadow of the Almighty. We leave you under the brow of that protective hill. We wish to work with the one known as Jim through vibration, and so we leave in order that one of our brothers may speak. I am known to you as Oxal. My peace to you, in the love and the light of the infinite Creator. I am Hatonn. Adonai, my friends.

(Unknown channeling

I am Oxal, and I also greet you in the love and the light of our infinite Creator. We are very pleased to have *(inaudible)* this contact with this instrument. We are aware that he is learning our vibration and will therefore benefit from continued exposure to our vibration. We would say a few words before transferring our contact. We always are delighted to be able to speak a few words through a new instrument through our vibrations.

We are having some difficulty at this time transferring our concepts. We would therefore suggest that this instrument relax and refrain from analysis. It is not always possible to remain free of interfering thoughts, but we assure this instrument that our vibration shall be easier to receive with practice. We would now transfer this contact. I am Oxal.

(Unknown channeling

I am Oxal, and I greet you once again. We wished to follow the directive of our brothers in speaking to you about a second method of advancing your discipleship along the path. Our suggestion has to do with simple self-confidence. To be unsure of oneself is to not be free. If you are not free, it is difficult for you to allow others to be free. Therefore, acknowledging that you and yourself are grass that withers and dies at the end of the season of greening, realize that you carry within you such perfection as you can never fully understand [while] you are in your vibration.

In all humility, my friends, carry out your plans. Actualize your dreams and in all of your contacts with your fellow beings, see them in the same gentle light of love. If they be a rapist, a killer, a robber, a tax collector, they still are perfect. Grant them therefore the freedom that you grant yourself. It begins within you. In our work [we express a preference] that you do not, in your anxiety, distress yourself over your feelings towards your deepest goals. It continues as you view a world gone quite mad, when many goals seem to you to be distinctly without merit. We will speak at a later time about the work that you may do in hearing those who are unhappy, but first give to each the love and the acceptance that you have given to yourself, knowing in all humility that it is the Creator in yourself Whom you love and Whom you must nurture.

Before I leave, I will gratefully open this meeting to any question from the one known as Jim.

Jim: I am curious about the strong feeling of comradeship that I feel with Don and Carla here. We seem to feel together. I am wondering if that's based solely on our mutual interest of being of service or if there might be more to it. Can you shed any light on that?

I am Oxal. I would not wish to interfere with the free will of you, my brother. The path ahead lies open in more than one direction. It is probable that the path concerning the entities known as Don and Carla will remain open. It is also possible for us to confirm that there is the possibility of not only work on the spiritual plane but a life experience of integrating all of the planes now available to you in this context. Nevertheless, another path open to you also draws you. We can only say to you that in your free will you must in all humility follow to the best of your ability the will of the Creator, for those of whom you speak are well aware of free will, and you may trust that understanding.

We cannot speak without infringement of several possible futures which you may encounter in your travels. We cannot speak of these things because we may influence you and you, my brother, must journey upon your own inner path, in your heart that which feels to be the will of the Creator. You must abide. You have the strength to be wrong. You have the will to press on. There are no doors closing behind you, for both paths will lie open for some time. More than this we cannot say, therefore, we leave you in peace, for that which you are to do will come to you, will feel the way that you await. We are sorry that we cannot answer you further, my brother.

Is there another question at this time?

Jim: No, thank you. That was fine. That's all I have to say.

I am Oxal. I speak as a shadow, a ripple upon the ocean. My words like water, gently cascade through you. They are words born in love and in light, and though we refrain now from speaking, that love and that light shall sustain you. I am Oxal. Adonai vasu borragus.

Sunday Meditation
September 4, 1980

(September 4, 1980, was not a Sunday, but a Thursday. It is not certain at this time whether the transcript title or date is correct.)

(Carla channeling

… vibration, thanking this instrument for the privilege of this work. I am Hatonn.

(N channeling

I am Hatonn, speaking from this instrument with greetings of love and light to my brothers and sisters. For the receptivity of this *(inaudible)* is such that our vibrations may be shared more readily due to the willingness of this oneness. From that point of light within we are one and in that love which we extend we bid you adieu. I am Hatonn.

(Carla channeling

I am Hatonn, and am again with this instrument. We thank the one known as N for the flexibility and desire to serve which enabled our contact. We would at this time share our vibration with the one known as *(inaudible)*, offering to her also our humble thanks that we may share with this new instrument in service to the infinite Creator. I am Hatonn.

(Carla channeling

I am Hatonn, and am again with this instrument. May we thank all of those present for the desire to serve and for your patience as we do this careful work with the new instruments. We are very happy as we begin to blend various tonalities and vibrations of the Confederation with the somewhat more complex vibratory needs of capacities of each new instrument here present. We have been able to blend with those energies already existing in what seems to us to be a most satisfactory manner using the fellowship of those entities with whom each new instrument had already been in contact, sharing concepts and allowing the one great message of love to find [the] new channels. We shall be with each at any time that you may mentally request our presence.

We would at this time transfer in order that queries may be had. I am Hatonn.

(Jim channeling

I am Hatonn, and greet you all once again in love and light. At this time it is our privilege to attempt the answering of questions which those present might have upon their minds. Is there a question at this time?

Questioner: Hatonn, was it your vibration that I felt this morning in this morning's meditation or was it Laitos? Is there anything you can say?

I am Hatonn. My brother, during the meditation of which you speak you were experiencing the vibration of our brothers and sisters of Laitos. For it is their task to work with the new instruments in familiarizing the new instruments with the lighter band of the Confederation vibration. We of Hatonn have blended our vibrations with you on a specific basis this afternoon for the first time and shall at any time in your future in which you request our assistance be most honored to blend them at that time.

May we answer you further, my brother?

Questioner: No. Thank you very much.

I am Hatonn. We are most grateful to you my brother, as well. May we answer another question at this time?

Questioner: Is the difference between channeling we receive now and that experience that might be shared with what I will term a recording angel different only in functioning and the type of sharing that is involved or is there a difference?

I am Hatonn. My brother, we might be of most service in this regard by suggesting that all messengers of love and light are one. There are within your illusion certain relationships which would seem to make a difference between such messengers. These supposed and apparent differences are only in the type of relationship which the one serving as instrument has to the one serving as the messengers. Those entities of whom you speak are more closely related to this planetary influence, if we may use this misnomer, than are most of those of the Confederation since these entities of whom you speak have been in incarnation at times long past on this sphere.

May we answer you further, my brother?

Questioner: No. Thank you for your clearing *(inaudible)*.

We are grateful once again to you. May we answer another question at this time?

(Pause)

I am Hatonn. My friends, it has been a great honor to join you in your meditation. We of Hatonn feel the greatest joy and love with each opportunity to blend our vibrations with yours. Again we remind each that we are available for assistance in deepening meditation at any time in your future and need only a simple request for our presence and we shall happily respond. If at any time our vibrational contact becomes uncomfortable we ask that you request a lessening of the contact. If this is not successful in removing the discomfort, we again remind you that you need only ask us to depart and we shall depart and look forward to a future joining.

At this time we shall take our leave of this group and leave you in the love and in the light of the one infinite Creator. Peace be with you, my friends. I am Hatonn.

(Continuation of tape entitled "UFO Meditation, September 4, 1980—Hatonn Earth Changes." The following could be a recording that was on the tape, the beginning of which was erased by the September 4, 1980 recording. It could also be a recording of a subsequent meditation in which the recording began without preamble.)

(Jim channeling

… their fellow creatures and we would suggest for this reason plans for survival on the physical level might be made.

May we answer you further?

Questioner: No questions here.

Then we would now leave this instrument and transfer this contact to be able to answer any further questions. I am Hatonn.

(Carla channeling

I am Hatonn, and again I greet you in the love and the light of the infinite Creator. Within the boundaries of our ability, it is my pleasure to ask if there are other questions at this time?

Don: What causes the weather changes in the Earth right now?

I am Hatonn. We would like to confirm your opinion concerning the causes of these things. As you know, all that is is caused by thought. There is therefore nothing that is not caused by thought, up to and including changes in density including difficult changes in density. The reason that the transition will include difficult Earth changes for your peoples is that the thinking of this planetary consciousness is very awry. There are many upon this planet that are of highest caliber of service to others. However, there are just as many who are very strongly polarized towards separation. As a buffer zone you have an extremely weak, though large, segment of the population that cares about very little, learns very little, and contributes very little to the planetary consciousness. Therefore there is the battle of which you have spoken yourself many times between the forces of light and the forces of darkness. And as the battle rages in thought, so its shadows must cross the Earth's path. As disharmony enters year after year after bloody year into the planetary crust, so the mantle of the Earth must adjust to the disarrangement of harmony. This is the basic cause of the difficulties that you are now in the middle of experiencing, as you well know. We feel that you know these things and desire confirmation from an outside source for you fear that you are too opinionated. However, you have been receiving the correct information and we must simply ask you to use it with the wisdom and the grace that comes with years of dealing with this sort of information. We need not remind you of the caution with which this information must be offered.

May we answer you further, my brother?

Don: Will you give me a general idea of the progression of the problems?

Again, my brother, your understanding of the probabilities is correct although we cannot discover which of the parallel possibilities will be chosen until now is then. The great probability is that by your 1986 your west continent will be a block of islands and your Great Lakes will be the beginnings of a great inland waterway. It is probable that between that time and the next seven years there will be devastation economically and politically that may cause the rest of the Earth changes to be irrelevant.

By the beginning of the 1990's—we have difficulty with time; you must forgive us for pausing—you may pray to the Creator each and every day that you are not destroyed by your own creations before you can build anew in thought for the new age. Approximately 1992, if you have survived the crucial period for warfare, including civil war, you will begin to experience the worldwide changes of which the Americas, the lower Americas and the Pacific experiences are but the beginning. The entire world will be in some disarray for some time.

At approximately the year 2010, by probabilities at this moment, you will have experienced the shifting of the poles and very few shall survive. However, as it has always been promised, a remnant shall remain. It may be that you in this group will train those who aid the survivors. Therefore the timetable, extensive as it is, is a challenge to each person who has chosen to come here with a mission to serve. That challenge is to do what that person may do, what that person is best at doing, always keeping in mind the will of the Creator, for …

(Tape ends.)

Saturday Morning Meditation
September 6, 1980

(Unknown channeling

I am Hatonn, and I greet you in the love and the light of the infinite Creator. We have been with you in meditation and enjoying the serene gentleness of your vibrations. We wish only to say a few words to hopefully aid you in your thinking this day and, of course, to answer any questions that you may wish to have sent out as streams of light from the living fountain, with crystal purity in your very heart.

Each of your souls have traveled infinite dimensions and taken many, many directions to reach this point in your evolution of spirit. You could have passed by this vibration and chosen another, for your travels have been extensive and your journeys many. This one plucked your attention and in the end plucked you from the one true fountain into a smaller fountain, a shadow of the water of the Creator. And as you move about in this water that is half Creator and half made by man, you know that it is not the true living water of the Creator's fountain. Yet know within yourself that your stream of life runs clear. True and free from blemish or stain. You desire to cleanse yourself, then do so, my friends, from the inside to the out, cleansing your thoughts and purifying your emotions. Let your actions then be a delight unto you and a service to the Creator.

At this time we would transfer to the one known as Don. I am Hatonn.

(Don channeling)

I am Hatonn, and I am with this instrument. I shall continue using this instrument. As you journey, through what you call time and space, you will [have], as you have had, many experiences. These experiences, as you know, mold what you call your personalities. It is necessary, if you are to become what you wish to be, to aid the experiences in molding your personalities. This is the path of the master. This is a very important step. If you can remember to aid the experiences that you have, regardless of how trivial, to effect the complete mold [of] what you wish to become then you will become that thing.

I shall repeat this. It is very difficult to remember all of the time. If you can remind yourself of this simple process, each time you speak, act or think, my friends, your progress will be *(inaudible)*. Do not underestimate the consequence of thought. Apply this principle to each thought you have. Decide whether it is a thought of a master. If it is not, correct it. Do the same for each action and each word you speak. Self-analysis is a continuing and all-important step in your self-education. You are now at the position your self education is possible and necessary. We are also at the same position in the evolution of our thought.

We will at this time transfer this contact.

(Unknown channeling

I am Hatonn, and am with this instrument. We have been speaking about the journey which each of you are proceeding upon, the journey towards mastering of your own being. We hope that we may further inspire your efforts by our simple thoughts, for we wish to be of service on this most important of journeys.

It is necessary at this time for your people to experience the urgency of making such a journey, of making such an investment of effort, for the investments which most of your people have made in this world of yours will not pay great dividends. We hope to be able to point a direction for future investments for the journey inward.

The path of mastering is that effort, is that investment of energy which shall reap the only rewards which sustain the true self. Each of your people seeks in some way to build a firm foundation of being that will sustain their consciousness, that will provide a source of security. We would suggest that the journey of the one known as Jesus is the example that has been placed before your people. We would hope that such a journey, such an example, would inspire each upon your plane to reproduce that effort.

Unfortunately, my friends, it has been seldom attempted by your people. We are hopeful that as the times of change draw ever nearer, more of your people will become aware of the urgency of making the inner journey, the inner preparations for transition. The world in which you live provides constant impetuses to remind you that each person you meet is as yourself, as each is as sacred and divine as the original Thought from which each springs.

We would at this time ask if there are any questions which we might attempt to answer through this instrument. Are there any questions?

Carla: Yes, Hatonn, I would like to know the significance of the two hawks that we saw this morning.

I am Hatonn, and would answer you, my sister, by saying that these particular hawks are as emissaries of the divine Being from which we also are sprung. And these particular emissaries were sent to wish you well and to communicate the blessings upon your new center and residence and the efforts which you shall make in this new location as emissaries yourselves of this divine Being as the One from which we all originate.

May we answer you further?

Carla: Yes, two more questions. Was there any significance to their mating?

The significance of the mating is the creation of the new effort, the effort to help those within your world who seek light but have known only darkness. The mating is the blending of the old with the new resulting in the offspring that is your work.

May we answer you further, my sister?

Carla: Yes, if it would not be beyond the right of me to know, I would like to know whether these hawks are biological or mechanical in construct.

We would answer you simply by saying these were biological creatures, in service to the divine Creator.

Carla: Thank you, Hatonn.

Is there another question?

Carla: Not from me, thank you.

I am Hatonn. If there are no further questions, we would take our leave of this instrument and leave, as always, in the love and the light of the infinite Creator. I am Hatonn. Adonai, my friends.

L/L Research

L/L Research is a subsidiary of Rock Creek Research & Development Laboratories, Inc.

P.O. Box 5195
Louisville, KY 40255-0195

www.llresearch.org

Rock Creek is a non-profit corporation dedicated to discovering and sharing information which may aid in the spiritual evolution of humankind.

ABOUT THE CONTENTS OF THIS TRANSCRIPT: This telepathic channeling has been taken from transcriptions of the weekly study and meditation meetings of the Rock Creek Research & Development Laboratories and L/L Research. It is offered in the hope that it may be useful to you. As the Confederation entities always make a point of saying, please use your discrimination and judgment in assessing this material. If something rings true to you, fine. If something does not resonate, please leave it behind, for neither we nor those of the Confederation would wish to be a stumbling block for any.

CAVEAT: This transcript is being published by L/L Research in a not yet final form. It has, however, been edited and any obvious errors have been corrected. When it is in a final form, this caveat will be removed.

© 2009 L/L RESEARCH

SATURDAY EVENING MEDITATION
SEPTEMBER 6, 1980

(Unknown channeling)

I am known to you as Hatonn. I am here tonight to work with the love vibration, to answer any question that you may have, and was hoping to have started this contact through the other instrument. It is a matter of gaining confidence. We feel that you will find it easier, my brother, when you are the only contact in a group. It is then not subject to your concern as to whether another shall speak at the same time, although we do not send messages to more than one instrument at a time.

We are aware of the physical plane problems of your planet. We know that young children lie naked in the streets of some cities in Africa and South America and other places, their bellies swollen and the flies buzzing about their closing eyes. We know the injustice of the wasteful man who takes what he cannot use and does not give it away. My friends, although we are of the Confederation of Planets, we are not blind. We do not paint a rosy picture where there is no rosy picture. Left to your own devices, you would soon become nothing but ghosts, my friends, ghosts in a living machine. We hope that you will do something about it.

I would open the meeting at this time to any questions from my brother, Jim.

Jim: Hatonn, I am wondering when the subject of those who are called "seeds" or wanderers, if there are wanderers from other Confederations than the Confederation to which you belong.

Yes, my brother, there is such a Confederation although it is much smaller than our own. It is a very uneasy combination of shifting influences and patterns, and tends towards the negative side of polarity. It does not intend to be negatively polarized, however, the way the organization works causes them to seem very negative to you. We have never paid a great deal of attention to them other than acting as your guardians and placing the planet under quarantine. However, such ships do slip through, and these vehicles do what they can to disrupt an already chaotic society.

May we answer you further?

Jim: I am wondering with those which the Space Confederation have seated here as wanderers or "apples," if at the end of this age that is now ending, that the transition into the New Age, if these wanderers will be returning their home planets or if there will be need for some to remain yet *(inaudible)*.

My brother, it is difficult for us to answer that for we do not yet know whether you will have the man-made catastrophe which will destroy your culture rather than the God-created catastrophe which only destroys portions of your geography. If you are in a full-scale war, one of our concerns will be to recover enough records to serve as a kind of Rosetta Stone to those who came after you, so they may translate our works if they wish instead of feeling completely without aid in this area.

May we speak further for you, my brother?

Jim: No, I don't believe so tonight. Thank you very much.

Is there another question at this time?

Jim: No, those are the two questions that I had, thank you.

In that case, I shall transfer this contact to the other instrument. I am Hatonn.

(Unknown channeling

I am Hatonn, and am with this instrument. We are pleased to greet you once again in the love and the light of our infinite Creator. We have said many times that it is necessary for the people of our planet to realign themselves with the plan of the Father. And we would say again, as each day passes, that your days are well spent when spent in the realization of the oneness that you share with all of Creation. We would hope that more of your people will seek to fulfill the yearning desire that most feel in one way or another with the pursuit of the inner being. We have said many times, such a pursuit is the only type of fulfillment that endures and yields fruit of the Father's creation.

We would hope that these messages which we are privileged and honored to be able to transmit through instruments such as these have been of aid and will continue to be of aid in this quest for your people. We are aware that, at the present, few value such messages, few value the method of contacts, but we say to you that instruments such as yourselves, and meditation groups such as this one, are precious tools and avenues for the sharing in the transmitting of the light from the infinite Creator, this light that shines within all creation.

We hope you will pour your efforts into and feed this light that it might burn ever brighter, covering more and more of your tired and weary world. This light is the light which illuminates the darkness that hangs so heavily upon your plane and your planet at this time. Such meditations as this one are invaluable tools for lighting yet one more candle to illuminate the darkness. And we thank those that are gathered here tonight for their efforts in preparing a way for yet more of their fellow creatures to share in the bounty and the harvest of the Father's creation.

We would now close this contact and, as always, leave you in the love and the light of the One Who is All. I am Hatonn. Adonai, my friends. Vasu borragus. ❦

Sunday Meditation
September 7, 1980

(Carla channeling)

I am Hatonn, and I greet each of you in the love and the light of the infinite Creator. We send special love to all of those who are present tonight, especially those who are new to this group or whom we have not seen for some time. It is a great privilege to blend our vibrations with yours. May we give our thanks to the one known as W, for had he not removed the young one from your midst, we would not have been able to speak, for he did not desire our presence at this time.

We would talk to you this evening about desire. Perhaps, my friends, you have heard of those who go on safari and [to] exotic places, discover remote islands, find new frontiers of learning, and it is an open question why some people do these things and others do not. Few are the people who are driven and this, my friends, is one of your planet's deepest problems. For you are all conscious beings and your desire, whatever it may be, should hopefully be clear enough to you that you are literally driven to pursue it. We are not speaking here of one type of desire being better than another for we find no elite among your peoples. All are one with the Creator. All are equal. We can, however, see simple differences in the patterns and the energies that surround some of your peoples, some of your peoples who have decided to pursue that which they desire.

And what, my friends, might be the mechanism for discovering your true desire? You can think and conjugate and plan and it will come to very little. To know your true desire, you must know yourself. And so, my friends, the journey is not to an exotic island or on a safari. The journey is inward to your heart, to that spark of love which holds the plan for you and for your universe and for your journey.

At this time, I would transfer this contact to the one known as Jim. I am Hatonn.

(Jim channeling)

I am Hatonn, and I am with this instrument and greet you once again in the love and light of the infinite Creator.

It has been our privilege and pleasure to address groups such as this one for some time now. In our messages, we seek to share that vibration of love which lies within each of your beings. We seek through these messages to serve each of your people, for service is our way of expressing the love of the Creator and we hope in these meditations and messages that we might be of some inspiration to each who hears our message; that each might for one more moment seek ever more deeply inward. For that is a journey which so few of your people have sought to make but which so many are in need of sharing and experiencing with each other.

We look upon your planet and see great turmoil. We see the seeking and the striving every day in the material world for the things which many think will bring them peace of mind. We look and we see that such seeking offers so little in the final analysis. For how much of the things of your world are required before peace of mind is achieved?

My friends, great things have been built and won and gathered in one empire or another and yet those in whose rule the empire rests have found no peach of mind. My friends, we would once again suggest that meditation upon the inner journey might serve you well as you seek peace of mind; as you seek your source; as you seek love. We have spoken many times upon this subject, for we believe that love, though so obvious in its power, is so little understood by your people. And we hope that upon your journey you will include daily meditation to seek inward for that spark of the divine Creator which we all share, each with the other.

At this time we will leave this instrument and transfer contact back to the one known as Carla. I am Hatonn.

(Carla channeling

I am Hatonn, and I am again with this instrument. My friends, so often you discount your own worth. We do not wish to praise you for your humanity, your personality, your intellect, but for yourself. Those things which I have just described are as clothing as you go into meditation. As you desire to know yourself and the Creator, strip off those things which limit you. Remove them gently, for they serve you well. Then bathe in the clean waters of the tranquil silence of the universal Thought. And come to rest in the heart of love. There you will find food and drink for your spirit. Parched and hungry though it may be, there is a never-ending supply of love for each of you—of courage, of innocence, of kindness, of all those things that you would like to add to your wardrobe.

But, my friends, they are not clothing, they must come from the heart. They must come from yourself. Your ego, your personality, your intellect, can never display to others that which you wish. Therefore, my friends, let it all go and rest in love, with no name, no reputation, no learning, for love is the greatest force and the greatest knowledge that you can possibly attain and you cannot reach it with your mind, with your ego, with your personality. It is a matter of desire.

We who are travelers upon that path hold our hand out to you. Many of us come from a distance. Some of us from other dimensions. But we are all here for one purpose, to hold out that hand to you and to say, "Fellow traveler, be not so weary that you forget to desire love."

I will leave this instrument now, for my brother Latwii is waiting eagerly to speak. I leave you in the love and the light of our infinite Creator. I am known to you as the consciousness of Hatonn. Adonai, my friends. Adonai vasu.

I am Latwii, and I greet each of you in the love and the light of our infinite Creator. I was attempting to contact the one known as Jim, however, there was some difficulty due to the imagination of his mind, therefore we will try again and hopefully speak to you now through the one known to you as Jim. I am Latwii.

(Jim channeling

I am Latwii, and I am with this instrument and we greet you in the love and the light of our infinite Creator. It is a pleasure and a privilege to be able to speak a few words through this instrument. We would now like to ask if any of you listening to our words would have questions to ask. If so we would be most happy to attempt to answer. Is there any question?

Questioner: I would like to know if on your plane or level of existence, if there's male and female entities?

I am Latwii, and we would assure you my sister, that upon our level of vibration we do, indeed, have what are termed male and female entities, though in a somewhat different mode than upon your plane. We are paired according to our vibratory similarities, for as we exist as vibrations of light we are able through our perceptions to discern the vibrations of our mates and the similarity or match, so to speak, so that we are mated in a very harmonious manner.

May we answer you further?

Questioner: I would like to know if you think there is any significance to astrology as it is practiced on Earth as far as finding the right mate?

I am Latwii, and I am aware of your question. We would answer you, my sister, by saying that, indeed, the science of astrology is quite useful as a tool for selecting a mate when used with precision. Unfortunately, as with all tools, it is quite easy to misuse a tool and therefore we would suggest to those who would seek to use astrology for any particular purpose to search carefully within their own being for the harmonious feeling of unity with whatever interpretation that you are using or experimenting with. For many have grains of truth but are wrought with some distortion. We would suggest that to find the most precise and effective means of using astrology, to seek within your own being and to ask if your technique is meant for you.

May we answer you further?

Questioner: No, that's fine, thank you.

Questioner: Can you recommend a good book on astrology?

I am Latwii. My brother, we would answer by suggesting that the research into the particular book might best be made by the individual seeking, for that is an important part of the journey, to seek and to sort between one interpretation and another. It would not be proper for us to make this selection for you.

May we answer you further?

Questioner: No, thank you.

We thank you. Is there another question?

Questioner: Can you tell me anything about the person or the being that came to the barn Friday night? Just came to the door and left?

I am Latwii. My sister, we cannot at this time give any information concerning the particular situation but again would suggest that you seek within for the answer which you seek. We are sorry when we are unable to give a specific piece of information but we value highly the individual free will in the experiencing of your reality and are quite careful to choose those pieces of information which we may share without violating your free will.

Is there another question?

Questioner: Does my friend R know anything about reading Tarot cards?

I am Latwii. Again, my brother, we must suggest that it would not be proper to comment upon one's abilities as they may be manifested. It is for those who wish to enjoy this individual in his activities to decide whether he has ability.

Questioner: Thank you.

We thank you. Is there another question?

Questioner: Would it be possible for Earth people to become like you are in possibly another reincarnation?

I am Latwii, and I am aware of your question. My sister, we would say to you that, indeed, for all of the inhabitants of Earth such an opportunity is being held wide open, that the opportunity to advance in your manifestation and experiencing of the love of the infinite Creator is within each of your beings. That is why we feel it is of utmost importance for each of your people to seek within for that spark of love which shall light the way on their journey. And their journey shall take them many places; and their journey shall indeed result in the reaping of a harvest for each. For it is the time upon your plane for the harvest of the crop. The seeds long have been sown, the seeds of the divine Creator, the seeds within all of Creation. Many have fallen on barren ground. Many have fallen on ground which has been tended somewhat, yet some weeds grow. Few have fallen on fertile ground, but we assure you that within each of your beings the fertile ground to sow such seeds exists and the opportunity to more fully and completely experience the love of the Creator is available.

May we answer you further, my sister?

Questioner: Thank you. Not right now.

We thank you. Is there another question?

Carla: I had an unusual occurrence in choir practice this morning and contemplated and wondered if you could confirm my analysis of it?

I am Latwii. And, my sister, we would answer you by saying that your own analysis is indeed your correct answer.

Carla: Thank you.

Is there another question?

Questioner: I saw what is called a "crazer" last night and would like to know if you can say anything about that?

I am Latwii. My brother, we would answer you by saying it would not be proper at this time to describe the phenomenon which you are aware of. We are again sorry not to be able to give specific information of this nature.

Is there another question?

Questioner: I have been reading a lot about the Illuminati and hearing about international bankers. Do they exist, are they the same, are they different? Are their motives what are supposedly given them by the writers?

I am Latwii, and am aware of your question and we would answer by saying that upon the stage of your planet there are many players. Some have roles which appear to be very heavy, very dark and to be of the nature of darkness, of that which you refer to as the Illuminati. There are many who are swayed and polarized toward the dark part of the spectrum, toward the dark experience of separation from the Father, many in your world.

Indeed, each within your planetary vibration at one time or another does experience and express this dark force. Each time you meet a fellow creature and fail to recognize the divinity that resides within, each time you turn your face from the light of the infinite Creator, you are polarized in the direction of darkness or negativity. And this does indeed create an energy which can be tapped into, so to speak, and used to lure others in that direction.

We would suggest that should such beings indeed exist upon your plane, a most important consideration is how you, yourself, live your own life; how you are able to manifest the vibration of love. For, my friends, love is that force which encompasses all.

May we answer you further, my sister?

Questioner: No, Latwii. It's a great relief to know that I don't have to get paranoid.

We are very happy to ease your mind. May we answer another question?

(Someone blows their nose in the background, followed by laughter.)

We are greatly enjoying the vibrations of this group. We enjoy laughter quite heartily and join you in your mirth.

Questioner: Latwii, I have a question. As a community, we are about to embark in a cooperative manner together. Could you advise us relative to this endeavor? Are we acting at the right time? In other words, are we acting too soon? Are we acting too late? Is it the right time to be doing what we are doing?

I am Latwii, and I am aware of your question. My brother, we would suggest it is never too soon, never too late to join in love, to join in cooperation, that whatever endeavor you seek to carry out together, that you join your energies as closely as possible with each other, with the infinite Creator that you seek amongst yourselves, the council of your wisdom. That you seek to manifest to the best of your ability the love that resides in each of your beings.

Ask yourselves these question and within your cooperative experience the answers will become very apparent. We cannot council you specifically for you have the answers within your shared experience.

May we answer you further?

Questioner: Thank you.

We thank you. Is there another question?

Questioner: I would like to know more about the nature of the type of life or nervous system or whatever you are manifesting in relation to what we experience here.

I am Latwii, and am aware of your question. We would have great difficulty explaining precisely our experience of reality through this particular instrument for his mind is not furnished with the necessary concepts and it is also limiting to be forced to use words, but can only answer by saying that we exist as vibration of light and our experience is one which enables us to create by thought all that we need in the way of material things or things of a mass nature.

Questioner: What kind of things of a material nature do you need?

We occasionally make transitions to lower densities such as your own and are able to materialize any object that we need in order to navigate through such densities.

May we answer you further?

Questioner: Well, could you do that now? I mean, if you wanted to.

If there was such a need, it would indeed be possible. May we answer you further?

Questioner: I was just wondering. Thank you. Do you occasionally manifest bodies in order to perform things here? Perform actions here on Earth?

Yes. May we answer you further?

Questioner: Have you done this yourself recently?

We have been long absent from your third dimension. May we answer you further?

Questioner: Well, come on down!

We appreciate the invitation. May we take what this instrument would call a rain check?

Questioner: Well that would be fine. I understand if you are busy and all.

Our business frequently takes us on jaunts and we will keep this particular destination in mind for future journeys.

Questioner: OK. We could also use some help on our workshop.

Is there another question that we might attempt to [answer?]

Questioner: Is there a cure to allergies?

I am Latwii, and we would suggest that allergies are indeed difficult to deal with upon your plane and we sympathize greatly. Is there another question?

(Pause)

I am Latwii, and we would suggest that if there are no further questions we would take our leave of this instrument. We wish to express our great gratitude and happiness at being able to share a few of our thoughts with your meditation group. It has been a joy to blend our vibrations with yours. I am known to you as Latwii and I leave you in the love and the light of the infinite Creator. Adonai vasu borragus.

Monday Meditation
September 8, 1980

(Carla channeling

I am Laitos, and I greet you in the love and the light of the infinite Creator. As though we are one with you, a part of you, we love you, my friends; as we would love our own bodies, our own hearts and our own thoughts, we love you, my friends. Look around you. Who else in the creation of the Father loves you? Feast your eyes. Look at the rose that blooms in its enormous wealth of color and scent and form—because it loves. There is nowhere that you can truly look in the Creation of the Father that you cannot find love.

We realize that there is much to be said for the difficult nature of the task of the pilgrim for a pilgrim is one who sets himself to journey consciously. All beings journey unconsciously, but a few in any generation begin to journey in a consciousness understanding of the process of pilgrimage. This makes your existence at once more blessed and more difficult. Blessed, my friends, because you have all the company of heaven to surround you in angelic chorus. Difficult because you know that you cannot react as do those who are unconscious of the process of learning to those things which would undo you but must aim to remain centered.

We give you the idea of the rose, for truly, my friends, your life in this density is very like it. Your bloom and your form and your scent will please and glorify the Creator and then be gone. What remains, my friends, if you have shown as much love as a simple rose climbing towards the light, your scent, the odor of your spiritual being will remain. Certainly, you have examples of this in some of your great teachers. Their thoughts, their beings, remaining fresh in memory for many hundreds of your years. All else is and shall be consumed in time.

We are aware that each of you wishes to do what this instrument would call worldly work but each of you is consciously aware that these needs involve working for the good of the planet to which you have given your beings in this effort. Remember always to first center yourself, to feel the beauty of your own unfolding, the delicate scent of the love of the Creator that emanates from you in many, many, ways. Do not see yourself in any way except as a channel for love, the love of the Creator, my friends. If you can maintain that connection in sincerity, that which you need shall be given unto you.

I would like to leave this instrument at this time so that one of our brothers in the Confederation of Planets in the Service of the Infinite Creator may use the other instrument. I am Hatonn. Adonai, my friends.

I am Oxal, and I greet you in the love and light of the infinite Creator. We are very pleased and privileged to be able to make this contact with this instrument tonight. We have been waiting to reestablish this contact and to help this instrument to recognize our vibrations. We are very pleased when we are able to speak a few words through a new instrument.

We have been observing the content of your meditation and are very pleased that we are able to join our vibrations with yours, for your vibrations this evening are of quite angelic nature. We are aware that both of the instruments here this evening are in pursuit of what our brother Hatonn has described as world work and we would add our blessings and assurances to this efforts. We wish to assure each instrument that there are great needs in your world today which you will be asked by your own choice to help meet. There is a crying need for those [with] the light and experience of the light of the infinite Creator to share and shine this light with your people who are bathed in darkness.

We are aware that many of your people seek sincerely yet inefficiently as they make their own journeys into consciousness. Their inability to fully recognize the light that shines [in] their being stems in some part from a lack of what might be called examples of your fellow creatures, for by example much is [communicated.] Unfortunately, there are too few examples of the light of the infinite Creator as you travel about in your daily activities. Shine that light forth with every opportunity that presents itself to you, as you meet and deal with your fellow creatures daily. Be noticed as one who radiates the love and the peace of the Father to those who are harried and worried and unable to find the center of *(inaudible)* within their own being. By your example you shall remind these that they also are capable of being such sources of light.

It is a noble endeavor to be as an example. It is not always easy but is one of the most effective methods of teaching, for it says in an action what a thousand words may fail to say. Therefore, we urge each of you to be as the shining light that is your source and to shine your light about you as you become beacons for your fellow creatures who are lost on dark and stormy seas.

We would now leave this instrument. It has been a pleasure and a privilege to be able to share our thoughts with you this evening. I am Oxal. Adonai, my friends. Vasu borragus.

I am Latwii and I greet you both in love and light and am here for the purpose of attempting to answer any question that you may have if you have not yet run out of questions. So I open myself to you at this time. Do you have a question, my brother?

Jim: Latwii, I was wondering about the concept of tithing and how it works for the individual to give part of the fruits of his or her labors to the larger community or a church. Could you share some of the underlining principles of tithing and who it benefits and how?

I am Latwii, and would be glad to share with you our limited ability to speak on this subject for it has been distorted by many of what this instrument would call fundraising activities until it is barely recognizable as the spiritual exercise which it once was.

The original concept as this instrument herself has stated recently is that all things come from the Creator and that any supply material that you may receive is the Creator's 100%. In giving part of that bounty back to the Creator, no matter how little or how much you can afford to give, you are blessing yourself, for the principle of giving is that those who give shall have a thousand-fold added [unto] them, but those who keep and hoard will lose all that they have.

The, shall we say, industrialized church business had caused tithing to become a means of being respectable within the society devised by those who attend a meeting on Sundays which makes them feel good. As far as we can tell, your peoples do not feel blessed at giving to the Creator who gave them the other 90 or 95% of what they have received as material supplies. Instead they are concerned at the loss of the 5% or the 10%.

The basic principle, however, is that tithing helps only one person and that is you, for it puts you in a right relationship between your work and your Creator. For work is a way of manifesting the original Thought of love and these manifestations may then be turned to whatever end you feel is closest to working toward the ends which you feel the Creator would have His centers of prayer and light approach.

The money itself cannot help anyone but you. The organization to which you offer your manifested energy and work and money must then feel the conscious aliveness of this gift from the heart and work with it to fulfill the desires of the participants in this giving. Then and only then do you find the organization itself multiplying as does the fortune of the giver. Then and only then do you find the exchange of love that erases any hint of money-raising, and instead observes tithing or giving some portion of your worldly bounty as a form of recognition that if the Creator has given you 100% of all that you are and all that you have, it is a right relationship with the Creator to give back to Him, then, a certain amount of that which, through His grace, you have garnered and reaped.

May we answer you further my brother?

Jim: That was very enlightening, Latwii. I appreciate that. I just have one other question of another nature. Um. It is of a personal nature and you may not be able to give me any information on this, but I'll ask anyway.

Somewhere within my being, I remember being in a state of bliss, moving into a state of what seemed to be disharmony and almost Hell in comparison and I was fearful that I would get lost in this hellish state and I remember a voice saying, "It is OK. You won't get lost, you can come back." I am wondering if you can shed any light on the origin of that feeling within my being?

Yes, my brother. We understand and we feel that you already understand enough of the answer that we will not infringe upon your free will by dealing with this question at this time.

Jim: I understand. I thank you, and that's the only question that I have for this evening. Thank you very much.

You are very welcome, my brother. At this time, if there are no more questions from you I would transfer this contact to you in order that this instrument may ask a question of me through you. I am Latwii.

(Jim channeling

I am with this instrument and would be very pleased to attempt to answer a question from our sister. Do you have a question?

Carla: Yes, Latwii, I do. As you know, I am working with a friend to attempt to help him to get as much as I can offer him of lessons that I have learned from working with the energies of the Brotherhood over a period of years. Is it possible for you to suggest to me things of which I may not have thought that I may be able to help him further?

I am Latwii, and am aware of your question and would answer by suggesting that your own efforts in this sharing which you have undertaken have been of a very positive and productive nature. We feel that you have truly given of yourself and have done so in an unselfish manner. Our only suggestion for further sharing would be to continue your true concern for the welfare of this entity and to consider carefully how your future sharing will affect this entity's right of free will to learn by his own efforts so that your sharings are in harmony with his right of free will.

We would attempt to state this somewhat more clearly through this instrument. We would suggest entering more of the concept of personal direction for this entity and less dependence upon your efforts.

May we answer you further?

Carla: Could you be more specific?

I am Latwii, and we will attempt to be more specific without infringing upon your own free will. We have suggested that your sharings have been quite positive and of an uplifting nature. We would now suggest that future sharings, to be also of an uplifting nature, might concentrate more upon helping the entity to help himself rather than to depend upon your efforts.

Carla: That is what I wish to do but I'm not sure how to go about it.

We wish that we could be more specific with the details of your sharing efforts but we must suggest that the very specific particulars must be of your own origination.

Carla: Possibly talking with the one known as Jim might be fruitful.

Yes.

Carla: Thank you, Latwii.

And we thank you. Did you have another question?

Carla: No, that was it for the night. Thank you very much.

I am Latwii and would now leave this instrument. As always, we leave you in the love and the light of the infinite Creator. I am Latwii. Adonai, my friends. ✣

Meeting with Jim McCarty
September 9, 1980

(Unknown channeling

[I am Hatonn, and] we greet you, my friends, in the love and light of the infinite Creator. It is a privilege to join our vibrations with you this evening. We are especially pleased to be able to make our initial contact through this instrument for that is an important part of his efforts in channeling at this time.

We would speak with you this evening a few words on the subject of the Earth changes which you have been discussing this evening. We are aware of your great interest in this phenomenon which has begun upon your planet. We would suggest that those people who shall survive the Earth changes which are approaching rapidly will be in great need of guidance, even more than they are now, for your reality shall, in the twinkling of an eye, be changed radically and such an event will have drastic effects upon the mass consciousness of your people.

We would suggest that at such time it will be critical for the survivors to be aware of a greater reality, the reality of our unity each with the other that none are cast out alone on stormy seas, that even when the worst imaginable events have been played to their finale upon your Earth's stage that even then and especially then we are all one. Such survivors will be in great need of those who have traveled this path of peace, this path of seeking the truth. These pilgrims who are well acquainted with that path will be of invaluable service to those who are fortunate, shall we say, to survive the changes imminent upon your plane. These people will be in great need of the light which those such as are gathered here this evening will be able to share in their efforts to share the light that has been sparked within their being.

We are hopeful that the messages which we are transmitting at this time concerning Earth changes might be of help to those such as yourselves to prepare not only your own beings but to prepare for the showing of the way inward to those who shall need such directions greatly.

We would at this time transfer this contact to another channel. I am Hatonn.

(Carla channeling

I am Hatonn, and am now with this instrument. I greet you again in love and light. We were attempting to communicate through the one known as Don for he needs the practice in order to regain his fluency as a channel. However, he is somewhat fatigued and quite disinterested in making the effort to communicate as a channel at this time. Therefore we gladly move on to this instrument.

In the days ahead you will find that the decisions which you as spiritual beings make will be the keynotes to the decisions upon the physical plane which you then must make in order to carry out your spiritual plan. For those of you who have consciously worked on seeking out your own identity, whatever happens to you will therefore be of a much different timbre and feeling than it will be to others for it will be seen differently by you. You will find yourself being changed and, since growth is always painful, you will experience some discomfort emotionally and mentally as you adjust to new conditions of living. But those of you who are destined to live through the first changes and to be some of those who are as rocks amid the quicksand will be able to view and deal with these discomforts in such a manner as would befit your state of mind.

As you know, we are a planetary consciousness and therefore it is not surprising that we suggest that those of you who desire to aid the planet during these times of change find groups of like-minded people and work as a community. For it is in community that your best abilities both to survive and to be a center of light will be realized. We would not be so specific as to indicate that we can see into the future and say which of you will and which of you will not be existing in this density at any particular time. We are attempting to give you guidelines to follow so that the vibrational change and its after-effects that you are already experiencing will not seem overly traumatic, in fact, will seem to be in some ways a ray of hope. For you will see people turning from their previous sleep and awakening to the brevity of their physical lives and to the next obvious question: "Will I survive the demise of my own physical vehicle?" This concern alone in a time of difficulty will have many seeking answers. Therefore, we encourage you in your dedication and are with you whenever you ask.

We would leave this instrument at this time. I leave you in the love and the light of our infinite Creator. I am Hatonn. Adonai vasu borragus.

Sunday Meditation
September 14, 1980

(Carla channeling

I am Hatonn, and I greet you this evening in the love and the light of the infinite Creator. We who are in His service do thank you most heartily for allowing us to be with you this evening. This evening we would touch briefly upon an aspect of service. We have been concentrating in our talks with you upon the discovery of your inner self and of the seed of love within you. This evening we would talk about love in action, for there is no tree planted without help, and crop gathered without reapers. We have cautioned you many times not to be aggressive or abrasive in your contacts with others. But we would speak to you this evening about the confidence of the knowledge of who you are and whose glory you may manifest in this Earth world.

It is a responsibility to know, for then you must serve, and we would like you to be aware that in each contact that you make you are manifesting the Creator in some manner. When you think back, my friends, to the point in time when you yourself became aware of the kingdom of the Father and of all that there was to gain from the knowledge and the being of it, you will understand how precious it is to be able to share that experience with others. It is written that there is great joy when one lost sheep has been brought back into the fold. More joy than all ninety-nine of the other sheep engendered for they were already found. We encourage you not to be elite or apart from the world in which you live. You may see yourselves as somewhat different only because you have become conscious of who you are. Use your being to allow those about you to dwell in such an atmosphere that they too have the potential of realizing who they are also.

If you see those about you as perfect beings, you are seeing them clearly. If you see and react [to] them in their emotional, mental and physical illusory patterns, you are not seeing them clearly. You are not then allowing them the freedom to reach the point which was so precious to you when you reached it. It is true, my friends, there is often nothing that you can say, little that you can do to help those whom you meet. But there is much that you can be and much that you can conceive in your mind as the identity of those people who may to the outer eye be less than perfect.

To your inner eye, my friends, to that patient, timeless, inner eye, each being is perfect, manifesting in the eternal present. Give that gift in love, for you are disciples of a path of service. And to expend all of your energy upon yourself will block you from gaining more understanding. You must use what you have learned until it becomes a part of you, until it becomes second nature.

We would like at this time to transfer this contact to the one known as Jim. I am Hatonn.

(Jim channeling)

I am Hatonn, and am with this instrument. We have been speaking of the pathway of service and we would say to you that this is a path which few of your people have chosen to travel. The path which is most frequently traveled is the one which seeks only self-gratification, the attempt to fill what is understood to be the self with the material wealth of your people and of your culture. The filling of the self with things which have matter …

We would suggest a pause for …

(Pause)

I am Hatonn, and am again with this instrument. We welcome the new members of our group this evening, and hope that they will forgive us for beginning in the middle of our presentation. We have been speaking of the pathway of service that so few of your people have chosen to follow, the pathway which we suggest for your serious consideration, for to serve is to allow that gift of the infinite Creator the energy which courses through your various bodies to continue its flow and to be shared by your fellow creatures. So few of your people have been able to discern the nature of service, for their ways have been circling round, shall we say, unto themselves so that the energy which is their daily gift of the Creator stays only within their being as they seek to fill themselves with the various material rewards of your third-dimensional world.

It would seem to the surface observer that the things of your world are indeed worth pursuing, for so many pursue them and so much is made of their possessions. But we would suggest to you that as you go forth in your daily round of activities that you consider the fact that each person you meet is the Creator and what else can one do, when one knows that he or she is also of the Creator, other than serve the Creator? My friends, what else can one do other than serve the Creator?

We would leave you with this question. We would now transfer this contact to the one known as Carla. I am Hatonn.

(Carla channeling)

I am Hatonn, and I am again with this instrument, and greet you all in love and light. We give you but very poor food, my friends, for we must speak to you in words. But as we have said, we hope you have food for thought for the path of service as opposed to the path of non-service is an illusion and one which you must only come to grips with within yourself. We cannot express to you the paradoxes of your illusion, the difference between that which seems and that which is, for many are the actions which look the same and yet are diametrically opposed in intention and in effect in the thought world.

Therefore, my friends, look to your thoughts and let your thoughts create your actions, not the other way around. Above all realize that you are in a divine flow of perfect love into which you may tap as into an ever-flowing fountain cascading, scintillating, full of light, full of energy. It is easiest to do so in meditation, although there are other ways having to do with service to your fellow beings and a realization of the unity of us all. We ask you this: choose. At any moment that you can, stop and choose. It is your path, it is your illusion, it is your thought, it is your action. Refresh yourself in meditation on a daily basis and live the joyous life of love in action.

Before I leave this instrument I would like to pass among you aided by my brother Laitos, in order that we may make each of you aware of our presence and offer you our conditioning. If you would appreciate our help in deepening your meditation or in strengthening your ability to do channeling work in the future, please ask mentally for our presence, for we are in the room at this time and will pass among you. We will pause at this time. I am Hatonn.

(Pause)

(Carla channeling)

I am Hatonn, and will speak through this instrument just long enough to say that I and my brother Laitos thank you for the privilege of working with you. We would leave you now that one of our brothers in the Confederation of Planets in the Service of the Infinite Creator may speak. We leave you in the love and light of the infinite One. I am Hatonn. Adonai vasu.

I am Latwii, and am with this instrument and greet each of you in the love and light of the infinite Creator. We have been waiting eagerly to be able to speak to your group this evening and would like to ask if there are any questions which we might attempt to answer? Are there any questions?

Questioner: Yes Latwii. I have been confused with the idea of whether … I've been chanting a few years, you know, high mantra and which I call the maha mantra, and I was speaking with some Jesus followers, and there is always this conflict in my mind. Is mantra OK, and is the eastern path OK, or should I just surrender with being a follower of Jesus Christ as the master? And then in my mind I go, well, I guess it's the same path, there is no different path. But I have always this conflict, and I hear so many things about, oh, [it] is devil worship in meditations, and then the Jesus people say, Jesus [has] already been through all this so you don't have to believe in karma and past deeds. And so could you please help me in my mind to ease it up, the confusion?

I am Latwii, and am aware of your question, my sister. We would suggest that the path which you would most benefit following is the path of your own choosing, that if you choose to do one exercise or another matters really very little, for that knowledge which you seek, that source of energy within your being is where it is, and it calls to you for you are one with it. And if you follow that inner voice you shall arrive at that destination.

Your path may wind around various trees in the woods, around various incantations or postures or beliefs, but shall surely bring you to that center of yourself. All of the various foliage, shrubbery of the woods, is there for you to enjoy along your path as you choose. You may pick one or another or many or various ways in which to enrich your journey according to your own interests. There are not what might be called right or wrong choices, for all will bring you to the destination which you seek.

What we would suggest in easing your conflict of mind is to simply experience that which is of interest, experience that which seems of value and examine it with your own thinking. Meditate on it within your own being. Ask sincerely which path is most beneficial for you to follow and you will have your answers, for you are at this moment one with your answers.

May we answer you further, my sister?

Questioner: Thank you, Latwii.

And we thank you. Is there another question?

Questioner: I have a question, Latwii. I've read that greenhouses can be used to improve a person's health, and specifically I've read that incorporating a seventh part of blue glass, with the rest being clear, has a beneficial effect on the health of plants and animals. Can you tell me anything about this?

I am Latwii, and am aware of your question. We will do the best that we can through this instrument to make an answer for you, my brother. We would suggest that the color blue is, indeed, a beneficial color for growing living organisms, for the blue provides what might be called a coolness to the light of your sun, which is in its unaltered form of a hot nature, that there is a need by most living creatures to experience a combination of cool and hot light. To provide a balance in their growing cycles which is not available when the plant is in the open sunlight unshaded, we would suggest that adding the blue part of the color spectrum to a greenhouse would indeed be of value for any plants which you would grow therein. As we have mentioned before through another instrument, this would be more properly termed a bluehouse.

May we answer you further?

Questioner: Yes. I'd like to know if there would be any benefits for elderly people, particularly arthritic, in such an environment.

I am Latwii, and would answer you, my brother, in the affirmative, for all living creatures would benefit by a closer interplay of their lives with various life-forms, for each life-form, plant or animal or mineral, has certain ingredients, shall we say, that are somewhat lacking in the other life-forms, and by combining various types of life-forms in one location there is a balanced exchange of various chemicals and vibrations of light, shall we say.

And the elderly of your people are especially in need of an expanded contact with various life-forms, for the elderly of your people are most frequently excluded from experiencing a variety of life-forms, and are most frequently placed in seclusion, so to speak, and therefore would benefit greatly by experiencing the vibrations and energy of plants and animals and the natural environment.

May we answer you further, my brother?

Questioner: No, thank you.

We thank you. Is there another question?

Questioner: Yes, Latwii. Of course you are aware of the movie, "Close Encounters," and is that *(inaudible)*, is that what you people use to express? How much of that movie was the true thing, and also the part of the Indian chanting, is that a special chanting you people … you know, that sequence with the sounds, it's real pretty. Is that for real? I mean the whole thing was real, that's the way it happened, that's the way it goes?

I am Latwii, and would answer you, my sister, by saying that movies such as the one which you have mentioned, "Close Encounters," have utilized a variety of the data, shall we say, available to those who study the UFO phenomenon, as your people call it. There have been many ways that your people have been contacted by beings from dimensions and other parts of your universe. Many of these have been documented over long periods of time and are well known to many of your people.

We would suggest that those which were used in this movie were a compilation of various contact methods and our own Confederation of Planets in Service to the Infinite Creator have used a number of contact methods, most frequently the telepathic contact which is now being used, and those used within the movie are not very frequently used by our Confederation but are contacts of other beings.

May we answer you further?

Questioner: No, thank you.

Questioner: What sorts would the other beings be?

I am Latwii, and would answer you, my brother, simply by saying that for thousands of your Earth years we of the Space Confederation have been observing your people. We have been observing the interaction of your people with other beings as well and have attempted to, shall we say, quarantine your planet so that various negative energies could be worked out, so to speak, upon your plane. These energies are not just from the outside, shall we say, but have been attracted to your planet by the condition of your people on its surface, and there is the necessity for certain energies to find their fruition and to find reconciliation. Therefore, we can only say that the other beings are other beings not of the Confederation.

May we answer you further?

Questioner: No, that's fine.

Is there another question?

Questioner: I have another question, Latwii. I've recently heard that there is another group of entities that are known as the Nines and I would like to know whether or not, having an affinity for knowing myself, it would be useful for me to get in touch with them or in contact with that *(inaudible)*?

I am Latwii, and would answer you, my brother, by saying that your decision to contact any group or any resource must come from within your own being, and is best made there within your own knowing and being. Therefore, we cannot suggest that you do or do not make an attempt to contact those beings of the Nines. We hope that you will consider all such choices carefully, for they are your own choices.

May we answer you further?

Questioner: Yes. How would I go about contacting those entities known as the Nines?

I am Latwii, and would suggest that any contact with any group begins simply by being open to that group or concept. This is all we can suggest in this matter.

Can we answer you further? May we answer you further?

Questioner: No. I think I've about had it for awhile.

Is there another question?

Questioner: Yes, Latwii. I'm curious on the subject that I read myself and speculated on—immortality. Like, I understand that there is the mind and your mind sort of creates the body that you reside in. So if that is so, why do we choose to die? Why [is] there the urge in men that we create this body, and the Creator gave us this body, and then it had to perish with disease and old age? Can you explain that?

I am Latwii, and would answer you, my sister, by simply saying that it is an illusion that you live within and an illusion that you die when you leave, for while you are upon this stage in third dimension of material reality you play many parts. Each requires certain basic costuming. Your physical vehicle is a requirement for this particular stage and this particular drama. When you leave this stage and pass from this third dimension you will no longer be required to continue carrying certain burdensome costumes, your physical vehicle being one of these, that you are indeed at this moment immortal, that you have been for all time and beyond all time immortal and existing within the creation of the infinite Creator and that when you pass from this particular illusion, this particular stage, you will merely change roles and costumes as you have done so many, many times before.

May we answer you further, my sister?

Questioner: Yeah, there's one thing. What if somebody is so diseased, you know, the illusion of disease, and they choose, for instance, to self-destruct their own body and pass on. Is there sort of like a punishment, or is the choice being that somebody choose to leave their body by means of suicide, or is that a way to go that is a safe way, or is that playing games, or can [you] explain suicide and that sort of illusion?

I am Latwii, and would answer you, my sister, by saying that of the various illusions and games and roles and learnings which each of your people undertake upon your plane, all are illusion, yet do teach. All are chosen by each of your people for their own unique and personal reason, reasons which vary widely from one to another. That within this range of learnings of illusions, of games which are played upon your stage, some teach one thing and some another. And some teach different lessons to different entities depending upon the reasons which the entities [have that] began that illusion.

That, in general, it may be said that each choice which a person makes is the choice which will teach the perfect lesson for that moment. We would suggest that many stresses, so to speak, are encountered by your people as each plays their chosen role, and that each moment each person has an infinity of choices of how to continue that role. Some become overwhelmed by the heaviness and the burden which they have created in their role, stepping too far into the unknown, so to speak, or taking on too much of a challenge it would seem and thereby respond by the path which is described as suicide or the taking …

(Tape ends.)

Advanced Meeting
September 16, 1980

(Carla channeling)

I am Hatonn. And I greet each of you in the light and the love of the infinite Creator. May we thank you for inviting us into your circle to share your love and your light.

May we also inject a piece of pertinent information which we feel that the newer channel and the one who is relearning old skills might find helpful. It is the custom of our channeling preparations to use the most experienced channel as a sort of battery to enable the less experienced channel or one who is rusty to achieve more distinctive contact with us. Therefore, we urge each of those who are working on their channeling at this time to make use of the battery of this psychic generator known as Carla in order that when you are working by yourself you will have gained the confidence that you need. We are very interested in creating an atmosphere in which you feel very comfortable with the vibrations of the various entities of the Confederation and feel able to discern them. If you pray aright in the name of the one known as Christ you shall receive a properly tuned contact. Therefore, we leave this instrument and again, work with another instrument. I am Hatonn.

(Unknown channeling)

I am Hatonn. And I am with this instrument. And greet you once again in the love and the light of our infinite Creator. It has been our practice to begin our contact sessions with an opening message which is of general concern to those which are gathered to hear our thoughts. That this evening we would speak a few words on the subject of love as it is experienced or as it may be experienced in your daily life.

We would suggest that you carefully examine a concept which you now know within your being as love. We would ask each of you if that concept is clear to your own thinking and feeling. We would ask you to examine your concept to consider whether it is free of conditions. To examine, to discover, does the energy known as love flow freely through your being? Does it flow as the river, without interference? And if, in your examinations, you perchance discover blockages in the flow here or there, from whence come these blockages? Examine carefully, my friends, for though love is the basic power and motivating source of the universe, still it may be blocked by individual perceptions and behaviors.

And it is not always easy to allow a concept or the energy of love to course through one's being and wash all perceptive blocks away, for frequently we would wish as individuals that it would flow one way or another. But as you examine within your own being how it is that it flows through you, we would suggest examining the course and the channel and the way in which you allow it to flow. Are there constrictions? Are there blockages? If so, how best removed?

For, my friends, we would suggest that though preconceived ideas of the world might make the mind feel better, the unimpeded flow of the energy of the Creator is the greatest feeling of freedom which an entity can experience, for the flow has within it the wisdom of the Creator. And each of the creations of the Father is as a vessel which holds and allows this energy to be. Each of you people are as vessels, are as channels which allow or restrict the flow of this energy of the Father.

We would at this time transfer this contact. I am Hatonn.

(Unknown channeling

I am Hatonn. I'm with this instrument. What you call the beginning of the Creation *(inaudible)*. The creative energy creates all there is. It is channeled through each individual, controlled only by an individual's thought. This is the natural or normal way. Creation, all the planets, all of the vegetation upon the planets, all of the animals that inhabit the planets, all of the birds that fly in the sky, are all thought forms brought into what you call reality by direction of original creative energy directed through the co-creators that inhabit the universe.

Each of you has this power and always has had it and always will have it. All of your fellow beings on the planet you call Earth have this ability. One thing, my friends, is necessary. To act as the perfect modulator or filter. The all-inclusive force is the creation. Only one thing, my friends, is necessary: that is to think as your Creator. Many lessons have been given those of your peoples who dwell upon the surface of the planet. Lessons to bring them back *(inaudible)* to that place, to the original *(inaudible)* state of perfection of things that's normal.

There are things that have occurred that the people of your planet have called miracles. And yet these are normal activities. If you wish to perform a miracle, all that is necessary is that you do so. Each of you, like everyone that exists, has the ability to do anything *(inaudible)*. All that is necessary is for you to think the original Thought, become one with that Thought, to open yourself as a channel to the infinite energy of the universe. Become in tune with its song. My friends, that song is a song of love. That is the song of the universe. Become receptive to that song. Hear it. Be one with it.

(Tape ends.) ♣

Sunday Meditation
September 28, 1980

(Carla channeling)

I am Latwii. Ho, ho, ho, this was intended to come through another channel. However, we needed to begin with this channel in order to give confidence to the one known as Jim. We greet you through this instrument in the love and the light of our infinite Creator. We are at the same time extremely glad and extremely sorry to be speaking to you instead of the brothers and sisters of your special teachers, the ones of Hatonn. However, this group entity has again returned to its duty, working in the Far East, as you would call it, working against the spread of disharmony upon your planet.

We have been conditioning the one known as Jim while we have been speaking through this instrument and we would again attempt to speak through the one known as Jim. We leave this instrument, in gratitude for her quick senses of inner listening, and in hopes of speaking through her many times in the future. We thank this instrument. I will now leave this instrument. I am called by your group, Latwii.

(Jim channeling)

I am Latwii, and am with this instrument and we greet you, once again, in the love and the light of the infinite Creator.

We are pleased to be able to make this contact through this instrument, for we are aware that this instrument shall be away from this group in the near future, and is desirous of being able to continue this service as he embarks upon his journey. And it will be necessary for this instrument to be able to initiate contacts with the Confederation and with our vibration when he is on his own.

We would speak a few words this evening upon the subject of harmony, for the vibration and condition of harmony is one which is not frequently found upon your planet, as is evidenced by the condition of your world situation at the present.

Harmony is that state of being in tune with the infinite Creator, which is achieved by desire, a desire for unification, a desire for knowing and experiencing that fullness of being which is the Creator within. Harmony is that force which helps to unite people in their relationships with each other, but it must be sought before it can be found, and it is unfortunate, but it appears that few upon your planet seek harmony, for it is an endeavor which includes the welfare of those around you, and most of your people are pointed in the direction of their own interests and meeting them as best they can, fearing there will not be enough to go round.

The state of being, within the individual, which leads to harmony, is the same state which opens doors to any step of growth within the individual, and that is the receptivity, the openness, and the desire for attaining such a state. It is often too easy to think only of the personal needs, desires, wishes, beliefs and other codes which we set up for ourselves as we judge our lives. It is far too easy to consider only what one wants for oneself, instead of how to blend one's being with another in the state of harmony. We would suggest to those who are desirous of attaining that state of harmony to consider that it is a state which is achieved *with* others; a state which is achieved in cooperative effort as individual entities blend their energies with each other; a path which usually entails a type of compromise of positions, so that each may share with the other a common position, and the sharing of the position, the belief, or the place, is that which is harmony within that concept.

We would suggest to those seeking such a balanced point with themselves and with those around them that the first step is to give: to recognize the needs, rights and position of those close about you. And that this state of giving, and accepting, and recognizing, will be reciprocated by those with whom you are in close contact. For the state of giving is based upon the concept of love; that to give is to share that which is love, and that which is love is recognized by the inner being of those to whom it is given, even though it may not be given directly as a gift of love, but may begin in more modest ways by the simple recognition of another person's needs. We would suggest that harmony is that process whereby people in close communication join their beings even closer by agreeing to accept each other as they are and to work from that beginning point in a constant balancing of the needs, ideas and beliefs of each party.

We would, at this time, pause for a moment as our brother Laitos passes among each in your group and makes his vibration available to those in need of deepening their meditation and of becoming familiar with the vibrations of the Confederacy. We speak specifically of the one known as L, who has expressed this evening a desire to become a channel.

We pause for a moment as our brother, Laitos, passes among you.

(Pause)

I am Latwii, and am once again with this instrument. We would, at this time, like to open the meeting to any questions. If any present would have a question, we would do our best to make an answer. Are there any questions?

Questioner: I was reading some cosmic awareness communications ideas, which have been run down by some people in the East, and I really have no doubt as to the truth of it. But I know that they are not, precisely, in the same company with you guys, and I was wondering what view was among your particular branch of the Confederation of [as to] what's happening here. What about the great concern for the survival of leaders? Does that have some kind of implication as to what will happen at the New Age vibrations, with a lot of old vibration people surviving?

I am Latwii, and am aware of your question, and would answer you, my sister, simply by saying that the most appropriate phrase for this particular phase which your nation and those individuals who lead it are going through would perhaps be that the first shall be last, and the last shall be first; for those who would seek to gain the whole world and yet lose their souls, what in truth and in spirit have they gained?

For to hold onto that which is of the material world, that which has, up to this point in the evolution of human history, been unable to completely fulfill human entities upon your plane, to hold on so tightly to that which is of the material, is to focus the energies of one's being in a direction which is likened unto building a house upon sand. And we would suggest that those who engage in such activities and have no concern for the welfare for those whom they are governing—or those whom they have been chosen to serve, those whom it a privilege to serve—these shall find that not only shall they not be serving such people or be in such high positions, but shall find themselves at the bottom of the pit of their own being, which they have dug with their own hands.

And we would suggest that the new age shall see many different responses to the flow of energy which is now sweeping over your planet. And you may expect to see the most absurd of dramas appearing upon your world's stage, for all the energies of the universe, it would seem, shall be sweeping across the stage of your planet and you shall see many wonders. But those energies may be channeled and focused into creative elements and centers by those who are truly concerned with serving those who are their brothers and sisters. And to focus in the direction of the spirit is the means by which true survival shall be attained.

May we answer you further, my sister?

Questioner: Well, I had a couple of other questions, which you may answer at your discretion, of course. I was—I've been very impressed by the Cosmic Awareness things that I've read, and I was wondering what your relationship in the Confederation was to this particular source. Is it a planetary source within the Confederation? Is it another source? What is the relationship between the two?

I am Latwii, and am aware of your question. And can answer best by suggesting that the source of which you speak is a source which is most well known to those who are familiar with the works of Edgar Cayce.

The source which is known as Cosmic Awareness appears to be simply that; an awareness of the being—the state of being—which is described as Cosmic, or of the Consciousness of all being. And this source of information is now proceeding to reveal unto those of your people who are concerned about the new age the pathway or process by which each may attune to these universal forces which we have spoken of as proceeding into your reality with such great speed at the present time, so to speak.

We cannot say whether the information revealed by this source is correct or incorrect, for it can never be known at the moment information is given whether it is correct or not, for the mere giving of information alters the situation which is being described.

We would suggest with all sources of information, including especially our own, that those who are contacted with information of this nature consider carefully within themselves what they themselves believe, to evaluate carefully on your own concerning what you are reading or hearing, and to make those judgments in light of competing or opposing information. For, within your world, you will discover there are infinite sources of information, and it is your task as entities upon your planet to sort and sift through the infinite variety of information available, and to choose that which speaks within your own being.

May we answer you further?

Questioner: Yes, my brother. Then I see that confirms what I thought about Cosmic Awareness. It did seem to be a planetary vibration in that, like the Cayce vibration, it comes from a much higher plane, inner plane, of our own planet, close to the akashic records. I was—I had pretty much of an idea in my head as to the type of information that they were giving and why they gave that type of information, as opposed to the philosophy that you give, and I was just wondering if you would care to say anything on that subject in confirmation, or changing, of what I had basically thought.

I am Latwii, and would add only that information of a specific nature is most difficult to express clearly, for the future, as you know, is never fixed. Directions, propensities, tendencies and likelihoods of directions of energy, are the most easily pinpointed and transmitted information, but to say where an infinite variety of energies will eventually coincide is very difficult and is a task which we of the Space Confederation do not attempt with these types of contacts, for the distortion factor would soon cause our information to become nearly worthless.

It is for this reason that we attempt to give the basic groundwork and basic philosophy of love and light which we feel are so important to your people at this time. We do not feel that the revealing of specific names, and dates, and places, and events is most beneficial to those in your meditation group, for this information can be attained elsewhere and we would be most pleased if we could, in our effort, plant the seeds of meditation, of love, of light, and of the seeking of the divinity within each of your peoples' being. We would suggest that sources which are focusing in the area of more specific information can be of great value, but must be carefully evaluated upon their performance, and we would suggest being very cautious in the area of accepting without further investigation any specific information which is attained, wherever it might be obtained.

May we answer you further, my sister?

Question: Well, just a little bit. I would like to thank you because I think you do work with the basic things and teach us love and light. But I just I wanted to check out the Cosmic Awareness people, because I was interested in them at this point. I made a few basic assumptions: number one, that they were planetary; number two, that they were giving more precise information because, being planetary, they had a right to do so; and number three, that they were able to put their probability guesses through because of the particular configuration of one channel, Paul Shokely. A lighter trance, the type of contact that we have with you, would never work for that type of information, that it would take a different vibration.

If you want to confirm any of the three—you already confirmed the first one—I just wondered about the second two.

I am Latwii, and we would conclude our comments upon this subject simply by saying that the particular type of trance which is used in this contact of the Space Confederation is most beneficial to the type of message we have to offer, and [we] are also appreciative of the efforts of those who would use the trance medium, for such an entity is indeed able to transmit information of a much different frequency or nature than that which we are able to transmit through our light trances, as you have spoken of them. We would suggest to those who wish to become more familiar with the contact situation to investigate the nature of meditation on their own, so that they may themselves discover what varieties and types of information are available within their own being.

Are there any other questions?

Questioner: No, thank you.

Questioner: I have a question. You are aware of my desire to learn more about channeling and to serve as a channel. I would ask for advice on how to proceed on this path.

I am Latwii, and, my brother, we will answer you simply by saying that to desire this type of service is the most important ingredient for those who wish to become channels. For it is indeed a service that you render, and within your own being it is necessary to search and to seek that you might be made an instrument, and might kindle within yourself that desire to share the love and the light of the infinite Creator, which resides within your being.

And we would suggest as well a daily system of meditation of your own design. We would suggest meditating at the same time each day, so that you might develop a pattern of relaxation and communication within your own being, so that you might find within yourself that point of centering from which you might be of service.

We would also suggest that a simple prayer might be used to ask that divine guidance be with you as you serve, and that you might be made an instrument of that service of the infinite Creator. We would also suggest that frequent experiences with a channel who has experience, such as those present this evening, might be of use in making the vibration of the Confederation more familiar to you.

May we be of further service?

Questioner: You've answered my questions.

We thank you. Is there another question?

Questioner: No, thank you.

We are very pleased to have been able to speak these few words and to share our thoughts through this instrument with you this evening. We would at this time take our leave of this instrument and, as always, we leave you in the love and the light of the infinite Creator. I am Latwii. Adonai, my friends. Vasu borragus. ♣

Intermediate Meeting
October 5, 1980

(Carla channeling

I am Latwii, and I greet you in the love and the light of our infinite Creator. The desire for our words is strong this evening and we have been called in quickly. Therefore, we will pause in the middle of our message that you may as a group yet attain a deeper state of oneness. We speak to you because of your need to hear and because of our growing understanding of the difficulties of your peoples at this time. When we first spoke to you as a group we did not understand these difficulties. We knew that the people of your planet dwell within a heavy chemical illusion, but our previous study had been of the various vibrations of what you would call your heaven worlds. They too are troubled, color fading into color, the qualities sometimes distressed, as you would call it, muddying the water of your higher plane. But as we come into your minds, as we enter your domicile and join you in meditation, it is as though we were inside a deep well. And we understand the claustrophobia of those like you who, knowing there are other ways to live, must live in this well, this deep well of sorrow, limitation and lack.

This instrument does not understand why I am giving you this message at this time, for she herself is not sorrowful. Yet she is a faithful channel and will speak what I ask and what I give. We sound this somber note because we wish to tell you that although we can only be your companions in sorrow, lack or limitation, we do know of a reality that dwarfs the illusion in which you now live, and that is available to you through meditation. We know a very simple truth. It is so simple that we are laughable for speaking it to you, for all we have to tell you is what you already know. Many have said it before us. Love is all that there is. Light is the manifestation of love and each of you are vibrating in some area of light, not only in your physical body, but in your thought body and your emotional body and in your spiritual body.

Some of you are more harmonious than others at this time, and we can see you as the song you have just listened to said, as a kind of chord of being. And yet all of you, my friends, emanate it and will return to the one perfect light, the one beingness of love. In fact, you have not left. This trip, this journey, is an illusion which you have created because you have chosen not to be aware of the original Thought of love. This is your right and you have a great deal of help within the illusion which you now enjoy.

There are almost no people to whom you may speak of simple things. Almost all of those who attempt to speak wisdom unto you speak a complex wisdom, one that breaks down so that reality forever recedes before you. The truth, my friends, is simple. Through this instrument and others we of the Confederation have many times urged you to meditate daily. We do not do this because we feel that a ritual is helpful. We do not do this because we desire to convert any being from any path that he or she may be upon. We do this because this is all that we can do that is not a complete distortion of the truth, for in meditation you simply listen. It is written in your holy works, "The place whereon you stand is holy ground." You carry your tabernacle and your meaning with you. It is a bag you can never leave behind when you pack. It is an item you will never have forgotten when you unpack. All that you are able to forget is how to find that simplicity which is yours in meditation.

When there is something that is troubling you in the physical world, it is often very handy to take an implement such as a pocket knife and remove it, be it the hanging thread or whatever else has begun to seem shabby and extraneous to your needs. There is a great deal in your thoughts that is of the same quality, and meditation has the same effect as a good sharp pocket knife. It cuts through a good deal that you would not be able to cut through by the use of your intellect, in order to bring you to the present, to infinity, to love.

I would pause at this time that you may experience in silence the force of that love. I am Latwii.

(Pause)

I am again with this instrument. I am Latwii. We are continuing to use this instrument in order that the one known as Jim may be more fresh when we get to the questions. This instrument is well suited to our message this evening.

We speak to your planet of sorrow. If we could, we would be upon our knees with our hands outstretched to you, for it is time. If you are going to pursue the life of a student of reality, if you are going to attempt to be one who loves with the love of the Creator, it is time now for you to decide and to do it. We realize that we have been speaking for many years of those things which are to come, and we cheerfully admit to you our inadequacy in understanding your time frame. But we cannot see any more daylight, as you would say, between the events that have been triggered by your planetary consciousness and your own paths. It is time, my friends, for you to be what you will be. There will be an hour in the not-so-distant future when you will be what you have become. And, like it or not, my friends, that will be your time. Becoming will temporarily be at an end and whatever you have developed up until that point will be your sensitivity, your resource, and your sanctuary.

We see down into a well. We do not see very well. Therefore, we ask you to come into the kingdom now and each day in meditation that you may spend as much time as possible in the light and the love of the infinite Creator, for in those days which are to come you will be called upon to be what you hoped to be. We offer you every assistance, as we of the Confederation wish nothing more than to aid you in your realization of the illusion and the way out. We will speak to you many times, for we have infinity. But we speak to you now in your bodies heavy with physical matter, and we send you our sympathy and our urgent message: seek love.

I will again pause that the one known as Laitos may touch each of you who requests it with his presence. I am Latwii.

(Pause)

(Carla channeling

I am Latwii. I am again with this instrument, and greet you once again in love and light. Having delivered myself of such a solemn message, I was looking forward to answering some questions and perhaps being able to spread a bit more cheer. However, we are having difficulty contacting the one known as Jim. If he would relax and allow our thoughts to flow through him, we will again attempt to contact him. I am Latwii.

(Jim channeling

I am Latwii, and am with this instrument, and greet you all once [again] in the love and light of the infinite Creator. We are very pleased to be able to make this contact at this time and would ask if there are any questions which we might attempt to answer. Are there any questions?

Questioner: I have a question. In the time I have attended these meditations I have never known you to seem depressed—what we would call depressed— or to feel the sense of urgency that you seem to project tonight. Are there events here on our planet which have prompted this that you can tell us of or events in the near future that we would wish to be aware of?

I am Latwii, and am aware of your question, and we would answer you, my brother, by saying that there are, indeed, events occurring upon your planet which require an urgent attention. But they are not events which have happened only recently, for the history of your planet is one of strife, is one of sorrow, is one of struggling for the material rewards which your reality has to offer. Your planet's history, the history of your people, is now culminating in the dramas which you may observe occurring upon your plane each day of your existence. You need only look carefully at those sources which are available to each of your people as the bearers of news and the occurrence of events around your world, to know that things are not right, so to speak, that there is a great growing of tensions among the various peoples of your world, that these tensions have as their roots thousands of years of motion, and this motion, this energy, this direction is now coming to its full bloom, so to speak.

There will be days in your future in which you will have to ask yourselves whether you have changed realities or if you are still existing within what you thought was your world, for the events occurring upon your plane at this time are of such a nature that they are changing the reality of your people very greatly and very quickly. We suggest that each of your people look carefully at what is occurring, that you make your decisions as to your path of action at this time, for in the very near future there shall not be the time for consideration and careful reflection.

Therefore, we bring this message of a solemn note it would seem to you this evening that you might prepare the way in which your spirit shall travel, for we wish that each of your people might know love and know that love for each other, for that simple action of love is the action which has so long been absent from your planet and your people.

May we answer you further, my brother?

Questioner: I have further questions, but I'm not sure what they are. I'd like to wait until later. Thank you.

We thank you. Are there any other questions?

Questioner: Yes. I'd like to know in relation to what you've just expressed if there are any signs that you can tell us that would signal us to run for cover, so to speak?

I am Latwii, and am aware of your question, my brother. We again would make the suggestion which we have made so often to your meditation group, that you engage yourselves in meditation daily, that you look within your own being for the signs, the directions and the answers which are necessary for your survival, that daily meditation is the most efficient means for tuning in to the energy of what might be called the flow of events, and that by so tuning your energy and your vibration into your planetary vibration you might most accurately decide which direction you shall proceed in.

May we answer you further, my brother?

Questioner: Yeah. I'd like to know more specifically what you were referring when you said that there would be a time when whatever we had would be all we have, and we would be more or less frozen in that position. It wasn't very clear to me what you meant, and I'd like elaboration on that.

I am Latwii, and would answer simply by saying that as you progress upon your own spiritual path, you also are a part of the collective consciousness of your planet, and that there will be a time in your future in which the vibrations of the consciousness of your people shall receive an input of energy, and this input of energy shall signal the end of the old age and the beginning of the new. And within this experiencing of the energy, if you have chosen the path of light, you shall be catapulted, so to speak, in that direction. If you have chosen the direction of darkness, of separation from your own people, from your planet, the direction that so many of your people now seek, those so seeking shall also be catapulted in that direction, that whichever choice you have made you shall receive that choice manyfold by the increase of vibrations of energy that shall be made available and is being made available daily more and more upon your planet.

May we answer you further, my brother?

Questioner: Yes. I just want to ask one more question and then I'll be quiet, and that is how is Hatonn doing?

I am Latwii, and would report to you that the efforts of your most beloved teacher, Hatonn, are realizing more of their purpose, but there is still great difficulty in making the leaders of the various nations aware of the possibility of love becoming a part of their foreign policy.

May we answer you further?

Questioner: No, thank you.

Is there another question?

Questioner: Yes, Latwii. I'm being kind of split lately with the idea of having to return to my country, Brazil, due to the fact that my father is ill and I feel the need to be there right now and also I feel the need of being here. And it flashed on me a few times that I might have a strong purpose of going there more than just my father being ill, and if that is so would you give me some light on that or reassure me that I'm right, or would that be a good time for me to leave right now, and why is it that I feel so much strong power about being there in that part of the country, of the world, right now?

I am Latwii, and am aware of your query, my sister, and can only answer by saying that the feelings which you express as coming from within your being are those feelings which you must follow according to their strength, that we cannot give you directions as to where you must be but again may only refer you to the wisdom that resides within your own being, for as you yourself express, you are aware of that wisdom and have begun to tap into its energy, and we encourage you to continue to follow your feelings and to consider carefully within meditation the direction which is right for you to follow at this time. We are sorry that we cannot be more specific, but it would be an infringement upon your free will, your right to make this choice yourself.

May we answer you further, my sister?

Questioner: No, thank you, Latwii.

We thank you. Is there another question?

Carla: I have a question. From what you were saying to E, I have a whole new thought that what you're basically saying may be that already, since the new age has already begun and is growing stronger every day, already the time for contemplation and the potential for choosing and for growth is diminishing and the time for action is more and more so that we begin to learn more and more through service and have less of a potential difference between where we are and where meditation will take us. Is this true? Is our understanding beginning even now to be based on our actions?

I am Latwii, and we would answer by saying that you are correct, and, to amplify, we would also suggest the analogy of the gardener, that to reap the desired harvest one must plant the seeds; that seeds, whatever their character, do take that illusion time to grow, and there is a season for growth and a season for harvest. Previous to this time your people have had many seasons in which to sow the seeds of love. Too often other seeds have been sown, too often weeds have been allowed to grow, too often the flower of love has gone unwatered. And now we suggest once again that the season grows short, and those who have not sown the seeds of love, have not made the decision within their being, deep within their being, to follow the path of light and to serve their fellow creatures as best they can, that the time for such to decide is now, for there is only what appears to be a single season remaining for the seeds of love to be sown.

May we answer you further?

Carla: No, thank you.

We thank you. Is there another question?

Questioner: I do not have a question, but I would like to know if it is appropriate to react, to share my feelings about what you are saying?

I am Latwii, and we would be most privileged to experience your understanding and your feelings.

Questioner: I found myself reacting as I heard your answer to what E was asking. I could not accept what you were saying. I hear part of it, and it is beautiful, the growing new age, but what I have mainly difficulty to get into is that I hear [Latwii] dividing the world, the universe, into good forces and bad forces. I just cannot get into this idea that there is something evil or wrong that we have to overcome. I think there is just nothing evil, and somehow it is our illusion *(inaudible)* our *(inaudible)* and that everything, everything is love, everything is light, and we don't have to do anything special, you know, it is just really nice, and I would like to be able to meditate every day, but I do not think that we have to tell everybody to do that because working, even fighting, just all this must be done. And just *(inaudible)* out a word like "weed," you know, what is a weed? A farmer looks at something as a crop and something else as a weed, but a doctor or somebody who is in herbs will look at something like, you know, an unusual or not useable plant and look at something else as something really useable. So …

(Side one of tape ends.)

(Jim channeling)

… to our message to consider what part of the message has value for them, and to take that part and to use it and to nourish that that they hold within their [own] being to be of love, and to take the part which they do not feel and to simply brush it aside as the chaff is brushed aside from the berry of wheat.

And we are very grateful to you, my brother, for your sharing of your feeling, for it is very important, we feel, for each of your people to be able to share openly that which is within their being, and we encourage each of you in this endeavor.

May we ask at this time if there are any other questions which we might attempt to answer?

Questioner: I have another question. Am I correct in assuming that the division of humanity in the near future that you refer to will result in a physical death for part or all of humanity?

I am Latwii, and would answer you, my brother, by saying that the division of humanity which you have mentioned is a division that is not preordained. It is a choice that each of your people make, a choice which each of your people have a right to make, and there shall be many experiences each on an individual level, each occurring in unique ways to each of the people of your planet. The experiences which each of you shall go through shall be chosen by you, by the way you choose to live your life; that there are many events which await your people. Many on the physical level in the realm of Earth changes shall indeed result in what is called the physical death of many of your people, but these changes and these experiences as well shall also be by the choice of those, each and every one who experience them, for free will is a foundation stone upon which creation rests.

May we answer you further, my brother?

Questioner: Can you give us a time frame within which the physical occurrences will begin?

I am Latwii, and would answer simply by saying that the physical changes in the surface of your planet have already begun and shall accelerate in intensity as time goes on. As we have said many times in these messages, we are unable to pinpoint the exact time that any event shall happen, for your future is never fixed, and it is only possible for us to see the direction of energies as they flow, as your people individually and collectively make their choices for how they shall live their lives.

We have suggested before that the decade of the eighties which you have just entered shall be the decade of great changes. As the midpoint of the decade is passed and as the decade of the nineties approaches even greater changes, with more frequency of the various Earth disturbances, shall occur and that some time after the year 2000 your planet shall experience the great change which is known as the polar shift. Beyond this we cannot give more specific information for we are unable to see that clearly or that far into what you would call your future.

May we answer you further, my brother?

Questioner: No, you have placed it in a perspective where I can deal with it now. I thank you.

We thank you again. Is there another question?

Questioner: I have another question, and that is that there is more and more talk of war these days, and what I'd like to know, is it possible that we are close to nuclear war?

I am Latwii, and am aware of your question. We would suggest, my brother, that there have been many times which your people have been close to that which you call nuclear war and there will be more such occasions, and as you have correctly assumed, such an occasion is upon you now. But we would suggest it is nothing new, but is now more visible so that more of your people may see this possibility and may work in their own way to resolve the tensions which bring this possibility onto the center stage.

May we answer you further, my brother?

Questioner: No, I don't think I have to ask any more questions.

Is there another question?

(Pause)

I am Latwii, and if there are no further questions we would take this opportunity to thank each and every one of you for allowing us the privilege and the pleasure of speaking to you in your meditation this evening. We are always honored to be asked to share our vibrations with your people and would gladly resume such transmission at a future date. We would suggest a pause for a moment.

(Pause)

I am Latwii, and would close by saying that should any of you desire our presence in your meditation we would be most happy to blend our vibrations with yours. We are creatures of service and seek to serve in whatever way is made available to us. I am known to you as Latwii, and I leave you in the love and the light of the infinite Creator. Adonai, my friends. Vasu borragus. ☥

L/L Research

Advanced Meeting
October 15, 1980

(Carla channeling

I am with this instrument. I am new to this group. I and my brothers are members of the Confederation of Planets of Service to the Infinite Creator. We have been having difficulty giving our name to this instrument. She is aware of this name and does not believe it. However, I am Monka. We are aware that this instrument feels that previous communications which she has heard from our source were unsatisfactorily legitimate. However, this was due to the editing of your peoples of a real transmission.

We are what you might call sociologists; we would not call it that. We share with you now what we would call it, insofar as words can be messengers of concepts, too deep for the bearing of words. We share with you a looking into the mirror. Yes, my friends, you cannot look away from the mirror. Look away from your mirror and up to the stars. The stars are a mirror. Look away from the stars and in the face of the person you like the least. Aha! A mirror. Look into the eyes of those you consider robots and thieves. Look into the mechanisms of you government. Behold the mirror.

How little you know of yourself, my friends, if you do not know that all things are you. When you study, what do you study? Whatever it is, you are studying yourself. Stare deeply into yourself. Leap at that mirror. What do you feel? What do you deny? You are looking in a mirror. You are looking at your shadow. Drink it. We know that each of you is concerned for this planet. And we have great concerns for your peoples also. We have attempted through other instruments to give you an idea of proper society, proper economics, the proper raising of children, the proper structures of a society based on the love and the light of the infinite Creator. We do not say that we have failed, for we are looking in the mirror, also. And we know that our image is infinite, and failure is far too finite of a concept to consider. Unfortunately, at this time, so is success. I am Monka.

I introduce myself to you and offer what little I have to say. I am as wordless as a fly upon the wall. But I can only urge you to continue to be both merciless and idealistic, both fierce and tender, for those who love mankind must indeed use the sword and the embrace. Look always straight and without sympathy at yourself wherever you may find that manifestation in the mirror of your existence.

We have probed both of the other instruments and find that perhaps it would be better if we worked a bit more before we attempted contact. Therefore, we will pause for a brief moment and reestablish contact with another instrument if he will accept our somewhat different form of vibration. We pause in love. I am Monka.

(Carla channeling)

I am again with this instrument. I am Monka. We will return to this group if it is desired by those of you who are here. We do not feel that we can come to all of those in your group, however, this group has the proper tuning. Would you desire for us to return at another time, my brothers?

Several: Yes.

We are gratified to find our poor presence requested again and therefore will indeed again come to you. It is our honor to leave you with all of our love and light, as messengers of the one infinite Creator of the universe of one Being. I am Monka. Peace to you, my brothers, and love.

(Carla channeling)

I am with this instrument. I am Latwii, and greet you in the love and the light of the infinite Creator.

We have been attempting to speak through the one known as Jim, however, we find that his attention is somewhat divided at this time. And we feel that perhaps we could be of some service to him, by offering ourselves to him in case he would like to ask any questions at this time.

Jim: I am having some difficulty in picking up your vibration. Last night I had some difficulty with E and B. I am wondering if there is something I could concentrate on or if there is any special interference on my part that is occurring. Could you shed some light on that, perhaps?

My brother, that is our business, and indeed our very nature. However, we will also attempt to make some sense as well as shed light. The difficulty you are having is transient and has to do with the feelings involved in departing and beginning a new phase of existence. Perhaps this has already occurred to you on the conscious level, however, it may not have been clear to you at this time what is occurring to you at this time on the unconscious level in your character.

You are setting the stage for your own act to come with some precision and a realization that the curtain rings down on the previous act. In one's life this is a momentous time and you are in the fortunate happenstance of being aware of it and even enjoying it. You may have noticed that those about you who are not as consciously developed on some of the finer realms as you in disciplines of the personality have been quite upset. This will occur when you consciously make changes in your existence. Those who understand will simply flow with your experiences. You are fortunate in having fellow pilgrims. It is possible that this difficulty may occur again, and we would forewarn you that you not be upset. If it occurs in the future you must not doubt your contact but must instead be aware that there will be those to whom you may speak who seem very interested but who do not wish to know that which is not already known to them.

We cannot speak where there is resistance, whether it is conscious or unconscious. We are, however, always with you and if you cannot receive us verbally you can always feel our love and our light, as you feel it at this moment, my brother. We are aware you are having difficulty receiving these words. But can you indeed feel the power of the Creator's love at this moment? We ask you then to remember and trust our contact. And know that the difficulty you are having at this moment will pass quickly. The difficulties you will have in the future are the difficulties shared by any instrument. That is our absolute desire, never to infringe upon the free will of any individual.

May we answer any other questions you may have?

Jim: I have a question concerning the message we just received from the contact Monka. It was a very interesting message and one statement was made that we should look into the mirror without sympathy for the reflection of ourselves that we see. I was wondering if it was possible for you to explain that or shed a little more light on that? I'm thinking in the realm of having affection for ourselves and accepting ourselves also as we look into the mirror. I'm having some difficulty balancing looking into the mirror without sympathy but also looking with affection.

I am Latwii. We are glad you speak of balance. The one known to you as Monka was attempting in the way of your world to give you some idea of the eye of the Creator as it is filtered through the tree of life, which is the tree of duality. When there abounds too much sympathy, when sympathy becomes too sentimental, when sympathy becomes self-pity, when sympathy becomes denial of a part of oneself, it is then that the surgeon's knife must come out. You must cut away that part of yourself that cannot be merciless in accepting all that there is in yourself.

When you deal with that which has no sympathy, with that which is indeed merciless, with the murderer, with the rapist, with the terrorizer, then, my brother, balance with sympathy.

The one known as Monka spoke of a cosmic mirror and the eye as the symbol of all that there is. If you look into the mirror, you see yourself as you really are. But most cannot look into that mirror, even into their own eyes, for they become quite frightened. Therefore, it is a very strong allegory for the great oneness of mankind. To love oneself fully is to know without mercy the folly of the depths of one's heart. It is to know and accept without mercy the deepest and most degrading parts of one's being.

For they are not fantasies, my brother. They are all being acted out against the stage of this experience on your sphere of existence at this time. As we speak to you in cosmic gentleness, many terrible things occur. At this very moment, can you cry mercy? No, my brother. You must stand without sympathy and accept the totality of your being, and then pour love from the Creator into that world, into that merciless darkness, with every iota of your being.

For only when you know total mercilessness, in your estimation of the situation of your being, can you be truly a channel for love. Spirits are lovely but the sturdy who stand astride the world of illusion, of pain, of limitations of all kinds, and against that illusion take up the sword of love. Ah, my brother, there is the soldier that shall conquer in the name of love. We hope that this elucidates the theme of our brother of Monka.

May we answer you further?

Jim: No, Latwii, that was very beautiful. Thank you very much.

(A dog is howling outside.)

We thank you and the dog thanks you. Is there another question at this time?

Jim: Not at this time. You have answered my questions very thoroughly.

We are glad, my brother. We will at this time surround you in our vibration that you may carry a charge with you and fear no more that you could ever lose our contact.

I will leave this instrument at this time. I leave you in love and light. I am a fool called Latwii, poor messenger of the infinite Creator. Adonai vasu.

(Tape ends.)

Intensive Meditation
October 16, 1980

(Unknown channeling)

I am Laitos, and I greet you in the love and light of our infinite Creator. It is a privilege to be with this group this afternoon and we thank the one known as Jim for joining us and the one known as L for making use of our contact.

This afternoon we would like to work in two ways. We would like to work with the new instrument, using the one known as Jim, in order that he may gain experience in the type of work which may be done with the newer instrument in order to familiarize him with our contact. The one known as L has already made some very impressive progress, for a newer instrument, and we are very pleased to work with each of you. At this time we would like to transfer to the one known as Jim. I am Laitos.

(Jim channeling)

I am Laitos, and am with this instrument and greet you once again in the love and light of the infinite Creator.

We are pleased to have made this contact for this instrument has been experiencing some difficulty of late in receiving our vibrations and it is most pleasing to see that this difficulty has been dissolved. We would say to those who wish to experience our contact for the first time or on a new basis, so to speak, that our vibration is somewhat less intense, so to speak, than is the vibration of Latwii and we work always with those who request conditioning in meditation for it is our purpose to serve as intermediaries, so to speak, between the newer instruments and the Confederation.

We are able to make our vibration known to any who request it because we have what might be termed a more simple wavelength that is easily perceived by those who are able to quiet their minds for a few moments and who wish to receive this type of contact. We are most pleased in every instance to be asked to join in each person's meditation and are always honored to be asked to join in meditation such as this.

We would at this time make our vibration known to the one known as L, if he would relax and refrain from analysis and simply speak the thoughts that appear in his mind. We will now transfer this contact to the one known as L. I am Laitos.

(L channeling)

I am Laitos, and I greet you in the love and light of the infinite Creator. *(Inaudible).*

(Jim channeling)

I am Laitos, and am once again with this instrument. We are most pleased to have been able to make this excellent contact with the one known as L and we encourage him in his endeavor to become an instrument that will be of service to his fellow creatures upon this planet. We are always overjoyed to be able to speak our words through yet another instrument, for, as you all well know, the people of your planet are in great need of words of love and of light and we are especially honored to be able to provide even our limited understanding of the love and the light of the infinite Creator. Therefore, we are always overjoyed at the prospect of being able to utilize one more instrument in this service to the people of your [planet.]

We would, at this time, transfer our contact to the one known as Carla. I am Laitos.

(Carla channeling

I am again with this instrument. We had to bring this instrument back from a trance too deep for our use. We please ask pardon for the delay. As you know, it is especially important that we establish good contacts at this particular time and not only that, but [in] those who are grounded in themselves as seekers, who cannot be moved. There will come times in which your faith will be shaken and it will seem that you have too great a task to accomplish, too many unanswerable questions to deal with. However, that which is needed will be provided. That which is to be, will be. Although there will be miracles, we shall not safeguard the physical lives and the artificial values of each of those who seek our information. Our concern is for the things of the spirit and that is why we urge you, who seek to be the shepherds, to know that it is only important to have a state of mind in which the Creator is remembered as the center, as the giver, as the source, and as the identity of the self. You must have covering for your feet and protection against the cold and food to fill your bellies while you are in the physical. We ask you not to be overly concerned but simply to work upon yourselves, your desire, and your sense of will.

It is not understood in your culture that man can be born with a mission. It is taken, indeed, as a sign of mental aberration that such a belief could be held, yet your higher self planned certain things for you to accomplish, to seek them, to know the Creator, the channel through which your higher self speaks to you, that you may know in each day the service and the action and the manifestation of that day and in each experience the lesson and the import of that experience. If you cannot be shaken from the faith in things unseen, those things which you can see will never shake you.

We thank each of you for your dedication and we join you with our whole hearts in the love and in the light of the infinite Creator. Before we leave, we would simply make sure that we cannot be of further service by answering any questions that you may have.

Is there a question at this time?

(Pause)

Very well, then. We are aware of several questions that are beneath the surface and are content to await their maturity, for, after all, the answers are within you; this instrument is only part of yourself. We leave you in oneness, my brothers. I am known to you as Laitos. We leave you in the love and the light of the infinite Creator. Adonai, my friends. Adonai.

(Tape ends.)

Intensive Meditation
October 19, 1980

(Unknown channeling)

We of Latwii have been attempting to send energy to this group for its use and balance the energies so that we may speak through this instrument for a brief period. We greet you in the love and light of our infinite Creator.

As you know, my friends, our love is always with you and we are very grateful that you desire that we speak with you at this time. We have very little in words to share with you this evening for we understand that we are, at this time, speaking to a group whose understanding of the basic truths of existence is fairly strong. We could attempt to deepen your understanding, but at this time we feel that you simply need to rest and that your minds have been all too active and so we ask you to come with us on a journey, floating up from your physical vehicles as you would float in the water, light as a bubble. There are no more limitations. There is no more ugliness, for you are now seeing reality and the light is very bright. You may pass through many, many dimensions and colors and glimpse many universes being born and existing in ways far unlike your own. You may do this for infinity, my friends, but this is only a short trip, for we know that you will desire, in the end, to arrive back in your physical vehicle, refreshed and ready again to take up the task of loving and living consciously and well.

As always, we ask you to be aware of each other as the Creator, and to be aware of yourself as the Creator. As always, we ask you to forgive others but far more, we ask you to forgive yourself. For though you may have many times heard and made mistakes, yet you have learned from these mistakes, and, my friends, how else can you learn when that is the entire reason for this experience which you are now sharing: education, the education of your soul. Do not worry about your grade, as a spirit, but simply enjoy what you can and when there is not the simple enjoyment, take conscious enjoyment in the knowledge that you are learning.

There will come a time in the not-too-distant future when you will not be burdened with the difficulties and limitations of your density of existence and you will be far more able to see the love and the light of the Creator at work in your lives. Meanwhile, there is an element of faith in living well and we encourage you to refresh it by cleansing yourselves in the waters of meditation.

I would, at this time, open the meeting to questions.

Questioner: I was wondering—I feel guilty to do meditation. I think sometimes I have come to that point of feeling a strong union with a being or a high consciousness and I feel sometimes that I want to—just like—[let] my whole being just fly away and go, you know, like an astral projection or something, but I feel that I hold back and am kind of scared to release and let go. Could you give me some advice on that, how can I release that eagerness of my soul to just go on traveling, doing astral projection, to be more in union, to be more released with that energy?

I am Latwii, and am aware of your question. My sister, the separation of your astral body, as you would call it, from your physical is done by you each time that you sleep, consequently it is not an alien or an unusual occurrence in your life, it is simply somewhat unusual for entities to have the ability to do it consciously. There are physiological reactions, which can cause discomfort, such as the sounds and the vibrations of the astral body leaving the physical body in an imperfectly symmetrical manner. This often causes fear. However, there is no, shall we say, astral "boogey man."

The places which you wish to go are created by your desire and you will go where your desire is to go and visit whom or what your desire is to visit. Therefore, we feel that it is proper to reassure you that you have no fear, that you will be waylaid by some astral [monster] and stripped of whatever astral belongings you may have. This will not happen unless you have been calling it to yourself. If you desire to work with your guides or to simply examine the experience of what this instrument would call "distant vision," that is precisely what you will do.

Your desire shapes your experience. That is a law of the universe. If you are indeed feeling very cautious about such experiments, it is a reassuring thing to work with a group who is in meditation with you. Thus, they act as batteries strengthening your own desire for the truth, the good, and the beautiful. This is what is necessary in the astral or inner realms of experience, for in those realms, your thoughts are the only reality.

As your thoughts are, so shall your astral body go. Maintain your true desire for love and light and you will not be placed in a difficult situation. However, we assure you that it is not necessary to experience any unusual phenomenon in order to experience the release and the freedom which the love and the light of the infinite Creator can bring. This can be experienced in any condition. It requires only a state of mind capable of grasping love. Cultivate, then, freedom in whatever state you may find yourself and choose freely what you wish to experience, according to your desires.

May we answer you further, my sister?

Questioner: No, thanks. Interesting.

We are pleased to share with you our thoughts, my sister.

If there are no more questions that you wish to enunciate at this time, we would pause before we leave, that the one known as Laitos may work with each of you. I am Latwii.

(Pause)

I am again with this instrument. I am Latwii. It has been a great pleasure to speak with you and we are very, very happy to share in your vibrations at this time. We wish that your life streams may flow evenly and sweetly. We are always with you at any time you request our presence and you must always be sure that the teachers of Hatonn are with you in spirit even though their work calls them elsewhere at this time. We are their stand-ins, and it is our great pleasure to be with you. We leave you, through this instrument now, in the love and the light of the infinite Creator. I am Latwii. Adonai, my friends.

(Tape ends.)

L/L Research

Sunday Meditation
October 26, 1980

(Unknown channeling)

I am Latwii, and I greet you, my friends, in the love and the light of our infinite Creator. It is a great privilege to be able to share this meditation with you, and we thank you for the opportunity. We see the calm that is growing within your minds as you begin to rest in meditation, as though it were the surface of a quiet pond which had been tossed by storms, and blown by the wind, and now it begins to calm under sunny skies, and to reflect, more accurately, the beauty of the foliage which surrounds the pond.

The minds of your people are so often disturbed by the waves and the storms of emotion, emotion which has been developed by the sense of separateness of one being from another. My friends, if we could but give to you the understanding of the one simple concept that underlies all of reality, the waters of your mind would ever be calm, and the springs of your inspiration would flow clear and sweet.

That simple truth is one Thought; it is written in your holy works as one word. That word is love. In those works, it was written that love came into the world, this love which is light. And the world was full of darkness—which we would call separation—and the darkness did not understand the light. And so, my friends, it will always be. The complex will never understand the simple. The simple truth, as we know it, is that love, manifesting itself in your world as light, is the source of all matter, all consciousness, and all energy. All the beauty that you see is a living embodiment of love.

Would that we could say to all of your peoples who live upon your troubled sphere at this time, "Please, beloved planet whom we serve, can you but calm your minds, and see the beauty of love."

People find their minds to be like stone, their opinions and their biases etched in the stony surface with great deliberations and therefore people do not change. Yet in truth, my friends, all living things are in constant state of change, and thus the mind is water, not stone. For water can adapt itself to any circumstance, and in the end is stronger than any rock. For you can see, as you look about you at your rivers and your canyons, that given time, as you call it, water erodes that hard and unforgiving stone, absorbing life-giving minerals, and [is] flowing, always flowing, giving beauty and life, rain from the sky, waves along the shore.

That is the secret of your consciousness, my friends. Your mind is much stronger than you may think. Not because of its firmness, but because of its incredible ability to learn, to change, to adapt, and to transform itself, just as water becomes part of the air and is then reformed as a life-giving substance watering the crops.

As you rest, as your mind is clear, rejoice that you are part of a consciousness which is all one consciousness of being, of all living things in all the universe. You can no more be separate from each other than can one drop of water be separate from the ocean. We are all one, my sisters. And in this may we humbly rejoice and give thanks to the Father who created us, to share His love and His light.

I would pause at this time, in order that the one known as Laitos may work with each of you at this time. I am Latwii.

(Pause)

I am again with this instrument. I am Latwii, and again I greet you in the love and the light of the infinite Creator. Our brothers and sisters of Hatonn send you their greetings, and we come to the part of the meditation which is reserved for any questions you might have. We are grateful to you for allowing us to share our thoughts with you. We have become better at keeping our minds upon communication with you. For when we began speaking to your group, it was our first interaction with the consciousness of the people of your planet, and we found ourselves constantly drawn away by what we found to be the humor of the situation, as each of you has a vibration which dances and shimmers, and looks to us in a certain way, and we would become involved in watching those vibrations, and we would become distracted and end up making jokes which we found did not precisely add to the inspirational tone of our message.

We are grateful for the chance to work with this group and develop an ability to give to you some of the philosophical basis of our understanding, which in all seriousness we do wish to share with you. It is simply that, for those of us who deal almost completely in telepathy and do not speak, it is very difficult to work through language without finding that process somewhat hilarious. We wanted to especially thank you for being patient with us.

Now, we would be very happy if we could answer any questions you might have at this time. Is there a question?

Questioner: Could you tell me if the dizziness that I've felt since the beginning of the meditation—is it physical, a physical problem, or is it something more on a psychic level?

I am Latwii. We are with the instrument. We have been scanning your physical vehicle and we find that you do not have a basic physical problem at this time which would account for dizziness. However, this room is quite charged with the vibration of a sincere desire for understanding, and the contact which you have experienced has perhaps been a bit strong, since several of the Confederation of Planets in the Service of the Infinite Creator have been with us this evening without announcing their presence.

The dizziness seems to be associated with the vibration of the one whom you know as Nona, who has been with you during this meditation, for she wishes to send you strength and healing at this time.

We will at this time allow this vibration to modify so that you will not experience discomfort. We will pause at this time for that purpose.

(Pause)

We are adjusting the vibration at this time, my sister. Are you feeling better at this time?

Questioner: Yes, I am.

We are very pleased. We will use more caution, for we realize that you desire and need healing of a *(inaudible)*. And that is what you are here for. However, we do not wish to cause you *(inaudible)* while we are attempting to help you.

Is there another question at this time?

(Pause)

Very well then, my sisters. If there are no more questions, I will leave you with a simple thought that I hope will help you in the days to come.

Say, my sisters, that your neighbor had a very, very large garden, and yours was very, very small. But in your garden, you planted with balance, and an understanding of the position of sun and *(inaudible)* each other, and colors, and beauty, and the needs of your *(inaudible)*. And your garden *(inaudible)* weeded, and fed, and harvested in *(inaudible)* and flowers *(inaudible)* about its edges.

And your neighbor's garden, large as it may be, was planted without regard to the needs of plants, was allowed to grow wildly, weeds growing along with the food. Your neighbors planted no flowers, had no eye for beauty. Which garden, my sisters, would be the beautiful garden? Indeed, it would be the small one. It is not how great the deeds are that we do, in our day-by-day existence, it is the grace and the understanding with which we do them. Keep your heart full of love, and your mind acquainted with beauty. And no matter how great, how intellectual, how ambitious are the people with whom you deal, the quality will be judged only by the grace with which each of you meets the small requirements of the day, the tiny moments when you can be graceful, and kind, and appreciative. Never, ever lose confidence in the beauty and the grace and, if we may use this word, the importance of yourself. For you are the Creator. You have all that anyone has, within you. Perhaps your lot in life, this particular time, is not dramatic. But if you are graceful in the smallest thing, you are a better channel for love than the greatest individual who does not look to love for his actions.

We leave you in remembrance and constant acquaintance with that love, and with the light of the infinite Creator. I am known to you as Latwii. Adonai, my friends. Adonai vasu borragus.

(Tape ends.)

Sunday Meditation
November 9, 1980

(Unknown channeling

I am Hatonn, and I greet you in the love and the light of the infinite Creator. It is a great blessing to be back with you. Indeed, we have been back for several days, and have been looking forward to the opportunity of speaking to this group, and are very pleased that you are meeting.

We have had some success in causing some of the leaders of those peoples whom you call Russians to envision a more spiritual view. However, we are sorry to report that on the whole we have met with what this instrument would call a resounding rebuff. And [this] causes us to become very [weary,] as we have our energy reflected back to us with much negative energy added. We have been retired from that particular duty once again, and are able to return to you.

Although this instrument is somewhat puzzled at the change in program, we would like to open the meeting to questions at this time. Is there a question that we may answer for you?

Questioner: *(Inaudible).*

I am Hatonn. We were aware this was very centrally upon your mind at this time, and we feel that it is one of the central questions, because it adds into one of the central occurrences of the dawning of the new age. Therefore, we wished to focus upon this.

This instrument is experiencing some difficulty, partially due to the depleted state of her physical energy, also partially due to her lack of personal understanding of this problem. However, we shall continue through this instrument, for we have a good contact. And we caution this instrument to be calm, and do her usual job without regard to the nature of her communications.

If you can picture with me the formation of mineral crystals, you will be aware that there is a great deal of rock that is not at all crystallized, and is therefore relatively insensitive to delicate vibrations. This is analogous to a large portion of the peoples of your planet, who feel the new vibrations of what you may call the "golden age," but whose crystallization of purpose or intent in seeking the path of truth and the love of the Creator is so truncated that it does not matter to them and they go about their business and lead the lives that they would lead, their relationships being guided almost entirely by their needs for procreation, companionship and financial aid. This governs the relationships of most of those among your peoples.

When these conditions are not met—when finances are inadequate, the procreative instinct of one does not suit the other, or the need of companionship is not agreeable to both—this type of union will cease.

Now we move on to your question. There are seeded among your peoples more crystallized souls or spirits who are much more oriented towards reflecting and refracting the light and the love of the Creator. These are people of magnetism and illumination to some degree or another, and are committed each in his or her own way to the path of righteousness, as this instrument would call it.

However, it is the nature of most crystals to be flawed, and the delicate vibrations of the golden age are such that each crystal will begin to disintegrate to a certain extent along the flawed line. It is within the free will of each of these entities to rebuild their crystallized entity in such a manner that the flaw no longer exists. However, this is extremely painful. It is much more common for the individual not totally understanding the purification that he or she is going through to blame the pain of transformation upon those nearest the entity.

Thus, many who are undergoing personal and individual purifications in order to become purely crystallized and free of flaws on the path to what you would call mastery are interpreting this pain as having to do with a relationship, rather than recognizing that the problem is completely personal, and is no reflection upon any partner, child or situation. This is the great contributing cause to the many seemingly synchronous relationship difficulties that you are now observing and indeed experiencing.

May we answer you further, my brother?

Questioner: *(Inaudible).*

I am Hatonn, and I understand your question, my brother. You must address yourself to the fact that each individual has a path of his own. The individual who spoke in this wise to you is an individual whose nature sees things in a very simplistic way. Having once experienced relationships, and again experienced relationships, and again, this individual has determined to his own satisfaction, by simple experiment, as he would put it, that spiritual union does not exist for him, and that it is his fate to be alone. He may well be surprised when fate offers him a spiritual partner whose energy balances his own.

The simple truth is that each individual comes into this illusion that you have in third density to learn specific lessons. Some of them involve a large degree of loneliness. This does not have to do with the new age, this has to do with the choice of lessons by the individual. There are some individuals who have a great need to balance the love vibration with a wisdom vibration. Thus, they spend time alone working to become more self-disciplined and more wise. They are therefore unable at some particular point or perhaps for a large amount of time in the illusion to experience true spiritual union. Others spend their entire lives involved in spiritual union with partners due to the fact that their orientation attracts such partnership.

There is no right or wrong path. There are two poles to the love and the light of the infinite Creator. One is love, the other wisdom. Love is a female vibration, and wisdom male, if you would use those terms. We feel it will be helpful to you to understand what we are saying for us to use those terms. It is more characteristic of the male energy to be wise, and more characteristic of the female energy to be loving. Neither will be of service in becoming a channel for the love and the light of the infinite Creator without some balancing agent of the other. And in order to achieve mastery, the two must come into balance so that each male has the female energy totally balanced within his nature, and the female the male energy totally balanced within her nature.

It is basically, shall we say, nearly impossible to achieve mastery alone. Those who achieve it, for the most part, work with a partner. This is the true basis of spiritual union. This is the true yoga, for the female and the male to work out together the lessons of love and wisdom. For love without wisdom is wasted on foolish things. And wisdom without love is hollow, and foolish also.

Thus, at the end of this illusion, as you begin to achieve a mastery of this illusion, you will undoubtedly have done so through the unions that you have experienced in your lives during this cycle. Therefore, it is of course incorrect to say that there is no such thing as a spiritual union in the new age. Indeed, spiritual union is what the new age is all about. However, there are those individuals who must experience solitude, until they have reached the point at which they are ready to open themselves. Then the opener, that is to say the partner, will appear, and they will be caught up without doubts or prejudice.

For such is true union, that it is impossible to ignore. It is a characteristic of your peoples, that bitterness, as you were pointing out earlier in your conversation, is a by-product of age. It is unfortunate that some distill this from their experience, for it is not a healthy drink. Far better indeed, to let the bitterness go, and enjoy the beauty of each moment.

The entity who has spoken to you is indeed cleansing himself at this very moment, day by day, and will in time not be bitter, for his soul is a sweet one. He is simply discouraged over what he sees as failure on his part. However, when the entity has vibratory difficulties, it is not failure; it is simply the pain of growing. It is sometimes unfortunate that during the growth process, that which could be saved is lost, but almost always, this loss is for the purpose of freeing the individual for a relationship or an understanding that he needs more.

Therefore, what this instrument would call initiation through purification exists for those entities who are ready to work upon themselves. And the currency of this work is most often pain. It is in time balanced by joy. The nature of this illusion is polarity. Thus, your perception that spiritual union with a partner is not obsolete is certainly a proper one. However, this does not indicate that everyone will always have a partner, for there are times when solitude is necessary for growth process.

Remember that you are a continuing soul or spirit, and that this particular incarnation, in this particular illusion, in this particular space/time, is merely one small part of the circle of yourself. Thus, it does not always make sense day by day, but you must look at the greater picture and see the greater cycles that you experience knowing that that which you need will come to you and be unmistakable.

May we answer you further, my brother?

Questioner: *(Inaudible)*.

We of Hatonn thank you, my brother. We are pleased that you will work with what we have said. It is our greatest blessing to share our humble thoughts with you. Please know always that what we say to you is not infallible, and never trust anything that we say above your own instincts, anymore than you would trust the voicings of the opinions of a brother or a sister, for that is all that we are.

We would, before we leave this group, attempt contact with the one known as L, that he may experience our vibrations, not through computer, but directly. Thus, we will close through the one known as L. I am Hatonn.

(Tape ends.)

Sunday Meditation
November 16, 1980

(Unknown channeling)

[I am Hatonn.] Tonight we have been successful in contacting a new instrument and we are pleased that he was going to step out on his faith. We of Hatonn are willing to adjust our being if it is difficult to discern for this instrument. We will pause for this purpose. I am Hatonn.

(Pause)

I am Hatonn, and I am again with you. We have adjusted our being and we feel that we are more closely aligned with this instrument. At this time, we would like to share with you a story of our past.

At one time, we of Hatonn were a warlike nation in that, although united as one planet, we were divided into many sects that strove to dominate or control the planet. We chose to combat one another in our efforts to achieve this control, however, none were able to dominate and all were weakened by the struggle. Finally a point was reached in which we of Hatonn were destitute. We had destroyed all of the resources that our planet had to offer and were unable to kill one another simply because we no longer possessed the raw materials from which to construct further weaponry. At this point, we had also destroyed our food chain and were near starvation. In many ways we were, at that time, very similar to you as your planet is today, fixed upon oblivion.

We discovered that our survival as a priority superseded all other priorities and that the requirements for survival became very obvious: regard each man or woman as one's own brother and share with that brother as you would with your wife or husband or child. Our decimation became, in this manner, our strength. In our choice, in our choosing to reduce our planet's ability to support life, we inadvertently chose a very strenuously spiritual path, that of loving through forced sharing. Perhaps this may not sound very spiritual to those listening to our words, however, then we learned that sharing was more valuable than surviving. We obtained a vibration level that enabled us to both sustain our bodies and at the same time, progress beyond physical needs.

We share this story with you not in pride, obviously, but in encouragement. Small though your numbers may be, those of you who have grown beyond your brothers in your desire to love and share will be able in destitution and poverty and in starvation to mold and guide the growth of your race but only if you keep faith with your feelings. We feel that it is necessary to encourage you at this point because the time draws near when your strengths will be called upon and tested severely. Many of those strengths in many of you are already being tested at this time.

We love you in the manner of brothers who can only watch and encourage and advise you as you grow and we desire that your growth be rapid and as painless as is possible. However, what you call growing pains will occur and are occurring now that you may adapt yourselves to the experience of pain without taking the pain within and clinging to it as one would a valuable jewel or possession. All things pass, as will your pains even if they pass as a result of your death on the physical plane. Do not let this death or these pains worry you. They are merely tools with which the universe shapes the final product which you so desire to become. I am Hatonn.

I am Latwii, and I greet you also, my brothers, in the love and light of our infinite Creator, in whom the hope of consciousness lies. We are grateful to our brothers and sisters of Hatonn for enabling us to visit with you once more for we are very, very fond of this group and greet each of you. We are here for the purpose of answering any questions that you might have at this time. Is there a question at this time?

Questioner: Latwii, I have a question or more correctly a group of questions. I have some friends who receive information of a teacher such as possibly yourself, however the advice they receive often conflicts with what I receive from you. This has aroused my curiosity. I therefore ask you about their teachers and about the level of competence of these teachers and how much they should be believing.

I am Latwii. My brother, may we answer the last question first for it is the most important. You are not to believe any teacher. You must believe your heart. This is a simple truth but important to your advancement. There is no true teacher but yourself, for there is no one but yourself. All the information that comes your way does so for a purpose. Out of it you take what vibrates to you as proper. The rest you discard. This is true of all information, including the owner's manual of your car. You must not separate any information from any other information or treat some information as priority. This is only information that we are giving you. We do not consider ourselves, shall we say, a higher source. We are your brothers. We have had experience. We share it. It may not help you. It is as simple as that. We now go backwards and answer the first question.

We are a source that is not connected karmically, shall we say, with your physical planet or its finer planes. We are messengers or angels, if you will, in the service of the infinite Creator. We are a variety, but we are all one in His service. We do not have the right by the law of the creation to interfere with the free will of any of those upon your planet, although, in an advanced group, we can sometimes give information or confirm information for those in that group, knowing as we do that those advanced students will not believe us unless they wished to and if they believe us they already believed when they asked the question. Therefore, we are not infringing upon free will.

Those connected with the Cosmic Awareness Group and others whose information you have been acquainted with are a planetary source. This source is not a bad one at all, but you must understand it is no more to be believed than the owner's manual of your car, which most often will get you out of tight spots but is sometimes incorrect due to misprint, a torn-out page, or the book being for the wrong model.

This often happens with planetary consciousness such as this Awareness Consciousness. It is aware, in part, of the akashic record. However, it is filtered through the egoic vibrations of the interpreter. Therefore, there is an element of human awareness in this awareness and that particular human is somewhat alarmed about the practical side of things.

It is perfectly all right to consider any information that you may wish to. How much better it is to follow your heart and do not give the slightest amount of worry to various bits of data as they occur but merely be intelligent and knowledgeable of the only tool that you have for analysis upon the physical plane, to use it correctly. That is, use your intellect correctly. Collect and store data and observe further data to see if it fits various patterns. This will inform you [that] by far the most important group of data in your life is your thoughts and actions. The printed page, the spoken word, may be paranoid, inspiring, extremely interesting or dull, but it is basically irrelevant compared to the data of yourself, your thoughts, your beliefs, your biases and the actions that you take towards those about you.

You are like a web shining in the light and you weave yourself moment by moment. Do not compare teachers. They are all lacking. Listen to the wind, and attentively weave your life from the strands of love and light the Creator has placed at your momentary disposal.

As to your second question of the three, we do not feel that it is necessary for us to evaluate sources of information. Perhaps you do not agree with this and would like to question further, but we feel sure that you are following our drift, as it were, and understand that it is not interesting to us to evaluate our brothers who are attempting to be of service but who have a different point of view, terrestrial rather than, shall we say, heavenly for our kingdom is the universe and that which is upon your ball in space is of interest to us only as it affects you in your growth and evolution.

May be answer you further my brother?

Questioner: I have a different question now. In examining my understanding of the concept of reincarnation and karma, I felt that in each situation one encounters, there may be a lesson which is confusing. The lesson itself might be more clear if I understood some of the things that I had returned to learn. For example, if I had returned to this Earth with one lesson as objective to learn not to kill and I were consciously aware of this, it would be perhaps easier to complete the lesson or to learn it fully.

Is it possible for you, first of all, to determine what an individual's lessons are for this lifetime and second, if it is possible, are you allowed to share that information with the individual to help them further their growth?

I am Latwii, and I am with this instrument. It is possible, my brother, for us to scan the various bodies that you possess and to discover thereby the patterns which you brought into this incarnation. It is not permissible for us to give you the answers to the examination before you have taken it. We are not in the business of crib sheets, and you must view your lessons as just what they are: things to be learned.

There is a shortcut and you know it well. Release all the lessons, all the worries, all the distress, and all the confusion and meditate. We cannot emphasize your daily surrender to the Infinite enough times. If you have that much faith in yourself to work upon yourself by opening yourself to yourself, your confusion, your problems, your karma will take care of itself. You may notice that you are foolish quite a lot and spend a good bit of time regretting it. That is because you are on a third-density planet. It, in effect, goes with the territory. Do not worry about it but turn instead once more to the Infinite and be enabled by contact with love to face with joy the total folly of your existence, if it seems so to you. Enjoy yourself, my brother. That is the highest advice that we can think of to give you. Laugh and love and be. What you came here to learn you will only learn by embracing this life with love.

The other part of your question has to do with karma and much is partly understood about it, which makes it very difficult to explain. It is commonly understood to be another way of saying that as you sow, so shall you reap. It is much more clearly seen in the context of forgiveness.

Karma is, very simply, action. There is a law in your physics that says there is an equal and opposite reaction and this can be true unless a higher law of creation is invoked. And that law is forgiveness. If you can forgive yourself or if you can forgive another you have eliminated that much karma. You have nulled the action and there will be no reaction. This is what the master known as Jesus was exemplifying. He stopped the wheel of karma and so may you, without being quite so dramatic.

We thank you. Is there another question at this time?

(Pause)

We would find it difficult to answer a snore, therefore, we will leave this instrument, wishing you only the infinite capacity to laugh as you tread the path of spirit. We leave you in the love and light of the infinite Creator. I am Latwii. Adonai vasu borragus.

(Tape ends.)

Sunday Meditation
November 30, 1980

(Unknown channeling

I am Hatonn, and I greet you, my friends, in the love and the light of the infinite Creator. It gives us great pleasure to welcome the ones known as C and D to the group once again for we have not had the pleasure of meditating with you for some time in this group although, of course, we are always with you. We may make it known at this time that we appreciate those who meditate at this time in other places to join this group in its meditations and are with them also.

It is said, my friends, that the one known as Jesus was incarnate by a virgin and was made man and dwelt among men and by them was crucified. This, my friends, is a much misunderstood story, a much misunderstood example, and a vastly underrated life. Around it has been built a great organization, all too lacking in the one thing that the entity known as Jesus to you desired and that is, my friends, the experience of being one with the Creator.

The one whom we call Amira and whom you call Jesus did not desire to eliminate from his disciples' lives cares and concerns about the state of their spiritual wellbeing. Indeed, he constantly urged his disciples to become more close to perfection. And it is written in your holy works that he said, "Be perfect as your Father is perfect," and again, "It is not I that do these things, but my Father."

My friends, as you go through your daily lives, so much of your attention is consumed with the needs of your physical vehicles, the security, your comfort, the enjoyment of your personality. But let us look at what is known as the virgin birth, that event which is celebrated every year by your peoples and that event which almost no one believes and even fewer understand. You, yourselves, my friends, are at some stage of holy conception by the inspirited self, that self who you really are. This self was not conceived by man but came to this plane of existence and to the human race asleep in a body, the physical vehicle.

The physical conception was, of course, not immaculate but the spiritual conception which each of you who seek are attempting to further is totally immaculate and takes place within what we may call your heart of hearts, within your deepest inner self. And like an infant, the spiritual self must be nurtured, loved and nourished through meditation and through as much right action as you can possibly interject into your daily lives.

We realize that this seems to be an inhumanly difficult thing many times but once an understanding of the love of the infinite Creator has been realized, that which is difficult will become obvious. That which is crooked will be made straight.

At this time, I would transfer this contact to the one known as L.

(L channeling)

I am Hatonn, and I greet you with the love and the light of our Creator. This evening is a special time for all who work for the cause of enlightenment. *(Inaudible).*

We of Hatonn are able to see progress that has been made by meditating but, unfortunately, we must tell you that it is only slight. The special occasion we spoke of is an event of communication, for we are now able to speak and be heard by several others simultaneously. This is due both to the synchronization of the meditations of the various groups, and also to the level of competence or achievement that these groups have attained.

For the first time the scattered energies of the small varying groups scattered across the face of your geographic area are united, thus making our contact with you and them and your contact with them much stronger. We of Hatonn described your progress with your brothers as woefully short and that of the many-calling, [who] have been [chosen] by themselves to carry a level of learning and understanding forward among your brothers. Although we cannot urge you to contact your brothers and publicize our communications for our connections with your race must be through the warmth of an almost magnetic current of drawing seekers to light. We urge you to pursue physically a type of life that exemplifies true correct living that your light may be a beacon to those who seek.

As we of Hatonn share our knowledge, our love, and our strength with you, so also must you share with your brothers. It is only in this manner that you appear. You cannot take your plan to the universe, just as on this night the various groups that we mentioned have attuned themselves to one another.

We of Hatonn share our love with you at this moment and we ask the blessings of good nature upon you and upon your planet on this night and may you all rest in peace. I am Hatonn.

(Unknown channeling)

I am again with this instrument. I am Hatonn, and again I greet you in love and light. Take heed, my friends, for you have within you the most precious thing in the creation. Take heed to your spirits. Nourish them and hearken to the faint music of the angelic choirs as they resound throughout the heavens of the creation. For each realized soul is a cause of great rejoicing among our peoples, for the harvest draws near and we grow closer to you. Draw on us if you need us but more than any, draw upon the love within you, the truth that resides within you, the one original Thought that created you. All of these things you bear within yourself. Let them be born. We rejoice with you in the here and now that is eternity. That we seekers of the Creator can even now know the joy of being part of the creation and in concert with all those who seek, we sing a joyful hallelujah, for to love and to know love is beyond all joy that can be known in the brief shadow that is your physical illusion. We leave you in the sunlight, my friends. The shadow of your physical vehicles is not a lasting one. Never let its limitation distract you from the perfect beauty of that which is born within you, the seed of creation—love.

I leave you in that love and in that light. I am known to you as Hatonn. Adonai, my friends.

I am Latwii, and I am very glad to be with you. My brother Laitos is also here and she asks me to ask you to request her presence if you wish to have some conditioning at this time. I will pause while she works with each of you who requests it. I am Latwii.

(Pause)

I am again with this instrument. I am again having to adjust our vibration, for we are blowing this channel's circuits. If you will pause just a moment, we will step down our intensity, for this is a sensitive instrument. We sometimes come on a little strong.

(Pause)

There, my friends, we think that will be a little easier on the instrument. We are here at the invitation of Hatonn to offer ourselves at your service in order that we may share with you any information that we may have, if you have a question at this time. Does anyone have a question at this time?

Questioner: Oh yes, a friend wants information on the issue of astral travel and out of body experiences. What can I tell him?

My brother, I am Latwii. I am aware of your question. Your friend knows more than is known to you at this time. However, we would say to you at this time, you may say that the higher self, with a number of more highly vibrational bodies at the moment of incarnation—which is not necessarily the moment of conception—becomes attached to the physical vehicle of an infant by means of what those of the so-called occult world call the silver cord. This silver cord is retained. It shapes the physical vehicle and those illnesses and other limitations which you experience during your physical existence occur due to the fact that the higher selves functioning through the silver cord are not able to allow that energy to flow unimpeded into the physical shell which it has created. These blockages cause these problems.

Those who are able by nature to travel astrally are those whose attachments to the physical vehicles are not taken as totally integrated either consciously or unconsciously. There are some souls who seem to know and consciously be able to leave the body and travel in the higher bodies. There are others who are unconscious of this ability but who have it happen spontaneously due to a misalignment of the physical body with the higher bodies or because of some trauma which occurs, whether it be joyful or sorrowful.

It is not particularly helpful to experience astral travel unless it is needed by the individual in order to prove to himself the subjective truth of the fact that consciousness does not reside in the physical vehicle. In that context, astral travel is very valuable. In and of itself, however, it is not inclined to be a valuable experience unless the entity is very highly trained in what this instrument would call magic.

If trained in the western traditions of magic, it is possible to reach through the astral body guides who may then instruct you while you are completely conscious. This is seen by those who work in these realms to be of great benefit. In the Eastern tradition, there is much the same consideration of the benefits of astral travel, although it is taken much more for granted in that tradition which is, of course, much older and therefore less structured and more complex.

Is there anything more that we may tell you about this subject that you feel may be helpful to your friend?

Questioner: I don't know. He's talked to me about it before because I listened and had some knowledge that would be some encouragement. Should he be encouraged? Is he ready to be? Should he be encouraged at this point?

My brother, I am Latwii. You should neither encourage or discourage a person who is in pursuit of a phenomenon. Encourage only that the Creator may be known. The entity himself may choose the route by which he finds the Creator. For this entity, it might be the experience of astral travel. However, it is not the perquisite of any individual to give advice to another on these matters, but only to witness to one's own feelings and knowledge of the Creator and of the methods by which he has experienced a change in his feelings, in his life, or in his work of a positive nature, due to his involvement in [a] spiritual path.

We do not mean to denigrate or, as you might say, put down astral travel. It is a natural thing to do rendered unnatural only because those of your peoples are very largely sleeping in their spirit and unaware of the possibility of separating the higher bodies from the physical body connected only by the silver cord. It is not to be encouraged any more than any other experiential phenomenon should be encouraged simply because it is unknown to anyone whether his brother may be ready for such an experience. It is impossible to judge the state of a brother or sister; therefore, it is impossible to give advice. For some this experience might be very beneficial. For others it might be terrifying due to an unfamiliarity with the process, for there are physical sensations connected with the leaving and returning to the body that are somewhat alarming to some who experience them.

Therefore, you see you are more or less in a position where you may give information but without any emotional bias. You may say, "This is what I have heard. This is information that I have been able to share but I do not know what you must do. You must seek inside yourself for the answer to that question." In this way your friend will know you to be a person of integrity, as well as a friend who attempts to hate, to help—we will correct this instrument—a friend who attempts to help when asked.

May be answer you further, my brother?

Questioner: Thank you. I'll just keep an open ear to him and share love. Thank you.

That is good, my brother, and we thank you. An open ear is the greatest blessing a friend can have.

Is there another question?

Questioner: I've been experiencing some unusual physical sensations as you've been speaking.

There is an extremely good contact this evening, my brother, and this instrument we have had to be very careful with, for she is experiencing physical sensations herself having to do with enormous amounts of heat. At least we are able to speak through her, for when we began we were hardly able to control her vocal mechanisms. We are sorry for any stray vibrations that may be disturbing you and will ask the one known as Laitos to adjust your vibrations in such a way that you are more comfortable. We will pause at this time.

(Pause)

I am Latwii. I am again with this instrument. Are you feeling more comfortable, my brother?

Questioner: I was just thinking, now I know how a radio feels when it's turned down.

We are very glad that we have been able to adjust your dials. Is there another question at this time?

Questioner: Hatonn earlier spoke of understanding and the love of the infinite Creator. The statements reminds me of a kibbutz. I felt as though I were a finite being trying to understand the Infinite. Can you expand upon this statement?

Yes, my brother. Your concept of yourself as a finite being is essentially incorrect. You are an infinite being able to experience an infinite Creator. In fact, you are the infinite Creator, as is each person into whose eyes you may gaze at any moment in your existence. The finity or limited nature of your vehicle confuses almost all of your peoples, and it is because of this very concept in your mind that our brother of Hatonn spoke upon this subject earlier. It was intended to share with you our thinking upon this subject.

We of the Confederation see each entity, each man and woman of your planet as infinite. It is written in your holy works, "Before the world was, I AM." There is no past, there is no future. There is an infinite present and I AM. You and we of Latwii and this instrument, those in the room, and each of those upon your planet are part of the great I AM. You are awareness. You are consciousness. You are. Your being is infinite and preceded the making of this incredibly vast galaxy, solar system, and Earth. How many eons have you been infinite? And yet there is no duration, for in reality you are. And to understand your being is to understand love. For it was the love of the Creator that generated awareness. I AM. That is you and that is infinite. You are not a finite being and your brain, with all of its limitations, its overloads and its confusions, is merely a tool that you have sometimes used poorly. Never let it tell you what to do. Let your heart and your will express itself so that your mind performs the tasks given it by love, working as a servant to you who work as a servant to the Creation.

May we answer you further, my brother?

Questioner: *(Inaudible).*

We thank you, my brother. May we answer the one known as C at this time?

C: I really didn't have a question. I just wanted to send a thank you *(inaudible).*

We have relayed this to our brothers who are very, very pleased that they were able to share with you in such a way that it enabled you to feel more at home in yourselves, for you are truly only at home within yourself.

We have one more question that we must answer for one who is absent, but before that we wish to make sure there are no more questions. Is there another question at this time?

(Pause)

Very well then, we do not like to deal with this type of information because it is so boring, but we have been asked to deal with the earthquake situation. The one known as Don wishes to know about earthquakes. Unfortunately, he is not here but if he were, we would say to him that he already knows about earthquakes and has been talking about earthquakes for the last two decades of your time, as you count time. He may have noticed that there have been earthquakes. These are the earthquakes which he has been talking about. He is probably wondering whether there really are going to be more earthquakes. Has he not talked about more earthquakes? Yes, my brother there will be more earthquakes. The scenario is being played out due to the fact that although there has been great improvement in large segments of your population, although love and light has increased to what we would call a great extent in the light centers which we have started and among self-aware people all over your planet, it has not been enough to generate the positive love energy necessary to totally remove the necessity for the expression of disharmony which the Earth must now manifest, and so it will occur.

We are happy to say and this the entity also realizes, although he has not spoken of it to this instrument, that these occurrences will be less harmful than they would have been had the scenario not subtly changed due to the love that has been generated by people such as yourselves.

(Note: In the original printed transcript of November 30, 1980 that was converted to a text file a total of three more pages were attached. However, these same pages appear at the end of the December 7, 1980 transcript and are in context in that transcript to previous questioning about prayer. It is surmised that the last three pages in the November 30 transcript do not belong to that session and that some final pages are missing from it.)

Pearl Harbor Day
December 7, 1980

(Unknown channeling

I am Latwii, and I greet you, my friends, in the love and the light of our infinite Creator. It is a very great pleasure to welcome each of you to this group and we hope that our humble words may be of some service to you.

We wish to depart from our normal activities this evening by reversing the order of events, for we feel that there are questions in this group that we would like to have the opportunity to offer our thoughts upon and so we will begin with them and perhaps our messages will spring therefrom. Thus, may we ask each of you if you have a question for us and if so please feel free to ask it at this time.

Questioner: I would like to ask the contact if Jesus Christ was real in peoples' hearts?

I am Latwii. My brother, we are aware of your question and may we say to you that many things are real in people's hearts, not only the vibrational essence of the master known as Jesus but many other entities real and unreal, shall we say, as well. Kris Kringle, for instance, and other imaginary entities. What is perhaps more important is that the master known to you as Jesus is real as a vibrational entity, an individual essence independent of the knowledge of those who may be aware of him, who may deny him, or who may accept him as real, for this being, this very illuminated being, is an entity, real truly to the heart, to the understanding, and to the Creation of which he is a part.

May we answer you further, my brother?

Questioner: Is there also one known in the Bible as Satan that also lives?

There is, my brother, an entity in people's hearts known as Satan to them. However, this entity is part of the illusion of your density. The reality or seeming reality of evil is as natural to those who dwell in your polarized density as the darkness.

The vibration in which you live is made of many pairs of opposites and the interplay between these causes movement. To live is to move and the principle which has been called Satan is something within consciousness which repels and thus causes growth and movement.

There are some drawn to the negative or evil principle who may be said perhaps to be fond of the Satanic and these people are truly not pleasant. But they simply have chosen a path of separation from the Father, a path of belief in the importance of the self. This leads such people to desire power, especially over others. Those polarized towards the good desire power over themselves, so that they may better serve others.

There is no being known as Satan on your physical plane nor has there ever been. However, the vibrational principle from which this concept received its ancient name is a thought form which is a reality of your illusion. We wish to distinguish this from the reality of the one known as Jesus or, as we know him, Amira, who is an entity who lives and dwells in love. He is a thought form only to those who do not realize that he is a real being.

The one known as Satan is merely the shadow of evil thoughts. Given fear enough, evil thoughts can do harm, can cause fear and pain and anguish. This power is given to the Satanic principle only through the fear of the one who is feeling the difficulty. There is no reality to the fear and thus it is said love casteth out fear. The one principle called Satan is a lonely and sad thought form and we would say to you, accept this principle as part of yourself, as that within you, if you will, which spurs you on to growth, to new understandings, and to desire for truth. Love this entity therefore, and take all strength from this mere shadow.

May we answer you further, my brother?

Questioner: Is there a war between Latwii and the one you just mentioned?

I am Latwii, and we understand your question. You are speaking of what this instrument knows as Armageddon. This battle has been underway for some time and, in truth, is proceeding towards its conclusion. However, only the shadows of its fierce antagonisms reach the physical plane, for this is a battle between light and darkness.

There are many, many hosts of those in the service of the infinite Creator. We ourselves are in the service of the infinite Creator and have formed a Confederation in order to do just what we are doing now: to speak to those who desire whatever knowledge we may have to share. These forces of light, of whom we count ourselves, an humble and unworthy number stand, as it has been said, in your Holy works, in the armor of light.[2]

---

[2] *Holy Bible*, Romans 13:11-13: "Besides this you know what hour it is, how it is full time now for you to wake from sleep. For salvation is nearer to us now than when we first believed; the night is far gone, the day is at hand. Let us then cast off the works of darkness and put on the armor of light; let us conduct ourselves becomingly as in the day …"

Also, from Ephesians 6:11-13: "Put on the whole armor of God, that you may be able to stand against the wiles of the devil. For we are not contending against flesh and blood, but against the principalities, against the powers, against the world

We are given power first from the Creator Who is beyond light and darkness and from Whom we derive love. Secondly, from those upon your planet, who are praying, meditating and living to be loving, sincere, understanding and valuing the good and the beautiful. We face those of us on the physical, the etheric, and the [cosmic] forces which derive their substance from the belief and separation from the Creator and from each other.

Unfortunately, many of your peoples, their tempers sharpened through many, many generations of wars and territorial arguments, contribute to the negative quality of the forces of darkness. Anger, intense frustration, and the negative emotions associated with greed and envy add also to the aid that the etheric thought forms that are forces of darkness may draw upon and so the battle plan stands arrayed.

But whereas we have one Creator to guide us and one great truth to sustain us, the forces of darkness will always be scattered, for they do not trust one another but wish only to have power over one another as well as over all else. Therefore, as soon as enough of the people of your planet can stand behind us who are merely messengers of light, the battle gallantly joined will be over for this harvest and the harvest will be complete and those who stood in the light will avail themselves of that light.

We feel very positive about the coming of this harvest, for it pleases us that many have turned to that light and to that love to seek understanding. Even as the world seems to polarize itself more and more to negativity and separation yet you will find more and more of those people whom you personally know beginning to seek in some form of spiritual truth the light and the love of the Father.

Thus this battle. Whatever occurs upon your plane has already been joined and it is fought with the heart and the minds and the spirits of mankind, not with their physical bodies. This is a great lesson to learn

May we answer you further my brother?

Questioner: Yes, what I would like to know of one person known as Benjamin Franklin and if he was the antichrist?

---

rulers of this present darkness, against the spiritual hosts of wickedness in the heavenly places."

My brother, I am Latwii, and I am aware of your question. We are attempting to remain serious, however, we must tell you that the antichrist is a thought form. There will be several who will be called antichrists, however, it is a concept. Inasmuch as there are no gods, shall we say, of the darkness, but only one Creator and that a Creator of love, so there can be no son of such a god of darkness and thus no antichrist.

There is, however, a thought form in people's minds. And there will be those who are powerful, rich and negatively oriented who will seem to many as the antichrist as, indeed, candidates have been put up already.

The entity known as Ben Franklin was a humorous chap and one who was considerably more valuable to society, shall we say, than the antichrist would have been. He was involved in some intellectual scheming, this is true, but then so is Henry Kissinger and he is not the antichrist either. Basically, the one known as Franklin was what you might call a wanderer, someone who came from another civilization to this planet, incarnated therein, and brought through several inventions which facilitated the civilization of the country in which you live and of the world in general.

We realize that you cannot see the humor of the idea of the antichrist, but from our vantage point we exist in a sea of perfect love, and although mistaken ideas occur to people, and we are beginning to understand the great sorrows that you must bear because you cannot see the love about you all the time, we cannot imagine being so convinced of the shadows that we could give them a name. We are sorry in our inability to fully enter into the understanding of your peoples but we hope that what we have to say may in some way be of help.

May we answer you further, my brother?

Questioner: That is all that I can honestly say that I can ask about Ben.

Very well, my friend, we would add one thing for the general edification of those who attend. There were several of the, shall we say, "fathers of our country," as this entity would say, although we do not fully understand the meaning of that term, who took part in a somewhat negative plan together. It may be called a club. It has been called by your peoples, "Illuminati." They actually did not mean harm but to improve mankind. What has occurred since then was not in the plans of those such as your Jefferson, your Madison, and your Franklin, those who were a part of this organization and whose imprint can to this day be seen upon your currency as this instrument would call it.

May we ask if there are questions from anyone else at this time?

Questioner: I would like to know about prayer and how does prayer function?

My brother, I am Latwii, and I would ask you how does your question function to cause an answer from me as I listen to you? It is self-evident, is it not, my brother? Prayer is a conversation. Sometimes you ask for things for yourself. Sometimes you ask intercession for others. Sometimes you only wish to say a thanksgiving to the Creator and do not have any questions to ask. Sometimes, you merely say, "What should I do today, Father?" and then you listen, that also being a prayer. A prayer is a rather privileged conversation held inwardly betwixt yourself and the one whose spirit will fill your life if you request it.

You are guarded by what you would call angels so that in any situation wherein you are in a prayerful, penitential or meditative attitude, the forces about you will concentrate and grow brighter. The Creator being within you has no trouble hearing you for the Creator is the entire creation within everything, the substance of everything, omnipresent and therefore knowing everything. Thus, you cannot speak too softly for the Creator. However, my brother, one of the sad things about prayer is that the Creator often speaks more softly than the one who prays can hear. Then he who prays will say, "My prayer was not answered." But, my brother, prayer is always answered. Perhaps the answer is "no," when you wished it to be "yes," but always there is a contact that is infallible, the still, small voice, as your holy writings would call it. We realize that there are many different ways with which we could attack this particular question and would appreciate it if we have not spoken clearly enough, if you would guide us further that we may be of service.

Questioner: You spoke very clearly and I have one further area of confusion. Would you explain to me the statement, "Ask and you shall receive." From the statement the answer to a prayer might be "no." I'm confused. It seems to be a contradiction.

Yes, my brother, it does seem to be a contradiction and you will find in your spiritual life that you are constantly running up against paradoxes. This is one of the signs of spiritual progress. We are not the most unconfused people that you will ever speak with, we are sure, but perhaps we can shed some light upon your question.

Let us look at the situation of a person who prays and the will of the Father is not what is being prayed for. The answer which is awaiting is the will of the Father, which may well be not at all what is desired. However, the Father wills this only that His beloved son or daughter may learn and grow.

Sometimes it is necessary for the understanding [of] the spiritual entity that certain burdens be carried. It is also written that no burden will be made too heavy to bear, and this you may rely upon at all times. You will not be overburdened, for there is always a comforter. However, seeking is indeed finding. That which you ask you shall receive. However, if your basic desire is to know the truth, to know the will of the Creator in your life, that is what you may find. And what you—we will correct this instrument—and what you thought that you prayed for you may find indeed you did not pray for as much as you prayed for [the] understanding, love and presence of the infinite Creator in your life.

"Knock and it shall be opened unto you," but which door are you knocking upon? Do you believe not only in prayer but in the infallibility of your own praying? Or in your heart of hearts is your basic prayer to do the will of the Creator? If that is the truth, you cannot help but find your life opening, changing, moving according to laws of love.

We do not know if we have explained this seeming paradox to you, however, we may say to you as brothers, be careful what you pray for, for sometimes the Creator in His wisdom will give it to you just so that you will find out what to truly pray for.

May we answer you further upon this, my brother?

Questioner: You answered, thank you.

We thank you my brother. Is there another question at this time?

(Pause)

If there are no more questions at this time that you wish to ask, we will leave your delightful company and your meditation so that our brother may speak to you. I am most privileged to have been able to share our thoughts with you. I am of the entity Latwii, and I leave you in the love and the light of the infinite Creator. Adonai, my friends.

I am Hatonn and I greet you in the love and the light of our infinite Creator. In answer to the one known as Carla who carries messages of our brother Latwii, I speak now through this instrument *(inaudible)*.

It is our wish to share with you the story of a world much like your own. At one time the world of which we speak was covered with [a] great force which screened out the light of day from the crowd below. Those who lived on this planet were able only to live in a world of shadows and thus were not familiar with the light of day.

There came a time, however, their planet began to evolve just as yours is now perched upon the edge of an evolution. The grounds of the forest …

(Inaudible)

(Tape ends.) ♣

Sunday Meditation
December 14, 1980

(Unknown channeling

I am with this instrument. I am Hatonn, and I greet you in the love and the light of the infinite Creator, of whom we are all one of an infinite number of parts. Tonight, my friends, I am impressing this instrument with the subject that has not often been dealt with in these meetings, but we feel it would be of help to those of you here at this time, and so we would like to share some thoughts with you upon the anger that you may feel at times towards your Creator.

We realize that you live and breathe and experience your existence in a world which is full of seeming injustice and cruelty, that things occur within your own lives which are quite simply unfair. We realize that there is nowhere that you can look where this pattern is not repeated endlessly, whether it be the picture in this instrument's mind of the innocent deer cleaving his way through the burning forest, out onto the road in the country where wicked men sit, waiting, with guns; or whether it be a friend who unfairly has been taken from you, or hurt; or whether it be sadness for your planet—and the feeling of frustration that you can do nothing.

It is only natural that you should become angry, but to whom should you direct your anger? You can only direct it at the Creator, and we would suggest to you that, at times, it is healthy to do so, to express your anger and your frustration and your grief, to remove it from your system, to purge it as if it were an unhealthy substance, for the Creator is able to absorb this energy. As this instrument would say, "He can take it." You cannot damage the Creator.

Now that we have said that, let us work a bit with these feelings. Who is the Creator, my friends? He is, of course, yourself, ourselves, this instrument, your friends, those whom you prefer not to associate with—all of those who are conscious upon your planet, all of those who share consciousness in the creation. In short, yourself—the creator is yourself. As you are angry at the Creator, so you become angry at yourself. And again we say to you, be angry at yourself, you can take it. It is well to purge yourself, with the fullest conscious understanding of the nature of your anger and of the source to which you must direct that anger.

We urge you to face those things that make you angry, straight on, never blinking, for this is your school, this is where you will learn compassion, balance and understanding of love. This is where you will learn who you are. This is the only understanding that matters, and you cannot come to it by blinking at those things that make you frustrated or angry or fearful. As you look at the world about you, you see an illusion, largely man-made at this point in your history. It has been woven and embroidered many, many of your years and your cycle is coming to an end, and your piece of work is almost finished. And you know, each of you, that your planetary work leaves much to be desired.

May we say to you, my friends, before you condemn yourselves totally, that there have been so many instances throughout this cycle, and especially in the past few years, of those beings turning towards the light, towards love and towards service, and veritably shining with the love of the Creator, that much that could have been terrible upon your planet has been softened and ameliorated by the quality of the beings that dwell among you. Light groups such as this one have aided enormously. Catastrophes, including, my friends, nuclear war, that seemed almost inevitable a year ago seem less inevitable now.

We still see much turmoil upon your plane. We see war, but we no longer see the certainty of nuclear war; the probabilities have shifted. And before you become too angry at yourself, look with solemnity and joy upon the work of your hearts and your hands. You think, my friends, that you do nothing through your meditations, through your smiles, through noticing the difficulties of others and aiding them when it is not necessary. But, my friends, this is not true. The planetary consciousness is changed by such acts of conscious positivity.

We will never, ever encourage you to visit a never-never land, because you have all creation within you. You have nowhere to visit, you are within the boundaries of heaven. Cast a firm eye upon the hell which your peoples have made in many cases of the planetary vibration, but look also at the love that shines in the eyes of special ones about you, and in the hearts of yourselves and your loved ones. Seek always to be a light bearer, to be a light sharer, drop the seeds of light and love, asking no return, but casting, as your holy works would say, "your bread upon the waters."

We hope that these thoughts have been of some aid to you at this time. You must remember that the perfect symbol of love, the rose, is surrounded with thorns. The creation is a creation of polar opposites; the one without the other would not be complete. Cherish, then, the rose; avoid the thorns, but recognize them and love them as part of the rose. Look at the pearl and cherish it, but respect also the terrible irritation of sand which a small animal had to bear in order to build up this beauteous substance. Bless the rain as it falls sweetly from heaven upon the dry land, but know also that, in order for rain to fall, there must be a particle of dust.

Earth and heaven, my friends, they are about you. You dwell with Earthly things day by day, and this is necessary. These must be dealt with first, for you cannot teach a hungry man to love. The hunger is being dealt with, it is time to move on to the spiritual, and to dwell in the realms of truth, excellence and beauty. Turn your back neither on those things that make you angry or the redemption of a world by the heaven which permeates it. You are at this moment in that heaven, and the love of the Creator is so close to you that you cannot breathe without inhaling it. Rest, therefore, my friends, in that love, and stay centered as you gaze with compassion on a troubled world.

We will leave this instrument now. I am known to you as Hatonn, and I leave you in the love and the light of our infinite Creator. Adonai, my friends.

I am Latwii, and I am with this instrument. We would pause for a moment while our brother *(inaudible)* works with the ones known as D and C. I am Latwii.

I am again with this instrument. I will have to adjust to this instrument. We keep forgetting that she is more sensitive than we expect. We are adjusting. I am Latwii, and I greet you, my friends, in the love and the light of the One Who is All.

It is very kind of our brothers and sisters of Hatonn to allow us to come and speak with you, for it is our joy to share our thoughts with you on any subject which you may care to discuss. May we ask if you have a question at this time?

(Pause)

I am Latwii. Since there are no questions, we will merely give you our love and assure you that we will be with you whenever you wish to meet. It is our privilege to share this meditation with you. I will leave this instrument now. I leave you in love and light. Adonai, my friends. Adonai.

I am Nona. I would like to share with you this evening our healing sounds. We feel that it is possible that we may be able to share them through the one known as C. If he will open himself to our vibrations, we will attempt to, as you would call it, sing through him, as it is very difficult for us to speak since it involves translation from our language, which is singing. We will attempt to transfer to the one known as C. I am Nona.

(C sings)

(Note: This session, recorded on side one of the tape dated December 14, 1980, ends at this point. The following session was recorded on side two of the tape. It is assumed that that session was also recorded on the same date.)

(Unknown channeling

I am Hatonn, and I greet you in the love and the light of the infinite Creator. We who are in the Confederation of Planets in the Service of the Infinite Creator can never thank you enough for making yourselves available to us, that we may share our thoughts with you.

We trust that some of the events that have transpired for you in the past days have enabled you to feel more subjectively assured of our presence, but we would wish to say at this time that it is supremely unimportant to us whether the issue of our objective reality is ever resolved, for the simple reason that we are here to share the information that we have concerning love and light which love creates. Thus, we ourselves have no attachment to making your peoples aware of our presence. We have in the past attempted to do this in a much more open manner, and have found the results to be extremely unsatisfactory. Thus, we remain elusive, but we will continue with our small hints and notices of our being, as before.

We ask you now to become fully aware of your physical vehicle, and to realize that you sail within this combination of chemicals forming the complex of muscles and bone and nerves and other types of cells. You sail this as you would a ship from port to port along many a stormy sea, and you behold many and wondrous things with your physical eyes. Consider, my friends, all the wonders that you have seen on this very day and perhaps may have taken somewhat for granted.

Reach down into what you know of the universe, what is known by your science at this time, the vibrations that are called matter. Each leaf, my friends, that whirls in the wind, each tiny increment that in totality gives you a momentary scene as you move along one of your roadways or gaze from the window of your domicile, is a creation of an infinity of infinitesimally small parts. The physical vehicle in which you move is itself miraculous, each muscle and tendon moving in obedience to your wishes, the bio-computer, as this instrument would call it, processing information, sorting, distributing, remembering, retrieving that information as needed.

Consider the food that you have eaten this day, my friends: whence came it? In what earth did it grow? What hands harvested it, shipped it, unpacked it, prepared it, and served it to you? What a miraculous chain of love and service exists that you may eat. Consider your relationships, my friends, the kindnesses that you do, and those that are done to you. Are these not miracles also, my friends?

And yet how many have said this day, "What a rainy day! What a terrible day!" My friends, we ask you not to waste one moment; never lose sight of the fact that you are doing the impossible. You are aware in such a complex fashion of so many things in such an infinite creation filled with such beauty that it simply seems impossible. And yet, my friends, we say again, it is simple, it is love, and it is one. To understand this paradox is to understand enough to become silent.

We will pause for a moment in meditation to share with you, and then we will transfer to the other instrument. I am Hatonn.

(Pause)

I am Hatonn, and I greet you again in the love of our Creator. We have shared many thoughts with you in the past but now we are able to share more than simple thoughts, now we are able to share our minds, our love, and our compassion because we have learned much of your race and of your hearts. We *(inaudible)* Hatonn are of oneness with you in that we share many of your experiences as we watch you day by day, *(inaudible)* and follow you as your day passes and your hearts surge with love for one another *(inaudible)* as one of you as treats his brother.

There are times when we feel that we do not deserve this honor that the Creator has bestowed upon us, much more than our simple minds and hearts are worthy of, for we of Hatonn have never experienced many of the complex emotions that you take for granted because they have always been a part of your life. We have recently learned that this is a part of *our* lesson, that we of Hatonn are to grow from our contact with your race, not only through service but because of that service we of Hatonn, in helping you in our meager fashion, have learned and grown in our perceptions of emotions.

This may not seem to be a great gift to you of the Earth, but for us it is equivalent to a person from Earth suddenly going from being color-blind to perceiving color. We are overjoyed at the depth of emotion that we can now perceive and experience and this, my brothers, we owe to you.

It is true that perceiving the depths of emotion such as feeling disheartened, frustrated, heartbroken, jealous, jealousy, envy, greed and many of the other feelings, are emotions that you often term and sense as not pleasant. Yet we learn from these as well, for now we can empathize even with the greedy who perceive property as not yet theirs, or the glutton who sees the meal. In its own way, each of these *(inaudible)* is merely a convolution or defective form of love, and we are able to perceive the crystal teardrop of love within the experience or emotion, and are able to rejoice in that feeling.

And when we of Hatonn are able, through your hearts and eyes, through your tears and your touch, to experience that which you call love, our joy is boundless. To feel enthralled with a beautiful day, to worship from afar a wonderful person, to respect, to share, to regret a parting with the comforting knowledge of an imminent sharing, all of these we perceive through your eyes and hearts, and through our perception have grown boundlessly in our ability to appreciate the universe and our Creator as given us, and to appreciate in boundless gratitude our Creator Himself.

We wish to express to you *(inaudible)* our infinite love for you, our teachers, and our *(inaudible)* regret for we can find no way in which our puny efforts can begin to offer repayment for the beauty you have shared with us. We love you, you are our brothers and sisters. Our world and our lives are enriched from the experience of knowing you. We of Hatonn would thank you for *(inaudible)* and for accepting our feeble efforts of help *(inaudible)* our lack of experience. May our Creator bless you with many wonders and may you find your way *(inaudible)* into the heart of our Creator *(inaudible)*.

(Pause)

I am again with this instrument. I am Hatonn. I return to this instrument for the purpose of sharing with you any information that we might have if you have a question at this time.

Questioner: I have a question. I've noticed periodically a pain in my lower right leg that is almost similar to a headache. I feel that there must be a reason for this pain recurring *(inaudible)* and it's pointless for me to try to dispose of the pain. Could you give me some guidelines or suggestions that I can determine why I'm causing this pain?

I am Hatonn, and I am aware of your question. As you know, my brother, we do not give specific information. However, perhaps we could share a thought with you which might be helpful, in a general sense. Most of the imbalances that manifest in your physical vehicle as pains, limitations, etc., are the result of some form of tension, fear and anxiety, anger or resentment. It is not to your discredit that these things occur. That is why you are in the physical body, so that you may go through the catalyst of the experience of these things, and from them learn. However, it would be well to examine your tensions and the other expressions which we listed, going from the most ethereal manifestation of these to the most physical. The nervous system is only the lowest manifestation of the several bodies that make up your physical being.

May we answer you further, my brother?

Questioner: No.

Do you have another question at this time?

Questioner: It is my understanding that Carla would like to ask you a question.

This entity now has the question. We will repeat the question for the purpose of enlightening the one known as L who otherwise would probably be somewhat confused. The question has to do with the method of removing from one's aura or being the type of entity that is known in the occult sciences among your peoples as a subtle. The answer is as simple as it is difficult.

Those thought forms or subtles or, as some call them, devas, which may at times attach themselves to you, may have done so for a variety of reasons. It may be a thought form which you yourself have generated. It may be a thought form or an elemental which is connected to you because of the substance which you call blood, which you have given from your healthy body and which has been put into the veins of one who is quite ill and afflicted with elementals.

This occult connection can sometimes be very detrimental to the healthy person. However this occurs is immaterial. What is material is your understanding that, in all of this creation and in all of the infinite spheres and sub-spheres and dualities and differences that you may experience, you experience the illusion. The reality is that all things are one. In order to be removed from the darkening difficulties of association with a subtle entity, you must take that entity into your heart and love it, knowing that it is yourself under other circumstances—in another vibration, in another time and space, part of yourself. Accept the world as it is and take it to your heart.

In this way, and in this way only, can the power of love defeat, conquer or simply remove the separations that manifest themselves to you as difficulties that darken the aura, the dream, the feelings, or the thoughts. Whatever your fear, whatever your special thought difficulty, face it not in confrontation but in the knowledge that it is part of the creation and therefore a part of yourself. You are protected by a white light of the Creator. There is no other vibration for those who call upon it, for it contains all of the infinity of vibrations that color the many-hued rainbow of existence in the galaxies of mind, thought and space.

We trust that this is a sufficient answer, as it is being recorded and will be shared with him who asks. If our brother wishes to ask further, we most humbly invite any questions that he may have.

Is there another question at this time?

Questioner: No, thank you.

We thank you, my brother. We leave you, gazing at the brilliant sky that fills our dimension at this time. We are not far from you, however we are not in your density, and for us the world is washed in golden light, the golden light of the central sun. May this sun bless you in your meditations and in your daily life, as it is the symbol of the one infinite Creator in Whose love and in Whose light we now leave you. I am *(inaudible)* Hatonn. Adonai, my friends. Adonai.

L/L Research

L/L Research is a subsidiary of Rock Creek Research & Development Laboratories, Inc.

P.O. Box 5195
Louisville, KY 40255-0195

www.llresearch.org

Rock Creek is a non-profit corporation dedicated to discovering and sharing information which may aid in the spiritual evolution of humankind.

ABOUT THE CONTENTS OF THIS TRANSCRIPT: This telepathic channeling has been taken from transcriptions of the weekly study and meditation meetings of the Rock Creek Research & Development Laboratories and L/L Research. It is offered in the hope that it may be useful to you. As the Confederation entities always make a point of saying, please use your discrimination and judgment in assessing this material. If something rings true to you, fine. If something does not resonate, please leave it behind, for neither we nor those of the Confederation would wish to be a stumbling block for any.

CAVEAT: This transcript is being published by L/L Research in a not yet final form. It has, however, been edited and any obvious errors have been corrected. When it is in a final form, this caveat will be removed.

© 2009 L/L Research

Sunday Meeting
December 28, 1980

(Carla channeling

I am Latwii, and I greet you, my friends, in the love and light of the infinite Creator. Please be patient while we step the energy down for this instrument, as usual. She is more sensitive than the one we were attempting to reach known as L.

I am with this instrument. I am Latwii. We have a more comfortable contact for the instrument now. May we say to you how glad we are to welcome each of you to the group this evening, and especially those that have been absent for a little while, such as the one known as Jim. We thank each of you for the privilege of sharing our meditation, for we in the Confederation in Service to the Infinite Creator are here only to be the mirrors wherein you find your own soul's wisdom. And it is only by your invitation that we may be with you. We greet you in love and in light.

The light of this particular time of the year is so bright that it is harsh to many of your peoples, and there are many among your peoples at this particular time in the cycle that will leave this incarnation and pass on to other things. There are others who are very unhappy or sick or sick at heart or uncertain in many ways. If you are among the fortunate who have been caught up in the joy of this particular celebration which you call Christmas, may we ask your especial meditation and sending of light to those about you whom you may or may not know, for there are so many that it is necessary at this time that they be helped if at all possible for you to do so. Simply share the Creator with them by holding the love and the light of the Creator in your heart and releasing it to the world's use. This is all you need to do. You do not need to know details.

We say to you, my friends, you are under the earth. This is your time of growing, of knowing and realizing who you are. This is, in your cycle of what this instrument would call seasons, the winter, the quiet time. Therefore, my friends, bring quiet to your souls as they rest in the darkness of the earth, gathering the strength to move and to blossom in season. This is the time to be patient with yourself. This is the time to feel the light within rather than looking for the light without. This is the seed time.

You may look at this earth time as a prison, for indeed it is not a time wherein your being can make the transformations of color and harmony that it will make in its season. However, my friends, you have the key to that prison and that key once used opens the door to more color and more harmony than you shall ever experience as manifestation. As you meditate in your seed time, as you discover the love that is your essence, realize the source of that love, the original Thought that created that love, and revel in the harmony and the beauty and the blooming of that reality. Your manifestations can only occur in as much fullness as you prepare for at this time by the strength and the solidarity with which you ground yourself in your own being.

I will transfer at this tine. You will have to pardon the slight pause while we again step up the energy. I am Latwii.

(L channeling

I am Latwii, and I greet you *(inaudible)*. It is often said *(inaudible)* will receive yet how often do we find that the object of our desires is rarely as attractive as it was in our imagination. So it is, my brothers, with many of the desires of the heart. Often we *(inaudible)* thinking we know where it leads us. With all our hearts desiring an end, yet once we've achieved it and followed the path to its conclusion *(inaudible)* for our desires *(inaudible)*. My brothers, the path has no *(inaudible)* and like the universe goes on and on and on and on *(inaudible)* that the prayer of your hearts be not for ends but for growth, not for sights but for lights, not for *(inaudible)* but for strength, for of such is the road to the kingdom constructed *(inaudible)*.

(Inaudible) any questions at this time *(inaudible)*.

(Pause)

My brothers, I would share with you a simple thought at this time *(inaudible)*.

My brothers, it has been said to you, and I will say again the light of the universe goes on and on and on and on. We of Hatonn realize that this is confusing yet is important that you understand *(inaudible)* importance of meditation on this message. We of Hatonn realize that you find little of value upon your first examination of this message, yet we would encourage you *(inaudible)* further meditation *(inaudible)* your understanding *(inaudible)* the love and light of the Creator. Adonai, my friends *(inaudible)*. I am Hatonn.

(Carla channeling

(Chanting) Ami-Ra.

I greet you, my children, in the name of my Father. I lift up my heart to you for are you not of my Father? This little one through whom I speak calls herself by my name. My children, it is not necessary for I am and you are of my Father. I ask you to husband the creation in which you walk your ways this day, and to wait the precious gift of your love as it wakes toward the kingdom of love. And shall you not go where you have sought to go? Yea, you shall; I am with you as my Father is with you; as I am called, I speak. For as there is no time, I am always and you with me are part of that which is always. Thank you, my children, for thinking of me and requesting my vibration. Yours are as pleasing to me as the sweetest flowers, for are you not my Father? Peace to you, my children.

Carla: There's somebody else in the room. Did anyone request Nona? C, you don't feel it, do you? I do. OK.

(Carla channels a song from Nona until the end of the tape.)

Advanced Messages, New Year's Eve
December 31, 1980

(Unknown channeling

I am Latwii. I am getting through to this instrument with more ease than usual due to her relaxed state due to the ingestion of some alcohol. Normally this is a great difficulty in achieving contact but with this instrument, our vibrations are significantly stepped up from hers that, as she has stepped down her vibrations toward what is normally found on your planet, we are able to contact her without difficulty, using our normal strength.

We wish to greet the one known as B, with whom we have spoken several times. It is a tremendous pleasure to confirm to her that it is indeed our contact which she has been receiving. Our love is beyond measure and we are most, most grateful for the return love of you people in this deep and dense density. We do not understand how you can overcome so much and love so much for we are beginning to understand the limitations of your sphere of illusion and we are amazed that you are able to deal with it as well as you are given the limitations of your senses.

We would like to open the meeting to questions at this time, for we feel that perhaps we may be of more help in moving from interest to interest than we be in giving what may be called an inspirational message, for each of those present are most inspired and are inspiring us at this time and we do not feel that we would add to your inspiration where happiness in each other and your harmony is that which causes joy among those of us who are in the Confederation.

Is there a question at this time that we may perhaps share some information upon?

Jim: Latwii, how do you feel that Don and Carla and I can best serve the planet and fulfill our mission *(inaudible)*?

My brother, you have one mission above all others and that is, as you already know, which we are only confirming, to realize your true nature. As it happens, you have managed to arrive into a position where the mirror in which you look to determine your true character is a true mirror given support by those who will not lie to you in any way or give you a false image. This is true of each of the three of you, and as you work together, that will be your chief work: the improvement of the understanding of your own personality and the disciplines necessary to complete the understanding of that personality. Each of you will help the other. Each of you will learn. This is your most important task. The other tasks are within your free will and we cannot comment upon them at this time for we can only go as far as free will allows and you, at this time, and your comrades, are at a state of choosing what you will do of your own free will. Thus, we ask you to meditate and learn from yourselves what it is that you must do. We are always with you and commend you to the love of the Creator.

May we answer you further, my brother?

Jim: Not at this time, thank you.

We thank you, my brother. Is there another question at this time?

Questioner: There is a difficulty that has arisen with one in our group and my family, that may make it necessary for me to leave the group to keep harmony in my house, and I don't feel good about this. Do you have any suggestion?

Yes, my sister. You must realize that you are a completely free entity. You must detach yourself from all supposed entanglements, including those of your family, and those of the person in your group. You are a star. Your radiance lights many. Your decisions must be made on the basis of your ability to shine and that which causes you to be able to function properly. Whatever temporary difficulties may arise from any inharmonious action on the basis of those who do not understand, one way or another, your main concern must always be yourself. For without yourself, you do not have the heart, the center, from which to move.

Center yourself, therefore, without reference to those who would pull upon you and ask from you to play roles. You do not play a role. You are an eternal spirit and you have your work. Determine, therefore, what you can best do to help in the most high sense that you know. In this way, any mistakes that you make will be canceled by the simple fact that your intention was of the highest nature, not attached to feelings of universal law of the illusion but attached instead to the universal law of the Creator, which come within you alone, for you, which come to each of us, from us.

You cannot live in anyone else's understanding of life, it must be your own, therefore, remove yourself from both sides and know, within yourself, what you must do to be of service. Whatever service you feel is the highest, do. You may, perhaps, be mistaken in practice but it would not matter less, because your intention is of the highest. When one's intention is consistently of the highest nature, the fruits will be known upon the planes that affect the thought forms of this planet and eventually they will come back to you in such a way that these problems will disappear.

May we aid you further, my sister?

Questioner: Thank you, not now.

We thank you. As you know, my sister, we enjoy talking with you.

Is there another question at this time?

(Pause)

Well, my brother and my sisters, since we do not think the world is going to blow up tonight, we would like to share a bit more philosophical information to the other instruments. Therefore, at this time, I will transfer this contact. I am Latwii.

I am Latwii. It is my pleasure to speak with you this evening, a joy *(inaudible)* to feel the heartbeat and love that flows around you. We are always with you and rejoice at moments such as these and your light touches us so brilliantly. We are glad to be of service in any way that we can. My brothers and sisters, we [are] always with you. As you know, there are moments when your awareness of us is like a *(inaudible)*) and a celebration, and another time we feel your urgent desire to sift through the clouds of illusion that *(inaudible)*.

We are always with you and our love surpasses the words this channel can speak tonight, or any words. Feel our love in the radiance of this woman that we share as a part of the creation, as part of the oneness that is the Creator. We will leave this instrument with love. I am Latwii.

I am Latwii, and am with this instrument. It is with great pleasure that we greet you again. It has been a long time, as you reckon time, since we have had the privilege of utilizing this instrument. We wish to inform this instrument that we have been with him in his meditations and have been available for contact at any time. This is the offer and invitation which we make to each who wishes to become an instrument and allow the vibrations of love and light [to] flow through their being.

We are most grateful for each opportunity to utilize instruments such as are gathered here this evening. We realize that each of those present this evening have strong desire to be of service. We understand and appreciate this desire, for, my friends, we share this desire with you. The blending of our vibrations at times such as these are of great significance and inspiration to us as well as to those here who hear our humble messages, for we are sure you know, to be of service to the infinite Creator in each person which *(inaudible)* in each activity which you engage, is the greatest joy and the greatest love which we can imagine and to be of such service is our constant desire and we urge each of you to continue in your devotion to fulfill the desire to serve the infinite Creator, for we have found no other activity to be of such a fulfilling venture.

We would wish for each of you present tonight a wish for the New Year. A wish that the love and the light of the infinite Creator might light the way that each of you travel as you journey homeward and that that light might shine upon each you meet on this journey, and that light of the recognition of the Creator in each face might remain where you have passed, to illuminate the way for others to travel that same path homeward.

We would, at this time, transfer this contact for our closing message. I am Latwii.

I am Latwii. We have probed the one known as Don and discovered that he is not able to channel due to some difficulties of a physical nature. Each one of you is a radiant beam, far more well-realized than some of your brothers and sisters. We urge you to pay no attention to what others say. To remain simple, to remain humble, and in whatever situation you find yourself, to radiate the Creator and to know that you are doing your Father's work and not your own.

That is the key to simplicity, contentment and understanding. We know that each of you intends to work, that each of you has desires for the year ahead, as you would call it. So be it, my brothers and sisters, but let it be the Creator's year and do not confuse in your mind the gift of channeling with the gift of sure knowledge, for we are your brothers and our knowledge is not sure but only given to provoke thought.

And as you give it, give it to suggest pathways of thought that these pathways might perhaps help those to whom you speak. We ask you to remain simple, loving, charitable, kind, and above all, humble, for that is the key to a pure channel. We are grateful that you tuned to us on this powerful night. We share our laughter and our joys with you. We are capable, also, of sharing each moment that you may feel. If you do not laugh, call us anyway, for we love with the love that the Creator has given us as messengers and we are yours as companions whenever you wish us. We leave you in love and light. I am Latwii. Adonai, my friends. Adonai vasu borragus. ☙

Year 1981
January 4, 1981 to April 5, 1981

Sunday Meditation
January 4, 1981

(L channeling)

My brothers and sisters, it is a great pleasure for all of us to greet and be with so many of you. Often we find that there are but few who would contact us. Often we feel that our task is a difficult one and that our labors seem to go so often unrewarded and are even met with rejection, therefore, perhaps you can understand the deep pleasure and satisfaction that we feel in receiving communication from so large a group. At this time we would like to transfer the contact to another channel. I am Laitos.

(B channeling)

I am Laitos. I am now with this instrument. As always, it is a pleasure, as I would say. Often, my friends, it seems our efforts go unrewarded, but, my friends, when we see a group of people of this size dwelling into truth, it truly strengthens us.

Now, my friends, for some of you who have not been here before may I ask why exactly are we here? Partial answers to that question being: by offering ourselves as a spiritual channel through which we are hoping to spread the knowledge of love and its energy to those of you who are truly searching, my friends, but essentially we are speaking of at the spiritual growth of each one of you in this room. Now, at a later time, you will find through your explorations many chances to help others with questions, such as we help you. My friends, as with ourselves, we in return gain a more spiritual understanding through the helping of others that then another in the long line of the universal laws. We are also here, my friends, to spread the understanding of meditation through which you will find it easier to grow. I will now transfer this contact to another instrument. I am Laitos.

(Jim channeling)

I am Laitos, and am with this instrument and we greet you all once again. As we were saying, our purpose for being among your peoples at this time has to do with providing a wider understanding of the concept of love to your people. We have only limited means for being of this type of service, for we respect each individual's rights, each individual's free will choices and many would not wish to hear the message which we bring or experience the means by which we communicate it. Therefore, though we wish to be of the most possible service, we are especially grateful to be asked to join the vibrations of groups such as this so that our means of sharing the Creator's love might be experienced by your people and so that we might learn more ways to express the infinite love and understanding of the One who made us all, for are we not all children within that kingdom of creation?

Some have wandered from the "flock," so to speak. Some have chosen, as is the right of each, to turn their backs upon the Creator, for awhile, so that individual expression in some area might be experienced. Each creation, each entity within the universe, makes a journey throughout their existence. This journey is a path of learning. Much may be learned in many fields. Much may be experienced at many times. The possibilities are infinite. Our purpose at this time is to offer the understanding that is the foundation of all learning, the learning eventually by each within creation that each is the Creator, that each has within the divine spark of the One who made us all. We seek to share our simple understanding of this basic fact with those of your people who wish to learn more of the secrets of their own existence.

We would transfer this contact at this time. I am Laitos.

(Carla channeling

I am Laitos. My brother Latwii is very impatient. We have asked her to wait while we work with this group a little while longer. We wish you to understand the utter simplicity in which we come. We do not have a complex story to tell. We speak one word and that is love. The original Thought that created all that there is, is love. This simple and consuming fire is the fire of creation, is the fire of change, of transformation and of infinity. There is no end to love. You may think of love in many ways. There are many words for love—in many languages. And many different words have been used by your peoples to attempt to express the plenitude of the original Thought, for love is all that there is. Thus, we are not only your brothers and sisters, we and you are one for we are love. Look into the face of the one next to you, my friends. You are seeing love. Perhaps the mirror has been distorted. Perhaps sometimes the face next to yours does not know that it is a face of love, but there is no consciousness that is not love. There is a consciousness that touches each of you. One word for it is "Christ Consciousness." Another word is love. You may feel it personally as the touch of a loved one. Hand on your shoulder. Close. Near. Never away. You cannot flee from love, You cannot be separated from love. For you are love. Love is closer to you than your body. Each breath is farther from your being than is love. This is what we come to share. For we of the Confederation, of those in service to the infinite Creator, have one desire: to serve you by offering you the only information that is worthwhile. We will answer any question that you may have, but the simple truth is that all questions dissolve into a dying fall as they reach the ocean of infinite and all-encompassing love.

I would at this time pause and move among you. If you wish to feel our presence, please request it mentally and we will work with each of you. After a pause, my impatient sister will be glad to answer your questions. I am Laitos.

(Carla channeling

I am Latwii. I am very glad to be with you. We are stepping our energy down as usual. We keep forgetting about this instrument. Please be patient. That is better. It is a great privilege to be able to speak with each of you and we were not in truth so impatient because we were enjoying our brother, Laitos. Also, because we feel that men's lib is important we should add that there is a woman and a man here and we are working together so that he should not be talking about sisters without mentioning brothers.

We of Latwii greet you in the love and the light of the infinite Creator. It is a wonderful thing to be able to share this meditation with you and to let each of you feel a bit of the light that we dwell in. We very much enjoy your vibration also. We come to offer ourselves in case you may have a question or two. Does anyone have a question at this time?

(Pause)

There are two in the room who would like to ask questions, but they are somewhat shy. We would urge them to voice their questions or perhaps frame them more carefully mentally as we will be answering all night if we attempt to answer the general questions that are in your minds at this time. It would aid the group in general if you could voice them aloud. We would greatly appreciate it. Otherwise we will have to take a flyer in general and hope to hit the main points.

Do you wish, my brothers, to ask a specific question at this time?

C: I have a question. I'm curious about what it's like where you live—your relation to your environment—the people of the planet Earth have abused the Earth a lot and a lot of us are concerned—*don't* abuse it and try to love the Earth—and I just wonder what … if your planet, if you have to deal at all with abuse of your environment?

I understand, my sister. Because we are answering you we give you a different answer than others of the Confederation. Please understand that some of our members come from very different vibrations. Our situation is, however, as follows. We are our environment. We are a sun body as a community. The body of the sun being the male population of our sphere, the beams being what some call photon energy and what others call angelic energy. Thus, we live in a light vibration and form our environment, which in your terms is a very simple one since our entire society radiates in light and our, shall we say, families are products of the polarity between the compactness of the light body and the great receptivity and expansiveness of, what you would perhaps call, a sunbeam. Thus, we perpetuate ourselves in a manner not understood by your scientists and this is true of many of your sun bodies.

Although we are not in your density, in our density what is perceived as heat in your density, does not exist. Unfortunately, beings such as yourself who have come to realize the oneness of being which they share with their planetary sphere, you are in a vibration in which you are encased in a heavy chemical vehicle. You cannot hear the flowers and the trees speak nor understand the song of the wind. And it is not apparent to many of your peoples that each part of the creation of the Father that exists upon your planet dwells in service. Thus, as you attempt to be of service to the planetary sphere that aided you in living, it is difficult for you to see with calmness and peace the great abuse of others.

However, my sister, that's the third density for you. That's, unfortunately, the way it is. People will, because of a lack of ability to feel the connections between their body and their minds, their minds and the Earth, their minds and the minds of each other and so forth, you will see abuses going on of all types. People abusing their own body by feeding them improperly, people abusing the Earth by using it improperly, people abusing each other by failing to see clearly the face of love in each entity.

So be it, my sister, that you yourself do what you can, feel what you can, love as best you can, is a great deal in the third density. To do this is to exceed understanding and move into the area of love. To do this is an exercise in what you may call faith, for in an environment where not everyone lives in this wise, this becomes a matter of choice. Thus, you have your choice, you have your understanding, you have your lesson, and the rest of the world must have its also. To deal with your own is truly your service.

May we answer you further, my sister?

C: No, I don't think so. Thank you.

We thank you. Is there another question at this time?

K: Do you have information about the coming conjunction of the planets in our solar system and ways that we *(inaudible)* or be wise to perhaps steel ourselves …

I am Latwii, and I am sending this instrument probabilities, for you must understand that the only area of which we can be certain is the area of the immediate nowness. The consciousness of each of you upon the planet determines the future, thus we cannot give you certainty. However, the Jupiter Effect, as it has been called by your scientists, promises to be somewhat of a strain for your Earth's crust. What is unclear to us is the state of your planet prior to this, for as has been the case all too often in the past few months, it is not clear to us whether or not your peoples are attempting to alter certain configurations of your planet due to nuclear war.

The Jupiter Effect has nothing on nuclear war. Thus, we are, as always, asking each of you to remember in your meditation the cause of peace and to offer up your own visualization of a world at peace. The danger, you understand, does not seem to be immediate, however there are several probabilities that do not look particularly good. As to the 1982 probabilities of Earth changes and your wisdom in, as you say, steeling yourself for them, we may say that whatever you feel to do is correct for you, or as this instrument would say, choose your poison. It is very noteworthy and praiseworthy for those of you who have the feelings to do so to prepare for difficulty, having to do with the transportation of food and other of your merchant services by forming self-sufficient households and communities. This will be helpful to you, not only during this time but into the future for some time, for this area does not look to be an early victim of earth changes, however it will not last forever and you may simply look to your conscience and your heart for you will be guided to do what you feel is best.

Some will not feel the need to make preparation to survive and will instead find their survival due to the law which states that no shepherd shall be without his staff. It is those who follow the kingdom who then have all else added unto them. We would like to encourage you, therefore, not to do one thing or the other, not to homestead or not to homestead, but instead listen to your heart and seek the wisdom of the spirit in meditation. The answers for you have been programmed from your, shall we say, higher self. And you have access to the information about your decisions as they occur as it is needed if you but have patience to seek the Creator, to tabernacle with His presence on a regular basis. Each has free will and you, my brother, are free. Thus, we can only say to you it is quite feasible to prepare for Earth changes and sensible and [is] a certainly suitable and appropriate action if it is what your heart tells you to do. Wherever you are you will have the opportunity to be of service and we know that you will find that a blessing.

May we answer you further, my brother?

K: No, thank you.

We thank you also. Is there another question at this time?

(Pause)

I am Latwii. We will speak for a short time—winging it, as it were—and attempting to touch on the basis of an unspoken question which is within this group. When we attempt to speak of who we are, it is a confusing thing, for we are in fact a vibration communicating through the mind of this instrument. We are, in your density, quite insubstantial. To attempt to give you our origin is very impractical and would be an occasion for general hilarity among this group due to this instrument's total lack of geographical sense. We do not lay any emphasis upon who we are but ask you only to consider us as messengers bringing certain information for your consideration and discrimination, urging you always to use your powers of discrimination to take that which we say [which] may be of use and to toss away the rest without a second thought. We are not infallible. We are your brothers and sisters. We see a bit further than you do. We are somewhat more displaced from, as this instrument would say, some of the more difficult games that your peoples are involved in. We are not bound by so many restrictions, but we are brothers and sisters because we share consciousness and that, my friends, is a gift of the One Who is All. We as a Confederation have been with you for many thousands of your years. We have attempted to serve you, protect you and to nurture you. There are special reasons for our being here at this time which the questioner already knows, but our relationship to all that our brother has learned is very simple. We are not …

(Tape ends.) ☙

Wednesday Advanced Meeting
January 5, 1981

(Unknown channeling

I am Hatonn. I greet you, my friends, in the love and light of our infinite Creator. It is a very great privilege to greet you this morning and speak through this instrument. It is always a great privilege to be able to communicate to any of those of your peoples who will listen to what we have to bring them. You know, my friends, we have said many times, we have a very simple truth to bring your peoples. It is the truth, however, that seems somewhat difficult to convey. In its simplicity, it lacks this ability, ease of conveyance. We are continually searching for methods to convey the simple concepts of the greater *(inaudible)*. We have found without the spoken word, there is very little understood, therefore, we have to resort to the other vehicles of communication.

We are, at this time, initiating several, what you would call modes, for sending these messages which we have for your people. One of these programs has to do with your radio communications. We are, at this time, preparing certain communications to be substituted for some of your programming. This, I am sure, is a surprise to each of you, as it is to the instrument to which I am speaking through, but let me assure you, in the very near future that we will be using your radio communication to influence, shall I say, the thinking, without infringing upon those *(inaudible)* but we will bring them, without pain, to the limits of what you call *(inaudible)* of our reality or existence. We will, however, be blessed with *(inaudible)* because it will be a definite *(inaudible)*. The radio *(inaudible)* experience.

I will now transfer this contact.

(Unknown channeling

I am with the instrument. I am Hatonn. Due to the previous information, this instrument is not in a good state of concentration and we ask your patience while we deepen her contact.

We are capable of many things which we have never done and due to the extreme biases of your peoples, in relation to our purposes. A few of your years previous to this message, the basic concepts of this group with whom we have the relationship of love and service, began to change dramatically, due in part to our presence and our continued information which suggest the same sort of emphasis on the information which we have come to aid in conveying to your peoples. Therefore, our path has been cleared to have a more direct role in this culture's awareness. We are not, at this point, fearful of being guilty of infringement of free will by doing things which previously we would not have been able to consider.

The other reason, of course, for our plans at this time, is a reasoned and careful inspection, the configuration of probabilities having to do with the harvest that you are so involved in being the workers within. Because the harvest approaches and because the effectiveness of our attempt to lighten the darker forces, which have been trapped in this illusion, we are more capable of, shall we say, a more comprehensive means of indicating to your peoples certain sources of information by means of visual aids which may certainly spark the imagination without infringing upon free will. It is necessary that the energy given to and from this planet by the relationship between peoples, such as yourselves and us, be concretized so that you may begin to share some of the more inner teachings that we may share with you about our relationship to your identity, your relationship to others, and both of our relationships to the Creator. We will attempt, through the purer channels available in a more tuned, or as this instrument has called it, advanced group, information which may be needed by this group. Some of this information is not designed for publication.

At this time we would move on to a completely different subject having to do with the thought-forms which you are busily creating having to do with your service to mankind. We have consulted amongst ourselves in the Confederation and feel that we are glad to be of service by making available information tailored, to the best of our ability, for what you may call the one new to the concept of a personal identity that goes beyond the physical illusion and the other forms of life, which by means of the procreative aspects of your physical illusion, are tied to these entities. We hope to be able to aid you in furnishing information that can be used to advantage in such a campaign.

At this time, we would transfer to the other instrument. I am Hatonn.

(Unknown channeling

I am Hatonn and am with this instrument. We greet you once again in love and light. We have been sharing what may be considered a new line of thought and action with this group this evening. It is our desire in each of our sharings with your people to provide information and inspiration of a nature that stretches or steps up the awareness and the consciousness—the vibrations—of those who would listen to our messages. It is a difficult task for your people—those who would listen to our messages—are each located at various points in their evolution of understanding. Therefore, our methods of providing information must take into account many different variables so that there is as little infringement as possible of the wills of those who would listen.

We feel, at this time, that it is of utmost importance to make the information that we have at our disposal available to your people in as many manners, as many vehicles, as possible, for the time of listening and considering grows short. The time of the great changes which long have been spoken of in the cultures and religions and folk stories of your planet, the time is close at hand when this great transformation shall occur. We will undertake every possible means for making our simple message of love and understanding available to each entity upon your plane, for each is of the fold of the Father. Each must have the opportunity to finally decide whether he or she wishes to return to the fold or wishes to continue upon a path which takes the entity further away from that state of unity which is the birthright of each within the creation of the Father.

As beings who wish to be of service, we are pledged to provide this message of love to every last being upon your planet. In order to do this, there may have to be, in some cases, a certain shocking of the senses, a certain reflecting of consciousness upon itself in manners which previously we would not have considered, this related to our initial message concerning the use of radio transmission of our thoughts as a substitution for the normal programming of certain of your radio transmissions. Such may also be used in the field of your televised pictures over your television stations. From time to time there will appear various images and messages which will have no other explainable source than our transmission. It is our hope that such anomalies will shake the perceptions of those who view them to a proper degree where internal questioning will be followed by internal seeking and the outward manifestation of those who would become a seeker of truth.

We realize that it will be unavoidable in such cases to infringe on the rights of some who will witness these events. We have carefully considered this possibility and are willing to take these actions in the hopes that opening the hearts and the minds and the souls of the few who still are able to seek inwardly, that this action will provide such entities with the opportunities which they so richly deserve.

We would at this time transfer this contact for our closing message. I am Hatonn.

(The rest of the tape is inaudible.)

Sunday Meditation
January 11, 1981

(L channeling)

I am Laitos. And I greet you, my brothers, in the name of the Creator. We are pleased that you have chosen to take time away from your daily pursuits, from your happinesses and anguish, to contact us and share your love and attention with us. In return, my brothers, we hope to offer some advice, our love and, hopefully, a glimpse into intentions for which the Creator placed you on your planet. Our small efforts are never equal to the task, yet we will try, my brothers, to meet your needs as far as we are able.

My brothers, at this time I would share with you a small story. At one time in the past of your planet, a man came from a small town in a poor country proclaiming that he was able to hear the words and the voice of a father who existed in another realm from his own physical, [visible] father. Naturally, his neighbors knew he was crazy, for this, they knew, was not the way the universe worked. Still the man persisted. He was very insistent. He claimed that his father, of all things, was everyone's father and that, for this reason, everyone was brothers and sisters. Surely, my brothers, this was a calamity, for how could one hate or cheat or kill his own brother or sister? There was but one thing to do: the man must be silenced.

Many efforts were made to silence him. He was ridiculed, shamed, cursed and eventually beaten. He was held as an object of derision before his own countrymen. His own relatives and even his friends, who had followed him and listened to him preach his madness through endless days and nights, finally saw the error of their ways and abandoned him. Still this fool would not desist and in disgust his countrymen killed him.

Then, as if intent on making matters worse, he came back and continued his foolishness. By now his words, like a disease, had begun to spread. It was too late to check the infection and regrettably (or so it seemed to his countrymen) the disease was to continue and flourish until the situation exists as it does today, in which the foolishness of this man who claimed all to be his family, to be his brothers and his sisters, has become known—not believed—throughout his world.

My brothers, you probably wonder at the fact that we refer to this man as a fool and to his teachings as foolishness. Yet, my brothers, who but a fool could step out into oblivion and trust the truth to bear him up? Who but a fool would risk his earthly life in the belief that more existed than earthly life? And again, who but a fool would trust in an invisible father?

My brothers, we of Laitos are thankful for your foolishness, for the universe is desperately short of such fools. We would encourage you to trust in your foolishness, to step out off of the precipice into space and rely upon your foolish belief that what is real will bear you up and sustain you and maintain your real life.

At this time we would transfer our contact to another instrument. I am Laitos.

(Unknown channeling)

I am Laitos, and again I greet you in the love and the light of the infinite Creator. Yes, my friends, to make the leap of faith, as it has been called, to be the fool for the Creator, to seek what is most popularly known as foolishness instead of seeking personal power and glory and riches, this is indeed appreciated. For in your vibration, all of the signs point the other way if you can distract yourself enough. It is only when you have stopped distracting yourself with the things that man has made and the walls that man has put up against man that you can see the creation at work and the laws of the creation in practice, and thus have an inner feeling that to be a fool, to seek the truth, may have the most important basis of all in your thinking, that of an inner feeling of rightness.

We would add to you, my brothers, that it is most important as you unfold in the newness of your spiritual growth from day-to-day, that you refrain in the beginning from speaking with great detail about your path to others. For just as seedlings are fragile until they have taken root, so is the path that you take growing spiritually step-by-step. Each step is first taken with a very light treading of the foot and gradually, as you put into practice what you have learned in meditation and in seeking, that step becomes firm and you can push off from that onto the next. To avoid playing the hypocrite, which is never a desired role for a seeker, it is very precious to you to keep nurtured quietly and carefully, as a small plant in a hotbed, those new understandings into which you have come, those realizations which you have begun to understand and become one with.

Know that you are one of a great communion, a great fellowship of seekers, and that each positive thought, each positive deed, each prayer and meditation, is witnessed and emphasized by those who are tuned to that vibration of love and light. You have many helpers, and awareness of them will aid you in your own seeking. For as you are aware that they, in their, as you would call it, angelic presence, underscore and emphasize your own spiritual vibrations, you then can find a deeper and clearer level of meditation.

At this time I would like to work briefly with the one known as C. I will condition this instrument and attempt to contact him by speaking a few words through him, if you will relax. I am Laitos.

(Pause)

I am again with this instrument. We had a good contact with the one known as C, and wish to reassure him that all that lies between that feeling which he just experienced and channeling itself is simply the thought process whereby that instrument asks of himself whether the movements and feelings were coming from elsewhere or whether he was imagining them. Once that roadblock is removed and analysis ceases and you speak without thought, having tuned yourself to the proper spiritual vibration, you then will be able to perceive our contact.

We would like to work now with the one known as D, and give her some conditioning and a little healing from our sister, Nona. I am Laitos.

(Pause)

At this time we would work with the one known as N, if he would relax and request mentally that we be with him, we will work with his conditioning and attempt to make ourselves known unto him in some way.

(Pause)

I am again with this instrument. I am Laitos. Now if the instrument known as Jim would accede to the service of being used as a channel at this time, we would like to close this message through him. I am Laitos.

(Jim channeling)

I am Laitos, and am with this instrument. We are very pleased to have been asked to join your meditation this evening. It is a rare privilege to be able to share our simple thoughts and perceptions with people who seek to know more of the truth of their reality. We of Laitos have experienced no truth greater than love, the love of the infinite Creator, for each entity, each particle of creation. And are we not all united as a family in love, bound by our desire to speak, to know the Father of us all? Each of you in your daily lives encounter the Creator in every endeavor in which you enter. Each moment the opportunity is made for you to travel yet one step closer to experiencing the love of the Father, for each moment holds a message, ere it would not exist. The message, disguised in infinite ways, speaks the song of love, the lesson of life. Listen closely, my brothers, for the Father sings to you in each moment and speaks the infinite languages of life to your hearts. We of Laitos have heard this song and would share what we can of its melody and message with those of your people who desire to hear such music.

We would now leave this instrument and this group, as always, in the love and the light of the infinite Creator. Adonai, my friends.

(Carla channeling

I am Latwii. I am next on the cosmic hit parade tonight. I must step this vibration down for this instrument, if you will be patient. I … I … I … I am Latwii. I believe this is the most comfortable level for this instrument. We do apologize to this instrument. Somehow we always overestimate the necessary vibration for contacting this instrument. She is somewhat sensitive to our vibration. We apologize. We think we just broke her high A.

We are very pleased to be here and have asked for the privilege of answering any questions that you may have at this time. As you know, that is our favorite thing to do as we are somewhat new to this game of speaking to your peoples and it is difficult for us to know how to inspire you by telling you stories, facts and other embroideries about love because it is such a simple matter. We seem to do better with the questions, so if you would be so kind as to voice any that you may have at this time, we will be glad to answer them.

C: Last week a question came up after the meditation about—concerning Hatonn, what he's doing now or if he's still on a special mission or somewhere else—just exactly what he is up to these days.

[I am Latwii.] We will attempt to speak through this instrument, for this information is perfectly all right for you to know but somewhat different and she may have difficulty.

The vibration of Hatonn is working in a new pattern, which is not along any particular geographical frontier or area, for at this particular time the problem is, as it were, a kind of metastasized illness and exists in many parts of the Earth's body. Therefore, the ones of Hatonn have tuned themselves to a certain energy of negativity and are working on the mass consciousness of that particular part of your planet's entities. These entities include many which are, as this instrument would call them, the movers and the shakers.

Thus, Hatonn has moved [to the] eighth or final or covering layer or dimension of this particular octave, stretched itself until it covers the entire planet and is tuning in and attempting to ameliorate by love that particular vibration which is doing the most harm to your peoples. This is a vibration of thought, not of deed.

May we answer you further, my brother?

C: No, that's fine. Thank you.

The brothers of Hatonn have spent a great deal of energy working with certain entities and groups of entities, but we have not found this to be in any one case the appropriate action for this particular energy. Thus, the change of, shall we say, strategy attempting to make the best use of those of Hatonn's special vibration, which is a very, very strong love vibration, and which has had much experience with your Earth's sphere.

Is there another question at this time?

L: Recently in meditation a new or special project was referred to concerning advanced communication. The impression I received was that our involvement was somehow necessary for this to be accomplished. Is my understanding of this correct, and, if so, how can we best facilitate the effort?

I am Latwii. I understand your question, my brother. Essentially you are correct, however there are two completely different means of effecting such communication. One has already been used and we have not found it satisfactory; that is, impressing those people who are sensitive to our message to arrange for the technology necessary to jam one broadcast and substitute another. This involves money, people, time, and can ultimately be ignored since the means of its being done by mere humans, as you would put it, can be discovered or, at least, surmised. The other way is for people, such as this group contains, to make available with all sincerity, and with as much humor as possible, the information of which they are the surest and with which they are the most comfortable. That is, of course, the information having to do with the basic philosophy and something about our basic reasons for working with your peoples.

Cosmology enters in, but we do not expect people to find cosmology an interesting way of being introduced to our message. Thus, the other way of aiding our ability to use your mass media is to make enough of an impression by your own creative efforts on the mass mind of the society in which you live that enough people desire to know more about not only the existence of our being but what message we might be bringing to you, that we could then, without infringing upon the free will of these peoples, feed small bits of information about love and light through these media. If people are not in the majority greatly desirous of this information, we would be infringing upon free will and we would not wish to do this. We are not, as you would call it, gods; we are your brothers, and what we have to say is only for your consideration, not for you to believe. What you believe must come from within.

May we answer you further, my brother?

L: I would ask that you speak to me about the value of humor.

My brother, the value of humor is a pale shadow of reality. Reality, as we understand it, is likened unto what this instrument would call an orgasm. That is, the basic ecstasy or joy of the universe. That is, the energy that is love. It is existent in all levels of being. Laughter is one outward expression of the emotional state of what you may call orgasm, however, it would not be advisable for you to call it this during your working hours while speaking to your workmates, or they might think you a little strange.

You must understand that this particular word is known clearly to you as a common human experience, whereas it has never been understood that laughter, when entered into totally and wholly rather than nervously or embarrassedly, is another form of the same energy. Laughter is available to all. Laughter is a healing, comforting, lovely energy and indeed is one of the most highly prized of all states of being. We find the universe to be full of the laughter—or the song—of joy.

May we answer you further about this or have we simply hilariously confused you?

L: You explained it well to me. Thank you.

We thank you, my brother. Is there another question at this time?

(Pause)

My brothers and sisters, we hope that we have been of service to you and we hope that you find joy in your hearts and in your lives and in each other, for all of those things are the Creator. There is nothing outside the Creator. There is nowhere to trip or fall, to stumble or fear. You are in the universe of love. Rejoice therefore. We shall rejoice with you. I am Latwii. I leave you in that love and that light of the infinite Creator. Adonai, my friends. Adonai.

L/L Research

L/L Research is a subsidiary of Rock Creek Research & Development Laboratories, Inc.

P.O. Box 5195
Louisville, KY 40255-0195

www.llresearch.org

Rock Creek is a non-profit corporation dedicated to discovering and sharing information which may aid in the spiritual evolution of humankind.

ABOUT THE CONTENTS OF THIS TRANSCRIPT: This telepathic channeling has been taken from transcriptions of the weekly study and meditation meetings of the Rock Creek Research & Development Laboratories and L/L Research. It is offered in the hope that it may be useful to you. As the Confederation entities always make a point of saying, please use your discrimination and judgment in assessing this material. If something rings true to you, fine. If something does not resonate, please leave it behind, for neither we nor those of the Confederation would wish to be a stumbling block for any.

CAVEAT: This transcript is being published by L/L Research in a not yet final form. It has, however, been edited and any obvious errors have been corrected. When it is in a final form, this caveat will be removed.

© 2009 L/L Research

Intensive Meditation
January 15, 1981

(The editing changes made to this transcript while readying it for publishing in the Law of One books have been included. However, portions of the original transcript that were removed for the Law of One publications have been retained in this version.)

(Carla channeling

I am Ra. I have not spoken through this instrument before. We had to wait until she was precisely tuned, as we send a narrow band vibration. We greet you in the love and in the light of our infinite Creator.

We have watched your group. We have been called to your group, for you have a need for the diversity of experiences in channeling which go with a more intensive, or as you might call it, advanced approach to the system of studying the pattern of the illusions of your body, your mind, and your spirit, which you call seeking the truth. We hope to offer you a somewhat different slant upon the information which is always and ever the same.

The Confederation of Planets in the Service of the Infinite Creator has only one important statement. That statement, my friends, as you know is that all things, all life, all of the creation is part of one original Thought.

We will exercise each channel if we are able to. The reception of our beam is a somewhat more advanced feat than some of the more broad vibration channels opened by other members for more introductory and intermediate work.

Let us for a moment consider thought. What is it, my friends, to take thought? Took you then thought today? What thoughts did you think today? What thoughts were part of the original Thought today? In how many of your thoughts did the creation lie? Was love contained? And was service freely given? You are not part of a material universe. You are part of the Thought. You are dancing in a ballroom in which there is no material. You are dancing thoughts. You move your body, your mind, and your spirit in somewhat eccentric patterns for you have not completely grasped the concept that you are part of the original Thought.

We would at this time transfer to an instrument known as Don. I am Ra.

(Pause)

(Carla channeling

I am Ra. I am again with this instrument. We are close to initiating a contact but we are having difficulty penetrating a certain mental tension and distraction that are somewhat characteristic of this channel. We will therefore describe the type of vibration which is being sent. The instrument will find us entering the energy field at a slight angle towards the back of the top of the head in a narrow but strong area of intensity. We are not able to offer any conditioning due to our own transmitting limitations, therefore, if the instrument can feel this particular effect he may then speak our thoughts as they come to him. We will again attempt this contact. I am Ra.

(Pause)

(Carla channeling

This instrument is resisting our contact. However, we assure that we are satisfied that contact with the one known as Don is not preferable to that instrument. We will therefore move on to the one known as L. Again we caution the instrument that it is a narrow band of communication which is felt as a vibration entering the aura. We will now transfer this contact. I am Ra.

(Pause)

(Carla channeling

I am Ra. We greet once more in the love and the light of our infinite Creator. We ask that you be patient with us. We are a difficult channel to receive. We may perhaps add some dimensions to your understanding. At this time we would be glad to attempt to speak to any subject or question which those entities in the room may have potential use in the questing.

L: Do you have a specific purpose, and if so, could you tell us something of what your purpose is?

I am Ra. We communicate now. We too have our place. We are not those of the love or the light. We are those who are of the Law of One. In our vibration the polarities are harmonized; the complexities are simplified; the paradoxes have a solution; we are one. That is our nature and our purpose. We are old upon your planet and have served with varying degrees of success in transmitting the Law of One, of Unity of Singleness to your peoples. We have walked your planet. We have seen the faces of your peoples. This is not so with many of the entities of the Confederation. We found that it was not efficacious, however we now feel the great responsibility of staying in the capacity of removing the distortions and powers that have been given to the Law of One. We will continue in this until, shall we say, your cycle is appropriately ended. If not this one, then the next. We are not a part of time and thus are able to be with you in any of your times.

Does this give you enough information from which to extract our purpose, my brother?

L: Yes. Thank you.

I am Ra. We appreciate your vibrations. Is there another query?

L: I've heard of the name "Ra" in connection with the Egyptians. Are you connected with that Ra in any way?

I am Ra. Yes, the connection is congruency. May we elucidate? What do you not understand?

L: Could you give me a little more detail about your role with the Egyptians?

I am Ra. The identity of the vibration Ra is our identity. We as a group, or what you would call a social memory complex, made contact with a race of your planetary kind which you call Egyptians. Others from our density made contact at the same time in South America, and the so-called "lost cities" were their attempts to contribute to the Law of One.

We spoke to one who heard and understood and was in a position to decree the Law of One. However, the priests and peoples of that era quickly distorted our message, robbing it of the, shall we say, compassion with which unity is informed by its very nature. Since it contains all, it cannot abhor any.

When we were no longer able to have appropriate channels through which to enunciate the Law of One, we removed ourselves from the now hypocritical position which we had allowed ourselves to be placed in. Other myths, shall we say, having more to do with polarity and the things of your vibration that are complex, again took over in that particular society/complex.

Does this form a sufficient amount of information, or could we speak further?

Don: *(Inaudible)*.

Is there another query?

Don: *(Inaudible)*.

I am Ra. Consider, if you will, that the universe is infinite. This has yet to be proven or disproven, but we can assure you that there is no end to yourselves, your understanding, what you would call your journey of seeking, or your perceptions of the creation.

That which is infinite cannot be many, for many-ness is a finite concept. To have infinity you must identify or define the infinity as unity; otherwise, the term does not have any referent or meaning. In an infinite Creator there is only unity. You have seen simple examples of unity. You have seen the prism which shows all colors stemming from the sunlight. This is a simplistic example of unity.

In truth there is no right or wrong. There is no polarity for all will be, as you would say, reconciled at some point in your dance through the mind/body/spirit complex which you amuse yourself by distorting in various ways at this time. This distortion is not in any case necessary. It is chosen by each of you as an alternative to understanding the complete unity of thought which binds all things. You are not speaking of similar or somewhat like entities or things. You are every thing, every being, every emotion, every event, every situation. You are unity. You are infinity. You are love/light, light/love. You are. This is the Law of One.

May we enunciate in more detail?

Don: No.

I am Ra. Is there another query at this time?

Don: Can you comment on the coming planetary changes in our physical reality?

I am Ra. I preferred to wait til this instrument had again reached a proper state of depth of singleness or one-pointedness before we spoke.

The changes are very, very trivial. We do not concern ourselves with the conditions which bring about harvest.

Don: If an individual makes efforts to act as a catalyst in general to increase the awareness of planetary consciousness, is he of any aid in that direction, or is he doing nothing but acting upon himself?

I am Ra. We shall answer your question in two parts, both of which are important equally.

Firstly, you must understand that the distinction between yourself and others is not visible to us. We do not consider that a separation exists between the consciousness-raising efforts of the distortion which you project as a personality and the distortion that you project as another personality. Thus, to learn is the same as to teach unless you are not teaching what you are learning; in which case you have done you/them little good. This understanding should be pondered by your mind/body/spirit complex as it is a distortion which plays a part in your experiences at this nexus.

To turn to the second part of our response may we state our understanding, limited though it is.

Group-individuated consciousness is that state of sharing understanding with the other distortions of mind/body/spirit complexes which are within the evident reach of the mind/body/spirit complex individual or group. Thus, we are speaking to you and accepting both our distortions and your own in order to enunciate the laws of creation, more especially the Law of One. We are not available to many of your peoples, for this is not an easily understood way of communication or type of philosophy. However, our very being is hopefully a poignant example of both the necessity and the near-hopelessness of attempting to teach.

Each of those in this group is striving to use, digest and diversify the information which we are sending this instrument into the channels of the mind/body/spirit complex without distortion. The few whom you will illuminate by sharing your light are far more than enough reason for the greatest possible effort. To serve one is to serve all. Therefore, we offer the question back to you to state that indeed it is the only activity worth doing: to learn/teach or teach/learn. There is nothing else which is of aid in demonstrating the original Thought except your very being, and the distortions that come from the unexplained, inarticulate, or mystery-clad being are many. Thus, to attempt to discern and weave your way through as many group mind/body/spirit distortions as possible among your peoples in the course of your teaching is a very good effort to make. We can speak no more valiantly of your desire to serve.

May we speak in any other capacity upon this subject?

Don: Will you be available for communication? Can we call on you in the future?

I am Ra. We have good contact with this instrument because of her recent experiences with trance. She is to be able to communicate our thoughts in your future. However, we advise care in disturbing the channel for a few moments and then the proper procedure for aiding an instrument who has, to some extent, the need of re-entering the mind/body/spirit complex which the instrument has chosen for the life experience of this time/space. Do you understand how to nurture this instrument?

Don: No. Could you explain it?

We suggest first a brief period of silence. Then the repetition of the instrument's vibratory complex of sound in your density which you call name. Repeat until an answer is obtained. Then the laying on of the hands at the neck region for a brief period so that the instrument may recharge batteries which are not, shall we say, full of the essence of this particular field at this time. And finally, a gift of water into which the love of all present has been given. This will restore this entity, for her distortions contain great sensitivity towards the vibrations of love and the charged water will effect comfort. Do you now understand?

Don: Not completely.

I am Ra. We search your mind to find the vibration Lrac. It is this vibration from you which contains the largest amount of what you would call love. Others would call this entity Carla. The charging of the water is done by those present placing their hands over the glass and visualizing the power of love entering the water. This will charge that very effective medium with those vibrations.

Don: *(Inaudible).*

Lastly.

Don: *(Inaudible).*

This instrument is, at this time, quite fatigued. However, her heart is such that she continues to remain open to us and useful as a channel. This is why we have spent the time/space explaining how the distortions of what you may call fatigue may be ameliorated.

Don: *(Inaudible).*

Under no circumstances should this instrument be touched until she has responded to her name. I do not wish to take this instrument beyond her capacity for physical energy. It grows low. Therefore, I must leave this instrument. I leave you in the glory and peace of unity. Go forth in peace, rejoicing in the power of the one Creator. I am Ra.

L/L Research

L/L Research is a subsidiary of Rock Creek Research & Development Laboratories, Inc.

P.O. Box 5195
Louisville, KY 40255-0195

www.llresearch.org

Rock Creek is a non-profit corporation dedicated to discovering and sharing information which may aid in the spiritual evolution of humankind.

ABOUT THE CONTENTS OF THIS TRANSCRIPT: This telepathic channeling has been taken from transcriptions of the weekly study and meditation meetings of the Rock Creek Research & Development Laboratories and L/L Research. It is offered in the hope that it may be useful to you. As the Confederation entities always make a point of saying, please use your discrimination and judgment in assessing this material. If something rings true to you, fine. If something does not resonate, please leave it behind, for neither we nor those of the Confederation would wish to be a stumbling block for any.

© 2009 L/L Research

The Law of One, Book I, Session 1
January 15, 1981

Ra: I am Ra. I have not spoken through this instrument before. We had to wait until she was precisely tuned, as we send a narrow band vibration. We greet you in the love and in the light of our infinite Creator.

We have watched your group. We have been called to your group, for you have a need for the diversity of experiences in channeling which go with a more intensive, or as you might call it, advanced approach to the system of studying the pattern of the illusions of your body, your mind, and your spirit, which you call seeking the truth. We hope to offer you a somewhat different slant upon the information which is always and ever the same.

At this time we would be glad to attempt to speak to any subject or question which those entities in the room may have potential use in the requesting.

Questioner: Do you have a specific purpose, and if so, could you tell us something of what your purpose is?

Ra: I am Ra. We communicate now. We are those who are of the Law of One. In our vibration the polarities are harmonized; the complexities are simplified; the paradoxes have a solution. We are one. That is our nature and our purpose.

We are old upon your planet and have served with varying degrees of success in transmitting the Law of One, of Unity, of Singleness to your peoples. We have walked your planet. We have seen the faces of your peoples. However, we now feel the great responsibility of staying in the capacity of removing the distortions and powers that have been given to the Law of One. We will continue in this, until, shall we say, your cycle is appropriately ended. If not this one, then the next. We are not a part of time and, thus, are able to be with you in any of your times.

Does this give you enough information from which to extract our purpose, my brother?

Questioner: Yes. Thank you.

Ra: I am Ra. We appreciate your vibrations. Is there another query?

Questioner: I've heard of the name "Ra" in connection with the Egyptians. Are you connected with that Ra in any way?

Ra: I am Ra. Yes, the connection is congruency. May we elucidate? What do you not understand?

Questioner: Could you give me a little more detail about your role with the Egyptians?

Ra: I am Ra. The identity of the vibration Ra is our identity. We as a group, or what you would call a social memory complex, made contact with a race of your planetary kind which you call Egyptians. Others from our density made contact at the same time in South America, and the so-called "lost cities" were their attempts to contribute to the Law of One.

We spoke to one who heard and understood and was in a position to decree the Law of One. However, the priests and peoples of that era quickly distorted our message, robbing it of the, shall we say, compassion with which unity is informed by its very nature. Since it contains all, it cannot abhor any.

When we were no longer able to have appropriate channels through which to enunciate the Law of One, we removed ourselves from the now hypocritical position which we had allowed ourselves to be placed in. Other myths, shall we say, having more to do with polarity and the things of your vibration that are complex, again took over in that particular society/complex.

Does this form a sufficient amount of information, or could we speak further?

Is there another query?

Questioner: *(The question was lost because the questioner was sitting too far from the tape recorder to be recorded.)*

Ra: I am Ra. Consider, if you will, that the universe is infinite. This has yet to be proven or disproven, but we can assure you that there is no end to your selves, your understanding, what you would call your journey of seeking, or your perceptions of the creation.

That which is infinite cannot be many, for many-ness is a finite concept. To have infinity you must identify or define the infinity as unity; otherwise, the term does not have any referent or meaning. In an infinite Creator there is only unity. You have seen simple examples of unity. You have seen the prism which shows all colors stemming from the sunlight. This is a simplistic example of unity.

In truth there is no right or wrong. There is no polarity for all will be, as you would say, reconciled at some point in your dance through the mind/body/spirit complex which you amuse yourself by distorting in various ways at this time. This distortion is not in any case necessary. It is chosen by each of you as an alternative to understanding the complete unity of thought which binds all things. You are not speaking of similar or somewhat like entities or things. You are every thing, every being, every emotion, every event, every situation. You are unity. You are infinity. You are love/light, light/love. You are. This is the Law of One.

May we enunciate in more detail?

Questioner: No.

Ra: I am Ra. Is there another query at this time?

Questioner: Can you comment on the coming planetary changes in our physical reality?

Ra: I am Ra. I preferred to wait till this instrument had again reached a proper state of depth of singleness or one-pointedness before we spoke.

The changes are very, very trivial. We do not concern ourselves with the conditions which bring about harvest.

Questioner: If an individual makes efforts to act as a catalyst in general to increase the awareness of planetary consciousness, is he of any aid in that direction, or is he doing nothing but acting upon himself?

Ra: I am Ra. We shall answer your question in two parts, both of which are important equally.

Firstly, you must understand that the distinction between yourself and others is not visible to us. We do not consider that a separation exists between the consciousness-raising efforts of the distortion which you project as a personality and the distortion that you project as another personality. Thus, to learn is the same as to teach unless you are not teaching what you are learning; in which case you have done you/them little good. This understanding should be pondered by your mind/body/spirit complex as it is a distortion which plays a part in your experiences at this nexus.

To turn to the second part of our response may we state our understanding, limited though it is.

Group-individuated consciousness is that state of sharing understanding with the other distortions of mind/body/spirit complexes, which are within the evident reach of the mind/body/spirit complex individual or group. Thus, we are speaking to you and accepting both our distortions and your own in order to enunciate the laws of creation, more especially the Law of One. We are not available to many of your peoples, for this is not an easily understood way of communication or type of philosophy. However, our very being is hopefully a poignant example of both the necessity and the near-hopelessness of attempting to teach.

Each of those in this group is striving to use, digest, and diversify the information which we are sending this instrument into the channels of the mind/body/spirit complex without distortion. The few whom you will illuminate by sharing your light are far more than enough reason for the greatest possible effort. To serve one is to serve all. Therefore, we offer the question back to you to state that indeed it is the only activity worth doing: to learn/teach or teach/learn. There is nothing else which is of aid in demonstrating the original thought except your very being, and the distortions that come from the unexplained, inarticulate, or mystery-clad being are many. Thus, to attempt to discern and weave your way through as many group mind/body/spirit distortions as possible among your peoples in the course of your teaching is a very good effort to make. We can speak no more valiantly of your desire to serve.

May we speak in any other capacity upon this subject?

Questioner: Will you be available for communication? Can we call on you in the future?

Ra: I am Ra. We have good contact with this instrument because of her recent experiences with trance. She is to be able to communicate our thoughts in your future. However, we advise care in disturbing the channel for a few moments and then the proper procedure for aiding an instrument who has, to some extent, the need of re-entering the mind/body/spirit complex which the instrument has chosen for the life experience of this time/space. Do you understand how to nurture this instrument?

Questioner: No. Could you explain it?

Ra: We suggest first a brief period of silence. Then the repetition of the instrument's vibratory complex of sound in your density which you call name. Repeat until an answer is obtained. Then the laying on of the hands at the neck region for a brief period so that the instrument may recharge batteries which are not, shall we say, full of the essence of this particular field at this time. And finally, a gift of water into which the love of all present has been given. This will restore this entity, for her distortions contain great sensitivity towards the vibrations of love and the charged water will effect comfort. Do you now understand?

Questioner: Not completely.

Ra: I am Ra. We search your mind to find the vibration *(nickname)*. It is this vibration from you which contains the largest amount of what you would call love. Others would call this entity *(first name)*. The charging of the water is done by those present placing their hands over the glass and visualizing the power of love entering the water. This will charge that very effective medium with those vibrations.

This instrument is, at this time, quite fatigued. However, her heart is such that she continues to remain open to us and useful as a channel. This is why we have spent the time/space explaining how the distortions of what you may call fatigue may be ameliorated.

Under no circumstances should this instrument be touched until she has responded to her name. I do not wish to take this instrument beyond her capacity for physical energy. It grows low. Therefore, I must leave this instrument. I leave you in the glory and peace of unity. Go forth in peace, rejoicing in the power of the one Creator. I am Ra.

L/L Research

L/L Research is a subsidiary of Rock Creek Research & Development Laboratories, Inc.

P.O. Box 5195
Louisville, KY 40255-0195

www.llresearch.org

Rock Creek is a non-profit corporation dedicated to discovering and sharing information which may aid in the spiritual evolution of humankind.

ABOUT THE CONTENTS OF THIS TRANSCRIPT: This telepathic channeling has been taken from transcriptions of the weekly study and meditation meetings of the Rock Creek Research & Development Laboratories and L/L Research. It is offered in the hope that it may be useful to you. As the Confederation entities always make a point of saying, please use your discrimination and judgment in assessing this material. If something rings true to you, fine. If something does not resonate, please leave it behind, for neither we nor those of the Confederation would wish to be a stumbling block for any.

© 2009 L/L Research

The Law of One, Book V, Session 1, Fragment 1
January 15, 1981

Jim: The beginning of Session 1 appears here precisely as it was received. In our first private printing of Book One of *The Law Of One* we omitted a portion of this first session because Don felt that, compared with the other twenty-five sessions of Book One, it was anomalistic—and perhaps too confusing as such—for first-time readers. That omission was reproduced when the mass market edition was printed by The Donning Company under the title of *The Ra Material*.

This is the only session in which Ra delivered anything close to what Brad Steiger has called a "cosmic sermonette" before beginning with the question and answer format that was used exclusively throughout the remainder of the Ra contact. Ra preferred the question and answer format because it allowed our free will to decide what information we would seek rather than their determining that choice for us by using the lecture method of teach/learning.

And it was interesting to us that Ra mentioned in this first session that they were not able to offer any "conditioning" to any instrument due their own transmitting limitations. This conditioning often involves seemingly involuntary movement of some part of the vocal cords, mouth, lip, jaw, or some other physiological sensation which the one serving as instrument identifies with the approach of the contact. This session also marks the last time that Ra ever attempted to speak through any instrument other than Carla.

Since the channeling phenomenon has become so commonplace we would like to make an additional comment on the conditioning vibration. Many who serve as instruments feel that they recognize the entities who speak through them by the conditioning vibration and need no other identification to be sure that they are channeling whom they think they are channeling. We have found that this is not always so because negative entities of the same relative vibration will feel just like the familiar positive entity to the one serving as instrument when the negative entity wishes to call itself by another name and mimic the positive entity as a part of the process of tricking the instrument and then detuning the positive work done by the group receiving its information. This is standard procedure for those of the path of service to self. The fundamental concept involved is that the opportunity for positive entities to speak through instruments and groups must be balanced by the same opportunity being offered to negative entities. This need not be a difficulty for any instrument, however, if it and its support group utilizes the twin processes of tuning the group and challenging the contact each time channeling occurs.

Tuning the group is the process whereby each individual in the group refines the desire to serve others and puts it first and foremost in the mind and heart. The group may accomplish this tuning by any method which has meaning to each within the group whether that be by singing sacred songs, chanting, praying, telling jokes, sharing information, visualizing light surrounding the group, or whatever blends each present into one unified source of seeking.

Then when the instrument feels the entities which wish to channel through it are present the challenge is mentally given, again in whatever way that feels appropriate to the instrument and in whatever way that the instrument can get behind with every fiber of its being. The instrument will demand to know if the entities wishing to channel through it come in the name of whatever principle the instrument feels is the highest and best in its own life. One may challenge the entity wishing to speak in the name of Jesus the Christ, the Christ consciousness, the positive polarity, service to others or in the name of one of the archangels or in whatever represents the center of one's life, that for which the instrument lives and would gladly die. This forms a wall of light through which an entity of negative polarity has as much trouble passing through as you and I would discover with a solid brick wall.

Negative entities stand ready to fill in any lapse of care in this regard with their offering of service in their own way; that is, mimicking the positive contact only as much as necessary to maintain the channel and then giving false information whenever possible, usually having to do with dates and descriptions of upcoming cataclysmic earth changes which, when made public by the group receiving such information makes the group lose credibility since the dates are never correct. Thus the negative entity takes the spiritual strength of the light which the group had been able to share in service-to-others work.

Carla used this method of challenging Ra for the first two sessions. This was and is her normal method, as she usually does conscious channeling. But in the Ra contact she involuntarily went into trance, and could not tune in that way, so we were glad when, at the end of the second session, Ra gave us the ritual of walking the Circle of One to replace the challenging procedure used in telepathic channeling since in all sessions after the first two Carla was immediately in the trance state, out of her body, and unaware of any activity whatsoever. None of us ever discovered how she was able to accomplish this trance state and the leaving of her body. It was apparently a pre-incarnatively chosen ability chosen to aid in the contact with Ra. Our meditation before each session was our group process of tuning.

We used what Don called "tuned trance telepathy" to communicate with those of Ra. This is to say that while the contact was ongoing neither Carla nor those of Ra inhabited Carla's body. Carla's spirit was apparently in the care of those of Ra while Ra used Carla's body from a distance to form the words that responded to Don's questions. Ra mentioned many times that they had only the grossest control over her body and had difficulty, for example, in repositioning her hands when one of them was experiencing pain flares due to her arthritic condition. Carla could not feel these pain flares, but repositioning them was sometimes necessary since the pain was like static on the line. This occurred only occasionally and was always noted in the text.

Don and Carla had been working together for twelve years channeling, researching, and had written two books in the area of metaphysics before I joined them in December of 1980. Unsure of what to do as the first project together, we considered re-writing one of those books, *Secrets Of The Ufo*, and I had begun background reading and taking notes. Three weeks later the first Ra contact occurred and was totally unexpected. It happened when Carla was conducting a teaching session in which one of the Sunday meditation group members was learning how to channel. Don sat in on the session, but I was out shopping and happened to walk in through the front door loaded with sacks of groceries just as Don was asking about the earth changes that were anticipated at the end of this cycle of growth. At that point Ra requested a moment to deepen Carla's trance state before continuing. Such an interruption never happened again because after the second session we prepared another room especially for the Ra contact and continued to use the living room for all other meditations and teaching sessions. This first session is one of only four of the total 106 sessions with Ra in which anyone besides Don, Carla, and I attended. Since the three of us lived together the harmony that we developed between us was very stable and was a critical ingredient in establishing and maintaining the contact.

Carla: These days, I am teaching very few people to channel. Through the years, I have seen the kind of havoc an opened and untuned channel can wreak in the personality of the seeker who channels just for a while, or just for the fun of it. The basic problem with channeling tends to be that the channel needs to be actively attempting to live the message she is receiving. In spiritual work, no one has the luxury of saying "Do as I say, not as I do." If we do not embody the principles we offer to others, we receive often dramatic and life-shaking catalyst that points up the divergence of ideals from true intention. I have seen people lose their sanity when carelessly involved with channeling. So I take the responsibility of taking students very, very seriously. For the most part, I now work with people who come to me already channeling, and having difficulties with that. This has involved me with people being moved around the world by signals from Indians, UFO contactees with strange stories, and all manner of diverse folks who are in some way at risk in the "new age" sea of confusion. The phrase "spiritual counselor" has a smug, know-it-all feeling to it, which I hope I do not reflect, but it's pretty much what I am doing these days. Perhaps "spiritual listener" is more accurate. With e-mail there has come a wider opportunity to relate with seekers personally. We welcome anyone's communication here at L/L Research, and have never failed to answer any mail sent to us, so please feel free to address questions to us. We're delighted to help in any way we can. Our web site address is www.llresearch.org.

Session 1, January 15, 1981

Ra: I am Ra. I have not spoken through this instrument before. We had to wait until she was precisely tuned as we send a narrow band vibration. We greet you in the love and in the light of our infinite Creator.

We have watched your group. We have been called to your group, for you have a need for the diversity of experiences in channeling which go with a more intensive, or as you might call it, advanced, approach to the system of studying the pattern of illusions of your body, your mind, and your spirit, which you call seeking the truth. We hope to offer you a somewhat different slant upon the information which is always and ever the same.

The Confederation of Planets in the Service of the infinite Creator has only one important statement. That statement, my friends, as you know, is that all things, all life, all of the creation is part of one original thought.

We will exercise each channel if we are able to. The reception of our beam is a somewhat more advanced feat than some of the more broad vibration channels opened by other members for more introductory and intermediate work.

Let us for a moment consider thought. What is it, my friends, to take thought? Took you then thought today? What thoughts did you think today? What thoughts were part of the original thought today? In how many of your thoughts did the creation lie? Was love contained? And was service freely given? You are not part of a material universe. You move your body, your mind, and your spirit in somewhat eccentric patterns for you have not completely grasped the concept that you are part of the original thought.

We would at this time transfer to the instrument known as Don. I am Ra.

(Pause)

Ra: I am Ra. I am again with this instrument. We are close to initiating a contact but we are having difficulty penetrating a certain mental tension and distraction that are somewhat characteristic of this channel. We will therefore describe the type of vibration which is being sent. The instrument will find us entering the energy field at a slight angle towards the back of the top of the head in a narrow but strong area of intensity. We are not able to offer any conditioning due to our own transmitting limitations, therefore, if the instrument can feel this particular effect he may then speak our thoughts as they come to him. We will again attempt this contact. I am Ra.

(Pause)

Ra: This instrument is resisting our contact. However, we assure you that we are satisfied that contact with the one known as Don is not preferable to that instrument. We will, therefore, move on to the one known as Leonard. Again we caution the instrument that it is a narrow band of communication which is felt as a vibration entering the aura. We will now transfer this contact. I am Ra.

(Pause)

Ra: I am Ra. We greet you once more in the love and the light of our infinite Creator. We ask that you be patient with us. We are a difficult channel to receive. We may perhaps add some dimensions to your understanding. At this time we would be glad to attempt to speak to any subject or question which those entities in the room may have potential use in the requesting.

L/L Research

L/L Research is a subsidiary of Rock Creek Research & Development Laboratories, Inc.

P.O. Box 5195
Louisville, KY 40255-0195

www.llresearch.org

Rock Creek is a non-profit corporation dedicated to discovering and sharing information which may aid in the spiritual evolution of humankind.

ABOUT THE CONTENTS OF THIS TRANSCRIPT: This telepathic channeling has been taken from transcriptions of the weekly study and meditation meetings of the Rock Creek Research & Development Laboratories and L/L Research. It is offered in the hope that it may be useful to you. As the Confederation entities always make a point of saying, please use your discrimination and judgment in assessing this material. If something rings true to you, fine. If something does not resonate, please leave it behind, for neither we nor those of the Confederation would wish to be a stumbling block for any.

CAVEAT: This transcript is being published by L/L Research in a not yet final form. It has, however, been edited and any obvious errors have been corrected. When it is in a final form, this caveat will be removed.

© 2009 L/L Research

Sunday Meeting
January 18, 1981

(Carla channeling

I am Oxal. I greet you in the love and the light of the infinite Creator, and am delighted to be able to be with you this evening. I do not often speak through this channel and am privileged to be able to share this meeting with you at this time. I wish only to share with you the image, my friends, of the center of all things. When there is that which spins, you may call it a top or a gyroscope, there is always a center which allows the whirling to continue to be balanced. As you are light beings, the energy which spins you is called love. The balance must come from the coordination of light and the polarities of love. Therefore, please think upon the virtues of the balanced gyroscope, which is always aware of the level and true path. And in your meditation seek always to know your own center.

I am very grateful to have had the chance to exercise this instrument for a short time. I will leave you in the love and the light of the infinite Creator. I am Oxal.

(Pause)

I am Latwii. You see, my friends, at how good we are at being able to contact this instrument without blowing her circuits. We greet you in love and the light and apologize for the delay, but we had a desire to initiate contact through the channel known as Jim and were persistent in our attempts. Therefore, we shall leave this instrument to again make our contact with the one known as Jim. I am Latwii.

(Jim channeling

I am Latwii, and greet you once again in love and light. We are very pleased to have been able to make this contact. It is always a joy to be allowed to speak to your meditation group. We are always interested in joining our vibrations with those who seek to know what is the center of creation. We are simple beings for such a mighty task but in our way, simple and foolish though it may be, we would seek to share our understanding of the center of creation with you tonight. We do not mean to say that we have a complete understanding of any part of creation, for what is creation but the Infinite Father Who Is all and Who Is filled with mystery. But, in our searching we have found within the mystery clues and hints as to the central feature, shall we say, that composes all of creation. Of course, as you might suspect, love is to be found within each instance and experience that you might encounter in your lives, but we also have found that love may manifest in an infinite number of ways, many of which are not apparent at first glance.

We would refer each of you to your own library of experiences for analogies in this area for have not each of you had an experience which seemed to be cloaked in mystery for the duration of the experience and even after the experience passed? And as you ponder the situation, did you not uncover layer after layer [of] those lessons, those learnings, which revolved once again to the central theme of love, to the acceptance of the lesson, whatever it might be and in that acceptance learning to love the experience and all that it represented? But have you not also found that in many experiences which you have pondered long and solved to a degree, have you not also found that there remains still some measure of mystery?

My friends, we would suggest that this mystery that remains, this incompleteness of the understanding, is that central feature that resides with love within each experience and this mystery, this incompleteness, will draw one forth into the next experience, into the next adventure, into the next learning. We would suggest that those things which can be known are valuable, for they teach wisdom, but we would also suggest that those things which remain a mystery are equally as valuable, for they teach seeking and wisdom must always include seeking. Love, therefore, grows more fully by its residence, shall we say, in the same experience with mystery.

We would at this time transfer our contact to the one known as L. I am Latwii.

(L channeling

I am Latwii, and again I greet you, my brothers, in the love and the light of our Creator. My brothers, my friends, it is interesting to we of Latwii that many of the events of your lives seem to revolve not around your own central axis of love but rather around an avoidance of love. We find this difficult to understand, both in how you are able to accomplish this and also—and why you are willing to attempt it.

My brothers, it is necessary that the people of your planet realize that each, as an entity of energy, must revolve around that axis of love, thus making it the central point of their lives. To avoid doing so, especially on a large scale—for many of your people to avoid doing so—can only have the effect of placing your entire planet out of balance, for how can a spinning top revolve around an axis outside its perimeter? It's impossible, yet so many of your people continue to attempt this.

My brothers, we have spoken many times, and on so many occasions as to make this subject, we are sure, a boring one to you, yet we must again reiterate the fact that your planet, its people, are out of balance. And if they do not choose consciously to return to their given axis, then a new axis will be found.

My brothers, we sense at this time it would be best to transfer this contact. … I am Latwii.

(Pause)

(Carla channeling

I am Latwii, and I am again with this instrument. I greet you once more in the love and the light of the infinite Creator. It is my privilege to be open to questions at this time and as I scan you, I realize there are many questions which we might answer. However, we would prefer to let you pick among them yourselves. Therefore, we will wait for the spoken questions that you might have voice at this time and we would be glad to share what information we have. Does anyone have a question at this time?

L: Latwii, it is my understanding that the instrument through whom we are channeling has a question she would like to ask.

I am Latwii. That is correct, however we do not feel that the information she seeks should be given through this instrument due to the fact that she would doubt the answer since she channeled it herself and the question concerns channeling, therefore it is not possible for us to channel through this instrument with any degree of accuracy that [will] be appreciated by this instrument on this particular question. We thank you for your thoughtfulness.

Is there another question at this time?

L: What can you tell us of contacting people who have physically died on this planet?

Ah, but my brother, what do you want to know? We can tell you many things, the most pertinent of which is that it is, of course, possible, depending upon the desires of the departed, as you would euphemistically put it.

L: First, would it be possible for us to contact them through channeling and, second, would they be in a position to advise or counsel us? And to a degree beyond that of a normal living person?

I am Latwii, and am aware of your question. It is possible to contact one who wishes to speak with the appropriate medium. The channeling that you are aware of at this time is very efficient compared to the amount of tuning needed for the vibration of your own human worlds[3]. The information you might seek through such a contact would not be any greater in wisdom than that of a normal living person. A person does not become wise by dying. A person becomes two things: one, a shell of the personality which he or she has left behind; that is what you are in contact with. This shell is somewhat informed but does not have the creative independence of the living being, for the living being that he or she truly is[4] is moving onward and gradually further and further away from the density which he or she has left. Thus, the shell will grow weaker and weaker, until the thought form is no longer requested. It is in no case wise to take advice from the departed if you can consult your own wisdom instead, for you are undoubtedly more up-to-date in your information.

May we answer you further, my brother?

L: Yes, on a different subject. Recently in discussing hypnotic regression the statement was made to me that in some instances it was possible to contact what was referred to as the higher self of an individual so as to ascertain information about current karmic debts and whether they have been completed or not. Is it possible for us to use channeling to accomplish this?

I am Latwii. It is perhaps more to the point to suggest that you use the powers of your own will and use what this instrument would call autohypnosis, thus depending upon yourself to seek understanding of your own relationships and circumstances. I would not recommend that channeling of this type be used, due to the fact that in personal uses it can became quite full of the ego needs of the individual channeling and is much better used in a group situation. Thus, if autohypnosis fails, it is best to seek qualified hypnotherapists.

Is there another question at this time?

C: It seems at times that some people are subjected to great physical or emotional suffering, seemingly more so than others, and I've always had trouble understanding whether some people undergo this by some design or is it just a chance that it happened to them or is it caused by—do we bring it on to ourselves or … what I'm asking, is it part of a design or do we bring it on or is it just merely by chance that these people undergo this extreme suffering?

(Pause)

[I am Latwii.] I am with the instrument. Please pardon the delay but this contact is growing somewhat weak. The universe is a grand design in which free will is the great cosmic circumstance. This is paradoxical but true. You yourself, in your higher or more conscious self, program certain lessons that you feel that you need. You then incarnate and forget. However, these lessons are programmed. It is not a rigid program. It is a program that is marvelously flexible so that if you at first do not succeed in learning a lesson, you will be given more and more chances to learn the same lesson. Knowing this is a great aid to the seeker, for thus he or she becomes conscious of the process of learning and is able to take charge of it and use the experience as a teacher. The experiences are unequal because various persons have chosen for themselves various lessons to learn. Some of them have, shall we say, bitten off quite a hunk. Others have decided to take R and R. That is the free will of those who have obtained the right to choose their own incarnations. Most, to be serious, are indeed attempting to learn lessons as quickly as they feel their higher self can absorb them. The lessons of this cycle have to deal with love and its manifestations in a social sphere.

May we answer you further, my brother?"

C: Yes, 'cause I'm thinking of particular situations that just happened. That we program these things *(inaudible)* this situation *(inaudible)* how do you program *(inaudible)* I can't see the death of someone else can be programmed *(inaudible)* as used as a lesson. This person was married. There was the death of the father on the day of the marriage. Just this week, their child was killed. Surely we don't program other's death, or do they program *(inaudible)* I don't understand how deaths at key times could happen to one person.

I am Latwii. This contact is very weak, however we are able to keep it open somewhat. Each entity comes with lessons to learn. When those lessons are through, that entity no longer needs the heavy cloak of the physical being and is freed from it. The living one who experiences deaths has not programmed

---

[3] Latwii is speaking about the inner planes; they consider themselves outer-planes contacts.

[4] In other words, the second thing that a person becomes, or is.

death, but has programmed the lessons that such events may teach us. These lessons may be learned by many different kinds of losses, however, it seems to be a strong lesson for the particular entity of whom you speak that loss will be met with fortitude and an understanding of the loss as a gain. When this is seen, when the joy of the situation is seen, this lesson will have been learned. Then the entity may move on.

The individual is responsible for that individual and for no other. It is the truth as we know it that no one can aid another except by being and witnessing that being as a channel for love and light. We ask you not to stress in your mind the fine lines of intellectual rationalization of love. There will be in this illusion pain, loss, limitation—other negative effects. This is an illusion; there will be unequalness because there is harmony rather than unison on this density. Be you then prepared to show love and understanding in your gains and in your losses.

May we answer you further?

C: Well, I hate to keep straining the channel. I know she's tired. Then all events occur in a harmonious blend. Is it designed that these two particular entities work together to learn and grow? Was this designed for them to be together?

I am Latwii. One moment; we must scan. Yes, my brother, in this instance it was agreed between the two in both cases that this would occur and that nurturing would take place in its time. We see you are still not understanding the agreement was reached before the father incarnated. Time is not the same in all dimensions.

We fear that we must close at this time. The sound of snoring is heard in the room and we feel that we perhaps are not being scintillating enough, so we shall greet those named S and R with joy and welcome them to our meeting and leave you in the creation of the Father, the creation of love and light. I am known to you as Latwii. Adonai. ✻

L/L Research

L/L Research is a subsidiary of Rock Creek Research & Development Laboratories, Inc.

P.O. Box 5195
Louisville, KY 40255-0195

www.llresearch.org

Rock Creek is a non-profit corporation dedicated to discovering and sharing information which may aid in the spiritual evolution of humankind.

ABOUT THE CONTENTS OF THIS TRANSCRIPT: This telepathic channeling has been taken from transcriptions of the weekly study and meditation meetings of the Rock Creek Research & Development Laboratories and L/L Research. It is offered in the hope that it may be useful to you. As the Confederation entities always make a point of saying, please use your discrimination and judgment in assessing this material. If something rings true to you, fine. If something does not resonate, please leave it behind, for neither we nor those of the Confederation would wish to be a stumbling block for any.

© 2009 L/L Research

The Law of One, Book I, Session 2
January 20, 1981

Ra: I am Ra. I greet you in the love and the light of our infinite Creator. I am with this mind/body/spirit complex which has offered itself for a channel. I communicate with you.

Queries are in order in your projections of mind distortion at this time/space. Thusly would I assure this group that my own social memory complex has one particular method of communicating with those few who may be able to harmonize their distortions with ours, and that is to respond to queries for information. We are comfortable with this format. May the queries now begin.

Questioner: I'm guessing that there are enough people who would understand what you are saying, who would be interested enough in it, for us to make a book of your communications and I wondered if you would agree to this?

If so, I was thinking that possibly a bit of historical background of yourself might be in order.

Ra: I am Ra. The possibility of communication, as you would call it, from the One to the One, through distortion, acceptable for meaning is the reason we contacted this group. There are few who will grasp, without significant distortion, that which we communicate through this connection with this mind/body/spirit complex. However, if it be your desire to share our communications with others we have the distortion towards a perception that this would be most helpful in regularizing and crystallizing your own patterns of vibration upon the levels of experience which you call the life. If one is illuminated, are not all illuminated? Therefore, we are oriented towards speaking for you in whatever supply of speakingness you may desire. To teach/learn is the Law of One in one of its most elementary distortions.

Questioner: Could you tell us something of your historical background and your contact with earlier races on this planet? Then we would have something to start with.

Ra: I am Ra. We are aware that your mind/body is calculating the proper method of performing the task of creating a teach/learning instrument. We are aware that you find our incarnate, as you call it, state of interest. We waited for a second query so as to emphasize that the time/space of several thousand of your years creates a spurious type of interest. Thus in giving this information, we ask the proper lack of stress be placed upon our experiences in your local space/time. The teach/learning which is our responsibility is philosophical rather than historical. We shall proceed with your request which is harmless if properly evaluated.

We are those of the Confederation who eleven thousand of your years ago came to two of your planetary cultures which were at that time closely in touch with the creation of the one Creator. It was our naive belief that we could teach/learn by direct contact and that the free will distortions of individual feeling or personality were in no danger.

We had no thought of their being disturbed, as these cultures were already closely aligned with an all-embracing belief in the live-ness or consciousness of all. We came and were welcomed by the peoples whom we wished to serve. We attempted to aid them in technical ways having to do with the healing of mind/body/spirit complex distortions through the use of the crystal, appropriate to the distortion, placed within a certain appropriate series of ratios of time/space material. Thus were the pyramids created.

We found that the technology was reserved largely for those with the effectual mind/body distortion of power. This was not intended by the Law of One. We left your peoples. The group that was to work with those in the area of South America, as you call that portion of your sphere, gave up not so easily. They returned. We did not. However, we have never left your vibration due to our responsibility for the changes in consciousness we had first caused and then found distorted in ways not relegated to the Law of One. We attempted to contact the rulers of the land to which we had come, that land which you call Egypt, or in some areas, the Holy Land.

In the Eighteenth Dynasty, as it is known in your records of space/time distortions, we were able to contact a pharaoh, as you would call him. The man was small in life-experience on your plane and was a … what this instrument would call, Wanderer. Thus, this mind/body/spirit complex received our communication distortions and was able to blend his distortions with our own. This young entity had been given a vibratory complex of sound which vibrated in honor of a prosperous god, as this mind/body complex, which we call instrument for convenience, would call "Ammon." The entity decided that this name, being in honor of one among many gods, was not acceptable for inclusion in his vibratory sound complex. Thus, he changed his name to one which honored the sun disc. This distortion, called "Aten," was a close distortion to our reality as we understand our own nature of mind/body/spirit complex distortion. However, it does not come totally into alignment with the intended teach/learning which was sent. This entity, Ikhnaton, became convinced that the vibration of One was the true spiritual vibration and thus decreed the Law of One.

However, this entity's beliefs were accepted by very few. His priests gave lip service only, without the spiritual distortion towards seeking. The peoples continued in their beliefs. When this entity was no longer in this density, again the polarized beliefs in the many gods came into their own and continued so until the one known as Mohammed delivered the peoples into a more intelligible distortion of mind/body/spirit relationships.

Do you have a more detailed interest at this time?

Questioner: We are very interested in the entire story that you have to tell and getting in to the Law of One in quite some detail. There will be several questions that I'll ask as we go along that may or may not be related directly to understanding the Law of One. However, I believe that the proper way of presenting this as a teach/learning vehicle is to investigate different facets of what you tell us. You spoke of crystal healing. (One other thing I want to mention is that when the instrument becomes fatigued we want to cut off communication and continue questions at a later time when the instrument is recharged.) If the instrument is suitable at this time we would like a little information about the crystal healing that you mentioned.

Ra: I am Ra. The principle of crystal healing is based upon an understanding of the hierarchical nature of the structure of the illusion which is the physical body, as you would call it. There are crystals which work upon the energies coming into the spiritual body; there are crystals which work upon the distortions from spirit to mind; there are crystals which balance the distortions between the mind and the body. All of these crystal healings are charged through purified channels. Without the relative crystallization of the healer working with the crystal, the crystal will not be properly charged. The other ingredient is the proper alignment with the energy fields of the planet upon which you dwell and the holistic or cosmic distortions or streamings which enter the planetary aura in such a manner that an appropriate ratio of shapes and placement within these shapes is of indicated aid in the untangling or balancing process.

To go through the various crystals to be used would be exhaustive to this instrument, although you may ask us if you wish in another session. The delicacy, shall we say, of the choosing of the crystal is very critical and, in truth, a crystalline structure such as a diamond or ruby can be used by a purified channel who is filled with the love/light of One, in almost any application.

This, of course, takes initiation, and there never have been many to persevere to the extent of progressing through the various distortion leavings which initiation causes.

May we further inform you in any fairly brief way upon this or another subject?

Questioner: Yes. You mentioned that the pyramids were an outgrowth of this. Could you expand a little on that? Were you responsible for the building of the pyramid, and what was the purpose of the pyramid?

Ra: I am Ra. The larger pyramids were built by our ability using the forces of One. The stones are alive. It has not been so understood by the mind/body/spirit distortions of your culture. The purposes of the pyramids were two:

Firstly, to have a properly oriented place of initiation for those who wished to become purified or initiated channels for the Law of One.

Two, we wished then to carefully guide the initiates in developing a healing of the people whom they sought to aid, and of the planet itself. Pyramid after pyramid charged by the crystal and Initiate were designed to balance the incoming energy of the One Creation with the many and multiple distortions of the planetary mind/body/spirit. In this effort we were able to continue work that brothers within the Confederation had effected through building of other crystal-bearing structures and thus complete a ring, if you will, of these about the Earth's, as this instrument would have us vibrate it, surface.

This instrument begins to lose energy. We ask for one more query or subject and then we shall take our leave for this time/space.

Questioner: You might mention that originally there was a capstone on the pyramid at the top, what was it made of and how you moved the heavy blocks to build the pyramid. What technique was used for that?

Ra: I am Ra. I request that we be asked this question in our next worktime, as you would term the distortion/sharing that our energies produce.

If you have any questions about the proper use of this mind/body/spirit, we would appreciate your asking them now.

Questioner: Consider them asked. I don't have anything to go on. What is the proper use of this instrument? What should we do? What should we do to maximize her ability and her comfort?

Ra: I am Ra. We are pleased that you have asked this question for it is not our understanding that we have the right/duty to share our perceptions on any subject but philosophy without direct question. However, this mind/body/spirit is not being correctly used and therefore is experiencing unnecessary distortions of body in the area of fatigue.

The vibrations may well be purified by a simple turning to the circle of One and the verbal vibration while doing so of the following dialogue:

Question: "What is the Law?"

Answer: "The Law is One."

Question: "Why are we here?"

Answer: "We seek the Law of One."

Question: "Why do we seek Ra?"

Answer: "Ra is an humble messenger of the Law of One."

Both Together: "Rejoice then and purify this place in the Law of One. Let no thought-form enter the circle we have walked about this instrument, for the Law is One."

The instrument at this time should be in trance. The proper alignment is the head pointed twenty degrees north-by-northeast. This is the direction from which the newer or New Age distortions of love/light, which are less distorted, are emanating, and this instrument will find comfort therein. This is a sensitive instrument, by which we mean the distortions which enter her mind/body/spirit complex come from any of her senses. Thus, it is well to do the following:

Place at the entity's head a virgin chalice of water.

To the center, the book most closely aligned with the instrument's mental distortions which are allied most closely with the Law of One, that being the Bible that she touches most frequently.

To the other side of the Bible, a small amount of cense, or incense, in a virgin censer.

To the rear of the book symbolizing One, opened to the Gospel of John, Chapter One, a white candle.

The instrument would be strengthened by the wearing of a white robe. The instrument shall be covered and prone, the eyes covered.

We feel that, though this is a complex of activity/circumstance and may seem very distorted from a purposeful teach/learning experience, these elaborations on the technique of trance will ease the mind distortions of those about the instrument as they perceive improvement in the instrument's distortions with regard to fatigue. We add only that if these teach/learning sessions are held during time/space during which your sun-body does not light your room that it is best to call the instrument before the lighting of the illuminatory mechanism.

I am Ra. I leave you in the glory and the peace of the one Creator. Rejoice in the love/light, and go forth in the power of the one Creator. In joy, we leave you. Adonai.

Intensive Meditation
January 21, 1981

(Carla channeling)

[I am Laitos] … the love and in the light of our infinite Creator. It is with joy that we metaphorically raise our glasses to you in a toast to greeting. We have not had the privilege of working in a group such as this with you for some small period and have been conscious of your call to us. I and my brothers have been with you but very much appreciate the ability at this time to speak what humble words we can to share our message with you and to offer whatever service we may.

The gifts that you give us are infinitely precious to us and our thanks can never be sufficient, for you give to us a constant deepening of our understanding of love, and it is through this understanding that we ourselves are attempting to refine what you would call wisdom. Love we have; wisdom we are seeking. Thus, as we reach to you, who so sorely seek love, let us assure you that that which you offer us is greatly dear to us and aids us in our own spiritual seeking.

My friends, we wish to reassure you about the nature of love, for in many cases it seems as fragile as a newborn rose in the snow—beautiful but transient. As you continue in your seeking you will find that the rose may wither, the preserved odor may fade but the memory and the knowledge of that beauty is as infinite as your being. You hold each perception within you and you assign to it that value which seems proper. Look then to each moment, for in even the most difficult or confused circumstance love resides, and not as a fragile thing but as the very heart of your experience.

At this time, after a period of conditioning, we would like to transfer this contact to the one known as S. I am Laitos.

(S channeling)

I am Laitos, and I greet you, my friends, in the love and in the light of the one infinite Creator. We are pleased to be able to speak through this instrument once again. We are happy to be with your group today and we find it always a pleasure to be among those of your planet who are seeking the knowledge which we humbly try to express through instruments such as this. We are pleased to be called upon to aid those of your planet who seek to expand their awareness of the Creator. We are always privileged to be with those who seek our aid. We find it a great honor to serve in this manner.

We would at this time transfer this contact. I am Laitos.

(Carla channeling)

I am Laitos, and I am once again with this instrument, but this instrument keeps requesting that the contact be shifted to the one known as Jim due to her fondness for his channeling. We wish to close through this instrument that one of our sisters may speak through the one known as Jim. We would again pause and offer the conditioning vibration to the one known as R. I am Laitos.

(Carla channeling

I am Laitos, and am again with this instrument. We thank the one known as R for the privilege of working with him and we thank each of you for calling us. We shall be with you at any time you may request it in the future, as you call it. Meanwhile, we leave you with an attempt to emphasize the sturdy and unquenchable spirit of love. It may seem that love can be shattered. It may seem that love can be damaged. It may seem that misunderstandings and confusions can cause harm. If this be so, my friends, then you must search more deeply in your understanding for the essence of love, for naught can undo its everlasting beauty and strength. The power of your being and the power of the universe are one thing and that thing, my friends, is love.

I am Laitos. I leave you in the invisible and infinite love and in the manifested light of the one Creator. Adonai my friends, adonai.

(Jim channeling

I am Latwii, and am with this instrument and greet you all most joyfully in love and light. It has been some period of your time since we have had the honor of speaking to your group and we embrace that joyful opportunity at this time with great and heartfelt gratitude. May we at this time offer ourselves in the capacity of answering questions which those present might have the value in the asking. Is there a question at this time?

S: I have a question. In a couple of my meditations I've received what seemed to be telepathic messages. Is this possible, and if so, do they come from the entities who I believe they're coming from?

I am Latwii, and, my sister, we may say first of all, all things are quite possible, and in specific may we say with the experience you have recalled in your meditation, these contacts are of the nature of which you have surmised. We cannot speak very specifically, for this would not be proper in our estimation at this time, but we confirm your hypothesis.

May we answer you further, my sister?

S: Yes. Is there any harm in seeking out these messages as far as maybe obtaining erroneous information or receiving an entity disguising itself as another entity?

I am Latwii, and, my sister, in this regard may we say that it is always helpful in such a seeking to provide yourself with a shield of light to gird yourself, shall we say, in the light and love of the one Creator, to seek then from this point in that same light and love for further understanding of your being as it is congruent with the one Creator, to seek always the union of yourself with the great Self that is the Creator of all, to seek, to learn, to know, and to be the one Creator and to serve that one Creator in all ways that are possible and open as opportunities to you.

If the seeking or any type of contact or knowledge veers in any degree from this pure seeking for oneness, then the seeker may experience that which is a more distorted contact. Seek always the oneness that is the foundation of your being. Seek to serve that oneness, to know it, and in this seeking in love and in light shall you find that which you seek and so shall that love and light be your protection in the seeking.

May we answer you further, my sister?

S: No. Thank you for your help.

We are most grateful as well to you. Is there another question at this time?

Carla: I have two questions that someone has sent me. And I was wondering if it would be acceptable to you if I read them to you since it is daylight now and I can read without having to turn on a light?

I am Latwii. We are always glad to hear from you, my sister. Please read us your queries.

Carla: Thank you. These questions are from M in Denver, Colorado. Firstly she says, "I have difficulty in determining lessons I feel I am in the midst of. It seems experiences are resistant or chronic, which tells me I must be thick-skinned. One area is of the health of my family. I feel totally impotent that I cannot remove their afflictions. One day I believe it is food for the soul and the next the burden feels that it is too great. What is health, or rather ill health, a chosen path or an inability of the body/spirit to find balance on the physical plane? Knowing this could, I think, help my attitude and the problems."

I am Latwii, and am aware of your question, my sister, asked for your sister. May we say first of all in responding to this most thoughtful query, that what is defined as health within your culture is a term which is quite narrow in its scope, for it implies the smooth functioning of each body part with no hindrance no where and complete vitality at all times. This, of course, may be a pleasant condition for an entity in the third density to experience but is not a condition which clearly reflects the nature of the experiencing of catalyst which is the purpose of your being within the third density.

May we say in responding to another portion of this query that the condition of health and what is called ill health may be a result of a variety of choices made by the entity experiencing the condition. These choices most frequently are made during the incarnation and are results of utilizing the catalyst of this density either poorly or well or in combination, for each experience an entity encounters within the incarnation has the potential of teaching a lesson or many lessons. When these lessons are learned there [may be], shall we say, the smooth sailing for awhile until the next lesson is encountered.

Many conditions of the dysfunction of the body and mind complexes are the results of, shall we say, turbulent waters, difficulties experienced in the assimilating of the lessons by the entity when the mind is unable or unwilling to face that which is the lesson of the moment and continues in this ignoring, shall we say, of the lesson. Then the lesson must be passed on to the body complex so that it is more easy to recognize and in its symbolic form then might be pondered, might be meditated upon and might be unraveled as to its origin, which is the lesson needing learning.

There is also the great possibility at this time upon your planet that certain entities have placed upon themselves before the current incarnation certain conditions of physical and mental health or ill health, may we say, for very specific purposes. These purpose vary widely. An entity, for example, in one previous incarnation may have experienced the giving of love in great abundance to others about it, but may not have allowed these entities to give love to it and may decide before another incarnation to experience the giving of love from another by, shall we say, by making its physical vehicle somewhat crippled or, shall we say, less than perfectly functioning so that attention from others is necessary for the maintaining of the comfort and life systems.

Many are the reasons chosen before incarnation for the limiting of the physical and mental complexes. These choices are great lessons, lessons which could well take an entire incarnation to assimilate. It might be the case with such an entity that this would be the last lesson needing to be learned before the graduation.

May we say in responding to another part of this query that the entity seeing loved ones in conditions that are described as …

(Side one of tape ends.)

(Jim channeling

I am Latwii, and am once again with this instrument. As we were saying, an entity seeing loved ones in poor or ill health often wishes to be able to heal these loved ones, for such an entity feels the pain that is experienced by those around it and so, loving them, wishes to alleviate this pain. Often such an entity, after periods of meditation and struggling to understand the reasons for such afflictions, will find deeper levels of meaning to such conditions and will see that there is a great possibility that such conditions could be enabling the ones experiencing them to learn great lessons. This knowledge is often soothing and of comfort to the entity seeing pain in loved ones.

But when the pain is of a constant nature and the health continues to deteriorate and does not seem to respond in a lasting manner to treatment, the entity may once again burn with a desire to heal. May we say that this great love may be just that ingredient which is needed by the one experiencing the ill health. It may also be true that the understanding by all involved that such pain and suffering can indeed be teaching great lessons is most helpful in accepting the conditions as they are.

May we close this particular response by suggesting that in all cases, whether there is an understanding of the condition or not, it is most helpful to accept that condition and to feel the love that each moment of that condition offers to all involved. It is not useful to worry endlessly about conditions which persist. It is most helpful to find the love in each moment and to accept that which is given, for, my friends, may we say that there are no mistakes in any incarnation or experience. Each experience is a gift, a treasure, a gem from the one Creator who created each being to the one Creator that is each being so that the Creator might know Itself. Seek there, my friends, in the heart of your being for the Creator in each moment.

May we answer you further, my sister?

Carla: Yes. Since these questions are written down, I won't ask further on that question. I would like to thank you for a most inspiring answer, speaking as a slightly gimpy person myself.

M goes on then to ask another question here. She says, "G has playmates who have filled his thoughts with fire under the ground. This has me distraught. G started on a path I would not wish him to go. He wants to see the pictures in the Bible and seems quite interested. It all seems to be motivation from fear of punishment from God and an inclination for the morbid. I feel his spiritual seeking is his own but I am unsure if I should aggressively work to alter his newfound ideas just because I don't embrace them. I have tried to point out to him that everyone knows God differently and we don't know God that way, that is, N and I. Part of me says he is only [five years] old so I should take charge here but then again want him to feel his seeking is his own journey. Any comments or suggestions would be appreciated.

I am Latwii, and am aware of your query, my sister. May we say in this regard that indeed each entity of whatever the age is indeed the one which is responsible for the journey of seeking which it undertakes. It may be that many ports of call are necessary before the ship finally reaches the home port. Many experiences will aid each seeker in the seeking, for if all answers were known at once, would there be any need for the incarnations and experiences those of your planet have experienced for many thousands of your years?

Each entity in each incarnation travels a path laid out quite carefully before the incarnation, always allowing for free will to change or alter that path at any time. The traveling is of a nature that experience might be had. To taste of many flavors is to know the creation in greater depth and richness. Few upon your planet remain with one flavor, shall we say, for their entire incarnation. Each entity grows from the experience of a variety of flavors, a variety of patterns of thought, a variety of orientations and attitudes. In this way each entity reproduces the Creator experiencing Itself, for it must not be forgotten that all is one. Each entity, each experience, each thought, each turn, each port is the Creator.

Those who love the small ones of their bodies and being and family do feel the need from time to time to give the fruits of their own seeking in as pure a form as possible to the young ones entrusted to their care. This great feeling of love is not always possible nor is it always desirable, for if the young entity had all answers placed before him without the need to seek them for the self then where would come the strength that is born of the arduous journey? Where would come the wisdom of tasting many flavors? Where would come the ability to discern the wheat from chaff. In each seeking and experience that the young entity encounters there is the opportunity for those in whose care it is placed to provide yet another view, aspect or attitude concerning that which is the current experience of the young entity. Thereby shall both grow and learn respect each for the other, realizing both are seekers, both know very little, both seek to know the Creator.

May we answer further, my sister?

Carla: No, thank you Latwii. I know M will thank you.

I am Latwii. We are most grateful as well to you and to your sister, M. May we answer yet another question at this time?

(Pause)

I am Latwii, and since we have no answers for the growling stomach, may we say what a great honor and privilege it has been to join this group once again. We are with you always in your meditations, in your daily round of activities. You need only request our presence to become aware of it. Always are we with you. We leave you now in the love and in the light of the one infinite Creator. Rejoice in your being. I am Latwii. Adonai.

The Law of One, Book I, Session 3
January 21, 1981

Ra: I am Ra. I greet you in love and the light of the one infinite Creator. I communicate with you now.

Questioner: My first question is, did we correctly perform the ritual for starting the communication?

Ra: I am Ra. The placement of the artifacts designated to balance the instrument should be placed at the instrument's head for the least distortion of effect. The remainder of the beginning account of purpose is quite acceptable, for those speaking desire to serve. Otherwise, the attendant emphasis in mind complexities would not have been affected properly. We caution you to guard against those who are not wishing to serve others above all else, from taking part in the beginning or in lending their distortions of mind/body/spirit complex to any session as we should then be unable to properly blend our distortions with those of this instrument.

Questioner: Should I move the Bible, candle, and incense at this time?

Ra: I am Ra. This would be appropriate.

Questioner: *(After moving the items.)* Is this the proper position?

Ra: I am Ra. Please correct the angle of the incense so that it is perpendicular to the plane of twenty degrees north-by-northeast.

Questioner: *(After making the correction.)* Is this satisfactory?

Ra: I am Ra. Please check by eye to make fine correction. We will explain the process by which this becomes a significant distortion balancer. The incense acts as energizer to the physical body of this instrument, signifying its humanity. This is, therefore, a necessity that the wafted smoke is perceived from the same relative angle as the instrument perceives the opened Bible balanced by the lighted candle signifying love/light and light/love and, therefore, give the mental and emotional, shall we call it, distortion complex of this instrument the sight of paradise and peace which it seeks. Thus energized from the lower to the higher, the instrument becomes balanced and does not grow fatigued.

We appreciate your concern, for this will enable our teach/learning to proceed more easily.

Questioner: Does everything appear correctly aligned now?

Ra: I am Ra. I judge it within limits of acceptability.

Questioner: At the last session we had two questions that we were saving for this session: one having to do with the possible capstone on top of the Great Pyramid at Giza; the other having to do with how you moved the heavy blocks that make up the pyramid. I know these questions are of no importance with respect to the Law of One, but it was my judgment—and please correct me if I am wrong, and make the necessary suggestions—that this would provide an easy entry for those who would read the material that will eventually become a book. We are very grateful for your contact and will certainly take any suggestions as to how we should receive this information.

Ra: I am Ra. I will not suggest the proper series of questions. This is your prerogative as free agent of the Law of One having learned/understood that our social memory complex cannot effectually discern the distortions of the societal mind/body/spirit complex of your peoples. We wish now to fulfill our teach/learning honor/responsibility by answering what is asked. This only will suffice for we cannot plumb the depths of the distortion complexes which infect your peoples.

The first question, therefore, is the capstone. We iterate the unimportance of this type of data.

The so-called Great Pyramid had two capstones. One was of our design and was of smaller and carefully contrived pieces of the material upon your planet which you call "granite." This was contrived for crystalline properties and for the proper flow of your atmosphere via a type of what you would call "chimney."

At a time when we as a people had left your density, the original was taken away and a more precious one substituted. It consisted, in part, of a golden material. This did not change the properties of the pyramid, as you call it, at all, and was a distortion due to the desire of a few to mandate the use of the structure as a royal place only.

Do you wish to query further upon this first question?

Questioner: What did you mean by chimney? What was its specific purpose?

Ra: I am Ra. There is a proper flow of your atmosphere which, though small, freshens the whole of the structure. This was designed by having air-flow ducts, as this instrument might call them, situated so that there was a freshness of atmosphere without any disturbance or draft.

Questioner: How were the blocks moved?

Ra: I am Ra. You must picture the activity within all that is created. The energy is, though finite, quite large compared to the understanding/distortion by your peoples. This is an obvious point well known to your people, but little considered.

This energy is intelligent. It is hierarchical. Much as your mind/body/spirit complex dwells within a hierarchy of vehicles and retains, therefore, the shell or shape or field, and the intelligence of each ascendingly intelligent or balanced body, so does each atom of such a material as rock. When one can speak to that intelligence, the finite energy of the physical, or chemical rock/body is put into contact with that infinite power which is resident in the more well-tuned bodies, be they human or rock.

With this connection made, a request may be given. The intelligence of infinite rock-ness communicates to its physical vehicle and that splitting and moving which is desired is then carried out through the displacement of the energy field of rock-ness from finity to a dimension which we may conveniently call, simply, infinity.

In this way, that which is required is accomplished due to a cooperation of the infinite understanding of the Creator indwelling in the living rock. This is, of course, the mechanism by which many things are accomplished, which are not subject to your present means of physical analysis of action at a distance.

Questioner: I am reminded of the statement—approximately—that if you had faith to move a mountain, the mountain would move. This seems to be approximately what you were saying. That if you are fully aware of the Law of One, you would be able to do these things. Is that correct?

Ra: I am Ra. The vibratory distortion of sound, faith, is perhaps one of the stumbling blocks between those of what we may call the infinite path and those of the finite proving/understanding.

You are precisely correct in your understanding of the congruency of faith and intelligent infinity; however, one is a spiritual term, the other more acceptable perhaps to the conceptual framework distortions of those who seek with measure and pen.

Questioner: Then if an individual is totally informed with respect to the Law of One and lives the Law of One, then such things as the building of the pyramids by direct mental effort would be commonplace. Is that what I am to understand?

Ra: I am Ra. You are incorrect in that there is a distinction between the individual power through the Law of One and the combined, or societal memory complex mind/body/spirit understanding of the Law of One.

In the first case only the one individual, purified of all flaws, could move a mountain. In the case of mass understanding of unity, each individual may contain an acceptable amount of distortion and yet the mass mind could move mountains. The progress is normally from the understanding which you now seek to a dimension of understanding which is governed by the laws of love, and which seeks the laws of light. Those who are vibrating with the Law of Light seek the Law of One. Those who vibrate with the Law of One seek the Law of Foreverness.

We cannot say what is beyond this dissolution of the unified self with all that there is, for we still seek to become all that there is, and still are we Ra. Thus our paths go onward.

Questioner: Was the pyramid then built by the mutual action of many?

Ra: I am Ra. The pyramids which we thought/built were constructed thought-forms created by our social memory complex.

Questioner: Then the rock was created in place rather than moved from some place else? Is that correct?

Ra: I am Ra. We built with everlasting rock the Great Pyramid, as you call it. Other of the pyramids were built with stone moved from one place to another.

Questioner: What is everlasting rock?

Ra: I am Ra. If you can understand the concept of thought-forms you will realize that the thought-form is more regular in its distortion than the energy fields created by the materials in the rock which has been created through thought form from thought to finite energy and being-ness in your, shall we say, distorted reflection of the level of the thought-form.

May we answer you in any more helpful way?

Questioner: This is rather trivial, but I was wondering why the pyramid was built with many blocks rather than creating the whole thing as one form created at once?

Ra: I am Ra. There is a law which we believe to be one of the more significant primal distortions of the Law of One. That is the Law of Confusion. You have called this the Law of Free Will. We wished to make an healing machine, or time/space ratio complex which was as efficacious as possible. However, we did not desire to allow the mystery to be penetrated by the peoples in such a way that we became worshipped as builders of a miraculous pyramid. Thus it appears to be made, not thought.

Questioner: Well, then you speak of the pyramid, the Great Pyramid, I assume, as primarily a healing machine, and also you spoke of it as a device for initiation. Are these one and the same concept?

Ra: I am Ra. They are part of one complex of love/light intent/sharing. To use the healing properly it was important to have a purified and dedicated channel, or energizer, for the love/light of the infinite Creator to flow through; thus the initiatory method was necessary to prepare the mind, the body, and the spirit for service in the Creator's work. The two are integral.

Questioner: Does the shape of the pyramid have a function in the initiation process?

Ra: I am Ra. This is a large question. We feel that we shall begin and ask you to re-evaluate and ask further at a later session, this somewhat, shall we say, informative point.

To begin. There are two main functions of the pyramid in relation to the initiatory procedures. One has to do with the body. Before the body can be initiated, the mind must be initiated. This is the point at which most adepts of your present cycle find their mind/body/spirit complexes distorted from. When the character and personality that is the true identity of the mind has been discovered, the body then must be known in each and every way. Thus, the various functions of the body need understanding and control with detachment. The first use of the pyramid, then, is the going down into the pyramid for purposes of deprivation of sensory input so that the body may, in a sense, be dead and another life begin.

We advise, at this time, any necessary questions and a fairly rapid ending of this session. Have you any query at this time/space?

Questioner: The only question is, is there anything that we have done wrong, or that we could do to make the instrument more comfortable?

Ra: I am Ra. We scan this instrument.

This instrument has been much aided by these precautions. We suggest only some attention to the neck which seems in this body/distortion to be distorted in the area of strength/weakness. More support, therefore, to the neck area may be an aid.

Questioner: Should we have the instrument drink the water from the chalice behind her head, or should we have her drink from another glass after we charge it with love?

Ra: I am Ra. That and only that chalice shall be the most beneficial as the virgin material living in the chalice accepts, retains, and responds to the love vibration activated by your being-ness.

I am Ra. I will now leave this group rejoicing in the power and peace of the one Creator. Adonai. ❦

The Law of One, Book I, Session 4
January 22, 1981

Ra: I am Ra. I greet you in the love and the light of the infinite Creator. I communicate with you now.

Questioner: When we finished the last session, I had asked a question that was too long to answer. It had to do with the shape of the pyramid, its relationship to the initiation. Is this the appropriate time to ask this question?

Ra: I am Ra. Yes, this is an appropriate time/space to ask that question.

Questioner: Does the shape of the pyramid have an effect upon the initiation?

Ra: I am Ra. As we began the last session question, you have already recorded in your individual memory complex the first use of the shape having to do with the body complex initiation. The initiation of spirit was a more carefully designed type of initiation as regards the time/space ratios about which the entity to be initiated found itself.

If you will picture with me the side of the so-called pyramid shape and mentally imagine this triangle cut into four equal triangles, you will find the intersection of the triangle, which is at the first level on each of the four sides, forms a diamond in a plane which is horizontal. The middle of this plane is the appropriate place for the intersection of the energies streaming from the infinite dimensions and the mind/body/spirit complexes of various interwoven energy fields. Thus it was designed that the one to be initiated would, by mind, be able to perceive and then channel this, shall we say, gateway to intelligent infinity. This, then, was the second point of designing this specific shape.

May we provide a further description of any kind to your query?

Questioner: Yes. As I understand it then, the initiate was to be on the center line of that pyramid, but at an altitude above the base as defined by the intersection of the four triangles made by dividing each side. Is that correct?

Ra: I am Ra. This is correct.

Questioner: Then at this point there is a focusing of energy that is extra-dimensional in respect to our dimensions. Am I right?

Ra: I am Ra. You may use that vibratory sound complex. However, it is not totally and specifically correct. There are no "extra" dimensions. We would prefer the use of the term multi-dimensional.

Questioner: Is the size of the pyramid a function of the effectiveness of the initiation?

Ra: I am Ra. Each size pyramid has its own point of streaming in of intelligent infinity. Thus, a tiny pyramid that can be placed below a body or above a body will have specific and various effects depending upon the placement of the body in relationship to the entrance point of intelligent infinity.

For the purposes of initiation, the size needed to be large enough to create the impression of towering size so that the entrance point of multi-dimensional intelligent infinity would completely pervade and fill the channel, the entire body being able to rest in this focused area. Furthermore, it was necessary for healing purposes that both channel and the one to be healed be able to rest within that focused point.

Questioner: Is the large pyramid at Giza still usable for this purpose, or is it no longer functional?

Ra: I am Ra. That, like many other pyramid structures, is like the piano out of tune. It, as this instrument would express it, plays the tune but, oh, so poorly. The disharmony jangles the sensitivity. Only the ghost of the streaming still remains due to the shifting of the streaming points which is in turn due to the shifting electromagnetic field of your planet; due also to the discordant vibratory complexes of those who have used the initiatory and healing place for less compassionate purposes.

Questioner: Would it be possible to build a pyramid and properly align it and use it today from the materials that we have available?

Ra: I am Ra. It is quite possible for you to build a pyramid structure. The material used is not critical, merely the ratios of time/space complexes. However, the use of the structure for initiation and healing depends completely upon the inner disciplines of the channels attempting such work.

Questioner: My question then would be, are there individuals incarnate upon the planet today who would have the inner disciplines to, using your instructions, construct and initiate in a pyramid they built? Is this within the limits of what any one on the planet today can do? Or is there no one available for this?

Ra: I am Ra. There are people, as you call them, who are able to take this calling at this nexus. However, we wish to point out once again that the time of the pyramids, as you would call it, is past. It is indeed a timeless structure. However, the streamings from the universe were, at the time we attempted to aid this planet, those which required a certain understanding of purity. This understanding has, as the streamings revolved and all things evolve, changed to a more enlightened view of purity. Thus, there are those among your people at this time whose purity is already one with intelligent infinity. Without the use of structures, healer/patient can gain healing.

May we further speak to some specific point?

Questioner: Is it possible for you to instruct in these healing techniques if we could make available an individual who had the native ability?

Ra: I am Ra. It is possible. We must add that many systems of teach/learning the healing/patient nexus are proper given the various mind/body/spirit complexes. We ask your imagination to consider the relative simplicity of the mind in the earlier cycle and the less distorted, but often overly complex, views and thought/spirit processes of the same mind/body/spirit complexes after many incarnations. We also ask your imagination to conceive of those who have chosen the distortion of service and have removed their mind/body/spirit complexes from one dimension to another, thus bringing with them in totally latent form many skills and understandings which more closely match the distortions of the healing/patient processes.

Questioner: I would very much like to continue investigation into the possibility of this healing process, but I'm a little lost as to where to begin. Can you tell me where my first step would be?

Ra: I am Ra. I cannot tell you what to ask. I may suggest that you consider the somewhat complex information just given and thus discover several avenues of inquiry. There is one "health," as you call it, in your polarized environment, but there are several significantly various distortions of types of mind/body/spirit complexes. Each type must pursue its own learn/teaching in this area.

Questioner: Would you say, then, that the first step would be to find an individual with ability brought with him into this incarnation? Is this correct?

Ra: I am Ra. This is correct.

Questioner: Once I have selected an individual to perform the healing, it would be helpful to receive instruction from you. Is this possible?

Ra: I am Ra. This is possible given the distortions of vibratory sound complexes.

Questioner: I'm assuming, then, that the selected individual would be one who was very much in harmony with the Law of One. Even though he may not have any intellectual understanding of it, he should be living the Law of One?

Ra: I am Ra. This is both correct and incorrect. The first case, that being correctness, would apply to one such as the questioner himself who has the distortions towards healing, as you call it.

The incorrectness which shall be observed is the healing of those whose activities in your space/time illusion do not reflect the Law of One, but whose ability has found its pathway to intelligent infinity regardless of the plane of existence from which this distortion is found.

Questioner: I'm a little confused. I partially understand you, but I'm not sure that I fully understand you. Could You restate that in another way?

Ra: I am Ra. I can restate that in many ways, given this instrument's knowledge of your vibratory sound complexes. I will strive for a shorter distortion at this time.

Two kinds there are who can heal: those such as yourself who, having the innate distortion towards knowledge-giving of the Law of One, can heal but do not; and those who, having the same knowledge, but showing no significant distortions toward the Law of One in mind, body, or spirit, yet, and nevertheless, have opened a channel to the same ability.

The point being that there are those who, without proper training, shall we say, nevertheless, heal. It is a further item of interest that those whose life does not equal their work may find some difficulty in absorbing the energy of intelligent infinity and thus become quite distorted in such a way as to cause disharmony in themselves and others and perhaps even find it necessary to cease the healing activity. Therefore, those of the first type, those who seek to serve and are willing to be trained in thought, word, and action are those who will be able to comfortably maintain the distortion toward service in the area of healing.

Questioner: Then would it be possible for you to train us in healing awareness?

Ra: I am Ra. It is possible.

Questioner: Will you train us?

Ra: I am Ra. We will.

Questioner: I have no idea how long this would take. Is it possible for you to give a synopsis of the program of training required? I have no knowledge of what questions to ask at this point.

Ra: I am Ra. We consider your request for information, for as you noted, there are a significant number of vibratory sound complexes which can be used in sequence to train the healer.

The synopsis is a very appropriate entry that you might understand what is involved.

Firstly, the mind must be known to itself. This is perhaps the most demanding part of healing work. If the mind knows itself then the most important aspect of healing has occurred. Consciousness is the microcosm of the Law of One.

The second part has to do with the disciplines of the body complexes. In the streamings reaching your planet at this time, these understandings and disciplines have to do with the balance between love and wisdom in the use of the body in its natural functions.

The third area is the spiritual, and in this area the first two disciplines are connected through the attainment of contact with intelligent infinity.

Questioner: I believe I have a little idea of the accomplishment of the first step. Can you elaborate a little bit on the other two steps which I am not at all familiar with.

Ra: I am Ra. Imagine the body. Imagine the more dense aspects of the body. Proceed therefrom to the very finest knowledge of energy pathways which revolve and cause the body to be energized. Understand that all natural functions of the body have all aspects from dense to fine, and can be transmuted to what you may call sacramental. This is a brief investigation of the second area.

To speak to the third, if you will, imagine the function of the magnet. The magnet has two poles. One reaches up. The other goes down. The function of the spirit is to integrate the upreaching yearning of the mind/body energy with the downpouring and streaming of infinite intelligence. This is a brief explication of the third area.

Questioner: Then would this training program involve specific things to do, specific instructions and exercises?

Ra: I am Ra. We are not at this time incarnate among your peoples; thus, we can guide and attempt to specify, but we cannot, by example, show. This is an handicap. However, there should indeed be fairly specific exercises of mind, body, and spirit during the teach/learning process we offer. It is to be once more iterated that healing is but one distortion of the Law of One. To reach an undistorted understanding of that law, it is not necessary to heal or to show any manifestation but only to exercise the discipline of understanding.

We would ask that one or two more questions be the ending of this session.

Questioner: My objective is primarily to discover more of the Law of One, and it would be very helpful to discover the techniques of healing. I am aware of your problem with respect to free will. Can you state the Law of One and the laws of healing to me?

Ra: I am Ra. The Law of One, though beyond the limitation of name, as you call vibratory sound complexes, may be approximated by stating that all things are one, that there is no polarity, no right or wrong, no disharmony, but only identity. All is one, and that one is love/light, light/love, the infinite Creator.

One of the primal distortions of the Law of One is that of healing. Healing occurs when a mind/body/spirit complex realizes, deep within itself, the Law of One; that is, that there is no disharmony, no imperfection; that all is complete and whole and perfect. Thus, the intelligent infinity within this mind/body/spirit complex re-forms the illusion of body, mind, or spirit to a form congruent with the Law of One. The healer acts as energizer or catalyst for this completely individual process.

One item which may be of interest is that a healer asking to learn must take the distortion understood as responsibility for that ask/receiving. This is an honor/duty which must be carefully considered in free will before the asking.

Questioner: I assume that we should continue tomorrow.

Ra: I am Ra. Your assumption is correct unless you feel a certain question is necessary. This instrument is nurtured by approximately this length of work.

Questioner: I have one more short question. Is this instrument capable of two of these sessions per day, or should we remain with one?

Ra: I am Ra. This instrument is capable of two sessions a day. However, she must be encouraged to keep her bodily complex strong by the ingestion of your foodstuffs to an extent which exceeds this instrument's normal intake of your foodstuffs, this due to the physical material which we use to speak.

Further, this instrument's activities must be monitored to prevent overactivity, for this activity is equivalent to a strenuous working day on the physical level.

If these admonishments are considered, the two sessions would be possible. We do not wish to deplete this instrument.

Questioner: Thank you, Ra.

Ra: I am Ra. I leave you in the love and the light of the one Infinite Intelligence which is the Creator. Go forth rejoicing in the power and the peace of the One. Adonai. ♣

L/L Research is a subsidiary of Rock Creek Research & Development Laboratories, Inc.

P.O. Box 5195
Louisville, KY 40255-0195

www.llresearch.org

Rock Creek is a non-profit corporation dedicated to discovering and sharing information which may aid in the spiritual evolution of humankind.

ABOUT THE CONTENTS OF THIS TRANSCRIPT: This telepathic channeling has been taken from transcriptions of the weekly study and meditation meetings of the Rock Creek Research & Development Laboratories and L/L Research. It is offered in the hope that it may be useful to you. As the Confederation entities always make a point of saying, please use your discrimination and judgment in assessing this material. If something rings true to you, fine. If something does not resonate, please leave it behind, for neither we nor those of the Confederation would wish to be a stumbling block for any.

© 2009 L/L Research

The Law of One, Book I, Session 5
January 23, 1981

Ra: I am Ra. I greet you in the love and the light of the infinite Creator. I communicate now.

Questioner: The last time that we communicated we were speaking of the learning of healing. It is my impression from what you gave to us in the earlier session that it is necessary to first purify the self by certain disciplines and exercises. Then in order to heal a patient, it is necessary, by example, and possibly certain exercises, to create the mental configuration in the patient that allows him to heal himself. Am I correct?

Ra: I am Ra. Although your learn/understanding distortion is essentially correct, your choice of vibratory/sound complex is not entirely as accurate as this language allows.

It is not by example that the healer does the working. The working exists in and of itself. The healer is only the catalyst, much as this instrument has the catalysis necessary to provide the channel for our words, yet by example or exercise of any kind can take no thought for this working.

The healing/working is congruent in that it is a form of channeling some distortion of the intelligent infinity.

Questioner: We have decided to accept, if offered, the honor/duty of learning/teaching the healing process. I would ask as to the first step which we should accomplish in becoming effective healers.

Ra: I am Ra. We shall begin with the first of the three teachings/learnings.

We begin with the mental learn/teaching necessary for contact with intelligent infinity. The prerequisite of mental work is the ability to retain silence of self at a steady state when required by the self. The mind must be opened like a door. The key is silence.

Within the door lies an hierarchical construction you may liken unto geography and in some ways geometry, for the hierarchy is quite regular, bearing inner relationships.

To begin to master the concept of mental disciplines it is necessary to examine the self. The polarity of your dimension must be internalized. Where you find patience within your mind you must consciously find the corresponding impatience and vice versa. Each thought a being has, has in its turn an antithesis. The disciplines of the mind involve, first of all, identifying both those things of which you approve and those things of which you disapprove within yourself, and then balancing each and every positive and negative charge with its equal. The mind contains all things. Therefore, you must discover this completeness within yourself.

The second mental discipline is acceptance of the completeness within your consciousness. It is not for a being of polarity in the physical consciousness to pick and choose among attributes, thus building the roles that cause blockages and confusions in the already distorted mind complex. Each acceptance smoothes part of the many distortions that the faculty you call judgment engenders.

The third discipline of the mind is a repetition of the first but with the gaze outward toward the fellow entities that it meets. In each entity there exists completeness. Thus, the ability to understand each balance is necessary. When you view patience, you are responsible for mirroring in your mental understandings, patience/impatience. When you view impatience, it is necessary for your mental configuration of understanding to be impatience/patience. We use this as a simple example. Most configurations of mind have many facets, and understanding of either self polarities, or what you would call other-self polarities, can and must be understood as subtle work.

The next step is the acceptance of the other-self polarities, which mirrors the second step. These are the first four steps of learning mental disciplines. The fifth step involves observing the geographical and geometrical relationships and ratios of the mind, the other mind, the mass mind, and the infinite mind.

The second area of learn/teaching is the study/understanding of the body complexes. It is necessary to know your body well. This is a matter of using the mind to examine how the feelings, the biases, what you would call the emotions, affect various portions of the body complex. It shall be necessary to both understand the bodily polarity and to accept them, repeating in a chemical/physical manifestation the work you have done upon the mind bethinking the consciousness.

The body is a creature of the mind's creation. It has its biases. The biological bias must be first completely understood and then the opposite bias allowed to find full expression in understanding. Again, the process of acceptance of the body as a balanced, as well as polarized, individual may then be accomplished. It is then the task to extend this understanding to the bodies of the other-selves whom you will meet.

The simplest example of this is the understanding that each biological male is female; each biological female is male. This is a simple example. However, in almost every case wherein you are attempting the understanding of the body of self or other-self, you will again find that the most subtle discernment is necessary in order to fully grasp the polarity complexes involved.

At this time we would suggest closing the description until the next time of work so that we may devote time to the third area commensurate with its importance.

We can answer a query if it is a short one before we leave this instrument.

Questioner: Is the instrument comfortable? Is there anything that we can do to increase the comfort of the instrument?

Ra: I am Ra. The candle could be rotated clockwise approximately 10° each session to improve the flow of spiraled energy through the being's receiving mechanisms. This particular configuration is well otherwise. But we ask that the objects described and used be centered with geometric care and checked from time to time. Also that they not be exposed to that space/time in which work is not of importance.

I am Ra. I leave this instrument in the love and in the light of the one infinite Creator. Go forth rejoicing in the power and the peace of the one Creator. Adonai.

L/L Research

L/L Research is a subsidiary of Rock Creek Research & Development Laboratories, Inc.

P.O. Box 5195
Louisville, KY 40255-0195

www.llresearch.org

Rock Creek is a non-profit corporation dedicated to discovering and sharing information which may aid in the spiritual evolution of humankind.

ABOUT THE CONTENTS OF THIS TRANSCRIPT: This telepathic channeling has been taken from transcriptions of the weekly study and meditation meetings of the Rock Creek Research & Development Laboratories and L/L Research. It is offered in the hope that it may be useful to you. As the Confederation entities always make a point of saying, please use your discrimination and judgment in assessing this material. If something rings true to you, fine. If something does not resonate, please leave it behind, for neither we nor those of the Confederation would wish to be a stumbling block for any.

© 2009 L/L Research

The Law of One, Book I, Session 6
January 24, 1981

Ra: I am Ra. I greet you in the love and the light of the infinite Creator. I communicate now.

Questioner: We would like to continue the material from yesterday.

Ra: I am Ra. This is well with us.

We proceed now with the third part of the teach/learning concerning the development of the energy powers of healing.

The third area is the spiritual complex which embodies the fields of force and consciousness which are the least distorted of your mind/body/spirit complex. The exploration and balancing of the spirit complex is indeed the longest and most subtle part of your learn/teaching. We have considered the mind as a tree. The mind controls the body. With the mind single-pointed, balanced, and aware, the body comfortable in whatever biases and distortions make it appropriately balanced for that instrument, the instrument is then ready to proceed with the greater work.

That is the work of wind and fire. The spiritual body energy field is a pathway, or channel. When body and mind are receptive and open, then the spirit can become a functioning shuttle or communicator from the entity's individual energy/will upwards, and from the streamings of the creative fire and wind downwards.

The healing ability, like all other, what this instrument would call, paranormal abilities, is affected by the opening of a pathway or shuttle into intelligent infinity. There are many upon your plane who have a random hole or gateway in their spirit energy field, sometimes created by the ingestion of chemicals such as, what this instrument would call LSD, who are able, randomly and without control, to tap into energy sources. They may or may not be entities who wish to serve. The purpose of carefully and consciously opening this channel is to serve in a more dependable way, in a more commonplace or usual way, as seen by the distortion complex of the healer. To others there may appear to be miracles. To the one who has carefully opened the door to intelligent infinity this is ordinary; this is commonplace; this is as it should be. The life experience becomes somewhat transformed. The great work goes on.

At this time we feel these exercises suffice for your beginning. We will, at a future time, when you feel you have accomplished that which is set before you, begin to guide you into a more precise understanding of the functions and uses of this gateway in the experience of healing.

Questioner: I think this might be an appropriate time to include a little more background on yourself, possibly information having to do with where you came from prior to your involvement with planet Earth, if this is possible.

Ra: I am Ra. I am, with the social memory complex of which I am a part, one of those who voyaged outward from another planet within your own solar system, as this entity would call it. The planetary influence was that you call Venus. We are a race old in your measures. When we were at the sixth dimension our physical beings were what you would call golden. We were tall and somewhat delicate. Our physical body complex covering, which you call the integument, had a golden luster.

In this form we decided to come among your peoples. Your peoples at that time were much unlike us in physical appearance, as you might call it. We, thus, did not mix well with the population and were obviously other than they. Thus, our visit was relatively short, for we found ourselves in the hypocritical position of being acclaimed as other than your other-selves. This was the time during which we built the structures in which you show interest.

Questioner: How did you journey from Venus to this planet?

Ra: I am Ra. We used thought.

Questioner: Would it have been possible to have taken one of the people of this planet at that time and placed him on Venus? Would he have survived? Were conditions on Venus hospitable?

Ra: I am Ra. The third-density conditions are not hospitable to the life-forms of your peoples. The fifth and sixth dimensions of that planetary sphere are quite conducive to growing/learning/teaching.

Questioner: How were you able to make the transition from Venus? Did you have to change your dimension to walk upon the Earth?

Ra: I am Ra. You will remember the exercise of the wind. The dissolution into nothingness is the dissolution into unity, for there is no nothingness. From the sixth dimension, we are capable of manipulating, by thought, the intelligent infinity present in each particle of light or distorted light so that we were able to clothe ourselves in a replica visible in the third density of our mind/body/spirit complexes in the sixth density. We were allowed this experiment by the Council which guards this planet.

Questioner: Where is this Council located?

Ra: I am Ra. This Council is located in the octave, or eighth dimension, of the planet Saturn, taking its place in an area which you understand in third-dimension terms as the rings.

Questioner: Are there any people such as you find on Earth on any of the other planets in our solar system?

Ra: I am Ra. Do you request space/time present information or space/time continuum information?

Questioner: Both.

Ra: I am Ra. At one time/space, in what is your past, there was a population of third-density beings upon a planet which dwelt within your solar system. There are various names by which this planet has been named. The vibratory sound complex most usually used by your peoples is Maldek. These entities, destroying their planetary sphere, thus were forced to find room for themselves upon this third density which is the only one in your solar system at their time/space present which was hospitable and capable of offering the lessons necessary to decrease their mind/body/spirit distortions with respect to the Law of One.

Questioner: How did they come here?

Ra: I am Ra. They came through the process of harvest and were incarnated through the processes of incarnation from your higher spheres within this density.

Questioner: How long ago did this happen?

Ra: I am Ra. I am having difficulty communicating with this instrument. We must deepen her state.

This occurred approximately 500,000 of your years ago.

Questioner: Is all of the Earth's human population then originally from Maldek?

Ra: I am Ra. This is a new line of questioning, and deserves a place of its own. The ones who were harvested to your sphere from the sphere known before its dissolution as other names, but to your peoples as Maldek, incarnated, many within your Earth's surface rather than upon it. The population of your planet contains many various groups harvested from other second-dimension and cycled third-dimension spheres. You are not all one race or background of beginning. The experience you share is unique to this time/space continuum.

Questioner: I think that it would be appropriate to discover how the Law of One acts in this transfer of beings to our planet and the action of harvest?

Ra: I am Ra. The Law of One states simply that all things are one, that all beings are one. There are certain behaviors and thought-forms consonant with the understanding and practice of this law. Those who, finishing a cycle of experience, demonstrate grades of distortion of that understanding of thought and action will be separated by their own choice into the vibratory distortion most comfortable to their mind/body/spirit complexes. This process is guarded or watched by those nurturing beings who, being very close to the Law of One in their distortions, nevertheless, move towards active service.

Thus, the illusion is created of light, or more properly but less understandably, light/love. This is in varying degrees of intensity. The spirit complex of each harvested entity moves along the line of light until the light grows too glaring, at which time the entity stops. This entity may have barely reached third density or may be very, very close to the ending of the third-density light/love distortion vibratory complex. Nevertheless, those who fall within this octave of intensifying light/love then experience a major cycle during which there are opportunities for the discovery of the distortions which are inherent in each entity and, therefore, the lessening of these distortions.

Questioner: What is the length, in our years, of one of these cycles?

Ra: I am Ra. One major cycle is approximately 25,000 of your years. There are three cycles of this nature during which those who have progressed may be harvested at the end of three major cycles. That is, approximately between 75 and 76,000 of your years. All are harvested regardless of their progress, for during that time the planet itself has moved through the useful part of that dimension and begins to cease being useful for the lower levels of vibration within that density.

Questioner: What is the position of this planet with respect to the progression of cycles at this time?

Ra: I am Ra. This sphere is at this time in fourth-dimension vibration. Its material is quite confused due to the society memory complexes embedded in its consciousness. It has not made an easy transition to the vibrations which beckon. Therefore, it will be fetched with some inconvenience.

Questioner: Is this inconvenience imminent within a few years?

Ra: I am Ra. This inconvenience, or disharmonious vibratory complex, has begun several of your years in your past. It shall continue unabated for a period of approximately thirty of your years.

Questioner: After this period of thirty years I am assuming that this will be a fourth-density planet. Is this correct?

Ra: I am Ra. This is so.

Questioner: Is it possible to estimate what percent of the present population will inhabit the fourth-density planet?

Ra: I am Ra. The harvesting is not yet, thus, estimation is meaningless.

Questioner: Does the fact that we are in this transition period now have anything to do with the reason that you have made your information available to the population?

Ra: I am Ra. We have walked among your people. We remember. We remember sorrow: have seen much. We have searched for an instrument of the proper parameters of distortion in mind/body/spirit complex and supporting and understanding of mind/body/spirit complexes to accept this information with minimal distortion and maximal desire to serve for some of your years. The answer, in short, is yes. However, we wished you to know that in our memory we thank you.

Questioner: The disc-shaped craft that we call UFOs—some have been said to have come from the planet Venus. Would any of these be your craft?

Ra: I am Ra. We have used crystals for many purposes. The craft of which you speak have not been used by us in your space/time present memory complex. However, we have used crystals and the bell-shape in the past of your illusion.

Questioner: How many years in the past did you use the bell-shaped craft to come to earth?

Ra: I am Ra. We visited your peoples 18,000 of your years ago and did not land; again, 11,000 years ago.

Questioner: Photographs of bell-shaped craft and reports of contact of such from Venus exist from less than thirty years ago. Do you have any knowledge of these reports?

Ra: I am Ra. We have knowledge of Oneness with these forays of your time/space present. We are no longer of Venus. However, there are thought-forms created among your peoples from our time of walking among you. The memory and thought-forms created, therefore, are a part of your society-memory complex. This mass consciousness, as you may call it, creates the experience once more for those who request such experience. The present Venus population is no longer sixth-density.

Questioner: Do any of the UFOs presently reported at this time come from other planets, or do you have this knowledge?

Ra: I am Ra. I am one of the members of the Confederation of Planets in the Service of the Infinite Creator. There are approximately fifty-three civilizations, comprising approximately five hundred planetary consciousness complexes in this Confederation. This Confederation contains those from your own planet who have attained dimensions beyond your third. It contains planetary entities within your solar system, and it contains planetary entities from other galaxies.[5] It is a true Confederation in that its members are not alike, but allied in service according to the Law of One.

Questioner: Do any of them come here at this time in spacecraft? In the past, say, thirty years?

Ra: I am Ra. We must state that this information is unimportant. If you will understand this, we feel that the information may be acceptably offered. The Law of One is what we are here to express. However, we will speak upon this subject.

Each planetary entity which wishes to appear within your third dimension of space/time distortion requests permission to break quarantine, as you may call it, and appear to your peoples. The reason and purpose for this appearance is understood and either accepted or rejected. There have been as many as fifteen of the Confederation entities in your skies at any one time. The others are available to you through thought.

At present there are seven which are operating with craft in your density. Their purposes are very simple: to allow those entities of your planet to become aware of infinity which is often best expressed to the uninformed as the mysterious or unknown.

Questioner: I am fully aware that you are primarily interested in disseminating information concerning the Law of One. However, it is my judgment, and I could be wrong, that in order to disseminate this material it will be necessary to include questions such as the one I have just asked. If this is not the objective, then I could limit my questions to the application of the Law of One. But I understand that at this time it is the objective to widely disseminate this material. Is this correct?

Ra: I am Ra. This perception is only slightly distorted in your understand/learning. We wish you to proceed as you deem proper. That is your place. We, in giving this information, find our distortion of understanding of our purpose to be that not only of the offering of information, but the weighting of it according to our distorted perceptions of its relative importance. Thus, you will find our statements, at times, to be those which imply that a question is unimportant. This is due to our perception that the given question is unimportant. Nevertheless, unless the question contains the potential for answer-giving which may infringe upon free will, we offer our answers.

Questioner: Thank you very much. We do not want to overtire the instrument. We have gone considerably over our normal working time. Could you tell me what condition the instrument is in?

Ra: I am Ra. The instrument is balanced due to your care. However, her physical vehicle is growing stiff.

Questioner: In that case perhaps we should continue at a later time.

Ra: I am Ra. I leave you in the love and the light of the one infinite Creator. Go forth rejoicing in the power and the peace of the one Creator. Adonai.

---

[5] Ra often uses the word "galaxy" where we would say planetary system. This meaning is listed in the unabridged dictionary but is not in common use.

L/L Research

L/L Research is a subsidiary of Rock Creek Research & Development Laboratories, Inc.

P.O. Box 5195
Louisville, KY 40255-0195

www.llresearch.org

Rock Creek is a non-profit corporation dedicated to discovering and sharing information which may aid in the spiritual evolution of humankind.

ABOUT THE CONTENTS OF THIS TRANSCRIPT: This telepathic channeling has been taken from transcriptions of the weekly study and meditation meetings of the Rock Creek Research & Development Laboratories and L/L Research. It is offered in the hope that it may be useful to you. As the Confederation entities always make a point of saying, please use your discrimination and judgment in assessing this material. If something rings true to you, fine. If something does not resonate, please leave it behind, for neither we nor those of the Confederation would wish to be a stumbling block for any.

© 2009 L/L Research

The Law of One, Book V, Session 6, Fragment 2
January 24, 1981

Jim: The following material in Session 6 concerns the basic requirement for the Ra contact; that is, harmony. During the 106 sessions with Ra there were only three people who ever attended a Ra session besides the three of us, and in each case it was Ra's recommendation that each entity needed not only to have the appropriate attitude in its personal means of seeking but that each person needed to be in harmony with each of us before attending any session. In Tom's case this was achieved by Don's explaining to Tom the meaning that the Bible, candle, incense, and chalice of water held for us as triggering mechanisms or signals to our subconscious minds that a session was about to take place and that from all levels of our being we should begin the process of purifying our desires to serve others above all else and to surround ourselves with the joy-filled light of praise and thanksgiving. The harmony that this process produced among our group, then, was much as a musical chord with which those of Ra could blend their vibrations, and upon that harmonious blend of vibrations information of a metaphysical nature could be transmitted by being drawn to those which sought it.

Carla: *Tom is one of the members of L/L Research's spiritual family who attended our meditation group's Sunday meetings for some years. It is impossible to say how many "members" have come to our sessions over the years since 1962, when we began. Like many of these dear souls, he has kept in touch, although his personal path has taken him elsewhere. We have always attempted to "tune" our circle before we begin to meditate together, so Tom was perfectly clear on what we needed.*

That altar, with its Christian accouterments, may well puzzle some who think that it takes a new-age channel to produce new-age information. Not so for me, unless one counts Jesus Christ as a new-age channel himself! I was a cradle Anglican, and have attended Episcopal churches my whole life. That those of Ra worked with these deeply ingrained biases within me is, to me, a signal characteristic of this unique source. I felt loved, accepted and cherished by having these items placed near me, and that they thought this out was a constant blessing during this contact.

Session 6, January 24, 1981

Questioner: I would like to ask if it is possible for Tom to attend one of these sessions tomorrow. Are you familiar with the entity, Tom?

Ra: I am Ra. This mind/body/spirit complex, sound vibration "Tom," is acceptable. We caution you to instruct this entity in the frame of mind and various appurtenances which it must understand before it is conducted into the circle.

Questioner: I'm not quite sure what you mean by appurtenances.

Ra: I was referring to the symbolic objects which trigger this instrument's distortions towards love/light. The placement and loving acceptance of them by all present is important in the nurturing of this instrument. Therefore, the appurtenances involved must be described and their presence explained in your own words of teach/learning, for you have the proper attitude for the required results.

Questioner: The only question that I have is that I will assume that since Leonard was here when you first made contact that it is suitable for him to be here as well as Tom.

Ra: This is correct and completes the number of those at this time able to come who are suitable. Again, remember the instructions given for the preparation of the vibratory sound complex, Tom. ☥

L/L Research

Sunday Meeting
January 25, 1981

(Don channeling)

I am Hatonn. I greet you, my friends, in the love and in the light of the infinite Creator. It is a very great privilege to be with you once more. I speak through this instrument. I will condition this instrument. Please bear with me. I am sorry for the delay. We have contact now. I was saying that I speak to you through this instrument, the first time in some time. It is a very great privilege to be with you. I am Hatonn. We of the Confederation of Planets in the Service of the Infinite Creator are always very pleased to serve those who seek our service. We are at all times available to you—at all times, my friends. It is only necessary that you think of us. Avail yourself to us in meditation and we are there. This is our service to you. This is our privilege and our pleasure. We are constantly with you. We are with those, the peoples of the planet Earth, who seek our service and we are with only those who seek our service. We cannot in any way offer our aid to those who do not seek our service, for this is our understanding of the principle of free will.

Unfortunately, many of your peoples at this time do not understand the service we offer [the] service we offer, my friends, is the service toward that which, not only you, but also they seek. For all of the people of this planet in truth seek the same thing. They seek development of their mind and spirit. This development, my friends, is in truth all that there is. This development, my friends, in truth is all that there is to develop. Any other development [will] stay transient. That will be left in the memory of your being during that very short time that you walk the surface of this planet. We offer aid to those who seek that development which they seek. Many times we have come to you. Many times we have stated the importance of daily meditation. For only in this way can you truly understand that which we offer.

We do not have a language adequate to give to you the concepts which we offer. Those concepts are not complex but very simple. Simplicity, my friends, defies description in your language. The beauty defies description in your language. The truth defies description in your language. For your language, my friends, is not based in the system of thought which encompasses reality. The creation which all of us exist in are one. Avail yourselves, therefore, in meditation and begin to know without speaking. Begin to see without looking. Begin to hear without listening, that small voice that is all and ever present, for it is not only without you, it is within you. For it is all things, my friends—[and] you are all things. Become one with all that there is. Rejoice [in] the harmonious symphony that speaks to you from every part [of] the infinite, all being, all knowing creation.

(Jim channeling)

I am Hatonn, and I am with this instrument. We must apologize for our delay. We lost our contact with the one known as Don for he has been himself under somewhat of a strain of late and is feeling the resulting fatigue. We would simply close this part of our sharing with you this evening by saying that we always enjoy the opportunity of joining our vibrations with those of your people who seek to know more of the law of love, for this is the vibration in which we dwell and the service which we offer is that of familiarizing those seekers of love with its vibration. We at this time thank each of those present for asking for our service for this evening. We are simple creatures of service and desire only to serve the one Creator. As always, we leave you in the love and the light of the one infinite Creator. We are known to you as Hatonn. Adonai, my friends.

(Carla channeling)

I am Latwii. I am with this instrument. I greet you in the love and the light of our infinite Creator. I am being very careful with this instrument and do not appreciate all the levity about how I always blow this instrument's circuits. That is no longer true. I have learned to be delicate. The love and the light of the infinite Creator, my friends—this is what we greet you with. And we rest in it awaiting any questions that you might have at this time. Do you have a question at this time that we may share what information we have with you on?

C: I'm still having a hard time understanding things we talked about last week. I asked about a person that I knew that suffered so much personal loss in their life: why that they suffered it, why did so such happen to one, and you talked to me about how we set up our own lessons to be learned in this plane. You said that we could … that it's possible that some entities worked in conjunction to help each other with their lesson and that it was all part of a harmony.

It's just not quite soaking in for some reason. How is it … where are we coming from, where are we planning these things at … that we want to learn? How did we know what was necessary?

I am Latwii. That is quite a question, my brother. We will answer in several parts. The first part is a general concept. Consider yourself upon the floor of a terminal building. You are planning a trip. You look at all of the schedules and you decide your destination. You may need to go a short distance, in a relatively convenient way. You may decide to go a very long distance, and the difficulty of getting there may be quite great. You choose your destination. This destination, in spiritual terms, is the sum total of lessons you wish yourself to learn. This is done by yourself prior to incarnation and during incarnation it is extremely unlikely that you will, without help, remember picking such a destination if it happens to be difficult. Thus, the problems, the losses, the limitations you meet are preprogrammed by yourselves in order that you may learn whatever lessons these difficulties cause you to face more squarely.

That is often a challenging task for the soul body due to the fact that your peoples seem endlessly able to avoid seeing things clearly by deciding various rationalizations of them. Secondly, the cooperation between entities is not only common, it is the usual pattern for those advanced enough to choose their own incarnations. The path, shall we say, to mastering the lessons of this planet is a path where one entity is of great help in balancing another. It is extraordinarily difficult to learn the lessons completely alone, for you then have no feedback, as this instrument would call it, and must rely upon your own thinking. This is like shaving without a mirror and is not particularly easy.

May we answer you further, my brother?

C: Each of us has chosen the lesson that they wish to learn in this incarnation? Does the fact that we have free will in this incarnation … does it … do we many times bypass the road we have chosen for an easier path and miss our lesson? Or do many of us miss our lesson in this incarnation and have to repeat?

I am Latwii. I am with the instrument. Yes, my brother, many miss their lessons, but not because they do not receive them again and again. Free will is always in effect. You chose your lesson, each of you in this room. Not all of your peoples are able to do this. Some must incarnate randomly until they have reached a certain level of understanding. However, each of you has programmed certain lessons in order to learn the ways of love.

There are many, many times that each of you has decided not to learn a particular lesson. This lesson immediately returns in another form. You again may choose. You are never hopelessly lost. This instrument has the expression in her mind, "All roads lead to Rome." This is true of your journey in this lifetime. If you miss a turn, there is always another turning that will bring you back to the correct path. Perhaps a few detours have been experienced by each of you. This is not a cause for discouragement.

When you see a person such as the one of whom you spoke who has had a great deal of stimulus for learning, you see a person who has chosen to go from New York to Tanganyika by ark. This is difficult, but the lessons are rewarding. In the life of the soul, that is what is important, not the ease of the journey.

Do you have another question?

C: I get the feeling at times there is something giving us a nudge or helping hand or a blocking. Is that just the entities on this level? Is that just part of the harmony? Is something directing us? Helping us maybe with our lessons?

I am Latwii. My brother, you have as much help as you request. You yourself guide your own learning but there is always comfort. The blockages come by far most of the time from within your own thoughts. Thus, welcome a helping hand but know the responsibility lies with you.

Is there another question at this time?

C: No.

I am Latwii. We are glad to be able to use this instrument. We wish you very well and send you the light in which we dwell and the love of the Creator. I am Latwii.

The Law of One, Book I, Session 7
January 25, 1981

Ra: I am Ra. I greet you in the love and the light of our infinite Creator. I communicate now.

Questioner: You mentioned that there were a number of members of the Confederation of Planets. What avenues of service, or types of service, are available to the members of the Confederation?

Ra: I am Ra. I am assuming that you intend the service which we of the Confederation can offer, rather than the service which is available to our use.

The service available for our offering to those who call us is equivalent to the square of the distortion/need of that calling divided by, or integrated with, the basic Law of One in its distortion indicating the free will of those who are not aware of the unity of creation.

Questioner: From this, I am assuming that the difficulty that you have in contacting this planet at this time is the mixture of people here, some being aware of the unity, and some not, and for this reason you cannot come openly or give proof of your contact. Is this correct?

Ra: I am Ra. As we just repeated through this instrument, we must integrate all of the portions of your social memory complex in its illusory disintegration form. Then the product of this can be seen as the limit of our ability to serve. We are fortunate that the Law of Service squares the desires of those who call. Otherwise, we would have no beingness in this time/space at this present continuum of the illusion. In short, you are basically correct. The thought of not being able is not a part of our basic thought-form complex towards your peoples, but rather it is a maximal consideration of what is possible.

Questioner: By squared, do you mean that if ten people call you can count that, when comparing it to the planetary ratio, as 100 people, squaring ten and getting 100?

Ra: I am Ra. This is incorrect. The square is sequential—one, two, three, four, each squared by the next number.

Questioner: If only ten entities on earth required your services how would you compute their calling by using this square method?

Ra: I am Ra. We would square one ten sequential times, raising the number to the tenth square.

Questioner: What would be the result of this calculation?

Ra: I am Ra. The result is difficult to transmit. It is 1,012, approximately. The entities who call are sometimes not totally unified in their calling and, thus, the squaring slightly less. Thus, there is a statistical loss over a period of call. However, perhaps you may see by this statistically corrected information the squaring mechanism.

Questioner: About how many entities at present on planet Earth are calling for your services?

Ra: I am Ra. I am called personally by 352,000. The Confederation, in its entire spectrum of entity-complexes, is called by 632,000,000 of your mind/body/spirit complexes. These numbers have been simplified.

Questioner: Can you tell me what the result of the application of the Law of Squares is to those figures?

Ra: I am Ra. The number is approximately meaningless in the finite sense as there are many, many digits. It, however, constitutes a great calling which we of all creation feel and hear as if our own entities were distorted towards a great and overwhelming sorrow. It demands our service.

Questioner: At what point would this calling be great enough for you to come openly among the people on Earth? How many entities on Earth would have to call the Confederation?

Ra: I am Ra. We do not calculate the possibility of coming among your peoples by the numbers of calling, but by a consensus among an entire societal-memory complex which has become aware of the infinite consciousness of all things. This has been possible among your peoples only in isolated instances.

In the case wherein a social memory complex which is a servant of the Creator sees this situation and has an idea for the appropriate aid which can only be done among your peoples, the social memory complex desiring this project lays it before the Council of Saturn. If it is approved, quarantine is lifted.

Questioner: I have a question about that Council. Who are the members, and how does the Council function?

Ra: I am Ra. The members of the Council are representatives from the Confederation and from those vibratory levels of your inner planes bearing responsibility for your third density. The names are not important because there are no names. Your mind/body/spirit complexes request names and so, in many cases, the vibratory sound complexes which are consonant with the vibratory distortions of each entity are used. However, the name concept is not part of the Council. If names are requested, we will attempt them. However, not all have chosen names.

In number, the Council that sits in constant session, though varying in its members by means of balancing, which takes place, what you would call irregularly, is nine. That is the Session Council. To back up this Council, there are twenty-four entities which offer their services as requested. These entities faithfully watch and have been called Guardians.

The Council operates by means of, what you would call, telepathic contact with the oneness or unity of the nine, the distortions blending harmoniously so that the Law of One prevails with ease. When a need for thought is present, the Council retains the distortion-complex of this need, balancing it as described, and then recommends what it considers as appropriate action. This includes: One, the duty of admitting social memory complexes to the Confederation; Two, offering aid to those who are unsure how to aid the social memory complex requesting aid in a way consonant with both the call, the Law, and the number of those calling (that is to say, sometimes the resistance of the call); Three, internal questions in the Council are determined.

These are the prominent duties of the Council. They are, if in any doubt, able to contact the twenty-four who then offer consensus/judgment/thinking to the Council. The Council then may reconsider any question.

Questioner: You mentioned the nine who sit on the Council. Is this "nine" the same nine as those mentioned in this book? *(Questioner gestures to* Uri.*)*

Ra: I am Ra. The Council of Nine has been retained in semi-undistorted form by two main sources, that known in your naming, as Mark and that known in your naming as Henry. In one case, the channel became the scribe. In the other, the channel was not the scribe. However, without the aid of the scribe, the energy would not have come to the channel.

Questioner: The names that you spoke of. Were they Mark Probert and Henry Puharich?

Ra: I am Ra. This is correct.

Questioner: I am interested in the application of the Law of One as it pertains to free will with respect to what I would call the advertising done by UFO contacts with the planet Earth. The Council seems to have allowed the quarantine to be lifted many times over the past thirty years. This seems to me to be a form of advertising for what we are doing right now, so that more people will be awakened. Am I correct?

Ra: I am Ra. It will take a certain amount of untangling of conceptualization of your mental complex to reform your query into an appropriate response. Please bear with us.

The Council of Saturn has not allowed the breaking of quarantine in the time/space continuum you mentioned. There is a certain amount of landing taking place. Some are of the entities known to you as the group of Orion.

Secondly, there is permission granted, not to break quarantine by dwelling among you, but to appear in thought form capacity for those who have eyes to see.

Thirdly, you are correct in assuming that permission was granted at the time/space in which your first nuclear device was developed and used for Confederation members to minister to your peoples in such a way as to cause mystery to occur. This is what you mean by advertising and is correct. The mystery and unknown quality of the occurrences we are allowed to offer have the hoped-for intention of making your peoples aware of infinite possibility. When your peoples grasp infinity, then and only then, can the gateway be opened to the Law of One.

Questioner: You said that Orion was the source of some of these contacts with UFOs. Can you tell me something of that contact, its purpose?

Ra: I am Ra. Consider, if you will, a simple example of intentions which are bad/good. This example is Adolf. This is your vibratory sound complex. The intention is to presumably unify by choosing the distortion complex called elite from a social memory complex and then enslaving, by various effects, those who are seen by the distortion as not-elite. There is then the concept of taking the social memory complex thus weeded and adding it to a distortion thought of by the so-called Orion group as an empire. The problem facing them is that they face a great deal of random energy released by the concept of separation. This causes them to be vulnerable as the distortions amongst their own members are not harmonized.

Questioner: What is the density of the Orion group?

Ra: I am Ra. Like the Confederation, the densities of the mass consciousnesses which comprise that group are varied. There are a very few third density, a larger number of fourth density, a similarly large number of fifth density, and very few sixth-density entities comprising this organization. Their numbers are perhaps one-tenth ours at any point in the space/time continuum as the problem of spiritual entropy causes them to experience constant disintegration of their social memory complexes. Their power is the same as ours. The Law of One blinks neither at the light nor the darkness, but is available for service to others and service to self. However, service to others results in service to self, thus preserving and further harmonizing the distortions of those entities seeking intelligent infinity through these disciplines.

Those seeking intelligent infinity through the use of service to self create the same amount of power but, as we said, have constant difficulty because of the concept of separation which is implicit in the manifestations of the service to self which involve power over others. This weakens and eventually disintegrates the energy collected by such mind/body/spirit complexes who call the Orion group and the social memory complexes which comprise the Orion group.

It should be noted, carefully pondered, and accepted, that the Law of One is available to any social memory complex which has decided to strive together for any seeking of purpose, be it service to others or service to self. The laws, which are the primal distortions of the Law of One, then are placed into operation and the illusion of space/time is used as a medium for the development of the results of those choices freely made. Thus all entities learn, no matter what they seek. All learn the same, some rapidly, some slowly.

Questioner: Using as an example the fifth density concerning the social memory complex of the Orion group, what was their previous density before they became fifth density?

Ra: I am Ra. The progress through densities is sequential. A fifth-density social memory complex would be comprised of mind/body/spirit complexes harvested from fourth density. Then the conglomerate or mass mind/body/spirit complex does its melding and the results are due to the infinitely various possibilities of combinations of distortions.

Questioner: I'm trying to understand how a group such as the Orion group would progress. How it would be possible, if you were in the Orion group, and pointed toward self-service, to progress from our third density to the fourth. What learning would be necessary for that?

Ra: I am Ra. This is the last question of length for this instrument at this time.

You will recall that we went into some detail as to how those not oriented towards seeking service for others yet, nevertheless, found and could use the gateway to intelligent infinity. This is true at all densities in our octave. We cannot speak for those above us, as you would say, in the next quantum or octave of beingness. This is, however, true of this octave of density. The beings are harvested because they can see and enjoy the light/love of the appropriate density. Those who have found this light/love, love/light without benefit of a desire for service to others nevertheless, by the Law of Free Will, have the right to the use of that light/love for whatever purpose. Also, it may be inserted that there are systems of study which enable the seeker of separation to gain these gateways.

This study is as difficult as the one which we have described to you, but there are those with the perseverance to pursue the study just as you desire to pursue the difficult path of seeking to know in order to serve. The distortion lies in the effect that those who seek to serve the self are seen by the Law of One as precisely the same as those who seek to serve others, for are all not one? To serve yourself and to serve others is a dual method of saying the same thing, if you can understand the essence of the Law of One.

At this time we would answer any brief questions you may have.

Questioner: Is there anything that we can do to make the instrument more comfortable?

Ra: I am Ra. There are small adjustments you may make. However, we are now able to use this instrument with minimal distortion and without depleting the instrument to any significant extent.

Do you wish to ask further?

Questioner: We do not wish to tire the instrument. Thank you very much. That was very helpful and we would like to continue in the next session from this point.

Ra: I am Ra. I leave you in the love and the light of the one infinite Creator. Go forth then rejoicing in the power and the peace of the one Creator. Adonai.

L/L Research

L/L Research is a subsidiary of Rock Creek Research & Development Laboratories, Inc.

P.O. Box 5195
Louisville, KY 40255-0195

www.llresearch.org

Rock Creek is a non-profit corporation dedicated to discovering and sharing information which may aid in the spiritual evolution of humankind.

ABOUT THE CONTENTS OF THIS TRANSCRIPT: This telepathic channeling has been taken from transcriptions of the weekly study and meditation meetings of the Rock Creek Research & Development Laboratories and L/L Research. It is offered in the hope that it may be useful to you. As the Confederation entities always make a point of saying, please use your discrimination and judgment in assessing this material. If something rings true to you, fine. If something does not resonate, please leave it behind, for neither we nor those of the Confederation would wish to be a stumbling block for any.

© 2009 L/L Research

The Law of One, Book I, Session 8
January 26, 1981

Ra: I am Ra. I greet you in the love and the light of the infinite Creator. I communicate now.

Questioner: I have a question regarding what I call the advertising of the Confederation. It has to do with free will. There have been certain contacts allowed, as I understand, by the Confederation, but this is limited because of free will of those who are not oriented in such a way as to want contact. Many people on our planet want this material, but even though we disseminate it many will not be aware that it is available. Is there any possibility of creating some effect which I would call advertising, or is this against the principle of free will?

Ra: I am Ra. Consider, if you will, the path your life-experience complex has taken. Consider the coincidences and odd circumstances by which one thing flowed to the next. Consider this well.

Each entity will receive the opportunity that each needs. This information source-beingness does not have uses in the life-experience complex of each of those among your peoples who seek. Thus the advertisement is general and not designed to indicate the searching out of any particular material, but only to suggest the noumenal aspect of the illusion.

Questioner: You said that some of the landings at this time were of the Orion group. Why did the Orion group land here? What is their purpose?

Ra: I am Ra. Their purpose is conquest, unlike those of the Confederation who wait for the calling. The so-called Orion group calls itself to conquest. As we have said previously, their objective is to locate certain mind/body/spirit complexes which vibrate in resonance with their own vibrational complex, then to enslave the un-elite, as you may call those who are not of the Orion vibration.

Questioner: Was the landing at Pascagoula in 1973 when Charlie Hixson was taken aboard this type of landing?

Ra: I am Ra. The landing of which you speak was what you would call an anomaly. It was neither the Orion influence nor our peoples in thought-form, but rather a planetary entity of your own vibration which came through quarantine in all innocence in a random landing.

Questioner: What did they do to Charlie Hixson when they took him on board?

Ra: I am Ra. They used his mind/body/spirit complex's life experience, concentrating upon the experience of the complexes of what you call war.

Questioner: How did they use them?

Ra: I am Ra. The use of experience is to learn. Consider a race who watches a movie. It experiences a story and identifies with the feelings, perceptions, and experiences of the hero.

Questioner: Was Charlie Hixson originally of the same social memory complex of the ones who picked him up?

Ra: I am Ra. This entity of vibratory sound complex did not have a connection with those who used him.

Questioner: Did those who used him use his war experiences to learn more of the Law of One?

Ra: I am Ra. This is correct.

Questioner: Did the entities who picked him up have the normal configuration? His description of them was rather unusual.

Ra: I am Ra. The configuration of their beings is their normal configuration. The unusualness is not remarkable. We ourselves, when we chose a mission among your peoples, needed to study your peoples for had we arrived in no other form than our own, we would have been perceived as light.

Questioner: What density were the entities who picked up Charlie Hixson from?

Ra: I am Ra. The entities in whom you show such interest are third-density beings of a fairly advanced order. We should express the understanding to you that these entities would not have used the mind/body/spirit complex, Charlie, except for the resolve of this entity before incarnation to be of service.

Questioner: What was the home or origin of the entities who picked up Charlie?

Ra: I am Ra. These entities are of the Sirius galaxy.

Questioner: Would it be possible for any of us to have contact with the Confederation in a more direct way?

Ra: I am Ra. In observing the distortions of those who underwent this experiential sequence we decided to gradually back off, shall I say, from direct contact in thought-form. The least distortion seems to be available in mind-to-mind communication. Therefore, the request to be taken aboard is not one we care to comply with. You are most valuable in your present orientation.

May we ask at this time if you have a needed short query before we end this session?

Questioner: Is there anything that we can do to make the instrument more comfortable?

Ra: I am Ra. The instrument is well balanced. It is possible to make small corrections in the configuration of the spine of the instrument that it be straighter. Continue also to continually monitor the placement and orientation of the symbols used. This particular session, the censer is slightly off and, therefore, this instrument will experience a slight discomfort.

Questioner: Is the censer off in respect to angle or in respect to lateral displacement?

Ra: I am Ra. There is an approximate three degrees' displacement from proper perpendicularity.

I am Ra. I leave you in the love and the light of the one infinite Creator. Go forth, therefore, rejoicing in the power and the peace of the one Creator. Adonai.

L/L Research is a subsidiary of Rock Creek Research & Development Laboratories, Inc.

P.O. Box 5195
Louisville, KY 40255-0195

L/L Research

www.llresearch.org

Rock Creek is a non-profit corporation dedicated to discovering and sharing information which may aid in the spiritual evolution of humankind.

ABOUT THE CONTENTS OF THIS TRANSCRIPT: This telepathic channeling has been taken from transcriptions of the weekly study and meditation meetings of the Rock Creek Research & Development Laboratories and L/L Research. It is offered in the hope that it may be useful to you. As the Confederation entities always make a point of saying, please use your discrimination and judgment in assessing this material. If something rings true to you, fine. If something does not resonate, please leave it behind, for neither we nor those of the Confederation would wish to be a stumbling block for any.

© 2009 L/L Research

The Law of One, Book V, Session 8, Fragment 3
January 26, 1981

Jim: Early in the Ra contact we received answers to our questions which fell into a controversial portion of our third-density illusion. Almost everyone, at some point within the study of the paranormal, spends some time being fascinated by the so-called "conspiracy theories" which have generally to do with the supposedly unseen groups and individuals who are said to be the real powers behind governments and their activities in the world today. Such theories usually hold that the news reports that we hear and read concerning politics, economics, the military, and so forth are but the tip of a very large iceberg that has mainly to do with various schemes for world domination and which function through the secret activities of this small, elite group of human beings and their alien allies.

The following information falls into this category and resulted from a follow-up question Don asked about UFOs and their sources. You will note Don's incredulous attitude throughout this portion of his questioning. It was our decision to remove this information from Book One of *The Law Of One* because we felt it to be entirely unimportant and of a transient nature since knowing it adds nothing to one's ability or desire to seek the truth and the nature of the evolutionary process, whether the information is true or not. In fact, knowing and continuing to seek this kind of information can become a major stumbling block to one's spiritual journey because it removes one's attention from the eternal truths which may serve anyone's journey—at any time—and places it upon that which is only of fleeting interest and of little use spiritually. Concentrating on conspiracy theories and their participants tends to reinforce the illusion of separation and ignores the love that binds all things as One Being. If we had continued to pursue this particular line of questioning, or any other line of questioning of a transient nature, we would soon have lost the contact with those of Ra because, as Ra mentioned in the very first session, Ra communicated with us through a "narrow band" of vibration or wave length.

Through various clues that Ra gave us when Don asked about the alignments at the end of each session, we were able to determine that this "narrow band" meant that only information of the purest and most precise nature concerning the process of the evolution of mind, body, and spirit could be successfully transmitted on a sustainable basis through our instrument. To ask Ra questions of a transient nature would be like trying to run a finely-tuned engine on crude petroleum.

Many groups become fascinated with transient information of a specific, mundane nature and have their information polluted by negative entities who gradually replace the positive entities that began their contact. Pursuing information of this kind is like moving the dial on your radio so that you end up with another station altogether from the one with which you began. This change in desire for the kind of information that the group seeks from its contact is the signal to that contact that what it has to offer is no longer desired, and the Law of Free Will requires that only hints of this de-tuning process be given to the group so that all choices that the group makes are totally a product of its free will. When a group continues to seek the transient information, the positive contact gives hints here and there that such information is not of importance, but when the group persists in seeking this kind of information, the positive contact, in order to observe the free will of the group, must slowly withdraw and is then eventually replaced by a negative contact which is only too happy to give this kind of information, but with less desire for accuracy and with maximal desire to remove the group from the ranks of those who serve others. When the group has been discredited by false information—such as dates of future disasters which are publicized by the group and then do not occur—then the negative entities have been successful in removing the power of the group's light and have gathered it for themselves.

We still feel that this information is totally unimportant, and the only reason that we include it now is to show how easy it is for a group to get off the track, shall we say, and to lose the focus of desire for that which is important and that with which the group began: the desire to serve others by gathering information which may aid in the evolution of mind, body, and spirit. Ten thousand years from now it will not matter one whit who did what to whom on this tiny speck of whirling dust. All that will matter is that love may be found at any time in every person and particle of the one creation, or any illusion thereof. Hopefully information gained through any effort such as the Ra contact will help some other third-density entities to discover more of that truth and to move one step further on their evolutionary journey to the one Creator.

Carla: All I can add to this is a plea to all official sources: we do not know anything, we are not in on any conspiracies, and please, please don't tap our telephones … again! When Don and I joined Andrija Puharich for a mind-link in 1977, we caught the attention of some agency who played havoc with our telephone system. And how utterly without use to listen in to our converse! Mystics seldom plot! We honestly don't care about this stuff, and just stumbled into it by accident.

I'd like to point out the way those of Ra seem here somewhat off-balance compared to their usual steady selves. It is subtle, but easy to see—the opening to each answer is normally "I am Ra." Several times in this fragment, however, that signature is missing. The contact was going slightly out of tune here, I think, due to the information's transient nature.

Session 8, January 26, 1981

Questioner: There was a portion of the material from yesterday which I will read where you say "there is a certain amount of landing taking place. Some of these landings are of your own people; some are of the group known to you as Orion." My first question is what did you mean that some of the landings are of your peoples?

Ra: I am Ra. Your peoples have, at this time/space present, the technological achievement, if you would call it that, of being able to create and fly the shape and type of craft known to you as unidentified flying objects. Unfortunately for the social memory complex vibratory rate of your peoples, these devices are not intended for the service of mankind, but for potential destructive use. This further muddles the vibratory nexus of your social memory complex, causing a situation where neither those oriented towards serving others nor those oriented towards serving self can gain the energy/power which opens the gates to intelligent infinity for the social memory complex. This in turn causes the harvest to be small.

Questioner: Are these craft that are from our peoples from what we call planes that are not incarnate at this time? Where are they based?

Ra: I am Ra. These of which we spoke are of third density and are part of the so-called military complex of various of your peoples' societal divisions or structures.

The bases are varied. There are bases, as you would call them, undersea in your southern waters near the Bahamas as well as in your Pacific seas in various places close to your Chilean borders on the water. There are bases upon your moon, as you call this satellite, which are at this time being reworked. There are bases which move about your lands. There are bases, if you would call them that, in your skies. These are the bases of your peoples, very numerous and, as we have said, potentially destructive.

Questioner: Where do the people who operate these craft come from? Are they affiliated with any nation on Earth. What is their source?

Ra: These people come from the same place as you or I. They come from the Creator.

As you intend the question, in its shallower aspect, these people are those in your and other selves' governments responsible for what you would term national security.

Questioner: Am I to understand then that the United States has these craft in undersea bases?

Ra: I am Ra. You are correct.

Questioner: How did the United States learn the technology to build these craft?

Ra: I am Ra. There was a mind/body/spirit complex known to your people by the vibratory sound complex, Nikola. This entity departed the illusion and the papers containing the necessary understandings were taken by mind/body/spirit complexes serving your security of national divisional complex. Thus your people became privy to the basic technology. In the case of those mind/body/spirit complexes which you call Russians, the technology was given from one of the Confederation in an attempt, approximately twenty seven of your years ago, to share information and bring about peace among your peoples. The entities giving this information were in error, but we did many things at the end of this cycle in attempts to aid your harvest from which we learned the folly of certain types of aid. That is a contributing factor to our more cautious approach at this date, even as the need is power upon power greater, and your peoples' call is greater and greater.

Questioner: I'm puzzled by these craft which have undersea bases. Is this technology sufficient to overshadow all other armaments? Do we have the ability to just fly in these craft or are they just craft for transport? What is the basic mechanism of their power source? It's really hard to believe is what I'm saying.

Ra: I am Ra. The craft are perhaps misnamed in some instances. It would be more appropriate to consider them as weaponry. The energy used is that of the field of electromagnetic energy which polarizes the Earth sphere. The weaponry is of two basic kinds: that which is called by your peoples psychotronic and that which is called by your peoples particle beam. The amount of destruction which is contained in this technology is considerable and the weapons have been used in many cases to alter weather patterns and to enhance the vibratory change which engulfs your planet at this time.

Questioner: How have they been able to keep this a secret? Why aren't these craft in use for transport?

Ra: The governments of each of your societal division illusions desire to refrain from publicity so that the surprise may be retained in case of hostile action from what your peoples call enemies.

Questioner: How many of these craft does the United States have?

Ra: I am Ra. The United States has 573 at this time. They are in the process of adding to this number.

Questioner: What is the maximum speed of one of these craft?

Ra: I am Ra. The maximum speed of these craft is equal to the Earth energy squared. This field varies. The limit is approximately one-half the light speed, as you would call it. This is due to imperfections in design.

Questioner: Would this type of craft come close to solving many of the energy problems as far as transport goes?

Ra: I am Ra. The technology your peoples possess at this time is capable of resolving each and every limitation which plagues your social memory complex at this present nexus of experience. However, the concerns of some of your beings with distortions towards what you would call powerful energy cause these solutions to be withheld until the solutions are so needed that those with the distortion can then become further distorted in the direction of power.

Questioner: You also said that some of the landings at this time were of the Orion group. Why did the Orion group land here? What is their purpose?

Ra: I am Ra. Their purpose is conquest, unlike those of the Confederation who wait for the calling. The so-called Orion group calls itself to conquest.

Questioner: Specifically, what do they do when they land?

Ra: There are two types of landings. In the first, entities among your peoples are taken on their craft and programmed for future use. There are two or three levels of programming. First, the level that will be discovered by those who do research. Second, a triggering program. Third, a second and most deep triggering program crystallizing the entity thereby rendering it lifeless and useful as a kind of beacon. This is a form of landing.

The second form is that of landing beneath the Earth's crust which is entered from water. Again, in the general area of your South American and Caribbean areas and close to the so-called northern pole. The bases of these people are underground.

Questioner: The most startling information that you have given me, which I must admit that I'm having difficulty believing, is that the United States has 573 craft of the type which you described. How many people of United States designation are aware of these craft, including those who operate them?

Ra: I am Ra. The number of your peoples varies, for there are needs to communicate at this particular time/space nexus so that the number is expanding at this time. The approximate number is 1,500. It is only approximate for as your illusory time/space continuum moves from present to present at this nexus many are learning.

Questioner: Where are these craft constructed?

Ra: These craft are constructed one by one in two locations: in the desert or arid regions of your so-called New Mexico and in the desert or arid regions of your so-called Mexico, both installations being under the ground.

Questioner: Am I to believe that the United States actually has a manufacturing plant in Mexico?

Ra: I am Ra. I spoke thusly. May I, at this time, reiterate that this type of information is very shallow and of no particular consequence compared to the study of the Law of One. However, we carefully watch these developments in hopes that your peoples are able to be harvested in peace.

Questioner: I am totally aware that this line of questioning is of totally no consequence at all, but this particular information is so startling to me that it makes me question your validity on this. Up until this point I was in agreement with everything you had said. This is very startling to me. It just does not seem possible to me that this secret could have been kept for twenty-seven years, and that we are operating these craft. I apologize for my attitude, but I thought that I would be very honest. It is unbelievable to me that we would operate a plant in Mexico, outside of the United States, to build these craft. Maybe I'm mistaken. These craft are physical craft built by physical people? Could I go get in one and ride in one? Is that correct?

Ra: I am Ra. This is incorrect. You could not ride one. The United States, as you call your society divisional complex, creates these as a type of weapon.

Questioner: There are no occupants then? No pilot, shall I say?

Ra: I am Ra. This is correct.

Questioner: How are they controlled?

Ra: I am Ra. They are controlled by computer from a remote source of data.

Questioner: Why do we have a plant in Mexico?

Ra: I am Ra. The necessity is both for dryness of the ground and for a near total lack of population. Therefore, your so-called government and the so-called government of your neighboring geographical vicinity arranged for an underground installation. The government officials who agreed did not know the use to which their land would be put, but thought it a governmental research installation for use in what you would call bacteriological warfare.

Questioner: Is this the type of craft that Dan Frye was transported in?

Ra: I am Ra. The one known as Daniel was, in thought-form, transported by Confederation thought-form vehicular illusion in order to give this mind/body/spirit complex data so that we might see how this type of contact aided your people in the uncovering of the intelligent infinity behind the illusion of limits.

Questioner: The reason that I have questioned you so much and so carefully about the craft which you say the United States government operates is that if we include this in the book it will create numerous problems. It is something that I am considering leaving out of the book entirely, or I am going to have to question you in considerable detail about it. It's difficult to even question in this area, but I would like to ask a few more questions about it with the possible option of leaving it in the book. What is the diameter of the craft which the United States has?

Ra: I am Ra. I suggest that this be the last question for this session. We will speak as you deem fit in further sessions, asking you to be guided by your own discernment only.

The approximate diameter, given several model changes, is twenty-three of your feet, as you measure.

❧

L/L Research

L/L Research is a subsidiary of Rock Creek Research & Development Laboratories, Inc.

P.O. Box 5195
Louisville, KY 40255-0195

www.llresearch.org

Rock Creek is a non-profit corporation dedicated to discovering and sharing information which may aid in the spiritual evolution of humankind.

ABOUT THE CONTENTS OF THIS TRANSCRIPT: This telepathic channeling has been taken from transcriptions of the weekly study and meditation meetings of the Rock Creek Research & Development Laboratories and L/L Research. It is offered in the hope that it may be useful to you. As the Confederation entities always make a point of saying, please use your discrimination and judgment in assessing this material. If something rings true to you, fine. If something does not resonate, please leave it behind, for neither we nor those of the Confederation would wish to be a stumbling block for any.

© 2009 L/L Research

The Law of One, Book I, Session 9
January 27, 1981

Ra: I am Ra. I greet you in the love and the light of our infinite Creator. We communicate now.

Questioner: The healing exercises that you gave us are of such a nature that it is best to concentrate on a particular exercise at a certain time. I would like to ask what exercise that I should concentrate on tonight?

Ra: I am Ra. Again, to direct your judgment is an intrusion upon your space/time continuum distortion called future. To speak of past or present within our distortion/judgment limits is acceptable. To guide rather than teach/learn is not acceptable to our distortion in regards to teach/learning. We, instead, can suggest a process whereby each chooses the first of the exercises given in the order in which we gave them, which you, in your discernment, feel is not fully appreciated by your mind/body/spirit complex.

This is the proper choice, building from the foundation, making sure the ground is good for the building. We have assessed for you the intensity of this effort in terms of energy expended. You will take this in mind and be patient for we have not given a short or easy program of consciousness learn/teaching.

Questioner: The way that I understand the process of evolution is that our planetary population has a certain amount of time to progress. This is generally divided into three 25,000-year cycles. At the end of 75,000 years the planet progresses itself. What caused this situation to come about with the preciseness of the years in each cycle?

Ra: I am Ra. Visualize, if you will, the particular energy which, outward flowing and inward coagulating, formed the tiny realm of the creation governed by your Council of Saturn. Continue seeing the rhythm of this process. The living flow creates a rhythm which is as inevitable as one of your timepieces. Each of your planetary entities began the first cycle when the energy nexus was able in that environment to support such mind/body experiences. Thus, each of your planetary entities is on a different cyclical schedule as you might call it. The timing of these cycles is a measurement equal to a portion of intelligent energy.

This intelligent energy offers a type of clock. The cycles move as precisely as a clock strikes your hour. Thus, the gateway from intelligent energy to intelligent infinity opens regardless of circumstance on the striking of the hour.

Questioner: The original, first entities on this planet—what was their origin? Where were they before they were on this planet?

Ra: I am Ra. The first entities upon this planet were water, fire, air and earth.

Questioner: Where did the people who are like us who were the first ones here, where did they come from? From where did they evolve?

Ra: I am Ra. You speak of third-density experience. The first of those to come here were brought from another planet in your solar system called by you the Red Planet, Mars. This planet's environment became inhospitable to third-density beings. The first entities, therefore, were of this race, as you may call it, manipulated somewhat by those who were guardians at that time.

Questioner: What race is that, and how did they get from Mars to here?

Ra: I am Ra. The race is a combination of the mind/body/spirit complexes of those of your so-called Red Planet and a careful series of genetical adjustments made by the guardians of that time. These entities arrived, or were preserved, for the experience upon your sphere by a type of birthing which is non-reproductive, but consists of preparing genetic material for the incarnation of the mind/body/spirit complexes of those entities from the Red Planet.

Questioner: I assume from what you are saying that the guardians transferred the race here after the race had died from the physical as we know it on Mars. Is that correct?

Ra: I am Ra. This is correct.

Questioner: The guardians were obviously acting within an understanding of the Law of One in doing this. Can you explain the application of the Law of One in this process?

Ra: I am Ra. The Law of One was named by these guardians as the bringing of the wisdom of the guardians in contact with the entities from the Red Planet, thus melding the social memory complex of the guardian race and the Red Planet race. It, however, took an increasing amount of distortion into the application of the Law of One from the viewpoint of other guardians and it is from this beginning action that the quarantine of this planet was instituted, for it was felt that the free will of those of the Red Planet had been abridged.

Questioner: Were the entities of the Red Planet following the Law of One prior to leaving the Red Planet?

Ra: I am Ra. The entities of the Red Planet were attempting to learn the Laws of Love which form one of the primal distortions of the Law of One. However, the tendencies of these people towards bellicose actions caused such difficulties in the atmospheric environment of their planet that it became inhospitable for third-density experience before the end of its cycle. Thus, the Red Planet entities were unharvested and continued in your illusion to attempt to learn the Law of Love.

Questioner: How long ago did this transfer occur from the Red Planet to Earth?

Ra: I am Ra. In your time this transfer occurred approximately 75,000 years ago.

Questioner: 75,000 years ago?

Ra: I am Ra. This is approximately correct.

Questioner: Were there any entities of the form that I am now—two arms, two legs—on this planet before this transfer occurred?

Ra: I am Ra. There have been visitors to your sphere at various times for the last four million of your years, speaking approximately. These visitors do not affect the cycling of the planetary sphere. It was not third-density in its environment until the time previously mentioned.

Questioner: Then there were second-density entities here prior to approximately 75,000 years ago. What type of entities were these?

Ra: I am Ra. The second density is the density of the higher plant life and animal life which exists without the upward drive towards the infinite. These second-density beings are of an octave of consciousness just as you find various orientations of consciousness among the conscious entities of your vibration.

Questioner: Did any of these second-density entities have shapes like ours—two arms, two legs, head, and walk upright on two feet?

Ra: I am Ra. The two higher of the sub-vibrational levels of second-density beings had the configuration of the biped, as you mentioned. However, the erectile movement which you experience was not totally effected in these beings who were tending towards the leaning forward, barely leaving the quadrupedal position.

Questioner: Where did these beings come from? Were they a product of evolution as understood by our scientists? Were they evolved from the original material of the earth that you spoke of.

Ra: I am Ra. This is correct.

Questioner: Do these beings then evolve from second density to third density?

Ra: I am Ra. This is correct, although no guarantee can be made of the number of cycles it will take an entity to learn the lessons of consciousness of self which are the prerequisite for transition to third density.

Questioner: Is there any particular race of people on our planet now who were incarnated here from second density?

Ra: I am Ra. There are no second-density consciousness complexes here on your sphere at this time. However, there are two races which use the second-density form. One is the entities from the planetary sphere you call Maldek. These entities are working their understanding complexes through a series of what you would call karmic restitutions. They dwell within your deeper underground passageways and are known to you as "Bigfoot."

The other race is that being offered a dwelling in this density by guardians who wish to give the mind/body/spirit complexes of those who are of this density at this time appropriately engineered physical vehicles, as you would call these chemical complexes, in the event that there is what you call nuclear war.

Questioner: I didn't understand what these vehicles or beings were for that were appropriate in the event of nuclear war.

Ra: I am Ra. These are beings which exist as instinctual second-density beings which are being held in reserve to form what you would call a gene pool in case these body complexes are needed. These body complexes are greatly able to withstand the rigors of radiation which the body complexes you now inhabit could not do.

Questioner: Where are these body complexes located?

Ra: I am Ra. These body complexes of the second race dwell in uninhabited deep forest. There are many in various places over the surface of your planet.

Questioner: Are they Bigfoot-type creatures?

Ra: I am Ra. This is correct although we would not call these Bigfoot, as they are scarce and are very able to escape detection. The first race is less able to be aware of proximity of other mind/body/spirit complexes, but these beings are very able to escape due to their technological understandings before their incarnations here. These entities of the glowing eyes are those most familiar to your peoples.

Questioner: Then there are two different types of Bigfoot. Correct?

Ra: I am Ra. This will be the final question.

There are three types of Bigfoot, if you will accept that vibratory sound complex used for three such different races of mind/body/spirit complexes. The first two we have described.

The third is a thought-form.

Questioner: I would like to ask if there is anything that we can do to aid the instrument's comfort.

Ra: I am Ra. This instrument will require some adjustment of the tender portions of her body complex. The distortions are due to the energy center blockage you would call pineal.

I leave you in the love and the light of the one infinite Creator. Go forth, therefore, rejoicing in the power and the peace of the one Creator. Adonai.

L/L Research

L/L Research is a subsidiary of Rock Creek Research & Development Laboratories, Inc.

P.O. Box 5195
Louisville, KY 40255-0195

www.llresearch.org

Rock Creek is a non-profit corporation dedicated to discovering and sharing information which may aid in the spiritual evolution of humankind.

ABOUT THE CONTENTS OF THIS TRANSCRIPT: This telepathic channeling has been taken from transcriptions of the weekly study and meditation meetings of the Rock Creek Research & Development Laboratories and L/L Research. It is offered in the hope that it may be useful to you. As the Confederation entities always make a point of saying, please use your discrimination and judgment in assessing this material. If something rings true to you, fine. If something does not resonate, please leave it behind, for neither we nor those of the Confederation would wish to be a stumbling block for any.

© 2009 L/L Research

The Law of One, Book I, Session 10
January 27, 1981

Ra: I am Ra. I greet you in the love and light of the infinite Creator. I communicate now.

Questioner: I think that it would clarify things for us if we went back to the time just before the transfer of souls from Maldek to see how the Law of One operated with respect to this transfer and why this transfer was necessary. What happened to the people of Maldek that caused them to lose their planet? How long ago did this event occur?

Ra: I am Ra. The peoples of Maldek had a civilization somewhat similar to that of the societal complex known to you as Atlantis in that it gained much technological information and used it without care for the preservation of their sphere following to a majority extent the complex of thought, ideas, and actions which you may associate with your so-called negative polarity or the service to self. This was, however, for the most part, couched in a sincere belief/thought structure which seemed to the perception of the mind/body complexes of this sphere to be positive and of service to others. The devastation that wracked their biosphere and caused its disintegration resulted from what you call war.

The escalation went to the furthest extent of the technology this social complex had at its disposal in the space/time present of the then time. This time was approximately 705,000 of your years ago. The cycles had begun much, much earlier upon this sphere due to its relative ability to support the first-dimensional life forms at an earlier point in the space/time continuum of your solar system. These entities were so traumatized by this occurrence that they were in what you may call a social complex knot or tangle of fear. Some of your time passed. No one could reach them. No beings could aid them.

Approximately 600,000 of your years ago the then-existing members of the Confederation were able to deploy a social memory complex and untie the knot of fear. The entities were then able to recall that they were conscious. This awareness brought them to the point upon what you would call the lower astral planes where they could be nurtured until each mind/body/spirit complex was able to finally be healed of this trauma to the extent that each entity was able to examine the distortions it had experienced in the previous life/illusion complex.

After this experience of learn/teaching, the group decision was to place upon itself a type of what you may call karma alleviation. For this purpose they came into incarnation within your planetary sphere in what were not acceptable human forms. This then they have been experiencing until the distortions of destruction are replaced by distortions towards the desire for a less distorted vision of service to others. Since this was the conscious decision of the great majority of those beings in the Maldek experience, the transition to this planet began approximately 500,000 of your years ago and the type of body complex available at that time was used.

Questioner: Was the body complex available at that time what we refer to as the ape body?

Ra: I am Ra. That is correct.

Questioner: Have any of the Maldek entities transformed since then? Are they still second-density now or are some of them third-density?

Ra: I am Ra. The consciousness of these entities has always been third-density. The alleviation mechanism was designed by the placement of this consciousness in second-dimensional physical chemical complexes which are not able to be dextrous or manipulative to the extent which is appropriate to the working of the third-density distortions of the mind complex.

Questioner: Have any of the entities moved on now, made a graduation at the end of a cycle and made the transition from second-density bodies to third-density bodies?

A: I am Ra. Many of these entities were able to remove the accumulation of what you call karma, thus being able to accept a third-density cycle within a third-density body. Most of those beings so succeeding have incarnated elsewhere in the creation for the succeeding cycle in third density. As this planet reached third density some few of these entities became able to join the vibration of this sphere in third-density form. There remain a few who have not yet alleviated through the mind/body/spirit coordination of distortions the previous action taken by them. Therefore, they remain.

Questioner: Are these the Bigfoot that you spoke of?

Ra: I am Ra. These are one type of Bigfoot.

Questioner: Then our human race is formed of a few who originally came from Maldek and quite a few who came from Mars. Are there entities here from other places?

Ra: I am Ra. There are entities experiencing your time/space continuum who have originated from many, many places, as you would call them, in the creation, for when there is a cycle change, those who must repeat then find a planetary sphere appropriate for this repetition. It is somewhat unusual for a planetary mind/body/spirit complex to contain those from many, many various loci, but this explains much, for, you see, you are experiencing the third-dimension occurrence with a large number of those who must repeat the cycle. The orientation, thus, has been difficult to unify even with the aid of many of your teach/learners.

Questioner: When Maldek was destroyed, did all the people of Maldek have the fear problem or were some advanced enough to transfer to other planets?

Ra: I am Ra. In the occurrence of planetary dissolution none escaped, for this is an action which redounds to the social complex of the planetary complex itself. None escaped the knot or tangle.

Questioner: Is there any danger of this happening to Earth at this time?

Ra: I am Ra. We feel this evaluation of your planetary mind/body/spirit complexes' so-called future may be less than harmless. We say only the conditions of mind exist for such development of technology and such deployment. It is the distortion of our vision/understanding that the mind and spirit complexes of those of your people need orientation rather than the "toys" needing dismantlement, for are not all things that exist part of the Creator? Therefore, freely to choose is your own duty.

Questioner: When graduation occurs at the end of a cycle, and entities are moved from one planet to another, by what means do they go to a new planet?

Ra: I am Ra. In the scheme of the Creator, the first step of the mind/body/spirit/totality/beingness is to place its mind/body/spirit complex distortion in the proper place of love/light. This is done to ensure proper healing of the complex and eventual attunement with the totality/beingness complex. This takes a very variable length of your time/space. After this is accomplished the experience of the cycle is dissolved and filtered until only the distillation of distortions in its pure form remains. At this time, the harvested mind/body/spirit/totality/beingness evaluates the density needs of its beingness and chooses the more appropriate new environment for either a repetition of the cycle or a moving forward into the next cycle. This is the manner of the harvesting, guarded and watched over by many.

Questioner: When the entity is moved from one planet to the next, is he moved in thought or by a vehicle?

Ra: I am Ra. The mind/body/spirit/totality/beingness is one with the Creator. There is no time/space distortion.

Therefore, it is a matter of thinking the proper locus in the infinite array of time/spaces.

Questioner: While an entity is incarnate in this third density at this time he may either learn unconsciously without knowing what he is learning, or he may learn after he is consciously aware that he is learning in the ways of the Law of One. By the second way of learning consciously, it is possible for the entity to greatly accelerate his growth. Is this correct?

Ra: I am Ra. This is correct.

Questioner: Then although many entities are not consciously aware of it, what they really desire is to accelerate their growth, and it is their job to discover this while they are incarnate. Is it correct that they can accelerate their growth much more while in the third density than in between incarnations of this density?

Ra: I am Ra. This is correct. We shall attempt to speak upon this concept.

The Law of One has as one of its primal distortions the free will distortion, thus each entity is free to accept, reject, or ignore the mind/body/spirit complexes about it and ignore the creation itself. There are many among your social memory complex distortion who, at this time/space, engage daily, as you would put it, in the working upon the Law of One in one of its primal distortions; that is, the ways of love. However, if this same entity, being biased from the depths of its mind/body/spirit complex towards love/light, were then to accept the responsibility for each moment of the time/space accumulation of present moments available to it, such an entity can empower its progress in much the same way as we described the empowering of the call of your social complex distortion to the Confederation.

Questioner: Could you state this in a little different way … how you empower this call?

Ra: I am Ra. We understand you to speak now of our previous information. The call begins with one. This call is equal to infinity and is not, as you would say, counted. It is the cornerstone. The second call is added. The third call empowers or doubles the second, and so forth, each additional calling doubling or granting power to all the preceding calls. Thus, the call of many of your peoples is many, many-powered and overwhelmingly heard to the infinite reaches of the One Creation.

Questioner: For the general development of the reader of this book, could you state some of the practices or exercises to perform to produce an acceleration toward the Law of One?

Ra: I am Ra.

Exercise One. This is the most nearly centered and useable within your illusion complex. The moment contains love. That is the lesson/goal of this illusion or density. The exercise is to consciously see that love in awareness and understanding distortions. The first attempt is the cornerstone. Upon this choosing rests the remainder of the life-experience of an entity. The second seeking of love within the moment begins the addition. The third seeking empowers the second, the fourth powering or doubling the third. As with the previous type of empowerment, there will be some loss of power due to flaws within the seeking in the distortion of insincerity. However, the conscious statement of self to self of the desire to seek love is so central an act of will that, as before, the loss of power due to this friction is inconsequential.

Exercise Two. The universe is one being. When a mind/body/spirit complex views another mind/body/spirit complex, see the Creator. This is an helpful exercise.

Exercise Three. Gaze within a mirror. See the Creator.

Exercise Four. Gaze at the creation which lies about the mind/body/spirit complex of each entity. See the Creator.

The foundation or prerequisite of these exercises is a predilection towards what may be called meditation, contemplation, or prayer. With this attitude, these exercises can be processed. Without it, the data will not sink down into the roots of the tree of mind, thus enabling and ennobling the body and touching the spirit.

Questioner: I was wondering about the advent of the civilizations of Atlantis and Lemuria, when these civilizations occurred, and where did they come from?

Ra: I am Ra. This is the last question of this working. The civilizations of Atlantis and Lemuria were not one but two. Let us look first at the Mu entities.

They were beings of a somewhat primitive nature, but those who had very advanced spiritual distortions. The civilization was part of this cycle, experienced early within the cycle at a time of approximately 53,000 of your years ago. It was an helpful and harmless place which was washed beneath the ocean during a readjustment of your sphere's tectonic plates through no action of their own. They sent out those who survived and reached many places in what you call Russia, North America, and South America. The Indians of whom you come to feel some sympathy in your social complex distortions are the descendants of these entities. Like the other incarnates of this cycle, they came from elsewhere. However, these particular entities were largely from a second-density planet which had some difficulty, due to the age of its sun, in achieving third-density life conditions. This planet was from the galaxy Deneb.

The Atlantean race was a very conglomerate social complex which began to form approximately 31,000 years in the past of your space/time continuum illusion. It was a slow growing and very agrarian one until approximately 15,000 of your years ago. It reached quickly a high technological understanding which caused it to be able to use intelligent infinity in an informative manner. We may add that they used intelligent energy as well, manipulating greatly the natural influxes of the indigo or pineal ray from divine or infinite energy. Thus, they were able to create life forms. This they began to do instead of healing and perfecting their own mind/body/spirit complexes, turning their distortions towards what you may call negative.

Approximately 11,000 of your years ago, the first of the, what you call, wars, caused approximately forty percent of this population to leave the density by means of disintegration of the body. The second and most devastating of the conflicts occurred approximately 10,821 years in the past according to your illusion. This created an earth-changing configuration and the large part of Atlantis was no more, having been inundated. Three of the positively-oriented of the Atlantean groups left this geographical locus before that devastation, placing themselves in the mountain areas of what you call Tibet, what you call Peru, and what you call Turkey.

Do you have any brief questions before we close this meeting?

Questioner: Only one, other than what we can do to make the instrument more comfortable. I would like to have your definition of galaxy, the word "galaxy" as you have used it.

Ra: I am Ra. We use the term known to your people by the sound vibration "galaxy." We accept that some galaxies contain one system of planetary and solar groups. Others contain several. However, the importance of the locus in infinite time/space dimensionality is so little that we accept the distortion implicit in such an ambiguous term.

Questioner: Then the nine planets and sun which we have here in our system, would you refer to that as a galaxy?

Ra: I am Ra. We would not.

Questioner: How many stars would be—approximately—in a galaxy?

Ra: I am Ra. It depends upon the galactic system. Your own, as you know, contains many, many, millions of planetary entities and star bodies.

Questioner: I was just trying to get to the definition that you were using for galaxy. You mentioned a couple of times the term galaxy in reference to what we call a planetary system and it was causing some confusion. Is there any way that we can make the instrument more comfortable?

Ra: I am Ra. This instrument could be made somewhat more comfortable if more support were given the body complex. Other than this, we can only repeat the request to carefully align the symbols used to facilitate this instrument's balance. Our contact is narrow-banded and thus the influx brought in with us must be precise.

I am Ra. I leave you in the love and the light of the one infinite Creator. Go forth, therefore, rejoicing in the power and peace of the one Creator. Adonai. ✦

The Law of One, Book V, Session 9, Fragment 4
January 27, 1981

Jim: None of us was ever greatly interested in previous incarnational experiences. Again, it's easy to lose the focus on the present moment's opportunities for growth if one becomes overly interested in one's lives before this one. The one query of this nature that we did ask of Ra elicited an answer that seemed to support our lack of interest in past lives.

Carla: I do personally believe that we incarnate many times, and that we fashion, through these cycles of manifestation, complex and meaningful relationships that root deeply within our beings. When Don and I met, he has said he knew for certain that we would be together. Since what immediately thereafter ensued for me was a four-year marriage to a fellow who wished not to be married, I once braced him for not having told me this home truth right then in 1962, and saved me that difficult four years. "What? And have you miss all that good catalyst?" he said.

Both Donald and Jim had a loving and generous regard of me that is amazing unless one introduces the concept of previous connections. I have no doubt that we have served together before, in other lives and other times. An interesting bit of possible past history was expressed years ago to Jim in a psychic reading: it was suggested that in the American great plains frontier of the nineteenth century, Don and Jim were brothers living together as farmers. I was Jim's child, Don's nephew, and I lived only to the age of five, being sickly from birth. This was suggested as being preparation for their taking care of me in this life, as I dealt with disability, limitation and especially psychic greeting during the time of the Ra contact. It rings true at some level with me. However, I also feel that we do not need to know anything of our past associations in order to learn and serve together at this present moment. We have all we need to meet the present moment. The rest is just details.

Session 9, January 27, 1981

Questioner: Is it possible for you to tell us anything about our past experiences, our past incarnations before this incarnation?

Ra: I am Ra. It is possible. However, such information as this is carefully guarded by your mind/body/spirit being totality so that your present space/time experiences will be undiluted.

Let us scan for harmless material for your beingness. I am, in the distortion of desire for your freedom from preconception, able to speak only generally. There have been several times when this group worked and dwelt together. The relationships varied. There is balanced karma, as you call it; each thus teacher of each. The work has involved healing, understanding the uses of the earth energy, and work in aid of civilizations which called just as your sphere has done and we have come. This ends the material which we consider harmless. ☙

Intensive Meditation
January 28, 1981

(Unknown channeling

[I am Hatonn,] and I greet you in the light and in the love of the one great infinite Creator, Whose name is written in the heavens and Whose being encompasses all that there is. I greet you, my friends, against this backdrop of unimaginable immensity and scale. I am the voice of the Creator and you the creation. I realize, my friends, that it is extremely difficult to imagine that which you seem to be as being in analogy the immense infinity of creation. But you are all that there is. Your culture has offered you silence which pretends to know yet does not question. And scientists look at the boundlessness of the universe and upon remarking at its immensity proceed immediately back to their studies, starting petty arguments defining and redefining unknowns.

We of the Confederation of Planets in the Service of the Infinite Creator do not ask you to believe. We ask you to question. We do not pretend to have *the* answers although we do have information to share. We are not those who know, we are those who seek. And when we speak to you we ask you to join us in that seeking, but not against the backdrop of those things which your people wish to limit themselves by defining as the limits for seeking. We ask you to seek against the backdrop that to us is meaningful. That is the backdrop of the infinite creation, the one Creator. It is our understanding that this one Creator is the very core of each and every thing that exists, and that each ear that hears these words is part of some of the Creator. We are one being. This is our simple explanation *(inaudible)*. It is our further understanding that this one being, this one point *(inaudible)* is love. We do not ask you to believe this, we ask you to seek. As we join in your meditations, as we join in this paramount of all ways of seeking, we give thanks both for the opportunity to speak through this instrument and we thank you for both of you and would at this time transfer this contact to another instrument. I am Hatonn.

(Inaudible)

I am trying to exercise the instrument at this time for it is a good thing to, shall we say, stay in practice. One wishes to retain the techniques necessary for reception. We will continue to offer conditioning to the one known as D while we transfer contact to the one known as S1. I am Hatonn.

(S1 channeling

I am Hatonn. And I am with your instrument. It is indeed a pleasure to greet you, my friends, through this instrument once more. We of Hatonn are indeed honored to be able to speak through those amongst your people who offer themselves in service through what you call channeling. We are always happy to be of service to those who would request our presence during meditation. We are available at any time to those who request. We do so. We of Hatonn are greatly pleased with the progress of this instrument and wish to assure her that she is correctly receiving those words which we are sending. We have not been able to speak through this instrument for some time, though we have been with her and given her our conditioning vibrations during her meditations. We are always happy when we are able to serve in this manner. We hope to be able to experience the sharing of love and light with this group in the near future as we are quite happy when we feel the closeness which we share with you today. We would at this time transfer this contact to another instrument. I am Hatonn.

(Unknown channeling

I am Hatonn, and I am again with this instrument. We are sorry that we have not made contact with the one known as D but appreciate each person's free will and assure this instrument that we are available at any time she may request our services. We leave you, my friends, in the love and the light of the infinite Creator. I am Hatonn. Adonai.

(Unknown channeling

I am Latwii, and am with this instrument. I greet you in the love and in the light of our infinite Creator. It is really great to be with you and to be speaking through this instrument of whom we are very fond. We do not get a chance to blend our vibrations with this instrument these days as we are handling the questions and answers and she is abstaining from same. We would like to work with the new instrument to acquaint this instrument further with our particular vibratory pattern, and will attempt to say a few words through her. I am Latwii.

(S2 channeling

I am Latwii. We are here with this instrument. We were able to contact this instrument without knocking her on the floor. She is happy about that. It is a pleasure to speak through this instrument again for we rarely have the opportunity to do so. We would like to assure her that we are indeed here. She is somewhat skeptical of our presence. We, nevertheless, are pleased to be here. We are going to leave this instrument now so that we may speak through another. I am Latwii.

(Unknown channeling

I am Latwii. And greet you all once again in love and light. We are very pleased to have made our contact with the one known as S2 and to have spoken the words through her that it was our pleasure to speak.

May we at this time ask if there are any questions which we might attempt to respond to?

Questioner: Yes, I have a question, Latwii. Is meditation the best way to get in contact with the higher self and does the higher self express itself through meditation?

I am Latwii, and am aware of your question, my sister. First of all, may we say that meditation is the most accessible way to most of the people of your planet to obtain contact with their inner being, their higher self, and the many guides which wait upon the seeking of the seeker. That it is the best way cannot be said for certain for many ways there are for those known as the *(inaudible)* to make such contact. But many steps of preparation are necessary for the utilization of these other techniques. So, we feel we might be most accurate in our response by suggesting that meditation is the most accessible means at this time for obtaining a contact with your deeper, or shall we say, higher levels of being including your higher self.

In response to the second portion of your query may we say that intuition is one of the many means utilized by the higher self and the other entities who form the inner resources available to each seeker through which this contact might be expressed. Intuition, dreams, meditation, hunches or insights of a sudden appearance are techniques, situations utilized to make such contact with entities of your planet who for the most part are unable to receive a contact from the, shall we say, inner planes by any conscious means.

May we answer you further, my sister?

Questioner: Yes. You spoke of other steps for making contact with the higher self or other beings besides meditation. Can you give any more information on this at this point?

I am Latwii, and am aware of your question, my sister, and may respond only in general by suggesting that long preparation of the entity who seeks such contact by means which utilize deep meditative states in the what has come to be known to this group as the balancing process, is necessary for the seeker upon the path of what is called by your peoples the white magical ritual, to prepare the self for this type of seeking of contact with the higher self. These techniques have been outlined to a basic degree in the text which this group has had the honor in the preparing that is known to you as the Law of One.

May we answer you further, my sister?

Questioner: No, thank you.

We are most grateful to you as well. Is there another question at this time?

(Pause)

I am Latwii. We are most grateful for this opportunity to speak to this group. We assure each that we shall at any time in the future be available for the conditioning contact. Simply request our presence and we shall be most honored to join you in your meditations. We leave you now in the love and in the light of the one infinite Creator. I am known to you as Latwii. Adonai, my friends. ☙

The Law of One, Book I, Session 11
January 28, 1981

Ra: I am Ra. I greet you in the love and the light of the infinite Creator. I communicate now.

Questioner: Should we include the ritual that you have suggested that we use to call you in the book that will result from these sessions?

Ra: I am Ra. This matter is of small importance for our suggestion was made for the purpose of establishing contact through this instrument with this group.

Questioner: Is it of any assistance to the instrument to have *(name)* and *(name)* present during these sessions? Does the number in the group make any difference in these sessions?

Ra: I am Ra. The most important of the entities are the questioner and the vibratory sound complex, *(name)*. The two entities additional aid the instrument's comfort by energizing the instrument with their abilities to share the physical energy complex which is a portion of your love vibration.

Questioner: You said yesterday that Maldek was destroyed due to warfare. If Maldek hadn't destroyed itself due to warfare would it have become a planet that evolved in self-service and would the entities involved have increased in density, and gone on to say the fourth density in the negative sense or the sense of self-service?

Ra: I am Ra. The planetary social memory complex, Maldek, had in common with your own sphere the situation of a mixture of energy direction. Thus it, though unknown, would most probably have been a mixed harvest—a few moving to fourth density, a few moving towards fourth density in service to self, the great majority repeating third density. This is approximate due to the fact that parallel possibility/probability vortices cease when action occurs and new probability/possibility vortices are begun.

Questioner: Is there a planet opposite our sun, in relation to us, that we do not know about?

Ra: I am Ra. There is a sphere in the area opposite your sun of a very, very cold nature, but large enough to skew certain statistical figures. This sphere should not properly be called a planet as it is locked in first density.

Questioner: You say that entities from Maldek might go to fourth density negative. Are there people who go out of our present third density to places in the universe and serve, which are fourth-density self-service negative type of planets?

Ra: I am Ra. Your question is unclear. Please restate.

Questioner: As our cycle ends and graduation occurs, is it possible for anyone to go from our third density to a fourth-density planet that is of a self-service or negative type?

Ra: I am Ra. We grasp now the specificity of your query. In this harvest the probability/possibility vortex is an harvest, though small, of this type. That is correct.

Questioner: Can you tell us what happened to Adolf (Hitler)?

Ra: I am Ra. The mind/body/spirit complex known as Adolf is at this time in an healing process in the middle astral planes of your spherical force field. This entity was greatly confused and, although aware of the circumstance of change in vibratory level associated with the cessation of the chemical body complex, nevertheless, needed a great deal of care.

Questioner: Is there anyone in our history who is commonly known who went to a fourth-density self-service or negative type of planet or any who will go there?

Ra: I am Ra. The number of entities thus harvested is small. However, a few have penetrated the eighth level which is only available from the opening up of the seventh through the sixth. Penetration into the eighth or intelligent infinity level allows a mind/body/spirit complex to be harvested if it wishes at any time/space during the cycle.

Questioner: Are any of these people known in the history of our planet by name?

Ra: I am Ra. We will mention a few. The one known as Taras Bulba, the one known as Genghis Khan, the one known as Rasputin.

Questioner: How did they accomplish this? What was necessary for them to accomplish this?

Ra: I am Ra. All of the aforementioned entities were aware, through memory, of Atlantean understandings having to do with the use of the various centers of mind/body/spirit complex energy influx in attaining the gateway to intelligent infinity.

Questioner: Did this enable them to do what we refer to as magic? Could they do paranormal things while they were incarnate?

Ra: I am Ra. This is correct. The first two entities mentioned made little use of these abilities consciously. However, they were bent single-mindedly upon service to self, sparing no efforts in personal discipline to double, re-double and so empower this gateway. The third was a conscious adept and also spared no effort in the pursuit of service to self.

Questioner: Where are these three entities now?

Ra: I am Ra. These entities are in the dimension known to you as fourth. Therefore the space/time continua are not compatible. An approximation of the space/time locus of each would net no actual understanding. Each chose a fourth-density planet which was dedicated to the pursuit of the understanding of the Law of One through service to self, one in what you know as the Orion group, one in what you know as Cassiopeia, one in what you know as Southern Cross; however, these loci are not satisfactory. We do not have vocabulary for the geometric calculations necessary for transfer of this understanding to you.

Questioner: Who went to the Orion group?

Ra: I am Ra. The one known as Genghis Khan.

Questioner: What does he presently do there? What is his job or occupation?

Ra: I am Ra. This entity serves the Creator in its own way.

Questioner: Is it impossible for you to tell us precisely how he does this service?

Ra: I am Ra. It is possible for us to speak to this query. However, we use any chance we may have to reiterate the basic understanding/learning that all beings serve the Creator.

The one you speak of as Genghis Khan, at present, is incarnate in a physical light body which has the work of disseminating material of thought control to those who are what you may call crusaders. He is, as you would term this entity, a shipping clerk.

Questioner: What do the crusaders do?

Ra: I am Ra. The crusaders move in their chariots to conquer planetary mind/body/spirit social complexes before they reach the stage of achieving social memory.

Questioner: At what stage does a planet achieve social memory?

Ra: I am Ra. A mind/body/spirit social complex becomes a social memory complex when its entire group of entities are of one orientation or seeking. The group memory lost to the individuals in the roots of the tree of mind then becomes known to the social complex, thus creating a social memory complex. The advantages of this complex are the relative lack of distortion in understanding the social beingness and the relative lack of distortion in pursuing the direction of seeking, for all understanding/distortions are available to the entities of the society.

Questioner: Then we have crusaders from Orion coming to this planet for mind control purposes. How do they do this?

Ra: I am Ra. As all, they follow the Law of One observing free will. Contact is made with those who call. Those then upon the planetary sphere act much as do you to disseminate the attitudes and philosophy of their particular understanding of the Law of One which is service to self. These become the elite. Through these, the attempt begins to create a condition whereby the remainder of the planetary entities are enslaved by their free will.

Questioner: Can you name any names that may be known on the planet that are recipients of the crusaders' efforts?

Ra: I am Ra. I am desirous of being in nonviolation of the free will distortion. To name those involved in the future of your space/time is to infringe; thus, we withhold this information. We request your contemplation of the fruits of the actions of those entities whom you may observe enjoying the distortion towards power. In this way you may discern for yourself this information. We shall not interfere with the, shall we say, planetary game. It is not central to the harvest.

Questioner: How do the crusaders pass on their concepts to the individuals on Earth?

Ra: I am Ra. There are two main ways, just as there are two main ways of, shall we say, polarizing towards service to others. There are those mind/body/spirit complexes upon your plane who do exercises and perform disciplines in order to seek contact with sources of information and power leading to the opening of the gate to intelligent infinity. There are others whose vibratory complex is such that this gateway is opened and contact with total service to self with its primal distortion of manipulation of others is then afforded with little or no difficulty, no training, and no control.

Questioner: What type of information is passed on from the crusaders to these people?

Ra: I am Ra. The Orion group passes on information concerning the Law of One with the orientation of service to self. The information can become technical just as some in the Confederation, in attempts to aid this planet in service to others, have provided what you would call technical information. The technology provided by this group is in the form of various means of control or manipulation of others to serve the self.

Questioner: Do you mean to say then that some scientists receive technical information, shall we say, telepathically that comes out then as useable gadgetry?

Ra: I am Ra. That is correct. However, very positively, as you would call this distortion, oriented scientists have received information intended to unlock peaceful means of progress which redounded unto the last echoes of potential destruction due to further reception of other scientists of a negative orientation/distortion.

Questioner: Is this how we learned of nuclear energy? Was it mixed with both positive and negative orientation?

Ra: I am Ra. That is correct. The entities responsible for the gathering of the scientists were of a mixed orientation. The scientists were overwhelmingly positive in their orientation. The scientists who followed their work were of mixed orientation including one extremely negative entity, as you would term it.

Questioner: Is this extremely negative entity still incarnate on Earth?

Ra: I am Ra. This is correct.

Questioner: Then I would assume that you can't name him. So I will ask you where Nikola Tesla got his information?

Ra: I am Ra. The one known as Nikola received information from Confederation sources desirous of aiding this extremely, shall we say, angelically positive entity in bettering the existence of its fellow mind/body/spirit complexes. It is unfortunate, shall we say, that like many Wanderers the vibratory distortions of third-density illusion caused this entity to become extremely distorted in its perceptions of its fellow mind/body/spirit complexes so that its mission was hindered and in the result, perverted from its purposes.

Questioner: How was Tesla's work supposed to benefit man on Earth, and what were its purposes?

Ra: I am Ra. The most desired purpose of the mind/body/spirit complex, Nikola, was the freeing of all planetary entities from the darkness. Thus, it attempted to give to the planet the infinite energy of the planetary sphere for use in lighting and power.

Questioner: By freeing the planetary entities from darkness, precisely what do you mean?

Ra: I am Ra. *(Most of the following answer was lost due to tape recorder malfunction. The core of the response was as follows.)* We spoke of freeing people from darkness in a literal sense.

Questioner: Would this freeing from darkness be commensurate with the Law of One or does this have any real product?

Ra: I am Ra. The product of such a freeing would create two experiences.

Firstly, the experience of no need to find the necessary emolument for payment, in your money, for energy.

Secondly, the leisure afforded, thereby exemplifying the possibility and enhancing the probability of the freedom to then search the self, the beginning of seeking the Law of One.

Few there are working physically from daybreak to darkness, as you name them, upon your plane who can contemplate the Law of One in a conscious fashion.

Questioner: What about the Industrial Revolution in general. Was this planned in any way?

Ra: I am Ra. This will be the final question of this session.

That is correct. Wanderers incarnated in several waves, as you may call them, in order to bring into existence the gradual freeing from the demands of the diurnal cycles and lack of freedom of leisure.

Questioner: That was the last question, so I will do as usual and ask if there is anything that we can do to make the instrument more comfortable?

Ra: I am Ra. You are doing well. The most important thing is to carefully align the symbols. The adjustment made this particular time/space present will aid this instrument's physical complex in the distortion towards comfort.

May we ask if you have any short questions which we may resolve before closing the session?

Questioner: I don't know if this is a short question or not, so we can save it till next time, but my question is, why do the crusaders from Orion do this? What is their ultimate objective? This is probably too long to answer.

Ra: I am Ra. This is not too long to answer. To serve the self is to serve all. The service of the self, when seen in this perspective, requires an ever-expanding use of the energies of others for manipulation to the benefit of the self with distortion towards power.

If there are further queries to further explicate this subject we shall be with you again.

Questioner: There was one thing that I forgot. Is it possible to have another session later on today?

Ra: I am Ra. It is well.

Questioner: Thank you.

Ra: I am Ra. I leave you in the love and the light of the one infinite Creator. Go forth, then, rejoicing in the power and the peace of the one Creator. Adonai. ♣

The Law of One, Book I, Session 12
January 28, 1981

Ra: I am Ra. I greet you in the love and the light of the infinite Creator. I communicate now.

Questioner: In the last session you mentioned that the Orion crusaders came here in chariots. Could you describe the chariots?

Ra: I am Ra. The term chariot is a term used in warfare among your peoples. That is its significance. The shape of the Orion craft is one of the following: firstly, the elongated, ovoid shape which is of a darker nature than silver but which has a metallic appearance if seen in the light. In the absence of light, it appears to be red or fiery in some manner.

Other craft include disc-shaped objects of a small nature approximately twelve feet in your measurement in diameter, the box-like shape approximately forty feet to a side in your measurement. Other craft can take on a desired shape through the use of thought control mechanisms. There are various civilization complexes which work within this group. Some are more able to use intelligent infinity than others. The information is very seldom shared; therefore, the chariots vary greatly in shape and appearance.

Questioner: Is there any effort on the part of the Confederation to stop the Orion chariots from arriving here?

Ra: I am Ra. Every effort is made to quarantine this planet. However, the network of guardians, much like any other pattern of patrols on whatever level, does not hinder each and every entity from penetrating quarantine, for if request is made in light/love, the Law of One will be met with acquiescence. If the request is not made, due to the slipping through the net, then there is penetration of this net.

Questioner: Who makes this request?

Ra: I am Ra. Your query is unclear. Please restate.

Questioner: I don't understand how the Confederation stops the Orion chariots from coming through the quarantine?

Ra: I am Ra. There is contact at the level of light-form or lightbody-being depending upon the vibratory level of the guardian. These guardians sweep reaches of your Earth's energy fields to be aware of any entities approaching. An entity which is approaching is hailed in the name of the one Creator. Any entity thus hailed is bathed in love/light and will of free will obey the quarantine due to the power of the Law of One.

Questioner: What would happen to the entity if he did not obey the quarantine after being hailed?

Ra: I am Ra. To not obey quarantine after being hailed on the level of which we speak would be equivalent to your not stopping upon walking into a solid brick wall.

Questioner: What would happen to the entity if he did this? What would happen to his chariot?

Ra: I am Ra. The Creator is one being. The vibratory level of those able to breach the quarantine boundaries is such that upon seeing the love/light net it is impossible to break this Law. Therefore, nothing happens. No attempt is made. There is no confrontation. The only beings who are able to penetrate the quarantine are those who discover windows or distortions in the space/time continua surrounding your planet's energy fields. Through these windows they come. These windows are rare and unpredictable.

Questioner: Does this account for what we call "UFO Flaps" where a large number of UFOs show up like in 1973?

Ra: I am Ra. This is correct.

Questioner: Are most of the UFOs which are seen in our skies from the Orion group?

Ra: I am Ra. Many of those seen in your skies are of the Orion group. They send out messages. Some are received by those who are oriented toward service to others. These messages then are altered to be acceptable to those entities while warning of difficulties ahead. This is the most that self-serving entities can do when faced with those whose wish is to serve others. The contacts which the group finds most helpful to their cause are those contacts made with entities whose orientation is towards service to self. There are many thought-form entities in your skies which are of a positive nature and are the projections of the Confederation.

Questioner: You mentioned that the Orion crusaders, when they get through the net, give both technical and non-technical information. I think I know what you mean by technical information, but what type of non-technical information do they give? And am I right in assuming that this is done by telepathic contact?

Ra: I am Ra. This is correct. Through telepathy the philosophy of the Law of One with the distortion of service to self is promulgated. In advanced groups there are rituals and exercises given and these have been written down just as the service-to-others oriented entities have written down the promulgated philosophy of their teachers. The philosophy concerns the service of manipulating others that they may experience service towards the other self, thus through this experience becoming able to appreciate service to self. These entities would become oriented towards service to self and in turn manipulate yet others so that they in turn might experience the service towards the other self.

Questioner: Would this be the origin of what we call black magic?

Ra: I am Ra. This is correct in one sense, incorrect in another. The Orion group has aided the so-called negatively oriented among your mind/body/spirit complexes. These same entities would be concerning themselves with service to self in any case and there are many upon your so-called inner planes which are negatively oriented and thus available as inner teachers or guides and so-called possessors of certain souls who seek this distortion of service to self.

Questioner: Is it possible for an entity here on Earth to be so confused as to call both the Confederation and the Orion group in an alternating way, first one, then the other, and then back to the first again?

Ra: I am Ra. It is entirely possible for the untuned channel, as you call that service, to receive both positive and negative communications. If the entity at the base of its confusion is oriented toward service to others, the entity will begin to receive messages of doom. If the entity at the base of the complex of beingness is oriented towards service to self, the crusaders, who in this case, do not find it necessary to lie, will simply begin to give the philosophy they are here to give. Many of your so-called contacts among your people have been confused and self-destructive because the channels were oriented towards service to others but, in the desire for proof, were open to the lying information of the crusaders who then were able to neutralize the effectiveness of the channel.

Questioner: Are most of these crusaders fourth-density?

Ra: I am Ra. There is a majority of fourth-density. That is correct.

Questioner: Is an entity in the fourth density normally invisible to us?

Ra: I am Ra. The use of the word "normal" is one which befuddles the meaning of the question. Let us rephrase for clarity. The fourth density is, by choice, not visible to third density. It is possible for fourth density to be visible. However, it is not the choice of the fourth-density entity to be visible due to the necessity for concentration upon a rather difficult vibrational complex which is the third density you experience.

Questioner: Are there any Confederation or Orion entities living upon the Earth and operating visibly among us in our society at this time?

Ra: I am Ra. There are no entities of either group walking among you at this time. However, the crusaders of Orion use two types of entities to do their bidding, shall we say. The first type is the thought-form; the second, a kind of robot.

Questioner: Could you describe the robot?

Ra: I am Ra. The robot may look like any other being. It is a construct.

Questioner: Is the robot what is normally called the "Men in Black"?

Ra: I am Ra. This is incorrect.

Questioner: Who are the Men in Black?

Ra: I am Ra. The Men in Black are a thought-form type of entity which have some beingness to their make-up. They have certain physical characteristics given them. However, their true vibrational nature is without third-density vibrational characteristics and, therefore, they are able to materialize and dematerialize when necessary.

Questioner: Are all of these Men in Black then used by the Orion crusaders?

Ra: I am Ra. This is correct.

Questioner: You spoke of Wanderers. Who are Wanderers? Where do they come from?

Ra: I am Ra. Imagine, if you will, the sands of your shores. As countless as the grains of sand are the sources of intelligent infinity. When a social memory complex has achieved its complete understanding of its desire, it may conclude that its desire is service to others with the distortion towards reaching their hand, figuratively, to any entities who call for aid. These entities whom you may call the Brothers and Sisters of Sorrow move toward this calling of sorrow. These entities are from all reaches of the infinite creation and are bound together by the desire to serve in this distortion.

Questioner: How many of them are incarnate on Earth now?

Ra: I am Ra. The number is approximate due to an heavy influx of those birthed at this time due to an intensive need to lighten the planetary vibration and thus aid in harvest. The number approaches sixty-five million.

Questioner: Are most of these from the fourth density? Or what density do they come from?

Ra: I am Ra. Few there are of fourth density. The largest number of Wanderers, as you call them, are of the sixth density. The desire to serve must be distorted towards a great deal of purity of mind and what you may call foolhardiness or bravery, depending upon your distortion complex judgment. The challenge/danger of the Wanderer is that it will forget its mission, become karmically involved, and thus be swept into the maelstrom of which it had incarnated to avert the destruction.

Questioner: What could one of these entities do to become karmically involved? Could you give an example of that?

Ra: I am Ra. An entity which acts in a consciously unloving manner in action with other beings can become karmically involved.

Questioner: Do many of these Wanderers have physical ailments in this third-density situation?

Ra: I am Ra. Due to the extreme variance between the vibratory distortions of third density and those of the more dense densities, if you will, Wanderers have as a general rule some form of handicap, difficulty, or feeling of alienation which is severe. The most common of these difficulties are alienation, the reaction against the planetary vibration by personality disorders, as you would call them, and body complex ailments indicating difficulty in adjustment to the planetary vibrations such as allergies, as you would call them.

Questioner: Thank you. Is there anything that we can do to make the instrument more comfortable?

Ra: I am Ra. We ask you to realign the object upon which the symbols sit. It is not a significant distortion for only one session, but you will find upon measuring the entire assemblage that the resting place is 1.4° from the correct alignment, the resting place an additional .5° away from proper orientation. Do not concern yourselves with this in the space/time nexus present, but do not allow these distortions to remain over a long period or the contact will be gradually impaired.

I am Ra. I leave you in the love and in the light of the one infinite Creator. Go forth rejoicing in the power and the peace of the one Creator. Adonai.

The Law of One, Book V, Session 12, Fragment 5
January 28, 1981

Jim: In the first paragraph of the next section one can see how easy it is for even the most serious of seekers occasionally to lose the proper attitude for finding the heart of the evolutionary process. Properly attuning one's being for efficient seeking has far less to do with what one does than with how one does it and how one balances it or seats it within one's being with meditation and contemplation. Without the balance of the meditative attitude the mind tends to become distracted by the mundane repetition of events, and one's lessons tend to orbit the periphery of one's being without becoming seated in the center of the being, there to provide a deeper grasp of the nature of this illusion and a sense of how to navigate one's self through it in a more harmonious fashion. We also see in Ra's next response that it is imperative that all such navigational movements of one's being be a product of one's free will choices, never to be abridged by any other being. That point is echoed again in Ra's response to Don's query about the metaphysical implications of attempting to lock an Man In Black in one's closet, an opportunity that we never had, incidentally!

This is another good example of a line of questioning veering off into transient and unimportant information. Note how Ra ends Session 12 in Book I, also titled *The Ra Material*, with hints that the "correct alignment" and "proper orientation" of the Bible, candle, censer and water are somewhat askew. It took us twelve sessions to determine that Ra was not actually speaking of the physical placement of the Bible and so forth, but Ra was giving us a hint that our metaphysical alignment was off. Our line of questioning was misplaced from the heart of the evolutionary process. Since our contact with Ra was "narrow band" that meant that Ra could not long respond to questions which were off the target. If we had allowed these distortions to remain over a long period of time the contact would have been impaired and eventually we would have lost the contact..

The last portion of this session deals with the concept of what is called the Wanderers and their frequently shared characteristics of exhibiting physical ailments such as allergies and personality disorders which, in the deeper sense, seem to be a reaction against this planet's vibrational frequency. This is apparently a side-effect that is due to such entities having another planetary influence in a higher density as their home vibration. They incarnate on this third-density planet in order to be of service in whatever way is possible to help the population of this planet to become more aware of the evolutionary process and to move in harmony with it. These Wanderers go through the same forgetting process that every other third-density being who incarnates here goes through, and they become completely the third-density being—even as they slowly begin to remember why it is that they have been born here. Apparently, about one in every seventy people on Earth is of such an origin.

It almost seems to be in vogue now to say that one is from this or that planet, this or that higher density, and that one is really this or that exalted being come down to Earth to be a great teacher. It is embarrassing to us to see such a magnificent opportunity for rendering a humble service cheapened to a game of who has the most spiritual sergeant's stripes. We do not hide the possibility that we may be of such origins, but neither do we nor those of Ra feel that such an origin is particularly remarkable. As Don used to say, "You've got to be somewhere doing something. You might as well be here doing this."

Carla: *I think one thing to keep in mind, if we are Wanderers from elsewhere, is that we came here for a reason: to serve at this time right here in this very shadow world of Earth's third density. Yes, we suffer the results of trying to live in a vibratory range that is difficult for us, and yes, we somehow remember a "better way" to live. With this in mind, it becomes clearer that our main mission here is simply to live, to breathe the air and to let the love within us flow. Just the simple living of an everyday life is sacramental when the person is living with that consciousness of "all is love" humming its tune beneath our words and thoughts. To live devotionally does not mean, necessarily, that one becomes a hermit or a wandering pilgrim, although if you feel called to it, blessings on your way. To me, at least, the daily things are the most holy, the washing up, the chores, the errands. All moves in rhythm, and we are just part of that symphony of all life that shares energy back and forth.*

I know one of the great hopes a Wanderer has is to find its service. The living of a devotional life, right in the busy midst of everything, is ample and perfect service. It is what we came here to do. As we let love flow through us, others change, and as they open their hearts, the circle of light grows. We are now at a stage where the light sources are beginning to connect … do I hear the sound of global mind being born?

The global mind is a very real concept to me, as well, especially since the advent of e-mail and the world-wide web. With information being exchanged without pen or paper, we are basically working with light, surely one of the purer ways to communicate. As I collect stories of Wanderers' blues, I am struck by how intense and constant is the general desire for a spiritual home, an identity, and a way of service. I encourage all those who experience themselves as Wanderers to link up and "network" with other awakened consciousnesses, to live in the open heart together and allow the light to come through us all into the "world-wide web" of planetary consciousness. As Jim says, there is no greater service than being yourself in this sometimes refractory world.

Don loved Andrija Puharich and was a loyal and generous friend to him for many years. We met Andrija in 1974, after we read the book, URI, which he wrote, and identified him as one of the characters in our oddly prophetic novel, THE CRUCIFIXION OF ESMERELDA SWEETWATER, which we had written in 1968 and 1969. We helped with the now-historic "Mind Link" of 1977, and heard from him from far and wide as he dodged bullets and various agents of various governments who thought he was up to something. Puharich was a person of immense hospitality and kindness of character, although quite insensitive to and unaware of the world and its requirements outside his work. This was a guy who got up in the morning and worked steadily, only stopping for grabbing some food, literally, until time for bed. He rather ran through people, using their talents and donations as they aided the work, and unaware of depleting people's resources or time, because he focused on the work before him, never on making money. This was a born scholar and a brilliant man, and much occurred in his ken, It is a loss to the world of ideas that his carefully kept journals were confiscated at the time of his death and have disappeared. I admit readily to feeling oftimes that he was "using" Don. I felt he was a man of more energy, but less wisdom, than Don. I felt he should have followed Don's sage council at times. Don himself never felt anything like this. He was glad to help. I celebrate Andrija. What a singular and remarkable fellow, and what a contribution he made in so many ways!

George Hunt Williamson was a channel we greatly admired; indeed, we used his channeling of Brother Philip in our tape, MESSAGES FROM THE UFOs. We were in telephone contact with him only, and like Andrija, he never made it to our sessions. It's likely he was not too pleased at Ra's request for him to prepare! He is one of the great pioneers in UFO and related metaphysical research, and I think the first to name Wanderers. He called them "apples," quoting the radio-channeled UFO message, "To the apples we salt, we shall return."

Session 12, January 28, 1981

Questioner: I got a call from Henry Puharich this afternoon and he will be here next month. I would like to ask if it is permissible for him to join in our circle and ask questions? I would also like to ask if Michael D'brenovic, also known as George Hunt Williamson, could join our circle as well?

Ra: I am Ra. These entities, at present, are not properly attuned for the particular work due to vibrational distortions which in turn are due to a recent lack of time/space which you call busy-ness. It would be requested that the entities spend a brief time/space in each diurnal cycle of your planet in contemplation. At a future time/space in your continuum you are requested to ask again. This group is highly balanced to this instrument's vibratory distortions due to, firstly, contact with the instrument on a day-to-day basis. Secondly, due to contact with the instrument through meditation periods. Thirdly, through a personal mind/body/spirit complex distortion towards contemplation which in sum causes this group to be effective.

Questioner: Which group was it that contacted Henry Puharich in Israel around 1972?

Ra: I am Ra. We must refrain from answering this query due to the possibility/probability that the one you call Henry will read this answer. This would cause distortions in his future. It is necessary that each being use free and complete discernment from within the all-self which is at the heart of the mind/body/spirit complex.

Questioner: Would that also keep you from answering who it was that the group I was in, in 1962, contacted then?

Ra: I am Ra. This query may be answered. The group contacted was the Confederation.

Questioner: Did they have any of their craft in our area at that time?

Ra: I am Ra. There was no craft. There was a thought-form.

Questioner: If an Man In Black were to visit me and I locked him in the closet could I keep him, or would he disappear?

Ra: I am Ra. It depends upon which type of entity you grab. You are perhaps able to perceive a construct. The construct might be kept for a brief period, although these constructs also have an ability to disappear. The programming on these constructs, however, makes it more difficult to remotely control them. You would not be able to grapple with a thought-form entity of the Man in Black, as you call it, type.

Questioner: Would this be against the Law of One? Would I be making a mistake by grabbing one of those entities?

Ra: I am Ra. There are no mistakes under the Law of One.

Questioner: What I mean to ask is would I be polarizing more towards self-service or service to others when I did this act of locking up the thought-form or construct?

Ra: I am Ra. You may consider that question for yourself. We interpret the Law of One, but not to the extent of advice.

Questioner: Is there a way for these Wanderers to heal themselves of their physical ailments?

Ra: I am Ra. This will be the last complete question of this time/space.

The self-healing distortion is effected through realization of the intelligent infinity resting within. This is blocked in some way in these who are not perfectly balanced in bodily complexes. The blockage varies from entity to entity. It requires the conscious awareness of the spiritual nature of reality, if you will, and the corresponding pourings of this reality into the individual mind/body/spirit complex for healing to take place.

Is there a short question before we close this session?

Questioner: Is it possible for you to tell us if any of the three of us are Wanderers?

Ra: I am Ra. In scanning each of the mind/body/spirit complexes present, we find an already complete sureness of this occurrence and, therefore, find no harm in recapitulating this occurrence. Each of those present are (sic) Wanderers pursuing a mission, if you will.

The Law of One, Book I, Session 13
January 29, 1981

Ra: I am Ra. I greet you in the love and the light of the infinite Creator. I communicate now.

Questioner: First of all I would like to apologize for asking so many stupid questions while searching for what we should do. I consider what we are doing to be a great honor and privilege to also be humble messengers of the Law of One. I now believe that the way to prepare this book is to start at the beginning of creation and follow through the evolution of man on Earth, investigating at all times how the Law of One was used. I would also like to make as the title of the book, *The Law of One*, and I would like to state as the author, Ra. Would you agree to this?

Ra: I am Ra. Your query is unclear. Would you please state as separate queries each area of agreement?

Questioner: First, I would like to start at the beginning of creation, as far back as we can go and follow the development of man to the present time. Is this agreeable?

Ra: I am Ra. This is completely your discernment/understanding/decision.

Questioner: Secondly, I would like to title the book, *The Law of One*, by Ra. Is this agreeable?

Ra: I am Ra. The title of the book is acceptable. The authorship by vibratory sound complex Ra is, in our distortion of understanding, incomplete. We are messengers.

Questioner: Can you state who then should author the book?

Ra: I am Ra. I can only request that if your discernment/understanding suggests the use of this vibratory sound complex, Ra, the phrase "An humble messenger of the Law of One" be appended.

Questioner: Thank you. Can you tell me of the first known thing in the creation?

Ra: I am Ra. The first known thing in the creation is infinity. The infinity is creation.

Questioner: From this infinity then must come what we experience as creation. What was the next step or the next evolution?

Ra: I am Ra. Infinity became aware. This was the next step.

Questioner: After this, what came next?

Ra: I am Ra. Awareness led to the focus of infinity into infinite energy. You have called this by various vibrational sound complexes, the most common to your ears being "Logos" or "Love." The Creator is the focusing of infinity as an aware or conscious principle called by us as closely as we can create understanding/learning in your language, intelligent infinity.

Questioner: Can you state the next step?

Ra: I am Ra. The next step is still at this space/time nexus in your illusion achieving its progression as you may see it in your illusion. The next step is an infinite reaction to the creative principle following the Law of One in one of its primal distortions, freedom of will. Thus many, many dimensions, infinite in number, are possible. The energy moves from the intelligent infinity due first to the outpouring of randomized creative force, this then creating patterns which in holographic style appear as the entire creation no matter which direction or energy is explored. These patterns of energy begin then to regularize their own local, shall we say, rhythms and fields of energy, thus creating dimensions and universes.

Questioner: Then can you tell me how the galaxy and planetary systems were formed?

Ra: I am Ra. You must imagine a great leap of thought in this query, for at the last query the physical, as you call, it, universes were not yet born.

The energies moved in increasingly intelligent patterns until the individualization of various energies emanating from the creative principle of intelligent infinity became such as to be co-Creators. Thus the so-called physical matter began. The concept of light is instrumental in grasping this great leap of thought as this vibrational distortion of infinity is the building block of that which is known as matter, the light being intelligent and full of energy, thus being the first distortion of intelligent infinity which was called by the creative principle.

This light of love was made to have in its occurrences of being certain characteristics, among them the infinite whole paradoxically described by the straight line, as you would call it. This paradox is responsible for the shape of the various physical illusion entities you call solar systems, galaxies, and planets of revolving and tending towards the lenticular.

Questioner: I think I made an error in getting ahead of the process you were describing. Would it be helpful to fill in that great leap due to the mistake I made?

Ra: I am Ra. I attempted to bridge the gap. However, you may question me in any manner you deem appropriate.

Questioner: Taking the question just before the one I asked about the galaxies and planets and tell me what the next step was from there?

Ra: I am Ra. The steps, as you call them, are, at the point of question, simultaneous and infinite.

Questioner: Can you tell me how intelligent infinity became, shall we say (I'm having difficulty with the language), how intelligent infinity became individualized from itself.

Ra: I am Ra. This is an appropriate question.

The intelligent infinity discerned a concept. This concept was discerned to be freedom of will of awareness. This concept was finity. This was the first and primal paradox or distortion of the Law of One. Thus the one intelligent infinity invested itself in an exploration of many-ness. Due to the infinite possibilities of intelligent infinity there is no ending to many-ness. The exploration, thus, is free to continue infinitely in an eternal present.

Questioner: Was the galaxy that we are in created by the infinite intelligence or was it created by a portion of the infinite intelligence?

Ra: I am Ra. The galaxy and all other things of material of which you are aware are products of individualized portions of intelligent infinity. As each exploration began, it, in turn, found its focus and became co-Creator. Using intelligent infinity each portion created an universe and allowing the rhythms of free choice to flow, playing with the infinite spectrum of possibilities, each individualized portion channeled the love/light into what you might call intelligent energy, thus creating the so-called Natural Laws of any particular universe.

Each universe, in turn, individualized to a focus becoming, in turn, co-Creator and allowing further diversity, thus creating further intelligent energies regularizing or causing Natural Laws to appear in the vibrational patterns of what you would call a solar system. Thus, each solar system has its own, shall we say, local coordinate system of illusory Natural Laws. It shall be understood that any portion, no matter how small, of any density or illusory pattern contains, as in an holographic picture, the one Creator which is infinity. Thus all begins and ends in mystery.

Questioner: Can you tell me how the individualized infinity created our galaxy and if the same portion created our planetary system and, if so, how this came about?

Ra: I am Ra. We may have misperceived your query. We were under the distortion/impression that we had responded to this particular query. Would you restate the query?

Questioner: I am wondering if the planetary system that we are in now was all created at once or if our sun was created first and the planets later?

Ra: I am Ra. The process is from the larger, in your illusion, to the smaller. Thus the co-Creator, individualizing the galaxy, created energy patterns which then focused in multitudinous focuses of further conscious awareness of intelligent infinity. Thus, the solar system of which you experience inhabitation is of its own patterns, rhythms, and so-called natural laws which are unique to itself. However, the progression is from the galaxy spiraling energy to the solar spiraling energy, to the planetary spiraling energy, to the experiential circumstances of spiraling energy which begin the first density of awareness of consciousness of planetary entities.

Questioner: Could you tell me about this first density of planetary entities?

Ra: I am Ra. Each step recapitulates intelligent infinity in its discovery of awareness. In a planetary environment all begins in what you would call chaos, energy undirected and random in its infinity. Slowly, in your terms of understanding, there forms a focus of self-awareness. Thus the Logos moves. Light comes to form the darkness, according to the co-Creator's patterns and vibratory rhythms, so constructing a certain type of experience. This begins with first density which is the density of consciousness, the mineral and water life upon the planet learning from fire and wind the awareness of being. This is the first density.

Questioner: How does this first density then progress to greater awareness?

Ra: I am Ra. The spiraling energy, which is the characteristic of what you call "light," moves in a straight line spiral thus giving spirals an inevitable vector upwards to a more comprehensive beingness with regards to intelligent infinity. Thus, first dimensional beingness strives towards the second-density lessons of a type of awareness which includes growth rather than dissolution or random change.

Questioner: Could you define what you mean by growth?

Ra: I am Ra. Picture, if you will, the difference between first-vibrational mineral or water life and the lower second-density beings which begin to move about within and upon its being. This movement is the characteristic of second density, the striving towards light and growth.

Questioner: By striving towards light, what do you mean?

Ra: I am Ra. A very simplistic example of second-density growth striving towards light is that of the leaf striving towards the source of light.

Questioner: Is there any physical difference between first and second density? For instance if I could see both a first and second-density planet side by side, in my present condition, could I see both of them? Would they both be physical to me?

Ra: I am Ra. This is correct. All of the octave of your densities would be clearly visible were not the fourth through the seventh freely choosing not to be visible.

Questioner: Then how does the second density progress to the third?

Ra: I am Ra. The second density strives towards the third density which is the density of self-consciousness or self-awareness. The striving takes place through the higher second-density forms who are invested by third-density beings with an identity to the extent that they become self-aware mind/body complexes, thus becoming mind/body/spirit complexes and entering third density, the first density of consciousness of spirit.

Questioner: What is the density level of our planet Earth at this time?

Ra: I am Ra. The sphere upon which you dwell is third density in its beingness of mind/body/spirit complexes. It is now in a space/time continuum, fourth density. This is causing a somewhat difficult harvest.

Questioner: How does a third-density planet become a fourth density planet?

Ra: I am Ra. This will be the last full question.

The fourth density is, as we have said, as regularized in its approach as the striking of a clock upon the hour. The space/time of your solar system has enabled this planetary sphere to spiral into space/time of a different vibrational configuration. This causes the planetary sphere to be able to be molded by these new distortions. However, the thought-forms of your people during this transition period are such that the mind/body/spirit complexes of both individual and societies are scattered throughout the spectrum instead of becoming able to grasp the needle, shall we say, and point the compass in one direction.

Thus, the entry into the vibration of love, sometimes called by your people the vibration of understanding, is not effective with your present societal complex. Thus, the harvest shall be such that many will repeat the third-density cycle. The energies of your Wanderers, your teachers, and your adepts at this time are all bent upon increasing the harvest. However, there are few to harvest.

Questioner: I would like to apologize for sometimes asking inappropriate questions. It's difficult sometimes to ask precisely the right question. I don't wish to go over any ground that we've already covered. I notice that this period is slightly shorter than previous work sessions. Is there a reason for this?

Ra: I am Ra. This instrument's vital energy is somewhat low.

Questioner: I am assuming from this that it would be a good idea not to have another session today. Is that correct?

Ra: I am Ra. It is well to have a session later if it is acceptable that we monitor this instrument and cease using it when it becomes low in the material which we take from it. We do not wish to deplete this instrument.

Questioner: This is always acceptable in any session. I will ask my final question. Is there anything that we can do to make the instrument more comfortable or aid in this communication?

Ra: I am Ra. It is well. Each is most conscientious. Continue in the same.

I am Ra. I leave you in the love and the light of the one infinite Creator. Go forth, therefore, rejoicing in the power and the peace of the one Creator. Adonai.

The Law of One, Book I, Session 14
January 29, 1981

Ra: I am Ra. I greet you in the love and the light of the infinite Creator. We communicate now.

Questioner: After going over this morning's work, I thought it might be helpful to fill in a few things. You said that the second density strives towards the third density which is the density of self-consciousness, or self-awareness. The striving takes place through higher second-density forms being invested by third-density beings. Could you explain what you mean by this?

Ra: I am Ra. Much as you would put on a vestment, so do your third-density beings invest or clothe some second-density beings with self-awareness. This is often done through the opportunity of what you call pets. It has also been done by various other means of investiture. These include many so-called religious practice complexes which personify and send love to various natural second-density beings in their group form.

Questioner: When this Earth was second-density, how did the second-density beings on it become so invested?

Ra: I am Ra. There was not this type of investment as spoken but the simple third-density investment which is the line of spiraling light calling distortion upward from density to density. The process takes longer when there is no investment made by incarnate third-density beings.

Questioner: Then what was the second-density form—what did it look like—that became Earth-man in the third density? What did he look like in the second density?

Ra: I am Ra. The difference between second- and third-density bodily forms would in many cases have been more like one to the other. In the case of your planetary sphere the process was interrupted by those who incarnated here from the planetary sphere you call Mars. They were adjusted by genetic changing and, therefore, there was some difference which was of a very noticeable variety rather than the gradual raising of the bipedal forms upon your second-density level to third-density level. This has nothing to do with the so-called placement of the soul. This has only to do with the circumstances of the influx of those from that culture.

Questioner: I understand from previous material that this occurred 75,000 years ago. It was then that our third-density process of evolution began. Can you tell me the history, hitting only the points of development, shall I say, that occurred within this 75,000 years, any point when contact was made to aid this development?

Ra: I am Ra. The first attempt to aid your peoples was at the time 75,000. This attempt 75,000 of your years ago has been previously described by us. The next attempt was approximately 58,000 of your years ago, continuing for a long period in your measurement, with those of Mu as you call this race or mind/body/spirit social complex. The next attempt was long in coming and occurred approximately 13,000 of your years ago when some intelligent information was offered to those of Atlantis, this being of the same type of healing and crystal working of which we have spoken previously. The next attempt was 11,000 of your years ago. These are approximations as we are not totally able to process your space/time continuum measurement system. This was in what you call Egypt and of this we have also spoken. The same beings who came with us returned approximately 3,500 years later in order to attempt to aid the South American mind/body/spirit social complex once again. However, the pyramids of those so-called cities were not to be used in the appropriate fashion.

Therefore, this was not pursued further. There was a landing approximately 3,000 of your years ago also in your South America, as you call it. There were a few attempts to aid your peoples approximately 2,300 years ago, this in the area of Egypt. The remaining part of the cycle, we have never been gone from your fifth dimension and have been working in this last minor cycle to prepare for harvest.

Questioner: Was the Egyptian visit of 11,000 years ago the only one where you actually walked the Earth?

Ra: I am Ra. I understand your question distorted in the direction of selves rather than other-selves. We of the vibratory sound complex, Ra, have walked among you only at that time.

Questioner: I understood you to say in an earlier session that pyramids were built to ring the Earth. How many pyramids were built?

Ra: I am Ra. There are six balancing pyramids and fifty-two others built for additional healing and initiatory work among your mind/body/spirit social complexes.

Questioner: What is a balancing pyramid?

Ra: I am Ra. Imagine, if you will, the many force fields of the Earth in their geometrically precise web. Energies stream into the Earth planes, as you would call them, from magnetically determined points. Due to growing thought-form distortions in understanding of the Law of One, the planet itself was seen to have the potential for imbalance. The balancing pyramidal structures were charged with crystals which drew the appropriate balance from the energy forces streaming into the various geometrical centers of electromagnetic energy which surround and shape the planetary sphere.

Questioner: Let me make a synopsis and you tell me if I am correct. All of these visits for the last 75,000 years were for the purpose of giving to the people of Earth an understanding of the Law of One, and in this way allowing them to progress upward through the fourth, fifth, and sixth densities. This was to be a service to Earth. The pyramids were used also in giving the Law of One in their own way. The balancing pyramids, I'm not quite sure of. Am I right so far?

Ra: I am Ra. You are correct to the limits of the precision allowed by language.

Questioner: Did the balancing pyramid prevent the Earth from changing its axis?

Ra: I am Ra. This query is not clear. Please restate.

Questioner: Does the balancing refer to the individual who is initiated in the pyramid or does it refer to the physical balancing of the Earth on its axis in space?

Ra: I am Ra. The balancing pyramidal structures could be and were used for individual initiation. However, the use of these pyramids was also designed for the balancing of the planetary energy web. The other pyramids are not placed correctly for Earth healing but for healing of mind/body/spirit complexes. It came to our attention that your density was distorted towards, what is called by our distortion/understanding of third density on your planetary sphere, more of a time/space continuum in one incarnation pattern in order to have a fuller opportunity to learn/teach the Laws or Ways of the primal distortion of the Law of One which is Love.

Questioner: I want to make this statement and you tell me if I am correct. The balancing pyramids were to do what we call increase the life span of entities here so that they would gain more wisdom of the Law of One while they were in the physical at one time. Is this correct?

Ra: I am Ra. This is correct. However, the pyramids not called by us by the vibrational sound complex, balancing pyramids, were more numerous and were used exclusively for the above purpose and the teach/learning of healers to charge and enable these processes.

Questioner: George Van Tassel built a machine in our western desert called an integratron. Will this machine work for that purpose, of increasing the life span?

Ra: I am Ra. The machine is incomplete and will not function for the above-mentioned purpose.

Questioner: Who gave George the information on how to build it?

Ra: I am Ra. There were two contacts which gave the entity with the vibratory sound complex, George, this information. One was of the Confederation. The second was of the Orion group. The Confederation was caused to find the distortion towards non-contact due to the alteration of the vibrational mind complex patterns of the one called George. Thus, the Orion group used this instrument; however, this instrument, though confused, was a mind/body/spirit complex devoted at the heart to service to others, so the, shall we say, worst that could be done was to discredit this source.

Questioner: Would there be any value to the people of this planet now to complete this machine?

Ra: I am Ra. The harvest is now. There is not at this time any reason to include efforts along these distortions toward longevity, but rather to encourage distortions toward seeking the heart of self, for this which resides clearly in the violet-ray energy field will determine the harvesting of each mind/body/spirit complex.

Questioner: Going back to when we started this 75,000 year period, there was a harvest 25,000 years after the start which would make it 50,000 years ago. Can you tell me how many were harvested at that time?

Ra: I am Ra. The harvest was none.

Questioner: There was no harvest? What about 25,000 years ago?

Ra: I am Ra. A harvesting began taking place in the latter portion, as you measure time/space, of the second cycle, with individuals finding the gateway to intelligent infinity. The harvest of that time, though extremely small, was those entities of extreme distortion towards service to the entities who were now to repeat the major cycle. These entities, therefore, remained in third density although they could, at any moment/present nexus, leave this density through use of intelligent infinity.

Questioner: Then in the harvest 25,000 years ago, the entities who could have been harvested into the fourth density chose to remain here in service to this planetary population. Is this correct?

Ra: I am Ra. This is correct. Thus, there was no harvest, but there were harvestable entities who shall choose the manner of their entrance into fourth dimension.

Questioner: Then for the last 2,300 years you have been working to create as large a harvest as possible at the end of the total 75,000 year cycle. Can you state with respect to the Law of One why you do this?

Ra: I am Ra. I speak for the social memory complex termed Ra. We came among you to aid you. Our efforts in service were perverted. Our desire then is to eliminate as far as possible the distortions caused by those misreading our information and guidance. The general cause of service such as the Confederation offers is that of the primal distortion of the Law of One, which is service. The one Being of the creation is like unto a body, if you will accept this third-density analogy. Would we ignore a pain in the leg? A bruise upon the skin? A cut which is festering. No. There is no ignoring a call. We, the entities of sorrow, chose as our service the attempt to heal the sorrow which we are calling analogous to the pains of a physical body complex/distortion.

Questioner: Of what density level is Ra?

Ra: I am Ra. I am sixth density with a strong seeking towards seventh density. The harvest for us will be in only approximately two and one-half million of your years and it is our desire to be ready for harvest as it approaches in our space/time continuum.

Questioner: And you ready yourselves for this harvest through the service you can provide. Is this correct?

Ra: I am Ra. This is correct. We offer the Law of One, the solving of paradoxes, the balancing of love/light and light/love.

Questioner: How long is one of your cycles?

Ra: I am Ra. One of our cycles computes to 75 million of your years.

Questioner: 75 million years?

Ra: I am Ra. That is correct.

Questioner: In your service in giving the Law of One, do you work with any other planets than Earth at this time, or just Earth?

Ra: I am Ra. We work only with this planetary sphere at this time.

Questioner: You stated that you were called by 352,000 Earth entities. Does this mean that it is this number that will understand and accept the Law of One?

Ra: I am Ra. We cannot estimate the correctness of your statement for those who call are not in every case able to understand the answer to their calling. Moreover, those who were not calling previously may, with great trauma, discover the answers to the call nearly simultaneously with their late call. There is no time/space in call. Therefore, we cannot estimate the number of your mind/body/spirit complexes which will, in your space/time continuum/distortion, hear and understand.

Questioner: How do you normally perform your service of giving the Law of One? How have you done this over the last 2,300 years? How have you normally given this to Earth people?

Ra: I am Ra. We have used channels such as this one, but in most cases the channels feel inspired by dreams and visions without being aware, consciously, of our identity or existence. This particular group has been accentuatedly trained to recognize such contact. This makes this group able to be aware of a focal or vibrational source of information.

Questioner: When you contact the entities in their dreams and otherwise, these entities first have to be seeking in the direction of the Law of One. Is this correct?

Ra: I am Ra. This is correct. For example, the entities of the nation Egypt were in a state of pantheism, as you may call the distortion toward separate worship of various portions of the Creator. We were able to contact one whose orientation was toward the One.

Questioner: I assume that as the cycle ends and inconveniences occur, there will be some entities who start seeking or be catalyzed into seeking because of the trauma and will then hear your words telepathically or in written form such as this book. Is this correct?

Ra: I am Ra. You are correct except in understanding that the inconveniences have begun.

Questioner: Can you tell me who was responsible for transmitting the book *Oahspe*?

Ra: I am Ra. This was transmitted by one of Confederation social memory complex status whose idea, as offered to the Council, was to use some of the known physical history of the so-called religions or religious distortions of your cycle in order to veil and partially unveil aspects or primal distortions of the Law of One. All names can be taken to be created for their vibrational characteristics. The information buried within has to do with a deeper understanding of love and light, and the attempts of infinite intelligence through many messengers to teach/learn those entities of your sphere.

Questioner: Have there been any other books that you can name that are available for this purpose that have been given by the Confederation?

Ra: I am Ra. We cannot share this information, for it would distort your discernment patterns in your future. You may ask about a particular volume.

Questioner: Who transmitted the *Urantia Book*?

Ra: I am Ra. This was given by a series of discarnate entities of your own Earth planes, the so-called inner planes. This material is not passed by the Council.

Questioner: Who spoke through Edgar Cayce?

Ra: I am Ra. No entity spoke through Edgar Cayce.

Questioner: Where did the information come from that Edgar Cayce channeled?

Ra: I am Ra. We have explained before that the intelligent infinity is brought into intelligent energy from eighth density or octave. The one sound vibratory complex called Edgar used this gateway to view the present, which is not the continuum you experience but the potential social memory complex of this planetary sphere. The term your peoples have used for this is the "Akashic Record" or the "Hall of Records." This is the last question which you may now ask.

Questioner: Is there anything that we can do to make the instrument more comfortable or to help during the transmission?

Ra: I am Ra. We only reiterate the importance of alignment. This instrument is placed .2° away from the direction of the resting place, which is correct. This may be "eyed," shall we say, by sight and the instrument reminded. You are being conscientious. Is there any brief question we may answer before this session is closed?

Questioner: Can you tell me if we are accomplishing our effort reasonably well?

Ra: I am Ra. The Law is One. There are no mistakes.

I am Ra. I leave this instrument in the love and the light of the one infinite Creator. Go forth, therefore, rejoicing in the power and the peace of the one Creator. Adonai.

The Law of One, Book I, Session 15
January 30, 1981

Ra: I am Ra. I greet you in the love and the light of the infinite Creator. I communicate now.

Questioner: I would like to apologize for any past and future stupid questions. They are due to the fact that I am searching for the proper entry into the investigation of the Law of One.

I would like to ask about the use of the instrument, if it is a function of the time we use the instrument or the amount of words or information the instrument gives? In other words, do I have to hurry and ask questions, or can I take my time to ask questions?

Ra: I am Ra. There are two portions to your query. Firstly, this instrument's reserve of vital energy which is a product of body, mind, and spirit distortions in the various complexes, is the key to the length of time which we may expend using this instrument. We searched your group and we contacted you for each in your group possesses significantly more vital energy of the body complex. However, this instrument was tuned most appropriately by the mind/body/spirit complex distortions of its beingness in this illusion. Therefore, we remained with this instrument.

Secondly, we communicate at a set rate which is dependent upon our careful manipulation of this instrument. We cannot be more, as you would say, quick. Therefore, you may ask questions speedily but the answers we have to offer are at a set pace given.

Questioner: This isn't exactly what I meant. If it takes me, say forty-five minutes to ask my questions, does that give the instrument only fifteen minutes to answer, or could the instrument go over an hour, all totaled, with her answers?

Ra: I am Ra. The energy required for this contact is entered into this instrument by a function of time. Therefore, the time is the factor, as we understand your query.

Questioner: Then I should ask my questions rapidly so that I do not reduce the time. Is this correct?

Ra: I am Ra. You shall do as you deem fit. However, we may suggest that to obtain the answers you require may mean that you invest some of what you experience as time. Although you lose the answer-time, you gain thereby in the specificity of the answer. At many times in the past, we have needed clarification of hastily phrased questions.

Questioner: Thank you. The first question is this: Why does rapid aging occur on this planet?

Ra: I am Ra. Rapid aging occurs upon this third-density planet due to an ongoing imbalance of receptor web complex in the etheric portion of the energy field of this planet. The thought-form distortions of your peoples have caused the energy streamings to enter the planetary magnetic atmosphere, if you would so term this web of energy patterns, in such a way that the proper streamings are not correctly imbued with balanced vibratory light/love from the, shall we say, cosmic level of this octave of existence.

Questioner: Do I assume correctly that one of your attempts in service to this planet was to help the population more fully understand and practice the Law of One so that this rapid aging could be changed to normal aging?

Ra: I am Ra. You assume correctly to a great degree.

Questioner: What is the greatest service that our population on this planet could perform individually?

Ra: I am Ra. There is but one service. The Law is One. The offering of self to Creator is the greatest service, the unity, the fountainhead. The entity who seeks the one Creator is with infinite intelligence. From this seeking, from this offering, a great multiplicity of opportunities will evolve depending upon the mind/body/spirit complexes' distortions with regard to the various illusory aspects or energy centers of the various complexes of your illusion.

Thus, some become healers, some workers, some teachers, and so forth.

Questioner: If an entity were perfectly balanced with respect to the Law of One on this planet would he undergo the aging process?

Ra: I am Ra. A perfectly balanced entity would become tired rather than visibly aged. The lessons being learned, the entity would depart. However, this is appropriate and is a form of aging which your peoples do not experience. The understanding comes slowly, the body complex decomposing more rapidly.

Questioner: Can you tell me a little more about the word, "balancing," as we are using it?

Ra: I am Ra. Picture, if you will, the One Infinite. You have no picture. Thus, the process begins. Love creating light, becoming love/light, streams into the planetary sphere according to the electromagnetic web of points or nexi of entrance. These streamings are then available to the individual who, like the planet, is a web of electromagnetic energy fields with points or nexi of entrance.

In a balanced individual each energy center is balanced and functioning brightly and fully. The blockages of your planetary sphere cause some distortion of intelligent energy. The blockages of the mind/body/spirit complex further distort or unbalance this energy. There is one energy. It may be understood as love/light or light/love or intelligent energy.

Questioner: Am I correct to assume that one of the blockages of the mind/body/spirit complex might be, shall we say, ego, and this could be balanced using a worthiness/unworthiness balance. Am I correct?

Ra: I am Ra. This is incorrect.

Questioner: Can you tell me how you balance the ego?

Ra: I am Ra. We cannot work with this concept as it is misapplied and understanding cannot come from it.

Questioner: How does an individual go about balancing himself? What is the first step?

Ra: I am Ra. The steps are only one; that is, an understanding of the energy centers which make up the mind/body/spirit complex. This understanding may be briefly summarized as follows. The first balancing is of the Malkuth, or Earth, vibratory energy complex, called the red-ray complex. An understanding and acceptance of this energy is fundamental. The next energy complex, which may be blocked is the emotional, or personal complex, also known as the orange-ray complex. This blockage will often demonstrate itself as personal eccentricities or distortions with regard to self-conscious understanding or acceptance of self.

The third blockage resembles most closely that which you have called ego. It is the yellow-ray or solar plexus center. Blockages in this center will often manifest as distortions toward power manipulation and other social behaviors concerning those close and those associated with the mind/body/spirit complex. Those with blockages in these first three energy centers, or nexi, will have continuing difficulties in ability to further their seeking of the Law of One.

The center of heart, or green-ray, is the center from which third-density beings may springboard, shall we say, to infinite intelligence. Blockages in this area may manifest as difficulties in expressing what you may call universal love or compassion.

The blue-ray center of energy streaming is the center which, for the first time, is outgoing as well as inpouring. Those blocked in this area may have difficulty in grasping the spirit/mind complexes of its own entity and further difficulty in expressing such understandings of self. Entities blocked in this area may have difficulties in accepting communication from other mind/body/spirit complexes.

The next center is the pineal or indigo-ray center. Those blocked in this center may experience a lessening of the influx of intelligent energy due to manifestations which appear as unworthiness. This is that of which you spoke. As you can see, this is but one of many distortions due to the several points of energy influx into the mind/body/spirit complex. The indigo-ray balancing is quite central to the type of work which revolves about the spirit complex, which has its influx then into the transformation or transmutation of third density to fourth density, it being the energy center receiving the least distorted outpourings of love/light from intelligent energy and also the potential for the key to the gateway of intelligent infinity.

The remaining center of energy influx is simply the total expression of the entity's vibratory complex of mind, body, and spirit. It is as it will be, "balanced" or "imbalanced" has no meaning at this energy level, for it gives and takes in its own balance. Whatever the distortion may be, it cannot be manipulated as can the others and, therefore, has no particular importance in viewing the balancing of an entity.

Questioner: You previously gave us information on what we should do in balancing. Is there any publishable information you can give us now about particular exercises or methods of balancing these energy centers?

Ra: I am Ra. The exercises given for publication seen in comparison with the material now given are in total a good beginning. It is important to allow each seeker to enlighten itself rather than for any messenger to attempt in language to teach/learn for the entity, thus being teach/learner and learn/teacher. This is not in balance with your third density. We learn from you. We teach to you. Thus, we teach/learn. If we learned for you, this would cause imbalance in the direction of the distortion of free will. There are other items of information allowable. However, you have not yet reached these items in your line of questioning and it is our belief/feeling complex that the questioner shall shape this material in such a way that your mind/body/spirit complexes shall have entry to it, thus we answer your queries as they arise in your mind complex.

Questioner: Yesterday you stated that "the harvest is now. There is not at this time any reason to include efforts along this line of longevity, but rather to encourage efforts to seek the heart of self. This which resides clearly in the violet-ray energy field will determine the harvest of the mind/body/spirit complex." Could you tell us the best way to seek the heart of self?

Ra: I am Ra. We have given you this information in several wordings. However, we can only say the material for your understanding is the self: the mind/body/spirit complex. You have been given information upon healing, as you call this distortion. This information may be seen in a more general context as ways to understand the self. The understanding, experiencing, accepting, and merging of self with self and other-self, and finally with the Creator, is the path to the heart of self. In each infinitesimal part of your self resides the One in all of Its power. Therefore, we can only encourage these lines of contemplation or prayer as a means of subjectively/objectively using or combining various understandings to enhance the seeking process. Without such a method of reversing the analytical process, one could not integrate into unity the many understandings gained in such seeking.

Questioner: I don't mean to ask the same question twice, but there are some areas that I consider so important that possibly a greater understanding may be obtained if the answer is restated a number of times in other words. I thank you for your patience. Yesterday, you also mentioned that when there was no harvest at the end of the last 25,000 year period, "there were harvestable entities who shall choose the manner of their entrance into the fourth density." Could you tell me what you mean by "they shall choose the manner of their entry into the fourth density"?

Ra: I am Ra. These shepherds, or, as some have called them, the "Elder Race," shall choose the time/space of their leaving. They are unlikely to leave until their other-selves are harvestable also.

Questioner: What do you mean by their "other-selves" being harvestable?

Ra: I am Ra. The other-selves with whom these beings are concerned are those which did not attain harvest during the second major cycle.

Questioner: Could you tell me just a small amount of the history of what you call the Elder Race?

Ra: I am Ra. The question is unclear. Please restate.

Questioner: I ask this question because I have heard of the Elder Race before in a book, *Road in the Sky*, by George Hunt Williamson, and I was wondering if this Elder Race was the same that he talked about?

Ra: I am Ra. The question now resolves itself, for we have spoken previously of the manner of decision-making which caused these entities to remain here upon the closing of the second major cycle of your current master cycle. There are some distortions in the descriptions of the one known as Michel; however, these distortions have to do primarily with the fact that these entities are not a social memory complex, but rather a group of mind/body/spirit complexes dedicated to service. These entities work together, but are not completely unified; thus, they do not completely see each the other's thoughts, feelings, and motives. However, their desire to serve is the fourth-dimensional type of desire, thus melding them into what you may call a brotherhood.

Questioner: Why do you call them the Elder Race?

Ra: I am Ra. We called them thusly to acquaint you, the questioner, with their identity as is understood by your mind complex distortion.

Questioner: Are there any Wanderers with this Elder Race?

Ra: I am Ra. These are planetary entities harvested—Wanderers only in the sense that they chose, in fourth-density love, to immediately reincarnate in third density rather than proceeding towards fourth density. This causes them to be Wanderers of a type, Wanderers who have never left the Earth plane because of their free will rather than because of their vibrational level.

Questioner: In yesterday's material you mentioned that the first distortion was the distortion of free will. Is there a sequence, a first, second, and third distortion of the Law of One?

Ra: I am Ra. Only up to a very short point. After this point, the many-ness of distortions are equal one to another. The first distortion, free will, finds focus. This is the second distortion known to you as Logos, the Creative Principle or Love. This intelligent energy thus creates a distortion known as Light. From these three distortions come many, many hierarchies of distortions, each having its own paradoxes to be synthesized, no one being more important than another.

Questioner: You also said that you offered the Law of One which is the balancing of love/light with light/love. Is there any difference between light/love and love/light?

Ra: I am Ra. This will be the final question of this time/space. There is the same difference between love/light and light/love as there is between teach/learning and learn/teaching. Love/light is the enabler, the power, the energy giver. Light/love is the manifestation which occurs when light has been impressed with love.

Questioner: Is there anything we can do to make the instrument more comfortable? Can we have two sessions today?

Ra: I am Ra. This instrument requires a certain amount of manipulation of the physical or body complex due to a stiffness. Other than this, all is well, the energies being balanced. There is a slight distortion in the mental energy of this instrument due to concern for a loved one, as you call it. This is only slightly lowering the vital energies of the instrument. Given a manipulation, this instrument will be well for another working.

Questioner: By manipulation, do you mean that she should go for a walk or that we should rub her back?

Ra: I am Ra. We meant the latter. The understanding must be added that this manipulation be done by one in harmony with the entity.

I am Ra. I leave you in the love and the light of the infinite Creator. Go forth, then, rejoicing in the power and the peace of the one infinite Creator. Adonai.

L/L Research

The Law of One, Book V, Session 15, Fragment 6
January 30, 1981

Jim: However, our curiosity did periodically return. And, once again, we see the importance of maintaining one's free will by not diluting the present incarnational experience with too much information concerning one's previous experiences. Meditations and lives tend to be more efficient if they remain focused upon one point or moment.

Carla: We have spent a few moments of our lives thinking about who was fifth-density and who was sixth, but it has never been clear, nor have we been much pushed to figure it out!

Session 15, January 30, 1981

Questioner: Is it possible, since we are Wanderers, for you to tell us anything about which our last density was, which density we came from?

Ra: I scan each and find it acceptable to share this information. The Wanderers in this working are of two densities, one the density of five; that is, of light; one the density of love/light, or unity. To express the identity of which came from which density, we observe this to be an infringement upon the free will of each. Therefore, we state simply the two densities, both of which are harmoniously oriented towards work together.

L/L Research

The Law of One, Book I, Session 16
January 31, 1981

Ra: I am Ra. I greet you in the love and the light of the infinite Creator. We communicate now.

Questioner: I would like to ask, considering the free will distortion of the Law of One, how can the Guardians quarantine the Earth? Is this quarantine within free will?

Ra: I am Ra. The Guardians guard the free will distortion of the mind/body/spirit complexes of third density on this planetary sphere. The events which required activation of quarantine were interfering with the free will distortion of mind/body/spirit complexes.

Questioner: I may be wrong, but it seems to me that it would be the free will of, say the Orion group, to interfere. How is this balanced with the information which you just gave?

Ra: I am Ra. The balancing is from dimension to dimension. The attempts of the so-called Crusaders to interfere with free will are acceptable upon the dimension of their understanding. However, the mind/body/spirit complexes of this dimension you call third form a dimension of free will which is not able to, shall we say, recognize in full, the distortions towards manipulation. Thus, in order to balance the dimensional variances in vibration, a quarantine, this being a balancing situation whereby the free will of the Orion group is not stopped but given a challenge. Meanwhile, the third group is not hindered from free choice.

Questioner: Could these "windows" that occur to let the Orion group come through once in a while have anything to do with this free will balancing?

Ra: I am Ra. This is correct.

Questioner: Could you tell me how that works?

Ra: I am Ra. The closest analogy would be a random number generator within certain limits.

Questioner: What is the source of this random number generator? Is it created by the Guardians to balance their guarding? Or is it a source other than the Guardians?

Ra: I am Ra. All sources are one. However, we understand your query. The window phenomenon is an other-self phenomenon from the Guardians. It operates from the dimensions beyond space/time in what you may call the area of intelligent energy. Like your cycles, such balancing, such rhythms are as a clock striking. In the case of the windows, no entities have the clock. Therefore, it seems random. It is not random in the dimension which produces this balance. That is why we stated the analogy was within certain limits.

Questioner: Then this window balancing prevents the Guardians from reducing their positive polarization by totally eliminating the Orion contact through shielding. Is this correct?

Ra: I am Ra. This is partially correct. In effect, the balancing allows an equal amount of positive and negative influx, this balanced by the mind/body/spirit distortions of the social complex. Thus in your particular planetary sphere, less negative, as you would call it, information or stimulus is necessary than positive due to the somewhat negative orientation of your social complex distortion.

Questioner: In this way, total free will is balanced so that individuals may have an equal opportunity to choose service to others or service to self. Is this correct?

Ra: I am Ra. This is correct.

Questioner: This is a profound revelation, I believe, in the Law of Free Will. Thank you.

This is a minor question further to make an example of this principle, but if the Confederation landed on Earth, they would be taken as gods, breaking the Law of Free Will and thus reducing their polarization of service to all. I assume that the same thing would happen if the Orion group landed. How would this affect their polarization of service to self if they were able to land and became known as gods?

Ra: I am Ra. In the event of mass landing of the Orion group, the effect of polarization would be strongly toward an increase in the service to self, precisely the opposite of the former opportunity which you mentioned.

Questioner: If the Orion group was able to land, would this increase their polarization? What I am trying to get at is, is it better for them to work behind the scenes to get recruits, shall we say, from our planet, the person from our planet going strictly on his own using free will, or is it just as good for the Orion group to land on our planet and demonstrate remarkable powers and get people like that?

Ra: I am Ra. This first instance is, in the long run, shall we put it, more salubrious for the Orion group in that it does not infringe upon the Law of One by landing and, thus, does its work through those of this planet. In the second circumstance, a mass landing would create a loss of polarization due to the infringement upon the free will of the planet. However, it would be a gamble. If the planet were then conquered and became part of the Empire, the free will would then be re-established. This is restrained in action due to the desire of the Orion group to progress towards the one Creator. This desire to progress inhibits the group from breaking the Law of Confusion.

Questioner: You mentioned the word "Empire" in relation to the Orion group. I have thought for some time that the movie *Star Wars* was somehow an allegory for what is actually happening. Is this correct?

Ra: I am Ra. This is correct in the same way that a simple children's story is an allegory for physical/philosophical/social complex distortion/understanding.

Questioner: Is there a harvest of entities oriented toward service to self like there is a harvest of those oriented toward service to others?

Ra: I am Ra. There is one harvest. Those able to enter fourth density through vibrational complex levels may choose the manner of their further seeking of the one Creator.

Questioner: Then as we enter the fourth density there will be a split, shall we say, and part of the individuals who go into the fourth density will go into planets or places where there is service to others and part will go into places where there is service to self.

Is this correct?

Ra: I am Ra. This is correct.

Questioner: Can you tell me the origin of the Ten Commandments?

Ra: I am Ra. The origin of these commandments follows the law of negative entities impressing information upon positively oriented mind/body/spirit complexes. The information attempted to copy or ape positivity while retaining negative characteristics.

Questioner: Was this done by the Orion group?

Ra: I am Ra. This is correct.

Questioner: What was their purpose in doing this?

Ra: I am Ra. The purpose of the Orion group, as mentioned before, is conquest and enslavement. This is done by finding and establishing an elite and causing others to serve the elite through various devices such as the laws you mentioned and others given by this entity.

Questioner: Was the recipient of the commandments positively or negatively oriented?

Ra: I am Ra. The recipient was one of extreme positivity, thus accounting for some of the pseudo-positive characteristics of the information received. As with contacts which are not successful, this entity, vibratory complex, Moishe, did not remain a credible influence among those who had first heard the philosophy of One and this entity was removed from this third-density vibratory level in a lessened or saddened state, having lost, what you may call, the honor and faith with which he had begun the conceptualization of the Law of One and the freeing of those who were of his tribes, as they were called at that time/space.

Questioner: If this entity was positively oriented, how was the Orion group able to contact him?

Ra: I am Ra. This was an intensive, shall we say, battleground between positively oriented forces of Confederation origin and negatively oriented sources. The one called Moishe was open to impression and received the Law of One in its most simple form. However, the information became negatively oriented due to his people's pressure to do specific physical things in the third-density planes. This left the entity open for the type of information and philosophy of a self-service nature.

Questioner: It would be wholly unlike an entity fully aware of the knowledge of the Law of One to ever say "Thou shalt not." Is this correct?

Ra: I am Ra. This is correct.

Questioner: Can you give me some kind of history of your social memory complex and how you became aware of the Law of One?

Ra: I am Ra. The path of our learning is graven in the present moment. There is no history, as we understand your concept. Picture, if you will, a circle of being. We know the alpha and omega as infinite intelligence. The circle never ceases. It is present. The densities we have traversed at various points in the circle correspond to the characteristics of cycles: first, the cycle of awareness; second, the cycle of growth; third, the cycle of self-awareness; fourth, the cycle of love or understanding; fifth, the cycle of light or wisdom; sixth, the cycle of light/love, love/light or unity; seventh, the gateway cycle; eighth, the octave which moves into a mystery we do not plumb.

Questioner: Thank you very much. In previous material, before we communicated with you, it was stated by the Confederation that there is actually no past or future … that all is present. Would this be a good analogy?

Ra: I am Ra. There is past, present, and future in third density. In an overview such as an entity may have, removed from the space/time continuum, it may be seen that in the cycle of completion there exists only the present. We, ourselves, seek to learn this understanding. At the seventh level or dimension, we shall, if our humble efforts are sufficient, become one with all, thus having no memory, no identity, no past or future, but existing in the all.

Questioner: Does this mean that you would have awareness of all that is?

Ra: I am Ra. This is partially correct. It is our understanding that it would not be our awareness, but simply awareness of the Creator. In the Creator is all that there is. Therefore, this knowledge would be available.

Questioner: I was wondering how many inhabited planets there are in our galaxy and if they all reach higher density by the Law of One? It doesn't seem that there would be any other way to reach higher density? Is this correct?

Ra: I am Ra. Please restate your query.

Questioner: How many inhabited planets are there in our galaxy?

Ra: I am Ra. We are assuming that you intend all dimensions of consciousness or densities of awareness in this question. Approximately one-fifth of all planetary entities contain awareness of one or more densities. Some planets are hospitable only for certain densities. Your planet, for instance, is at this time hospitable for densities one, two, three, and four.

Questioner: Roughly how many total planets in this galaxy of stars that we are in are aware regardless of density?

Ra: I am Ra. Approximately 67 million.

Questioner: Can you tell me what percentage of those are third, fourth, fifth, sixth etc., density?

Ra: I am Ra. A percentage seventeen for first density, a percentage twenty for second density, a percentage twenty-seven for third density, a percentage sixteen for fourth density, a percentage six for fifth density. The other information must be withheld.

Questioner: Of these first five densities, have all of the planets progressed from the third density by knowledge and application of the Law of One?

Ra: I am Ra. This is correct.

Questioner: Then the only way for a planet to get out of the situation that we are in is for the population to become aware of and start practicing the Law of One. Is this correct?

Ra: I am Ra. This is correct.

Questioner: Can you tell me what percentage of the third-, fourth-, and fifth-density planets which you have spoken of here are polarized negatively towards service to self?

Ra: I am Ra. This is not a query to which we may speak given the Law of Confusion.

We may say only that the negatively or self-service oriented planetary spheres are much fewer. To give you exact numbers would not be appropriate.

Questioner: I would like to make an analogy as to why there are fewer negatively oriented, and then ask you if the analogy is good.

In a positively oriented society with service to others, it would be simple to move a large boulder by getting everyone to help move it. In a society oriented towards service to self, it would be much more difficult to get everyone to work for the good of all to move the boulder; therefore, it is much easier to get things done to create the service to others principle and to grow in positively oriented communities than in negatively oriented communities. Is this correct?

Ra: I am Ra. This is correct.

Questioner: Thank you very much.

Can you tell me how the Confederation of Planets was formed and why?

Ra: I am Ra. The desire to serve begins, in the dimension of love or understanding, to be an overwhelming goal of the social memory complex.

Thus, those percentiles of planetary entities, plus approximately four percent more of whose identity we cannot speak, found themselves long, long ago in your time seeking the same thing: service to others. The relationship between these entities as they entered an understanding of other beings, other planetary entities, and other concepts of service was to share and continue together these commonly held goals of service. Thus, each voluntarily placed the social memory complex data in what you may consider a central thought complex available to all. This then created a structure whereby each entity could work in its own service while calling upon any other understanding needed to enhance the service. This is the cause of the formation and the manner of the working of the Confederation.

Questioner: With such a large number of planets in this galaxy you say that there are approximately five hundred planets in the Confederation. There seems to be a relatively small number of Confederation planets around. Is there a reason for it?

Ra: I am Ra. There are many Confederations. This Confederation works with the planetary spheres of seven of your galaxies, if you will, and is responsible for the callings of the densities of these galaxies.

Questioner: Would you define the word galaxy as you just used it?

Ra: I am Ra. We use that term in this sense as you would use star systems.

Questioner: I'm a little bit confused as to how many total planets the Confederation that you are in serves?

Ra: I am Ra. I see the confusion. We have difficulty with your language.

The galaxy term must be split. We call galaxy that vibrational complex that is local. Thus, your sun is what we would call the center of a galaxy. We see you have another meaning for this term.

Questioner: Yes. In our science the term galaxy refers to the lenticular star system that contains millions and millions of stars. There was a confusion about this in one of our earlier communications, and I'm glad to get it cleared up.

Using the term galaxy in the sense that I just stated, using the lenticular star system that contains millions of stars, do you know of evolution in other galaxies besides this one?

R: I am Ra. We are aware of life in infinite capacity. You are correct in this assumption.

Questioner: Can you tell me if the progression of life in other galaxies is similar to the progression of life in our galaxy?

Ra: I am Ra. The progression is somewhat close to the same, asymptotically approaching congruency throughout infinity. The free choosing of what you would call galactic systems causes variations of an extremely minor nature from one of your galaxies to another.

Questioner: Then the Law of One is truly universal in creating a progression towards the eighth density in all galaxies. Is this correct?

Ra: I am Ra. This is correct. There are infinite forms, infinite understandings, but the progression is one.

Questioner: I am assuming that it is not necessary for an individual to understand the Law of One to go from the third to the fourth density. Is this correct?

Ra: I am Ra. It is absolutely necessary that an entity consciously realize it does not understand in order for it to be harvestable. Understanding is not of this density.

Questioner: That is a very important point. I used the wrong word. What I meant to say was that I believed that it was not necessary for an entity to be consciously aware of the Law of One to go from the third to the fourth density.

Ra: I am Ra. This is correct.

Questioner: At what point in the densities is it necessary for an entity to be consciously aware of the Law of One in order to progress?

Ra: I am Ra. The fifth density harvest is of those whose vibratory distortions consciously accept the honor/duty of the Law of One. This responsibility/honor is the foundation of this vibration.

Questioner: Can you tell me a little more about this honor/responsibility concept?

Ra: I am Ra. Each responsibility is an honor; each honor, a responsibility.

Questioner: Thank you. Is it possible for you to give a short description of the conditions in the fourth density?

Ra: I am Ra. We ask you to consider as we speak that there are not words for positively describing fourth density. We can only explain what is not and approximate what is. Beyond fourth density our ability grows more limited until we become without words.

That which fourth density is not: it is not of words, unless chosen. It is not of heavy chemical vehicles for body complex activities. It is not of disharmony within self. It is not of disharmony within peoples. It is not within limits of possibility to cause disharmony in any way.

Approximations of positive statements: it is a plane of type of bipedal vehicle which is much denser and more full of life; it is a plane wherein one is aware of the thought of other-selves; it is a plane wherein one is aware of vibrations of other-selves; it is a plane of compassion and understanding of the sorrows of third density; it is a plane striving towards wisdom or light; it is a plane wherein individual differences are pronounced although automatically harmonized by group consensus.

Questioner: Could you define the word density as we have been using it?

Ra: I am Ra. The term density is a, what you call, mathematical one. The closest analogy is that of music, whereby after seven notes on your western type of scale, if you will, the eighth note begins a new octave. Within your great octave of existence which we share with you, there are seven octaves or densities. Within each density there are seven sub-densities. Within each sub-density, are seven sub-sub-densities. Within each sub-sub-density, seven sub-sub-sub-densities and so on infinitely.

Questioner: I noticed that the time of this session has gone slightly over an hour. I would like to ask at this time if we should go on? What is the condition of the instrument?

Ra: I am Ra. This instrument is in balance. It is well to continue if you desire.

Questioner: I understand that each density has seven sub-densities which again have seven sub-densities and so on. This is expanding at a really large rate as each is increased by powers of seven. Does this mean that in any density level anything that you can think of is happening?

Ra: I am Ra. From your confusion we select the concept with which you struggle, that being infinity/opportunity. You may consider any possibility/probability complex as having an existence.

Questioner: Do things like daydreams become real in other densities?

Ra: I am Ra. This depends upon the nature of the daydream. This is a large subject. Perhaps the simplest thing we can say is, if the daydream, as you call it, is one which attracts to self, this then becomes reality to self. If it is a contemplative general daydream, this may enter the infinity of possibility/probability complexes and occur elsewhere, having no particular attachment to the energy fields of the creator.

Questioner: To make this a little more clear, if I were to daydream strongly about building a ship, would this occur in one of these other densities?

Ra: I am Ra. This would/would have/or shall occur.

Questioner: Then if an entity daydreams strongly about battling an entity, would this occur?

Ra: I am Ra. In this case the entity's fantasy concerns the self and other-self, this binding the thought-form to the possibility/probability complex connected with the self which is the creator of this thought-form. This then would increase the possibility/probability of bringing this into third-density occurrence.

Questioner: Does the Orion group use this principle to create conditions favorable to suit their purpose?

Ra: I am Ra. We will answer more specifically than the question. The Orion group uses daydreams of hostile or other negative natures to feed back or strengthen these thought-forms.

Questioner: Are the many Wanderers who have and are coming to our planet subject to the Orion thoughts?

Ra: I am Ra. As we have said before, Wanderers become completely the creature of third density in mind/body complex. There is just as much chance of such influence to a Wanderer entity as to a mind/body/spirit complex of this planetary sphere. The only difference occurs in the spirit complex which, if it wishes, has an armor of light, if you will, which enables it to recognize more clearly that which is not as it would appropriately be desired by the mind/body/spirit complex. This is not more than bias and cannot be called an understanding.

Furthermore, the Wanderer is, in its own mind/body/spirit, less distorted toward the, shall we say, deviousness of third density positive/negative confusions. Thus, it often does not recognize as easily as a more negative individual the negative nature of thoughts or beings.

Questioner: Then would the Wanderers, as they incarnate here, be high-priority targets of the Orion group?

Ra: I am Ra. This is correct.

Questioner: If a Wanderer should be successfully infringed upon, shall I say, by the Orion group, what would happen to this Wanderer when harvest came?

Ra: I am Ra. If the Wanderer entity demonstrated through action a negative orientation towards other-selves it would be as we have said before, caught into the planetary vibration and, when harvested, possibly repeat again the master cycle of third density as a planetary entity. This shall be the last full question of this session.

Is there a short question we may answer before we close this session?

Questioner: Can the instrument be made more comfortable?

Ra: I am Ra. This instrument is as comfortable as it is possible for you to make it given the weakness distortions of its body complex. You are conscientious.

I am Ra. I leave you in the love and the light of the one infinite Creator. Go forth, then, rejoicing in the power and the peace. Adonai.

The Law of One, Book V, Session 9, Fragment 4, January 27, 1981

L/L Research

L/L Research is a subsidiary of Rock Creek Research & Development Laboratories, Inc.

P.O. Box 5195
Louisville, KY 40255-0195

www.llresearch.org

Rock Creek is a non-profit corporation dedicated to discovering and sharing information which may aid in the spiritual evolution of humankind.

ABOUT THE CONTENTS OF THIS TRANSCRIPT: This telepathic channeling has been taken from transcriptions of the weekly study and meditation meetings of the Rock Creek Research & Development Laboratories and L/L Research. It is offered in the hope that it may be useful to you. As the Confederation entities always make a point of saying, please use your discrimination and judgment in assessing this material. If something rings true to you, fine. If something does not resonate, please leave it behind, for neither we nor those of the Confederation would wish to be a stumbling block for any.

© 2009 L/L Research

The Law of One, Book V, Session 16, Fragment 7
January 31, 1981

Jim: The following material on "silver flecks" is curious in that these small, shiny pieces of what looked like silver rectangles would occasionally appear on or around us when we were discussing matters of a metaphysical nature. Apparently, if we were on the track of thinking that was felt appropriate by our subconscious minds, we would be given a sign of this correctness in the form of the "silver fleck." There are apparently many, many different ways in which people may receive such subconscious confirmations of the appropriateness of their thoughts or actions. The most common, of course, is that feeling of rightness that wells up from within when one is on the right track or receiving spiritually helpful information.

Carla: The awareness of this method of feedback from the winds of destiny is most helpful to one on a spiritual path. The natural world seems very open to the production of synchronicities that are subjectively meaningful. Once the seeker "gets" the presence of these signs, and begins consciously to watch for them, she can actually have influence in the creating of more subjective signs, until there are times when meaningful coincidence seems to take on a constant presence in her life. I certainly have found these signs most comforting and strengthening.

Session 16, January 31, 1981

Questioner: Can you tell me of the silver flecks that we have found sometimes on our faces or elsewhere?

Ra: I am Ra. These of which you speak are a materialization of a subjectively oriented signpost indicating to one mind/body/spirit complex, and no other, a meaning of subjective nature.

Questioner: Who creates these silver flecks?

Ra: I am Ra. Picture, if you will, the increasing potential for learn/teaching. At some point a sign will be given indicating the appropriateness or importance of that learn/teaching. The entity itself, in cooperation with the inner planes, creates whatever signpost is most understandable or noticeable to it.

Questioner: I understand then that we ourselves create this?

Ra: I am Ra. Entities consciously do not create these. The roots of mind complex, having touched in understanding, intelligent infinity, create them. ☙

The Law of One, Book I, Session 17
February 3, 1981

Ra: I am Ra. I greet you in the love and in the light of the infinite Creator.

Before we communicate by answer we shall correct an error which we have discovered in the transmission of our information to you. We have difficulty dealing with your time/space. There may again be errors of this type. Feel free to question us that we may recalculate in your time/space measurements.

The error we have discovered concerns one of the arrivals of both the Orion group into your planetary sphere of influence and the corresponding arrival of emissaries of the Confederation. We gave dates of 2,600 years for the Orion entry, 2,300 for Confederation entry. This is incorrect. The recalculation indicates numbers 3,600 for Orion entry, 3,300 for Confederation entry.

We communicate now.

Questioner: Thank you very much. I would like to say again that we consider it a great honor, privilege, and duty to be able to do this particular work. I would like to reiterate that some of my questions may seem irrelevant at times, but I am trying to ask them in a manner so as to gain a foothold into the application of the Law of One.

We are now in the fourth density. Will the effects of the fourth density increase in the next thirty years? Will we see more changes in our environment and our effect upon our environment?

Ra: I am Ra. The fourth density is a vibrational spectrum. Your time/space continuum has spiraled your planetary sphere and your, what we would call galaxy, what you call star, into this vibration. This will cause the planetary sphere itself to electromagnetically realign its vortices of reception of the in-streaming of cosmic forces expressing themselves as vibrational webs so that the Earth thus be fourth-density magnetized, as you may call it.

This is going to occur with some inconvenience, as we have said before, due to the energies of the thought-forms of your peoples which disturb the orderly constructs of energy patterns within your Earth spirals of energy which increases entropy and unusable heat. This will cause your planetary sphere to have some ruptures in its outer garment while making itself appropriately magnetized for fourth density. This is the planetary adjustment.

You will find a sharp increase in the number of people, as you call mind/body/spirit complexes, whose vibrational potentials include the potential for fourth-vibrational distortions. Thus, there will seem to be, shall we say, a new breed. These are those incarnating for fourth-density work.

There will also be a sharp increase in the short run of negatively oriented or polarized mind/body/spirit complexes and social complexes, due to the polarizing conditions of the sharp delineation between fourth-density characteristics and third-density self-service orientation.

Those who remain in fourth density upon this plane will be of the so-called positive orientation. Many will come from elsewhere, for it would appear that with all the best efforts of the Confederation, which includes those from your peoples' inner planes, inner civilizations, and those from other dimensions, the harvest will still be much less than this planetary sphere is capable of comfortably supporting in service.

Questioner: Is it possible by the use of some technique or other to help an entity to reach fourth-density level in these last days?

Ra: I am Ra. It is impossible to help another being directly. It is only possible to make catalyst available in whatever form, the most important being the radiation of realization of oneness with the Creator from the self, less important being information such as we share with you.

We, ourselves, do not feel an urgency for this information to be widely disseminated. It is enough that we have made it available to three, four, or five. This is extremely ample reward, for if one of these obtains fourth-density understanding due to this catalyst then we shall have fulfilled the Law of One in the distortion of service.

We encourage a dispassionate attempt to share information without concern for numbers or quick growth among others. That you attempt to make this information available is, in your terms, your service. The attempt, if it reaches one, reaches all.

We cannot offer shortcuts to enlightenment. Enlightenment is, of the moment, an opening to intelligent infinity. It can only be accomplished by the self, for the self. Another self cannot teach/learn enlightenment, but only teach/learn information, inspiration, or a sharing of love, of mystery, of the unknown that makes the other-self reach out and begin the seeking process that ends in a moment, but who can know when an entity will open the gate to the present?

Questioner: Thank you. Can you tell me who was the entity, before his incarnation on Earth, known as Jesus of Nazareth?

Ra: I am Ra. I have difficulty with this question as it is phrased. Can you discover another form for this query?

Questioner: What I meant to say was can you tell me if Jesus of Nazareth came from the Confederation before incarnation here?

Ra: I am Ra. The one known to you as Jesus of Nazareth did not have a name. This entity was a member of fifth density of the highest level of that sub-octave. This entity was desirous of entering this planetary sphere in order to share the love vibration in as pure a manner as possible. Thus, this entity received permission to perform this mission. This entity was then a Wanderer of no name, of Confederation origins, of fifth density, representing the fifth-density understanding of the vibration of understanding or love.

Questioner: Did you say the fifth vibration was that of love?

Ra: I am Ra. I have made an error. The fourth-density being is that which we intended to say, the highest level of fourth density going into the fifth. This entity could have gone on to the fifth but chose instead to return to third for this particular mission. This entity was of the highest sub-octave of the vibration of love. This is fourth density.

Questioner: When I am communicating with you as Ra, are you at times individualized as an entity or am I speaking to an entire social memory complex?

Ra: I am Ra. You speak with Ra. There is no separation. You would call it social memory complex thus indicating many-ness. To our understanding, you are speaking to an individualized portion of consciousness.

Questioner: Am I always speaking to the same individualized portion of consciousness in each of the sessions?

Ra: I am Ra. You speak to the same entity through a channel or instrument. This instrument is at times lower in vital energy. This will sometimes hamper our proceedings. However, this instrument has a great deal of faithfulness to the task and gives whatever it has to this task. Therefore, we may continue even when energy is low. This is why we usually speak to the ending of the session due to our estimation of the instrument's levels of vital energy.

Questioner: I would like to make a point clear now that I am sure of myself. The people of this planet, following any religion or no religion at all, or having no intellectual knowledge at all of the Law of One, can still be harvested into the fourth density if they are of that vibration. Is that not correct?

Ra: I am Ra. This is correct. However, you will find few who are harvestable whose radiance does not cause others to be aware of their, what you may call, spirituality, the quality of the mind/body/spirit complex distortion. Thus, it is not particularly probable that an entity would be completely unknown to his immediate acquaintances as an unusually radiant personality, even were this individual not caught up in any of the distortions of your so-called religious systems.

Questioner: When Jesus of Nazareth incarnated was there an attempt by the Orion group to discredit him in some way?

Ra: I am Ra. This is correct.

Questioner: Can you tell me what the Orion group did in order to try to cause his downfall?

Ra: I am Ra. We may describe in general what occurred. The technique was that of building upon other negatively oriented information. This information had been given by the one whom your peoples called "Yahweh." This information involved many strictures upon behavior and promised power of the third-density, service-to-self nature. These two types of distortions were impressed upon those already oriented to think these thought-forms.

This eventually led to many challenges of the entity known as Jesus. It eventually led to one, sound vibration complex "Judas," as you call this entity, who believed that it was doing the appropriate thing in bringing about or forcing upon the one you call Jesus the necessity for bringing in the third-density planetary power distortion of third-density rule over others.

This entity, Judas, felt that, if pushed into a corner, the entity you call Jesus would then be able to see the wisdom of using the power of intelligent infinity in order to rule others. The one you call Judas was mistaken in this estimation of the reaction of the entity, Jesus, whose teach/learning was not oriented towards this distortion. This resulted in the destruction of the bodily complex of the one known as Jesus.

Questioner: Then if the entity Jesus was fourth density and there are Wanderers on the planet today who came from fifth and sixth density, what was it that Jesus did that enabled him to be such a good healer and could these fifth- and sixth-density beings here now do the same?

Ra: I am Ra. Those who heal may be of any density which has the consciousness of the spirit. This includes third, fourth, fifth, sixth, and seventh. The third density can be one in which healing takes place just as the others. However, there is more illusory material to understand, to balance, to accept, and to move forward from.

The gate to intelligent infinity can only be opened when an understanding of the in-streamings of intelligent energy are opened unto the healer. These are the so-called Natural Laws of your local space/time continuum and its web of electromagnetic sources or nexi of in-streaming energy.

Know then, first, the mind and the body. Then as the spirit is integrated and synthesized, these are harmonized into a mind/body/spirit complex which can move among the dimensions and can open the gateway to intelligent infinity, thus healing self by light and sharing that light with others.

True healing is simply the radiance of the self causing an environment in which a catalyst may occur which initiates the recognition of self, by self, of the self-healing properties of the self.

Questioner: How did Jesus learn this during his incarnation?

Ra: I am Ra. This entity learned the ability by a natural kind of remembering at a very young age. Unfortunately, this entity first discovered his ability to penetrate intelligent infinity by becoming the distortion you call "angry" at a playmate. This entity was touched by the entity known as Jesus and was fatally wounded.

Thus the one known as Jesus became aware that there dwelt in him a terrible potential. This entity determined to discover how to use this energy for the good, not for the negative. This entity was extremely positively polarized and remembered more than most Wanderers do.

Questioner: How did this aggressive action against a playmate affect Jesus in his spiritual growth? Where did he go after his physical death?

Ra: I am Ra. The entity you call Jesus was galvanized by this experience and began a lifetime of seeking and searching. This entity studied first day and night in its own religious constructs which you call Judaism and was learned enough to be a rabbi, as you call teach/learners of this particular rhythm or distortion of understanding, at a very young age.

At the age of approximately thirteen and one-half of your years, this entity left the dwelling place of its earthly family, as you would call it, and walked into many other places seeking further information. This went on sporadically until the entity was approximately twenty-five, at which time it returned to its family dwelling, and learned and practiced the art of its earthly father.

When the entity had become able to integrate or synthesize all experiences, the entity began to speak to other-selves and teach/learn what it had felt during the preceding years to be of a worthwhile nature. The entity was absolved karmically of the destruction of an other-self when it was in the last portion of lifetime and spoke upon what you would call a cross saying, "Father, forgive them for they know not what they do." In forgiveness lies the stoppage of the wheel of action, or what you call karma.

Questioner: What density is the entity known as Jesus in now?

Ra: I am Ra. This information is harmless though unimportant. This entity studies now the lessons of the wisdom vibration, the fifth-density, also called the light vibration.

Questioner: In our culture there is a saying that he will return. Can you tell me if this is planned?

Ra: I am Ra. I will attempt to sort out this question. It is difficult. This entity became aware that it was not an entity of itself but operated as a messenger of the one Creator whom this entity saw as love. This entity was aware that this cycle was in its last portion and spoke to the effect that those of its consciousness would return at the harvest.

The particular mind/body/spirit complex you call Jesus is, as what you would call an entity, not to return except as a member of the Confederation speaking through a channel. However, there are others of the identical congruency of consciousness that will welcome those to the fourth-density. This is the meaning of the returning.

Questioner: Can you tell me why you say that the Earth will be fourth density positive instead of fourth density negative since there seems to be much negativity here now?

Ra: I am Ra. The Earth seems to be negative. That is due to the quiet, shall we say, horror which is the common distortion which those good or positively oriented entities have towards the occurrences which are of your time/space present. However, those oriented and harvestable in the ways of service to others greatly outnumber those whose orientation towards service to self has become that of harvestable quality.

Questioner: In other words there will be fewer negative entities than positive entities harvested into the fourth density. Is this correct?

Ra: I am Ra. This is correct. The great majority of your peoples will repeat third density.

Questioner: How did Taras Bulba, Genghis Khan, and Rasputin get harvested prior to the harvest?

Ra: I am Ra. It is the right/privilege/duty of those opening consciously the gate to intelligent infinity to choose the manner of their leaving of third density. Those of negative orientation who so achieve this right/duty most often choose to move forward in their learn/teaching of service to self.

Questioner: Am I to understand that the harvest is to occur in the year 2,011, or will it be spread out?

Ra: I am Ra. This is an approximation. We have stated we have difficulty with your time/space. This is an appropriate probable/possible time/space nexus for harvest. Those who are not in incarnation at this time will be included in the harvest.

Questioner: If an entity wants to be of service to others rather than service to self while he is in this third density, are there "best ways" of being of service to others, or is any way just as good as any other way?

Ra: I am Ra. The best way to be of service to others has been explicitly covered in previous material. We will iterate briefly.

The best way of service to others is the constant attempt to seek to share the love of the Creator as it is known to the inner self. This involves self knowledge and the ability to open the self to the other-self without hesitation. This involves, shall we say, radiating that which is the essence or the heart of the mind/body/spirit complex.

Speaking to the intention of your question, the best way for each seeker in third density to be of service to others is unique to that mind/body/spirit complex. This means that the mind/body/spirit complex must then seek within itself the intelligence of its own discernment as to the way it may best serve other-selves. This will be different for each. There is no best. There is no generalization. Nothing is known.

Questioner: I don't wish to take up extra time asking questions over again. Some areas I consider important enough in relation to the Law of One to ask questions in a different way in order to get another perspective in the answer.

In the book *Oahspe* it states that if an entity goes over fifty one percent service to others and is less than fifty percent service to self, then that entity is harvestable. Is this correct?

Ra: I am Ra. This is correct if the harvesting is to be for the positive fourth dimensional level.

Questioner: What is to be the entity's percentage if he is to be harvested for the negative?

Ra: I am Ra. The entity who wishes to pursue the path of service to self must attain a grade of five, that is five percent service to others, ninety-five percent service to self. It must approach totality. The negative path is quite difficult to attain harvestability upon and requires great dedication.

Questioner: Why is the negative path so much more difficult to attain harvestability upon than the positive?

Ra: I am Ra. This is due to a distortion of the Law of One which indicates that the gateway to intelligent infinity be a gateway at the end of a straight and narrow path as you may call it. To attain fifty-one percent dedication to the welfare of other-selves is as difficult as attaining a grade of five percent dedication to otherselves. The, shall we say, sinkhole of indifference is between those two.

Questioner: Then if an entity is harvested into the fourth density with a grade of fifty-one percent for others and forty-nine percent for self, what level of the fourth density would he go into? I am assuming that there are different levels of the fourth density.

Ra: I am Ra. This is correct. Each enters that sub-density which vibrates in accordance with the entity's understanding.

Questioner: How many levels do we have here in the third density at this time?

Ra: I am Ra. The third density has an infinite number of levels.

Questioner: I've heard that there are seven astral and seven devachanic levels. Is this correct?

Ra: I am Ra. You speak of some of the more large distinctions in levels in your inner planes. That is correct.

Questioner: Who inhabits the astral and devachanic planes?

Ra: I am Ra. Entities inhabit the various planes due to their vibration/nature. The astral plane varies from thought-forms in the lower extremities to enlightened beings who become dedicated to teach/learning in the higher astral planes.

In the devachanic planes, as you call them, are those whose vibrations are even more close to the primal distortions of love/light.

Beyond these planes there are others.

Questioner: Are there seven sub-planes to what we call our physical plane here?

Ra: I am Ra. You are correct. This is difficult to understand. There are an infinite number of planes. In your particular space/time continuum distortion there are seven sub-planes of mind/body/spirit complexes. You will discover the vibrational nature of these seven planes as you pass through your experiential distortions, meeting other-selves of the various levels which correspond to the energy influx centers of the physical vehicle.

The invisible, or inner, third-density planes are inhabited by those who are not of body complex natures such as yours; that is, they do not collect about their spirit/mind complexes a chemical body. Nevertheless these entities are divided in what you may call an artificial dream within a dream into various levels. In the upper levels, desire to communicate knowledge back down to the outer planes of existence becomes less, due to the intensive learn/teaching which occurs upon these levels.

Questioner: Is it necessary to penetrate one level at a time as we move through these planes?

Ra: I am Ra. It has been our experience that some penetrate several planes at one time. Others penetrate them slowly. Some in eagerness attempt to penetrate the higher planes before penetrating the energies of the so-called more fundamental planes. This causes energy imbalance.

You will find ill health, as you call this distortion, to frequently be the result of a subtle mismatch of energies in which some of the higher energy levels are being activated by the conscious attempts of the entity while the entity has not penetrated the lower energy centers or sub-densities of this density.

Questioner: Is there a "best way" to meditate?

Ra: I am Ra. No.

Questioner: At this time, near the end of the cycle, how are reincarnations into the physical allocated, shall we say, on this planet?

Ra: I am Ra. Entities wishing to obtain critically needed experience in order to become harvestable are incarnated with priority over those who will, without too much probable/possible doubt, need to re-experience this density.

Questioner: How long has this type of allocation been going on?

Ra: I am Ra. This has been going on since the first individual entity became conscious of its need to learn the lessons of this density. This was the beginning of what you may call a seniority by vibration.

Questioner: Can you explain what you mean by a seniority by vibration?

Ra: I am Ra. This will be the final question of this session of working.

The seniority by vibration is the preferential treatment, shall we say, which follows the ways of the Law of One which encourages harvestable individuals, each individual becoming aware of the time of harvest and the need on a self-level to bend mind/body/spirit towards the learn/teaching of these lessons, by giving them priority in order that an entity may have the best possible chance, shall we say, in succeeding in this attempt.

May we ask at this time if there are any brief questions?

Questioner: My only question is what can we do to make the instrument more comfortable?

Ra: I am Ra. This instrument is not wearing the appropriate apparel for this work. As inpourings occur in the regions of the, what you may call, seventh chakra as you speak of these energy centers, filtering through the sixth and so forth, the entity's other or base chakras become somewhat de-energized. Thus, this entity should be more careful in its selection of warm apparel for the part of the body complex you call the feet.

May we answer any other brief questions?

Questioner: Then we want to put heavier clothing on the feet. Is this correct?

Ra: I am Ra. This is correct.

I will leave this instrument now, I leave you in the love and the light of the one infinite Creator. Adonai.

The Law of One, Book V, Session 17, Fragment 8
February 3, 1981

Jim: Before each contact with those of Ra we conducted a meditation which we used as our tuning device; that is, our means of becoming as one in our seeking to be of service to others. Oftentimes, during this meditation, Don would get a hunch as to an addition to the line of questioning which we had decided upon the night before. In Session 17 such a hunch came to him concerning a crater in the Tunguska region of Russia which, it is speculated, was made by either a crashed UFO or a large meteor of some kind in 1908. There is also speculation that some scientists of the Soviet Union first became interested in the possibility of life in other parts of the galaxy and solar system as a result of their investigation of this crater and its possible origin.

After asking about this crater and following it up with questions concerning the development of nuclear energy on Earth and the odd and rarely reported phenomenon of spontaneous combustion of a human being, Don determined that this line of questioning would yield little of value.

Carla: Donald was a scientist, and he never could quite accept that Ra was in no position to chat with us about phenomena that can be measured. The desire that had brought Ra to our group was a true desire for non-transient material, and this desire fueled our sessions. When we departed from that level of information, Ra would remind us to get back on track in a subtle way: by telling us to watch our alignments. We at first took them literally and thought they were referring to the items on the altar, to getting them lined up rightly. Later, we figured out that they were grading our questions, not our Bible and candle placement. It's worth emphasizing that anything measurable is also transient. The human spirit, the force of creative love, the creation's essence: these things are unfindable, noumenal, always sensed and never penetrated by our fact-finding intellects. But we sense into them through living with an open heart, and by talking about them with sources such as Ra and Q'uo and other "universal" or "outer" energies and essences. The personal guides and other teachers of the inner planes of our planet have much more leeway in offering personal information, whenever their last incarnation. Go to them to get your readings on your health and other specific issues. Go to outer sources such as our confederation sources with questions that transcend space and time. If it will matter less in 10,000 years than it does now, it is probably not a universal question!

Session 17, February 3, 1981

Questioner: In meditation I got the question about the crater in Russia in the, I believe, Tunguska region. Can you tell me what caused the crater?

Ra: I am Ra. The destruction of a fission reactor caused this crater.

Questioner: Whose reactor?

Ra: I am Ra. This was what you may call a "drone" sent by Confederation which malfunctioned. It was moved to an area where its destruction would not cause infringement upon the will of mind/body/spirit complexes. It was then detonated.

Questioner: What was its purpose in coming here?

Ra: It was a drone designed to listen to the various signals of your peoples. You were, at that time, beginning work in a more technical sphere. We were interested in determining the extent and the rapidity of your advances. This drone was powered by a simple fission motor or engine as you would call it. It was not that type which you now know, but was very small. However, it has the same destructive effect upon third-density molecular structures. Thus as it malfunctioned we felt it was best to pick a place for its destruction rather than attempt to retrieve it, for the possibility/probability modes for this maneuver looked very, very minute.

Questioner: Was its danger both blast and radiation?

Ra: I am Ra. There is very little radiation, as you know of it, in this particular type of device. There is radiation which is localized, but the localization is such that it does not drift with the winds as does the emission of your somewhat primitive weapons.

Questioner: I believe that analysis has detected very little radiation in the trees in this area. Is this low level of radiation a result of what you are speaking of?

Ra: I am Ra. This is correct. The amount of radiation is very localized. However, the energy which is released is powerful enough to cause difficulties.

Questioner: Then was the Confederation responsible for the Earth receiving nuclear power?

Ra: I am Ra. It is a point which one cannot judge what is cause. The basic equation which preceded this work was an equation brought through by a Wanderer dedicated to service to the planet. That this work should have become the foundation for instruments of destruction was not intended and was not given.

Questioner: Can you tell me who this Wanderer was who brought through the equation?

Ra: I am Ra. This information seems harmless as this entity is no longer of your planetary third density. This entity was named, sound vibratory complex, Albert.

Questioner: Is this the reason for what we call spontaneous combustion of human beings?

Ra: I am Ra. This is not correct.

Questioner: Can you tell me what causes that phenomenon?

Ra: I am Ra. Picture, if you will, a forest. One tree is struck by lightening. It burns. Lightening does not strike elsewhere. Elsewhere does not burn. There are random occurrences which do not have to do with the entity, but with the window phenomenon of which we spoke.

Questioner: Are these entities uniquely the same, or are they random entities?

Ra: I am Ra. The latter is correct.

Intensive Meditation
February 4, 1981

(Carla channeling?)

[I am Hatonn,] and I greet you, my friends, in the love and in the light of our infinite Creator. We would like, at this time, to confirm that we have been conditioning the one known as S. If the instrument known as S had wished, it would have been possible for this instrument to initiate contact. This is a desirable ability, for there is not always an experienced instrument present during a time when one who wishes to be of service by offering itself as a vocal channel finds the opportunity to share in our thoughts.

We would speak a few words through this instrument before we work with the one known as S, for we sense the deprivation of some information which may perhaps be of service at this time. This deprivation is not due to any individual's efforts, rather, it is due, my friends, to the culture in which you find yourselves experiencing the great patterns of life which you weave day-by-day. It was intended by the Creator that you might experience your so-called work as a form of meditation and as an experience of love. It has been many centuries among your peoples since it was possible for many of your peoples to profoundly experience the combination of work and love. It has been said to work is to pray, and for those lucky enough, shall we say, to have found occupations which enable them to supply themselves with the necessities of survival which also feed the spirit, this is in the deepest sense true. You may find these people working with their hands to make beauty, working with their minds as channels of various forms of love, working among people in such a way that their very being is of service in a substantial manner.

But for so many, my friends, the connection between the daily life and love, between action and meditation, is not apparent. And in order for you to become able to link in any way the work of empty form which you find yourselves performing and the work which is love, it is recommended that you begin with the meditation rather than with the work. To move from one consciousness to another is like mounting the great hillside, the bottom of which is vanity, pollution, pettiness and distraction. In your spirit's garment you move in consciousness of this lovely hillside. You can feel that your garment, the garment of your spirit, is soiled from all that touches you that you perceive as being unclean. And so you remove the garment and cleanse yourself in the waters which you find falling down the hillside in a lovely waterfall, brilliant with crescents of *(inaudible)* and iridescent as it sprays the rocks, the moss, and the grass. Leaning into the water you can begin to see the purity of your true being, and you can cleanse yourself with the waters of [the lake.]

Taking up your fresh garment, a new washed linen, you move onward until you sit at the top of this hillside. The air about you is warm and redolent with the scent of wild flowers, pinks and roses and whites, all in profusion about you, and as you settle into meditation, this is your consciousness, this is who you are. All of creation breathes with you and desires to be of service to you, and you in turn offer up the rhythms of your body, your mind, and your spirit in service to this beautiful [place you're in,] loving and delighting in its beauty, its purity, and its gentle ever-present strength.

Yes, my friends, you come down again into the marketplace where you live the illusion, where your lessons [collect.] But you bring with you an unsoiled garment, a cleanliness of soul, and a new vision that begins to attempt to see the top of the hillside beneath the soiled garment of all labor, all conditions, and all relationships. You cannot and never shall function as a great [wise] one working in the valley. Within yourselves you must find a place in which in silence you find the creation offered unto you, and offer yourself unto the Creation, feeling the great beating rhythm, unity that binds all things together.

We ask that you never be discouraged if you fail to manifest what you have learned in your meditations, for this is the work of your life: to find who you are. That is, my friends, to find the Creator, that one great original Thought which is love and which when *(inaudible)*.

We are pleased at this time to transfer this contact to the one known as S, after pausing for a brief period in order to make our conditioning vibration *(inaudible)*, and to the one known as R, and to the one known as [Don.] I am Hatonn.

(Unknown channeling

I am Hatonn, and am with this instrument. We greet you, my friends, once more. It has been a pleasure to work with those who have requested our conditioning vibration. We are always pleased to join with those who seek our contact. We are honored to be with this group today, as it is indeed a joy to be of service to the one infinite Creator by aiding those who seek our help. We of Hatonn are always available to those who seek out aid. We ask that you simply mentally request our presence and we shall be with you. We are hoping to be with each of you in the near future, and would attempt to contact another instrument at this time. I am Hatonn.

(Unknown channeling

I am Hatonn, and am again with this instrument. And please excuse the pause, but we were attempting to initiate contact with another instrument, shall we say, an old friend of ours. May we say to the one known as S that her fidelity to our channeled communication is such that the degree of the instrument's own thoughts coming into the contact is very nearly nonexistent.

At this point in the training of the new instrument we do the opposite of that with which we start. We attempt to encourage the somewhat experienced instrument to feel more free to speak upon a subject about which the instrument does not have a prior recollection of, a subject matter from another contact. This type of channeling is the next step and requires that the instrument allow us to present her with images drawn from the treasure trove of her own experiences, recollections and thoughts. We use this framework in order that our extremely simple message may be offered in the greatest possible variety, or kaleidoscope, of patterns, for each various view of love, of the Creator, of the universe, of reality, may for the first time inspire one to whom all previous words were naught but chatter and foolishness.

The nature of inspiration is so personal and so unpredictable that we simply cannot expect to create parrots. We hope instead to create those who are able through practice in sessions such as these to recognize our vibrations, and to trust in our contact enough to sally forth into vistas about which they have not thought, and to describe concepts and stories the gist and outcome of which is not known to the instrument. This is the work of some time, as you call it. We say all this to assure the instrument that she is progressing very well. Well enough, in fact, to consider the possibility of launching forward on the next step at any contact at which she may feel comfortable in so doing.

The knowledge of the instrument that subjectively familiar material is being integrated into a meditation, causes all beginning channels, except those who are not excellent, to have doubts as to the origin of the channeled information. However, my sister, it is our way of insuring that each message is somewhat fresh. We thank the one known as S, and, as always, assure her that we and those of the Confederation in general, offer ourselves at any time we may be requested to accompany meditation.

I am Hatonn. We leave you on a hillside, my friends, gazing forth into a world of illusion, a world in which each illusion has a central core of purity and love. As this instrument would say, your mission is, impossible though it may seem, to find it. I leave you in the love and in light. I am Hatonn. Adonai vasu.

(Unknown channeling

I am Latwii, and greet you all in love and light. It is a great honor for us to be asked to join you this afternoon during your meditation. As always, we look forward to such adventures with glee and a happy anticipation. Before we would attempt to answer queries, we would attempt to offer our conditioning to the one known as R, and simultaneously to the one known as S. And then if the one known as S would care to speak out thoughts, we would speak a few words through this new instrument. I am Latwii.

(S channeling

I am Latwii, and am with this instrument. I greet you, my friends, in the love and in the light of the Creator. We are overjoyed to be speaking to you through this instrument once more. She is indeed a contact that we enjoy. We are happy to be with her at this time. We are always pleased to be able to speak through instruments such as this, for we are not often given the opportunity to do so. We find it a great deal of fun. We are sorry to say that we feel we should close this contact so that we may be of service to those who have questions on their minds. We would therefore sign off. I am Latwii.

(Unknown channeling

I am Latwii, and am with this instrument once again, and greet you all in love and light. May we at this time ask if any present might have a question which we would attempt to answer?

Questioner: Yes, Latwii. How can I, or how is it possible to increase receptiveness to the conditioning vibration?

I am Latwii, and, my brother, may we suggest that there is nothing in particular to do. Rather, it is that which is not done which is most helpful to the reception of, not only our conditioning vibration, but the conditioning vibration of any Confederation entity. That is, simply the relaxing of mind and body to the greatest degree possible, and the opening of the being as clearly and freely, shall we say, as is possible. This, of course, is predicated upon the assumption that the desire for such a contact is present, and we find that desire is quite present in your case. The many methods of relaxing the mind and body which have been written down among your peoples as the various methods of meditation are helpful, but we would also suggest that the concept of not doing and of simply seeking is the foundation stone upon which any technique is based.

May we answer you further, my brother?

Questioner: No, thank you.

I am Latwii. We are most grateful to you as well. Is there another question at this time?

S: Yes, Latwii, during one of my meditations I received what seemed to be very strong conditioning that I didn't ask for and was not able to get rid of for quite some time. It kind of frightened me. Can you give me any information about this?

I am Latwii, and am aware of your question, my sister. May we say in this regard that whenever you might feel a vibration which is not pleasant or desirable, at that time request that it be removed, and if the entity generating that vibration is of the Confederation of Planets in the Service of the Infinite Creator then you may be assured that the vibration shall be removed. If upon such request the vibration is not removed, we suggest the ceasing of the meditative state for a moment, the gathering of the self in concentrated thought, and the sending of love and light to all entities present, then the constructing, shall we say, of the shield of light about the self so that meditation may be resumed.

May we answer you further, my sister?

S: No, not on that subject, but I do have another question. Due to my feeling lately I've had a strong urge to proceed and go further, and against advice from the Confederation I proceeded to try channeling with just R and myself present. It did serve to confuse me as I was warned might happen, but I still feel somewhat compelled to continue so that I may be able to get more practice and therefore move along at a faster pace. Would you strongly advise against this or can I do anything more than I'm doing now to protect myself?

I am Latwii, and am aware of your question, my sister. It is always our advice to those …

(Side one of tape ends.)

(Unknown channeling

I am Latwii, and am once again with this instrument. As we were saying, we do not recommend that new instruments attempt to channel from any Confederation source without the presence of at least two other entities, one preferably being an instrument with some experience, so that the contact might be, shall we say, checked and balanced, so that there is reduced the possibility of the infringement of the contact by those entities which do seek to confuse positively-oriented instruments and do seek to sway such new instruments by giving information of what we might call a questionable and specific nature.

For those entities such as yourself who seek to speed their growth upon the spiritual path in general and the, shall we say, specific part of that path known to you as the channeling phenomenon, we recommend the intensive meditation periods, such as this period now occurring, with an experienced channel present. Also, we might recommend the additional meditation periods for the new instrument, at which time the instrument would request the conditioning vibration of the Confederation.

We would also suggest the lengthier, shall we say, meditation periods during which time the new instrument would attempt to increase the attention span, shall we say, that is the state of mind which is most receptive to a contact. This state of mind might be increased in its duration by the visualization technique, that is, the imaging [in] the mind during meditation of the new instrument of any symbol which has a particular meaning to that entity, whether it be the cross, the rose, the circle, the Buddha, or whatever. This is most helpful for the new instrument who wishes to improve its ability at receiving information as purely as possible.

To close this somewhat lengthy response, may we reiterate we are always available for the conditioning vibration to be experienced by any entity requesting it, and we further remind each present that it is most necessary to be accompanied in meditation that is directed toward the channeling phenomenon by at least two other entities. This is necessary, as we said, to preserve the purity of the contact.

May we answer you further, my sister?

S: No, thank you.

I am Latwii. We are most grateful to you as well. Is there another question at this time?

(Pause)

I am Latwii. We are most grateful to each present for inviting us to join this meditation. We of Latwii have a history, shall we say, of being somewhat more humorous in our contacts with this group, but have in recent contacts found the necessity, shall we say, to balance this particular distortion with the giving of information in response to queries of a, shall we say, more serious or intense nature, for we feel the entities within this group who have been seeking our service have sought the guideposts, shall we say, to direct them to the heart of their seeking, and it has been for this reason that we have attempted to deal in a more, shall we say, serious manner with these particular topics and our responses to them.

We do not mean by such gravity to suggest that the lightness and the humor which we are known for does not have a value is such situations, but we wish these entities to seek our service, to know without a doubt that we value their seeking, their questions, and their being greatly, and would honor each entity with the most purely formed response.

With this qualification made and recorded, we shall look forward to joining this group in the future in our more familiar mode of lightness and joy. We thank each entity for requesting our presence. We shall be with each at any time in the future that our presence is so requested. We are known to you as Latwii, and we leave you now in the light and the love and the humor of the one infinite Creator. Adonai vasu borragus. ☙

The Law of One, Book I, Session 18
February 4, 1981

Ra: I am Ra. I greet you in the love and the light of the infinite Creator. We communicate now.

Questioner: I was thinking last night that if I were in the place of Ra right now, the first distortion of the Law of One might cause me to mix some erroneous data with the true information that I was transmitting to this group. Do you do this?

Ra: I am Ra. We do not intentionally do this. However there will be confusion. It is not our intent in this particular project to create erroneous information, but to express in this confining ambiance of your language system the feeling of the Infinite Mystery of the One Creation in its infinite and intelligent unity.

Questioner: Thank you. I have a question here that I will read: "Much of the mystic tradition of seeking on Earth holds the belief that the individual self must be erased or obliterated and the material world ignored for the individual to reach 'nirvana,' as it is called, or enlightenment. What is the proper role of the individual self and its worldly activities to aid an individual to grow more into the Law of One?"

Ra: I am Ra. The proper role of the entity is in this density to experience all things desired, to then analyze, understand, and accept these experiences, distilling from them the love/light within them. Nothing shall be overcome. That which is not needed falls away.

The orientation develops due to analysis of desire. These desires become more and more distorted towards conscious application of love/light as the entity furnishes itself with distilled experience. We have found it to be inappropriate in the extreme to encourage the overcoming of any desires, except to suggest the imagination rather than the carrying out in the physical plane, as you call it, of those desires not consonant with the Law of One, thus preserving the primal distortion of free will.

The reason it is unwise to overcome is that overcoming is an unbalanced action creating difficulties in balancing in the time/space continuum. Overcoming, thus, creates the further environment for holding on to that which apparently has been overcome.

All things are acceptable in the proper time for each entity, and in experiencing, in understanding, in accepting, in then sharing with other-selves, the appropriate distortion shall be moving away from distortions of one kind to distortions of another which may be more consonant with the Law of One.

It is, shall we say, a shortcut to simply ignore or overcome any desire. It must instead be understood and accepted. This takes patience and experience which can be analyzed with care, with compassion for self and for other-self.

Questioner: Basically I would say that to infringe upon the free will of another entity would be the basic thing never to do under the Law of One. Can you state any other breaking of the Law of One than this basic rule?

Ra: I am Ra. As one proceeds from the primal distortion of free will, one proceeds to the understanding of the focal points of intelligent energy which have created the intelligences or the ways of a particular mind/body/spirit complex in its environment, both what you would call natural and what you would call man-made. Thus, the distortions to be avoided are those which do not take into consideration the distortions of the focus of energy of love/light, or shall we say, the Logos of this particular sphere or density. These include the lack of understanding of the needs of the natural environment, the needs of other-selves' mind/body/spirit complexes. These are many due to the various distortions of man-made complexes in which the intelligence and awareness of entities themselves have chosen a way of using the energies available.

Thus, what would be an improper distortion with one entity is proper with another. We can suggest an attempt to become aware of the other-self as self and thus do that action which is needed by other-self, understanding from the other-self's intelligence and awareness. In many cases this does not involve the breaking of the distortion of free will into a distortion or fragmentation called infringement. However, it is a delicate matter to be of service, and compassion, sensitivity, and an ability to empathize are helpful in avoiding the distortions of man-made intelligence and awareness.

The area or arena called the societal complex is an arena in which there are no particular needs for care for it is the prerogative/honor/duty of those in the particular planetary sphere to act according to their free will for the attempted aid of the social complex.

Thus, you have two simple directives: awareness of the intelligent energy expressed in nature, awareness of the intelligent energy expressed in self to be shared when it seems appropriate by the entity with the social complex, and you have one infinitely subtle and various set of distortions of which you may be aware; that is, distortions with respect to self and other-selves not concerning free will but concerning harmonious relationships and service to others as other-selves would most benefit.

Questioner: As an entity in this density grows from childhood, he becomes more aware of his responsibilities. Is there an age below which an entity is not responsible for his actions, or is he responsible from the time of his birth?

Ra: I am Ra. An entity incarnating upon the Earth plane becomes conscious of self at a varying point in its time/space progress through the continuum. This may have a median, shall we say, of approximately fifteen of your months. Some entities become conscious of self at a period closer to incarnation, some at a period farther from this event. In all cases responsibility becomes retroactive from that point backward in the continuum so that distortions are to be understood by the entity and dissolved as the entity learns.

Questioner: Then an entity four years old would be totally responsible for any actions that were against or inharmonious with the Law of One. Is this correct?

Ra: I am Ra. This is correct. It may be noted that it has been arranged by your social complex structures that the newer entities to incarnation are to be provided with guides of a physical mind/body/spirit complex, thus being able to learn quickly what is consonant with the Law of One.

Questioner: Who are these guides?

Ra: I am Ra. These guides are what you call parents, teachers, and friends.

Questioner: You stated yesterday that forgiveness is the eradicator of karma. I am assuming that balanced forgiveness for the full eradication of karma would require forgiveness not only of other-selves but also the forgiveness of self. Am I correct?

Ra: I am Ra. You are correct. We will briefly expand upon this understanding in order to clarify.

Forgiveness of other-self is forgiveness of self. An understanding of this insists upon full forgiveness upon the conscious level of self and other-self, for they are one. A full forgiveness is thus impossible without the inclusion of self.

Questioner: Thank you—a most important point.

You mentioned that there were a number of Confederations. Do all serve the infinite Creator in basically the same way, or do some specialize in some particular types of service?

Ra: I am Ra. All serve the one Creator. There is nothing else to serve, for the Creator is all that there is. It is impossible not to serve the Creator. There are simply various distortions of this service.

As in the Confederation which works with your peoples, each Confederation is a group of specialized individual social memory complexes, each doing that which it expresses to bring into manifestation.

Questioner: Can you tell me how Yahweh communicated to Earth's people?

Ra: I am Ra. This is a somewhat complex question.

The first communication was what you would call genetic. The second communication was the walking among your peoples to produce further genetic changes in consciousness. The third was a series of dialogues with chosen channels.

Questioner: Can you tell me what these genetic changes were and how they were brought about?

Ra: I am Ra. Some of these genetic changes were in a form similar to what you call the cloning process. Thus, entities incarnated in the image of the Yahweh entities. The second was a contact of the nature you know as sexual, changing the mind/body/spirit complex through the natural means of the patterns of reproduction devised by the intelligent energy of your physical complex.

Questioner: Can you tell me specifically what they did in this case?

Ra: I am Ra. We have answered this question. Please restate for further information.

Questioner: Can you tell me the difference between the sexual programming prior to Yahweh's intervention and after intervention?

Ra: I am Ra. This is a question which we can only answer by stating that intervention by genetic means is the same no matter what the source of this change.

Questioner: Can you tell me Yahweh's purpose in making the genetic sexual changes?

Ra: I am Ra. The purpose 75,000 years ago, as you measure time, was of one purpose only: that to express in the mind/body complex those characteristics which would lead to further and more speedy development of the spiritual complex.

Questioner: How did these characteristics go about leading to the more spiritual development?

Ra: I am Ra. The characteristics which were encouraged included sensitivity of all the physical senses to sharpen the experiences, and the strengthening of the mind complex in order to promote the ability to analyze these experiences.

Questioner: When did Yahweh act to perform the genetic changes?

Ra: I am Ra. The Yahweh group worked with those of the planet you call Mars 75,000 years ago in what you would call the cloning process. There are differences, but they lie in the future of your time/space continuum and we cannot break the free will Law of Confusion.

The 2,600, approximately, time was the second time—we correct ourselves: 3,600—approximately, the time of attempts by those of the Orion group during this cultural complex; this was a series of encounters in which the ones called Anak were impregnated with the new genetic coding by your physical complex means so that the organisms would be larger and stronger.

Questioner: Why did they want larger and stronger organisms?

Ra: I am Ra. The ones of Yahweh were attempting to create an understanding of the Law of One by creating mind/body complexes capable of grasping the Law of One. The experiment was a decided failure from the view of the desired distortions due to the fact that rather than assimilating the Law of One, it was a great temptation to consider the so-called social complex or subcomplex elite or different and better than other-selves, this one of the techniques of service to self.

Questioner: Then the Orion group produced this larger body complex to create an elite so that the Law of One could be applied in what we call the negative sense?

Ra: I am Ra. This is incorrect. The entities of Yahweh were responsible for this procedure in isolated cases as experiments in combating the Orion group.

However, the Orion group were able to use this distortion of mind/body complex to inculcate the thoughts of the elite rather than concentrations upon the learning/teaching of oneness.

Questioner: Was Yahweh then of the Confederation?

Ra: I am Ra. Yahweh was of the Confederation but was mistaken in its attempts to aid.

Questioner: Then Yahweh's communications did not help or create what Yahweh wished for them to create. Is this correct?

Ra: I am Ra. The results of this interaction were quite mixed. Where the entities were of a vibrational sum characteristic which embraced oneness, the manipulations of Yahweh were very useful. Wherein the entities of free will had chosen a less positively oriented configuration of sum total vibratory complex, those of the Orion group were able for the first time to make serious inroads upon the consciousness of the planetary complex.

Questioner: Can you tell me specifically what allowed the most serious of these inroads to be made by the Orion group?

Ra: I am Ra. This will be the final full question.

Specifically those who are strong, intelligent, etc., have a temptation to feel different from those who are less intelligent and less strong. This is a distorted perception of oneness with otherselves. It allowed the Orion group to form the concept of the holy war, as you may call it. This is a seriously distorted perception. There were many of these wars of a destructive nature.

Questioner: Thank you very much. As you probably know I will be working for the next three days, so we will possibly have another session tonight if you think it is possible. The next session after that would not be until four days from now. Do you believe another session tonight is possible?

Ra: I am Ra. This instrument is somewhat weak. This is a distortion caused by lack of vital energy. Thus, nurturing the instrument in physical balancing will allow another session. Do you understand?

Questioner: Not completely. What specifically shall we do for physical balancing?

Ra: I am Ra. One—take care with the foodstuffs. Two—manipulate the physical complex to alleviate the distortion toward pain. Three—encourage a certain amount of what you would call your exercise. The final injunction: to take special care with the alignments this second session so that the entity may gain as much aid as possible from the various symbols. We suggest you check these symbols most carefully. This entity is slightly misplaced from the proper configuration. Not important at this time. More important when a second session is to be scheduled.

I am Ra. I leave you in the love and the light of the one infinite Creator. Go forth, therefore, rejoicing in the power and the peace of the one Creator. Adonai.

THE LAW OF ONE, BOOK V, SESSION 18, FRAGMENT 9
FEBRUARY 4, 1981

Jim: At the beginning of Session 18, in response to a general query from Don concerning the information Ra was transmitting to our group, Ra innocently "told on" Carla. A good friend of hers had offered her the opportunity to experience the effects of LSD, which she had never experienced before. She used it twice in early February of 1981 as a programming device to attempt to achieve an experience of unity with the Creator, but she did not wish Don to know about these experiences since he was very much against the use of any illegal substances at any time and especially during the time during which our group was working with the Ra contact. In a later session it will be suggested by Ra that these two experiences were arranged by the negative entities monitoring our work with those of Ra in hopes that Carla's ability to serve in the Ra contact might be hindered. As a result of this particular session it was the determination of the three of us that there would be no further use of any illegal substances for as long as we were privileged to work with the Ra contact so that no chinks in our "armor of light" that we could eliminate would be present and so that the Ra contact could never be associated with the use of any such drugs.

The information on Aleister Crowley is self-explanatory and underlines again the caution that each seeker must take in moving carefully through its energy centers in a balanced fashion.

By chance, a few sessions earlier, we had discovered that sexual intercourse was an aid to Carla's vital energies during the trance state and would increase the length of a session if engaged in the night before a session was to be held. Thus at the end of Session 18, when Don asked how we might avoid further difficulties in the contact, Ra affirmed the aid which we had discovered sexual intercourse provided. We also found that the conscious dedication of the act of love-making to the service of others via the Ra contact increased its beneficial effects.

Carla: As a young college woman, I never dated or spent time with anyone who smoked marijuana or took LSD, or any other drugs. People all around me were experimenting, but I never was offered any drugs. It was the day of flower children and high ideals, a wonderful time to be young. The hippies ruled but I was only an honorary flower child, since I worked steadily throughout that decade. In 1981, I was 38. When an old friend offered to let me try LSD, I was tickled and eager to try it, for I had long been curious to see what this much-touted substance did to one's head. In the event, I thoroughly enjoyed the experiences—I tried LSD twice—and found that there really was a wonderful increase in the sense of rightness of things under its benign influence on me. Since then, I have heard from many people that my utterly positive experiences with LSD were somewhat atypical, in that most people deal with at least a little hallucination or departure from consensus reality, or even a negatively experienced "high," or bad trip. So I was either lucky, or my subconscious mind was more settled in its own skin than some others. I'd bet on luck!

Needless to say, I was not happy to learn that Ra had blithely told my secret to Don. I valued Don's opinion above all things, and he was not pleased with my judgment in taking illegal substances. But I did not, and do not, feel guilty or ashamed for satisfying my curiosity, under circumstances as safe as one could make them. I also have tried cigarettes and alcohol, both heavily addictive substances, but rarely drink and never use tobacco. (In cooking, however, I use many different spirits, as they offer such delightful notes when put into the harmony of cooking things.) My curiosity was satisfied, and I moved on. The freedom to do this, to know what is out there, is a valuable one, to my mind, if not abused. Moderation seems to me the key.

I have very fond memories of reading Aleister Crowley's autohagiography to Don. He did not like to read, so I frequently read to him. Once we got into this outrageous, brilliant man's work, we were fascinated. Crowley is a fine writer, regardless of what his polarity might have been fumbling around with. Our favorite poem of his is a perfectly ghoulish nursery rhyme he wrote as a precocious toddler. It begins, "In her hospital bed she lay, rotting away, rotting away, rotting by night and rotting by day, rotting and rotting and rotting away." Now that I have told you this, you may perhaps see why this character grew up to become … eccentric! But always interesting.

In working to fit myself into Don's requirements for a mate, I became a user of relative ethics, a practice that seems always to offer a challenge eventually. Don wished to be celibate, which became obvious to me within six months of our coming together in 1968. I always said that his inability to resist me for those first few months we lived together was my greatest compliment of all time! I attempted a celibate life, after we had talked this issue through, for a little over two years, before I concluded that celibacy was not for me. Don had also decided that we should not marry. This implied, to me, a relationship based on a commonality in a metaphysical rather than a physical sense. Always logical, I suggested to Don that we make an agreement: I would tell him before I took a lover, and when I had ceased seeing him. In between, there was no need to discuss it. This would preclude his hearing about such company from others. As he was gone flying about half the time, I had no difficulty in finding time for the lovers' relationship. My lover for most of the time Don and I spent together, ten of the sixteen years, was a trusted and much-loved buddy of mine ever since high school. We had thought of marriage years before, and then decided against it, but we'd remained close. He got the notion to come see me perhaps once a month. I stopped seeing him when he began to wish to take our relationship further, and I was celibate again for some four years before Jim. When Jim began coming to the group, we eventually got together, and he became my lover. All of this was done in the good mutual faith between Donald and me. He was genuinely happy for me to have these relationships, and they did not intrude upon our harmony.

However, in time, after Donald's death, it became clear to me that my relationship with Jim, especially the intimately sexual part of it, did bother Don at a level below the threshold of his awareness, or mine, for that matter. I doubt he ever realized or acknowledged the emotion. I certainly never saw any trace of it, and I am a sensitive person, able to pick up nuances of feeling. But he must have felt these things, and it led him, in the end, to lose faith in my allegiance. And that completely misplaced doubt was the weakness in his armor of light that resulted in his dying.

Long are the hours I have spent reflecting upon this matter. On the one hand, if I had been completely chaste and celibate, he would never have doubted me. He would have still been living, and with me. But we would not have had the contact with Ra that gave us the *Law Of One* material, because it was the combined energy of us three that contacted Ra, not myself as channel, or any one of us as L/L Research, or even L/L Research as an entity. This is clear from the simple dates: Jim came to L/L permanently on December 23, 1980, and we received our first contact from those of Ra on January 15, 1981, less than three weeks after Jim moved in. And Donald felt from the first session with Ra that this was his life's work, the culmination of all he had been through since the '50s, and his gift to the world. Logic fails in matters like these. One can hew completely and faithfully to the agreements one has made, and still err.

If one can move beyond the mythic tragedy of Donald's death, and believe me, one can, after a decade or so, barely, one begins to see the inherent humor in that human, prideful assumption that one can control one's destiny by doing only what is seen as right. One can certainly try to be without error or sin. My pride in myself as being one who always keeps her word blinded me to the suspicions Donald had, but kept completely to himself. His lack of faith in any opinion but his own, even when completely healthy of mind, made it more likely that when he became mentally ill, he would experience paranoia. It is a perfect tragedy.

Don wanted always and only my presence. He never asked for anything else, with the exception of the work we did together. He even begrudged me the time to work on his projects when he was at home. I did all the work for the books we wrote together while he was flying. When he was home, my job was to be in the same room he was in. I was delighted to do this. He could never bring himself to express it, but well I knew how devoted he was, and I felt the same. We had little choice in this; we both felt we were destined to be together, that we were truly star-crossed. Loving him was like breathing, and it did not matter how his needs impinged on mine. Indeed, my spiritual adviser said more than once that I was guilty of idolatry. I did not care what had to be lost to achieve his comfort. I knew these losses included marriage, home and children, things I valued highly and had hoped for. But we were "home" to each other in a way I cannot describe. He rested me, and I, him. I received two compliments from him, in our whole life together. He did not want to spoil me! The lessons were to see through the issues of home, family and reassurance to the ground of being that we shared, to the sensibility we had in common. I embraced them. He was worth whatever it cost. I look back and know I would not change anything. All our choices were made as well as we could make them.

This was the jigsaw puzzle within which we were living, in the world-drama, soap-opera consensus reality of our everyday lives. Carla and Don worked perfectly, as did Jim and Carla, and Don and Jim, who loved each other like family from the first meeting. These relationships were strong and true. Naught could have come between us except for doubt. It never occurred to me that Donald could mistake my fondness for Jim for any sort of alteration in Don's and my un-marriage version of being wed—and we were indeed truly wed, in spirit. You can imagine my wretchedness when one of his friends told me, long after the funeral, that Don had thought I had fallen out of love with him. I was flabbergasted, completely unaware of these doubts, so it never occurred to me to reassure him. How I wish I had! But I was grieving, for the man I knew was gone, and what took his place was a person in very bad need of help. And I was angry that he would not seek help, or follow any medical suggestions. He was my world, and without him, I felt I did not exist. I think most of my grieving was done before his death, in those surrealistic months when he was so very ill, and nothing I did to help was of avail. It took years after he died for me to come to a new sense of myself. That I have now done so is a gift of grace from the Creator, and has been greatly aided by Jim's sensitive treatment of me during the long years of confinement with debilitating episodes of arthritis and other troubles in the decade following Don's death, and during my rehab period in 1992. For the first six years after Don died, I actively felt I should kill myself, because I had "caused" his death, inadvertently, but surely. This was my longest walk in the desert until this present moment. I was resigned to having this basic mind-set for the rest of my life, and I was not aware that time had begun its healing work until I picked up something I'd written and forgot about. I read it anew, and thought, "you know, I like this person." Six years in the desert! Many were the times I was tempted to lay down my faith, but I could not, would not do that. So I survived, and waited for grace. The lesson here is simply that waiting does bring all things to one. Patience cannot be overvalued in the spiritual journey.

This world remains to me a sea of confusion. Knowing well how much I have erred, in what I have done and what I've left undone, and knowing how little I understand, I am well content to remain in the hands of destiny. One of my desires in publishing this personal material is to expose, with utter lack of modesty or fear, the humanness of the three of us. We were not "worthy" of the Ra contact, in the sense of being perfect people. We were three pilgrims who found comfort in each other, and who sought honestly and deeply to serve the light. The material is completely apart from who any of us was or is, and we are not to be confused with Ra, as having some sort of special excellence. This just is not so.

Are relative ethics OK? I still believe they are, and that keeping carefully made agreements is a real key to harmonious living and clear relationships. But it is just the best we can do. That doesn't make it perfect. Further, one cannot expect the universe to bless us with perfect peace just because we are keeping our agreements. We all are blindsided by life itself, and continue only by blunder, faith and a good humor in the face of all. There is an art to cooperating with destiny. And may I say, I am grateful to James Allen

McCarty for that selfsame good humor, and for deciding with me, three years after Don's death, to take hold of our friendship and create a marriage between us. He was most ill-suited to such, as I said, and his gallant cheer and courtesy in accommodating himself to this role has been and continues to be remarkable to me. Truly, he has been a good companion through many waters.

One thing is sure: in true love, the star-crossed kind, there is incredible sweetness, but also immense pain. Don was a hard man to love. Not communicative in the usual sense, he never said what he wanted of me, but just waited for me to guess right. I did not mind, and still am glad of every bit of pain I went through trying to be what he needed me to be, which was essentially without sexuality or the usual reassurance of words, yet greatly intimate. In the density we came from, we were already one, Ra said. So there was an ultimate satisfaction in being with Don, having to do much more with eternity than any particular time or space. What Jim and I had and have is the devoted love of old friends and lovers, who have an earthly pilgrimage together. Our time together is child's play after Don, as far as my being able to handle whatever happens with us. Jim will communicate until we find every bit of misunderstanding, and so we have an easy time of it and when we do have catalyst together, it is quickly worked through. Jim's never had that ultimate romance, and occasionally misses it. But what we do have is so good to us that we have found a considerable happiness with each other, and the good work we have between us.

We see ourselves as still working for and with Don, keeping L/L's doors open and our hearts as well, and living the devotional life that we have learned about from the Confederation teachings. These teachings are at one with universal wisdom as well as my Christian heritage, and have to do simply with living in love. This is such a simple teaching that it escapes many people. But that focus upon Love is one's access to truth, and one's willingness to keep the heart open, which one may call faith, is the energy that brings to us all that was meant for us, both of lessons to learn and of service to offer.

And above all, we may acknowledge, for once and for all, that we are but dust, unless we are living in Love. This helps one to deal with sorrows that inevitably visit our lives. We are not supposed to be in control, or perfect, or any particular thing, but just those who continue to love, through whatever confusion there is. Sheer persistence in faith, regardless of the illusion, is the key to many blessings.

Session 18, February 4, 1981

Questioner: I was thinking last night that if I was in the place of Ra right now, the first distortion of the Law of One might cause me to mix some erroneous data with the true information that I was transmitting to this group. Do you do this?

Ra: I am Ra. We do not intentionally do this. However, there will be confusion. The errors which have occurred have occurred due to the occasional variation in the vibrational complex of this instrument due to its ingestion of a chemical substance. It is not our intent in this particular project to create erroneous information but to express in the confining ambiance of your language system the feeling of the infinite mystery of the one creation in its infinite and intelligent unity.

Questioner: Can you tell me what the chemical substance is that, when ingested, causes poor contact?

Ra: I am Ra. This is not a clear query. Could you please restate.

Questioner: You just stated that you had some problems with the instrument because of the ingestion of some chemical substance by the instrument. Can you tell me what the chemical substance was?

Ra: I am Ra. The substance of which we speak is called vibration sound complex, LSD. It does not give poor contact if it is used in conjunction with the contact. The difficulty of this particular substance is that there is, shall we say, a very dramatic drop-off of the effect of this substance. In each case this instrument began the session with the distortion towards extreme vital energy which this substance produces. However this entity was, during the session, at the point where this substance no longer was in sufficient strength to amplify the entity's abilities to express vital energy. Thus, first the phenomenon of, shall we say, a spotty contact and then, as the instrument relies again upon its own vibrational complexes of vital energy, the vital energy in this case being very low, it became necessary to abruptly cut off communication in order to preserve and nurture the instrument. This particular chemical substance is both helpful and unhelpful in these contacts for the causes given.

Questioner: Are there any foods that are helpful or harmful that the instrument might eat?

Ra: I am Ra. This instrument has body complex distortion towards ill health in the distortion direction corrected best by ingestion of the foodstuffs of your grains and your vegetables as you call them. However, this is extremely unimportant when regarded as an aid with equality to other aids such as attitude which this instrument has in abundance. It, however, aids the vital energies of this instrument, with less distortion towards ill health, to ingest foodstuffs in the above manner with the occasional ingestion of what you call your meats, due to the instrument's need to lessen the distortion towards low vital energy.

Questioner: The entity Aleister Crowley wrote "Do what thou wilt is the whole of the law." He was obviously of some understanding of the Law of One. Where is this entity now?

Ra: I am Ra. This entity is within your inner planes. This entity is in an healing process.

Questioner: Did this entity, then, even though he intellectually understood the Law of One, misuse it and have to go through this healing process?

Ra: I am Ra. This entity became, may we use the vibration sound complex, overstimulated with the true nature of things. This over-stimulation resulted in behavior that was beyond the conscious control of the entity. The entity thus, in many attempts to go through the process of balancing, as we have described the various centers beginning with the red ray and moving upwards, became somewhat overly impressed or caught up in this process and became alienated from other-selves. This entity was positive. However, its journey was difficult due to the inability to use, synthesize, and harmonize the understandings of the desires of self so that It might have shared, in full compassion, with other-selves. This entity thus became very unhealthy, as you may call it, in a spiritual complex manner, and it is necessary for those with this type of distortion towards inner pain to be nurtured in the inner planes until such an entity is capable of viewing the experiences again with the lack of distortion towards pain.

Questioner: I just have two little questions here at the end. The instrument wanted to ask if there were any other substances foods, etc. that she should not eat or drink or things that she should not do because she does not wish to have poor contact for any reason.

Ra: I am Ra. There is no activity which this instrument engages in which affects abilities negatively. There is one activity which affects its abilities positively. This is the sexual activity, as you would call it. There are substances ingested which do not aid the individual in the service it has chosen, this being that which you would call the marijuana. This is due to the distortion towards chemical lapses within the mind complex causing lack of synaptic continuity. This is a chemical reaction of short duration. This instrument, however, has not used this particular substance at any time while performing this service. We believe we have covered the use of such chemical agents as LSD, this being positive to a certain extent due to the energizing or speeding up of the vital forces. However, it is not recommended for this instrument due to the toll it takes upon the vital energies once the substance wears off. This being true of any speeding-up chemical. ♣

The Law of One, Book I, Session 19
February 8, 1981

Ra: I am Ra. I greet you in the love and the light of the infinite Creator. We communicate now.

Questioner: We are concerned in this communication with the evolution of mind, body, and spirit. It seems to me that a good place to start would be the transition from the second to the third density, then to investigate in detail the evolution of third-density entities of Earth, paying particular attention to the mechanisms which help or hinder that evolution.

Do all entities make a transition from second to third density, or are there some entities who have never gone through this transition?

Ra: I am Ra. Your question presumes the space/time continuum understandings of the intelligent energy which animates your illusion. Within the context of this illusion we may say that there are some that do not transfer from one particular density to another, for the continuum is finite.

In the understanding which we have of the universe or creation as one infinite being, its heart beating as alive in its own intelligent energy, it merely is one beat of the heart of this intelligence from creation to creation. In this context each and every entity of consciousness has/is/will experienced/experiencing/experience each and every density.

Questioner: Let's take the point at which an individualized entity of second density is ready for transition to third. Is this second-density being what we would call animal?

Ra: I am Ra. There are three types of second-density entities which become, shall we say, enspirited. The first is the animal. This is the most predominant. The second is the vegetable, most especially that which you call, sound vibration complex, "tree." These entities are capable of giving and receiving enough love to become individualized. The third is mineral. Occasionally a certain location/place, as you may call it, becomes energized to individuality through the love it receives and gives in relationship to a third-density entity which is in relationship to it. This is the least common transition.

Questioner: When this transition from second to third density takes place, how does the entity, whether it be animal, [vegetable] tree, or mineral, become enspirited?

Ra: I am Ra. Entities do not become enspirited. They become aware of the intelligent energy within each portion, cell, or atom, as you may call it, of its beingness.

This awareness is that which is awareness of that already given. From the infinite come all densities. The self-awareness comes from within given the catalyst of certain experiences understanding, as we may call this particular energy, the upward spiraling of the cell or atom or consciousness.

You may then see that there is an inevitable pull toward the, what you may call, eventual realization of self.

Questioner: Then after the transition into the third density, am I correct in assuming—we'll take Earth as an example—the entities would then look like us? They would be in human form? Is this correct?

Ra: I am Ra. This is correct, taking your planetary sphere as an example.

Questioner: When the first second-density entities became third-density on this planet, was this with the help of the transfer of beings from Mars, or were there second-density beings who transferred into third density with no outside influence?

Ra: I am Ra. There were some second-density entities which made the graduation into third density with no outside stimulus but only the efficient use of experience.

Others of your planetary second density joined the third-density cycle due to harvesting efforts by the same sort of sending of vibratory aid as those of the Confederation send you now. This communication was, however, telepathic rather than telepathic/vocal or telepathic/written due to the nature of second-density beings.

Questioner: Who sent the aid to the second-density beings?

Ra: I am Ra. We call ourselves the Confederation of Planets in the Service of the Infinite Creator. This is a simplification in order to ease the difficulty of understanding among your people. We hesitate to use the term, sound vibration, understanding, but it is closest to our meaning.

Questioner: Then did this second-density to third-density transition take place 75,000 years ago? Approximately?

Ra: I am Ra. This is correct.

Questioner: Where did the second-density beings get physical vehicles of third-density type to incarnate into?

Ra: I am Ra. There were among those upon this second-density plane those forms which when exposed to third-density vibrations became the third-density, as you would call the sound vibration, human entities.

That is, there was loss of body hair, as you would call it, the clothing of the body to protect it, the changing of the structure of the neck, jaw, and forehead in order to allow the easier vocalization, and the larger cranial development characteristic of third-density needs. This was a normal transfiguration.

Questioner: Over how long a period of time was this transfiguration? It must have been very short.

Ra: I am Ra. The assumption is correct, in our terms at least—within a generation and one-half, as you know these things. Those who had been harvested of this planet were able to use the newly created physical complex of chemical elements suitable for third-density lessons.

Questioner: Can you tell me how this newly created physical complex was suited to third-density lessons and what those lessons were?

Ra: I am Ra. There is one necessity for third density. That necessity is self-awareness, or self-consciousness. In order to be capable of such, this chemical complex of body must be capable of abstract thought. Thus, the fundamental necessity is the combination of rational and intuitive thinking. This was transitory in the second-density forms operating largely upon intuition which proved through practice to yield results.

The third-density mind was capable of processing information in such a way as to think abstractly and in what could be termed "useless" ways, in the sense of survival. This is the primary requisite.

There are other important ingredients: the necessity for a weaker physical vehicle to encourage the use of the mind, the development of the already present awareness of the social complex. These also being necessary: the further development of physical dexterity in the sense of the hand, as you call this portion of your body complex.

Questioner: This seems to be a carefully planned or engineered stage of development. Can you tell me anything of the origin of this plan or its development?

Ra: I am Ra. We go back to previous information. Consider and remember the discussion of the Logos. With the primal distortion of free will, each galaxy developed its own Logos. This Logos has complete free will in determining the paths of intelligent energy which promote the lessons of each of the densities given the conditions of the planetary spheres and the sun bodies.

Questioner: I will make a statement then of my understanding and ask you if I am correct. There is a, what I would call, physical catalyst operating at all times upon the entities in third density. I assume this operates approximately the same way in second density. It is a catalyst which acts through what we call pain and emotion. Is the primary reason for the weakening of the physical body and the elimination of body hair, etc. so that this catalyst would act more strongly upon the mind and therefore create the evolutionary process?

Ra: I am Ra. This is not entirely correct, although closely associated with the distortions of our understanding.

Consider, if you will, the tree for instance. It is self-sufficient. Consider, if you will, the third-density entity. It is self-sufficient only through difficulty and deprivation. It is difficult to learn alone for there is a built-in handicap, at once the great virtue and the great handicap of third density. That is the rational/intuitive mind.

Thus, the weakening of the physical vehicle, as you call it, was designed to distort entities towards a predisposition to deal with each other. Thus, the lessons which approach a knowing of love can be begun.

This catalyst then is shared between peoples as an important part of each self's development as well as the experiences of the self in solitude and the synthesis of all experience through meditation. The quickest way to learn is to deal with other-selves. This is a much greater catalyst than dealing with the self. Dealing with the self without other-selves is akin to living without what you would call mirrors. Thus, the self cannot see the fruits of its being-ness. Thus, each may aid each by reflection. This is also a primary reason for the weakening of the physical vehicle, as you call the physical complex.

Questioner: Then we have second-density beings who have primarily motivation towards self and possibly a little motivation towards service to others with respect to their immediate family going into third density and carrying this bias with them but being in a position now where this bias will slowly be modified to one which is aimed toward a social complex and ultimately towards union with the all. Am I correct?

Ra: I am Ra. You are correct.

Questioner: Then the newest third-density beings who have just made the transition from second are still strongly biased towards self-service. There must be many other mechanisms to create an awareness of the possibility of service to others.

I am wondering, first about the mechanism and I am wondering when the split takes place where the entity is able to continue on the road to service to self that will eventually take him on to fourth density.

I'm assuming that an entity can start, say, in second density with service to self and continue right on through and just stay on what we would call the path of service to self and never be pulled over. Is this correct?

Ra: I am Ra. This is incorrect. The second-density concept of serving self includes the serving of those associated with tribe or pack. This is not seen in second density as separation of self and other-self. All is seen as self since in some forms of second-density entities, if the tribe or pack becomes weakened, so does the entity within the tribe or pack.

The new or initial third density has this innocent, shall we say, bias or distortion towards viewing those in the family, the society, as you would call, perhaps, country, as self. Thus though a distortion not helpful for progress in third density, it is without polarity.

The break becomes apparent when the entity perceives otherselves as other-selves and consciously determines to manipulate other-selves for the benefit of the self. This is the beginning of the road of which you speak.

Questioner: Then, through free will, some time within the third density experience, the path splits and the entity consciously chooses—or he probably doesn't consciously choose. Does the entity consciously choose this path of the initial splitting point?

Ra: I am Ra. We speak in generalities which is dangerous for always inaccurate. However, we realize you look for the overview; so we will eliminate anomalies and speak of majorities.

The majority of third density beings is far along the chosen path before realization of that path is conscious.

Questioner: Can you tell me what bias creates the momentum towards the chosen path of service to self?

Ra: I am Ra. We can speak only in metaphor. Some love the light. Some love the darkness. It is a matter of the unique and infinitely various Creator choosing and playing among its experiences as a child upon a picnic. Some enjoy the picnic and find the sun beautiful, the food delicious, the games refreshing, and glow with the joy of creation. Some find the night delicious, their picnic being pain, difficulty, sufferings of others, and the examination of the perversities of nature. These enjoy a different picnic.

All these experiences are available. It is the free will of each entity which chooses the form of play, the form of pleasure.

Questioner: I assume that an entity on either path can decide to change paths at any time and possibly retrace steps, the path changing being more difficult the farther along the path the change is made. Is this correct?

Ra: I am Ra. This is incorrect. The further an entity has, what you would call, polarized, the more easily this entity may change polarity, for the more power and awareness the entity will have.

Those truly helpless are those who have not consciously chosen but who repeat patterns without knowledge of the repetition or the meaning of the pattern.

Questioner: I believe we have a very important point here. It then seems that there is an extreme potential in this polarization the same as there is in electricity. We have a positive and negative pole. The more you build the charge on either of these, the more the potential difference and the greater the ability to do work, as we call it in the physical.

This would seem to me to be the same analogy that we have in consciousness. Is this correct?

Ra: I am Ra. This is precisely correct.

Questioner: Then it would seem that there is a relationship between what we perceive as a physical phenomenon, say the electrical phenomenon, and the phenomenon of consciousness in that they, having stemmed from the one Creator, are practically identical but have different actions. Is this correct?

Ra: I am Ra. Again we oversimplify to answer your query.

The physical complex alone is created of many, many energy or electromagnetic fields interacting due to intelligent energy, the mental configurations or distortions of each complex further adding fields of electromagnetic energy and distorting the physical complex patterns of energy, the spiritual aspect serving as a further complexity of fields which is of itself perfect but which can be realized in many distorted and unintegrated ways by the mind and body complexes of energy fields.

Thus, instead of one, shall we say, magnet with one polarity you have in the body/mind/spirit complex one basic polarity expressed in what you would call violet-ray energy, the sum of the energy fields, but which is affected by thought of all kinds generated by the mind complex, by distortions of the body complex, and by the numerous relationships between the microcosm which is the entity and the macrocosm in many forms which you may represent by viewing the stars, as you call them, each with a contributing energy ray which enters the electromagnetic web of the entity due to its individual distortions.

Questioner: Is this then the root of what we call astrology?

Ra: I am Ra. This will be the last full question of this session.

The root of astrology, as you speak it, is one way of perceiving the primal distortions which may be predicted along probability/possibility lines given, shall we say, cosmic orientations and configurations at the time of the entrance into the physical/mental complex of the spirit and at the time of the physical/mental/spiritual complex into the illusion.

This then has the possibility of suggesting basic areas of distortion. There is no more than this. The part astrology plays is likened unto that of one root among many.

Questioner: Is there anything that we can do to make the instrument more comfortable?

Ra: I am Ra. This instrument is well aligned. You are being very conscientious. We request you take more care in being assured that this instrument is wearing footwear of what you would call, vibratory sound complex, shoes.

I am Ra. I leave you in the love and the light of the one infinite Creator. Go forth, therefore, rejoicing in the power and the peace of the one Creator. Adonai.

The Law of One, Book I, Session 20
February 9, 1981

Ra: I am Ra. I greet you in the love and the light of the infinite Creator. I communicate now.

Questioner: To go back a bit, what happened to the second-density entities who were unharvestable when the third density began? I assume that there were some that did not make it into third density.

Ra: I am Ra. The second density is able to repeat during third density a portion of its cycle.

Questioner: Then the second-density entities who did not get harvested at the beginning of this 75,000 year period, some are still on this planet. Were any of these second-density entities harvested into the third density within the past 75,000 years?

Ra: I am Ra. This has been increasingly true.

Questioner: So more and more second-density entities are making it into third density. Can you give me an example of a second-density entity coming into the third density in the recent past?

Ra: I am Ra. Perhaps the most common occurrence of second-density graduation during third-density cycle is the so-called pet.

For the animal which is exposed to the individualizing influences of the bond between animal and third-density entity, this individuation causes a sharp rise in the potential of the second density entity so that upon the cessation of physical complex the mind/body complex does not return into the undifferentiated consciousness of that species, if you will.

Questioner: Then can you give me an example of an entity in third density that was just previously a second-density entity? What type of entity do they become here?

Ra: I am Ra. As a second-density entity returns as third-density for the beginning of this process of learning, the entity is equipped with the lowest, if you will so call these vibrational distortions, forms of third-density consciousness; that is, equipped with self-consciousness.

Questioner: This would be a human in our form then who would be beginning the understandings of third density. Is this correct?

Ra: I am Ra. This is correct.

Questioner: Speaking of the rapid change that occurred in the physical vehicle from second to third density: this occurred, you said, in approximately a generation and a half. Body hair was lost and there were structural changes.

I am aware of the physics of Dewey B. Larson, who states that all is motion or vibration. Am I correct in assuming that the basic vibration that makes up the physical world changes, thus creating a different set of parameters, shall I say, in this short period of time between density changes allowing for the new type of being? Am I correct?

Ra: I am Ra. This is correct.

Questioner: Is the physics of Dewey Larson correct?

Ra: I am Ra. The physics of sound vibrational complex, Dewey, is a correct system as far as it is able to go. There are those things which are not included in this system. However, those coming after this particular entity, using the basic concepts of vibration and the study of vibrational distortions, will begin to understand that which you know as gravity and those things you consider as "n" dimensions. These things are necessary to be included in a more universal, shall we say, physical theory.

Questioner: Did this entity, Dewey, then bring this material through for use primarily in the fourth density?

Ra: I am Ra. This is correct.

Questioner: Yesterday we were talking about the split that occurs when an entity either consciously or unconsciously chooses the path that leads to either service to others or service to self. The philosophical question of why such a split even exists came up. It was my impression that just as it is in electricity, if we have no polarity in electricity we have no electricity; we have no action. Therefore, I am assuming that it is the same in consciousness. If we have no polarity in consciousness we also have no action or experience. Is this correct?

Ra: I am Ra. This is correct. You may use the general term "work."

Questioner: Then the concept of service to self and service to others is mandatory if we wish to have work, whether it be work in consciousness or work of a mechanical nature in the Newtonian concept in the physical. Is this correct?

Ra: I am Ra. This is correct with one addendum. The coil, as you may understand this term, is wound, is potential, is ready. The thing that is missing without polarizing is the charge.

Questioner: Then the charge is provided by individualized consciousness. Is this correct?

Ra: I am Ra. The charge is provided by the individualized entity using the in-pourings and in-streamings of energy by the choices of free will.

Questioner: Thank you. As soon as the third-density started 75,000 years ago and we have incarnate third-density entities, what was the average human life span at that time?

Ra: I am Ra. At the beginning of this particular portion of your space/time continuum the average life span was approximately nine hundred of your years.

Questioner: Did the average life span grow longer or shorter as we progressed into third-density experience?

Ra: I am Ra. There is a particular use for the span of life in this density and, given the harmonious development of the learning/teachings of this density, the life span of the physical complex would remain the same throughout the cycle. However, your particular planetary sphere developed vibrations by the second major cycle which shortened the life span dramatically.

Questioner: Assuming a major cycle is 25,000 years, at the end of the first major cycle, what was the life span?

Ra: I am Ra. The life span at the end of the first cycle which you call major was approximately seven hundred of your years.

Questioner: Then in 25,000 years we lost two hundred years of life span. Is this correct?

Ra: I am Ra. This is correct.

Questioner: Can you tell me the reason for this shortening of life span?

Ra: I am Ra. The causes of this shortening are always an ineuphonious or inharmonious relational vibration between otherselves. In the first cycle this was not severe due to the dispersion of peoples, but there was the growing feeling complex/distortion towards separateness from other-selves.

Questioner: I am assuming that at the start of one of these cycles there could have been either a positive polarization that would generally occur over the 25,000 years or a negative polarization. Is the reason for the negative polarization and the shortening of the life span the influx of entities from Mars who had already polarized somewhat negatively?

Ra: I am Ra. This is incorrect. There was not a strong negative polarization due to this influx. The lessening of the life span was due primarily to the lack of the building of positive orientation. When there is no progress those conditions which grant progress are gradually lost. This is one of the difficulties of remaining unpolarized. The chances, shall we say, of progress become steadily less.

Questioner: The way I understand it, at the beginning of this 75,000 year cycle, then, we had a mixture of entities—those who had graduated from second density on Earth to become third-density and then a group of entities transferred from the planet Mars to continue third density here. Is this correct?

Ra: I am Ra. This is correct. You must remember that those transferred to this sphere were in the middle of their third density so that this third density was an adaptation rather than a beginning.

Questioner: What percentage of the entities who were here in third density at that time were Martian and what percentage were harvested from Earth's second density?

Ra: I am Ra. There were perhaps one-half of the third-density population being entities from the Red Planet, Mars, as you call it. Perhaps one-quarter from second density of your planetary sphere. Approximately one-quarter from other sources, other planetary spheres whose entities chose this planetary sphere for third-density work.

Questioner: When they incarnated here did all three of these types mix together in societies or groups or were they separated by groups and society?

Ra: I am Ra. They remained largely unmixed.

Questioner: Then did this unmixing lend to a possibility of warlike energy between groups?

Ra: I am Ra. This is correct.

Questioner: Did this help to reduce the life span?

Ra: I am Ra. This did reduce the life span, as you call it.

Questioner: Can you tell me why nine hundred years is the optimum life span?

Ra: I am Ra. The mind/body/spirit complex of third density has perhaps one hundred times as intensive a program of catalytic action from which to distill distortions and learn/teachings than any other of the densities. Thus the learn/teachings are most confusing to the mind/body/spirit complex which is, shall we say, inundated by the ocean of experience.

During the first, shall we say, perhaps 150 to 200 of your years as you measure time, a mind/body/spirit complex is going through the process of a spiritual childhood. The mind and the body are not enough in a disciplined configuration to lend clarity to the spiritual influxes. Thus, the remaining time span is given to optimize the understandings which result from experience itself.

Questioner: Then at present it would seem that our current life span is much too short for those who are new to third-density lessons. Is this correct?

Ra: I am Ra. This is correct. Those entities which have, in some way, learned/taught themselves the appropriate distortions for rapid growth can now work within the confines of the shorter life span. However, the greater preponderance of your entities find themselves in what may be considered a perpetual childhood.

Questioner: Back in the first 25,000 year period, or major cycle, what type of aid was given by the Confederation to the entities who were in this 25,000 year period so that they would have the opportunity to grow?

Ra: I am Ra. The Confederation members which dwell in inner-plane existence within the planetary complex of vibratory densities worked with these entities. There was also the aid of one of the Confederation which worked with those of Mars in making the transition.

For the most part, the participation was limited, as it was appropriate to allow the full travel of the workings of the confusion mechanism to operate in order for the planetary entities to develop that which they wished in, shall we say, freedom within their own thinking.

It is often the case that a third-density planetary cycle will take place in such a way that there need be no outside, shall we say, or other-self aid in the form of information. Rather, the entities themselves are able to work themselves towards the appropriate polarizations and goals of third-density learn/teachings.

Questioner: I make the assumption that if maximum efficiency had been achieved in this 25,000 year period the entities would have polarized either toward service to self or toward service to others, one or the other. This would have made them harvestable at the end of that 25,000 year period in which case they would have had to move to another planet because this one would have been third density for 50,000 more years. Is this correct?

Ra: I am Ra. Let us untangle your assumption which is complex and correct in part.

The original desire is that entities seek and become one. If entities can do this in a moment, they may go forward in a moment, and, thus, were this to occur in a major cycle, indeed, the third-density planet would be vacated at the end of that cycle.

It is, however, more towards the median or mean, shall we say, of third-density developments throughout the one infinite universe that there be a small harvest after the first cycle; the remainder having significantly polarized, the second cycle having a much larger harvest; the remainder being even more significantly polarized, the third cycle culminating the process and the harvest being completed.

Questioner: Was the Confederation watching to see and expecting to see a harvest at the end of the 25,000 year period in which a percentage would be harvestable fourth-density positive and a percentage harvestable fourth-density negative?

Ra: I am Ra. That is correct. You may see our role in the first major cycle as that of the gardener who, knowing the season, is content to wait for the spring. When the springtime does not occur, the seeds do not sprout; then it is that the gardener must work in the garden.

Questioner: Am I to understand, then, that there was neither a harvest of positive or negative entities at the end of that 25,000 years?

Ra: I am Ra. This is correct. Those whom you call the Orion group made one attempt to offer information to those of third density during that cycle. However, the information did not fall upon the ears of any who were concerned to follow this path to polarity.

Questioner: What technique did the Orion group use to give this information?

Ra: I am Ra. The technique used was of two kinds: one, the thought transfer or what you may call "telepathy"; Two, the arrangement of certain stones in order to suggest strong influences of power, this being those of statues and of rock formations in your Pacific areas, as you now call them, and to an extent in your Central American regions, as you now understand them.

Questioner: Were you speaking in part of the stone heads of Easter Island?

Ra: I am Ra. This is correct.

Questioner: How would such stone heads influence the people to take the path of service to self?

Ra: I am Ra. Picture, if you will, the entities living in such a way that their mind/body/spirit complexes are at what seems to be the mercy of forces which they cannot control. Given a charged entity such as a statue or a rock formation charged with nothing but power, it is possible for the free will of those viewing this particular structure or formation to ascribe to this power, power over those things which cannot be controlled. This, then, has the potential for the further distortion to power over others.

Questioner: How were these stone heads constructed?

Ra: I am Ra. These were constructed by thought after a scanning of the deep mind, the trunk of mind tree, looking at the images most likely to cause the experience of awe in the viewer.

Questioner: Did the Orion entities do this themselves? Did they do this in the physical? Did they land, or did they do it from mental planes?

Ra: I am Ra. Nearly all of these structures and formations were constructed at a distance by thought. A very few were created in later times in imitation of original constructs by entities upon your Earth plane/density.

Questioner: What density Orion entity did the construction of these heads?

Ra: I am Ra. The fourth density, the density of love or understanding, was the density of the particular entity which offered this possibility to those of your first major cycle.

Questioner: You use the same nomenclature for the fourth-density negative as for the fourth-density positive. Both are called the dimension of love or of understanding. Is this correct?

Ra: I am Ra. This is correct. Love and understanding, whether it be of self or of self toward other-self, is one.

Questioner: What was the approximate date in years past of the construction of these heads?

Ra: I am Ra. This approximately was 60,000 of your years in the past time/space of your continuum.

Questioner: What structures were built in South America?

Ra: I am Ra. In this location were fashioned some characteristic statues, some formations of what you call rock and some formations involving rock and earth.

Questioner: Were the lines at Nazca included in this?

Ra: I am Ra. This is correct.

Questioner: Since these can only be seen from an altitude, of what benefit were they?

Ra: I am Ra. The formations were of benefit because charged with energy of power.

Questioner: I'm a little confused. These lines at Nazca are hardly understandable for an entity walking on the surface. He cannot see anything but disruption of the surface. However, if you go up to a high altitude you can see the patterns. How was it of benefit to the entities walking on the surface?

Ra: I am Ra. At the remove of the amount of time/space which is now your present it is difficult to perceive that at the time/space 60,000 years ago the earth was formed in such a way as to be visibly arranged in powerful structural designs, from the vantage point of distant hills.

Questioner: In other words at that time there were hills overlooking these lines?

Ra: I am Ra. This will be the last full question of this session.

The entire smoothness, as you see this area now, was built up in many places in hills. The time/space continuum has proceeded with wind and weather, as you would say, to erode to a great extent both the somewhat formidable structures of earth designed at that time and the nature of the surrounding countryside.

Questioner: I think I understand then that these lines are just the faint traces of what used to be there?

Ra: I am Ra. This is correct.

Questioner: Thank you. We need to know whether or not it is possible to continue with another session today and whether there is anything that we can do to make the instrument more comfortable?

Ra: I am Ra. It is possible. We ask that you observe carefully the alignment of the instrument. Otherwise, you are conscientious.

Is there any short query before we close?

Questioner: I intend in the next session to focus upon the development of the positively oriented entities in the first 25,000 years. I know you can't make suggestions. Can you give me any comment on this at all?

Ra: I am Ra. The choices are yours according to your discernment.

I am Ra. I leave you in the love and the light of the one infinite Creator. Adonai.

The Law of One, Book I, Session 21
February 10, 1981

Ra: I am Ra. I greet you in the love and the light of the infinite Creator. I communicate now.

Questioner: I have a couple of questions that I don't want to forget to ask in this period, so I will ask them first.

The first question is: Would the future content of this book be affected in any way if the instrument reads the material that we have already obtained?

Ra: I am Ra. The future, as you measure in time/space, communications which we offer through this instrument have no connection with the instrument's mind complex. This is due to two things: first, the fidelity of the instrument in dedicating its will to the service of the infinite Creator; secondly, the distortion/understanding of our social memory complex that the most efficient way to communicate material with as little distortion as possible, given the necessity of the use of sound vibration complexes, is to remove the conscious mind complex from the spirit/mind/body complex so that we may communicate without reference to any instrument's orientation.

Questioner: Do you use the instrument's vocabulary or your own vocabulary to communicate with us?

Ra: I am Ra. We use the vocabulary of the language with which you are familiar. This is not the instrument's vocabulary. However, this particular mind/body/spirit complex retains the use of a sufficiently large number of sound vibration complexes that the distinction is often without any importance.

Questioner: So at the start of this 75,000 year cycle we know that the quarantine was fully set up. I am assuming then that the Guardians were aware of the infringements on the free will that would occur if they didn't set this up at that time and therefore did it. Is this correct?

Ra: I am Ra. This is partially incorrect. The incorrectness is as follows: those entities whose third-density experience upon your Red Planet was brought to a close prematurely were aided genetically while being transferred to this third density. This, although done in a desire to aid, was seen as infringement upon free will. The light quarantine which consists of the Guardians, or gardeners as you may call them, which would have been in effect was intensified.

Questioner: When the 75,000 year cycle started, the life span was approximately nine hundred years, average. What was the process and scheduling mechanism, shall I say, of reincarnation at that time, and how did the time in between incarnations into third-density physical apply to the growth of the mind/body/spirit complex?

Ra: I am Ra. This query is more complex than most. We shall begin. The incarnation pattern of the beginning third-density mind/body/spirit complex begins in darkness, for you may think or consider of your density as one of, as you may say, a sleep and a forgetting. This is the only plane of forgetting. It is necessary for the third-density entity to forget so that the mechanisms of confusion or free will may operate upon the newly individuated consciousness complex.

Thus, the beginning entity is one in all innocence oriented towards animalistic behavior using other-selves only as extensions of self for the preservation of the all-self. The entity becomes slowly aware that it has needs, shall we say, that are not animalistic; that is, that are useless for survival. These needs include: the need for companionship, the need for laughter, the need for beauty, the need to know the universe about it. These are the beginning needs.

As the incarnations begin to accumulate, other needs are discovered: the need to trade, the need to love, the need to be loved, the need to elevate animalistic behaviors to a more universal perspective.

During the first portion of third-density cycles, incarnations are automatic and occur rapidly upon the cessation of energy complex of the physical vehicle. There is small need to review or to heal the experiences of the incarnation. As, what you would call, the energy centers begin to be activated to a higher extent, more of the content of experience during incarnation deals with the lessons of love.

Thus the time, as you may understand it, between incarnations is lengthened to give appropriate attention to the review and the healing of experiences of the previous incarnation. At some point in third density, the green-ray energy center becomes activated and at that point incarnation ceases to be automatic.

Questioner: When incarnation ceases to be automatic I am assuming that the entity can decide when he needs to incarnate for the benefit of his own learning. Does he also select his parents?

Ra: I am Ra. This is correct.

Questioner: At this time in our cycle, near the end, what percentage of the entities incarnating are making their own choices?

Ra: I am Ra. The approximate percentage is fifty-four percent.

Questioner: Thank you. During this first 25,000 year cycle was there any industrial development at all, any machinery available to the people?

Ra: I am Ra. Using the term "machine" to the meaning which you ascribe, the answer is no. However, there were, shall we say, various implements of wood and rock which were used in order to obtain food and for use in aggression.

Questioner: At the end of this first 25,000 year cycle was there any physical change that occurred rapidly like that which occurs at the end of a 75,000 year cycle or is this just an indexing time for harvesting period?

Ra: I am Ra. There was no change except that which according to intelligent energy, or what you may term physical evolution, suited physical complexes to their environment, this being of the color of the skin due to the area of the sphere upon which entities lived; the gradual growth of peoples due to improved intake of foodstuffs.

Questioner: Then, at the end of the first 25,000 year period, I am guessing that the Guardians discovered that there was no harvest of either positively or negatively oriented entities. Tell me then what happened? What action was taken?

Ra: I am Ra. There was no action taken except to remain aware of the possibility of a calling for help or understanding among the entities of this density. The Confederation is concerned with the preservation of the conditions conducive to learning. This for the most part, revolves about the primal distortion of free will.

Questioner: Then the Confederation gardeners did nothing until some of the plants in their garden called them for help. Is this correct?

Ra: I am Ra. This is correct.

Questioner: When did the first call occur, and how did it occur?

Ra: I am Ra. The first calling was approximately 46,000 of your years ago. This calling was of those of Maldek. These entities were aware of their need for rectifying the consequences of their action and were in some confusion in an incarnate state as to the circumstances of their incarnation; the unconscious being aware, the conscious being quite confused. This created a calling. The Confederation sent love and light to these entities.

Questioner: How did the Confederation send this love and light? What did they do?

Ra: I am Ra. There dwell within the Confederation planetary entities who from their planetary spheres do nothing but send love and light as pure streamings to those who call. This is not in the form of conceptual thought but of pure and undifferentiated love.

Questioner: Did the first distortion of the Law of One then require that equal time, shall I say, be given to the self-service oriented group?

Ra: I am Ra. In this case this was not necessary for some of your time due to the orientation of the entities.

Questioner: What was their orientation?

Ra: I am Ra. The orientation of these entities was such that the aid of the Confederation was not perceived.

Questioner: Since it was not perceived it was not necessary to balance this. Is that correct?

Ra: I am Ra. This is correct. What is necessary to balance is opportunity. When there is ignorance, there is no opportunity. When there exists a potential, then each opportunity shall be balanced, this balancing caused by not only the positive and negative orientations of those offering aid but also the orientation of those requesting aid.

Questioner: Thank you very much. I apologize in being so stupid in stating my questions but this has cleared up my understanding nicely.

Then in the second 25,000 year major cycle was there any great civilization that developed?

Ra: I am Ra. In the sense of greatness of technology there were no great societies during this cycle. There was some advancement among those of Deneb who had chosen to incarnate as a body in what you would call China.

There were appropriately positive steps in activating the green-ray energy complex in many portions of your planetary sphere including the Americas, the continent which you call Africa, the island which you call Australia, and that which you know as India, as well as various scattered peoples.

None of these became what you would name great as the greatness of Lemuria or Atlantis is known to you due to the formation of strong social complexes and in the case of Atlantis, very great technological understandings.

However, in the South American area of your planetary sphere as you know it, there grew to be a great vibratory distortion towards love. These entities were harvestable at the end of the second major cycle without ever having formed strong social or technological complexes.

This will be the final question in completion of this session. Is there a query we may answer quickly before we close, as this instrument is somewhat depleted?

Questioner: I would just like to apologize for the confusion on my part in carrying on to this second 25,000 years.

I would like to ask if there is anything that we can do to make the instrument more comfortable? We would like to have a second session today.

Ra: I am Ra. You may observe a slight misalignment between book, candle, and perpendicularity of censer. This is not significant, but as we have said the cumulative effects upon this instrument are not well. You are conscientious. It is well to have a second session given the appropriate exercising and manipulation of this instrument's physical complex.

I am Ra. I leave you in the love and the light of the one infinite Creator. Go forth, therefore, rejoicing in the power and the peace of the one Creator. Adonai.

The Law of One, Book V, Session 21, Fragment 10
February 10, 1981

Jim: As we were preparing to welcome Dr. Puharich into our circle of working with Ra, we were reminded once again of the prerequisite of the tuning in the personal life that was necessary for all of those involved in the contact.

Carla: In the event, Andrija never visited us here in Kentucky. But it is worth noting that Ra frequently did respond to our questions by invoking the law of confusion. Those of Ra felt that the primary importance in personal ethics of allowing people to do their own learning, make their own mistakes, cannot be overemphasized.

Session 21, February 10, 1981

Questioner: Andrija Puharich will be visiting later this month. Can he read the unpublished healing material?

Ra: I am Ra. The entity of whom you speak has a knowledge of this material in its conscious memory in somewhat altered form. Therefore, it is harmless to allow this entity to become acquainted with this material. However, we request the mind/body/spirit complex, Henry, be sufficiently prepared by means of meditation, contemplation, or prayer before entering these workings. At present, as we have said before, this mind/body/spirit complex is not of proper vibrational distortion.

Questioner: I had already determined to exclude him from these workings. I had only determined to let him read the material. The only other thing that I have noticed within the material as it exists now there is a certain statement that will allow him to understand who I believe Spectra really was. It seems to be my duty to remove this from his knowledge to preserve the same free will that you attempted to preserve by not naming the origin of the Spectra contact in Israel. Am I correct?

Ra: I am Ra. This is a matter for your discretion.

Questioner: That's what I thought you'd say.

The Law of One, Book I, Session 22
February 10, 1981

Ra: I am Ra. I greet you in the love and in the light of the one infinite Creator. I communicate now.

Questioner: I will ask a couple of questions to clear up the end of the second major cycle. Then we will go on to the third and last of the major cycles.

Can you tell me what was the average life span at the end of the second major cycle?

Ra: I am Ra. By the end of the second major cycle the life span was as you know it, with certain variations among geographically isolated peoples more in harmony with intelligent energy and less bellicose.

Questioner: Can you tell me the length of the average life span in years at the end of the second major cycle?

Ra: I am Ra. The average is perhaps misleading. To be precise, many spent approximately thirty-five to forty of your years in one incarnation with the possibility not considered abnormal of a life span approaching one hundred of your years.

Questioner: Can I assume then that this drastic drop in average life span from seven hundred years to less than one hundred years in length during this second 25,000 years was caused by an intensification of a lack of service to others?

Ra: I am Ra. This is in part correct. By the end of the second cycle, the Law of Responsibility had begun to be effectuated by the increasing ability of entities to grasp those lessons which there are to be learned in this density. Thus, entities had discovered many ways to indicate a bellicose nature, not only as tribes or what you call nations but in personal relationships, each with the other, the concept of barter having given way to the concept of money; also, the concept of ownership having won ascendancy over the concept of nonownership on an individual or group basis.

Each entity then was offered many more subtle ways of demonstrating either service toward others or service to self with the distortion of the manipulation of others. As each lesson was understood, those lessons of sharing, of giving, of receiving in free gratitude—each lesson could be rejected in practice.

Without demonstrating the fruits of such learn/teaching the life span became greatly reduced, for the ways of honor/duty were not being accepted.

Questioner: Would this shortened life span help the entity in any way in that he would have more time in between incarnations to review his mistakes, or would this shortened life span hinder him?

Ra: I am Ra. Both are correct. The shortening of the life span is a distortion of the Law of One which suggests that an entity not receive more experience in more intensity than it may bear. This is only in effect upon an individual level and does not hold sway over planetary or social complexes.

Thus the shortened life span is due to the necessity for removing an entity from the intensity of experience which ensues when wisdom and love are, having been rejected, reflected back into the consciousness of the Creator without being accepted as part of the self, this then causing the entity to have the need for healing and for much evaluation of the incarnation.

The incorrectness lies in the truth that, given appropriate circumstances, a much longer incarnation in your space/time continuum is very helpful for continuing this intensive work until conclusions have been reached through the catalytic process.

Questioner: You spoke of the South American group which was harvestable at the end of the second cycle. How long was their average life span at the end of the second cycle?

Ra: I am Ra. This isolated group had achieved life spans stretching upwards towards the nine hundred year life span appropriate to this density.

Questioner: I am assuming that the planetary action that we are experiencing now, which it seems shortens all life spans here, was not strong enough then to affect them and shorten their life span. Is this correct?

Ra: I am Ra. This is correct. It is well to remember that at that nexus in space/time great isolation was possible.

Questioner: How many people populated the Earth totally at that time; that is, were incarnate in the physical at any one time?

Ra: I am Ra. I am assuming that you intend to query regarding the number of incarnate mind/body/spirit complexes at the end of the second major cycle, this number being approximately 345,000 entities.

Questioner: Approximately how many were harvestable out of that total number at the end of the cycle?

Ra: I am Ra. There were approximately 150 entities harvestable.

Questioner: Then as the next cycle started were these the entities who stayed to work on the planet?

Ra: I am Ra. These entities were visited by the Confederation and became desirous of remaining in order to aid the planetary consciousness. This is correct.

Questioner: What type of visit did the Confederation make to this group of 150 entities?

Ra: I am Ra. A light being appeared bearing that which may be called a shield of light. It spoke of the oneness and infinity of all creation and of those things which await those ready for harvest. It described in golden words the beauties of love as lived. It then allowed a telepathic linkage to progressively show those who were interested the plight of third density when seen as a planetary complex. It then left.

Questioner: Did all of these entities then decide to stay and help during the next 25,000 year cycle?

Ra: I am Ra. This is correct. As a group they stayed. There were those peripherally associated with this culture which did not stay. However, they were not able to be harvested either and so, beginning at the very highest, shall we say, of the sub-octaves of third density, repeated this density. Many of those who have been of the loving nature are not Wanderers but those of this particular origin of second cycle.

Questioner: Are all of these entities still with us in this cycle?

Ra: I am Ra. The entities repeating the third-density major cycle have, in some few cases, been able to leave. These entities have chosen to join their brothers and sisters, as you would call these entities.

Questioner: Are any of these entities names that we would know from our historical past?

Ra: I am Ra. The one known as sound vibration complex, Saint Augustine, is of such a nature. The one known as Saint Teresa of such a nature. The one known as Saint Francis of Assisi of such nature. These entities, being of monastic background, as you would call it, found incarnation in the same type of ambiance appropriate for further learning.

Questioner: As the cycle terminated 25,000 years ago, what was the reaction of the Confederation to the lack of harvest?

Ra: I am Ra. We became concerned.

Questioner: Was any action taken immediately, or did you wait for a call?

Ra: I am Ra. The Council of Saturn acted only in allowing the entry into third density of other mind/body/spirit complexes of third-density, not Wanderers, but those who sought further third-density experience. This was done randomly so that free will would not be violated for there was not yet a call.

Questioner: Was the next action taken by the Confederation when a call occurred?

Ra: I am Ra. This is correct.

Questioner: Who or what group produced this call, and what action was taken by the Confederation?

Ra: I am Ra. The calling was that of Atlanteans. This calling was for what you would call understanding with the distortion towards helping other-selves. The action taken is that which you take part in at this time: the impression of information through channels, as you would call them.

Questioner: Was this first calling then at a time before Atlantis became technologically advanced?

Ra: I am Ra. This is basically correct.

Questioner: Then did the technological advancement of Atlantis come because of this call? I am assuming that the call was answered to bring them the Law of One and the Law of Love as a distortion of the Law of One, but did they also then get technological information that caused them to grow into such a highly advanced technological society?

Ra: I am Ra. Not at first. At about the same time as we first appeared in the skies over Egypt and continuing thereafter, other entities of the Confederation appeared unto Atlanteans who had reached a level of philosophical understanding, shall we misuse this word, which was consonant with communication, to encourage and inspire studies in the mystery of unity.

However, requests being made for healing and other understanding, information was passed having to do with crystals and the building of pyramids as well as temples, as you would call them, which were associated with training.

Questioner: Was this training the same sort of initiatory training that was done with Egyptians?

Ra: I am Ra. This training was different in that the social complex was more, shall we say, sophisticated and less contradictory and barbarous in its ways of thinking. Therefore the temples were temples of learning rather than the attempt being made to totally separate and put upon a pedestal the healers.

Questioner: Then were there what we call priests trained in these temples?

Ra: I am Ra. You would not call them priests in the sense of celibacy, of obedience, and of poverty. They were priests in the sense of those devoted to learning.

The difficulties became apparent as those trained in this learning began to attempt to use crystal powers for those things other than healing, as they were involved not only with learning but became involved with what you would call the governmental structure.

Questioner: Was all of their information given to them in the same way that we are getting our information now, through an instrument such as this instrument?

Ra: I am Ra. There were visitations from time to time but none of importance in the, shall we say, historical passage of events in your space/time continuum.

Questioner: Was it necessary for them to have an unified social complex for these visitations to occur? What conditions were necessary for these visitations to occur?

Ra: I am Ra. The conditions were two: the calling of a group of people whose square overcame the integrated resistance of those unwilling to search or learn; the second requirement, the relative naiveté of those members of the Confederation who felt that direct transfer of information would necessarily be as helpful for Atlanteans as it had been for the Confederation entity.

Questioner: I see then. What you are saying is that these naive Confederation entities had had the same thing happen to them in the past so they were doing the same thing for the Atlantean entities. Is this correct?

Ra: I am Ra. This is correct. We remind you that we are one of the naive members of that Confederation and are still attempting to recoup the damage for which we feel responsibility. It is our duty as well as honor to continue with your peoples, therefore, until all traces of the distortions of our teach/learnings have been embraced by their opposite distortions, and balance achieved.

Questioner: I see. Then I will state the picture I have of Atlantis and you tell me if I am correct.

We have a condition where a large enough percentage of the people of Atlantis had started at least going in the direction of the Law of One and living the Law of One for their call to be heard by the Confederation. This call was heard because, using the Law of Squares, it overrode the opposition of the Atlantean entities who were not calling. The Confederation then used channels such as we use now in communication and also made contact directly, but this turned out to be a mistake because it was perverted by the entities of Atlantis. Is this correct?

Ra: I am Ra. This is correct with one exception. There is only one law. That is the Law of One. Other so-called laws are distortions of this law, some of them primal and most important for progress to be understood. However, it is well that each so-called law, which we also call "way," be understood as a distortion rather than a law. There is no multiplicity to the Law of One.

This will be the final question in length of this working. Please ask it now.

Questioner: Can you give me the average life span of the Atlantean population?

Ra: I am Ra. The average life span, as we have said, is misleading. The Atlanteans were, in the early part of their cultural experience, used to life spans from 70 to 140 years, this being, of course, approximate. Due to increasing desire for power, the lifetime decreased rapidly in the later stages of the civilization and, thus, the healing and rejuvenating information was requested.

Do you have any brief queries before we close?

Questioner: Is there anything that we can do to make the instrument more comfortable? Is there anything that we can do for her?

Ra: I am Ra. The instrument is well. It is somewhat less easy to maintain clear contact during a time when some or one of the entities in the circle of working is or are not fully conscious. We request that entities in the circle be aware that their energy is helpful for increasing the vitality of this contact. We thank you for being conscientious in the asking.

I am Ra. It is a great joy to leave you in the love and the light of the one infinite Creator. Go forth, therefore, rejoicing in the power and the peace of the one Creator. Adonai.

L/L Research

L/L Research is a subsidiary of Rock Creek Research & Development Laboratories, Inc.

P.O. Box 5195
Louisville, KY 40255-0195

www.llresearch.org

Rock Creek is a non-profit corporation dedicated to discovering and sharing information which may aid in the spiritual evolution of humankind.

ABOUT THE CONTENTS OF THIS TRANSCRIPT: This telepathic channeling has been taken from transcriptions of the weekly study and meditation meetings of the Rock Creek Research & Development Laboratories and L/L Research. It is offered in the hope that it may be useful to you. As the Confederation entities always make a point of saying, please use your discrimination and judgment in assessing this material. If something rings true to you, fine. If something does not resonate, please leave it behind, for neither we nor those of the Confederation would wish to be a stumbling block for any.

© 2009 L/L Research

The Law of One, Book V, Session 22, Fragment 11
February 10, 1981

Jim: Most of the personal information from Session 22 is self-explanatory. The prayer that Ra speaks of in relation to Carla is the Prayer of St. Francis which Carla has used as her own personal tuning mechanism since she began channeling in 1974. It further refines the tuning done by the support group and is always prayed mentally before any session, whether telepathic or trance.

The limitations which Ra speaks of in the second answer refers to Carla's rheumatoid arthritis which was apparently chosen before the incarnation to provide an inner focus for her meditative work rather than allow the ease of outer expression that might have dissipated the inner orientation. Thus not all disabilities are meant to yield to even the best efforts of healers, and when such a disability does not respond to any kind of healing effort, one may begin to consider what opportunities for learning and service are opened up by the disability. Ra even mentioned in the last sentence that her acceptance of her disabilities and limitations would ease the amount of pain that she suffered because of them.

Carla: *It was distinctly odd to be going about and walking into aromas which had no overt origin. It seemed to me throughout this time that I was being more and more sensitized, and less and less vibrating with my humanhood. I feel sure that the constant weight loss added to this Alice-in-Wonderland feeling. To the present day, I continue to have a very sensitized physical vehicle. However, my formerly tiny body has grown from size pre-teen 5/8 to its present position athwart 14/16, a weight gain of double the lightest weight reached during the contact. Just for a feel for where "normal" is for me, I used to weigh between 115 and 120, year after year. I looked quite normal at that weight. It's been interesting to feel the different weights I have been, to live with a more or less bulky vehicle. One feels stronger, the heavier one is. I was surprised at this, figuring that lighter weights would make one feel more toned and vital. It makes it easier to understand why we in America so often allow ourselves to eat to the point of obesity. It feels good! One doubts that it is a life-lengthening thing, however!*

The pre-incarnative choice which I made to have a body that would limit what I could do is one I have taken a long time to appreciate. It is frustrating at first not to be able to do the work one's trained to do. I loved being a librarian, I enjoyed researching for Don. When I could no longer work in these ways, I was profoundly puzzled and not a little upset. But then quiet years taught me so much. I learned the open heart although my body was declining; I found hope and faith although the physical picture grew steadily worse. After Donald died, I came close to dying too, and in 1992, when at last I was able to turn the boat around, I felt the grip of death loosen and fall away.

My present experience is of living in a barely-working physical vehicle. Taking no less than seven medications,

I walk the razor's edge between doing too much and not doing enough. The one thing that has never changed throughout this experience is my dedication to helping the Wanderers of this planet. All the various skills that I have had to give up have their place in my work with people who are having trouble with their spiritual path, and so I feel fully useful at last. And yet I know that we are all most useful, not by what we do or say, but in the quality of our being.

Session 22, February 10, 1981

Questioner: The instrument would like to ask a couple of questions of you. The instrument would like to know why she smells the incense at various times during the day at various places?

Ra: I am Ra. This instrument has spent a lifetime in dedication to service. This has brought this instrument to this nexus in space/time with the conscious and unconscious distortion towards service, with the further conscious distortion towards service by communication. Each time, as you would put it, that we perform this working our social memory complex vibrational distortion meshes more firmly with this instrument's unconscious distortions towards service. Thus we are becoming a part of this instrument's vibratory complex and it a part of ours. This occurs upon the unconscious level, the level whereby the mind has gone down through to the roots of consciousness which you may call cosmic. This instrument is not consciously aware of this slow changing of the meshing vibratory complex. However, as the dedication on both levels continues, and the workings continue, there are signals sent from the unconscious in a symbolic manner. Because this instrument is extremely keen in its sense of smell this association takes place unconsciously, and the thought-form of this odor is witnessed by the entity.

Questioner: Secondly, she would like to know why she feels more healthy now that she has begun these sessions and feels more healthy as time goes on?

Ra: I am Ra. This is a function of the free will of the entity. This entity has, for many of your years, prayed a certain set of sound vibration complexes before opening to communication. Before the trance state was achieved this prayer remained within the conscious portion of the mind complex and, though helpful, was not as effective as the consequence of this prayer, as you would call this vibrational sound complex, which then goes directly into the unconscious level, thus more critically affecting the communication from the spiritual complex. Also, this entity has begun, due to this working, to accept certain limitations which it placed upon itself in order to set the stage for services such as it now performs. This also is an aid to re-aligning the distortions of the physical complex with regard to pain.

The Law of One, Book I, Session 23
February 11, 1981

Ra: I am Ra. I greet you in the love and the light of the infinite Creator. We communicate now.

Questioner: You were speaking yesterday of the first contact made by the Confederation which occurred during our third major cycle. You stated that you appeared in the skies over Egypt at approximately the same time that aid was given to Atlantis. Can you tell me why you went to Egypt and your orientation of attitude and thinking when you first went to Egypt?

Ra: I am Ra. At the time of which you speak there were those who chose to worship the hawk-headed sun god which you know as vibrational sound complex, "Horus." This vibrational sound complex has taken other vibrational sound complexes, the object of worship being the sun disc represented in some distortion.

We were drawn to spend some time, as you would call it, scanning the peoples for a serious interest amounting to a seeking with which we might help without infringement. We found that at that time the social complex was quite self-contradictory in its so-called religious beliefs and, therefore, there was not an appropriate calling for our vibration. Thus, at that time, which you know of as approximately 18,000 of your years in the past, we departed without taking action.

Questioner: You stated yesterday that you appeared in the skies over Egypt at that time. Were the Egyptian entities able to see you in their skies?

Ra: I am Ra. This is correct.

Questioner: What did they see, and how did this affect their attitudes?

Ra: I am Ra. They saw what you would speak of as crystal powered bell-shaped craft.

This did not affect them due to their firm conviction that many wondrous things occurred as a normal part of a world, as you would call it, in which many, many deities had powerful control over supernatural events.

Questioner: Did you have a reason for being visible to them rather than being invisible?

Ra: I am Ra. This is correct.

Questioner: Can you tell me your reason for being visible to them?

Ra: I am Ra. We allowed visibility because it did not make any difference.

Questioner: Then at this time you did not contact them. Can you answer the same question that I just asked with respect to your next attempt to contact the Egyptians?

Ra: I am Ra. The next attempt was prolonged. It occurred over a period of time. The nexus, or center, of our efforts was a decision upon our parts that there was a sufficient calling to attempt to walk among your peoples as brothers.

We laid this plan before the Council of Saturn, offering ourselves as service-oriented Wanderers of the type which land directly upon the inner planes without incarnative processes. Thus we emerged, or materialized, in physical-chemical complexes representing as closely as possible our natures, this effort being to appear as brothers and spend a limited amount of time as teachers of the Law of One, for there was an ever-stronger interest in the sun body, and this vibrates in concordance with our particular distortions.

We discovered that for each word we could utter, there were thirty impressions we gave by our very being, which confused those entities we had come to serve. After a short period we removed ourselves from these entities and spent much time attempting to understand how best to serve those to whom we had offered ourselves in love/light.

The ones who were in contact with that geographical entity, which you know of as Atlantis, had conceived of the potentials for healing by use of the pyramid-shape entities. In considering this and making adjustments for the difference as in the distortion complexes of the two geographical cultures, as you would call them, we went before the Council again, offering this plan to the Council as an aid to the healing and the longevity of those in the area you know of as Egypt. In this way we hoped to facilitate the learning process as well as offer philosophy articulating the Law of One. Again the Council approved.

Approximately 11,000 of your years ago we entered, by thought-form, your—we correct this instrument. We sometimes have difficulty due to low vitality. Approximately 8,500 years ago, having considered these concepts carefully, we returned, never having left in thought, to the thought-form areas of your vibrational planetary complex and considered for some of your years, as you measure time, how to appropriately build these structures.

The first, the Great Pyramid, was formed approximately 6,000 of your years ago. Then, in sequence, after this performing by thought of the building or architecture of the Great Pyramid using the more, shall we say, local or earthly material rather than thought-form material to build other pyramidal structures. This continued for approximately 1,500 of your years.

Meanwhile, the information concerning initiation and healing by crystal was being given. The one known as "Ikhnaton" was able to perceive this information without significant distortion and for a time, moved, shall we say, heaven and earth in order to invoke the Law of One and to order the priesthood of these structures in accordance with the distortions of initiation and true compassionate healing. This was not to be long-lasting.

At this entity's physical dissolution from your third-density physical plane, as we have said before, our teachings became quickly perverted, our structures once again went to the use of the so-called "royal" or those with distortions towards power.

Questioner: When you spoke of pyramid healing, I am assuming that the primary healing was for the mind. Is this correct?

Ra: I am Ra. This is partially correct. The healing, if it is to be effectuated, must be a funneling without significant distortion of the in-streamings through the spiritual complex into the tree of mind. There are parts of this mind which block energies flowing to the body complex. In each case, in each entity, the blockage may well differ.

However, it is necessary to activate the sense of the spiritual channel or shuttle. Then whether the blockage is from spiritual to mental or from mental to physical, or whether it may simply be a random and purely physical trauma, healing may then be carried out.

Questioner: When you started building the pyramid at Giza using thought, were you at that time in contact with incarnate Egyptians and did they observe this building?

Ra: I am Ra. At that time we were not in close contact with incarnate entities upon your plane. We were responding to a general calling of sufficient energy in that particular location to merit action. We sent thoughts to all who were seeking our information.

The appearance of the pyramid was a matter of tremendous surprise. However, it was carefully designed to coincide with the incarnation of one known as a great architect. This entity was later made into a deity, in part due to this occurrence.

Questioner: What name did they give this deity?

Ra: I am Ra. This deity had the sound vibration complex, "Imhotep."

Questioner: What can you tell me about the overall success of the pyramid? I understand that the pyramids were not successful in producing a rise in consciousness that was hoped for, but there must have been some success that came from them.

Ra: I am Ra. We ask you to remember that we are of the Brothers and Sisters of Sorrow. When one has been rescued from that sorrow to a vision of the one Creator, then there is no concept of failure.

Our difficulty lay in the honor/responsibility of correcting the distortions of the Law of One which occurred during our attempts to aid these entities. The distortions are seen as responsibilities rather than failures; the few who were inspired to seek, our only reason for the attempt.

Thus, we would perhaps be in the position of paradox in that as one saw an illumination, we were what you call successful, and as others became more sorrowful and confused, we were failures. These are your terms. We persist in seeking to serve.

Questioner: Can you tell me what happened to Ikhnaton after his physical death?

Ra: I am Ra. This entity was then put through the series of healing and review of incarnational experiences which is appropriate for third-density experience. This entity had been somewhat in the distortions of power ameliorated by the great devotion to the Law of One. This entity thus resolved to enter a series of incarnations in which it had no distortions towards power.

Questioner: Can you tell me what the average life span was for the Egyptians at the time of Ikhnaton?

Ra: I am Ra. The average life span of these people was approximately thirty-five to fifty of your years. There was much, what you would call, disease of a physical complex nature.

Questioner: Can you tell me of the reasons for the disease? I think I already know, but I think it might be good for the book to state this at this time.

Ra: I am Ra. This is, as we have mentioned before, not particularly informative with regard to the Law of One. However, the land you know of as Egypt at that time was highly barbarous in its living conditions, as you would call them. The river which you call Nile was allowed to flood and to recede, thus providing the fertile grounds for the breeding of diseases which may be carried by insects. Also, the preparation of foodstuffs allowed diseases to form. Also, there was difficulty in many cases with sources of water and water which was taken caused disease due to the organisms therein.

Questioner: I was really questioning about the more basic cause of disease rather than the mechanism of its transmission. I was going back to the root of thought that created the possibility of disease. Could you briefly tell me if I am correct in assuming the general reduction of thought over the long time on planet Earth with respect to the Law of One created a condition whereby what we call disease could develop? Is this correct?

Ra: I am Ra. This is correct and perceptive. You, as questioner, begin now to penetrate the outer teachings.

The root cause in this particular society was not so much a bellicose action although there were, shall we say, tendencies, but rather the formation of a money system and a very active trading and development of those tendencies towards greed and power; thus, the enslaving of entities by other entities and the misapprehension of the Creator within each entity.

Questioner: I understand, if I am correct, that a South American contact was also made. Can you tell me of the nature of your contact with respect to the attitude about the contact, its ramifications, the plan for the contact, and why the people were contacted in South America?

Ra: I am Ra. This will be the final full question of this session. The entities who walked among those in your South American continent were called by a similar desire upon the part of the entities therein to learn of the manifestations of the sun. They worshipped this source of light and life.

Thus, these entities were visited by light beings not unlike ourselves. Instructions were given and they were more accepted and less distorted than ours. The entities themselves began to construct a series of underground and hidden cities including pyramid structures.

These pyramids were somewhat at variance from the design that we had promulgated. However, the original ideas were the same with the addition of a desire or intention of creating places of meditation and rest, a feeling of the presence of the one Creator; these pyramids then being for all people, not only initiates and those to be healed.

They left this density when it was discovered that their plans were solidly in motion and, in fact, had been recorded. During the next approximately 3,500 years these plans became, though somewhat distorted, in a state of near-completion in many aspects.

Therefore, as is the case of the breakings of the quarantine, the entity who was helping the South American entities along the South American ways you call in part the Amazon River went before the Council of Saturn to request a second attempt to correct in person the distortions which had occurred in their plans. This having been granted, this entity or social memory complex returned and the entity chosen as messenger came among the peoples once more to correct the errors.

Again, all was recorded and the entity rejoined its social memory complex and left your skies.

As in our experience the teachings were, for the most part, greatly and grossly perverted to the extent in later times of actual human sacrifice rather than healing of humans. Thus, this social memory complex is also given the honor/duty of remaining until those distortions are worked out of the distortion complexes of your peoples.

May we ask if there are any questions of a brief nature before we close?

Questioner: Is there anything we can do to make the instrument more comfortable? Since you stated that she seems to be low on energy, is it possible to have another session later on today?

Ra: I am Ra. All is well with alignments. However, this instrument would benefit from rest from the trance state for this diurnal period.

I am Ra. I leave this instrument now. I leave each of you in the love and the light of the one infinite Creator. Go forth, therefore, rejoicing in the power and the peace of the one Creator. Adonai.

The Law of One, Book V, Session 23, Fragment 12
February 11, 1981

Jim: Dr. Puharich never did visit us during the Ra contact, so all of our questions about how he should prepare for joining the contact were only for our information. His strong desire to solve riddles and puzzles and his desire to prove spiritual truth would have made it difficult for him to become a part of our circle, since it was supported by the opposite mental attitude, faith.

Carla: Once one starts watching for synchronicities, one can find many a book, movie, or any other object or event bringing repeated messages and reminders of our path. So often, Jim and I will be discussing an issue only to find that for the next day or two, we receive confirmations meaningful only to us.

And I do think that many wanderers here are making today's movies and songs. One has only to listen to the wonderful words to current songs, sung by people as diverse as Arlo Guthrie and Donavon, Black Oak Arkansas and Earth, Wind and Fire, the Rolling Stones … the list is as long as my legs! We have wonderful company, we who wander here on earth.

Session 23, February 11, 1981

Questioner: I can't answer this question but I will ask it anyway since we are in the area that I think that this occurred in. I feel this is somewhat of a duty to ask this question because Henry Puharich will be visiting us here later this month. Was this entity involved in any of these times of which you have just spoken?

Ra: I am Ra. You are quite correct in your assumption that we can speak in no way concerning the entity Henry. If you will consider this entity's distortions with regard to what you call "proof" you will understand/grasp our predicament.

Questioner: I had assumed before I asked the question that that would be the answer. I only asked it for his benefit because he wished for me to. This may be a dumb question. There is a movie called "Battle Beyond the Stars." I don't know if you are familiar with it or not. I guess you are. It just seemed to have what you are telling us included in the script. Is this correct?

Ra: I am Ra. This particular creation of your entities had some distortions of the Law of One and its scenario upon your physical plane. This is correct. ♣

The Law of One, Book I, Session 24
February 15, 1981

Ra: I am Ra. I greet you in the love and in the light of the infinite Creator. We communicate now.

Questioner: We are a little concerned about the physical condition of the instrument. She has a slight congestion. If you can tell me of the advisability of the session, I would appreciate it.

Ra: I am Ra. This instrument's vital energies of the physical complex are low. The session will be appropriately shortened.

Questioner: In the last session you mentioned that in this last 25,000 year cycle the Atlanteans, Egyptians, and those in South America were contacted and then the Confederation departed. I understand that the Confederation did not come back for some time. Could you tell me of the reasons, consequences, and attitudes with respect to the next contact with those here on planet Earth?

Ra: I am Ra. In the case of the Atlanteans, enlargements upon the information given resulted in those activities distorted towards bellicosity which resulted in the final second Atlantean catastrophe 10,821 of your years in the past, as you measure time.

Many, many were displaced due to societal actions both upon Atlantis and upon those areas of what you would call North African deserts to which some Atlanteans had gone after the first conflict. Earth changes continued due to these, what you would call, nuclear bombs and other crystal weapons, sinking the last great land masses approximately 9,600 of your years ago.

In the Egyptian and the South American experiments results, though not as widely devastating, were as far from the original intention of the Confederation. It was clear to not only us but also to the Council and the Guardians that our methods were not appropriate for this particular sphere.

Our attitude thus was one of caution, observation, and continuing attempts to creatively discover methods whereby contact from our entities could be of service with the least distortion and above all with the least possibility of becoming perversions or antitheses of our intention in sharing information.

Questioner: Thank you. Then I assume that the Confederation stayed away from Earth for a period of time. What condition created the next contact that the Confederation made?

Ra: I am Ra. In approximately 3,600 of your years in the past, as you measure time, there was an influx of those of the Orion group, as you call them. Due to the increasing negative influences upon thinking and acting distortions, they were able to begin working with those whose impression from olden times, as you may say, was that they were special and different.

An entity of the Confederation, many, many thousands of your years in the past, the one you may call "Yahweh," had, by genetic cloning, set up these particular biases among these peoples who had come gradually to dwell in the vicinity of Egypt, as well as in many, many other places, by dispersion after the down-sinking of the land mass Mu. Here the Orion group found fertile soil in which to plant the seeds of negativity, these seeds, as always, being those of the elite, the different, those who manipulate or enslave others.

The one known as Yahweh felt a great responsibility to these entities. However, the Orion group had been able to impress upon the peoples the name Yahweh as the one responsible for this elitism. Yahweh then was able to take what you would call stock of its vibratory patterns and became, in effect, a more eloquently effective sound vibration complex.

In this complex the old Yahweh, now unnamed, but meaning "He comes," began to send positively oriented philosophy. This was approximately, in your past, of 3,300 years. Thus, the intense portion of what has become known as Armageddon was joined.

Questioner: How did the Orion group get through the quarantine 3,600 years ago? The random window effect?

Ra: I am Ra. At that time this was not entirely so, as there was a proper calling for this information. When there is a mixed calling the window effect is much more put into motion by the ways of the densities.

The quarantine in this case was, shall we say, not patrolled so closely, due to the lack of strong polarity, the windows thus needing to be very weak in order for penetration. As your harvest approaches, those forces of what you would call light work according to their call. The ones of Orion have the working only according to their call. This calling is in actuality not nearly as great.

Thus, due to the way of empowering or squares there is much resistance to penetration. Yet free will must be maintained and those desiring negatively oriented information, as you would call it, must then be satisfied by those moving through by the window effect.

Questioner: Then Yahweh, in an attempt to correct what I might call a mistake (I know you don't want to call it that), started 3,300 years ago a positive philosophy. Were the Orion and Yahweh philosophies impressed telepathically, or were there other techniques used?

Ra: I am Ra. There were two other techniques used: one by the entity no longer called Yahweh, who still felt that if it could raise up entities which were superior to the negative forces, that these superior entities could spread the Law of One. Thus this entity, "Yod-Heh-Shin-Vau-Heh," came among your people in form according to incarnate being and mated in the normal reproductive manner of your physical complexes, thus birthing a generation of much larger beings, these beings called "Anak."

The other method used to greater effect later in the scenario, as you would call it, was the thought-form such as we often use among your peoples to suggest the mysterious or the sublime. You may be familiar with some of these appearances.

Questioner: Could you state some of those?

Ra: I am Ra. This is information which you may discover. However, we will briefly point the way by indicating the so-called wheel within a wheel and the cherubim with sleepless eye.

Questioner: Did the Orion group use similar methods for their impression 3,600 years ago?

Ra: I am Ra. The group or empire had an emissary in your skies at that time.

Questioner: Can you describe that emissary?

Ra: I am Ra. This emissary was of your fiery nature which was hidden by the nature of cloud in the day. This was to obliterate the questions of those seeing such a vehicle and to make it consonant with these entities' concept of what you may call the Creator.

Questioner: And then how was the information passed on to the entities after they saw this fiery cloud?

Ra: I am Ra. By thought transfer and by the causing of fiery phenomena and other events to appear as being miraculous through the use of thought-forms.

Questioner: Then are there any prophets that sprang from this era or soon after it that are recorded?

Ra: I am Ra. Those of the empire were not successful in maintaining their presence for long after the approximate three zero, zero, zero date in your history and were, perforce, left with the decision to physically leave the skies. The so-called prophets were often given mixed information, but the worst that the Orion group could do was to cause these prophets to speak of doom, as prophecy in those days was the occupation of those who love their fellow beings and wish only to be of service to them and to the Creator.

Questioner: Are you saying that the Orion group was successful in polluting some of the positively oriented prophets' messages with prophecies of doom?

Ra: I am Ra. This is correct. Your next query shall be the last full query for this session.

Questioner: Could you tell me why the Orion group had to leave after what figures to be a six hundred year period?

Ra: I am Ra. Although the impression that they had given to those who called them was that these entities were an elite group, that which you know as "Diaspora" occurred, causing much dispersion of these peoples so that they became an humbler and more honorable breed, less bellicose and more aware of the loving-kindness of the one Creator.

The creation about them tended towards being somewhat bellicose, somewhat oriented towards the enslavement of others, but they themselves, the target of the Orion group by means of their genetic superiority/weakness, became what you may call the underdogs, thereby letting the feelings of gratitude for their neighbors, their family, and their one Creator begin to heal the feelings of elitism which led to the distortions of power over others which had caused their own bellicosity.

Any short queries may be asked now.

Questioner: Is there anything that we can do to make the instrument more comfortable?

Ra: I am Ra. You are conscientious. Be careful to adjust this instrument's upper appendages if its upper body is elevated.

I am Ra. All is well. It is our joy to speak with you. We leave in the love and the light of the one infinite Creator. Go forth, therefore, rejoicing in the power and the peace of the one Creator. Adonai.

L/L Research

L/L Research is a subsidiary of Rock Creek Research & Development Laboratories, Inc.

P.O. Box 5195
Louisville, KY 40255-0195

www.llresearch.org

Rock Creek is a non-profit corporation dedicated to discovering and sharing information which may aid in the spiritual evolution of humankind.

ABOUT THE CONTENTS OF THIS TRANSCRIPT: This telepathic channeling has been taken from transcriptions of the weekly study and meditation meetings of the Rock Creek Research & Development Laboratories and L/L Research. It is offered in the hope that it may be useful to you. As the Confederation entities always make a point of saying, please use your discrimination and judgment in assessing this material. If something rings true to you, fine. If something does not resonate, please leave it behind, for neither we nor those of the Confederation would wish to be a stumbling block for any.

© 2009 L/L Research

The Law of One, Book V, Session 24, Fragment 13
February 15, 1981

Jim: The following information refers to two of the most widely rumored events in Ufology in this country. The first refers to the supposed face-to-face meeting between extraterrestrials and then President Dwight D. Eisenhower and some senior military staff at Edwards Air Force Base in California in February, 1954. The second incident refers to the supposed crash of a UFO outside of Roswell, NM, in which the ufonauts on board supposedly died. It is further rumored that their bodies were stored in Hangar #18 at Wright Patterson Air Base in Ohio. Once again we encountered the temptation to pursue information that seemed on the surface to be extremely interesting but which in truth would yield little or no information which might aid in the evolution of mind, body, or spirit. And we would have lost the Ra contact because Ra's "narrow band contact" was focused only on aiding our evolution and not on revealing the transient intricacies of how groups play games in this illusion.

Carla: In 1962, when I joined with Donald to help make up the initial meditation group which grew into L/L Research, there were several rumors being bruited about. Supposedly, the government knew all about UFOs, had had contact. There were alleged conspiracies that various sources warned the public about. To this day, there has continued a steady stream of such prophecies and doomsday warnings of all kinds. Only the dates of Armageddon have changed, usually predicting doom within the next two or three years.

It is not that I do not think UFOs are communicating with our government. They might be. Certainly they are here; the landing trace cases alone prove that something that makes dents in the ground is visiting us, and the many witnesses and abductees create a comprehensive picture of human-alien contact that is undeniable. It is that I feel that the real treasure the UFO entities have brought us are those of the spirit, not those of this world. Whatever the physical reality of UFOs and governmental doings, they remain part of the transient world picture: part of this heavy illusion. But the messages have a metaphysical content that 10,000 years would not make out of date or less meaningful. So I tend to respond to people's questions about such highjinks as these with a redirection, back from phenomena to metaphysical truth.

Session 24, February 15, 1981

Questioner: One thing that has been bothering me that I was just reading about is not too important, but I would really be interested in knowing if Dwight Eisenhower met with either the Confederation or the Orion group in the 1950s?

Ra: I am Ra. The one of which you speak met with thought-forms which are indistinguishable from third density. This was a test. We, the Confederation, wished to see what would occur if this extremely positively oriented and simple congenial person with no significant distortion towards power happened across peaceful information and the possibilities which might append therefrom. We discovered that this entity did not feel that those under his care could deal with the concepts of other beings and other philosophies. Thus an agreement reached then allowed him to go his way, ourselves to do likewise; and a very quiet campaign, as we have heard you call it, be continued alerting your peoples to our presence gradually. Events have overtaken this plan. Is there any short query before we close?

Questioner: Another question with that is: was there a crashed spaceship with small bodies now stored in our military installations?

Ra: I am Ra. We do not wish to infringe upon your future. Gave we you this information, we might be giving you more than you could appropriately deal with in the space/time nexus of your present somewhat muddled configuration of military and intelligence thought. Therefore, we shall withhold this information.

The Law of One, Book I, Session 25
February 16, 1981

Ra: I am Ra. I greet you in the love and the light of the infinite Creator. We communicate now.

Questioner: We shall now continue with the material from yesterday. You stated that about 3,000 years ago the Orion group left due to Diaspora. Was the Confederation then able to make any progress after the Orion group left?

Ra: I am Ra. For many of your centuries, both the Confederation and the Orion Confederation busied themselves with each other upon planes above your own, shall we say, planes in time/space whereby machinations were conceived and the armor of light girded. Battles have been and are continuing to be fought upon these levels.

Upon the Earth plane, energies had been set in motion which did not cause a great deal of call. There were isolated instances of callings, one such taking place beginning approximately 2,600 of your years in the past in what you would call Greece (at this time) and resulting in writings and understandings of some facets of the Law of One. We especially note the one known as Thales and the one known as Heraclitus, those being of the philosopher career, as you may call it, teaching their students. We also point out the understandings of the one known as Pericles.

At this time there was a limited amount of visionary information which the Confederation was allowed to telepathically impress. However, for the most part, during this time empires died and rose according to the attitudes and energies set in motion long ago, not resulting in strong polarization but rather in that mixture of the positive and the warlike or negative which has been characteristic of this final minor cycle of your beingness.

Questioner: You spoke of an Orion Confederation and of a battle being fought between the Confederation and the Orion Confederation. Is it possible to convey any concept of how this battle is fought?

Ra: I am Ra. Picture, if you will, your mind. Picture it then in total unity with all other minds of your society. You are then single-minded and that which is a weak electrical charge in your physical illusion is now an enormously powerful machine whereby thoughts may be projected as things.

In this endeavor the Orion group charges or attacks the Confederation armed with light. The result, a stand-off, as you would call it, both energies being somewhat depleted by this and needing to regroup; the negative depleted through failure to manipulate, the positive depleted through failure to accept that which is given.

Questioner: Could you amplify the meaning of what you mean by the "failure to accept that which is given"?

Ra: I am Ra. At the level of time/space at which this takes place in the form of what you may call thought-war, the most accepting and loving energy would be to so love those who wished to manipulate that those entities were surrounded and engulfed, transformed by positive energies.

This, however, being a battle of equals, the Confederation is aware that it cannot, on equal footing, allow itself to be manipulated in order to remain purely positive, for then though pure it would not be of any consequence, having been placed by the so-called powers of darkness under the heel, as you may say.

It is thus that those who deal with this thought-war must be defensive rather than accepting in order to preserve their usefulness in service to others. Thusly, they cannot accept fully what the Orion Confederation wishes to give, that being enslavement. Thusly, some polarity is lost due to this friction and both sides, if you will, must then regroup.

It has not been fruitful for either side. The only consequence which has been helpful is a balancing of the energies available to this planet so that these energies have less necessity to be balanced in this space/time, thus lessening the chances of planetary annihilation.

Questioner: Does a portion of the Confederation then engage in this thought-battle? What percent engages?

Ra: I am Ra. This is the most difficult work of the Confederation. Only four planetary entities at any one time are asked to partake in this conflict.

Questioner: What density are these four planetary entities?

Ra: I am Ra. These entities are of the density of love, numbering four.

Questioner: Would an entity of this density be more effective for this work than an entity of density five or six?

Ra: I am Ra. The fourth density is the only density besides your own which, lacking the wisdom to refrain from battle, sees the necessity of the battle. Thus it is necessary that fourth-density social memory complexes be used.

Questioner: Am I correct in assuming that both the Confederation and the Orion group utilize only their fourth densities in this battle, and that the fifth and sixth densities of the Orion group do not engage in this?

Ra: I am Ra. This will be the last full question as this entity's energies are low.

It is partially correct. Fifth- and sixth-density entities positive would not take part in this battle. Fifth-density negative would not take part in this battle. Thus, the fourth density of both orientations join in this conflict.

May we ask for a few short questions before we close?

Questioner: I will first ask if there is anything that we can do to make the instrument more comfortable. I would also really like to know the orientation of the fifth-density negative for not participating in this battle?

Ra: I am Ra. The fifth density is the density of light or wisdom. The so-called negative service-to-self entity in this density is at a high level of awareness and wisdom and has ceased activity except by thought. The fifth-density negative is extraordinarily compacted and separated from all else.

Questioner: Thank you very much. We do not wish to deplete the instrument. Is there anything that we can do to make the instrument more comfortable?

Ra: I am Ra. You are very conscientious. As we requested previously it would be well to observe the angles taken by the more upright posture of the entity. It is causing some nerve blockage in the portion of the body complex called the elbows.

I am Ra. I leave you in the love and in the light of the one infinite Creator. Go forth, then, rejoicing in the power and the peace of the one Creator. Adonai. ♣

The Law of One, Book V, Session 25, Fragment 14
February 16, 1981

Jim: The following information gave us some insight into how one's choices can be used in either the positive or the negative sense even when there is the seeming interference of negative entities in the manner of what many light workers call psychic attack and what we came to call psychic greetings. We chose the term greeting to emphasize that there does not have to be a negative experience on the part of the one who is greeted and that the experience that the one who is greeted actually has is in direct proportion to how that entity looks at the situation. If one wishes to see such a greeting as a difficult attack, then that becomes the experience. One can, however, also choose to see the Creator in all entities and events and can praise and seek the light within any situation, and then that will tend to become the experience.

When this latter choice is made the psychic greeting becomes a great blessing in that it presents to the one who is greeted an intensive opportunity to see the one Creator where it may be more difficult to see and which, when accomplished, develops a great deal more spiritual strength than may normally be developed without the negative entity's aid in pointing out the weaker areas of our magical personalities. Psychic greetings can only be offered by negative entities' enhancing our own free will choices that are distorted towards service-to-self thought and behavior. Our poor choices, usually reflecting a lack of love towards another or the self, get magnified by the negative entity and bleed away our efforts to seek the light and serve others until we are able to balance the situation with love, acceptance, compassion, tolerance, and the light touch. This is why Jesus said to "Resist not evil." To resist and fight is to see someone or something as other than the self, as other than the one Creator. That is the negative path. The positive path sees and loves all as the self and as the One.

Carla: The work that was perforce mine during this time of psychic greeting was, as Jim pointed out, very helpful in focusing my will and attention. I remember feeling tremendously uplifted and held in safe hands through all of the episodes. The key was the surrender to seeing one's own dark side. I think Dion Fortune's description of how to deal with a vampiric entity, in that case a wolf, still to be the most direct example of the understanding needed to move through such times. This wise soul had a wolf appearing at her bed, during training in white western ritual magic. The solution was to draw the wolf directly into the breast, loving it and accepting it as self. Against fearless love, the powers of negation and death are helpless, and melt away.

I think those of Ra were very careful of our group, compared to some sources, who did not show much concern that they were wearing the instrument out. Advice such as was given for me could well apply to anyone who must husband one's energy.

Session 25, February 16, 1981

Questioner: What cause or complex of causes has led to the instrument's chest cold, as it is called?

Ra: I am Ra. This distortion towards illness was caused by the free will of the instrument in accepting a chemical substance which you call LSD. This was carefully planned by those entities which do not desire this instrument to remain viable. The substance has within it the facility of removing large stores of vital energy from the ingestor. The first hope of the Orion entity which arranged this opportunity was that this instrument would become less polarized towards what you call the positive. Due to conscious efforts upon the part of this instrument, using the substance as a programmer for service to others and for thankfulness, this instrument was spared this distortion and there was no result satisfactory to the Orion group.

The second hope lay in the possible misuse of the most powerful means of transmission of energy between your peoples in the area of body complex distortions. We have not previously spoken of the various types of energy blockages and transfers, positive and negative, that may take place due to participation in your sexual reproductive complex of actions. This entity, however, is a very strong entity with very little distortion from universal green-ray love energy. Thus this particular plan was not effected either, as the entity continued to give of itself in this context in an open or green-ray manner rather than attempting to deceive or to manipulate other-self.

The only remaining distortion available, since this entity would not detune and would not cease sharing love universally under this chemical substance, was simply to drain this entity of as much energy as possible. This entity has a strong distortion towards busy-ness which it has been attempting to overcome for some time, realizing it not to be the appropriate attitude for this work. In this particular area the ingestion of this substance did indeed, shall we say, cause distortions away from viability due to the busy-ness and the lack of desire to rest; this instrument staying alert for much longer than appropriate. Thus much vital energy was lost, making this instrument unusually susceptible to infections such as it now experiences.

Questioner: The second question that the instrument requested is: How may I best revitalize my self not only now but in the future?

Ra: I am Ra. This instrument is aware of the basic needs of its constitution, those being meditation, acceptance of limitations, experiences of joy through association with others, and with the beauty as of the singing, and the exercising with great contact, whenever possible, with the life forces of second density, especially those of trees; this entity also needing to be aware of the moderate but steady intake of foodstuffs, exercise being suggested at a fairly early portion of the day and at a later portion of the day before the resting.

Questioner: The third question that she requested was: How may Don and Jim help to revitalize me?

Ra: I am Ra. This is not an appropriate question for full answer. We can say only that these entities are most conscientious. We may add that due to this instrument's distortion towards imbalance in the space/time nexus, it would be well were this entity accompanied during exercise.

The Law of One, Book I, Session 26
February 17, 1981

Ra: I am Ra. I greet you in the love and the light of the infinite Creator. I communicate now.

Questioner: Is any of the changing that we have done here going to affect communication with the instrument in any way? Is what we've set up here all right?

Ra: I am Ra. This is correct.

Questioner: Do you mean that everything is satisfactory for continued communication?

Ra: I am Ra. We meant that the changes affect this communication.

Questioner: Should we discontinue communication because of these changes, or should we continue?

Ra: I am Ra. You may do as you wish. However, we would be unable to use this instrument at this space/time nexus without these modifications.

Questioner: Assuming that it is all right to continue, we're down to the last 3,000 years of this present cycle, and I was wondering if the Law of One in its written or spoken form has been made available within this last 3,000 years in any complete way such as we are doing now? Is it available in any other source?

Ra: I am Ra. There is no possibility of a complete source of information of the Law of One in this density. However, certain of your writings passed on to you as your so-called holy works have portions of this law.

Questioner: Does the Bible that we know have portions of this law in it?

Ra: I am Ra. This is correct.

Questioner: Can you tell me if any of the Old Testament has any of the Law of One?

Ra: I am Ra. This is correct.

Questioner: Which has more of the Law of One in it, the Old Testament or the New Testament?

Ra: I am Ra. Withdrawing from each of the collections of which you speak the portions having to do with the Law of One, the content is approximately equal. However, the so-called Old Testament has a larger amount of negatively influenced material, as you would call it.

Questioner: Can you tell me about what percentage is of Orion influence in both the Old and New Testaments?

Ra: I am Ra. We prefer that this be left to the discretion of those who seek the Law of One. We are not speaking in order to judge. Such statements would be construed by some of those who may read this material as judgmental. We can only suggest a careful reading and inward digestion of the contents. The understandings will become obvious.

Questioner: Thank you. Have you communicated with any of our population in the third-density incarnate state in recent times?

Ra: I am Ra. Please restate, specifying "recent times" and the pronoun, "you."

Questioner: Has Ra communicated with any of our population in this century, in the last, say, eighty years?

Ra: I am Ra. We have not.

Questioner: Has the Law of One been communicated in the last eighty years by any other source to an entity in our population?

Ra: I am Ra. The ways of One have seldom been communicated, although there are rare instances in the previous eighty of your years, as you measure time.

There have been many communications from fourth density due to the drawing towards the harvest to fourth density. These are the ways of universal love and understanding. The other teachings are reserved for those whose depth of understanding, if you will excuse this misnomer, recommend and attract such further communication.

Questioner: Then did the Confederation step up its program of helping planet Earth some time late in this last major cycle? It seems that they did from previous data, especially with the Industrial Revolution. Can you tell me the attitudes and the reasonings behind this? is there any reason other than they just wanted to produce more leisure time in the last, say, one hundred years of the cycle? Is this the total reason?

Ra: I am Ra. This is not the total reason. Approximately two hundred of your years in the past, as you measure time, there began to be a significant amount of entities who by seniority were incarnating for learn/teaching purposes rather than for the lesser of the learn/teachings of those less aware of the process. This was our signal to enable communication to take place.

The Wanderers which came among you began to make themselves felt at approximately this time, firstly offering ideas or thoughts containing the distortion of free will. This was the prerequisite for further Wanderers which had information of a more specific nature to offer. The thought must precede the action.

Questioner: I was wondering if the one, Abraham Lincoln, could have been a Wanderer?

Ra: I am Ra. This is incorrect. This entity was a normal, shall we say, Earth being which chose to leave the vehicle and allow an entity to use it on a permanent basis. This is relatively rare compared to the phenomenon of Wanderers.

You would do better, considering the incarnations of Wanderers such as the one known as "Thomas," the one known as "Benjamin."

Questioner: I am assuming that you mean Thomas Edison and Benjamin Franklin?

Ra: I am Ra. This is incorrect. We were intending to convey the sound vibration complex, Thomas Jefferson. The other, correct.

Questioner: Thank you. Can you tell me where the entity who used Abraham Lincoln's body—what density he came from and where?

Ra: I am Ra. This entity was fourth-vibration.

Questioner: I assume positive?

Ra: I am Ra. That is correct.

Questioner: Was his assassination in any way influenced by Orion or any other negative force?

Ra: I am Ra. This is correct.

Questioner: Thank you. In the recent past of the last thirty to forty years the UFO phenomena have become known to our population. What was the original reason for the increase in what we call UFO activity in the past forty years?

Ra: I am Ra. Information which Confederation sources had offered to your entity, Albert [Einstein], became perverted, and instruments of destruction began to be created, examples of this being the Manhattan Project and its product.

Information offered through Wanderer, sound vibration, Nikola, also was experimented with for potential destruction: example, your so-called Philadelphia Experiment.

Thus, we felt a strong need to involve our thought-forms in whatever way we of the Confederation could be of service in order to balance these distortions of information meant to aid your planetary sphere.

Questioner: Then what you did, I am assuming, is to create an air of mystery with the UFO phenomenon, as we call it, and then by telepathy send many messages which could be accepted or rejected under the Law of One so that the population would start thinking seriously about the consequences of what it was doing. Is this correct?

Ra: I am Ra. This is partially correct. There are other services we may perform. Firstly, the integration of souls or spirits, if you will, in the event of use of these nuclear devices in your space/time continuum. This the Confederation has already done.

Questioner: I don't fully understand what you mean by that. Could you expand on that a little bit?

Ra: I am Ra. The use of intelligent energy transforming matter into energy is of such a nature among these weapons that the transition from space/time third density to time/space third density or what you may call your heaven worlds is interrupted in many cases.

Therefore, we are offering ourselves as those who continue the integration of soul or spirit complex during transition from space/time to time/space.

Questioner: Could you give us an example from Hiroshima or Nagasaki of how this is done?

Ra: I am Ra. Those who were destroyed, not by radiation, but by the trauma of the energy release, found not only the body/mind/spirit complex made unviable, but also a disarrangement of that unique vibratory complex you have called the spirit complex, which we understand as a mind/body/spirit complex, to be completely disarranged without possibility of re-integration. This would be the loss to the Creator of part of the Creator and thus we were given permission, not to stop the events, but to ensure the survival of the, shall we say, disembodied mind/body/spirit complex. This we did in those events which you mention, losing no spirit or portion or holograph or microcosm of the macrocosmic Infinite One.

Questioner: Could you tell me just vaguely how you accomplished this?

Ra: I am Ra. This is accomplished through our understanding of dimensional fields of energy. The higher or more dense energy field will control the less dense.

Questioner: Then you are saying that, in general, you will allow the population of this planet to have a nuclear war and many deaths from that war, but you will be able to create a condition where these deaths will be no more traumatic than entrance to what we call the heaven worlds or the astral world due to death by a bullet or by the normal means of dying by old age. Is this correct?

Ra: I am Ra. This is incorrect. It would be more traumatic. However, the entity would remain an entity.

Questioner: Can you tell me the condition of the entities who were killed in Nagasaki and Hiroshima at this time?

Ra: I am Ra. They of this trauma have not yet fully begun the healing process. They are being helped as much as is possible.

Questioner: When the healing process is complete with these entities, will this experience of death due to nuclear bomb cause them to be regressed in their climb towards fourth density?

Ra: I am Ra. Such actions as nuclear destruction affect the entire planet. There are no differences at this level of destruction, and the planet will need to be healed.

Questioner: I was thinking specifically if an entity was in Hiroshima or Nagasaki at that time and he was reaching harvestability at the end of our cycle, would this death by nuclear bomb create such trauma that he would not be harvestable at the end of the cycle?

Ra: I am Ra. This is incorrect. Once the healing has taken place the harvest may go forth unimpeded. However, the entire planet will undergo healing for this action, no distinction being made betwixt victim and aggressor, this due to damage done to the planet.

Questioner: Can you describe the mechanism of the planetary healing?

Ra: I am Ra. Healing is a process of acceptance, forgiveness, and, if possible, restitution. The restitution not being available in time/space, there are many among your peoples now attempting restitution while in the physical.

Questioner: How do these people attempt this restitution in the physical?

Ra: I am Ra. These attempt feelings of love towards the planetary sphere and comfort and healing of the scars and the imbalances of these actions.

Questioner: Then as the UFO phenomenon was made obvious to many of the population, many groups of people were reporting contact and telepathic contact with UFO entities and recorded the results of what they considered telepathic communication. Was the Confederation oriented to impressing telepathic communication on groups that were interested in UFOs?

Ra: I am Ra. This is correct although some of our members have removed themselves from the time/space using thought-form projections into your space/time, and have chosen, from time to time, with permission of the Council, to appear in your skies without landing.

Questioner: Then are all of the landings that have occurred with the exception of the landing that occurred when *(name)* was contacted of the Orion group or similar groups?

Ra: I am Ra. Except for isolated instances of those of, shall we say, no affiliation, this is correct.

Questioner: Is it necessary in each case of these landings for the entities involved to be calling the Orion group, or do some of these entities come in contact with the Orion group even though they are not calling that group?

Ra: I am Ra. You must plumb the depths of fourth-density negative understanding. This is difficult for you. Once having reached third-density space/time continuum through your so-called windows, these crusaders may plunder as they will, the results completely a function of the polarity of the, shall we say, witness/subject or victim.

This is due to the sincere belief of fourth-density negative that to love self is to love all. Each other-self which is thus either taught or enslaved thus has a teacher which teaches love of self. Exposed to this teaching, it is intended there be brought to fruition an harvest of fourth-density negative or self-serving mind/body/spirit complexes.

(The following material, from Session 53, May 25, 1981, was added for clarity.)

Questioner: Can you tell me of the various techniques used by the service-to-others positively oriented Confederation contacts with the people of this planet, the various forms and techniques of making contact?

Ra: I am Ra. We could.

Questioner: Would you do this, please?

Ra: I am Ra. The most efficient mode of contact is that which you experience at this space/time. The infringement upon free will is greatly undesired. Therefore, those entities which are Wanderers upon your plane of illusion will be the only subjects for the thought projections which make up the so-called "Close Encounters" and meetings between positively oriented social memory complexes and Wanderers.

Questioner: Could you give me an example of one of these meetings between a social memory complex and a Wanderer as to what the Wanderer would experience?

Ra: I am Ra. One such example of which you are familiar is that of the one known as Morris[6]. In this case the previous contact which other entities in this entity's circle of friends experienced was negatively oriented. However, you will recall that the entity, Morris, was impervious to this contact and could not see with the physical optical apparatus, this contact.

However, the inner voice alerted the one known as Morris to go by itself to another place and there an entity with the thought-form shape and appearance of the other contact appeared and gazed at this entity, thus awakening in it the desire to seek the truth of this occurrence and of the experiences of its incarnation in general.

The feeling of being awakened or activated is the goal of this type of contact. The duration and imagery used varies depending upon the subconscious expectations of the Wanderer which is experiencing this opportunity for activation.

Questioner: In a "Close Encounter" by a Confederation type of craft I am assuming that this "Close Encounter" is with a thought-form type of craft. Do Wanderers within the past few years have "Close Encounters" with landed thought-form type of craft?

---

[6] This refers to Case #1 in *Secrets of the UFO* by D. T. Elkins with Carla L. Rueckert, Louisville, L/L Research, 1976, pp 10-11.

Ra: I am Ra. This has occurred although it is much less common than the Orion type of so-called "Close Encounter."

We may note that in a universe of unending unity the concept of a "Close Encounter" is humorous, for are not all encounters of a nature of self with self? Therefore, how can any encounter be less than very, very close?

Questioner: Well, talking about this type of encounter of self to self, do any Wanderers of a positive polarization ever have a so-called "Close Encounter" with the Orion or negatively oriented polarization?

Ra: I am Ra. This is correct.

Questioner: Why does this occur?

Ra: I am Ra. When it occurs it is quite rare and occurs either due to the Orion entities' lack of perception of the depth of positivity to be encountered or due to the Orion entities' desire to, shall we say, attempt to remove this positivity from this plane of existence. Orion tactics normally are those which choose the simple distortions of mind which indicate less mental and spiritual complex activity.

Questioner: I have become aware of a very large variation in the contact with individuals. Could you give me general examples of the methods used by the Confederation to awaken or partially awaken the Wanderers they contact?

Ra: I am Ra. The methods used to awaken Wanderers are varied. The center of each approach is the entrance into the conscious and subconscious in such a way as to avoid causing fear and to maximize the potential for an understandable subjective experience which has meaning for the entity. Many such occur in sleep, others in the midst of many activities during the waking hours. The approach is flexible and does not necessarily include the "Close Encounter" syndrome, as you are aware.

Questioner: What about the physical examination syndrome? How does that relate to Wanderers and Confederation and Orion contacts?

Ra: I am Ra. The subconscious expectations of entities cause the nature and detail of thought-form experience offered by Confederation thought-form entities. Thus, if a Wanderer expects a physical examination, it will, perforce, be experienced with as little distortion towards alarm or discomfort as is allowable by the nature of the expectations of the subconscious distortions of the Wanderer.

Questioner: Well, are those who are taken on both Confederation and Orion craft then experiencing a seeming physical examination?

Ra: I am Ra. Your query indicates incorrect thinking. The Orion group uses the physical examination as a means of terrifying the individual and causing it to feel the feelings of an advanced second-density being such as a laboratory animal. The sexual experiences of some are a sub-type of this experience. The intent is to demonstrate the control of the Orion entities over the Terran inhabitant.

The thought-form experiences are subjective and, for the most part, do not occur in this density.

Questioner: Then both Confederation and Orion contacts are being made and "Close Encounters" are of a dual nature as I understand it. They can either be of the Confederation or of the Orion type of contact. Is this correct?

Ra: I am Ra. This is correct, although the preponderance of contacts is Orion-oriented.

Questioner: Well, we have a large spectrum of entities on Earth with respect to harvestability, both positively oriented and negatively oriented. Would the Orion group target in on the ends of this spectrum, both positively and negatively oriented, for contact with Earth entities?

Ra: I am Ra. This query is somewhat difficult to accurately answer. However, we shall attempt to do so.

The most typical approach of Orion entities is to choose what you might call the weaker-minded entity that it might suggest a greater amount of Orion philosophy to be disseminated.

Some few Orion entities are called by more highly polarized negative entities of your space/time nexus. In this case they share information just as we are now doing. However, this is a risk for the Orion entities due to the frequency with which the harvestable negative planetary entities then attempt to bid and order the Orion contact just as these entities bid planetary negative contacts. The resulting struggle for mastery, if lost, is damaging to the polarity of the Orion group.

Similarly, a mistaken Orion contact with highly polarized positive entities can wreak havoc with Orion troops unless these crusaders are able to depolarize the entity mistakenly contacted. This occurrence is almost unheard-of. Therefore, the Orion group prefers to make physical contact only with the weaker-minded entity.

Questioner: Then in general we could say that if an individual has a "Close Encounter" with a UFO or any other type of experience that seems to be UFO-related, he must look to the heart of the encounter and the effect upon him to determine whether it was Orion or Confederation contact. Is this correct?

Ra: I am Ra. This is correct. If there is fear and doom, the contact was quite likely of a negative nature. If the result is hope, friendly feelings, and the awakening of a positive feeling of purposeful service to others, the marks of Confederation contact are evident.

(End of material from Session 53, May 25, 1981.)

Questioner: Then I am assuming all of the groups getting telepathic contact from the Confederation are high-priority targets for the Orion crusaders, and I would assume that a large percentage of them are having their messages polluted by the Orion group. Can you tell me what percentage of them had their information polluted by the Orion group and if any of them were able to remain purely a Confederation channel?

Ra: I am Ra. To give you this information would be to infringe upon the free will or confusion of some living. We can only ask each group to consider the relative effect of philosophy and your so-called specific information. It is not the specificity of the information which attracts negative influences. It is the importance placed upon it.

This is why we iterate quite often, when asked for specific information, that it pales to insignificance, just as the grass withers and dies while the love and the light of the one infinite Creator redounds to the very infinite realms of creation forever and ever, creating and creating itself in perpetuity.

Why then be concerned with the grass that blooms, withers and dies in its season only to grow once again due to the infinite love and light of the one Creator? This is the message we bring. Each entity is only superficially that which blooms and dies. In the deeper sense there is no end to being-ness.

Questioner: As you have stated, it is a straight and narrow path. There are many distractions.

We have created an introduction to the Law of One, traveling through and hitting the high points of this 75,000 year cycle. After this introduction I would like to get directly to the main work, which is an investigation of evolution. I am very appreciative and feel a great honor and privilege to be doing this and hope that we can accomplish this next phase.

Ra: I am Ra. I leave you, my friends, in the love and the light of the one infinite Creator. Go forth, then, merry and glad and rejoicing in the power and the peace of the one Creator. Adonai.

The Law of One, Book V, Session 26, Fragment 15
February 17, 1981

Jim: The following information refers again to Carla's two experiences with LSD. We were very thankful that there were only two experiences with which she and we had to deal, for, as you can see, the debilitating effects apparently mount rapidly with each ingestion. The sessions in Book Two of *The Law Of One* were necessarily shortened in order to conserve the vital energy of the instrument which had been drained by the LSD.

Carla: I can only add the fact that this period of weakness did occur, and so Ra's suggestion not to mix any drugs with channeling seems to me a sound piece of advice that I have followed ever since.

Session 26, February 17, 1981

Questioner: The instrument asks how long will the debilitating effects that I am experiencing due to the LSD last, and is there anything that we can do to make the instrument more comfortable?

Ra: I am Ra. Firstly, the period of weakness of bodily complex is approximately three of your lunar cycles, the first ingestion causing approximately one of your lunar cycles; the second having a cumulative or doubling effect. ♣

The Law of One, Book II, Session 27
February 21, 1981

Ra: I am Ra. I greet you in the love and light of the one infinite Creator. I communicate now.

Questioner: This session I thought we would start Book Two of THE LAW OF ONE, which will focus on what we consider to be the only important aspect of our being. This, I assume, will be a much more difficult task than the first book. We want to focus on things that are not transient, and as questioner I may have difficulty at times.

When I do have this difficulty I may fall back on some transient questions simply because I will not be able to formulate what I really need, and I apologize for this. I will try my best to stay on the track and eliminate things of no value from the book if they do occur during my questioning.

The statement I will make to begin with is: In this density we tend to focus our minds on some transient condition or activity with little regard to its value or use as an aid or a tool for growth and understanding of the true and undistorted essence of the creation of which we are an integral part.

I will attempt, by starting at the beginning of creation, to establish an overview of ourselves in the creation, thereby arriving at a more informed viewpoint of what we consider to be reality. It is hoped that this will allow us to participate more effectively in the process of evolution.

I would like to start with definitions of words that we have been using that possibly we have not—and possibly cannot—understand totally, but since the first words that we use are intelligent infinity, I would like for you to define each of these words and give the definition of their combination.

Ra: I am Ra. Your vibrations of mind complex indicate a query. However, your vibrational sound complex indicate a preference. Please restate.

Questioner: Would you define the word intelligent in the context of intelligent infinity?

Ra: I am Ra. We shall address the entire spectrum of this question before defining as requested. Your language, using vibrational sound complexes, can be at best an approximation of that which is closer to an understanding, if you will, of the nature of conscious thought. Perceptions are not the same as sound vibration complexes and the attempt to define will therefore be a frustrating one for you, although we are happy to aid you within the limits of your sound vibration complexes.

To define intelligent apart from infinity is difficult, for these two vibration complexes equal one concept. It is much like attempting to divide your sound vibration concept, faith, into two parts. We shall attempt to aid you however.

Questioner: It is not necessary to divide it. The definition of intelligent infinity is sufficient. Could you define that please?

Ra: I am Ra. This is exponentially simpler and less confusing. There is unity. This unity is all that there is. This unity has a potential and kinetic. The potential is intelligent infinity. Tapping this potential will yield work. This work has been called by us, intelligent energy.

The nature of this work is dependent upon the particular distortion of free will which in turn is the nature of a particular intelligent energy of kinetic focus of the potential of unity or that which is all.

Questioner: I would like to expand a little on the concept of work. In Newtonian physics the concept of work is the product of force and distance. I am assuming that the work of which you speak is a much broader term including possibly work in consciousness. Am I correct?

Ra: I am Ra. As we use this term it is universal in application. Intelligent infinity has a rhythm or flow as of a giant heart beginning with the central sun as you would think or conceive of this, the presence of the flow inevitable as a tide of beingness without polarity, without finity; the vast and silent all beating outward, outward, focusing outward and inward until the focuses are complete. The intelligence or consciousness of foci have reached a state where their, shall we say, spiritual nature or mass calls them inward, inward, inward until all is coalesced. This is the rhythm of reality as you spoke.

Questioner: Then I think I have extracted an important point from this in that in intelligent infinity we have work without polarity, or a potential difference does not have to exist. Is this correct?

Ra: I am Ra. There is no difference, potential or kinetic, in unity. The basic rhythms of intelligent infinity are totally without distortion of any kind. The rhythms are clothed in mystery, for they are being itself. From this undistorted unity, however, appears a potential in relation to intelligent energy.

In this way you may observe the term to be somewhat two-sided, one use of the term, that being as the undistorted unity, being without any kinetic or potential side. The other application of this term, which we use undifferentiatedly for lack of other terms in the sense of the vast potential tapped into by foci or focuses of energy, we call intelligent energy.

Questioner: I understand that the first distortion of intelligent infinity is the distortion of what we call free will. Can you give me a definition of this distortion?

Ra: I am Ra. In this distortion of the Law of One it is recognized that the Creator will know Itself.

Questioner: Then am I correct in assuming that the Creator then grants for this knowing the concept of total freedom of choice in the ways of knowing? Am I correct?

Ra: I am Ra. This is quite correct.

Questioner: This then being the first distortion of the Law of One, which I am assuming is the Law of Intelligent Infinity, all other distortions which are the total experience of the creation spring from this. Is this correct?

Ra: I am Ra. This is both correct and incorrect. In your illusion all experience springs from the Law of Free Will or the Way of Confusion. In another sense, which we are learning, the experiences are this distortion.

Questioner: I will have to think about that and ask questions on it in the next session, so I will go on now to what you have given me as the second distortion which is the distortion of love. Is this correct?

Ra: I am Ra. This is correct.

Questioner: I would like for you to define love in its sense as the second distortion.

Ra: I am Ra. This must be defined against the background of intelligent infinity or unity or the one Creator with the primal distortion of free will. The term Love then may be seen as the focus, the choice of attack, the type of energy of an extremely, shall we say, high order which causes intelligent energy to be formed from the potential of intelligent infinity in just such and such a way. This then may be seen to be an object rather than an activity by some of your peoples, and the principle of this extremely strong energy focus being worshipped as the Creator instead of unity or oneness from which all Loves emanate.

Questioner: Is there a manifestation of love that we could call vibration?

Ra: I am Ra. Again we reach semantic difficulties. The vibration or density of love or understanding is not a term used in the same sense as the second distortion, Love; the distortion Love being the great activator and primal co-Creator of various creations using intelligent infinity; the vibration love being that density in which those who have learned to do an activity called "loving" without significant distortion, then seek the ways of light or wisdom. Thus in vibratory sense love comes into light in the sense of the activity of unity in its free will. Love uses light and has the power to direct light in its distortions. Thus vibratory complexes recapitulate in reverse the creation in its unity, thus showing the rhythm or flow of the great heartbeat, if you will use this analogy.

Questioner: I will make a statement that I have extracted from the physics of Dewey Larson which may or may not be close to what we are trying to explain. Larson says that all is motion which we can take as vibration, and that vibration is pure vibration and is not physical in any way or in any form or density, and the first product of that vibration is what we call the photon or particle of light. I am trying to make an analogy between this physical solution and the concept of love and light. Is this close to the concept of Love creating light?

Ra: I am Ra. You are correct.

Questioner: Then I will expand a bit more on this concept. We have the infinite vibration of Love which can occur, I am assuming, at varying frequencies.

I would assume that it begins at one basic frequency. Does this have any meaning?

Ra: I am Ra. Each Love, as you term the prime movers, comes from one frequency, if you wish to use this term. This frequency is unity. We would perhaps liken it rather to a strength than a frequency, this strength being infinite, the finite qualities being chosen by the particular nature of this primal movement.

Questioner: Then this vibration which is, for lack of better understanding, pure motion; it is pure love; it is nothing that is yet condensed, shall we say, to form any type of density of illusion. This Love then creates by this process of vibration a photon, as we call it, which is the basic particle of light. This photon then, by added vibrations and rotation, further condenses into particles of the densities we experience. Is this correct?

Ra: I am Ra. This is correct.

Questioner: Then this light which forms the densities has what we call color. This color is divided into seven categories. Can you tell me if there is a reason or explanation for these categories of color?

Ra: I am Ra. This will be the last complete question of this session as this instrument is low on vital energy. We will answer briefly and then you may question further in subsequent sessions.

The nature of the vibratory patterns of your universe is dependent upon the configurations placed upon the original material or light by the focus or Love using Its intelligent energy to create a certain pattern of illusions or densities in order to satisfy Its own intelligent estimate of a method of knowing Itself. Thus the colors, as you call them, are as straight, or narrow, or necessary as is possible to express, given the will of Love.

There is further information which we shall be happy to share by answering your questions. However, we do not wish to deplete this instrument. Is there a short query necessary before we leave?

Questioner: The only thing I need to know is if there is anything that we can do to make the instrument more comfortable or to help her or this contact?

Ra: I am Ra. This instrument is slightly uncomfortable. Perhaps a simpler configuration of the body would be appropriate given the instrument's improving physical complex condition.

I am Ra. You are conscientious in your endeavors. We shall be with you. We leave you now in the love and in the light of the one infinite Creator. Rejoice, therefore, in the power and the peace of the one infinite Creator. Adonai.

The Law of One, Book V, Session 27, Fragment 16
February 21, 1981

Jim: Just before I joined Don and Carla, at the end of 1980, I traveled to the Portland, Oregon, area to work with Paul Shockley and the Aquarian Church of Universal Service. It was a happy experience in itself, and it also provided the catalyst that eventually saw me return to Kentucky and join L/L Research. After two months in Oregon I decided to take a weekend alone to think about an opportunity to earn a great deal of money that had been presented to me by one of the members of the Aquarian Church. Thirty seconds into my first meditation of the weekend the very clear message to return to Don and Carla flashed across my inner sky. So I said good-bye to my new friends and returned to Louisville. Three weeks later the Ra contact began, and when Paul Shockley was informed of the nature of the contact he asked that two questions be asked for him of the social memory complex, Ra.

The answer to the second query is especially interesting to us because it seems to suggest the means by which some of the pyramids of Egypt were constructed.

Carla: *In 1986 we were invited to Shockley's "Friendship" conference, and I finally met this channel for a source called "Cosmic Awareness." He was a very sincere and valiant channel, pure in his desire to serve. I feel it unfortunate that the questions put to this channel, over a period of time, pretty much changed and worsened the quality of information received. As always when this occurs, the culprit was a fascination with transient material. I think that it was the questions put to this excellent channel that lessened the metaphysical level of this channeling.*

Session 27, February 21, 1981

Questioner: Jim has felt the obligation to ask two questions that were asked of him by Paul Shockley, and I will ask those two first, in case you are able to answer them before we get started. The first question: Paul Shockley is presently channeling the same source which Edgar Cayce channeled, and he has received information that he took part in the design and construction of the Egyptian pyramids. Can you tell us what his role was in that effort?

Ra: I am Ra. This was in your space/time continuum two periods and two lifetimes. The first of a physical nature working with Confederation entities in what you know of as Atlantis, this approximately 13,000 of your years ago. This memory, shall we say, being integrated into the unconscious of the mind/body/spirit complex of this entity due to its extreme desire to remember the service of healing and polarization possible by the mechanisms of the crystal and the charged healer.

The second experience being approximately 1,000 of your years later during which experience this entity prepared, in some part, the consciousness of the people of what you now call Egypt, that they were able to offer the calling that enabled those of our social memory complex to walk among your peoples. During this life experience this entity was of a priest and teaching nature and succeeded in remembering in semi-distorted form the learn/teachings of the Atlantean pyramidal experiences. Thus this entity became a builder of the archetypal thought of the Law of One with distortions towards healing which aided our people in bringing this through into a physical manifestation.

Questioner: The second question is: Paul has also received information that there were other beings aiding in the construction of the pyramids, but that they were not fully materialized in the third density. They were materialized from their waist up to their heads but were not materialized from their waist down to their feet. Did such entities exist and aid in the construction of the pyramids, and who were they?

Ra: I am Ra. Consider, if you will, the intelligent infinity present in the absorption of living-ness and being-ness as it becomes codified into intelligent energy, due to the thought impressions of those assisting the living stone into a new shape of being-ness The release and use of intelligent infinity for a brief period begins to absorb all the consecutive or interlocking dimensions, thus offering brief glimpses of those projecting to the material their thought. These beings thus beginning to materialize but not remaining visible. These beings were the thought-form or third-density visible manifestation of our social memory complex as we offered contact from our intelligent infinity to the intelligent infinity of the stone. ✣

The Law of One, Book II, Session 28
February 22, 1981

Ra: I am Ra. I greet you in the love and the light of the infinite Creator. I communicate now.

Questioner: I may be backtracking a little today because I think that possibly we are at the most important part of what we are doing in trying to make it apparent how everything is one, how it comes from one intelligent infinity. This is difficult, so please bear with my errors in questioning.

The concept that I have right now of the process, using both what you have told me and some of Dewey Larson's material having to do with the physics of the process, is that intelligent infinity expands outward from all locations everywhere. It expands outward uniformly like the surface of a bubble or a balloon expanding outward from every point everywhere. It expands outward at what is called unit velocity or the velocity of light. This is Larson's idea of the progression of what he calls space/time. Is this concept correct?

Ra: I am Ra. This concept is incorrect as is any concept of the one intelligent infinity. This concept is correct in the context of one particular Logos, or Love, or focus of this Creator which has chosen Its, shall we say, natural laws and ways of expressing them mathematically and otherwise.

The one undifferentiated intelligent infinity, unpolarized, full and whole, is the macrocosm of the mystery-clad being. We are messengers of the Law of One. Unity, at this approximation of understanding, cannot be specified by any physics but only become activated or potentiated intelligent infinity due to the catalyst of free will. This may be difficult to accept. However, the understandings we have to share begin and end in mystery.

Questioner: Yesterday we had arrived at a point where we were considering colors of light. You said: "The nature of the vibratory patterns of your universe is dependent upon the configurations placed upon the original material or light by the focus or Love using Its intelligent energy to create a certain pattern of illusions or densities in order to satisfy Its own intelligent estimate of a method of knowing Itself." Then after this you said that there was more material that you would be happy to share, but we ran out of time. Could you give us further information on that?

Ra: I am Ra. In discussing this information we then, shall we say, snap back into the particular methods of understanding or seeing that which the one, sound vibration complex, Dewey, offers; this being correct for the second meaning of intelligent infinity: the potential which then through catalyst forms the kinetic.

This information is a natural progression of inspection of the kinetic shape of your environment. You may understand each color or ray as being, as we had said, a very specific and accurate portion of intelligent energy's representation of intelligent infinity, each ray having been previously inspected in other regards.

This information may be of aid here. We speak now nonspecifically to increase the depth of your conceptualization of the nature of what is. The universe in which you live is recapitulation in each part of intelligent infinity. Thus you will see the same patterns repeated in physical and metaphysical areas; the rays or portions of light being, as you surmise, those areas of what you may call the physical illusion which rotate, vibrate, or are of a nature that may be, shall we say, counted or categorized in rotation manner in space/time as described by the one known as Dewey; some substances having various of the rays in a physical manifestation visible to the eye, this being apparent in the nature of your crystallized minerals which you count as precious, the ruby being red and so forth.

Questioner: This light occurred as a consequence of vibration which is a consequence of Love. I am going to ask if that statement is correct?

Ra: I am Ra. This statement is correct.

Questioner: This light then can condense into material as we know it into our density, into all of our chemical elements because of rotations of the vibration at quantized units or intervals of angular velocity. Is this correct?

Ra: I am Ra. This is quite correct.

Questioner: Thank you. I am wondering, what is the catalyst or the activator of the rotation? What causes the rotation so that light condenses into our physical or chemical elements?

Ra: I am Ra. It is necessary to consider the enabling function of the focus known as Love. This energy is of an ordering nature. It orders in a cumulative way from greater to lesser so that when Its universe, as you may call it, is complete, the manner of development of each detail is inherent in the living light and thus will develop in such and such a way; your own universe having been well-studied in an empirical fashion by those you call your scientists and having been understood or visualized, shall we say, with greater accuracy by the understandings or visualizations of the one known as Dewey.

Questioner: When does the individualization or the individualized portion of consciousness come into play? At what point does individualized consciousness take over working on the basic light?

Ra: I am Ra. You remain carefully in the area of creation itself. In this process we must further confuse you by stating that the process by which free will acts upon potential intelligent infinity to become focused intelligent energy takes place without the space/time of which you are so aware as it is your continuum experience.

The experience or existence of space/time comes into being after the individuation process of Logos or Love has been completed and the physical universe, as you would call it, has coalesced or begun to draw inward while moving outward to the extent that that which you call your sun bodies have in their turn created timeless chaos coalescing into what you call planets, these vortices of intelligent energy spending a large amount of what you would call first density in a timeless state, the space/time realization being one of the learn/teachings of this density of beingness.

Thus we have difficulty answering your questions with regard to time and space and their relationship to the, what you would call, original creation which is not a part of space/time as you can understand it.

Questioner: Thank you. Does a unit of consciousness, an individualized unit of consciousness, create a unit of the creation? I will give an example.

One individualized consciousness creates one galaxy of stars, the type that has many millions of stars in it. Does this happen?

Ra: I am Ra. This can happen. The possibilities are infinite. Thus a Logos may create what you call a star system or it may be the Logos creating billions of star systems. This is the cause of the confusion in the term galaxy, for there are many different Logos entities or creations and we would call each, using your sound vibration complexes, a galaxy.

Questioner: Let's take as an example the planet that we are on now and tell me how much of the creation was created by the same Logos that created this planet?

Ra: I am Ra. This planetary Logos is a strong Logos creating approximately 250 billion of your star systems for Its creation. The, shall we say, laws or physical ways of this creation will remain, therefore, constant.

Questioner: Then what you are saying is that the lenticular star system which we call a galaxy that we find ourselves in with approximately 250 billion other suns like our own was created by a single Logos. Is this correct?

Ra: I am Ra. This is correct.

Questioner: Since there are many individualized portions of consciousness in this lenticular galaxy, did this Logos then subdivide into more individualization of consciousness to create these consciousnesses?

Ra: I am Ra. You are perceptive. This is also correct although an apparent paradox.

Questioner: Could you tell me what you mean by an apparent paradox?

Ra: I am Ra. It would seem that if one Logos creates the intelligent energy ways for a large system there would not be the necessity or possibility of the further sub-Logos differentiation. However, within limits, this is precisely the case, and it is perceptive that this has been seen.

Questioner: Thank you. I'll call the lenticular galaxy that we are in the major galaxy just so we will not get mixed up in our terms. Does all the consciousness in individualized form that goes into what we are calling the major galaxy start out and go through all of the densities in order, one-two-three-four-five-six-seven and into the eighth, or are there some who start up higher in the rank so that there is always a mixture of intelligent consciousness in the galaxy?

Ra: I am Ra. The latter is more nearly correct. In each beginning there is the beginning from infinite strength. Free will acts as a catalyst. Beings begin to form the universes. Consciousness then begins to have the potential to experience. The potentials of experience are created as a part of intelligent energy and are fixed before experience begins.

However, there is always, due to free will acting infinitely upon the creation, a great variation in initial responses to intelligent energy's potential. Thus almost immediately the foundations of the, shall we call it, hierarchical nature of beings begins to manifest as some portions of consciousness or awareness learn through experience in a much more efficient manner.

Questioner: Is there any reason for some portions being much more efficient in learning?

Ra: I am Ra. Is there any reason for some to learn more quickly than others? Look, if you wish, to the function of the will … the, shall we say, attraction to the upward spiraling line of light.

Questioner: I am assuming that there are eight densities created when this major galaxy was created. Is this correct?

Ra: I am Ra. This is basically correct. However, it is well to perceive that the eighth density functions also as the beginning density or first density, in its latter stages, of the next octave of densities.

Questioner: Are you saying then that there are an infinite number of octaves of densities one through eight?

Ra: I am Ra. We wish to establish that we are truly humble messengers of the Law of One. We can speak to you of our experiences and our understandings and teach/learn in limited ways. However, we cannot speak in firm knowledge of all the creations. We know only that they are infinite. We assume an infinite number of octaves.

However, it has been impressed upon us by our own teachers that there is a mystery-clad unity of creation in which all consciousness periodically coalesces and again begins. Thus we can only say we assume an infinite progression though we understand it to be cyclical in nature and, as we have said, clad in mystery.

Questioner: Thank you. When this major galaxy is formed by the Logos, polarity then exists in a sense that we have electrical polarity. We do have electrical polarity existing at that time. Is that correct?

Ra: I am Ra. I accept this as correct with the stipulation that what you term electrical be understood as not only the one, Larson, stipulated its meaning but also in what you would call the metaphysical sense.

Questioner: Are you saying then that we have not only a polarity of electrical charge but also a polarity in consciousness at that time?

Ra: I am Ra. This is correct. All is potentially available from the beginning of your physical space/time; it then being the function of consciousness complexes to begin to use the physical materials to gain experience to then polarize in a metaphysical sense. The potentials for this are not created by the experiencer but by intelligent energy.

This will be the last full question of this session due to our desire to foster this instrument as it slowly regains physical complex energy. May we ask if you have one or two questions we may answer shortly before we close?

Questioner: I am assuming that the process of creation, after the original creation of the major galaxy, is continued by the further individualization of the consciousness of the Logos so that there are many, many portions of the individualized consciousness creating further items for experience all over the galaxy. Is this correct?

Ra: I am Ra. This is correct, for within the, shall we say, guidelines or ways of the Logos, the sub-Logos may find various means of differentiating experiences without removing or adding to these ways.

Questioner: Thank you. And since we are out of time I will ask if there is anything that we can do to make the instrument more comfortable or to help the contact?

Ra: I am Ra. This instrument is well adjusted. You are conscientious.

I am Ra. I leave you, my friends, in the love and the light of the one infinite Creator. Go forth then rejoicing in the power and the peace of the one Creator. Adonai.

The Law of One, Book II, Session 29
February 23, 1981

Ra: I am Ra. I greet you in the love and the light of the infinite Creator. I communicate now.

Questioner: Is our sun a sub-Logos or the physical manifestation of a sub-Logos?

Ra: I am Ra. This is correct.

Questioner: Then I am assuming that this sub-Logos created this planetary system in all of its densities. Is this correct?

Ra: I am Ra. This is incorrect. The sub-Logos of your solar entity differentiated some experiential components within the patterns of intelligent energy set in motion by the Logos which created the basic conditions and vibratory rates consistent throughout your, what you have called, major galaxy.

Questioner: Then is this sub-Logos which is our sun the same sub-Logos just manifesting in different parts through the galaxy, or is it all the stars in the galaxy?

Ra: I am Ra. Please restate.

Questioner: What I'm saying is that there are roughly 250 billion stars somewhat like ours in this major galaxy. Are they all part of the same sub-Logos?

Ra: I am Ra. They are all part of the same Logos. Your solar system, as you would call it, is a manifestation somewhat and slightly different due to the presence of a sub-Logos.

Questioner: Let me be sure I'm right then. Our sun is a sub-Logos of the Logos of the major galaxy?

Ra: I am Ra. This is correct.

Questioner: Are there any sub-sub-Logoi that are found in our planetary system that are "sub" to our sun?

Ra: I am Ra. This is correct.

Questioner: Would you give me an example of what I will call a sub-sub-Logos?

Ra: I am Ra. One example is your mind/body/spirit complex.

Questioner: Then every entity that exists would be some type of sub or sub-sub-Logos. Is that correct?

Ra: I am Ra. This is correct down to the limits of any observation, for the entire creation is alive.

Questioner: Then the planet which we walk upon here would be some form of sub-sub-Logos. Is this correct?

Ra: I am Ra. A planetary entity is so named only as Logos if It is working in harmonic fashion with entities or mind/body complexes upon Its surface or within Its electromagnetic field.

Questioner: Do the sub-Logoi such as our sun have a metaphysical polarity positive or negative as we have been using the term?

Ra: I am Ra. As you use the term, this is not so. Entities through the level of planetary have the strength of intelligent infinity through the use of free will, going through the actions of beingness. The polarity is not thusly as you understand polarity. It is only when the planetary sphere begins harmonically interacting with mind/body complexes, and more especially mind/body/spirit complexes, that planetary spheres take on distortions due to the thought complexes of entities interacting with the planetary entity. The creation of the one infinite Creator does not have the polarity you speak of.

Questioner: Thank you. Yesterday you stated that planets in first density are in a timeless state to begin with. Can you tell me how the effect that we appreciate as time comes into being?

Ra: I am Ra. We have just described to you the state of beingness of each Logos. The process by which space/time comes into continuum form is a function of the careful building, shall we say, of an entire or whole plan of vibratory rates, densities, and potentials. When this plan has coalesced in the thought complexes of Love, then the physical manifestations begin to appear; this first manifestation stage being awareness or consciousness.

At the point at which this coalescence is at the living-ness or being-ness point, the point or fountainhead of beginning, space/time then begins to unroll its scroll of living-ness.

Questioner: I believe that Love creates the vibration in space/time in order to form the photon. Is this correct?

Ra: I am Ra. This is essentially correct.

Questioner: Then the continued application of Love—I will assume that this is directed by a sub-Logos or a sub-sub-Logos—creates rotations of these vibrations which are in discrete units of angular velocity. This then creates chemical elements in our physical illusion and I will assume the elements in the nonphysical or other densities in the illusion. Is this correct?

Ra: I am Ra. The Logos creates all densities. Your question was unclear. However, we shall state the Logos does create both the space/time densities and the accompanying time/space densities.

Questioner: What I am assuming is that quantized incremental rotations of the vibrations show up as a material of these densities. Is this correct?

Ra: I am Ra. This is essentially correct.

Questioner: Then because of these rotations there is an inward motion of these particles which is opposite the direction of space/time progression as I understand it, and this inward progression then is seen by us as what we call gravity. Is this correct?

Ra: I am Ra. This is incorrect.

Questioner: Can you tell me how the gravity comes about?

Ra: I am Ra. This that you speak of as gravity may be seen as the pressing towards the inner light/love, the seeking towards the spiral line of light which progresses towards the Creator. This is a manifestation of a spiritual event or condition of living-ness.

Questioner: The gravity that we know of on our moon is less than it is on our planet. Is there a metaphysical principle behind this that you could explain?

Ra: I am Ra. The metaphysical and physical are inseparable. Thus that of which you spoke which attempts to explain this phenomenon is able to, shall we say, calculate the gravitational force of most objects due to the various physical aspects such as what you know of as mass. However, we felt it was necessary to indicate the corresponding and equally important metaphysical nature of gravity.

Questioner: I sometimes have difficulty in getting a foothold into what I am looking for. I am trying to seek out the metaphysical principles, you might say, behind our physical illusion.

Could you give me an example of the amount of gravity in the third density conditions at the surface of the planet Venus? Would it be greater or less than Earth's?

Ra: I am Ra. The gravity, shall we say, the attractive force which we also describe as the pressing outward force towards the Creator is greater spiritually upon the entity you call Venus due to the greater degree of success, shall we say, at seeking the Creator.

This point only becomes important when you consider that when all of creation in its infinity has reached a spiritual gravitational mass of sufficient nature, the entire creation infinitely coalesces; the light seeking and finding its source and thusly ending the creation and beginning a new creation much as you consider the black hole, as you call it, with its conditions of infinitely great mass at the zero point from which no light may be seen as it has been absorbed.

Questioner: Then the black hole would be a point at which the environmental material has succeeded in uniting with unity or with the Creator? Is this correct?

Ra: I am Ra. The black hole which manifests third density is the physical complex manifestation of this spiritual or metaphysical state. This is correct.

Questioner: Then when our planet is fully into fourth density, will there be a greater gravity?

Ra: I am Ra. There will be a greater spiritual gravity thus causing a denser illusion.

Questioner: This denser illusion then I would assume increases gravitational acceleration above the 32 feet per second squared that we experience. Is this correct?

Ra: I am Ra. Your entities do not have the instrumentation to measure spiritual gravity but only to observe a few of its extreme manifestations.

Questioner: This I know, that we can't measure spiritual gravity, but I was just wondering if the physical effect could be measured as an increase in the gravitational constant? That was my question.

Ra: I am Ra. The increase measurable by existing instrumentation would and will be statistical in nature only and not significant.

Questioner: OK. As the creation is formed, as the atoms form as rotations of the vibration which is light, they coalesce in a certain manner sometimes. They produce a lattice structure which we call crystalline. I am guessing that because of the formation from intelligent energy of the precise crystalline structure that it is possible by some technique to tap intelligent energy and bring it into the physical illusion by working through the crystalline structure. Is this correct?

Ra: I am Ra. This is correct only in so far as the crystalline physical structure is charged by a correspondingly crystallized or regularized or balanced mind/body/spirit complex.

Questioner: I don't wish to get off on subjects of no importance, but it is difficult sometimes to see precisely in what direction to go. I would like to investigate a little bit more this idea of crystals, how they are used. I am assuming then from what you said that in order to use the crystal to tap intelligent energy, it is necessary to have a partially undistorted mind/body/spirit complex. Is this correct?

Ra: I am Ra. This is specifically correct.

Questioner: There must be a point at which the removal of distortion reaches the minimum for use of the crystal in tapping intelligent energy. Is this correct?

Ra: I am Ra. This is correct only if it is understood, shall we say, that each mind/body/spirit complex has an unique such point.

Questioner: Can you tell me why each mind/body/spirit complex has this unique point of distortion-ridding?

Ra: I am Ra. Each mind/body/spirit complex is an unique portion of the one Creator.

Questioner: Then you are saying that there is no single level of purity required to tap intelligent energy through crystals but there can be a wide variation in the amount of distortion that an entity may have, but each entity has to reach his particular point of what I might call energizing the ability. Is this right?

Ra: I am Ra. This is incorrect. The necessity is for the mind/body/spirit complex to be of a certain balance, this balance thus enabling it to reach a set level of lack of distortion. The critical difficulties are unique for each mind/body/spirit complex due to the experiential distillations which in total are the, shall we say, violet-ray being-ness of each such entity.

This balance is what is necessary for work to be done in seeking the gateway to intelligent infinity through the use of crystals or through any other use. No two mind/body/spirit crystallized natures are the same. The distortion requirements, vibrationally speaking, are set.

Questioner: I see. Then if you are able to read the violet ray of an entity, to see that ray, is it possible to immediately determine whether the entity could use crystals to tap intelligent energy?

Ra: I am Ra. It is possible for one of fifth density or above to do this.

Questioner: Is it possible for you to tell me how an entity who has satisfactorily achieved the necessary violet ray qualification should use the crystal?

Ra: I am Ra. The gateway to intelligent infinity is born of, shall we say, the sympathetic vibration in balanced state accompanying the will to serve, the will to seek.

Questioner: Can you tell me precisely what the entity would do with the crystal to use it for the purpose of seeking the intelligent infinity?

Ra: I am Ra. The use of the crystal in physical manifestation is that use wherein the entity of crystalline nature charges the regularized physical crystal with this seeking, thus enabling it to vibrate harmonically and also become the catalyst or gateway whereby intelligent infinity may thus become intelligent energy, this crystal serving as an analog of the violet ray of the mind/body/spirit in relatively undistorted form.

Questioner: Is it possible for you to instruct us in the specific uses of crystals?

Ra: I am Ra. It is possible. There are, we consider, things which are not efficacious to tell you due to possible infringement upon your free will. Entities of the Confederation have done this in the past. The uses of the crystal, as you know, include the uses for healing, for power, and even for the development of life-forms. We feel that it is unwise to offer instruction at this time as your peoples have shown a tendency to use peaceful sources of power for disharmonious reasons.

Questioner: Is it possible for you to give me an example of various planetary developments in what I would call a metaphysical sense having to do with the development of consciousness and its polarities throughout the galaxy? In other words I believe that some of these planets develop quite rapidly into higher density planets and some take longer times. Can you give me some idea of that development?

Ra: I am Ra. This will be the final full query of this session.

The particular Logos of your major galaxy has used a large portion of Its coalesced material to reflect the being-ness of the Creator. In this way there is much of your galactic system which does not have the progression of which you speak but dwells spiritually as a portion of the Logos. Of those entities upon which consciousness dwells there is, as you surmise, a variety of time/space periods during which the higher densities of experience are attained by consciousness.

Is there any short query further before we close?

Questioner: Is there anything that we can do to make the instrument more comfortable or to improve the contact?

Ra: I am Ra. You are conscientious. The entity is well aligned

I am Ra. I leave you now in the love and the light of the one infinite Creator. Go forth, therefore, rejoicing in the power and the peace of the one infinite Creator. Adonai. ♣

The Law of One, Book V, Session 29, Fragment 17
February 23, 1981

Jim: Ra had advised Carla never to do any kind of physical healing because she was always very low on physical energy, and such healing would tend to drain her already low reserve in that area.

Carla: Since I was a child, I have had some sort of odd ability to sit with someone and, with our hands in contact, be able to clear some of the surface clutter away from the other person's mind or being. I have never investigated what I am doing, or how to do it better, trusting rather in my instinct for the right time to offer this. Perhaps I should, but it has always struck me as a very marginal gift, not one near my central path. I think that if I have any healing ability, it is in my listening. When someone comes to me for private counsel, I think of the time as a "listening session," and see myself as a spiritual listener. There is much healing in a person's talking something through with another in a supportive atmosphere. The listener simply enables the person to listen better to herself. And I have very deep instincts towards doing this. So this is where I have focused my own efforts to become a better healer. Listening is truly an art, and I think it begins with the way we listen to ourselves. There is a tremendous strength in knowing one's full self, the dark side as well as the one that sees the light of everyday behavior.

Once one has finally become able to bear one's own full nature and has gone through the painful process of surrendering the pride that would deny that wretchedness within, one becomes better able to love and forgive oneself. Often I think we feel our failure comes in being kind to another. But when this occurs, you can be sure the first and proximate cause of this outer ruthlessness lies within, in the self's refusal to reckon with the full-circle self.

Session 29, February 23, 1981

Questioner: The instrument had a question if we have time for a short question. I will read it. The instrument does not desire to do physical healing work. She already does spiritual balancing by hands. Can she read the private healing material without doing physical healing? I am assuming that she means can she read it without creating problems in her life pattern? She does not wish to incur lessening of positive polarity. Can she read the material under these conditions?

Ra: I am Ra. We shall speak shortly due to the fact that we are attempting to conserve this instrument's vital energies during the three month period of which we have spoken.

This entity has an experiential history of healing on levels other than the so-called physical. Thus it is acceptable that this material be read. However, the exercise of fire shall never be practiced by this instrument as it is used in the stronger form for physical healing.

The Law of One, Book II, Session 30
February 24, 1981

Ra: I am Ra. I greet you in the love and in the light of the one infinite Creator. We communicate now.

Questioner: I am going to make a statement and then let you correct it if I have made any errors. This is the statement: Creation is a single entity or unity. If only a single entity exists, then the only concept of service is the concept of service to self. If this single entity subdivides, then the concept of service of one of its parts to one of its other parts is born. From this springs the equality of service to self or to others. It would seem that as the Logos subdivided, parts would select each orientation. As individualized entities emerge in space/time then I would assume that they have polarity. Is this statement correct?

Ra: I am Ra. This statement is quite perceptive and correct until the final phrase in which we note that the polarities begin to be explored only at the point when a third density entity becomes aware of the possibility of choice between the concept or distortion of service to self or service to others. This marks the end of what you may call the unself-conscious or innocent phase of conscious awareness.

Questioner: Thank you. Would you define mind, body, and spirit separately?

Ra: I am Ra. These terms are all simplistic descriptive terms which equal a complex of energy focuses; the body, as you call it, being the material of the density which you experience at a given space/time or time/space; this complex of materials being available for distortions of what you would call physical manifestation.

The mind is a complex which reflects the in-pourings of the spirit and the up-pourings of the body complex. It contains what you know as feelings, emotions, and intellectual thoughts in its more conscious complexities. Moving further down the tree of mind we see the intuition which is of the nature of the mind more in contact or in tune with the total being-ness complex. Moving down to the roots of mind we find the progression of consciousness which gradually turns from the personal to the racial memory, to the cosmic influxes, and thus becomes a direct contactor of that shuttle which we call the spirit complex.

This spirit complex is the channel whereby the in-pourings from all of the various universal, planetary, and personal inpourings may be funneled into the roots of consciousness and whereby consciousness may be funneled to the gateway of intelligent infinity through the balanced intelligent energy of body and mind.

You will see by this series of definitive statements that mind, body, and spirit are inextricably intertwined and cannot continue, one without the other. Thus we refer to the mind/body/spirit complex rather than attempting to deal with them separately, for the work, shall we say, that you do during your experiences is done through the interaction of these three components, not through any one.

Questioner: Upon our physical death, as we call it, from this particular density and this particular incarnative experience, we lose this chemical body. Immediately after the loss of this chemical body do we maintain a different type of body? Is there still a mind/body/spirit complex at that point?

Ra: I am Ra. This is correct. The mind/body/spirit complex is quite intact; the physical body complex you now associate with the term body being but manifestation of a more dense and intelligently informed and powerful body complex.

Questioner: Is there any loss to the mind or spirit after this transition which we call death or any impairment of either because of the loss of this chemical body which we now have?

Ra: I am Ra. In your terms there is a great loss of mind complex due to the fact that much of the activity of the mental nature of which you are aware during the experience of this space/time continuum is as much of a surface illusion as is the chemical body complex.

In other terms nothing whatever of importance is lost; the character or, shall we say, pure distortion of emotions and biases or distortions and wisdoms, if you will, becoming obvious for the first time, shall we say; these pure emotions and wisdoms and bias/distortions being, for the most part, either ignored or underestimated during physical life experience.

In terms of the spiritual, this channel is then much opened due to the lack of necessity for the forgetting characteristic of third density.

Questioner: I would like to know how the mind/body/spirit complexes originate, going as far back as necessary. How does the origination occur? Do they originate by spirit forming mind and mind forming body? Can you tell me this?

Ra: I am Ra. We ask you to consider that you are attempting to trace evolution. This evolution is as we have previously described, the consciousness being first, in first density, without movement, a random thing. Whether you may call this mind or body complex is a semantic problem. We call it mind/body complex recognizing always that in the simplest iota of this complex exists in its entirety the one infinite Creator; this mind/body complex then in second density discovering the growing and turning towards the light, thus awakening what you may call the spirit complex, that which intensifies the upward spiraling towards the love and light of the infinite Creator.

The addition of this spirit complex, though apparent rather than real, it having existed potentially from the beginning of space/time, perfects itself by graduation into third density, When the mind/body/spirit complex becomes aware of the possibility of service to self or other-self, then the mind/body/spirit complex is activated.

Questioner: Thank you. I don't wish to cover ground that we have covered before but it sometimes is helpful to restate these concepts for complete clarity since words are a poor tool for what we do.

Just as a passing point, I was wondering—on this planet during the second density I believe there was habitation during the same space/time of bipedal entities and what we call the dinosaurs. Is this correct?

Ra: I am Ra. This is correct.

Questioner: These two types of entities seemed to be very incompatible, you might say, with each other. I don't know, but can you tell me the reason for both types of entities inhabiting the same space/time?

Ra: I am Ra. Consider the workings of free will as applied to evolution. There are paths that the mind/body complex follows in an attempt to survive, to reproduce, and to seek in its fashion that which is unconsciously felt as the potential for growth; these two arenas or paths of development being two among many.

Questioner: In second density the concept of bisexual reproduction first originates. Is this correct?

Ra: I am Ra. This is correct.

Questioner: Can you tell me the philosophy behind this method of propagation of the bodily complex?

Ra: I am Ra. The second density is one in which the groundwork is being laid for third density work. In this way it may be seen that the basic mechanism of reproduction capitulates into a vast potential in third density for service to other-self and to self; this being not only by the functions of energy transfer, but also by the various services performed due to the close contact of those who are, shall we say, magnetically attracted, one to the other; these entities thus having the opportunities for many types of service which would be unavailable to the independent entity.

Questioner: Was the basic reason for this to increase the opportunity of the experience of the one Creator?

Ra: I am Ra. This is not merely correct but is the key to that which occurs in all densities.

Questioner: Does the process of bisexual reproduction or the philosophy of it play a part in the spiritual growth of second density entities?

Ra: I am Ra. In isolated instances this is so due to efficient perceptions upon the part of entities or species. For the greater part, by far, this is not the case in second density, the spiritual potentials being those of third density.

Questioner: Thank you. Can you give me a brief history of the metaphysical principles of the development of each of our planets that surround our sun, their function with respect to the evolution of beings?

Ra: I am Ra. We shall give you a metaphysical description only of those planets upon which individual mind/body/spirit complexes have been, are, or shall be experienced. You may understand the other spheres to be a part of the Logos.

We take the one known as Venus. This planetary sphere was one of rapid evolution. It is our native earth and the rapidity of the progress of the mind/body/spirit complexes upon its surface was due to harmonious interaction.

Upon the entity known to you as Mars, as you have already discussed, this entity was stopped in mid-third density, thus being unable to continue in progression due to the lack of hospitable conditions upon the surface. This planet shall be undergoing healing for some of your space/time millennia.

The planet which you dwell upon has a metaphysical history well known to you and you may ask about it if you wish. However, we have spoken to a great degree upon this subject.

The planet known as Saturn has a great affinity for the infinite intelligence and thus it has been dwelled upon in its magnetic fields of time/space by those who wish to protect your system.

The planetary entity known to you as Uranus is slowly moving through the first density and has the potential of moving through all densities.

Questioner: Thank you. You stated yesterday that much of this major galactic system dwells spiritually as a part of the Logos. Do you mean that near the center of this major galactic system that the stars there do not have planetary systems? Is this correct?

Ra: I am Ra. This is incorrect. The Logos has distributed itself throughout your galactic system. However, the time/space continua of some of your more central sun systems are much further advanced.

Questioner: Well then, could you generally say that as you get closer to the center of this major system that there is a greater spiritual density or spiritual quality in that area?

Ra: I am Ra. This will be the last full question of this session as this instrument is somewhat uncomfortable. We do not wish to deplete the instrument.

The spiritual density or mass of those more towards the center of your galaxy is known. However, this is due simply to the varying timelessness states during which the planetary spheres may coalesce, this process of space/time beginnings occurring earlier, shall we say, as you approach the center of the galactic spiral.

Questioner: Is there anything that we can do to make the instrument more comfortable or to improve the contact?

Ra: This instrument is well balanced and the contact is as it should be. This instrument has certain difficulties of a distortion you would call the muscular spasm, thus making the motionless position uncomfortable. Thus we leave the instrument.

I am Ra. You are doing well, my friends. I leave you in the love and the light of the one infinite Creator. Go forth, then, rejoicing in the power and the peace of the one Creator. Adonai. ☥

L/L Research is a subsidiary of Rock Creek Research & Development Laboratories, Inc.

P.O. Box 5195
Louisville, KY 40255-0195

L/L Research

www.llresearch.org

Rock Creek is a non-profit corporation dedicated to discovering and sharing information which may aid in the spiritual evolution of humankind.

ABOUT THE CONTENTS OF THIS TRANSCRIPT: This telepathic channeling has been taken from transcriptions of the weekly study and meditation meetings of the Rock Creek Research & Development Laboratories and L/L Research. It is offered in the hope that it may be useful to you. As the Confederation entities always make a point of saying, please use your discrimination and judgment in assessing this material. If something rings true to you, fine. If something does not resonate, please leave it behind, for neither we nor those of the Confederation would wish to be a stumbling block for any.

© 2009 L/L Research

The Law of One, Book V, Session 30, Fragment 18
February 24, 1981

Jim: A fellow associated with Cosmic Awareness Communications in Washington state was developing and distributing a machine that was supposed to augment the general health and well-being of a person, and we asked Ra whether it might aid Carla. The response suggested Carla's magnetic field was somewhat unusual and very likely formed in such an unusual way as to permit contact with those of Ra specifically. This unusual magnetic field has been a source of frequent inconveniences with any electromagnetic equipment which Carla has used on a regular basis. She breaks it—just by touching it periodically. She can't wear any but quartz crystal watches, and we have many, many semi-functional tape recorders lying about different areas of our house.

Carla: It makes for a good story, but it can be frustrating to have electronically damaging energy—I am not amused when I break things. The last thing I want to do is destroy the very machines that allow me to communicate. And my tendency to feel various odd energies has at times been an unwelcome gift. I remember a couple of times when my being able to perceive some occult frequency or another put me in the way of very forceful people who decided that I was to work with them. Of course, I have withstood any requests for help which I felt uncomfortable accepting, but I really don't enjoy the process of convincing someone that I won't come out and play!

In all of the things, and there are a million or two, that we've tried to better my physical condition, we have not found anything of that nature that avails. However, the gifts of spirit and faith are far more efficacious. So I have become relatively uninterested in new modalities and gadgets—and rest in prayer and peace, knowing the perfect self within.

Session 30, February 24, 1981

Questioner: The instrument would like to know if you could tell her whether or not this item which is called Sam Millar's polarizer would help her physical well-being. Could you do that?

Ra: I am Ra. As we scan the instrument we find anomalies of the magnetic field which are distorted towards our abilities to find narrow band channel into this instrument's mind/body/spirit complex. The polarizer of which you speak, as it is, would not be helpful. A careful reading of this instrument's aura by those gifted in this area, and subsequent alterations of the magnetizing forces of this polarizer, would assist the entity, Sam, in creating such a polarizer that would be of some aid to the instrument. However, we would suggest that no electrical or magnetic equipment not necessary for the recording of our words be brought into these sessions, for we wish no distortions that are not necessary.

L/L Research

The Law of One, Book II, Session 31
February 25, 1981

Ra: I am Ra. I greet you in the love and in the light of the one infinite Creator. We communicate now.

Questioner: I have a question that the instrument has asked me to ask. It reads: You speak of various types of energy blockages and transfers, positive and negative, that may take place due to participation in our sexual reproductive complex of actions. Could you please explain these blockages and energy transfers with emphasis upon what an individual who is seeking to be in accordance with the Law of One may positively do in this area? Is it possible for you to answer this question?

Ra: I am Ra. It is partially possible, given the background we have laid. This is properly a more advanced question. Due to the specificity of the question we may give a general answer.

The first energy transfer is red ray. It is a random transfer having to do only with your reproductive system.

The orange and the yellow ray attempts to have sexual intercourse create, firstly, a blockage if only one entity vibrates in this area, thus causing the entity vibrating sexually in this area to have a never-ending appetite for this activity. What these vibratory levels are seeking is green ray activity. There is the possibility of orange or yellow ray energy transfer; this being polarizing towards the negative: one being seen as object rather than otherself; the other seeing itself as plunderer or master of the situation.

In green ray there are two possibilities. Firstly, if both vibrate in green ray there will be a mutually strengthening energy transfer, the negative or female, as you call it, drawing the energy from the roots of the being-ness through the energy centers, thus being physically revitalized; the positive, or male polarity, as it is deemed in your illusion, finding in its energy transfer an inspiration which satisfies and feeds the spirit portion of the body/mind/spirit complex, thus both being polarized and releasing the excess of that which each has in abundance by nature of intelligent energy, that is, negative/intuitive, positive/physical energies as you may call them; this energy transfer being blocked only if one or both entities have fear of possession or of being possessed, of desiring possession or desiring being possessed.

The other green ray possibility is that of one entity offering green ray energy, the other not offering energy of the universal love energy, this resulting in a blockage of energy for the one not green ray thus increasing frustration or appetite; the green ray being polarizing slightly towards service to others.

The blue ray energy transfer is somewhat rare among your people at this time but is of great aid due to energy transfers involved in becoming able to express the self without reservation or fear.

The indigo ray transfer is extremely rare among your people. This is the sacramental portion of the body complex whereby contact may be made through violet ray with intelligent infinity. No blockages may occur at these latter two levels due to the fact that if both entities are not ready for this energy it is not visible and neither transfer nor blockage may take place. It is as though the distributor were removed from a powerful engine.

Questioner: Could you define sexual energy transfer and expand upon its meaning, please?

Ra: I am Ra. Energy transfer implies the release of potential energies across, shall we say, a potentiated space. The sexual energy transfers occur due to the polarizations of two mind/body/spirit complexes, each of which have some potential difference one to the other. The nature of the transfer of energy or of the blockage of this energy is then a function of the interaction of these two potentials. In the cases where transfer takes place, you may liken this to a circuit being closed. You may also see this activity, as all experiential activities, as the Creator experiencing Itself.

Questioner: Could this then be the primal mechanism for the Creator to experience Itself?

Ra: I am Ra. This is not a proper term. Perhaps the adjectives would be "one appropriate" way of the Creator knowing Itself, for in each interaction, no matter what the distortion, the Creator is experiencing Itself. The bisexual knowing of the Creator by Itself has the potential for two advantages.

Firstly, in the green ray activated being there is the potential for a direct and simple analog of what you may call joy, the spiritual or metaphysical nature which exists in intelligent energy. This is a great aid to comprehension of a truer nature of being-ness. The other potential advantage of bisexual reproductive acts is the possibility of a sacramental understanding or connection, shall we say, with the gateway to intelligent infinity, for with appropriate preparation, work in what you may call magic may be done and experiences of intelligent infinity may be had. The positively oriented individuals concentrating upon this method of reaching intelligent infinity, then, through the seeking or the act of will, are able to direct this infinite intelligence to the work these entities desire to do, whether it be knowledge of service or ability to heal or whatever service to others is desired.

These are two advantages of this particular method of the Creator experiencing Itself. As we have said before, the corollary of the strength of this particular energy transfer is that it opens the door, shall we say, to the individual mind/body/spirit complexes' desire to serve in an infinite number of ways an otherself, thus polarizing towards positive.

Questioner: Can you expand somewhat on the concept that this action not only allows the Creator to know Itself better but also creates, in our density, an offspring or makes available the pathway for another entity to enter this density?

Ra: I am Ra. As we have previously said, the sexual energy transfers include the red ray transfer which is random and which is a function of the second-density attempt to grow, to survive, shall we say. This is a proper function of the sexual interaction. The offspring, as you call the incarnated entity, takes on the mind/body complex opportunity offered by this random act or event called the fertilization of egg by seed which causes an entity to have the opportunity to then enter this density as an incarnate entity.

This gives the two who were engaged in this bisexual reproductive energy transfer the potential for great service in this area of the nurturing of the small-experienced entity as it gains in experience.

It shall be of interest at this point to note that there is always the possibility of using these opportunities to polarize towards the negative, and this has been aided by the gradual building up over many thousands of your years of social complex distortions which create a tendency towards confusion, shall we say, or baffling of the service to others aspect of this energy transfer and subsequent opportunities for service to other selves.

Questioner: If a sexual energy transfer occurs in green ray—and I am assuming in this case that there is no red ray energy transfer—does this mean it is impossible for this particular transfer to include fertilization and the birthing of an entity?

Ra: I am Ra. This is incorrect. There is always the red ray energy transfer due to the nature of the body complex. The random result of this energy transfer will be as it will be, as a function of the possibility of fertilization at a given time in a given pairing of entities each entity being undistorted in any vital sense by the yellow or orange ray energies; thus the gift, shall we say, being given freely, no payment being requested either of the body, of the mind, or of the spirit. The green ray is one of complete universality of love. This is a giving without expectation of return.

Questioner: I was wondering if there was some principle behind the fact that a sexual union does not necessarily lead to fertilization. I'm not interested in the chemical or physical principles of it. I'm interested in whether or not there is some metaphysical principle that leads to the couple having a child or not, or is it purely random?

Ra: I am Ra. This is random within certain limits. If an entity has reached the seniority whereby it chooses the basic structure of the life experience, this entity may then choose to incarnate in a physical complex which is not capable of reproduction. Thus we find some entities which have chosen to be unfertile. Other entities, through free will, make use of various devices to insure nonfertility. Except for these conditions, the condition is random.

Questioner: Thank you. In the previous material you mentioned "magnetic attraction." Would you define and expand upon that term?

Ra: I am Ra. We used the term to indicate that in your bisexual natures there is that which is of polarity. This polarity may be seen to be variable according to the, shall we say, male/female polarization of each entity, be each entity biologically male or female. Thus you may see the magnetism which two entities with the appropriate balance, male/female versus female/male polarity, meeting and thus feeling the attraction which polarized forces will exert, one upon the other.

This is the strength of the bisexual mechanism. It does not take an act of will to decide to feel attraction for one who is oppositely polarized sexually. it will occur in an inevitable sense giving the free flow of energy a proper, shall we say, avenue. This avenue may be blocked by some distortion toward a belief/condition stating to the entity that this attraction is not desired. However, the basic mechanism functions as simply as would, shall we say, the magnet and the iron.

Questioner: We have what seems to be an increasing number of entities incarnate here now who have what is called a homosexual orientation. Could you explain and expand upon that concept?

Ra: I am Ra. Entities of this condition experience a great deal of distortion due to the fact that they have experienced many incarnations as biological male and as biological female. This would not suggest what you call homosexuality in an active phase were it not for the difficult vibratory condition of your planetary sphere. There is what you may call great aura infringement among your crowded urban areas in your more populous countries, as you call portions of your planetary surface. Under these conditions the confusions will occur.

Questioner: Why does density of population create these confusions?

Ra: I am Ra. The bisexual reproductive urge has as its goal, not only the simple reproductive function, but more especially the desire to serve others being awakened by this activity.

In an over-crowded situation where each mind/body/spirit complex is under constant bombardment from other-selves it is understandable that those who are especially sensitive would not feel the desire to be of service to otherselves. This would also increase the probability of a lack of desire or a blockage of the red ray reproductive energy.

In an uncrowded atmosphere this same entity would, through the stimulus of feeling the solitude about it, then have much more desire to seek out someone to whom it may be of service thus regularizing the sexual reproductive function.

Questioner: Roughly how many previous incarnations would a male entity in this incarnation have had to have had in the past as a female to have a highly homosexual orientation in this incarnation?

Ra: I am Ra. If an entity has had roughly 65% of its incarnations in the sexual/biological body complex, the opposite polarity to its present body complex, this entity is vulnerable to infringement of your urban areas and may perhaps become of what you call an homosexual nature.

It is to be noted at this juncture that although it is much more difficult, it is possible in this type of association for an entity to be of great service to another in fidelity and sincere green ray love of a nonsexual nature thus adjusting or lessening the distortions of its sexual impairment.

Questioner: Is there an imprint occurring on the DNA coding of an entity so that sexual biases are imprinted due to early sexual experiences?

Ra: I am Ra. This is partially correct. Due to the nature of solitary sexual experiences, it is in most cases unlikely that what you call masturbation has an imprinting effect upon later experiences.

This is similarly true with some of the encounters which might be seen as homosexual among those of this age group. These are often, instead, innocent exercises in curiosity.

However, it is quite accurate that the first experience in which the mind/body/spirit complex is intensely involved will indeed imprint upon the entity for that life experience a set of preferences.

Questioner: Does the Orion group use this as a gateway to impress upon entities preferences which could be of a negative polarization?

Ra: I am Ra. Just as we of the Confederation attempt to beam our love and light whenever given the opportunity, including sexual opportunities, so the Orion group will use an opportunity if it is negatively oriented or if the individual is negatively oriented.

Questioner: Is there any emotional bias that has nothing to do with male/female sexual polarity that can create sexual energy buildup in an entity?

Ra: I am Ra. The sexual energy buildup is extremely unlikely to occur without sexual bias upon the part of the entity. Perhaps we did not understand your question, but it seems obvious that it would take an entity with the potential for sexual activity to experience a sexual energy buildup.

Questioner: I was thinking more of the possibility of the Orion group influencing certain members of the Third Reich who I have read reports of having sexual gratification from the observation of the gassing and killing of entities in the gas chambers.

Ra: I am Ra. We shall repeat these entities had the potential for sexual energy buildup. The choice of stimulus is certainly the choice of the entity. In the case of which you speak, these entities were strongly polarized orange ray, thus finding the energy blockage of power over others, the putting to death being the ultimate power over others; this then being expressed in a sexual manner, though solitary. In this case the desire would continue unabated and be virtually unquenchable.

You will find, if you observe the entire spectrum of sexual practices among your peoples, that there are those who experience such gratification from domination over others either from rape or from other means of domination. In each case this is an example of energy blockage which is sexual in its nature.

Questioner: Would the Orion group be able, then, to impress on entities this orange ray effect? Is this the way that this came about? If we go back to the beginning of third-density there must be a primal cause of this.

Ra: I am Ra. The cause of this is not Orion. It is the free choice of your peoples. This is somewhat difficult to explain. We shall attempt.

The sexual energy transfers and blockages are more a manifestation or example of that which is more fundamental than the other way about. Therefore, as your peoples became open to the concepts of bellicosity and the greed of ownership, these various distortions then began to filter down through the tree of mind into body complex expressions, the sexual expression being basic to that complex. Thus these sexual energy blockages, though Orion influenced and intensified, are basically the product of the being-ness chosen freely by your peoples.

This will be the final question unless we may speak further upon this question to clarify, or answer any short queries before we close.

Questioner: I just need to know then if this works through the racial memory and infects the entire population in some way?

Ra: I am Ra. The racial memory contains all that has been experienced. Thus there is some, shall we say, contamination even of the sexual, this showing mostly in your own culture as the various predispositions to adversary relationships, or, as you call them, marriages, rather than the free giving one to another in the love and the light of the infinite Creator.

Questioner: That was precisely the point that I was trying to make. Thank you very much. I do not wish to overtire the instrument, so I will just ask if there is anything that we can do to make the instrument more comfortable or to improve the contact?

Ra: I am Ra. Please be aware that this instrument is somewhat fatigued. The channel is very clear. However, we find the vital energy low. We do not wish to deplete the instrument. However, there is, shall we say, an energy exchange that we feel an honor/duty to offer when this instrument opens itself. Therefore, counsel we this instrument to attempt to assess the vital energies carefully before offering itself as open channel.

All is well. You are conscientious.

I am Ra. I leave this instrument and you in the love and in the light of the one infinite Creator. Go forth, then, rejoicing in the power and the peace of the one Creator. Adonai. ☥

The Law of One, Book II, Session 32
February 27, 1981

Ra: I am Ra. I greet you in the love and the light of the one infinite Creator. We communicate now.

Questioner: We will now continue with the material from the day before yesterday. The subject is how sexual polarity acts as a catalyst in evolution and how to best make use of this catalyst. Going back to that material, I will fill in a few gaps that we possibly do not understand too well at this point.

Can you tell me the difference between orange and yellow ray activation? I am going to work up from the red ray right on through the violet. We have covered red ray, so I would like to ask now what the difference is between yellow and orange ray activation?

Ra: I am Ra. The orange ray is that influence or vibratory pattern wherein the mind/body/spirit expresses its power on an individual basis. Thus power over individuals may be seen to be orange ray. This ray has been quite intense among your peoples on an individual basis. You may see in this ray the treating of other-selves as non-entities, slaves, or chattel, thus giving otherselves no status whatever.

The yellow ray is a focal and very powerful ray and concerns the entity in relation to, shall we say, groups, societies, or large numbers of mind/body/spirit complexes. This orange—we correct ourselves—this yellow ray vibration is at the heart of bellicose actions in which one group of entities feels the necessity and right of dominating other groups of entities and bending their wills to the wills of the masters. The negative path, as would call it, uses a combination of the yellow ray and the orange ray in its polarization patterns. These rays, used in a dedicated fashion, will bring about a contact with intelligent infinity. The usual nature of sexual interaction, if one is yellow or orange in primary vibratory patterns, is one of blockage and then insatiable hunger due to the blockage. When there are two selves vibrating in this area the potential for polarization through the sexual interaction is begun, one entity experiencing the pleasure of humiliation and slavery or bondage, the other experiencing the pleasure of mastery and control over another entity. This way a sexual energy transfer of a negative polarity is experienced.

Questioner: From the material that you transmitted February 17th you stated: "In third ray there are two possibilities. Firstly, if both vibrate in third ray there will be a mutually strengthening energy transfer." What color is third ray in this material?

Ra: I am Ra. The ray we were speaking of in that material should be properly the green ray or fourth ray.

Questioner: So I should change that third to fourth or green?

Ra: This is correct. Please continue to scan for errors having to do with numbering, as you call them, as this concept is foreign to us and we must translate, if you will, when using numbers. This is an on-going weakness of this contact due to the difference between our ways and yours. Your aid is appreciated.

Questioner: Thank you. I believe for the time being we have amply covered green ray, so I am going to skip over green ray and go to blue ray. Could you tell me the difference that occurs between green ray and blue ray with the emphasis on blue ray?

Ra: I am Ra. With the green ray transfer of energy you now come to the great turning point sexually as well as in each other mode of experience. The green ray may then be turned outward, the entity then giving rather than receiving. The first giving beyond green ray is the giving of acceptance or freedom, thus allowing the recipient of blue ray energy transfer the opportunity for a feeling of being accepted, thus freeing that other-self to express itself to the giver of this ray. It will be noted that once green ray energy transfer has been achieved by two mind/body/spirits in mating, the further rays are available without both entities having the necessity to progress equally. Thus a blue ray vibrating entity or indigo ray vibrating entity whose other ray vibrations are clear may share that energy with the green ray other-self, thus acting as catalyst for the continued learn/teaching of the other-self. Until an other-self reaches green ray, such energy transfer through the rays is not possible.

Questioner: What is the difference between indigo and blue ray transfer?

Ra: I am Ra. The indigo ray is the ray of, shall we say, awareness of the Creator as self; thus one whose indigo ray vibrations have been activated can offer the energy transfer of Creator to Creator. This is the beginning of the sacramental nature of what you call your bisexual reproductive act. It is unique in bearing the allness, the wholeness, the unity in its offering to other-self.

Questioner: What is the difference between violet ray and the others?

Ra: I am Ra. The violet ray, just as the red ray, is constant in the sexual experience. Its experience by other-self may be distorted or completely ignored or not apprehended by other-self. However, the violet ray, being the sum and substance of the mind/body/spirit complex, surrounds and informs any action by a mind/body/spirit complex.

Questioner: Do the energy transfers of this nature occur in the fifth, sixth, and seventh-density—all the rays?

Ra: I am Ra. The rays, as you understand them, have such a different meaning in the next density and the next and so forth that we must answer your query in the negative. Energy transfers only take place in fourth, fifth, and sixth densities. These are still of what you would call a polarized nature. However, due to the ability of these densities to see the harmonies between individuals, these entities choose those mates which are harmonious, thus allowing constant transfer of energy and the propagation of the body complexes which each density uses. The process is different in the fifth and the sixth-density than you may understand it. However, it is in these cases still based upon polarity. In the seventh-density there is not this particular energy exchange as it is unnecessary to recycle body complexes.

Questioner: I am assuming we have on Earth today and have had in the past fourth, fifth, and sixth-density Wanderers. As they come into incarnation in the physical of this density for a period as a Wanderer, what types of polarizations with respect to these various rays do they find affecting them?

Ra: I am Ra. I believe I grasp the thrust of your query. Please ask further if this answer is not sufficient.

Fourth density Wanderers, of which there are not many, will tend to choose those entities which seem to be full of love or in need of love. There is the great possibility/probability of entities making errors in judgment due to the compassion with which other-selves are viewed.

The fifth-density Wanderer is one who is not tremendously affected by the stimulus of the various rays of other-self and in its own way offers itself when a need is seen. Such entities are not likely to engage in the, shall we say, custom of your peoples called marriage and are very likely to feel an aversion to childbearing and child-raising due to the awareness of the impropriety of the planetary vibrations relative to the harmonious vibrations of the density of light.

The sixth-density, whose means of propagation you may liken to what you call fusion, is likely to refrain, to a great extent, from the bisexual reproductive programming of the bodily complex and instead seek out those with whom the sexual energy transfer is of the complete fusion nature in so far as this is possible in manifestation in third-density.

Questioner: Can you expand a little bit on what you mean by "complete fusion nature"?

Ra: I am Ra. The entire creation is of the one Creator. Thus the division of sexual activity into simply that of the bodily complex is an artificial division, all things thusly being seen as sexual equally, the mind, the body, and the spirit; all of which are part of the polarity of the entity. Thus sexual fusion may be seen with or without what you may call sexual intercourse to be the complete melding of the mind, the body, and the spirit in what feels to be a constant orgasm, shall we say, of joy and delight each in the other's being-ness.

Questioner: Would many Wanderers of these densities have considerable problems with respect to incarnation in the third-density because of this different orientation?

Ra: I am Ra. The possibility/probability of such problems, as you call them, due to sixth-density incarnating in third is rather large. It is not necessarily a problem if you would call it thusly. It depends upon the unique orientation of each mind/body/spirit complex having this situation or placement of vibratory relativities.

Questioner: Can you give me an idea how the different colors … This is a difficult question to ask. I'm having trouble finding any words. What I'm trying to get at is how the different colors originate as the functions for the different expressions in consciousness? I don't know if this question is sufficient.

Ra: I am Ra. This question is sufficiently clear for us to attempt explanation of what, as you have observed, is not easily grasped material for the intellectual mind. The nature of vibration is such that it may be seen as having mathematically straight or narrow steps. These steps may be seen as having boundaries. Within each boundary there are infinite gradations of vibration or color. However, as one approaches a boundary, an effort must be made to cross that boundary. These colors are a simplistic way of expressing the boundary divisions of your density. There is also the time/space analogy which may be seen as the color itself in a modified aspect.

Questioner: Thank you. Is it possible for an entity in third-density physical to vary across the entire band of colors or is the entity pretty well zeroed in on one color?

Ra: I am Ra. This will be the last full question of this working. Please restate for clarity.

Questioner: I meant was it possible for a green ray person who is primarily of green ray activation to vary on both sides of the green ray in a large or a small amount in regards to energy activation, or is he primarily green ray?

Ra: I am Ra. We grasp the newness of material requested by you. It was unclear, for we thought we had covered this material. The portion covered is this: the green ray activation is always vulnerable to the yellow or orange ray of possession, this being largely yellow ray but often coming into orange ray. Fear of possession, desire for possession, fear of being possessed, desire to be possessed: these are the distortions which will cause the deactivation of green ray energy transfer.

The new material is this: once the green ray has been achieved, the ability of the entity to enter blue ray is immediate and is only awaiting the efforts of the individual. The indigo ray is opened only through considerable discipline and practice largely having to do with acceptance of self, not only as the polarized and balanced self but as the Creator, as an entity of infinite worth. This will begin to activate the indigo ray.

Questioner: Thank you.

Ra: I am Ra. Do you have any brief queries before we close?

Questioner: I think that anything I have would be too long, so I will just ask if there is anything that we can do to make the instrument more comfortable or to make the contact better?

Ra: I am Ra. All is well. We caution not only this instrument but each to look well to the vital energies necessary for nondepletion of the instrument and the contact level. You are most conscientious, my friends. We shall be with you. I leave you now in the love and in the light of the one infinite Creator. Go forth, then, rejoicing in the power and the peace of the one infinite Creator. Adonai.

L/L Research is a subsidiary of
Rock Creek Research &
Development Laboratories, Inc.

P.O. Box 5195
Louisville, KY 40255-0195

L/L Research

www.llresearch.org

Rock Creek is a non-profit
corporation dedicated to
discovering and sharing
information which may aid in
the spiritual evolution of
humankind.

ABOUT THE CONTENTS OF THIS TRANSCRIPT: This telepathic channeling has been taken from transcriptions of the weekly study and meditation meetings of the Rock Creek Research & Development Laboratories and L/L Research. It is offered in the hope that it may be useful to you. As the Confederation entities always make a point of saying, please use your discrimination and judgment in assessing this material. If something rings true to you, fine. If something does not resonate, please leave it behind, for neither we nor those of the Confederation would wish to be a stumbling block for any.

© 2009 L/L RESEARCH

THE LAW OF ONE, BOOK V, SESSION 32, FRAGMENT 19
FEBRUARY 27, 1981

Jim: Many people have written to us over the years telling us of what they call psychic attacks and asking how to protect themselves from them. It seems that one needn't perform any elaborate rituals or call upon any big league light bearers for assistance. Ra describes the manner in which anyone can provide all the protection that will ever be necessary in any situation. And it is very, very simple.

Carla: I will be 54 next birthday, and as I get older, I become more and more convinced that our path always lies in offering praise and thanksgiving for whatever is coming our way, no matter what we may humanly think about it. This is easy to do in good times, but it is a matter of some persistence of discipline to train the mind not to shrink away from trouble we perceive coming at us. However, I encourage in everyone that patient tenacity that refuses to doubt the Creator, no matter what. Once we have very clear the fact that we are safely in the Creator's hands and heart, this becomes easier. But the work is never fully done, for we fail again and again to witness to the light, and this causes confusion in our patterns of destiny.

Session 32, February 27, 1981

Questioner: I have a question that I will throw in at this point from Jim. I will read it. The instrument's physical vehicle is now in the process of recovery from the ingestion of a chemical. She was ignorant of the opening that she was creating. How may the three of us present be more aware of how such openings may be created in our actions and our thoughts? Is it possible that we can make such openings innocently as we question in different areas during these sessions? And what can we do to protect our selves from negative influences in general? Are there any rituals or meditations that we can do to protect our selves?

Ra: I am Ra. Although we are in sympathy with the great desire to be of service exemplified by the question, our answer is limited by the distortion of the Way of Confusion. We shall say some general things which may be of service in this area.

Firstly, when this instrument distorted its bodily complex towards low vital energy due to this occurrence, it was a recognizable substance which caused this. This was not a, shall we say, natural substance nor was the mind/body/spirit complex enough aware of its distortion towards physical weakness. The natural ways of, shall we say, everyday existence in which the entity without the distortions caused by ingestion of strongly effective chemicals may be seen to be of an always appropriate nature. There are no mistakes, including the action of this instrument.

Secondly, the means of protection against any negative or debilitating influence for those upon the positive path was demonstrated by this instrument to a very great degree. Consider, if you will, the potentials that this particular occurrence had for negative influences to enter the instrument. This instrument thought upon the Creator in its solitude and in actions with other-self, continually praised and gave thanksgiving to the Creator for the experiences it was having. This in turn allowed this particular self such energies as became a catalyst for an opening and strengthening of the other-self's ability to function in a more positively polarized state. Thus we see protection being very simple. Give thanksgiving for each moment. See the self and the other-self as Creator. Open the heart. Always know the light and praise it. This is all the protection necessary. ♣

L/L Research

www.llresearch.org

The Law of One, Book II, Session 33
March 1, 1981

Ra: I am Ra. I greet you in the love and in the light of the one infinite Creator. I communicate now.

Questioner: In our last session you said that each of us in these sessions should look well to the vital energies necessary for nondepletion of the instrument and the contact level. Did that mean that we should look at the instrument's vital energies or be careful of our own vital energies?

Ra: I am Ra. Each entity is responsible for itself. The mechanics of this process taking place involve firstly, the use of the physical bodily complex of third-density with its accompanying physical material in order to voice these words. Thus this instrument needs to watch its vital energies carefully, for we do not wish to deplete this instrument. Secondly, the function of the supporting group may be seen to be firstly, that of protection for this contact; secondly, that of energizing the instrument and intensifying its vital energies.

This supporting group has always, due to an underlying harmony, been of a very stable nature as regards protection in love and light, thus ensuring the continuation of this narrow band contact. However, the vital energies of either of the supporting members being depleted, the instrument must then use a larger portion of its vital energies, thus depleting itself more than would be profitable on a long-term basis.

Please understand that we ask your apology for this infringement upon your free will. However, it is our distortion/understanding that you would prefer this information rather than, being left totally to your own dedication/distortion, deplete the instrument or deplete the group to the point where the contact cannot be sustained.

Questioner: Can you give us advice on how to maintain the best possible condition for maintaining contact?

Ra: I am Ra. We have given information concerning the proper nurturing of this channel. We, therefore, repeat ourselves only in two ways in general. Firstly, we suggest that rather than being, shall we say, brave and ignoring a physical complex weakness/distortion it is good to share this distortion with the group and thus perhaps, shall we say, remove one opportunity for contact which is very wearying for the instrument, in order that another opportunity might come about in which the instrument is properly supported.

Secondly, the work begun in harmony may continue in harmony, thanksgiving and praise of opportunities and of the Creator. These are your protections. These are our suggestions. We cannot be specific for your free will is of the essence in this contact. As we said, we only speak to this subject because of our grasp of your orientation towards long-term maintenance of this contact. This is acceptable to us.

Questioner: Thank you very much. We have a device for so-called color therapy, and since we were on the concept of the different colors in the last session I was wondering if this would in some way apply to the principle of color therapy in the shining of particular colors on the physical body. Does this create a beneficial effect and can you tell me something about it?

Ra: I am Ra. This therapy, as you call it, is a somewhat clumsy and variably useful tool for instigating in an entity's mind/body/spirit complex an intensification of energies or vibrations which may be of aid to the entity. The variableness of this device is due firstly to the lack of true colors used, secondly, to the extreme variation in sensitivity to vibration among your peoples.

Questioner: I would think that you could achieve a true color by passing light through a crystal of the particular color. Is this correct?

Ra: I am Ra. This would be one way of approaching accuracy in color. It is a matter of what you would call quality control that the celluloid used is of a varying color. This is not of a great or even visible variation, however, it does make some difference given specific applications.

Questioner: Possibly you could use a prism breaking white light into its spectrum and screening off all parts of the spectrum except that which you wish to use by passing it through a slit. Would this be true?

Ra: I am Ra. This is correct.

Questioner: I was wondering if there is a programming of experiences that causes an individual to get certain catalysts in his daily life. For instance, as we go through our daily life there are many things which we can experience. We can look at these experiences as occurring by pure chance or by a conscious design of our own such as making appointments or going places. I was wondering if there was a behind-the-scenes, as you might call it, programming of catalyst to create the necessary experiences for more rapid growth in the case of some entities. Does this happen?

Ra: I am Ra. We believe we grasp the heart of your query. Please request further information if we are not correct.

The incarnating entity which has become conscious of the incarnative process and thus programs its own experience may choose the amount of catalyst or, to phrase this differently, the number of lessons which it will undertake to experience and to learn from in one incarnation. This does not mean that all is predestined, but rather that there are invisible guidelines shaping events which will function according to this programming. Thus if one opportunity is missed another will appear until the, shall we say, student of the life experience grasps that a lesson is being offered and undertakes to learn it.

Questioner: Then these lessons would be reprogrammed, you might say, as the life experience continues. Let's say that an entity develops the bias that he actually didn't choose to develop prior to incarnation. It is then possible to program experiences so that he will have an opportunity to alleviate this bias through balancing. Is this correct?

Ra: I am Ra. This is precisely correct.

Questioner: Thank you. From this I would extrapolate to the conjecture that the orientation in mind of the entity is the only thing that is of any consequence at all. The physical catalyst that he experiences, regardless of what is happening about him, will be a function strictly of his orientation in mind. I will use as an example *(example deleted)* this being a statement of the orientation in mind governing the catalyst. Is this correct?

Ra: I am Ra. We prefer not to use any well-known examples, sayings, or adages in our communications to you due to the tremendous amount of distortion which any well-known saying has undergone. Therefore, we may answer the first part of your query asking that you delete the example. It is completely true to the best of our knowledge that the orientation or polarization of the mind/body/spirit complex is the cause of the perceptions generated by each entity. Thus a scene may be observed in your grocery store. The entity ahead of self may be without sufficient funds. One entity may then take this opportunity to steal. Another may take this opportunity to feel itself a failure. Another may unconcernedly remove the least necessary items, pay for what it can, and go about its business. The one behind the self, observing, may feel compassion, may feel an insult because of standing next to a poverty-stricken person, may feel generosity, may feel indifference.

Do you now see the analogies in a more appropriate manner?

Questioner: I think that I do. Then from this I will extrapolate the concept which is somewhat more difficult because as you have explained before, even fourth-density positive has the concept of defensive action, but above the level of fourth-density the concept of defensive action is not in use. The concept of defensive action and offensive action are very much in use in our present density.

I am assuming that if an entity is polarized strongly enough in his thought in a positive sense that defensive action is not going to be necessary for him because the opportunity to apply defensive action will never originate for him. Is this correct?

Ra: I am Ra. This is unknowable. In each case, as we have said, an entity able to program experiences may choose the number and the intensity of lessons to be learned. It is possible that an extremely positively oriented entity might program for itself situations testing the ability of self to refrain from defensive action even to the point of the physical death of self or other-self. This is an intensive lesson and it is not known, shall we say, what entities have programmed. We may, if we desire, read this programming. However, this is an infringement and we choose not to do so.

Questioner: I will ask you if you are familiar with a motion picture called *The Ninth Configuration*. Are you familiar with this?

Ra: I am Ra. We scan your mind and see this configuration called The Ninth Configuration.

Questioner: This motion picture brought out the point about which we have been talking. The Colonel had to make a decision. I was wondering about his polarization. He could have knuckled under, you might say, to the negative forces, but he chose to defend his friend instead. Is it possible for you to estimate which is more positively polarizing: to defend the positively oriented entity, or to allow suppression by the negatively oriented entities?

Ra: I am Ra. This question takes in the scope of fourth-density as well as your own and its answer may best be seen by the action of the entity called Jehoshuah, which you call Jesus. This entity was to be defended by its friends. The entity reminded its friends to put away the sword. This entity then delivered itself to be put to the physical death. The impulse to protect the loved other-self is one which persists through the fourth-density, a density abounding in compassion. More than this we cannot and need not say.

Questioner: Thank you. As we near the end of this master cycle there may be an increasing amount of catalyst for entities. I am wondering if, as the planetary vibrations mismatch somewhat with the fourth-density vibrations and catalyst is increased, if this will create more polarization thereby getting a slightly greater harvest?

Ra: I am Ra. The question must be answered in two parts. Firstly, the planetary catastrophes, as you may call them, are a symptom of the difficult harvest rather than a consciously programmed catalyst for harvest. Thus we do not concern ourselves with it, for it is random in respect to conscious catalyst such as we may make available.

The second portion is this: the results of the random catalyst of what you call the earth changes are also random. Thus we may see probability/possibility vortices going towards positive and negative. However, it will be as it will be. The true opportunities for conscious catalyst are not a function of the earth changes but of the result of the seniority system of incarnations which at the time of the harvest has placed in incarnation those whose chances of using life experiences to become harvestable are the best.

Questioner: Is this seniority system also used in the service to self side for becoming harvestable on that side?

Ra: I am Ra. This is correct. You may ask one more full question at this time.

Questioner: What I would like for you to do is list all the major mechanisms designed to provide catalytic experience that do not include interaction with other-self. That is the first part.

Ra: I am Ra. We grasp from this question that you realize that the primary mechanism for catalytic experience in third-density is other-self. The list of other catalytic influences: firstly, the Creator's universe; secondly, the self.

Questioner: Can you list any sub-headings under self or ways the self is acted upon catalytically which would produce experience?

Ra: I am Ra. Firstly, the self unmanifested. Secondly, the self in relation to the societal self created by self and other-self. Thirdly, the interaction between self and the gadgets, toys, and amusements of the self, other-self invention. Fourthly, the self relationship with those attributes which you may call war and rumors of war.

Questioner: I was thinking possibly of the catalyst of physical pain. Does this go under this heading?

Ra: I am Ra. This is correct, it going under the heading of the unmanifested self; that is, the self which does not need other-self in order to manifest or act.

Questioner: Do we have enough time left to ask the second part of this question which is to list all major mechanisms designed to provide the catalyst that include action with other-self?

Ra: I am Ra. You have much time for this, for we may express this list in one of two ways. We could speak infinitely, or we could simply state that any interaction betwixt self and other-self has whatever potential for catalyst that there exists in the potential difference between self and other-self, this moderated and undergirded by the constant fact of the Creator as self and as other-self. You may ask to this question further if you wish specific information.

Questioner: I believe that this is sufficient for the time being.

Ra: I am Ra. Do you have a brief query or two before we close this working?

Questioner: Yes, here is one question. Is there any difference in violet ray activity or brightness between entities who are at entrance level both positive and negative to fourth-density?

Ra: I am Ra. This correct. The violet ray of the positive fourth-density will be tinged with the green, blue, indigo triad of energies. This tinge may be seen as a portion of a rainbow or prism, as you know it, the rays being quite distinct.

The violet ray of fourth-density negative has in its aura, shall we say, the tinge of red, orange, yellow, these rays being muddied rather than distinct.

Questioner: What would the rays of fifth and sixth-density look like?

Ra: I am Ra. We may speak only approximately. However, we hope you understand, shall we say, that there is a distinctive difference in the color structure of each density.

Fifth density is perhaps best described as extremely white in vibration.

The sixth-density of a whiteness which contains a golden quality as you would perceive it; these colors having to do with the blending into wisdom of the compassion learned in fourth-density, then in sixth the blending of wisdom back into an unified understanding of compassion viewed with wisdom. This golden color is not of your spectrum but is what you would call alive.

You may ask one more question briefly.

Questioner: Then I will ask if there is anything that we can do to make the instrument more comfortable or to improve the contact?

Ra: I am Ra. This working is well. You are attempting to be conscientious. We thank you. May we say we enjoyed your vision of our social memory complex drinking one of your liquids while speaking through this instrument.

I am Ra. I leave you in the love and in the light of the one infinite Creator. Go forth, then, rejoicing in the power and the peace of the one infinite Creator. Adonai.

The Law of One, Book II, Session 34
March 4, 1981

Ra: I am Ra. I greet you in the love and in the light of the one infinite Creator. We communicate now.

Questioner: You stated at an earlier time that penetration of the eighth level or intelligent infinity allows a mind/body/spirit complex to be harvested if it wishes at any time/space during the cycle. When this penetration of the eighth level occurs what does the entity who penetrates it experience?

Ra: I am Ra. The experience of each entity is unique in its perception of intelligent infinity. Perceptions range from a limitless joy to a strong dedication to service to others while in the incarnated state. The entity which reaches intelligent infinity most often will perceive this experience as one of unspeakable profundity. However, it is not usual for the entity to immediately desire the cessation of the incarnation. Rather the desire to communicate or use this experience to aid others is extremely strong.

Questioner: Thank you. Would you define karma?

Ra: I am Ra. Our understanding of karma is that which may be called inertia. Those actions which are put into motion will continue using the ways of balancing until such time as the controlling or higher principle which you may liken unto your braking or stopping is invoked. This stoppage of the inertia of action may be called forgiveness. These two concepts are inseparable.

Questioner: If an entity develops what is called karma in an incarnation, is there then programming that sometimes occurs so that he will experience catalysts that will enable him to get to a point of forgiveness thereby alleviating the karma?

Ra: I am Ra. This is, in general, correct. However, both self and any involved other-self may, at any time through the process of understanding, acceptance, and forgiveness, ameliorate these patterns. This is true at any point in an incarnative pattern. Thus one who has set in motion an action may forgive itself and never again make that error. This also brakes or stops what you call karma.

Questioner: Thank you. Can you give me examples of catalytic action from the last session beginning with the self unmanifested producing learning catalyst?

Ra: I am Ra. We observed your interest in the catalyst of pain. This experience is most common among your entities. The pain may be of the physical complex. More often it is of the mental and emotional complex. In some few cases the pain is spiritual in complex-nature. This creates a potential for learning. The lessons to be learned vary. Almost always these lessons include patience, tolerance, and the ability for the light touch.

Very often the catalyst for emotional pain, whether it be the death of the physical complex of one other-self which is loved or other seeming loss, will simply result in the opposite, in a bitterness and impatience, a souring. This is catalyst which has gone awry. In these cases then there will be additional catalyst provided to offer the unmanifested self further opportunities for discovering the self as all-sufficient Creator containing all that there is and full of joy.

Questioner: Do what we call contagious diseases play any part in this process with respect to the unmanifested self?

Ra: I am Ra. These so-called contagious diseases are those entities of second-density which offer an opportunity for this type of catalyst. If this catalyst is unneeded, then these second-density creatures, as you would call them, do not have an effect. In each of these generalizations you may please note that there are anomalies so that we cannot speak to every circumstance but only to the general run or way of things as you experience them.

Questioner: What part do what we call birth defects play in this process?

Ra: I am Ra. This is a portion of the programming of the mind/body/spirit complex totality manifested in the mind/body/spirit of third-density. These defects are planned as limitations which are part of the experience intended by the entity's totality complex. This includes genetic predispositions, as you may call them.

Questioner: Thank you. Can you give me the same type of information about the self in relation to the societal self?

Ra: I am Ra. The unmanifested self may find its lessons those which develop any of the energy influx centers of the mind/body/spirit complex. The societal and self interactions most often concentrate upon the second and third energy centers. Thus those most active in attempting to remake or alter the society are those working from feelings of being correct personally or of having answers which will put power in a more correct configuration. This may be seen to be of a full travel from negative to positive in orientation. Either will activate these energy ray centers.

There are some few whose desires to aid society are of a green ray nature or above. These entities, however, are few due to the understanding, may we say, of fourth ray that universal love freely given is more to be desired than principalities or even the rearrangement of peoples or political structures.

Questioner: If an entity were to be strongly biased toward positive societal effects, what would this do to his yellow ray in the aura as opposed to an entity who wanted to create an empire of society and govern it with an iron fist?

Ra: I am Ra. Let us take two such positively oriented active souls no longer in your physical time/space. The one known as Albert went into a strange and, to it, a barbaric society in order that it might heal. This entity was able to mobilize great amounts of energy and what you call money. This entity spent much green ray energy both as a healer and as a lover of your instrument known as the organ. This entity's yellow ray was bright and crystallized by the efforts needed to procure the funds to promulgate its efforts. However, the green and blue rays were of a toweringly brilliant nature as well. The higher levels, as you may call them, being activated, the lower, as you may call them, energy points remaining in a balance, being quite, quite bright.

The other example is the entity, Martin. This entity dealt in a great degree with rather negative orange ray and yellow ray vibratory patterns. However, this entity was able to keep open the green ray energy and due to the severity of its testing, if anything, this entity may be seen to have polarized more towards the positive due to its fidelity to service to others in the face of great catalyst.

Questioner: Could you give me the last names of Albert and Martin?

Ra: I am Ra. These entities are known to you as Albert Schweitzer and Martin Luther King.

Questioner: I thought that that was correct, but I wasn't sure. Can you give me the same type of information that we have been getting here with respect to the unmanifested interacting between self and gadgets and toys and inventions?

Ra: I am Ra. In this particular instance we again concentrate for the most part in the orange and in the yellow energy centers. In a negative sense many of the gadgets among your peoples, that is what you call your communication devices and other distractions such as the less competitive games, may be seen to have the distortion of keeping the mind/body/spirit complex unactivated so that yellow and orange ray activity is much weakened thus carefully decreasing the possibility of eventual green ray activation.

Others of your gadgets may be seen to be tools whereby the entity explores the capabilities of its physical or mental complexes and in some few cases, the spiritual complex, thus activating the orange ray in what you call your team sports and in other gadgets such as your modes of transport. These may be seen to be ways of investigating the feelings of power; more especially, power over others or a group power over another group of other-selves.

Questioner: What is the general overall effect of television on our society with respect to this catalyst?

Ra: I am Ra. Without ignoring the green ray attempts of many to communicate via this medium such information of truth and beauty as may be helpful, we must suggest that the sum effect of this gadget is that of distraction and sleep.

Questioner: Can you give me the same type of information that we are working on now with respect to war and rumors of war?

Ra: I am Ra. You may see this in relationship to your gadgets. This war and self relationship is a fundamental perception of the maturing entity. There is a great chance to accelerate in whatever direction is desired. One may polarize negatively by assuming bellicose attitudes for whatever reason. One may find oneself in the situation of war and polarize somewhat towards the positive activating orange, yellow, and then green rays by heroic, if you may call them this, actions taken to preserve the mind/body/spirit complexes of other-selves.

Finally, one may polarize very strongly third ray by expressing the principle of universal love at the total expense of any distortion towards involvement in bellicose actions. In this way the entity may become a conscious being in a very brief span of your time/space. This may be seen to be what you would call a traumatic progression. It is to be noted that among your entities a large percentage of all progression has as catalyst, trauma.

Questioner: You just used the term third ray in that statement. Was that the term you meant to use?

Ra: I am Ra. We intended the green ray. Our difficulty lies in our perception of red ray and violet ray as fixed; thus the inner rays are those which are varying and are to be observed as those indications of seniority in the attempts to form an harvest.

Questioner: Would the red ray, an intense red ray, then be used as an index for seniority in incarnation as well as an intense violet ray?

Ra: I am Ra. This is partially correct. In the graduation or harvesting to fourth-density positive, the red ray is seen only as that, which being activated, is the basis for all that occurs in vibratory levels, the sum of this being violet ray energy.

This violet ray is the only consideration for fourth-density positive. In assessing the harvestable fourth-density negative, the intensity of the red as well as the orange and the yellow rays is looked upon quite carefully as a great deal of stamina and energy of this type is necessary for the negative progression, it being extremely difficult to open the gateway to intelligent infinity from the solar plexus center. This is necessary for harvest in fourth-density negative.

Questioner: Is it possible for you to use as an example our General Patton and tell me the effect that war had on him in his development?

Ra: I am Ra. This will be the last full question of this working. The one of whom you speak, known as George, was one in whom the programming of previous incarnations had created a pattern or inertia which was irresistible in its incarnation in your time/space. This entity was of a strong yellow ray activation with frequent green ray openings and occasional blue ray openings. However, it did not find itself able to break the mold of previous traumatic experiences of a bellicose nature.

This entity polarized somewhat towards the positive in its incarnation due to its singleness of belief in truth and beauty. This entity was quite sensitive. It felt a great honor/duty to the preservation of that which was felt by the entity to be true, beautiful, and in need of defense. This entity perceived itself a gallant figure. It polarized somewhat towards the negative in its lack of understanding the green ray it carried with it, rejecting the forgiveness principle which is implicit in universal love.

The sum total of this incarnation vibrationally was a slight increase in positive polarity but a decrease in harvestability due to the rejection of the Law or Way of Responsibility; that is, seeing universal love, yet still it fought on.

Questioner: Do we have enough time for me to ask if the death, almost immediately after the cessation of war, of this entity could have been so that it could have immediately been reincarnated so that it could make harvest?

Ra: I am Ra. This is precisely correct.

Questioner: Thank you. Then I will just ask if there is anything that we can do to make the instrument more comfortable or to improve the contact?

Ra: I am Ra. All is well. We leave you, my friends, in the love and the light of the One which is All in All. I leave you in an ever-lasting peace. Go forth, therefore, rejoicing in the power and the peace of the one infinite Creator. Adonai.

L/L Research

L/L Research is a subsidiary of Rock Creek Research & Development Laboratories, Inc.

P.O. Box 5195
Louisville, KY 40255-0195

www.llresearch.org

Rock Creek is a non-profit corporation dedicated to discovering and sharing information which may aid in the spiritual evolution of humankind.

ABOUT THE CONTENTS OF THIS TRANSCRIPT: This telepathic channeling has been taken from transcriptions of the weekly study and meditation meetings of the Rock Creek Research & Development Laboratories and L/L Research. It is offered in the hope that it may be useful to you. As the Confederation entities always make a point of saying, please use your discrimination and judgment in assessing this material. If something rings true to you, fine. If something does not resonate, please leave it behind, for neither we nor those of the Confederation would wish to be a stumbling block for any.

© 2009 L/L Research

The Law of One, Book V, Session 34, Fragment 20
March 4, 1981

Jim: Because Carla's physical energy level was always very low and constantly being drained by the arthritic condition and the persistent presence of some degree of pain, it became necessary for her to engage in daily exercise in order to maintain the function of each portion of her body. We found that the more distorted or low on energy she was the greater was the need for this exercise. When her body was functioning most nearly normally, the exercise could be reduced in length until it also was normal. For Carla that was about one hour of rapid walking per day.

When Don queried about an experience that he had in 1964, the specificity of the answer was limited by Ra's desire to maintain Don's free will. Most events in our lives are a mystery in some degree or another. One way of looking at the process of evolution is to see it as the process of solving the mysteries all about us. All events are illusions or mysteries because each represents the one Creator in one disguise or another, offering us a greater or lesser opportunity to find love, joy, balance, and perfection in each moment. There is a spiritual strength that comes with unraveling such mysteries for one's self. It is not always a service for those with better trained eyes to tell another what he does not yet see for himself, but which he has the capacity to learn to see. Thus Ra often invoked the Law of Free Will, also known as the Law of Confusion.

Carla: When I was a child, I danced and swam and rode horses. I loved exercise, especially when it was rhythmic. The exercise that was my lot to do during this time was, though very hard, because I felt so tired, an energizing experience. Both Don and Jim helped me remember to get these periods in, and Jim made them easier still by joining me. It is always easier to do such things with a buddy! Don was not able to join me in these walks, as he had a painful condition of the feet brought on by working in tropical climes, and every step hurt. However, I witnessed, from time to time, a level of animal strength in Don that was miraculous. For instance, in 1977 Don and I went to join in a Mind Link held by Andrija Puharich. Gathered were a mixed bag of established psychics, all women, and other mid-aged supporters, and about an equal number of college-age kids who had identified themselves to Puharich as Wanderers. The kids loved soccer and played it when we weren't in session. Don joined in their first game. He did really well, impressing not only me but all the kids. They finally had to stop the game, red-faced and panting. Donald was not even breathing heavily. Needless to say, the kids warmed up to Don quickly! But they never could get him to play again.

Session 34, March 4, 1981

Questioner: The instrument would like to know if two short exercise periods per day would be better for her than one long one?

Ra: I am Ra. This is incorrect. The proper configuration of the physical complex exercising during the three month period wherein the instrument is vulnerable to physical complex distortion intensification, needs the strengthening of the physical complex. This may appropriately be seen to be one major period of the exercising followed late in your diurnal cycle before the evening meditation by an exercise period approximately one-half the length of the first. This will be seen to be wearing upon the instrument. However, it will have the effect of strengthening the physical complex and lessening the vulnerability which might be taken advantage of.

Questioner: Is it possible for you to tell me what I experienced, around 1964 I believe it was, when in meditation I became aware of what I considered a different density and different planet, and seemed to experience moving onto that planet? Is it possible for you to tell me what experience that was?

Ra: I am Ra. We see some harm in full disclosure due to infringement. We content ourselves with suggesting that this entity, which is not readily able to subject itself to the process of hypnotic regression instigated by others, nevertheless, has had its opportunities for understanding of its being-ness.

L/L Research

L/L Research is a subsidiary of Rock Creek Research & Development Laboratories, Inc.

P.O. Box 5195
Louisville, KY 40255-0195

www.llresearch.org

Rock Creek is a non-profit corporation dedicated to discovering and sharing information which may aid in the spiritual evolution of humankind.

ABOUT THE CONTENTS OF THIS TRANSCRIPT: This telepathic channeling has been taken from transcriptions of the weekly study and meditation meetings of the Rock Creek Research & Development Laboratories and L/L Research. It is offered in the hope that it may be useful to you. As the Confederation entities always make a point of saying, please use your discrimination and judgment in assessing this material. If something rings true to you, fine. If something does not resonate, please leave it behind, for neither we nor those of the Confederation would wish to be a stumbling block for any.

© 2009 L/L Research

The Law of One, Book II, Session 35
March 6, 1981

Ra: I am Ra. I greet you in the love and in the light of the one infinite Creator. We communicate now.

Questioner: I would like to say that we consider it a great privilege to be doing this work, and we hope that we will be questioning in the direction that will be of value to the readers of this material. I thought that in this session it might be helpful to inspect the effect of the rays of different well-known figures in history to aid in understanding how the catalyst of the illusion creates spiritual growth. I was making a list that I thought we might use to hit the high points on the workings of the catalysts on these individuals starting with the one we know as Franklin D. Roosevelt. Could you say something about that entity?

Ra: I am Ra. It is to be noted that in discussing those who are well-known among your peoples there is the possibility that information may be seen to be specific to one entity whereas in actuality the great design of experience is much the same for each entity. It is with this in mind that we would discuss the experiential forces which offered catalyst to an individual.

It is further to be noted that in the case of those entities lately incarnate much distortion may have taken place in regard to misinformation and misinterpretation of an entity's thoughts or behaviors.

We shall now proceed to, shall we say, speak of the basic parameters of the one known as Franklin.

When any entity comes into third-density incarnation, each of its energy centers is potentiated but must be activated by the self using experience.

The one known as Franklin developed very quickly up through red, orange, yellow, and green and began to work in the blue ray energy center at a tender age, as you would say. This rapid growth was due, firstly, to previous achievements in the activation of the rays, secondly, to the relative comfort and leisure of its early existence, thirdly, due to the strong desire upon the part of the entity to progress. This entity mated with an entity whose blue ray vibrations were of a strength more than equal to its own thus acquiring catalyst for further growth in that area that was to persist throughout the incarnation.

This entity had some difficulty with continued green ray activity due to the excessive energy which was put into the activities regarding other-selves in the distortion towards acquiring power. This was to have its toll upon the physical vehicle, as you may call it. The limitation of the nonmovement of a portion of the physical vehicle opened once again, for this entity, the opportunity for concentration upon the more, shall we say, universal or idealistic aspects of power; that is, the nonabusive use of power. Thus at the outset of a bellicose action this entity had lost some positive polarity due to excessive use of the orange and yellow ray energies at the expense of green and blue ray energies, then had regained the polarity due to the catalytic effects of a painful limitation upon the physical complex.

This entity was not of a bellicose nature but rather during the conflict continued to vibrate in green ray working with the blue ray energies. The entity who was the one known as Franklin's teacher also functioned greatly during this period as blue ray activator, not only for its mate but also in a more universal expression. This entity polarized continuously in a positive fashion in the universal sense while, in a less universal sense, developing a pattern of what may be called karma; this karma having to do with inharmonious relationship distortions with the mate/teacher.

Questioner: Two things I would like to clear up. First, then Franklin's teacher was his wife? Is this correct?

Ra: I am Ra. This is correct.

Questioner: Secondly, did Franklin place the physical limitation on his body himself?

Ra: I am Ra. This is partially correct. The basic guidelines for the lessons and purposes of incarnation had been carefully set forth before incarnation by the mind/body/spirit complex totality. If the one known as Franklin had avoided the excessive enjoyment of or attachment to the competitiveness which may be seen to be inherent in the processes of its occupation, this entity would not have had the limitation.

However, the desire to serve and to grow was strong in this programming and when the opportunities began to cease due to these distortions towards love of power the entity's limiting factor was activated.

Questioner: I would now like to ask for the same type of information with respect to Adolf Hitler. You have given a little of this already. It is not necessary for you to recover what you have already given. Could you complete that information?

Ra: I am Ra. In speaking of the one you call Adolf we have some difficulty due to the intense amount of confusion present in this entity's life patterns as well as the great confusion which greets any discussion of this entity.

Here we see an example of one who, in attempting activation of the highest rays of energy while lacking the green ray key, canceled itself out as far as polarization either towards positive or negative. This entity was basically negative. However, its confusion was such that the personality disintegrated, thus leaving the mind/body/spirit complex unharvestable and much in need of healing.

This entity followed the pattern of negative polarization which suggests the elite and the enslaved, this being seen by the entity to be of an helpful nature for the societal structure. However, in drifting from the conscious polarization into what you may call a twilight world where dream took the place of events in your space/time continuum, this entity failed in its attempt to serve the Creator in an harvestable degree along the path of service to self. Thus we see the so-called insanity which may often arise when an entity attempts to polarize more quickly than experience may be integrated.

We have advised and suggested caution and patience in previous communications and do so again, using this entity as an example of the over-hasty opening of polarization without due attention to the synthesized and integrated mind/body/spirit complex. To know your self is to have the foundation upon firm ground.

Questioner: Thank you. That is an important example I believe. I was wondering if any of those who were subordinate to Adolf at that time were able to polarize in a harvestable nature on the negative path?

Ra: I am Ra. We can speak only of two entities who may be harvestable in a negative sense, others still being in the physical incarnation: one known to you as Hermann; the other known, as it preferred to be called, Himmler.

Questioner: Thank you. Earlier we discussed Abraham Lincoln as a rather unique case. is it possible for you to tell us why the fourth-density being used Abraham Lincoln's body, what its orientation was, and when this took place with respect to the activities that were occurring in our society at that time?

Ra: I am Ra. This is possible.

Questioner: Would it be of value for the reader to know this in your estimation?

Ra: I am Ra. You must shape your queries according to your discernment.

Questioner: Well in that case I would like to know the motivation for this use of Abraham Lincoln's body at that time?

Ra: I am Ra. This shall be the last full query of this session as we find the instrument quite low in vital energies.

The one known as Abraham had an extreme difficulty in many ways and, due to physical, mental, and spiritual pain, was weary of life but without the orientation to self-destruction. In your time, 1853, this entity was contacted in sleep by a fourth-density being. This being was concerned with the battles between the forces of light and the forces of darkness which have been waged in fourth-density for many of your years.

This entity accepted the honor/duty of completing the one known as Abraham's karmic patterns and the one known as Abraham discovered that this entity would attempt those things which the one known as Abraham desired to do but felt it could not. Thus the exchange was made.

The entity, Abraham, was taken to a plane of suspension until the cessation of its physical vehicle much as though we of Ra would arrange with this instrument to remain in the vehicle, come out of the trance state, and function as this instrument, leaving this instrument's mind and spirit complex in its suspended state.

The planetary energies at this time were at what seemed to this entity to be at a critical point, for that which you know as freedom had gained in acceptance as a possibility among many peoples. This entity saw the work done by those beginning the democratic concept of freedom, as you call it, in danger of being abridged or abrogated by the rising belief and use of the principle of the enslavement of entities. This is a negative concept of a fairly serious nature in your density. This entity, therefore, went forward into what it saw as the battle for the light, for healing of a rupture in the concept of freedom.

This entity did not gain or lose karma by these activities due to its detachment from any outcome. Its attitude throughout was one of service to others, more especially to the downtrodden or enslaved. The polarity of the individual was somewhat, but not severely, lessened by the cumulative feelings and thought forms which were created due to large numbers of entities leaving the physical plane due to trauma of battle.

May we ask if this is the information you requested or if we may supply any further information?

Questioner: I will ask any further questions during the next working period which should occur in about four days. We do not want to overtire the instrument. I will only ask if there is anything that we can do to make the instrument more comfortable or to improve the contact?

Ra: I am Ra. All is well. I leave you, my friends, in the love and the light of the one infinite Creator. Go forth, therefore rejoicing in the power and the peace of the one Creator. Adonai.

Sunday Meditation
March 8, 1981

(Carla channeling

I am Hatonn. It is a great privilege and pleasure to greet you this evening. We have been with each of you in your meditations and we thank you for your continuing efforts to seek the path of truth. Our stories and our speeches are always and ever those attempting to give you an understanding that is very simple, an understanding of love. And once again we shall tell you, shall we say, a parable, in order that you may turn in your mind another facet of the understanding of love and its workings in your life as you live it at this time.

Imagine yourself, my friends, as a young man at the dawn of *(inaudible)*, contemplating with some despair the difficulties and limitations of responsibility and adulthood. Imagine then a guide, a guardian, coming to this young man and saying, "Come with me and I shall show you the alternative to your difficulties and your limitations."

And the young man awakes in an enchanted forest. He is cold and wishes himself better clothed, for it is somewhat chilly and immediately he is garbed in a warm and comfortable garment. He looks about and wonders if there might be water and suddenly a brook gurgles verily at his feet. Recklessly, he thinks to himself, "Well, I'll just think myself a house," and it is there. A comfortable, furnished cabin. Outside he finds beehives, gardens, all things as he would wish them to be. And it is many days before this young man begins to realize that he is not happy in this tremendous freedom from limitation and from responsibility. It is not many more days than that before he recalls his guardian. "Great Being," he says, "you have shown me what it is to be free of responsibility and limitation and I now understand. I wish to go back." And back he is in a world with responsibilities, sometimes of a crushing nature, of limitations of all kinds, and other people.

My friends, cherish each other and understand that in each entity you view the Creator. In each entity beginning with yourself and spreading outward through all of your life you meet a *(inaudible)* of love. Beings born and made of love. It is a responsibility to live in such a world, but, my friends, it is an honor to be able to share woe and *(inaudible)* alike with your fellow beings and a common understanding that you are one with the Creator, a Creator of infinite love.

How can you keep this in mind as your back bends under responsibilities you may not wish to bear, limitations and situations you might wish to be different? As always, my friends, we offer you the suggestion that time spent in meditation is time spent out of time and in the kingdom of heaven. These moments are with you through the days; as you need them you may call upon them if you but will.

At this time I would like to transfer this contact. I am Hatonn.

(Jim channeling)

I am Hatonn, and greet you once again in love and light. It is always a great privilege and honor to share our simple thoughts with your meditation group. We of Hatonn are simple messengers with a very simple message. A message which you know is a message of love. The experience of love, the recognition of love, the living of love, the sharing of love, the giving of love, for my friends, love is that force which binds all that is together in the one great Being that we serve and call the infinite Creator. We speak of love for there is nothing else that may be spoken of.

The love that is the source of your very being surrounds you each moment of every day that you experience in your lives upon this tiny planet that you call Earth. The infinite Creator has set in motion the force of love to carry each of His creations on a journey, a journey of awakening, a journey of realizing the oneness of self with all that is, with love, with the Creator. This journey has many routes available. Each of you in your own free will, by your own choices, may choose how to make this journey. Each of you in your daily activities as you go about that which is your work, your life, meets those who are like you, pilgrims upon this path of awakening. Each of you in your daily lives have infinite opportunities to realize that you share love with each other. Each of you has infinite opportunities to recognize the workings of love in your life, in each moment.

It is for this reason that we suggest again and again that you pause for a moment in each day to sit with yourself in the silence of meditation so that the realization of your oneness with all that is might be made more profoundly clear in your life, for amid the hustle and the bustle and the activity that are contained within each of your days in such great profusion it is easy, as you know, to lose the sight and the feeling and the realization of your oneness with all. It is easy to forget that the force which propels you through all your activities is simply the force of love. It is easy to overlook the most obvious of realities and, sadly to say, my friends, so often is love overlooked; so often is the Creator forgotten.

Though you meet the Creator in every activity in every face in every day, it is so easy to forget whom you meet. For this reason we suggest that meditation might be the means by which you make this connection with the foundation of your being on a daily basis. This meditation activity can became likened unto a fire, a light which burns within your being and illuminates your being burning brighter as you feed it the fuel of your attention. Burning brighter until those around you notice a change in your very being and are inspired by the light that shines from your being, from your words, from your thoughts, from your actions. In this way, the light and the love of the infinite Creator may find means of manifestation into your third-dimensional reality, a reality that contains the Creator in every degree. But a reality which, as all illusions, hides that which is its foundation.

We from Hatonn are privileged to be able to speak these simple words to your group and thank you for the opportunity that you offer for our service to you and to your fellow creatures as you open yourselves in meditation whenever possible. We shall be with you and shall be most happy to join you in your meditations whenever you have a moment, however long or short, to sit in the silence of the self at the throne of the Creator.

We would at this time transfer this contact to the one known as Carla. I am Hatonn.

(Carla channeling)

I am Hatonn. Before I leave you, my friends, I would like to allow our brothers and sisters of Laitos to join with us in greeting each of you personally with the vibration which we call the conditioning wave. We shall make this available first to the one known as N. If he will relax, we will deepen his state of meditation. And to the one known as D. To the one known as C. We give our thanks to each channel and we expand our love and our light to those others to whom these words, poor as they may be, shall be sent. We are only messengers, as we have said of the carrying of great news. You may feel the love. It does not come from us, but through us. May it also come through you, and bless the lives of all those whose lives you touch.

I leave you now in the love and the light of the infinite Creator, in the beauty of His great caring, in the joy of His creation. I am Hatonn. Adonai, my friends. Adonai vasu.

(Pause)

I am Nona. I am with this instrument and greet you in the love and in the light of the infinite Creator. We speak with difficulty but we are called by one of those of you, the one known as S. His request for healing does not go unheard and we share that healing with you now. We thank you for this opportunity to be of service.

I am Latwii. I am very happy to be with you. I greet you also in the love and in the light of the infinite Creator. It is a great joy to be here with you and to offer myself as one who would attempt to answer any questions that you may have at this time.

C: We were speaking earlier about a case that is currently in—well, it's in the paper this morning, and it dealt with a person claiming to have been possessed at the time of a violent act. But with the operation of free will, how can one be possessed by a negative influence, say as this one claims?

I am Latwii, and am aware of your question. We do not wish to make light of your negative entities, however, we ask you, my friend, is not anyone who is acting without rationality possessed by inspiration of some kind? The being that you are encompasses a, shall we say, dark side. This dark side may, in some cases, be extremely visible. The workings of the mind, as you call it, are such that many of the influences of your daily life are largely unknown to you. But they do exist in the individual, not in *(inaudible)*.

There are those who aid individuals wishing to be of a negative nature. But the wish must precede the deed. The cases of what you may call possession are so few that in discussing the greater number that are largely understood to be possessions we must simply say we see [a] darker side of the individual which has disintegrated from the whole. In some cases the disintegration is so great that what you would call a discarnate entity may actually be present. We ask you, my friends, not to think of devils but of negative and positive, for each of you has potentials for each so that you may be possessed by the thirst for beauty, truth, honor and faith, or by the lust for power, greed or destruction.

Does this answer your question, my brother?

C: Yes, so there's just a manifestation of a portion of ourselves and not external influences?

I am Latwii. In the majority of cases this is so. Is there another question at this time?

C: *(Inaudible).*

(Tape ends.)

The Law of One, Book II, Session 36
March 10, 1981

Ra: I am Ra. I greet you in the love and the light of the one infinite Creator. We communicate now.

Questioner: In previous communications you have spoken of the mind/body/spirit complex totality. Would you please give us a definition of the mind/body/spirit complex totality?

Ra: I am Ra. There is a dimension in which time does not have sway. In this dimension, the mind/body/spirit in its eternal dance of the present may be seen in totality, and before the mind/body/spirit complex which then becomes a part of the social memory complex is willingly absorbed into the allness of the one Creator, the entity knows itself in its totality.

This mind/body/spirit complex totality functions as, shall we say, a resource for what you perhaps would call the higher self. The higher self, in turn, is a resource for examining the distillations of third-density experience and programming further experience. This is also true of densities four, five, and six with the mind/body/spirit complex totality coming into consciousness in the course of seventh density.

Questioner: Then would the mind/body/spirit complex totality be responsible for programming changes in catalyst during a third-density experience of the mind/body/spirit complex so that the proper catalyst would be added, shall we say, as conditions for the complex changed during third-density experience?

Ra: I am Ra. This is incorrect. The higher self, as you call it, that is, that self which exists with full understanding of the accumulation of experiences of the entity, aids the entity in achieving healing of the experiences which have not been learned properly and assists as you have indicated in further life experience programming, as you may call it.

The mind/body/spirit complex totality is that which may be called upon by the higher self aspect just as the mind/body/spirit complex calls upon the higher self. In the one case you have a structured situation within the space/time continuum with the higher self having available to it the totality of experiences which have been collected by an entity and a very firm grasp of the lessons to be learned in this density.

The mind/body/spirit complex totality is as the shifting sands and is in some part a collection of parallel developments of the same entity. This information is made available to the higher self aspect. This aspect may then use these projected probability/possibility vortices in order to better aid in what you would call future life programming.

Questioner: Out of the Seth Material we have a statement in which Seth says that each entity here on Earth is one part of or aspect of a higher self or Oversoul which has many aspects or parts in many dimensions all of which learn lessons which allow the higher self to progress in a balanced manner. Am

I to understand from this that there are many experiences similar to the one which we experience in the third-density which are governed by a single higher self?

Ra: I am Ra. The correctness of this statement is variable. The more in balance an entity becomes, the less the possibility/probability vortices may need to be explored in parallel experiences.

Questioner: Do I understand from this then that the higher self or Oversoul may break down into numerous units if the experience is required to what we would call simultaneously experience different types of catalysts and then oversee these experiences?

Ra: I am Ra. This is a statement we cannot say to be correct or incorrect due to the confusions of what you call time. True simultaneity is available only when all things are seen to be occurring at once. This overshadows the concept of which you speak. The concept of various parts of the being living experiences of varying natures simultaneously is not precisely accurate due to your understanding that this would indicate that this was occurring with true simultaneity. This is not the case.

The case is from universe to universe and parallel existences can then be programmed by the higher self, given the information available from the mind/body/spirit complex totality regarding the probability/possibility vortices at any crux.

Questioner: Could you give an example of how this programming by the higher self would then bring about education through parallel experiences?

Ra: I am Ra. Perhaps the simplest example of this apparent simultaneity of existence of two selves, which are in truth one self at the same time/space, is this: the Oversoul, as you call it, or higher self, seems to exist simultaneously with the mind/body/spirit complex which it aids. This is not actually simultaneous, for the higher self is moving to the mind/body/spirit complex as needed from a position in development of the entity which would be considered in the future of this entity.

Questioner: Then the higher self operates from the future as we understand things. In other words my higher self would operate from what I consider to be my future? Is this correct?

Ra: I am Ra. From the standpoint of your space/time, this is correct.

Questioner: In that case my higher self would have a very large advantage in knowing what was needed since it would know, as far as I am concerned, what was going to happen. Is this correct?

Ra: I am Ra. This is incorrect, in that this would be an abrogation of free will. The higher self aspect is aware of the lessons learned through the sixth-density. The progress rate is fairly well understood. The choices which must be made to achieve the higher self as it is are in the provenance of the mind/body/spirit complex itself.

Thus the higher self is like the map in which the destination is known; the roads are very well known, these roads being designed by intelligent infinity working through intelligent energy. However, the higher self aspect can program only for the lessons and certain predisposing limitations if it wishes. The remainder is completely the free choice of each entity. There is the perfect balance between the known and the unknown.

Questioner: I'm sorry for having so much trouble with these concepts, but they are very difficult I am sure to translate into our understanding and language. Some of my questions may be rather ridiculous, but does this higher self have some type of vehicle like our physical vehicle? Does it have a bodily complex?

Ra: I am Ra. This is correct. The higher self is of a certain advancement within sixth-density going into the seventh. After the seventh has been well entered the mind/body/spirit complex becomes so totally a mind/body/spirit complex totality that it begins to gather spiritual mass and approach the octave density. Thus the looking backwards is finished at that point.

Questioner: Is the higher self of every entity of a sixth-density nature?

Ra: I am Ra. This is correct. This is an honor/duty of self to self as one approaches seventh density.

Questioner: Let me be sure that I understand this then. We have spoken of certain particular individuals. For instance we were speaking of George Patton in a previous communication. Then his higher self at the time of his incarnation here as George Patton about forty years ago was of sixth-density? is this correct?

Ra: I am Ra. This is correct. We make note at this time that each entity has several beings upon which to call for inner support. Any of these may be taken by an entity to be the mind/body/spirit complex totality. However, this is not the case. The mind/body/spirit complex totality is a nebulous collection of all that may occur held in understanding; the higher self itself a projection or manifestation of mind/body/spirit complex totality which then may communicate with the mind/body/spirit during the discarnate part of a cycle of rebirth or during the incarnation; may communicate if the proper pathways or channels through the roots of mind are opened.

Questioner: These channels would then be opened by meditation and I am assuming that the intense polarization would help in this. Is this correct?

Ra: I am Ra. This is partially correct. Intense polarization does not necessarily develop, in the mind/body/spirit complex, the will or need to contact the Oversoul. Each path of life experience is unique. However, given the polarization, the will is greatly enhanced and visa-versa.

Questioner: Let me take as an example the one that you said was called Himmler. We are assuming from this that his higher self was of the sixth-density and it was stated that Himmler had selected the negative path. Would his higher self then dwell in a sixth-density negative type of situation? Can you expand on this concept?

Ra: I am Ra. There are no negative beings which have attained the Oversoul manifestation, which is the honor/duty of the mind/body/spirit complex totality, of late sixth-density as you would term it in your time measurements. These negatively oriented mind/body/spirit complexes have a difficulty which to our knowledge has never been overcome, for after fifth-density graduation wisdom is available but must be matched with an equal amount of love. This love/light is very, very difficult to achieve in unity when following the negative path and during the earlier part of the sixth-density, society complexes of the negative orientation will choose to release the potential and leap into the sixth-density positive.

Therefore, the Oversoul which makes its understanding available to all who are ready for such aid is towards the positive. However, the free will of the individual is paramount, and any guidance given by the higher self may be seen in either the positive or negative polarity depending upon the choice of a mind/body/spirit complex.

Questioner: Then using Himmler as an example, was his higher self at the time he was incarnate in the 1940s a sixth-density positively oriented higher self?

Ra: I am Ra. This is correct.

Questioner: Was Himmler in any way in contact with his higher self at that time when he was incarnate during the 1940s?

Ra: I am Ra. We remind you that the negative path is one of separation. What is the first separation: the self from the self. The one known as Himmler did not choose to use its abilities of will and polarization to seek guidance from any source but its conscious drives, self-chosen in the life experience and nourished by previous biases created in other life experiences.

Questioner: Well then let's say that when Himmler reaches sixth-density negative, would he realize that his higher self was positively oriented and for that reason make the jump from negative to positive orientation?

Ra: I am Ra. This is incorrect. The sixth-density negative entity is extremely wise. It observes the spiritual entropy occurring due to the lack of ability to express the unity of sixth-density. Thus, loving the Creator and realizing at some point that the Creator is not only self but other-self as self, this entity consciously chooses an instantaneous energy reorientation so that it may continue its evolution.

Questioner: Then the sixth-density entity who has reached that point in positive orientation may choose to become what we call a Wanderer and move back. I am wondering if this ever occurs with a negatively oriented sixth-density entity? Do any ever move back as Wanderers?

Ra: I am Ra. Once the negatively polarized entity has reached a certain point in the wisdom density it becomes extremely unlikely that it will choose to risk the forgetting, for this polarization is not selfless but selfish and with wisdom realizes the jeopardy of such "Wandering." Occasionally a sixth-density negative becomes a Wanderer in an effort to continue to polarize towards the negative. This is extremely unusual.

Questioner: Then what is the mechanism that this unusual sixth-density entity would wish to gain to polarize more negatively through Wandering?

Ra: I am Ra. The Wanderer has the potential of greatly accelerating the density whence it comes in its progress in evolution. This is due to the intensive life experiences and opportunities of the third-density. Thusly the positively oriented Wanderer chooses to hazard the danger of the forgetting in order to be of service to others by radiating love of others. If the forgetting is penetrated the amount of catalyst in third-density will polarize the Wanderer with much greater efficiency than shall be expected in the higher and more harmonious densities.

Similarly, the negatively oriented Wanderer dares to hazard the forgetting in order that it might accelerate its progress in evolution in its own density by serving itself in third-density by offering to other-selves the opportunity to hear the information having to do with negative polarization.

Questioner: Are there any examples of sixth-density negatively polarized Wanderers in our historical past?

Ra: I am Ra. This information could be harmful. We withhold it. Please attempt to view the entities about you as part of the Creator. We can explain no further.

Questioner: It is very difficult at times for us to get more than a small percentage of under-standing of some of these concepts because of our limitation of awareness, but I think that some meditation on the information from today will help us in formulating some questions about these concepts.

Ra: I am Ra. May we ask for any brief queries before we leave this instrument?

Questioner: I'll just ask one short one before we close. Can you tell me what percentage of the Wanderers on Earth today have been successful in penetrating the memory block and have become aware of who they are, and finally, is there anything that we can do to make the instrument more comfortable or to improve the contact?

Ra: I am Ra. We can approximate the percentage of those penetrating intelligently their status. This is between eight and one-half and nine and three-quarters percent. There is a larger percentile group of those who have a fairly well defined, shall we say, symptomology indicating to them that they are not of this, shall we say, "insanity." This amounts to a bit over fifty percent of the remainder. Nearly one-third of the remainder are aware that something about them is different, so you see there are many gradations of awakening to the knowledge of being a Wanderer. We may add that it is to the middle and first of these groups that this information will, shall we say, make sense.

This instrument is well. The resting place is somewhat deleterious in its effect upon the comfort of the dorsal side of this instrument's physical vehicle. We have mentioned this before.

You are conscientious. We leave you now, my friends.

I am Ra. I leave you in the love and in the light of the infinite Creator. Go forth, then, rejoicing merrily in the power and the peace of the one Creator. Adonai.

L/L Research

L/L Research is a subsidiary of Rock Creek Research & Development Laboratories, Inc.

P.O. Box 5195
Louisville, KY 40255-0195

www.llresearch.org

Rock Creek is a non-profit corporation dedicated to discovering and sharing information which may aid in the spiritual evolution of humankind.

ABOUT THE CONTENTS OF THIS TRANSCRIPT: This telepathic channeling has been taken from transcriptions of the weekly study and meditation meetings of the Rock Creek Research & Development Laboratories and L/L Research. It is offered in the hope that it may be useful to you. As the Confederation entities always make a point of saying, please use your discrimination and judgment in assessing this material. If something rings true to you, fine. If something does not resonate, please leave it behind, for neither we nor those of the Confederation would wish to be a stumbling block for any.

© 2009 L/L RESEARCH

THE LAW OF ONE, BOOK V, SESSION 36, FRAGMENT 21
MARCH 10, 1981

Jim: Having only a faint but persistent idea that we had come to this planet in order to be of service to others was apparently a sufficient degree of the "penetrating of the forgetting process" that Don mentioned in Session 36, for we had little more than that with which to begin the Ra contact.

Any third-density entity apparently has a higher self or Oversoul which is at the mid-sixth density level of being. In addition, the Wanderer who is a member of a social memory complex also has another complex of consciousness upon which to call for assistance, for each social memory complex also seems to have the equivalent of its own Oversoul or what Ra calls a "mind/body/spirit complex totality."

Carla: *The forgetting process, or the veil, is a term used often by our sources. The basic thought is that when we take on flesh and become a manifested entity on the earth plane, that flesh shuts our metaphysical senses. All that we knew before birth is hidden in the deeper mind, and we set out on our earthly pilgrimage with only our naked selves and our heartfelt desires. It is no wonder then that Wanderers have some difficulty waking up within the illusion we call consensus reality. There is always the fear, as one enters incarnation, that one will not awaken at all, but be lost for the whole life experience. You who read this sentence are probably right in the midst of this awakening process, beginning more and more to identify with a new and larger concept of the self as an eternal and metaphysical being.*

As we all awaken and develop our truer selves, we can help each other, and I encourage each Wanderer to find ways to support fellow pilgrims of the light. People will come your way. They may not seem to be very "aware," or they may seem quite aware, but very confused or frightened. If the Creator put them in your way, then you are well equipped to aid them. Simply love and accept them.

This is much harder to do than to say. It involves first coming to love and accept yourself, forgiving yourself for the myriad imperfections and folly you find when gazing within. But all work is upon the self, speaking metaphysically. If you have trouble loving someone, look within for the place within self where you have rejected part of yourself, some slice of the dark side you'd rather not see or experience. As you work with this loving, accepting and forgiving of the dark side of self, you are working on service to all the other selves coming your way. I think the key to this acceptance of self is to see that to be in flesh is to be very imperfect and confused. There is no way to be without error when in the context of the world. Yet within us there is that self without the veil, with perfect memory of who we are and what we came to do. Once one is able to face one's wretched side, one becomes much more able to be transparent to that infinite love that comes not from us but through us, to bless all.

In this practice of loving, we have a wonderful source of strength and courage: the higher self. I call this self the Holy Spirit, because I am of the distortion called mystical Christianity. Other people refer to this higher self as inner guides, angelic beings, the higher nature, or simply Guidance. Whatever the term, this energy is quite dependable, always there, supporting and sustaining. One can practice becoming more aware of this energy, consciously opening to it within meditation, and calling upon it in times of challenge. I encourage each to see the self as an awakening being, with much support from the unseen forces. Lean into these sources of strength in silence and prayer. They will truly aid you.

Session 36, March 10, 1981

Questioner: I was wondering if qualification for contact with Ra might include penetrating this forgetting process? Is this correct?

Ra: I am Ra. This is quite correct.

Questioner: Otherwise the Law of Confusion would prohibit this? Is this correct?

Ra: This is correct.

Questioner: I was also wondering if three was the minimum number necessary for this type of working? Is this correct?

Ra: I am Ra. For protection of this instrument this is necessary as the minimum grouping and also as the most efficient number due to the exceptional harmony in this group. In other groups the number could be larger, but we have observed in this contact that the most efficient support is given by the individual mind/body/spirits present at this time.

Questioner: I'm a little fuzzy on a point with respect to the higher self. We each, I am assuming, have an individual higher self at sixth-density positive level. Is this correct? Each of us in the room here; that is, the three of us?

Ra: I am Ra. This shall be the last full question of this working. We shall attempt to aim for the intention of your query as we understand it. Please request any additional information.

Firstly, it is correct that each in this dwelling place has one Oversoul, as you may call it. However, due to the repeated harmonious interactions of this triad of entities there may be seen to be a further harmonious interaction besides the three entities' Higher Selves; that is, each social memory complex has an Oversoul of a type which is difficult to describe to you in words. In this group there are two such social memory complex totalities blending their efforts with your Higher Selves at this time. ♣

L/L Research

The Law of One, Book II, Session 37
March 12, 1981

Ra: I am Ra. I greet you in the love and in the light of the one infinite Creator. We communicate now.

Questioner: You said that each third-density entity has an higher self in the sixth-density which is moving to the mind/body/spirit complex of the entity as needed. Does this higher self also evolve in growth through the densities beginning with the first-density, and does each higher self have a corresponding higher self advanced in densities beyond it?

Ra: I am Ra. To simplify this concept is our intent. The higher self is a manifestation given to the late sixth-density mind/body/spirit complex as a gift from its future selfness. The mid-seventh density's last action before turning towards the allness of the Creator and gaining spiritual mass is to give this resource to the sixth-density self, moving as you measure time in the stream of time.

This self, the mind/body/spirit complex of late sixth-density, has then the honor/duty of using both the experiences of its total living bank of memory of experience, thoughts, and actions, and using the resource of the mind/body/spirit complex totality left behind as a type of infinitely complex thought-form.

In this way you may see your self, your higher self or Oversoul, and your mind/body/spirit complex totality as three points in a circle. The only distinction is that of your time/space continuum. All are the same being.

Questioner: Does each entity have an individual mind/body/spirit complex totality or do a number of entities share the same mind/body/spirit complex totality?

Ra: I am Ra. Both of these statements are correct given the appropriate time/space conditions. Each entity has its totality and at the point at which a planetary entity becomes a social memory complex the totality of this union of entities also has its Oversoul and its social memory complex totality as resource. As always, the sum, spiritually speaking, is greater than the sum of its parts so that the Oversoul of a social memory complex is not the sum of the Oversouls of its member entities but operates upon the way of what we have called squares and what we grasp you prefer to call doubling.

Questioner: Thank you. And thank you for that explanation of the mathematics too. Could you define spiritual mass?

Ra: I am Ra. This will be the last full question of this session.

Spiritual mass is that which begins to attract the out-moving and on-going vibratory oscillations of being-ness into the gravity, speaking in a spiritual sense, well of the great central sun, core, or Creator of the infinite universes.

Questioner: Since we don't want to tire the instrument I will just ask if there is anything that we can do to make the instrument more comfortable or to improve the contact?

Ra: I am Ra. All is well. We leave you now in the love and the light of the one infinite Creator. Go forth, then, rejoicing in the power and the peace of the one infinite Creator. Adonai.

L/L Research

L/L Research is a subsidiary of Rock Creek Research & Development Laboratories, Inc.

P.O. Box 5195
Louisville, KY 40255-0195

www.llresearch.org

Rock Creek is a non-profit corporation dedicated to discovering and sharing information which may aid in the spiritual evolution of humankind.

ABOUT THE CONTENTS OF THIS TRANSCRIPT: This telepathic channeling has been taken from transcriptions of the weekly study and meditation meetings of the Rock Creek Research & Development Laboratories and L/L Research. It is offered in the hope that it may be useful to you. As the Confederation entities always make a point of saying, please use your discrimination and judgment in assessing this material. If something rings true to you, fine. If something does not resonate, please leave it behind, for neither we nor those of the Confederation would wish to be a stumbling block for any.

© 2009 L/L Research

The Law of One, Book V, Session 37, Fragment 22
March 12, 1981

Jim: In March of 1981 we sent off the first ten sessions of the Ra contact to the Scott Meredith Literary Agency in New York City. We wanted to get the information out to as many people as we could, and we thought that a large literary agency could help us find a publisher. After considering the manuscript for about two weeks Mr. Meredith was kind enough to write us a four-page, single-spaced letter thanking us for sending him the material and telling us why it had no chance in the marketplace. The heart of the letter may be summarized by the following quote:

"No entity that wreaks such havoc with the English language is going to ingratiate himself with the general reading public. This has all the denseness of *The New England Journal Of Medicine*, or the *Journal Of English And German Philosophy* or a Ph.D. dissertation on epistemology … and for another thing, the dialogue form gets pretty tedious after a while. It was all the rage in Athens for a while, I know, and its popularity continued all the way through the neoclassic renaissance, but it died out shortly afterwards, and I don't think that it's about to be revived."

Ra's final comment on the topic of how to make the information available brought a somewhat humorous end to our earnestness. A few days earlier we had been sitting around the kitchen table wondering aloud what cosmic humor might be like, and Ra took this opportunity to give us an illustration. We would give the same basic advice to any group trying to disseminate information that it has collected so that it might be of service to others. Relax, and let the Law of Attraction work. Even if only one person is aided by the work, that is enough. At the very least, the benefit that the material provides to the group alone will become like unto a light which each in the group will radiate to all others met in the daily round of activities.

And, since we had discovered for ourselves the necessity of pursuing non-transient information, Ra clearly states that was a requirement for maintaining the contact in contrast to Don's estimate of the kind of information that usually attracts the attention of the marketplace.

Carla: It was always a hope of Don's that we would be able to communicate to a large number of people. He felt a real urgency at getting the word out, and as the contact with Ra persisted, his concern deepened. It was like a breath of fresh air to find Ra counseling us to be content with our "reasonable effort." As we write these comments, the first book of The Law Of One *series has sold about 30,000 copies. Our mail this week included queries from Poland, Romania, Malaysia and Japan, as well as the USA and Canada. I am sure that a little part of Don is sitting on my shoulder like the angel he is, content at last with his life's work and seeing it taken up by those who find it useful.*

The concept of sacrifice as part of the beginning of contact is not new at all. The channel for Oahspe *was told in a vision that he must live austerely for ten years before he could be of help, and he and a friend did just that, living monastically, waiting for the time of opportunity. When his decade of sacrifice was through, he was told to get a typewriter, new at the time. He did so. Over the next few years, he channeled the huge book, being put at the typewriter while he was asleep at night. He would awaken each morning to find his work lying by the machine. And Edgar Cayce had similar experiences with being told he needed to sacrifice in order to serve. In our case, Jim sacrificed his love of isolation and retreat from humankind, Don sacrificed his solitude with me, that happy and safe harbor we had made together. He let Jim into the very fabric of our lives, with never the first word of complaint. He also sacrificed himself by working in order to support us. I had the easiest sacrifice, that of myself as channel. The contact was hard on me, and I wasted away under the brilliant energy of Ra's vibration, losing two to three pounds per session. But I would gladly have died in this service, for during these sessions, Don was a happy man. This was the only time during which I knew him that he was not melancholy in his quiet way. To see him fulfilled and content was one of the greatest sources of pleasure in my whole life, for I knew that I'd been a part of that. It was worth everything, and I'd do it all again in a heartbeat, even the extremities of grief which we all felt as Donald sickened and perished, and I came closer and closer to death through the years following Don's suicide. My part of sacrifice has been turned into joy and satisfaction, and I know Don and Jim feel the same.*

That reviewer at the agency was quite right to view the language of Ra as technical. It represents the most balanced attempt I have ever read at creating a vocabulary for talking about metaphysical issues with neutral emotional words. It may be stilted at first read, but one always knows what Ra is trying to say, a real achievement in such subjects.

Session 37, March 12, 1981

Questioner: Is Ra familiar with the results of our efforts today to publish the first book that we did?

Ra: I am Ra. This is correct.

Questioner: I don't know if you can comment on the difficulty that we will have in making the Law of One available to those who would require it and want it. It is not something that is easy to disseminate to those who want it at this time. I am sure that there are many, especially the Wanderers, who want this information, but we will have to do something else in order to get it into their hands in the way of added material, I am afraid. Is it possible for you to comment on this?

Ra: I am Ra. It is possible.

Questioner: Will you comment on it?

Ra: I am Ra. We shall. Firstly, the choosing of this group to do some work to serve others was of an intensive nature. Each present sacrificed much for no tangible result. Each may search its heart for the type of sacrifice, knowing that the material sacrifices are the least; the intensive commitment to blending into an harmonious group at the apex of sacrifice. Under these conditions we found your vibration. We observed your vibration. It will not be seen often. We do not wish to puff up the pride, but we shall not chaffer with the circumstances necessary for our particular contact. Thus you have received and we willingly undertake the honor/duty of continuing to offer transmissions of concepts which are, to the best of our abilities, precise in nature and grounded in the attempt to unify many of those things that concern you.

Secondly, the use you make of these transmissions is completely at your discretion. We suggest the flowing of the natural intuitive senses and a minimum of the distortion towards concern. We are content, as we have said, to be able to aid in the evolution of one of your peoples. Whatever effort you make cannot disappoint us, for that number already exceeds one.

Questioner: I have been very hesitant to ask certain questions for fear that they would be regarded, as I regard them, as questions of unimportance or of too great a specificity and thereby reduce our contact with you. In order to disseminate some of the information that I consider to be of great importance; that is, the non-transient type of information, information having to do with the evolution of mind, body, and spirit, it seems almost necessary in our society to include information that is of little value simply because that is how our society works, how the system of distribution appraises that which is offered for distribution. Will you comment on this problem that I have?

Ra: I am Ra. We comment as follows: It is quite precisely correct that the level and purity of this contact is dependent upon the level and purity of information sought. Thusly, the continued request for specific information from this particular source is deleterious to the substance of your purpose. Moreover, as we scanned your mind to grasp your situation as regards the typescript of some of our words, we found that you had been criticized for the type of language construction used to convey data. Due to our orientation with regard to data, even the most specifically answered question would be worded by our group in such a way as to maximize the accuracy of the nuances of the answer. This, however, mitigates against what your critic desires in the way of simple, lucid prose. More than this we cannot say. These are our observations of your situation. What you wish to do is completely your decision and we remain at your service in whatever way we may be without breaking the Way of Confusion.

Questioner: We will attempt to work around these problems in the dissemination of the Law of One. It will take some careful work to do this. I personally will not cease while still incarnate to disseminate this. It will be necessary to write a book, probably about UFOs because the Law of One is connected with the phenomenon. It's connected with all phenomena, but this seems to be the easiest entry for dissemination. I plan firstly to use the UFO in the advertising sense as it was meant by the Confederation as an entry into an explanation of the process of evolution that is going on on this planet and how the rest of the Confederation has been involved in a more understandable way, shall I say, for the population that will read the book. We will use the Ra material in undistorted form just as it has been recorded here in various places throughout the book to amplify and clarify what we are saying in the book. This is the only way that I can see right now to create enough dissemination for the people who would like to have the Law of One for them to be able to get it. I could just print up the material that we have off of the tape recorder and publish it but we wouldn't be able to disseminate it very well because of distribution problems. Will you comment on my second idea of doing a general book on UFOs including the material from the Law of One?

Ra: I am Ra. We shall comment. We hope that your Ra plans materialize. This is a cosmic joke. You were asking for such an example of humor and we feel this is a rather appropriate nexus in which one may be inserted. Continue with your intentions to the best of your natures and abilities. What more can be done, my friends?

L/L Research

L/L Research is a subsidiary of Rock Creek Research & Development Laboratories, Inc.

P.O. Box 5195
Louisville, KY 40255-0195

www.llresearch.org

Rock Creek is a non-profit corporation dedicated to discovering and sharing information which may aid in the spiritual evolution of humankind.

ABOUT THE CONTENTS OF THIS TRANSCRIPT: This telepathic channeling has been taken from transcriptions of the weekly study and meditation meetings of the Rock Creek Research & Development Laboratories and L/L Research. It is offered in the hope that it may be useful to you. As the Confederation entities always make a point of saying, please use your discrimination and judgment in assessing this material. If something rings true to you, fine. If something does not resonate, please leave it behind, for neither we nor those of the Confederation would wish to be a stumbling block for any.

© 2009 L/L RESEARCH

THE LAW OF ONE, BOOK II, SESSION 38
MARCH 13, 1981

Ra: I am Ra. I greet you in the love and in the light of the one infinite Creator. We communicate now.

Questioner: Backtracking just a little bit today I would like to know if the reason nuclear energy was brought into this density forty or so years ago had anything to do with giving the entities who were here who had caused the destruction of Maldek another chance to use nuclear energy peacefully rather than destructively?

Ra: I am Ra. This is incorrect in that it places cart before horse, as your people say. The desire for this type of information attracted this data to your people. It was not given for a reason from outside influences; rather it was desired by your peoples. From this point forward your reasoning is correct in that entities had desired the second chance which you mentioned.

Questioner: What was the mechanism for fulfilling the desire for the information regarding nuclear energy?

Ra: I am Ra. As we understand your query the mechanism was what you may call inspiration.

Questioner: Would this inspiration be an entity impressing the person desiring the information with thoughts? Would this be the mechanism of inspiration?

Ra: I am Ra. The mechanism of inspiration involves an extraordinary faculty of desire or will to know or to receive in a certain area accompanied by the ability to open to and trust in what you may call intuition.

Questioner: Could you tell me how each of the rays, red through violet, would appear in a perfectly balanced and undistorted entity?

Ra: I am Ra. We cannot tell you this for each balance is perfect and each unique. We do not mean to be obscure.

Let us offer an example. In a particular entity, let us use as an example a Wanderer; the rays may be viewed as extremely even, red, orange, yellow. The green ray is extremely bright. This is, shall we say, balanced by a dimmer indigo. Between these two the point of balance resides, the blue ray of the communicator sparkling in strength above the ordinary. In the violet ray we see this unique spectrograph, if you will, and at the same time the pure violet surrounding the whole; this in turn, surrounded by that which mixes the red and violet ray, indicating the integration of mind, body, and spirit; this surrounded in turn by the vibratory pattern of this entity's true density.

This description may be seen to be both unbalanced and in perfect balance. The latter understanding is extremely helpful in dealing with other-selves. The ability to feel blockages is useful only to the healer. There is not properly a tiny fraction of judgment when viewing a balance in colors. Of course when we see many of the energy plexi weakened and blocked, we may understand that an entity has not yet grasped the baton and begun the race. However, the potentials are always there. All the rays fully balanced are there in waiting to be activated.

Perhaps another way to address your query is this: In the fully potentiated entity the rays mount one upon the other with equal vibratory brilliance and scintillating sheen until the surrounding color is white. This is what you may call potentiated balance in third-density.

Questioner: Is it possible for a third-density planet to form a social memory complex which operates in third-density?

Ra: I am Ra. It is possible only in the latter or seventh portion of such a density when entities are harmoniously readying for graduation.

Questioner: Could you give me an example of a planet of this nature, both a third-density service-to-others type and a third-density service-to-self type at this level of attainment?

Ra: I am Ra. As far as we are aware there are no negatively oriented third-density social memory complexes. Positively oriented social memory complexes of third-density are not unheard of but quite rare. However, an entity from the star Sirius' planetary body has approached this planetary body twice. This entity is late third-density and is part of a third-density social memory complex. This has been referred to in the previous material. The social memory complex is properly a fourth-density phenomenon.

Questioner: I was wondering if that particular social memory complex from the Sirius star evolved from trees?

Ra: I am Ra. This approaches correctness. Those second-density vegetation forms which graduated into third-density upon this planet bearing the name of Dog were close to the tree as you know it.

Questioner: I was also wondering, since action of a bellicose nature is impossible as far as I understand vegetation, would they not have the advantage as they move into third-density from second to not carry a racial memory of a bellicose nature and therefore develop a more harmonious society and accelerate their evolution in this nature?

Ra: I am Ra. This is correct. However, to become balanced and begin to polarize properly it is then necessary to investigate movements of all kinds, especially bellicosity.

Questioner: I am assuming, then, that their investigations of bellicosity were primarily of the type that they extracted from Hixson's memory rather than warfare among themselves?

Ra: I am Ra. This is correct. Entities of this heritage would find it nearly impossible to fight. Indeed, their studies of movements of all kinds is their form of meditation due to the fact that their activity is upon the level of what you would call meditation and thus must be balanced, just as your entities need constant moments of meditation to balance your activities.

Questioner: I believe that this is an important point for us in understanding the balancing aspect of meditation since we have here its antithesis in another type of evolution. These entities moved, we are told by Charlie Hixson, without moving their legs. I am assuming that they used a principle that is somewhat similar to the principle of movement of your crystal bells in the movement of their physical vehicles. Is this correct?

Ra: I am Ra. This is partially incorrect.

Questioner: I am assuming that their method of movement is not a function of mechanical leverage such as ours, but a direct function of the mind somehow connected with the magnetic action of a planet. Is this right?

Ra: I am Ra. This is largely correct. It is an electromagnetic phenomenon which is controlled by thought impulses of a weak electrical nature.

Questioner: Would their craft have been visible to anyone on our planet in that area at that time? Is it of a third-density material like this chair?

Ra: I am Ra. This is correct. Please ask one more full question before we close as this instrument has low vital energy at this space/time.

Questioner: Could you give me some idea of what conditions are like on a fourth-density negative or service to self planet?

Ra: I am Ra. The graduation into fourth-density negative is achieved by those beings who have consciously contacted intelligent infinity through the use of red, orange, and yellow rays of energy. Therefore, the planetary conditions of fourth-density negative include the constant alignment and realignment of entities in efforts to form dominant patterns of combined energy.

The early fourth-density is one of the most intensive struggle. When the order of authority has been established and all have fought until convinced that each is in the proper placement for power structure, the social memory complex begins. Always the fourth-density effect of telepathy and the transparency of thought are attempted to be used for the sake of those at the apex of the power structure.

This, as you may see, is often quite damaging to the further polarization of fourth-density negative entities, for the further negative polarization can come about only through group effort. As the fourth-density entities manage to combine, they then polarize through such services to self as those offered by the crusaders of Orion.

You may ask more specific questions in the next session of working. Are there any brief queries before we leave this instrument?

Questioner: I would just ask if there is anything that we can do to make the instrument more comfortable or to improve the contact?

Ra: I am Ra. All is well. We leave you in the love and light of the one infinite Creator. Go forth rejoicing in the power and in the peace of the one Creator. Adonai.

L/L Research is a subsidiary of
Rock Creek Research &
Development Laboratories, Inc.

P.O. Box 5195
Louisville, KY 40255-0195

L/L Research

www.llresearch.org

Rock Creek is a non-profit
corporation dedicated to
discovering and sharing
information which may aid in
the spiritual evolution of
humankind.

ABOUT THE CONTENTS OF THIS TRANSCRIPT: This telepathic channeling has been taken from transcriptions of the weekly study and meditation meetings of the Rock Creek Research & Development Laboratories and L/L Research. It is offered in the hope that it may be useful to you. As the Confederation entities always make a point of saying, please use your discrimination and judgment in assessing this material. If something rings true to you, fine. If something does not resonate, please leave it behind, for neither we nor those of the Confederation would wish to be a stumbling block for any.

© 2009 L/L RESEARCH

THE LAW OF ONE, BOOK V, SESSION 38, FRAGMENT 23
MARCH 13, 1981

Jim: Serving as the instrument for the Ra contact was very wearing on Carla. She would lose between two and three pounds per session, and the psychic greeting component of the contact often intensified her arthritic distortions to the point that her functioning on all levels was severely curtailed. Thus Don and I had hoped that one or the other of us could take her place from time to time in order to give her rest, but neither of us was properly prepared for this service. So rest was obtained by spacing the sessions out over a greater period of time, and we all contented ourselves with the fact that there was a price to be paid for being able to offer this kind of service, and Carla would have to bear the brunt of that price.

Carla: *I cannot express the amount of pleasure I felt at being able to serve in this way. To see Donald happy and inspired was a satisfaction of the heart that struck to the depths of my being. I adored Don, and wished to make him comfortable and happy. But he was not comfortable in this world, and so often felt painfully lonely and isolated, although this was never mentioned, nor did he show it in any way. For some reason, his pain and loneliness were always utterly apparent to me, and called forth my deepest sympathy and desire to nurture. The days of the Ra contact were golden indeed. I would have died quite gladly doing one last session, and rather expected to, and embraced that freely, but Don's death came first. So I remain! The years since his death have opened to me a wonderful path of service, as readers write in, and I have become counselor and friend to so many all over the world. It is as though I received a second life, for truly when Donald died, the Carla that was, was gone. He had taken a 25-year-old and molded her to his needs, with my willing aid. I became truly his creature. When I woke up from that life, 16 years later, I was neither that 25-year-old nor Don's. I really had to start from scratch to discover my current self.*

Session 38, March 13, 1981

Questioner: Will you tell us if there would be any hope or any purpose in either Jim or me taking the instrument's place as instrument by attempting the trance work ourselves?

Ra: I am Ra. This information is on the borderline of infringement upon free will. We shall, however, assume your desire to constitute permission to speak slightly beyond limits set by Confederation guidelines, shall we say.

At this space/time nexus neither the one known as Don nor the one known as Jim is available for this working. The one known as Don, by, shall we say, practicing the mechanics of contact and service to others by means of the channeling, as you call it, would in a certain length of your time become able to do this working. The one known as Jim would find it difficult to become a channel of this type without more practice also over a longer period of time. Then we should have to experiment with the harmonics developed by this practice. This is true in both cases. ☥

The Law of One, Book II, Session 39
March 16, 1981

Ra: I am Ra. I greet you in the love and in the light of the one infinite Creator. We communicate now.

Questioner: I noticed that most of the basic things seemed to be divided into units which total seven. In looking at a transcript by Henry Puharich of "The Nine" I found a statement by The Nine where they say, "If we get seven times the electrical equivalent of the human body then it would result in sevenon of the mass of electricity." Could you explain this?

Ra: I am Ra. To explain this is beyond the abilities of your language. We shall, however, make an attempt to address this concept.

As you are aware, in the beginning of the creations set up by each Logos, there are created the complete potentials, both electrical, in the sense the one you call Larson intends, and metaphysical. This metaphysical electricity is as important in the understanding, shall we say, of this statement as is the concept of electricity.

This concept, as you are aware, deals with potentiated energy. The electron has been said to have no mass but only a field. Others claim a mass of infinitesimal measure. Both are correct. The true mass of the potentiated energy is the strength of the field. This is also true metaphysically.

However, in your present physical system of knowledge it is useful to take the mass number of the electron in order to do work that you may find solutions to other questions about the physical universe. In such a way, you may conveniently consider each density of being to have a greater and greater spiritual mass. The mass increases, shall we say, significantly but not greatly until the gateway density. In this density the summing up, the looking backwards—in short—all the useful functions of polarity have been used. Therefore, the metaphysical electrical nature of the individual grows greater and greater in spiritual mass.

For an analog one may observe the work of the one known as Albert who posits the growing to infinity of mass as this mass approaches the speed of light. Thus the seventh-density being, the completed being, the Creator who knows Itself, accumulates mass and compacts into the one Creator once again.

Questioner: Then in the equation here I am assuming Mi is spiritual mass.

$$M_i = (m_0 C^2)/(1 - v^2 / c^2)^{\frac{1}{2}}$$

Ra: I am Ra. This is correct.

Questioner: Thank you. Can you tell me what this transmission from "The Nine" means. "CH is a principle which is the revealing principle of knowledge and of law"? Can you tell me what that principle is?

Ra: I am Ra. The principle so veiled in that statement is but the simple principle of the constant or Creator and the transient or the incarnate being and the yearning existing between the two, one for the other, in love and light amidst the distortions of free will acting upon the illusion-bound entity.

Questioner: Was the reason "The Nine" transmitted this principle in this form the first distortion?

Ra: I am Ra. This is incorrect.

Questioner: Can you tell me why they gave the principle in such a veiled form then?

Ra: I am Ra. The scribe is most interested in puzzles and equations.

Questioner: I see. "The Nine" describe themselves as the "nine principles of God." Can you tell me what they mean by that?

Ra: I am Ra. This is also a veiled statement. The attempt is made to indicate that the nine who sit upon the Council are those representing the Creator, the one Creator, just as there may be nine witnesses in a courtroom testifying for one defendant. The term principle has this meaning also.

The desire of the scribe may be seen in much of this material to have affected the manner of its presentation just as the abilities and preferences of this group determine the nature of this contact. The difference lies in the fact that we are as we are. Thus we may either speak as we will or not speak at all. This demands a very tuned, shall we say, group.

Questioner: I sense that there is fruitful ground for investigation of our development in tracing the evolution of the bodily energy centers because these seven centers seem to be linked with all of the sevens that I spoke of previously, and these seem to be central to our own development. Could you describe the process of evolution of these bodily energy centers starting with the most primitive form of life to have them?

Ra: I am Ra. This material has been covered previously to some extent. Therefore, we shall not repeat information upon which rays dwell in first and second density and the wherefores of this, but rather attempt to enlarge upon this information.

The basic pivotal points of each level of development; that is, each density beyond second, may be seen to be as follows: Firstly, the basic energy of so-called red ray. This ray may be understood to be the basic strengthening ray for each density. It shall never be condescended to as less important or productive of spiritual evolution, for it is the foundation ray.

The next foundation ray is yellow. This is the great steppingstone ray. At this ray the mind/body potentiates to its fullest balance. The strong red/orange/yellow triad springboards the entity into the center ray of green. This is again a basic ray but not a primary ray.

This is the resource for spiritual work. When green ray has been activated we find the third primary ray being able to begin potentiation. This is the first true spiritual ray in that all transfers are of an integrated mind/body/spirit nature. The blue ray seats the learnings/teachings of the spirit in each density within the mind/body complex animating the whole, communicating to others this entirety of being-ness.

The indigo ray, though precious, is that ray worked upon only by the adept, as you would call it. It is the gateway to intelligent infinity bringing intelligent energy through. This is the energy center worked upon in those teachings considered inner, hidden, and occult, for this ray is that which is infinite in its possibilities. As you are aware, those who heal, teach, and work for the Creator in any way which may be seen to be both radiant and balanced are those activities which are indigo ray.

As you are aware, the violet ray is constant and does not figure into a discussion of the functions of ray activation in that it is the mark, the register, the identity, the true vibration of an entity.

Questioner: In order to clarify a little bit I would like to ask this question: If we have a highly polarized entity polarized towards service to others and a highly polarized entity polarized towards service to self, what would be the difference in the red ray of these two entities?

Ra: I am Ra. This shall be the last full question of this working.

There is no difference in equally strongly polarized positive and negative entities as regards red ray.

Questioner: Is this also true of all of the other rays?

Ra: I am Ra. We shall answer briefly. You may question further at another working.

The negative ray pattern is the red/orange/yellow moving directly to the blue, this only being used in order to contact intelligent infinity.

In positively oriented entities the configuration is even, crystallinely clear, and of the seven ray description.

Are there any short queries before we leave this instrument?

Questioner: I would just ask if there is anything that we can do to make the instrument more comfortable and to improve the contact?

Ra: I am Ra. You are most conscientious. All is well. I leave you, my friends, in the love and in the light of the one infinite Creator. Go forth therefore rejoicing in the power and in the peace of the one Creator. Adonai.

L/L Research

The Law of One, Book V, Session 39, Fragment 24
March 16, 1981

Jim: The difficulties in recovering physical energy which Carla experienced as a result of the two experiences with LSD continued to shorten sessions and keep her condition somewhat fragile. We again saw not only the powerful effects of this chemical agent—which we do not recommend to anyone—but the even more powerful effects of unwise choices made by those who wish above all else to be of service to others. As time and experience with the Ra contact accumulated we became increasingly aware that the honor of providing this kind of service brought with it the need for just as much responsibility for providing the service with as much purity and harmony as one was capable of producing in every facet of the life experience. What was learned needed to be put to use in the daily life, or difficulties would result in the life pattern which were the means by which the subconscious mind would provide the opportunity to regain the balance and harmony which had been lost. These difficulties could then also be intensified by Orion crusaders in the form of psychic greetings designed to stop the contact with Ra.

We also discovered that every person which incarnates brings with him or her certain avenues, preferences, or ways of nurturing its inner beingness. This inner beingness is that which is the true enabler and ennobler of our daily lives. When we would ask Ra how best to aid the instrument we would often get more specific suggestions according to the situation, but we would always be reminded of those qualities which were Carla's ways of nurturing her inner beingness.

Carla: Data from the Ra contact indicates that I never had much actual physical energy at all, which fits with my own personal, subjective sense of myself as one who runs on spiritual and mental energy, and as one physically lazy. I call it laziness because I have such a hard time making myself do physical work, unless it is walking and wandering, dancing or swimming, rhythmic activities I love. Even as a young child I was easily able to sit and read, or sit and imagine, for hours. So the sessions we were doing completely exhausted my actual innate physical energy quite quickly. To this very day, I think since then I have always run on nerve alone, and the simple joy of being alive, which I have in abundance.

Don and Jim both were very upright persons of marked integrity and character, which helped tremendously as the process of psychic greeting could only work on our inherent distortions. They loved each other and treated each other with great respect, and did their utmost to care for me. They were wonderful in making sure that all was done as well as possible to make me more comfortable. I also had the advantage of being a straight-arrow kind of soul all my life. So the negative energy could only intensify my many physical "problems." Thusly the sessions were extremely wearing, but I gloried in them nevertheless, for seeing Don's pleasure in the talks with Ra was more than enough payment to me. I was and am careless of life force if by giving it I can see another live more fully.

I should note that I see the purity that Ra speaks of in myself not as a shining virtue, nor as a personal achievement, but rather as a gift of nature. I cannot remember a time when I was other than completely involved in the passion of my life: that life itself. I saw myself as a child of God, and wanted my life to be a gift to that deity. I was drawn to virtue as others are to gambling or drugs. This inexplicable condition still prevails—my hopes for this life remain simply the giving of all I have to the Creator. What this purity is not, is celibacy or retreat from the workings of the world. I have always followed my relationships and based my life around them, trusted my passion, and had an earthy, even vulgar side. I simply find life a wonder and a joy, and all the limitation, mess, loss and pain in this world have not changed my mind on that.

Session 39, March 16, 1981

Questioner: The instrument was wondering if the fragile feeling she has now is the result of the chemical ingestion of about six weeks ago?

Ra: I am Ra. This is correct. This instrument is now undergoing the most intensive period of physical complex debilitation/distortion due to the doubling effects of the two ingestions. This instrument may expect this extremity to proceed for a period of fifteen to twenty of your diurnal cycles. The weakness distortions will then begin to lift, however, not as rapidly as we first thought due to this instrument's weakness distortions. This instrument is very fortunate in having a support group which impresses upon it the caution necessary as regards these sessions at this time. This instrument is capable of almost instantaneously clearing the mental/emotional complex and the spiritual complex for the purity this working requires, but this instrument's distortion towards fidelity to service does not function to its best use of judgment regarding the weakness distortions of the physical complex. Thus we appreciate your assistance at space/times such as that in your most recent decision-making not to have a working. This was the appropriate decision and the guidance given this instrument was helpful.

Questioner: Is there anything that the instrument can do in addition to what she is attempting to do to help her condition get better faster? I know that she hasn't been able to exercise because of her foot problem for the last couple of days, but we are hoping to get back to that. Is there anything else that she could do?

Ra: I am Ra. As we have implied, the negative entities are moving all stops out to undermine this instrument at this time. This is the cause of the aforementioned problem with the pedal digit. It is fortunate that this instrument shall be greatly involved in the worship of the one infinite Creator through the vibratory complexes of sacred song during this period. The more active physical existence, both in the movements of exercise and in the sexual sense, are helpful. However the requirement of this instrument's distortions toward what you would call ethics have an effect upon this latter activity. Again, it is fortunate that this instrument has the opportunities for loving social intercourse which are of some substantial benefit. Basically, in your third density continuum, this is a matter of time.

Questioner: From your reading of the instrument's condition can you approximate how often and the length of workings we should plan on in future workings?

Ra: I am Ra. This query borders upon infringement. The information given sets up fairly followable guidelines. However, we are aware that not only can each of you not read this instrument's aura and so see conditions of the physical complex but also the instrument itself has considerable difficulty penetrating the precise distortion condition of its physical complex due to its constant dependence upon its will to serve. Therefore, we believe we are not infringing if we indicate that one working each alternate diurnal period in the matinal hours is most appropriate with the possibility of a shorter working upon the free matinal period if deemed appropriate. This is so not only during this period but in general. ♣

L/L Research is a subsidiary of Rock Creek Research & Development Laboratories, Inc.

P.O. Box 5195
Louisville, KY 40255-0195

L/L Research

www.llresearch.org

Rock Creek is a non-profit corporation dedicated to discovering and sharing information which may aid in the spiritual evolution of humankind.

ABOUT THE CONTENTS OF THIS TRANSCRIPT: This telepathic channeling has been taken from transcriptions of the weekly study and meditation meetings of the Rock Creek Research & Development Laboratories and L/L Research. It is offered in the hope that it may be useful to you. As the Confederation entities always make a point of saying, please use your discrimination and judgment in assessing this material. If something rings true to you, fine. If something does not resonate, please leave it behind, for neither we nor those of the Confederation would wish to be a stumbling block for any.

© 2009 L/L RESEARCH

THE LAW OF ONE, BOOK II, SESSION 40
MARCH 18, 1981

Ra: I am Ra. I greet you in the love and in the light of the infinite Creator. We communicate now.

Questioner: I thought that I would make a statement and let you correct it. I'm trying to make a simple model of the portion of the universe that we find ourselves in. Starting with the sub-Logos, our sun, we have white light emanating from this which is made up of the frequencies ranging from the red to the violet. I am assuming that this white light then contains the experiences through all of the densities and as we go into the eighth density we go into a black hole which becomes, on the other side, another Logos or sun and starts another octave of experience. Can you comment on this part of my statement?

Ra: I am Ra. We can comment upon this statement to an extent. The concept of the white light of the sub-Logos being prismatically separated and later, at the final chapter, being absorbed again is basically correct. However, there are subtleties involved which are more than semantic.

The white light which emanates and forms the articulated sub-Logos has its beginning in what may be metaphysically seen as darkness. The light comes into that darkness and transfigures it, causing the chaos to organize and become reflective or radiant. Thus the dimensions come into being.

Conversely, the blackness of the black hole, metaphysically speaking, is a concentration of white light being systematically absorbed once again into the one Creator. Finally, this absorption into the one Creator continues until all the infinity of creations have attained sufficient spiritual mass in order that all form once again the great central sun, if you would so imagine it, of the intelligent infinity awaiting potentiation by free will. Thus the transition of the octave is a process which may be seen to enter into timelessness of unimaginable nature. To attempt to measure it by your time measures would be useless.

Therefore, the concept of moving through the black hole of the ultimate spiritual gravity well and coming immediately into the next octave misses the subconcept or corollary of the portion of this process which is timeless.

Questioner: Our astronomers have noticed that light from spiral galaxies is approximately seventy times less than it should be, considering the calculated mass of the galaxy. I was wondering if that was due to the increase of spiritual mass in the galaxy in what we call white dwarf stars?

Ra: I am Ra. This is basically correct and is a portion of the way or process of creation's cycle.

Questioner: Thank you. I was also wondering if the first-density corresponded somehow to the color red, the second to the color orange, the third to the color yellow and so on through the densities corresponding to the colors in perhaps a way so that the basic vibration which forms the photon that forms the core of all atomic particles would have a

© 2009 L/L RESEARCH

367

relationship to the color in the density and that that vibration would step up for second, third, and fourth-density corresponding to the increase in the vibration of the colors. Is any of this correct?

Ra: I am Ra. This is more correct than you have stated. Firstly, you are correct in positing a quantum, if you will, as the nature of each density and further correct in assuming that these quanta may be seen to be of vibratory natures corresponding to color as you grasp this word. However, it is also true, as you have suspected but not asked, that each density is of the metaphysical characteristic complex of its ray. Thus in first-density the red ray is the foundation for all that is to come. In second density the orange ray is that of movement and growth of the individual, this ray striving towards the yellow ray of self-conscious manifestations of a social nature as well as individual; third-density being the equivalent, and so forth, each density being primarily its ray plus the attractions of the following ray pulling it forward in evolution and to some extent coloring or shading the chief color of that density.

Questioner: Then bodily energy centers for an individual, assuming that the individual evolves in a straight line from first through to eighth density, would then be activated to completion if everything worked as it should? Would each chakra be activated to completion and greatest intensity by the end of the experience in each density?

Ra: I am Ra. Hypothetically speaking, this is correct. However, the fully activated being is rare. Much emphasis is laid upon the harmonies and balances of individuals. It is necessary for graduation across densities for the primary energy centers to be functioning in such a way as to communicate with intelligent infinity and to appreciate and bask in this light in all of its purity. However, to fully activate each energy center is the mastery of few, for each center has a variable speed of rotation or activity. The important observation to be made once all necessary centers are activated to the minimal necessary degree is the harmony and balance between these energy centers.

Questioner: Thank you. Taking as an example the transition between second and third-density, when this transition takes place, does the frequency of vibration which forms the photon (the core of all the particles of the density) increase from a frequency corresponding to second density or the color orange to the frequency that we measure as the color yellow? What I am getting at is, do all the vibrations that form the density, the basic vibrations of the photon, increase in a quantum fashion over a relatively short period of time?

Ra: I am Ra. This is correct. Then you see within each density the gradual up-grading of vibratory levels.

Questioner: This is a guess. Would the frequency going from second to third increase from the middle orange or average orange frequency to the middle or average yellow frequency?

Ra: I am Ra. This query is indeterminate. We shall attempt to be of aid. However, the frequency that is the basis of each density is what may be called a true color. This term is impossible to define given your system of sensibilities and scientific measurements, for color has vibratory characteristics both in space/time and in time/space. The true color is then overlaid and tinged by the rainbow of the various vibratory levels within that density and the attraction vibrations of the next true color density.

Questioner: How long was the time of transition from second to third-density? A generation and a half I believe you said. Is that correct?

Ra: I am Ra. This is correct, the time measured in your years being approximately 1,350.

Questioner: Then what will be the time of transition on this planet from third to fourth-density?

Ra: I am Ra. This is difficult to estimate due to the uncharacteristic anomalies of this transition. There are at this space/time nexus beings incarnate which have begun fourth-density work. However, the third-density climate of planetary consciousness is retarding the process. At this particular nexus the possibility/probability vortices indicate somewhere between 100 and 700 of your years as transition period. This cannot be accurate due to the volatility of your peoples at this space/time.

Questioner: Has the vibration of the photon increased in frequency already?

Ra: I am Ra. This is correct. It is this influence which has begun to cause thoughts to become things. As an example you may observe the thoughts of anger becoming those cells of the physical bodily complex going out of control to become what you call the cancer.

Questioner: I am assuming that this vibratory increase began about twenty to thirty years ago. Is this correct?

Ra: I am Ra. The first harbingers of this were approximately forty-five of your years ago, the energies vibrating more intensely through the forty year period preceding the final movement of vibratory matter, shall we say, through the quantum leap, as you would call it.

Questioner: Starting then, forty-five years ago, and taking the entire increase of vibration that we will experience in this density change, approximately what percentage through this increase in vibrational change are we right now?

Ra: I am Ra. The vibratory nature of your environment is true color, green. This is at this time heavily over-woven with the orange ray of planetary consciousness. However, the nature of quanta is such that the movement over the boundary is that of discrete placement of vibratory level.

Questioner: You mentioned that the thoughts of anger now are causing cancer. Can you expand on this mechanism as it acts as a catalyst or its complete purpose?

Ra: I am Ra. The fourth-density is one of revealed information. Selves are not hidden to self or other-selves. The imbalances or distortions which are of a destructive nature show, therefore, in more obvious ways, the vehicle of the mind/body/spirit complex thus acting as a teaching resource for self revelation. These illnesses such as cancer are correspondingly very amenable to self-healing once the mechanism of the destructive influence has been grasped by the individual.

Questioner: Then you are saying that cancer is quite easily healed mentally and is a good teaching tool because it is easily healed mentally and once the entity forgives the other-self at whom he is angry the cancer will disappear. Is this correct?

Ra: I am Ra. This is partially correct. The other portion of healing has to do with forgiveness of self and a greatly heightened respect for the self. This may conveniently be expressed by taking care in dietary matters. This is quite frequently a part of the healing and forgiving process. Your basic premise is correct.

Questioner: In dietary matters, what would be the foods that one would include and what would be the foods that one would exclude in a general way for the greatest care of one's bodily complex?

Ra: I am Ra. Firstly, we underline and emphasize that this information is not to be understood literally but as a link or psychological nudge for the body and the mind and spirit. Thus it is the care and respect for the self that is the true thing of importance. In this light we may iterate the basic information given for this instrument's diet. The vegetables, the fruits, the grains, and to the extent necessary for the individual metabolism, the animal products. These are those substances showing respect for the self. In addition, though this has not been mentioned for this instrument is not in need of purification, those entities in need of purging the self of a poison thought-form or emotion complex do well to take care in following a program of careful fasting until the destructive thought-form has been purged analogously with the by-products of ridding the physical vehicle of excess material. Again you see the value not to the body complex but used as a link for the mind and spirit. Thus self reveals self to self.

Questioner: Thank you. A very important concept. Does the fact that the basic vibration that we experience now is green true color or fourth-density account for the fact that there are many mental effects upon material objects that are now observable for the first time in a mass way such as the bending of metal by mind?

Ra: I am Ra. This shall be the final query in total of this working. This is not only correct but we suggest you take this concept further and understand the great number of entities with the so-called mental diseases being due to the effect of this green ray true color upon the mental configurations of those unready mentally to face the self for the first time.

Are there any brief queries before we close?

Questioner: Just two. With respect to what you just said, would then people incarnating here by seniority of vibration who incarnate in the service-to-self path be ones who would have extreme difficulty mentally with this green ray vibration?

Ra: I am Ra. This is incorrect. It is rather the numbers who have distracted themselves and failed to prepare for this transition yet who are somewhat susceptible to its influence who may be affected.

Questioner: Thank you. Is there anything that we can do to make the instrument more comfortable or to improve the contact?

Ra: This instrument is well. You are conscientious. The appurtenances cause this instrument greater comfort in the distortion of the warmth of the body complex. I am Ra. I leave you, my friends, in the love and in the light of the one infinite Creator. Go forth then rejoicing in the power and in the peace of the one infinite Creator. Adonai.

The Law of One, Book II, Session 41
March 20, 1981

Ra: I am Ra. I greet you in the love and in the light of the one infinite Creator. We communicate now.

Questioner: I have one question of logistics to start with. I know that it is a dumb question, but I have to ask it to be sure. There is a possibility that we may have to move from this location. Will this have any effect at all on our contact with Ra?

Ra: I am Ra. This is not a foolish question. The location is meaningless, for are we not in the creation? However, the place of the working shall be either carefully adjudged by your selves to be of the appropriate vibratory levels or it shall be suggested that the purification of the place be enacted and dedication made through meditation before initial working. This might entail such seemingly mundane chores as the cleansing or painting of surfaces which you may deem to be inappropriately marred.

Questioner: I am familiar with the Banishing Ritual of the Lesser Pentagram. I was wondering if this ritual was of use in preparing a place for this type of working?

Ra: I am Ra. This is correct.

Questioner: In trying to build an understanding from the start, you might say, starting with intelligent infinity and getting to our present condition of being I think that I should go back and investigate our sun since it is the sub-Logos that creates all that we experience in this particular planetary system. Will you give me a description of our sun?

Ra: I am Ra. This is a query which is not easily answered in your language, for the sun has various aspects in relation to intelligent infinity, to intelligent energy, and to each density of each planet, as you call these spheres. Moreover, these differences extend into the metaphysical or time/space part of your creation.

In relationship to intelligent infinity, the sun body is, equally with all parts of the infinite creation, part of that infinity.

In relation to the potentiated intelligent infinity which makes use of intelligent energy, it is the offspring, shall we say, of the Logos for a much larger number of sub-Logoi. The relationship is hierarchical in that the sub-Logos uses the intelligent energy in ways set forth by the Logos and uses its free will to co-create the, shall we say, full nuances of your densities as you experience them.

In relationship to the densities, the sun body may physically, as you would say, be seen to be a large body of gaseous elements undergoing the processes of fusion and radiating heat and light.

Metaphysically, the sun achieves a meaning to fourth through seventh density according to the growing abilities of entities in these densities to grasp the living creation and co-entity, or other-self, nature of this sun body. Thus by the sixth density the sun may be visited and inhabited by those dwelling in time/space and may even be partially created from moment to moment by the processes of sixth density entities in their evolution.

Questioner: In your last statement did you mean that the sixth density entities are actually creating manifestations of the sun in their density? Could you explain what you meant by that?

Ra: I am Ra. In this density some entities whose means of reproduction is fusion may choose to perform this portion of experience as part of the beingness of the sun body. Thus you may think of portions of the light that you receive as offspring of the generative expression of sixth-density love.

Questioner: Then could you say that sixth-density entities are using that mechanism to be more closely co-Creators with the infinite Creator?

Ra: I am Ra. This is precisely correct as seen in the latter portions of sixth density seeking the experiences of the gateway density.

Questioner: Thank you. What I want to do now is investigate, as the first-density is formed, what happens and how energy centers are first formed in beings. Does it make any sense to ask you if the sun itself has a density, or is it all densities?

Ra: I am Ra. The sub-Logos is of the entire octave and is not that entity which experiences the learning/teachings of entities such as yourselves.

Questioner: I am going to make a statement of my understanding and ask you to correct me. I intuitively see the first-density being formed by an energy center which is a vortex. This vortex then causes these spinning motions that I have mentioned before of vibration which is light which then starts to condense into materials of the first-density. Is this correct?

Ra: I am Ra. This is correct as far as your reasoning has taken you. However, it is well to point out that the Logos has the plan of all the densities of the octave in potential completion before entering the space/time continuum in first-density. Thus the energy centers exist before they are manifest.

Questioner: Then what is the simplest being that is manifested? I am supposing that it might be a single cell or something like that. How does it function with respect to energy centers?

Ra: I am Ra. The simplest manifest being is light or what you have called the photon. In relationship to energy centers it may be seen to be the center or foundation of all articulated energy fields.

Questioner: When first-density is formed we have fire, air, earth, and water. There is at some time the first movement or individuation of life into a portion of consciousness that is self-mobile. Could you describe the process of the creation of this and what type of energy center it has?

Ra: I am Ra. The first or red-ray density, though attracted towards growth, is not in the proper vibration for those conditions conducive to what you may call the spark of awareness. As the vibratory energies move from red to orange the vibratory environment is such as to stimulate those chemical substances which lately had been inert to combine in such a fashion that love and light begin the function of growth.

The supposition which you had earlier made concerning single-celled entities such as the polymorphous dynaflagallate is correct. The mechanism is one of the attraction of upward spiraling light. There is nothing random about this or any portion of evolution.

Questioner: As I remember, the polymorphous dynaflagallate has an iron rather than a copper based cell. Could you comment on that?

Ra: I am Ra. This information is not central. The base of any metabolism, shall we say, is that which may be found in the chemical substances of the neighborhood of origin.

Questioner: I was just commenting on this because it has the motion of our animal life with copper based cells yet it has the iron based cell of plant life indicating a transition from possibly plant to animal life. Am I wrong? My memory is a little fuzzy on this.

Ra: I am Ra. It is not that you are incorrect but that no conclusions should be drawn from such information. There are several different types of bases for conscious entities not only upon this planetary sphere but to a much greater extent in the forms found on planetary spheres of other sub-Logoi. The chemical vehicle is that which most conveniently houses the consciousness. The functioning of consciousness is the item of interest rather than the chemical makeup of a physical vehicle.

We have observed that those whom you call scientists have puzzled over the various differences and possible interrelationships of various stages, types, and conditions of life-forms. This is not fruitful material as it is that which is of a moment's choice by your sub-Logos.

Questioner: I didn't mean to waste time with that question but you just happened to mention that particular single cell. Does this polymorphous dynaflagallate have an orange energy center?

Ra: I am Ra. This is correct.

Questioner: Is this energy center, then, on a very small scale related to the orange energy center in man?

Ra: I am Ra. The true color is precisely the same. However, the consciousness of the second-density beginning is primitive and the use of orange ray limited to the expression of self which may be seen to be movement and survival.

In third-density, at this time, those clinging to orange ray have a much more complex system of distortions through which orange ray is manifested. This is somewhat complicated. We shall endeavor to simplify.

The appropriate true color for third-density is, as you have ascertained, yellow. However, the influences of the true color, green, acting upon yellow ray entities have caused many entities to revert to the consideration of self rather than the stepping forward into consideration of other-self or green ray. This may not be seen to be of a negatively polarized nature, as the negatively polarized entity is working very intensively with the deepest manifestations of yellow ray group energies, especially the manipulations of other-self for service to self. Those reverting to orange ray, and we may add these are many upon your plane at this time, are those who feel the vibrations of true color green and, therefore, respond by rejecting governmental and societal activities as such and seek once more the self.

However, not having developed the yellow ray properly so that it balances the personal vibratory rates of the entity, the entity then is faced with the task of further activation and balancing of the self in relation to the self, thus the orange ray manifestations at this space/time nexus.

Thus true color orange is that which it is without difference. However, the manifestations of this or any ray may be seen to be most various depending upon the vibratory levels and balances of the mind/body or mind/body/spirit complexes which are expressing these energies.

Questioner: Could you tell me the simplest and first entity to have both orange and yellow ray energy centers?

Ra: I am Ra. Upon your planetary sphere those having the first yellow ray experiences are those of animal and vegetable natures which find the necessity for reproduction by bisexual techniques or who find it necessary to depend in some way upon otherselves for survival and growth.

Questioner: And then what entity would be the simplest that would have red, orange, yellow, and green rays activated?

Ra: I am Ra. This information has been covered in a previous session. To perhaps simplify your asking, each center may be seen to be activated potentially in third-density, the late second-density entities having the capability, if efficient use is made of experience, of vibrating and activating the green ray energy center.

The third-density being, having the potential for complete self-awareness, thus has the potential for the minimal activation of all energy centers. The fourth, fifth, and sixth densities are those refining the higher energy centers. The seventh density is a density of completion and the turning towards timelessness or foreverness.

Questioner: Then would an animal in second-density have all of the energy centers in some way in its being but just not activated?

Ra: I am Ra. This is precisely correct.

Questioner: Then the animal in second-density is composed of light as are all things. What I am trying to get at is the relationship between the light that the various bodies of the animal are created of and the relationship of this to the energy centers which are active and the ones which are not active and how this is linked with the Logos. It is a difficult question to ask. Can you give me some kind of answer?

Ra: I am Ra. The answer is to redirect your thought processes from any mechanical view of evolution. The will of the Logos posits the potentials available to the evolving entity. The will of the entity as it evolves is the single measure of the rate and fastidiousness of the activation and balancing of the various energy centers.

Questioner: Thank you. In the session from the day before yesterday you mentioned variable speed of rotation or activity of energy centers. What did you mean by that?

Ra: I am Ra. Each energy center has a wide range of rotational speed or as you may see it more clearly in relation to color, brilliance. The more strongly the will of the entity concentrates upon and refines or purifies each energy center, the more brilliant or rotationally active each energy center will be. It is not necessary for the energy centers to be activated in order in the case of the self-aware entity. Thusly entities may have extremely brilliant energy centers while being quite unbalanced in their violet ray aspect due to lack of attention paid to the totality of experience of the entity.

The key to balance may then be seen in the unstudied, spontaneous, and honest response of entities toward experiences, thus using experience to the utmost, then applying the balancing exercises and achieving the proper attitude for the most purified spectrum of energy center manifestation in violet ray. This is why the brilliance or rotational speed of the energy centers is not considered above the balanced aspect or violet ray manifestation of an entity in regarding harvestability; for those entities which are unbalanced, especially as to the primary rays, will not be capable of sustaining the impact of the love and light of intelligent infinity to the extent necessary for harvest.

Questioner: Could you tell me the difference between space/time and time/space?

Ra: I am Ra. Using your words, the difference is that between the visible and invisible or the physical and metaphysical. Using mathematical terms, as does the one you call Larson, the difference is that between s/t and t/s.

Questioner: You mentioned in the last session the concept of fasting for removing unwanted thought-forms. Can you expand on this process and explain a little bit more about how this works?

Ra: I am Ra. This, as all healing techniques, must be used by a conscious being; that is, a being conscious that the ridding of excess and unwanted material from the body complex is the analogy to the ridding of mind or spirit of excess or unwanted material. Thus the one discipline or denial of the unwanted portion as an appropriate part of the self is taken through the tree of mind down through the trunk to subconscious levels where the connection is made and thus the body, mind, and spirit, then in unison, express denial of the excess or unwanted spiritual or mental material as part of the entity.

All then falls away and the entity, while understanding, if you will, and appreciating the nature of the rejected material as part of the greater self, nevertheless, through the action of the will purifies and refines the mind/body/spirit complex, bringing into manifestation the desired mind complex or spirit complex attitude.

Questioner: Then would this be like a conscious reprogramming of catalyst? For instance, for some entities catalyst is programmed by the higher self to create experiences so that the entity can release itself from unwanted biases. Would this be analogous then to the entity consciously programming this release and using fasting as the method of communication to itself?

Ra: I am Ra. This is not only correct but may be taken further. The self, if conscious to a great enough extent of the workings of this catalyst and the techniques of programming, may through concentration of the will and the faculty of faith alone cause reprogramming without the analogy of the fasting, the diet, or other analogous body complex disciplines.

Questioner: I have a book, INITIATION, in which the woman describes initiation. Are you familiar with the contents of this book?

Ra: I am Ra. This is correct. We scan your mind.

Questioner: I have only read part of it, but I was wondering if the teachings in the book with respect to balancing were Ra's teachings?

Ra: I am Ra. This is basically correct with distortions that may be seen when this material is collated with the material we have offered.

Questioner: Why are the red, yellow, and blue energy centers called primary centers? I think from previous material I understand this, but is there some tracing of these primary colors back to intelligent infinity more profound than what you have given us?

Ra: I am Ra. We cannot say what may seem profound to an entity. The red, yellow, and blue rays are primary because they signify activity of a primary nature.

Red ray is the foundation; orange ray the movement towards yellow ray which is the ray of self-awareness and interaction. Green ray is the movement through various experiences of energy exchanges having to do with compassion and all-forgiving love to the primary blue ray which is the first ray of radiation of self regardless of any actions from another.

The green-ray entity is ineffectual in the face of blockage from other-selves. The blue ray entity is a co-Creator. This may perhaps simply be a restatement of previous activity, but if you consider the function of the Logos as representative of the infinite Creator in effectuating the knowing of the Creator by the Creator you may perhaps see the steps by which this may be accomplished.

May we ask for one final full question before we leave this working?

Questioner: This may be too long a question for this working, but I will ask it and if it is too long we can continue it at a later time. Could you tell me of the development of the social memory complex Ra, from its first beginnings and what catalysts it used to get to where it is now in activation of rays?

Ra: I am Ra. The question does not demand a long answer, for we who experienced the vibratory densities upon that planetary sphere which you call Venus were fortunate in being able to move in harmony with the planetary vibrations with an harmonious graduation to second, to third, and to fourth, and a greatly accelerated fourth-density experience.

We spent much time/space, if you will, in fifth-density balancing the intense compassion we had gained in fourth-density. The graduation again was harmonious and our social memory complex which had become most firmly cemented in fourth-density remained of a very strong and helpful nature.

Our sixth-density work was also accelerated because of the harmony of our social memory complex so that we were able to set out as members of the Confederation to even more swiftly approach graduation to seventh-density. Our harmony, however, has been a grievous source of naiveté as regards working with your planet. Is there a brief query before we leave this instrument?

Questioner: Is there anything that we can do to make the instrument more comfortable or to improve the contact?

Ra: I am Ra. All is well. I leave you, my friends, in the love and in the light of the one infinite Creator. Go forth, therefore, rejoicing in the power and the peace of the one infinite Creator. Adonai.

Sunday Meditation
March 22, 1981

(Carla channeling)

[I am Hatonn.] … in the light of our infinite Creator. It gives me great pleasure to greet each of you. Especially the one know as M for we have not seen him in this group for a short period. It is a great privilege to speak to you and we could not be more grateful for the opportunity to share our thoughts.

My friends, we have spoken to you often of love. We know that those to whom we speak are seeking that ineffable power and substance that is the creative force of all that there is, the simple, single substance of creation. And yet how hard it is, my friends, to constantly remember that we are seekers and that what we are seeking is love, for do we not seek other things, my friends, during each day? How many other things has each of you sought during this day? Many, many times my friends, it may seem to you that you are on a runaway freight train, as this instrument would put it, that you have begun a sequence of events, gotten on a track from which there is no removing yourself. My friends, this is not so and is a condition of the illusion which is reinforced only by your belief in it. There is no track that cannot be replaced with one which you more truly seek. The secret lies not in catching the right train but in knowing yourself; knowing enough about yourself to seek your deepest desires.

It has often been said that there are many things that simply cannot be expected to work out well, that this understanding is a part of becoming more mature. You have often heard from many sources a great variety of things that should be, ought to be, must be, and need to be the models on which to build your expectations of yourself and of others. And we come to you and suggest a substitute for all of these things, the substitute being love. There is a passage in one of your holy works where it states clearly: "Love is not puffed up." This is to be remembered, my friends, for part of the track of that freight train that you may sometimes feel yourself to be upon, part of what makes it complete in your existence, is your belief in a puffed up, proud sense of the rightness of certain ways of being.

If there is something within your existence that is not pleasing to you, reexamine those concepts of which you are proud of and evaluate them in the simple, single, all-encompassing light, love. Wash yourself clean in that love and, so purified, reexamine your concepts. You will find that the path you are on is not what is making you less than comfortable but rather your expectations, your preconceptions, and your feelings about how things should be. This, my friends, is why meditation is so centrally important to the seeker, for while you are bathed in this illusion you are susceptible to many, many influences and if the balance wheel of your central self has not been nourished in the silence of love and praise and thanksgiving, you will continually be generating freight trains and places you didn't want to go.

At this time I would like to transfer this contact. I am Hatonn.

(Carla channeling

I am Hatonn. I am again with this instrument. We have been attempting to contact the instrument known as Don. If he would relax, and open himself to our contact, we would be most grateful for the opportunity to speak through him at this time. I am Hatonn.

(Carla channeling

I am again with this instrument. I am Hatonn. We are having difficulty making an uninterrupted contact with the one known an Don. Therefore, we shall condition him while we transfer to the one known as Jim. I am Hatonn.

(Jim channeling

I am Hatonn. I am with this instrument and greet you once again in the love and light of the infinite Creator. It is always a pleasure to be able to utilize yet one more instrument in our humble attempt to speak the simple words of love, the simple words that are so often misunderstood, so often ignored by the people of your planet who need most to hear of love. We speak in groups such as this one with the hope that the simple words which we share might begin within this nucleus of entities who seek love, might kindle within their beings the seeking, the radiance, of the one infinite Creator; that they might take this kindled flame with them to their homes, to their work, to their family, to their friends, to strangers whom they meet on the street each day in their daily round of existence and might radiate yet one more small spark of love. Those upon your planet who seek this love and do not know that they seek, yet shall recognize when they come in contact with those such as yourselves, that they have been touched by love and they will in even a small way be nourished by this contact.

It is with this hope in our hearts that we send love to your group, to each of your beings to carry as vessels of the infinite Creator to all those whom you may come in contact with so that the desire that is so strong among your people to know the Creator, to experience the love of the Father, might be realized in even a small way. For when any realizes love of the Creator, are not all enriched thereby?

It is with this simple hope in our hearts that we rejoice at each instance and each meeting of your group which we are able to establish contact with. Each gathering such as this provides us with yet one more opportunity to share that which is the simplest, yet too often the rarest of delicacies upon your planet.

We would at this time attempt once again to contact the one known as Don. If he would relax, we would be most honored to speak a few words through this instrument. I am Hatonn.

(Don channeling

I am Hatonn. I am now with this instrument. We've had a small amount of difficulty making contact at this time, This instrument had changed his mind slightly off our channel, so to speak. He was investigating other perimeters, so to speak. We shall continue speaking through this instrument. As I have said, it is a very great privilege to contact this group at this time. My friends, this time is a very important time in the history of your planet. The lessons [that] have been learned are about to culminate. My friends, graduation is at hand. The lessons shall shortly change and you shall move to new lessons, lessons where love will be understood, not as an intellectual concept or expression of feeling or emotion toward others. My friends, love will be understood as a living being; will be understood in all of its essence as the foundation for everything that is.

As you become aware of this form of love you will then be aware of the true creation. My friends, the true creation is love. There is nothing else. Shortly, as I was saying, you will be fully into this vibration, fully into this new experience, or density, if you will, density of love. Many, many of the peoples that now inhabit the surface of your planet will not have the opportunity to enter this density at this time but will necessarily reexperience the lessons through which they have just passed. This is neither unfortunate for them or fortunate for you. It's just simply the condition of existence. For each it's the total freedom to choose the path that he walks.

For this reason we contact those who seek our teachings, who seek our understanding, who seek our love. For this reason we cannot contact those who do not seek. They seek what they desire. This, my friends, is their right and their privilege. They are in no way lesser than yourselves or us. They simply choose a different path. All of the creation, my friends, experiences the same path. Each walk it a slightly different way. We hold out our hands to those who would follow our footsteps. We hold out our hands to you at this time, try to express our understanding of the creation, our understanding of its essence, our understanding of its love.

Think on this very carefully, my friends, for if you have chosen this path and walk it carefully, it is a narrow path and misfootings are many. Be aware of your footsteps. Choose each step with accuracy. We will constantly be with you to guide you. This is our privilege and our purpose. We of Hatonn have but one mission, shall I say, to reach to those who would reach to us …

(Pause)

I shall continue. We're having some interference. As I was saying, my friends, we have but one purpose; to reach to those who would reach to us for our understanding. Our understanding, my friends, is, as you know, is simply stated. It is the creation is made of and is love. If you can at each moment of awareness see each being you meet as the total expression of love that is the Creator, if you can see yourself as that total expression of love that is the Creator, if you do these simple things, my friends, you have then found the Creator within yourself and within others. There is nothing else. Find that understanding in its complete totality, and you have found everything that exists. You have found your path and walking it becomes obvious. Practice this understanding. We are all one. I do not anymore speak through this instrument than I am this instrument and I am each of you that sit in this room, for each of us is the same being.

I will conclude this communication through another instrument at this time.

(Carla channeling)

I am Hatonn. I am again with this instrument. We have been attempting to close the message through the instrument know as L. If he wishes to make himself available we shall say but a few words through this instrument as this instrument is somewhat low in energy. I will again attempt this transfer. I am Hatonn.

(L channeling)

I am Hatonn and I greet you again, my brethren, in the love and the light of our Creator of our [own] oneness. My brothers, we are all the same in that we share each other. In your ceremonies of marriage, the statements, "for richer, for poorer, for better, for worse, in health and sickness," my brothers, what vows could possibly bind one more closely in the oneness that the universe shares with itself? As selves in one body we function. As each individual has a breath that feeds and nourishes the body of the universe, so are we all, both part of the whole and again all of the whole.

My brothers, be strong in your love for one another, in your love for yourselves, for it is that love that eliminates the clouds of confusion and disperses entanglements of the maya, the illusion. Be strong, my brothers, and remember that our love is always with yours. I am Hatonn.

(Carla channeling)

I am Latwii. I greet you in the love and the light of the infinite Creator. We were attempting to contact the instrument known as Jim, but find that this instrument is reluctant to take on the channeling of answers at this time. We shall give him another tumble next tine. If there are any questions that we could perhaps attempt to shed some light on for you we would be very pleased if you would ask them now.

M: Where did Joseph Smith get his information?

I am Latwii. This information is of a nature which we are reluctant to share. Much of the information was, may we say in general, not received as the story is told. However, the information, as all information, must stand upon its own recognizance, so that each may read and inwardly consider whether there be truth and virtue in any words. We do not wish to mince words about this particular source, but we do not wish to address ourselves to the questions of plates of gold and their reality when the true question is the possible virtue of the words themselves, regardless of the story.

We may say this much. This particular entity had a contact and attempted to share its results. We ask that you judge his efforts for yourself. Much too much reliance is placed upon the storybook or miraculous aspects of the gaining of information. Look instead into the heart of the information.

May we answer you further, my brother?

M: No.

Is there another question at this time?

L: I have noticed that a recent sleep disturbance that I received, that my son seemed to be also disturbed. I'm concerned that an outside influence may be periodically acting upon him. Is this true? And if it is what can I do to prevent it?

I am Latwii, and am aware of your question. My brother, there is no outside influence acting upon the entity known as E. There is some activity surrounding yourself at this time which you are fully capable of dealing with. The disturbance is due to strong empathic link betwixt yourself and the flesh of your flesh. This is as it should be and may be countered by the loving embrace of parent and child. No harm can come to those you love for you yourself are in the light and the love of the infinite Creator and are quite aware of this. This will pass itself along to your son. When you are disturbed, this entity will also be disturbed. When you comfort, this entity shall be comforted.

It is a great responsibility to be the one to whom a helpless child looks for love, but it is also a joy, which we know that you feel. If there is at any time any danger that you may feel, we ask that you feel free to call upon us and all of our brothers and sisters in the Confederation and we shall be with you, not only we, but the one whom we gather in service towards, the infinite Creator.

May we answer you further?

L: There are three individuals to whom it recently occurred to me may be receiving instruction from the Orion group …

(Tape ends.) ✣

The Law of One, Book II, Session 42
March 22, 1981

Ra: I am Ra. I greet you in the love and in the light of the one infinite Creator. We communicate now.

Questioner: I am going to make a statement and ask you to comment on its degree of accuracy. I am assuming that the balanced entity would not be swayed either towards positive or negative emotions by any situation which he might confront. By remaining unemotional in any situation, the balanced entity may clearly discern the appropriate and necessary responses in harmony with the Law of One for each situation. Is this correct?

Ra: I am Ra. This is an incorrect application of the balancing which we have discussed. The exercise of first experiencing feelings and then consciously discovering their antitheses within the being has as its objective not the smooth flow of feelings both positive and negative while remaining unswayed but rather the objective of becoming unswayed. This is a simpler result and takes much practice, shall we say.

The catalyst of experience works in order for the learn/teachings of this density to occur. However, if there is seen in the being a response, even if it is simply observed, the entity is still using the catalyst for learn/teaching. The end result is that the catalyst is no longer needed. Thus this density is no longer needed. This is not indifference or objectivity but a finely tuned compassion and love which sees all things as love. This seeing elicits no response due to catalytic reactions. Thus the entity is now able to become co-Creator of experiential occurrences. This is the truer balance.

Questioner: I will attempt to make an analogy. If an animal, shall I say, a bull, in a pen attacks you because you have wandered into his pen, you get out of his way rapidly but you do not blame him. You do not have much of an emotional response other than the response that he might damage you. However, if you encounter another self in his territory and he attacks you, your response may be more of an emotional nature creating physical bodily responses. Am I correct in assuming that when your response to the animal and to the other-self is that of seeing both as Creator and loving both and understanding their action in attacking you is the action of their free will then you have balanced yourself correctly in this area? Is this correct?

Ra: I am Ra. This is basically correct. However, the balanced entity will see in the seeming attack of an other-self the causes of this action which are, in most cases, of a more complex nature than the cause of the attack of the second-density bull as was your example. Thus this balanced entity would be open to many more opportunities for service to a third-density other-self.

Questioner: Would a perfectly balanced entity feel any emotional response in being attacked by the other-self?

Ra: I am Ra. This is correct. The response is love.

Questioner: In the illusion that we now experience it is difficult to maintain this response especially if the attack results in physical pain, but I assume that this response should be maintained even through physical pain or loss of life. Is this correct?

Ra: I am Ra. This is correct and further is of a major or principle importance in understanding, shall we say, the principle of balance. Balance is not indifference but rather the observer not blinded by any feelings of separation but rather fully imbued with love.

Questioner: In the last session you made the statement that "We, that is Ra, spent much time/space in the fifth-density balancing the intense compassion that we had gained in the fourth-density." Could you expand on this concept with respect to the material you just discussed?

Ra: I am Ra. The fourth-density, as we have said, abounds in compassion. This compassion is folly when seen through the eyes of wisdom. It is the salvation of third-density but creates a mismatch in the ultimate balance of the entity.

Thus we, as a social memory complex of fourth-density, had the tendency towards compassion even to martyrdom in aid of other-selves. When the fifth-density harvest was achieved we found that in this vibratory level flaws could be seen in the efficacy of such unrelieved compassion. We spent much time/space in contemplation of those ways of the Creator which imbue love with wisdom.

Questioner: I would like to try to make an analogy for third-density of this concept. Many entities here feel great compassion for relieving the physical problems of third-density other-selves by administering to them in many ways, with food if there is hunger as there is now in the African nations, by bringing them medicine if they feel that there is a need to minister to them medically, and being selfless in all of these services to a very great extent.

This is creating a vibration that is in harmony with green-ray or fourth-density but it is not balanced with the understanding of fifth-density that these entities are experiencing catalysts and a more balanced administration to their needs would be to provide them with the learning necessary to reach the state of awareness of fourth-density than it would be to minister to their physical needs at this time. Is this correct?

Ra: I am Ra. This is incorrect. To a mind/body/spirit complex which is starving, the appropriate response is the feeding of the body. You may extrapolate from this.

On the other hand, however, you are correct in your assumption that the green ray response is not as refined as that which has been imbued with wisdom. This wisdom enables the entity to appreciate its contributions to the planetary consciousness by the quality of its being without regard to activity or behavior which expects results upon visible planes.

Questioner: Then why do we have the extreme starvation problem in, generally, the area of Africa at this time? Is there any metaphysical reason for this, or is it purely random?

Ra: I am Ra. Your previous assumption was correct as to the catalytic action of this starvation and ill health. However, it is within the free will of an entity to respond to this plight of otherselves, and the offering of the needed foodstuffs and substances is an appropriate response within the framework of your learn/teachings at this time which involve the growing sense of love for and service to other-selves.

Questioner: What is the difference in terms of energy center activation between a person who represses emotional responses to emotionally charged situations and the person who is balanced and, therefore, truly unswayed by emotionally charged situations?

Ra: I am Ra. This query contains an incorrect assumption. To the truly balanced entity no situation would be emotionally charged. With this understood, we may say the following: The repression of emotions depolarizes the entity in so far as it then chooses not to use the catalytic action of the space/time present in a spontaneous manner, thus dimming the energy centers. There is, however, some polarization towards positive if the cause of this repression is consideration for other-selves. The entity which has worked long enough with the catalyst to be able to feel the catalyst but not find it necessary to express reactions is not yet balanced but suffers no depolarization due to the transparency of its experiential continuum. Thus the gradual increase in the ability to observe one's reaction and to know the self will bring the self ever closer to a true balance. Patience is requested and suggested, for the catalyst is intense upon your plane and its use must be appreciated over a period of consistent learn/teaching.

Questioner: How can a person know when he is unswayed by an emotionally charged situation or if he is repressing the flow of emotions, or if he is in balance and truly unswayed?

Ra: I am Ra. We have spoken to this point. Therefore, we shall briefly iterate that to the balanced entity no situation has an emotional charge but is simply a situation like any other in which the entity may or may not observe an opportunity to be of service. The closer an entity comes to this attitude the closer an entity is to balance. You may note that it is not our recommendation that reactions to catalyst be repressed or suppressed unless such reactions would be a stumbling block not consonant with the Law of One to an other-self. It is far, far better to allow the experience to express itself in order that the entity may then make fuller use of this catalyst.

Questioner: How can an individual assess what energy centers within its being are activated and in no immediate need of attention and which energy centers are not activated and are in need of immediate attention?

Ra: I am Ra. The thoughts of an entity, its feelings or emotions, and least of all its behavior are the signposts for the teaching/learning of self by self. In the analysis of one's experiences of a diurnal cycle an entity may assess what it considers to be inappropriate thoughts, behaviors, feelings, and emotions.

In examining these inappropriate activities of mind, body, and spirit complexes the entity may then place these distortions in the proper vibrational ray and thus see where work is needed.

Questioner: In the last session you said, "that when the self is conscious to a great enough extent of the workings of the catalyst of fasting, and the techniques of programming, it then may through concentration of the will and the faculty of faith alone cause reprogramming without the analogy of fasting, diet, or other analogous bodily complex disciplines." What are the techniques of programming which the higher self uses to insure that the desired lessons are learned or attempted by the third-density self?

Ra: I am Ra. There is but one technique for this growing or nurturing of will and faith, and that is the focusing of the attention. The attention span of those you call children is considered short. The spiritual attention span of most of your peoples is that of the child. Thus it is a matter of wishing to become able to collect one's attention and hold it upon the desired programming.

This, when continued, strengthens the will. The entire activity can only occur when there exists faith that an outcome of this discipline is possible.

Questioner: Can you mention some exercises for helping to increase the attention span?

Ra: I am Ra. Such exercises are common among the many mystical traditions of your entities. The visualization of a shape and color which is of personal inspirational quality to the meditator is the heart of what you would call the religious aspects of this sort of visualization.

The visualization of simple shapes and colors which have no innate inspirational quality to the entity form the basis for what you may call your magical traditions.

Whether you image the rose or the circle is not important. However, it is suggested that one or the other path towards visualization be chosen in order to exercise this faculty. This is due to the careful arrangement of shapes and colors which have been described as visualizations by those steeped in the magical tradition.

Questioner: As a youth I was trained in the engineering sciences which include the necessity for three dimensional visualization for the processes of design. Would this be helpful as a foundation for the type of visualization which you are speaking of, or would it be of no value?

Ra: I am Ra. To you, the questioner, this experience was valuable. To a less sensitized entity it would not gain the proper increase of concentrative energy.

Questioner: Then the less sensitized entity should use … What should he use for the proper energy?

Ra: I am Ra. In the less sensitized individual the choosing of personally inspirational images is appropriate whether this inspiration be the rose which is of perfect beauty, the cross which is of perfect sacrifice, the Buddha which is the All-being in One, or whatever else may inspire the individual.

Questioner: Using the teach/learning relationship of parent to child, what type of actions would demonstrate the activation of the energy centers in sequence from red to violet?

Ra: I am Ra. This shall be the last full query of this working.

The entity, child or adult, as you call it, is not an instrument to be played. The appropriate teach/learning device of parent to child is the open-hearted being-ness of the parent and the total acceptance of the beingness of the child. This will encompass whatever material the child entity has brought into the life experience in this plane.

There are two things especially important in this relationship other than the basic acceptance of the child by the parent. Firstly, the experience of whatever means the parent uses to worship and give thanksgiving to the one infinite Creator, should if possible be shared with the child entity upon a daily basis, as you would say. Secondly, the compassion of parent to child may well be tempered by the understanding that the child entity shall learn the biases of service-to-others or service-to-self from the parental other-self. This is the reason that some discipline is appropriate in the teach/learning. This does not apply to the activation of any one energy center for each entity is unique and each relationship with self and other-self doubly unique. The guidelines given are only general for this reason.

Is there a brief query before we leave this instrument?

Questioner: Is there anything that we can do to make the instrument more comfortable or to improve the contact?

Ra: I am Ra. The instrument is well. I leave you, my friends, in the love and the light of the infinite Creator. Go forth, then, rejoicing in the power and the peace of the one infinite Creator. Adonai.

L/L RESEARCH

L/L Research is a subsidiary of Rock Creek Research & Development Laboratories, Inc.

P.O. Box 5195
Louisville, KY 40255-0195

www.llresearch.org

Rock Creek is a non-profit corporation dedicated to discovering and sharing information which may aid in the spiritual evolution of humankind.

ABOUT THE CONTENTS OF THIS TRANSCRIPT: This telepathic channeling has been taken from transcriptions of the weekly study and meditation meetings of the Rock Creek Research & Development Laboratories and L/L Research. It is offered in the hope that it may be useful to you. As the Confederation entities always make a point of saying, please use your discrimination and judgment in assessing this material. If something rings true to you, fine. If something does not resonate, please leave it behind, for neither we nor those of the Confederation would wish to be a stumbling block for any.

© 2009 L/L RESEARCH

THE LAW OF ONE, BOOK V, SESSION 42, FRAGMENT 25
MARCH 22, 1981

Jim: Almost everyone on the path of consciously seeking the truth has had some kind of mystical experience that may or may not make much sense to the person. Most such experiences remain unfathomable to our conscious minds and accomplish their work in an unseen and incomprehensible fashion. Being inhabitants of the third density with the great veil of forgetting drawn over our ability to see and to truly know, we must content ourselves with the fact that we only make the barest beginnings upon understanding in this illusion. But we may also rest assured that there are no mistakes and that the events of our lives, whether ordinary or extraordinary, fall into the appropriate place at the appropriate time.

Carla: Don had several experiences of altered consciousness that were permanently etched into his mind. The initiation he spoke of here was received in 1968, while we were in meditation together. He suddenly found himself in a world where the colors were living. He said these colors made our earthly hues look like black and white photos. They were three-dimensional. He saw living waters, and a golden sunrise streaming over the sky. He could open his eyes and he was in his chair, then close them again and see the other world. This state lasted about half an hour. The other event that is notable, to me, was a night he was meditating and found his arm moving rapidly up and down from elbow to fingers as his arm rested upon the chair arm. A blue light began to emanate from his lower arm, and he was forever grateful that he had company who saw his arm turning blue and glowing. Later transmissions indicated that the UFO entities were winding his battery!

Session 42, March 22, 1981

Questioner: I had one experience in meditation which I spoke of before which was very profound approximately twenty years ago, a little less. What disciplines would be most applicable to create this situation and this type of experience?

Ra: I am Ra. Your experience would best be approached from the ceremonial magical stance. However, the Wanderer or adept shall have the far greater potential for this type of experience which, as you have undoubtedly analyzed to be the case, is one of an archetypal nature, one belonging to the roots of cosmic consciousness.

Questioner: Was that in any way related to the Golden Dawn in ceremonial magic?

Ra: I am Ra. The relationship was congruency.

Questioner: Then in attempting to reproduce this experience would I then best follow the practices for the Order of the Golden Dawn in reproducing this?

Ra: I am Ra. To attempt to reproduce an initiatory experience is to move, shall we say, backwards. However, the practice of this form of service to others is appropriate in your case working with your associates. It is not well for positively polarized entities to work singly. The reasons for this are obvious.

Questioner: Then this experience was a form of initiation? Is this correct?

Ra: I am Ra. Yes.

The Law of One, Book II, Session 43
March 24, 1981

Ra: I am Ra. I greet you in the love and in the light of the one infinite Creator.

Before we communicate may we request the adjustment, without the touching of this instrument's physical body complex, of the item which presses upon the instrument's head. This is causing some interference with our contact.

Questioner: Is that the pillow or something else? Do you speak of the pillow under the neck?

Ra: I am Ra. There is a line of interference crossing the crown of the head.

Questioner: Is it this? *(A two inch fold in the sheet is located three inches from the crown of the instrument's head and is laid flat on the bed.)* Is that it?

Ra: I am Ra. This is correct. Please increase the distance from the crown of the head.

Questioner: *(Ruffles in the sheet are smoothed all along the length of the sheet next to the instrument's head.)* Is this satisfactory?

Ra: I am Ra. Yes.

Questioner: I am sorry that we failed to notice that.

Ra: We communicate now.

Questioner: I don't know if it is of any importance, but it occurred to me that the parts removed from the cattle mutilations are the same every time, and I wondered if this is related to the energy centers and why they were important if that was so?

Ra: I am Ra. This is basically correct if you may understand that there is a link between energy centers and various thought-forms. Thus the fears of the mass consciousness create the climate for the concentration upon the removal of bodily parts which symbolize areas of concern or fear in the mass consciousness.

Questioner: Are you saying, then, that these parts that are removed are related to the mass consciousness of the third-density human form and that this fear is being used in some way by the thought-form entities in these mutilations?

Ra: I am Ra. This is correct. The thought-form entities feed upon fear; thus they are able to do precise damage according to systems of symbology. The other second-density types of which you speak need the, what you call, blood.

Questioner: These other second-density types need the blood to remain in the physical? Do they come in and out of our physical from one of the lower astral planes?

Ra: I am Ra. These entities are, shall we say, creatures of the Orion group. They do not exist in astral planes as do the thought-forms but wait within the Earth's surface. We, as always, remind you that it is our impression that this type of information is unimportant.

Questioner: I agree with you wholeheartedly, but I sometimes am at a loss before investigation into an area as to whether it is going to lead to a better understanding. This just seemed to be related somehow to the energy centers which we had been speaking of.

I am going to make a statement and have you comment on it for its correctness. The statement is: When the Creator's light is split or divided into colors and energy centers for experience, then in order to reunite with the Creator the energy centers must be balanced exactly the same as the split light was as it originated from the Creator. Is this correct?

Ra: I am Ra. To give this query a simple answer would be nearly impossible.

We shall simplify by concentrating upon what we consider to be the central idea towards which you are striving. We have, many times now, spoken about the relative importance of balancing as opposed to the relative unimportance of maximal activation of each energy center. The reason is as you have correctly surmised. Thusly the entity is concerned, if it be upon the path of positive harvestability, with the regularizing of the various energies of experience. Thus the most fragile entity may be more balanced than one with extreme energy and activity in service-to-others due to the fastidiousness with which the will is focused upon the use of experience in knowing the self. The densities beyond your own give the minimally balanced individual much time/space and space/time with which to continue to refine these inner balances.

Questioner: In the next density, the fourth density, is the catalyst of physical pain used as a mechanism for experiential balancing?

Ra: I am Ra. The use of physical pain is minimal, having only to do with the end of the fourth-density incarnation. This physical pain would not be considered severe enough to treat, shall we say, in third density. The catalysts of mental and spiritual pain are used in fourth density.

Questioner: Why is physical pain a part of the end of fourth density?

Ra: I am Ra. You would call this variety of pain weariness.

Questioner: Can you state the average lifespan in the fourth density of space/time incarnation?

Ra: I am Ra. The space/time incarnation typical of harmonious fourth density is approximately 90,000 of your years as you measure time.

Questioner: Are there multiple incarnations in fourth density with time/space experiences in between incarnations?

Ra: I am Ra. This is correct.

Questioner: How long is a cycle of experience in fourth density in our years?

Ra: The cycle of experience is approximately 30 million of your years if the entities are not capable of being harvested sooner. There is in this density a harvest which is completely the function of the readiness of the social memory complex. It is not structured as is your own, for it deals with a more transparent distortion of the one infinite Creator.

Questioner: Then the big difference in harvestability between third and fourth density is that at the end of the third density the individual is harvested as a function of individual violet ray, but it is the violet-ray for the entire social memory complex that must be of a harvestable nature to graduate to the fifth density. Is this correct?

Ra: I am Ra. This is correct although in fifth density entities may choose to learn as a social memory complex or as mind/body/spirit complexes and may graduate to sixth density under these conditions, for the wisdom density is an extremely free density whereas the lessons of compassion leading to wisdom necessarily have to do with other-selves.

Questioner: Then is sixth-density harvest strictly of a social memory complex nature because again we have wisdom and compassion blended back using wisdom?

Ra: I am Ra. This is quite correct.

Questioner: The physical vehicle that is used in fourth-density space/time is, I am assuming, quite similar to the one that is now used in third density. Is this correct?

Ra: I am Ra. The chemical elements used are not the same. However, the appearance is similar.

Questioner: Is it necessary to eat food in fourth density?

Ra: I am Ra. This is correct.

Questioner: The mechanism of, shall we say, social catalyst due to a necessity for feeding the body then is active in fourth-density. Is this correct?

Ra: I am Ra. This is incorrect. The fourth-density being desires to serve and the preparation of foodstuffs is extremely simple due to increased communion between entity and living foodstuff. Therefore, this is not a significant catalyst but rather a simple precondition of the space/time experience. The catalyst involved is the necessity for the ingestion of foodstuffs. This is not considered to be of importance by fourth-density entities and it, therefore, aids in the teach/learning of patience.

Questioner: Could you expand a little bit on how that aids in the teach/learning of patience?

Ra: I am Ra. To stop the functioning of service-to-others long enough to ingest foodstuffs is to invoke patience.

Questioner: I'm guessing that it is not necessary to ingest foodstuffs in fifth-density. Is this correct?

Ra: I am Ra. This is incorrect. However, the vehicle needs food which may be prepared by thought.

Questioner: What type of food would this be?

Ra: I am Ra. You would call this type of food, nectar or ambrosia, or a light broth of golden white hue.

Questioner: What is the purpose of ingesting food in fifth density?

Ra: I am Ra. This is a somewhat central point. The purpose of space/time is the increase in catalytic action appropriate to the density. One of the preconditions for space/time existence is some form of body complex. Such a body complex must be fueled in some way.

Questioner: In third density the fueling of our bodily complex is not only simply fueling of the bodily complex but gives us opportunities to learn service. In fourth density it not only fuels the complex but gives us opportunities to learn patience. In fifth density it fuels the complex but does it teach?

Ra: I am Ra. In fifth density it is comfort for those of like mind gathered together to share in this broth, thus becoming one in light and wisdom while joining hearts and hands in physical activity. Thus in this density it becomes a solace rather than a catalyst for learning.

Questioner: I am simply trying to trace the evolution of this catalyst that then, as you say, changes in fifth density. I might as well complete this and ask if there is any ingestion of food in sixth density?

Ra: I am Ra. This is correct. However, the nature of this food is that of light and is impossible to describe to you in any meaningful way as regards the thrust of your query.

Questioner: On this planet after the harvest is complete, will fourth-density beings be incarnate on the surface as we know it now?

Ra: I am Ra. The probability/possibility vortices indicate this to be most likely.

Questioner: Then will there be at that time any fifth-density or sixth-density beings on the surface of the planet?

Ra: I am Ra. Not for a fairly long measure of your time as fourth-density beings need to spend their learn/teaching space/time with their own density's entities.

Questioner: Then basically what you are saying is that at that point the teachings of fifth or sixth-density beings would not be too well understood by the new fourth-density beings?

Ra: I am Ra. Do you wish to query us upon this point?

Questioner: I guess I didn't state that correctly. Would the new fourth-density beings then need to evolve in their thinking to reach a point where fifth-density lessons would be of value?

Ra: I am Ra. We grasp the thrust of your query. Although it is true that as fourth-density beings progress they have more and more need for other density teachings, it is also true that just as we speak to you due to the calling, so the information called is always available. It is simply that fifth-density beings will not live upon the surface of the planetary sphere until the planet reaches fifth-density vibratory level.

Questioner: I was wondering, then, if the mechanism of teach/learning was the same relatively then in fourth density. From what you say, it is necessary first for a call to exist for the teach/learning of fifth density to be given to fourth just as a call must exist here before fourth-density lessons are given to third density. Is this correct?

Ra: I am Ra. This query is misguided, for experience in fourth density is emphatically not the same as third-density experience. However, it is correct that the same mechanism of calling predisposes the information received in a way consonant with free will.

You may ask one more full question at this working.

Questioner: You stated that the key to strengthening the will is concentration. Can you tell me the relative importance of the following aids to concentration? I have listed: silence, temperature control, comfort of body, screening as a Faraday cage would screen electromagnetic radiation, visible light screening, and a constant smell such as the use of incense. In other words, an isolation-type of situation. You mentioned that this was one of the functions of the pyramid.

Ra: I am Ra. The analogies of body complex to mind and spirit complex activities have been discussed previously. You may consider all of these aforementioned aids as those helpful to the stimulation of that which in actuality aids concentration, that being the will of the entity. This free will may be focused at any object or goal.

Questioner: I was really trying to get at whether it would be of great importance to construct a better place for our meditations. We have distractions here of the types which I mentioned, and I know that it is a function of our total free will as to whether we construct this or not, but I was trying to get at the principles behind and the relative importance of the Faraday cage. It would be quite a construction and I was wondering if it would be of any real value?

Ra: I am Ra. Without infringing upon free will we feel it possible to state that the Faraday cage and the isolation tank are gadgets.

The surrounding of self in a sylvan atmosphere, apart from distractions, in a place of working used for no other purpose, in which you and your associates agree to lay aside all goals but that of the meditative seeking of the infinite Creator is, shall we say, not gadgetry but the making use of the creation of the Father in second-density love, and in the love and support of otherselves. Are there any brief queries before this working is at an end?

Questioner: Is there anything that we can do to make the instrument more comfortable or to improve the contact?

Ra: I am Ra. All is well. I leave you in the love and the light of the one infinite Creator. Go forth, therefore, rejoicing in the power and the peace of the one infinite Creator. Adonai.

(Session #44, March 28, 1981, and Session #45, April 6, 1981, contain only personal material and were, for that reason, removed.) ♣

L/L Research

L/L Research is a subsidiary of Rock Creek Research & Development Laboratories, Inc.

P.O. Box 5195
Louisville, KY 40255-0195

www.llresearch.org

Rock Creek is a non-profit corporation dedicated to discovering and sharing information which may aid in the spiritual evolution of humankind.

ABOUT THE CONTENTS OF THIS TRANSCRIPT: This telepathic channeling has been taken from transcriptions of the weekly study and meditation meetings of the Rock Creek Research & Development Laboratories and L/L Research. It is offered in the hope that it may be useful to you. As the Confederation entities always make a point of saying, please use your discrimination and judgment in assessing this material. If something rings true to you, fine. If something does not resonate, please leave it behind, for neither we nor those of the Confederation would wish to be a stumbling block for any.

© 2009 L/L RESEARCH

THE LAW OF ONE, BOOK V, SESSION 44, FRAGMENT 26
MARCH 28, 1981

Jim: Session 44 was removed from Book Two because it is almost entirely a maintenance session. In querying as to how best to revitalize Carla's physical vehicle and aid the contact with Ra in general we did, however, discover a couple of fundamental principles which we found useful thereafter.

In the first answer we found that a strong desire to be of service is not enough when it is uninformed by wisdom. Carla, and our entire group as well, suffered in the first months of the Ra contact from an overactive desire to be of service through having more sessions with Ra than was helpful for the contact over the long run. Scheduling so many sessions in such a short period of time was overly draining on Carla's physical energy and would mean that the total number of sessions that was possible during her incarnation was probably being reduced.

The second principle which we found of interest was the power of dedication. If Carla dedicated herself to having a session with Ra she would expend an amount of energy equal to a full day's work—even if the session did not occur. Thus it was most important that her dedication be informed by wisdom, if not her own then that of the support group's. Thus, for any person, it is the will which drives the dedication, all thoughts, words, and actions depending therefrom. As one points the will, one's desires become manifest. It is important, therefore, that one use the will carefully.

Carla: My body has always been fragile. Born with birth defects, laid low by rheumatic fever at the age of 2 years and kidney failure at ages 13 and 15, I have since worked with an increasing amount of rheumatoid arthritic and other rheumatoid diseases. By 1981, when the contact with Ra began, I had had several operations on my wrists and finger joints, and was experiencing rheumatoid changes in virtually every joint in my body, the neck and back being the worst hit after the hands. I had worked as a librarian, a job I loved, and as a researcher and writer for Don, but 1976 was the last year I was able to manage a typewriter, and by 1981 I was on Social Security Disability and having grave problems physically, both organic and rheumatoid. I was in pain constantly. I tolerated this without much remark, and tried to appear well; indeed, I felt healthy. But the body was a weak one. And I think that the trance state was difficult because without my being able to move my body around, it simply lay in one position during the sessions. This meant that the bad joints were liable to become far more painful, especially in those joints of back, neck and wrist which were severely damaged. I would wake up in a world of hurt. There did not seem to be a way to avoid this, and it was easy for me to be discouraged at my imperfect physical vehicle. I felt as though I were letting the group down when Ra said they had to limit the session length, and always tried my hardest to maximize my time in trance.

*Donald and Jim never reproached me even the first time, and were endlessly patient in working with my limitations. However, I cried many a tear of frustration, for I wished so much to be able to continue with this channeling of Ra. It was fortunate for the contact that Jim and I were lovers, for apparently all the physical energy I had to give, after the first few sessions, was the energy transferred during lovemaking. How does a person called "pure" have a lover? Purely, of course. I tried celibacy for about two years when Don and I first got together. I found it extremely difficult and unsatisfying as a life choice. After talking this over with Donald, we agreed that I would take a lover if I wished. As he was gone fully half of the time flying for Eastern Air Lines, I was able to be completely discreet. He never saw the lover, who never saw him. When Jim began coming to meditations regularly, I had once again been celibate for about four years, not having anyone I felt good about to be a lover and friend. Jim was the answer to a maiden's prayers, being extremely fond of his solitude most of the time, but a marvelous companion and an amazing lover when he was in the mood. He wanted nothing from me in the everyday sense of having a constant companion. Don wanted only that companionship. The two men fitted into my life like puzzle pieces, just so. It was, for the time it lasted, a seamless and wonderful threesome of those who truly and entirely wished to serve.

I pondered Ra's words about martyrdom for some time, and eventually decided that I should take a vacation, the first one I had taken since 1971. Jim and I went to the seashore, and I rested and felt great healing. I see this as the first step I took away from the forces of death and towards an embrace of continued life. I wish that Don could also have done this, but it was not in him.

I think Ra's comments on how to treat psychic greeting are very wise. To look on these experiences of being "attacked" as less than vitally important was to invite their prolongation. When faced and given full consideration, without fear, just being with these energies and loving them, seeing them as the dark side of oneself, the greetings were simply experiences to have and to ponder, working towards acceptance of the full self. Jesus suggested that we not resist evil, and I think this is part of what He meant—to embrace the greeting as coming from the self, and as loved by the self, was to draw its teeth and neutralize its venom.

Donald had a long-standing interest in ritual magic, one that predated my arrival in his life. He was fascinated with the thought that somehow he could help me by dealing with the negative entities that were offering greetings. It has always been an uneasy thought that he, as he once discussed with Jim, might have tried to make a pact with the entity that was so persistently greeting me, to give himself instead of me.

Session 44, March 28, 1981

Ra: I am Ra. I greet you in the love and in the light of the one infinite Creator. We communicate now.

Questioner: The instrument had some question as to her vitality. We were having some difficulty in appraising it. Is it possible for you to comment on this?

Ra: I am Ra. We scan this instrument and find that we may be of service without infringement due to this instrument's decision to abide by the most careful appraisal possible rather than the most desired.

We have been surprised that we have been able to maintain contact on a regular basis during this most intense period of negatively influenced interference. Sexual energy transfers have at some workings given this instrument additional vital resources upon which to draw. However, this is not so at this working and, therefore, the will of the instrument drives its bodily complex. This instrument has no judgment about this service. The faculty of will, while recognized as most central and valuable, could in this application cause serious distortion in the bodily complex of the instrument. May we note that martyrdom is not necessarily helpful. We ask this instrument to examine these thoughts, judge, and discriminate the possible truth of them, and if they be deemed true we suggest this instrument release the power of judgment to the support group whose interests are balanced far more than this instrument's. Allow decisions to be made without expectation or attachment to the outcome. Our hopes, may we say, for long-term contact through this instrument depend upon its maturing ability to be of service to other-selves by accepting their help and thus remaining a viable instrument.

May we thank the questioner for allowing us to speak to this point, for we were aware of the distortions incumbent upon one whose will to serve is not regulated by knowledge of limitations of bodily complex distortion.

Questioner: Could you please terminate this contact as soon as necessary since we are not aware of the vitality of the instrument at this time?

Ra: I am Ra. In your way of speaking our hands are, to a certain extent, tied. This instrument has called upon inner reserves which are dearly bought. Therefore, we have the honor/duty of using this energy to the best of our ability. When it becomes low we shall most certainly, as always, express the need for ending the working. The only way of avoiding this sharing of service at whatever cost is to refrain from the working. It is a dilemma.

Questioner: Can you tell me what the tone was that I heard in my left ear when you started your communication?

Ra: I am Ra. This was a negatively oriented signal.

Questioner: Can you tell me how I would hear a positively oriented signal?

Ra: I am Ra. Two types there are of positive signal. First, in the right ear location the signal indicates a sign that you are being given some unworded message saying, "Listen. Take heed." The other positive sign is the tone above the head which is a balanced confirmation of a thought.

Questioner: Are there any other negatively oriented signals that I get?

Ra: I am Ra. This is correct. You are able to receive thought-forms, word-forms, and visions. However, you seem able to discriminate.

Questioner: Is there a reason that I am open to these signals of a negative nature?

Ra: I am Ra. Are you not all things?

Questioner: I think that it might be a good idea if we terminated the contact at this time to allow the instrument to gain more of the necessary energy before continuing these sessions. This is my decision at this time. I would very much like to continue the contact, but it seems to me, although I can't tell the instrument's level, that the instrument should not use up any more energy.

Ra: I am Ra. We are responding to an unasked query. However, it is most salient and therefore we beg your forgiveness for this infringement. The energy has been lost to the instrument, dedicated to this purpose only. You may do as you will, but this is the nature of the instrument's preparation for contact and is the sole reason we may use it.

Questioner: I am not sure if I fully understood you. Could you say that in a little different way? Could you explain more completely?

Ra: I am Ra. Each of you in this working has consciously dedicated the existence now being experienced to service to others. This instrument has refined this dedication through long experience with the channeling, as you term it, of Confederation philosophy, as you may say. Thus when we first contacted this instrument it had offered its beingness, not only to service to other-selves but service by communication of this nature. As this contact has developed, this dedication of beingness has become quite specific. Thus once the vital energy is dedicated by the instrument to our communications, even if the working did not occur, this vital energy would be lost to the day-by-day experience of the instrument. Thus we indicated the importance of the instrument's releasing of the will from the process of determining the times of working, for if the instrument desires contact, the energy is gathered and thus lost for ordinary or mundane purposes.

Questioner: In that case, since her energy is already lost, we might as well continue with this session, and we should very carefully monitor the instrument and be the sole judge of when the sessions should occur. Am I correct?

Ra: I am Ra. This is profoundly correct. This instrument's determination to continue contact during this period has already extended the low energy period.

Questioner: This is very revealing to us. Thank you. Each of us gets signals and dreams. I have been aware of clairaudient communication at least once in waking up. Can you suggest a method whereby we might be able, shall I say, to nullify the influence of that which we don't want of a negative source?

Ra: I am Ra. There are various methods. We shall offer the most available or simple. To share the difficult contact with the other-selves associated with this working and to meditate in love for these senders of images and light for self and other-selves is the most available means of nullifying the effects of such occurrences. To downgrade these experiences by the use of intellect or the disciplines of will is to invite the prolonging of the effects. Far better then to share in trust such experiences and join hearts and souls in love and light with compassion for the sender and armor for the self.

Questioner: Can you tell me the source of the instrument's dream this morning as soon as she woke up?

Ra: I am Ra. The feeling of the dream, shall we say, was Orion-influenced. The clothing of the dream revealing more the instrument's unconscious associative patterns of symbolism.

Questioner: In meditation a number of years ago my arm started to glow and to move rapidly involuntarily. What was that?

Ra: I am Ra. The phenomenon was an analogy made available to you from your higher self. The analogy was that the being that you were was living in a way not understood by, shall we say, physicists, scientists, or doctors.

Questioner: What I am trying to get at in this session is if there are any practices that we might be able to do to best revitalize the instrument, for it is going to be necessary to do all we can in order to maintain our contact. Can you tell us what we can do to increase the instrument's vitality for these contacts?

Ra: I am Ra. Your experience was a function of your ability to contact intelligent infinity. Therefore, it does not have a direct bearing upon this instrument's vital energy.

We have spoken before of those things which aid this instrument in the vital energy: the sensitivity to beauty, to the singing of sacred music, to the meditation and worship, to the sharing of self with self in freely given love either in social or sexual intercourse. These things work quite directly upon the vitality. This instrument has a distortion towards appreciation of variety of experiences. This, in a less direct way, aids vitality.

Questioner: I was looking at a diagram of the advancement of magical practices starting from Malkuth and ending at Kether. I was wondering if these corresponded to the colors or the densities with Malkuth as one, Yesod as two, Hod and Netzach being three, Tiphareth four, and so on. Is this correct?

Ra: I am Ra. This is basically incorrect although you are upon the correct track of thinking. Each of these stations has a complex number and shading of energy centers as well as some part in various balances; the lower, the middle, the high, and the total balance. Thus there are complex colors or rays and complex charges, if you will, in each station.

Questioner: Does the left-hand path of this represent the service-to-self path and the right-hand path the service-to-others?

Ra: I am Ra. This will be the last full query of this working.

This is incorrect. These stations are relationships. Each path has these relationships offered. The intent of the practitioner in working with these powerful concepts determines the polarity of the working. The tools are the tools.

Questioner: As an ending question I will just ask if it is possible for the Ipsissimus then to have either positive or negative polarity, or must he be neither?

Ra: I am Ra. We shall respond to the meaning of this term in a specialized sense. The Ipsissimus is one who has mastered the Tree of Life and has used this mastery for negative polarization.

Is there any brief query which we may respond to as we take leave of this instrument?

Questioner: I am sorry that we got a little off the track today. I think that the most important thing that we accomplished was discovering how to better regulate the instrument's sessions, and I would hope that you would bear with me for my inability to select questions properly at times. Sometimes I probe into areas to see if it is a direction in which we might go, and once entering, am then able to determine whether or not to continue in that direction.

Other than that, all I would like to ask is if there is anything that we can do to make the instrument more comfortable or to improve the contact?

Ra: I am Ra. There are no mistakes. Be at rest, my friend. Each of you is most conscientious. All is well. I leave you in the love and the light of the one infinite Creator. Go forth, therefore, rejoicing in the power and in the peace of the one infinite Creator. I am Ra. Adonai.

L/L Research

Sunday Meditation
March 29, 1981

(Carla channeling)

I am Hatonn. I greet you in the love and the light of the infinite Creator. It is a privilege to speak to you through this instrument. We ask your pardon for the delay, however, it was our attempt to initiate contact through the one known as L and then through the one known as Jim that they may have more experience in initiating contact. We wish to confirm to these two instruments that they had indeed been receiving conditioning.

We would at this time attempt again to contact the one known an L. I am Hatonn.

(L channeling)

I am Hatonn, and I again greet you, my brothers, in [the] love and the light of our infinite Creator. My brothers, it is a great pleasure for all of us to share with you our thoughts that we might be of service to those of your planet. In this manner we of Hatonn further our own development as well, for is it not through service that we all grow? Therefore, my brothers, be not hesitant to call upon us in your time of need, be it a need originating from indecision or a need in which you may feel yourself threatened either physically or spiritually. We cannot guarantee that we will be able to assist you in the manner you prefer, for it is not our will or our way to interfere with another's karmic responsibilities. But, my brothers, if the path is open to us we will surely take it.

At this time, my brothers, I would like to renew our contact through the one known as Jim. I am Hatonn.

(Jim channeling)

I am Hatonn, and am with this instrument and greet you all once again in love and light. It is our privilege, as always, to share our simple thoughts with your group. We of Hatonn are humble messengers of the message and the vibration of love. We have through many years attempted to share our simple message with the people of your planet. Unfortunately, we must say our attempts have fallen far short of our hopes, but yet we shall continue in this effort for as long as there is a calling for a desire on the part of any of the people of your planet to hear our message.

We know that those of you who have been attending these meditations for a period of time now are very familiar with the message which we have to offer. The message of love seems very simple to those who have heard it, but, my friends, we ask you in truth, how simple is the Creator? Is it not a simple thing to consider that the Creator is all about you? Is it not a simple thing to consider that the Creator, being all things, loves all things, each part of Its creation? Yes, my friends, it is simple, a simple thing to consider this simple truth, yet so many of your people find it so difficult to express such a simple truth, such a simple recognition in their daily lives. It seems, by observation, so much simpler for entities to consider only their own momentary interests as they go about their daily round of activities. It seems so much simpler to forget that the Creator is within each being that you meet, is within each experience that you encounter.

Yes, my friends, it is very simple, this thing which you call life. It is simply a matter of choice. A matter of knowing which direction you wish to point your life. Do you wish to see love, do you wish to experience the love of the Creator? Do you wish to express this love each moment of your life? Do you wish to experience the fullness and the oneness of the Creator all about you? It is a simple choice. A choice which we of Hatonn hope that we are able to aid you in some small way by the presentation of our variety of a simple message, the message of love, the message of understanding that all is the Creator, that you are the Creator. That you have the love of the Creator available each moment, each day of your lives and this love may be the energy upon which you draw to express your life in any way. We hope through these simple communications that we are able to share same small spark of this infinite light and love which is available at all times to all creatures in the creation of the Father.

We would at this time pause so that our brother, Laitos, may pass among those gathered here and should any request the conditioning vibration, our brother Laitos would be most pleased and privileged to aid each such request by sharing the conditioning vibration of the Confederation. I am Hatonn.

(Carla channeling

I am Hatonn. I am again with this instrument and again I greet you in the love and light. As we were saying, my friends, each and every part of the Creation is full of the love of the Creator. Let us consider two models of such love. Let us consider the differences which we may see with the intellect and perhaps find possibilities of thought. Let us consider the concern and love of the parent for the child. How careful the parent is, how concerned, how totally committed to the care of this being, this perfect entity which is a representation of the Creator. Of what service in this great love of parent to child.

Let us consider another model of love. Let us look at the first rose as it blooms, first a bud, then sweet smelling and fresh with the dew. It opens to the sun, sharing its scented beauty with the breeze and the glory of its radiant color with all who pass by or with no one at all if there is no one to pass by.

There is much to consider in these two models of love. One is a radiation; one a relationship. Consider, my friends the love of which we speak. Are you in a relationship with the Creator? Do you feel the radiance of the Creator? Is there a point at which it is necessary to understand the difference? We leave you these thoughts to ponder. I would close through the one known as Don. I am Hatonn.

(Carla channeling

I am again with this instrument. The one known as Don is not tuned to our vibratory level, thus we shall close through this instrument. It is our great privilege to be able to share our humble thoughts with you. We hope that there may be in some way a feeling of the radiance, of the love of the Creator within you at this moment; a feeling of the perfection of His love and His light. In this, I leave you. I am known to you as Hatonn. Adonai vasu borragus.

I am Latwii. I am with this instrument. I greet you in the love and the light of our infinite Creator. We said previously that we would attempt to give the one known as Jim another tumble, however he beat us to the mat three out of three. We will continue to attempt to establish contact with this instrument at a later time. Meanwhile, it is our pleasure to offer ourselves in the event that we may share our thoughts with you if you have any questions at this time.

N: What happens to persons who have crises in their life?

I am Latwii. I am aware of your question. The nature of the events following the premature ending of a life by conscious act or suicide are various, depending upon the state of mind and basic vibration of the entity. However, there are some common problems with this action. That is, the removal of the entity from the life experience it was unable to finish then causes this same entity to at some point re-travel the same path in another attempt to finish the life experience begun but not ended. However, because of the trauma of the physical death it is more difficult to solve the life experience upon the rerun, shall we say. This is perhaps the most salient, common experience associated with this action.

May we answer you further, my brother?

Don: What type of music should you use for tuning this group?

I am Latwii. The tuning mechanism is not important but rather the dedication of the group to using that period in order to form the feeling of unity of purpose in seeking the truth. It is not suggested that raucous or disharmonious sounds be proffered, however any harmonious sounds or inspirational words will suffice well if they allow the functioning of the unifying of the will of the group.

Is there another question at this time?

N: How does the Confederation look upon things like abortion?

I am Latwii. This area, like the previously mentioned area of suicide, is somewhat misunderstood among your peoples. Neither suicide nor abortion is recommended for those entities wishing to zoom to the head of the class of service to others, for such actions as abortion or the taking of one's own life indicate a feeling of being unable to cope. This is not a correct perception, however, there is such a thing upon your planet as what is called morals. These morals are used much like stones to hurt people. Unfortunately, morals enter greatly into discussions of both suicide and abortion as well as many other emotionally charged matters.

Abortion is that action which removes anything from an empty opportunity to a life. Whether the abortion removes only physical matter or an entity can be known only through meditation upon the part of the mother. The mother will know if a soul wishes to be born and wishes it as mother. If such an entity cannot feel the presence of a soul those morally against abortion are incorrect. If after careful meditation the presence of a spirit desiring the experience of an incarnation with this entity as mother is felt and then the entity removes that opportunity, this action is to some degree part of a reckoning. The relationship will then occur in the future and restitution made: love will find its balance in time.

Again, those with morals do not have the concept of the all-encompassing, all-embracing power of love to eventually balance all incorrectness. Morals do not apply precisely as those who jump up and down and are angry may think [they] do. This is difficult for us to speak of, for each case is unique. Each suicide, each murder, each abortion, each thought, my friends, of an unkind nature, these things cannot be judged by morals but can only be offered to love in the knowledge that love will truly conquer all.

May we answer you further, my brother?

(Pause)

I am Latwii. Is there another question at this time?

L: I am having difficulty emotionally with a past relationship. I ask whatever advice or counseling you can offer.

I am Latwii. My brother, we do not give advice but we can give you a thought or two. You are perfect. Forgive yourself. Let your friends comfort you. Listen in your heart for the love of the Father. Feel upon your shoulder the hand of a presence so near and so dear that you could not be separated from it, This presence may be called Christ consciousness or divine love. Seek and ye shall find. This is that which you will find. As always, we are with you.

May we answer you further, my brother?

L: Could you give some detail on what conditioning is?

I am Latwii. This is not our field, however we shall attempt the basics. The electrical, shall we say, characteristics of your mind are tunable in a way much like that of the radio. To strengthen the signal of a radio, such a thing as a carrier wave is given. We underscore your meditational vibration with such a carrier wave. This does not interfere with your free will in tuning beyond a certain point as our conditioning wave is broadly tuned over the positive spectrum, however, it enables the meditator to deepen the state of meditation. Some electrical experiences or symptoms may be observed when feeling this conditioning wave.

Those who wish to become instruments may also use this wave by request mentally as a means of exercising and making ready the mouth and vocal mechanism for channeling such as this instrument does.

Is there another question?

L: Yes. Is it beneficial to request conditioning immediately prior to going to sleep, with an understanding that an effort will be made on your part to work upon the instrument while they're in a relaxed sleeping condition?

I am Latwii. The hypnogogic state is a good state for conditioning. Therefore, it is beneficial, however, we do not work upon the sleeping entity. This would be an infringement of free will.

Is there another question at this time?

L: Would it be an infringement on free will if it were requested?

I am Latwii. When you request it in a dream it will not be an infringement upon free will. Your vulnerability during sleeping states is much different than the waking state. We do not intrude where we are not specifically requested. You would have to request our presence while asleep. This may be difficult to understand but a knowledge of the way the mind functions makes this point apparent.

Is there another question at this time?

(Pause)

I am Latwii. This instrument is a naughty girl. She wants to know who will win the basketball game. We think that it is time that we leave you in the love and in the light of the infinite Creator. Our love and light and comfort are always with you, my friends. I am Latwii. Enjoy each other and the universe for all is very beautiful, my friends. Adonai vasu. ☘

Sunday Meditation
April 5, 1981

(Carla channeling)

[I am Hatonn] … Creator. It is a great privilege to be with you this evening, and I especially greet those who have not been with this group for some time. May we send you our blessings and our peace and know that there is no treasure as great to us as the privilege of sharing our love and our thoughts with you.

My friends, it in written in your holy works: "I have waited for the Lord more than the watchman for the morning, more than the watchman for the morning." We would speak to you this evening of the love that manifests itself to you more slowly than you would perhaps wish. We would speak to you of patience and waiting. It is very difficult for your peoples to wait for anything for among your peoples it is understood that each entity has rights and privileges and these include prompt results from any energy output. And yet we say to you, my friends, that when your day is done and you look back upon it you find, perhaps, all too much of your precious time has been spent waiting for inconsequential and petty things, those things which shall not outlast this transient illusion nor even last until your next week, your next month, your next year.

We have suggested to you often that you spend time daily in meditation, for how else, my friends, can you discover that the waiting that is profitable for you to do is the waiting for the truth? Not the truth of a circumstance of an apparent problem or any evanescent phenomenon of who you really are and whence you truly came. This is worth much waiting, my friends. The Creator makes Itself known in an eternal present and as you in your experience live from the day-to-day you have little natural access to this wonderful sphere of celestial influence. It takes patience to set aside the time to wait upon the Creator. But one moment it will come to you, my friends, that you seek this Creator, not as a part of many other things which you do but as the bride seeks the bridegroom, as the sailor his home, as the lost sheep the fold, and you will watch with even more patience than the watchman for the morning.

For the light which you seek is the light wherein creation is illumined. That sun body which you may seek at the dawning is but a tiny prototype, for example, of the dawn of understanding of love, of oneness with the creation, yourself and the Creator. Wait, my friends, and be comfortable, for you are not alone and there is no end to the patience of He who waits for you.

At this time I would transfer this contact to the one known as Jim. I am Hatonn.

Sunday Meditation, April 5, 1981

(Jim channeling)

I am Hatonn, and am with this instrument. Once again it is our privilege to greet you in love and light. We have been speaking of patience, the patience of waiting for the goals which you seek, the illumination of the entirety of your being. It is a waking which each creature within the creation of the Father experiences as a necessary part of the life stream, for each within the creation is the Creator in one form or another likened unto the guests at a costume ball, each with their own mask and costume, each playing a part which in a certain way expresses the Creator for that individual in a way that has meaning for that entity.

Most at the ball know not that they wear costumes. Most believe that they are who they seem to be in their daily round of activities, but most also suspect that there is more to their expression of life than meets their own eyes. And each, on occasion, peers into the mirror of their own being to examine that which is the self. Each discovers certain parts of the costume and decides that perhaps these are parts of their personality. For most, they find contentment in assuming that they are many different things, that they have many different aspects to their personalities, and this, my friends, is true, for the Creator is all things. But each entity at the appointed hour of their own illumination shall discover that they are but one thing in truth: they are the Creator.

Upon that discovery they shall also realize that each of the other entities at the costume ball are also the Creator. They shall discover that there is nothing but the Creator and they shall take their place within the realm of the infinite and reign as the Creator. The patience of playing the parts is a prime requisite for playing the part well. Enjoy the ball. Enjoy your costume. Enjoy all the manifestations of the creation, for each expresses the Creator in an infinity of ways, but realize also that it is but a costume you wear, a play in which you partake, an illusion in which you are immersed. And know also that there is a truth in which you are an integral part—the truth of the love and the light of the infinite Creator that shines from deep within your very being. Have the patience and play your parts. And play them well, for much there is to learn of the Father's creation, and in many ways are these lessons learned.

We of Hatonn hope that in some small way our simple messages of love to your meditation group might serve as part of your infinite play and might help you learn yet one more small lesson, the lesson of love and light and oneness of all beings, of all creation.

We would at this time transfer our contact to the one known as L. I am Hatonn.

(L channeling)

I am Hatonn, and again I greet you, my brothers, in the love and the light of the Creator. My brothers, it is often seemingly that we repeat our messages concerning the subject of meditation. This is true and yet we would emphasize that this is the most important tool available to you for growth. My brothers, we do not deny your intention for growth or even your willingness to strive for growth, yet of what value are good intentions or a strong will with no guidance? It is like going on a trip in a powerful, well-tuned car with no road map and no destination in mind, Therefore, my brothers, we reiterate our seemingly endless message that meditation is the key for your understanding of the universe and your place, your role, within that universe.

We would now share with you what answers we might be able to provide to your questions, should you have any. Are there any questions?

Carla: Would you like to make a comment on our recent Ra contact?

I am Hatonn. I have received your question. The Ra contact that you received is of incomplete detail. The reason for this in not within our area of responsibility in that the Ra contacts are of a highly controlled nature. We would answer you in more detail if we could, however, it is not within the intention of the Ra contact for us to expand on that source of information. May we answer you further?

Carla: Just a few questions peripherally to that. By "incomplete," do you mean that answers to questions asked are incomplete or that some questions cannot be answered?

I am Hatonn. I understand your question. By incomplete we mean that the information you seek is more complex than you have ascertained. Therefore, when you ask a question not knowing the full extent of detail supporting the answer it is not possible to say that a simple phrase given in answer has given the entire answer. In other words, my brother, if you were to ask what is the weather like today the answer you sought would concern only your own geographic location yet would not completely answer the question, for the weather conditions vary widely on your planet, as you well know.

Does this answer your question?

Carla: I believe so. Let me try to clarify. Then the incompleteness of the contact is due to the limits of our understanding? And the language?

I am Hatonn. Yes, my brother, in conjunction with the fact that, as you know, not all may be revealed to you because of the requirements concerning your free will for your personal growth.

Carla: Yes, I'm aware of that stipulation. That's been mentioned many times by Ra. What is your relationship with the group Ra?

I am Hatonn. I understand your question. The Ra entity speaks frequently to you, my brother of oneness. Does this not answer your question?

Carla: To be more specific, I was wondering whether you had a special connection with this teaching group within the Confederation of Planets or whether you did not work closely, since you both had spoken to this group.

I an Hatonn. The Ra group on your planet has incurred specific responsibilities as a result of their actions. This you are already aware of. For this reason the Ra group has responsibilities for debts, if you will, that must be completed. These responsibilities are unique to the Ra group, that the Ra group are members of the Federation as a whole. It would not be correct to assume, however, that the Federation or its individual members share in those unique responsibilities. Where the Ra group is discharging previously incurred responsibilities prior to their own advancement, we of Hatonn work at this time solely for advancement through service.

Is this clear to you my brother?

Carla: Yes, thank you, my brother. I send you my love.

Don: What density is Hatonn?

I am Hatonn. My brother, you ask a question in an effort to test this instrument. We cannot answer this question because of the intention with which it is asked. This would violate the precept concerning free will, my brother.

May we answer you further?

Don: Expand on what you said about the responsibilities of Ra.

I am Hatonn. My brother, the Ra group has, in your distant past, attempted to accomplish specific works with your race. These efforts, although well intentioned, were not successful. Indeed, they resulted in setbacks for which the Ra group held itself responsible. In judging themselves responsible the Ra group obligated themselves to correct the deficiencies they caused.

Does this answer your question, my brother?

Don: Yes.

Is there another question?

Carla: Is there anything that this group could do, in your opinion, to aid in your contact?

I am Hatonn. My brothers, there is an atmosphere of disbelief which is causing difficulty for this instrument. Although we of Hatonn cannot initiate actions of proof we can only remind you that the quality of the contact is dependent upon atmosphere control.

May we answer you further?

Carla: I'm assuming that you're speaking of this particular meeting and that you're having this difficulty because of some tinge of disbelief along with open-mindedness, Is that correct?

I am Hatonn. That is correct, my brother.

Carla: My intent in asking had mostly to do with a general thought about our tuning. We have been doing many different kinds of tuning, everything from the Lord's prayer to chanting, to other prayers and oms. Is any method which gets the group in a unified tune seeking truth satisfactory or is one preferred?

I am Hatonn. It is not significant in which manner you tune your vibrations, as long as the attunement is of a positive nature and the attunement is accomplished.

Is there another question?

Carla: Thank you.

I am Hatonn. As there are no further questions, we bid you farewell in the love and the light of the Creator. I am Hatonn. ✣

www.ingramcontent.com/pod-product-compliance
Lightning Source LLC
Chambersburg PA
CBHW080420230426
43662CB00015B/2163